P9-DUJ-759

DATE DUE

DE 8 '95			
MY 10 '96			
DE 11 '96			
OC 31 97			
MY 17 99			
MR 6 '05			
AP 17 05			
AP 18 05			

DEMCO 38-296

MANAGEMENT

THIRD EDITION

MANAGEMENT

THIRD EDITION

ARTHUR G. BEDEIAN

LOUISIANA STATE UNIVERSITY

Riverside Community College
Library
4800 Magnolia Avenue
Riverside, California 92506

MAY '95

THE DRYDEN PRESS

HARCOURT BRACE JOVANOVICH

Fort Worth   Philadelphia   San Diego   New York   Orlando   Austin   San Antonio
Toronto   Montreal   London   Sydney   Tokyo

Editor-in-Chief   Robert A. Pawlik
Aquisitions Editor   Ruth E. Rominger
Developmental Editor   Carla D. Houx
Project Editor   Sheila M. Spahn
Production Manager   Jacqui Y. Parker
Book Designer   Garry Harman
Photo/Permissions Editor   Doris Milligan

Copyright © 1993 by
Harcourt Brace Jovanovich College Publishers.

All rights reserved. No part of this publication may be
reproduced or transmitted in any form or by any
means, electronic or mechanical, including photocopy,
recording, or any information storage and retrieval
system, without permission in writing from the
publisher.

Requests for permission to make copies of any part of
the work should be mailed to: Permissions
Department, Harcourt Brace Jovanovich College
Publishers, Orlando, FL 32887.

Address for Editorial Correspondence
The Dryden Press, 301 Commerce Street, Suite 3700,
Fort Worth, TX 76102

Address for Orders
The Dryden Press, 6277 Sea Harbor Drive,
Orlando, FL 32887
1-800-782-4479, or 1-800-433-0001 (in Florida)

ISBN: 0-03-074683-3

Library of Congress Catalogue Number: 92-075111

Printed in the United States of America

3456789012 036 987654321

The Dryden Press
Harcourt Brace Jovanovich

Again for Lynda, Katherine, and Tab

Anthony, Perrewe, and Kacmar
Strategic Human Resource Management

Bartlett
Cases in Strategic Management for Business

Bedeian
Management
Third Edition

Bedeian and Zammuto
Organizations: Theory and Design

Boone and Kurtz
Contemporary Business
Seventh Edition

Bowman and Branchaw
Business Report Writing
Second Edition

Bracker, Montanari, and Morgan
Cases in Strategic Management

Calvasina and Barton
Chopstick Company: A Business Simulation

Czinkota, Rivoli, and Ronkainen
International Business
Second Edition

Daft
Management
Second Edition

Higgins and Vincze
Strategic Management: Text and Cases
Fifth Edition

Hills
Compensation Decision Making

Hodgetts
Management: Theory, Process, and Practice

Hodgetts
Modern Human Relations at Work
Fifth Edition

Hodgetts and Kroeck
Personnel and Human Resource Management

Hodgetts and Kuratko
Effective Small Business Management
Third Edition

Hodgetts and Kuratko
Management
Third Edition

Holley and Jennings
The Labor Relations Process
Fourth Edition

Huseman, Lahiff, and Penrose
Business Communication: Strategies and Skills
Fourth Edition

Jauch and Coltrin
The Managerial Experience: Cases, Exercises, and Readings
Sixth Edition

Kemper
Experiencing Strategic Management

Kuehl and Lambing
Small Business: Planning and Management
Second Edition

Kuratko and Hodgetts
Entrepreneurship: A Contemporary Approach
Second Edition

Luthans and Hodgetts
Business
Second Edition

We live in a volatile world marked by domestic uncertainty and ever-increasing global competition. Old ways are virtually useless, as foreign competitors are becoming tougher, employees are clamoring to be empowered, and customers are demanding the highest quality products at minimum prices. Now, more than ever, no job is more vital to our future success than that of manager. Rarely, if ever, in human history has a job proven so indispensable so quickly.

This book has been written in response to the pressing need for world-class managers. It is designed for a one-semester or one-quarter course and for students who may or may not go on to take further management classes. Each chapter is intended to be a lively, enjoyable experience for both students and instructors. No previous academic knowledge of the subject is assumed.

In preparing this new edition, every attempt was made to maintain the readability and informal tone of the previous edition and to preserve an emphasis on management as an interdisciplinary field. Whenever possible, likely questions were anticipated and answered in such a way as to address the more significant and provocative issues that confront practicing managers. Every chapter has been thoroughly updated to convey the excitement and dynamism of management today. Contemporary examples are abundantly employed to illustrate the most current research and theories. Each example was carefully chosen on the basis of its significance and interest.

Designed to stimulate inquiry and clear thinking about management, the text is organized around the five major functions of management—planning, organizing, staffing and human resource management, leading and interpersonal influence, and controlling. Its style and content reflect extensive input from teaching colleagues, students, practicing managers, and leading researchers throughout the world. To the over 10,000 students whom

I've had the pleasure of instructing in the last 24 years, a special thanks for reporting favorably (and occasionally not so favorably) on their experiences with previous editions and for providing excellent ideas for how the text might be made even better.

Like its predecessors, the goal of *Management, 3/e,* is to enhance student learning by providing the most current, challenging, readable, and exciting survey of management knowledge possible. Every facet of its preparation has been guided by this ultimate purpose. While there is no simple substitute for direct experience for learning to be a manager, over two decades of teaching experience have bolstered the author's firm belief that a thorough understanding of the management process helps develop the perspective necessary for becoming a successful manager.

CONTENT

Like its predecessors, the part and chapter sequence of *Management* is consistent with the traditional management process. Each part is designed as a separate and virtually self-contained unit of study; substantial cross-referencing provides coherence and a central unifying theme. This format allows considerable latitude in scheduling class assignments, as well as in determining course coverage.

Part I, "Understanding the Managerial Task," introduces the reader to the world of professional management. The functions of management are identified, and the various levels of the management pyramid are examined. This section also presents a historical review of approaches to management, explores the changing environment of a typical contemporary organization, and examines management's ethical and social responsibilities.

Part II, "Planning," examines goal setting, strategy formulation and implementation, and managerial decision making.

Part III, "Organizing," covers how jobs are grouped to form work units and the design and analysis of individual jobs. Because change is a universal aspect of all organization, conditions for successfully introducing change are explained, as well as the reasons why people resist change, tactics for overcoming resistance to change, and different methods for introducing change. A new chapter on power and authority covers the types of power; line and staff authority; employee empowerment; management resistance to delegation; and types of coordination.

Part IV, "Staffing and Human Resource Management," focuses on how organizations can identify, hire, train, and retain employees. A new chapter on human resource development has been added. This chapter includes extensive coverage of employee training, performance appraisal, compensation programs, employee wellness, and labor relations. It also explains how an organization develops a managerial team, how to plan a managerial career, and what types of unique challenges managers encounter.

Part V, "Leading and Interpersonal Influence," discusses the interpersonal talents a manager must develop to be effective. It explains various approaches to motivation, different leadership theories, the nature of work group behavior, and the essence of managerial communication.

Part VI, "Controlling," concentrates on various methods of control and presents control guidelines for interpreting operating results. It also examines both the nature of information systems, as well as operations management and productivity.

Part VII, "Contemporary Challenges," examines the unique demands of international management and the so-called quality imperative.

LEARNING-ORIENTED FEATURES

An effort has been made throughout *Management* to combine both a theoretical and a practical perspective in the belief that neither is sufficient alone. Thus, the following learning-oriented features have been incorporated into each chapter in order to strike a proper balance between the presentation of management theory and the application of that theory.

LEARNING OBJECTIVES

Each chapter begins with a clear and attainable set of learning objectives. Keyed to main topics, the learning objectives are intended to serve as study guidelines as well as an introduction to the chapter. Any current study of management principles must include global competitiveness and the special challenges presented by crossing national boundaries. International aspects of managing are integrated throughout the textual material, in boxed features, and in a stand-alone chapter. Examples of global management issues are found throughout the text and are identified by a globe icon like the one on the margin of this page.

OPENING VIGNETTES

Chapter-opening vignettes capture student interest by applying ensuing material to a real-world organization or situation. They also provide relevant examples for classroom discussion and highlight topics such as international joint ventures, employee empowerment, valuing diversity, and quality improvement.

ART AND PHOTO PROGRAM

Each opening vignette is illustrated with a full-color supporting photograph. To further stimulate student interest and imagination, additional full-color photographs, as well as tables, figures, and other graphics of various types, are used extensively throughout the book. All artwork is specially designed to reiterate essential chapter material while creating a visually pleasing presentation. The photographs are accompanied by in-depth captions that provide additional examples of concepts discussed in the text.

CLOSE UP

Emerging issues such as valuing diversity, quality improvement, social responsibility, and international dimensions of management have been highlighted throughout the text in Close Up features. These thematic presentations provide additional examples to emphasize important concepts. Examples of topics addressed include:

- The need for Euro-managers
- Cultural barriers to communication
- Ringi: Japanese decision making techniques
- New career and business opportunities based on environmental preservation

SMART MANAGEMENT

These boxed features appear in every chapter and are carefully crafted to highlight the application of key managerial concepts, as well as provide additional examples. Smart Management features include:

- Corporate espionage
- Telecommuting advantages
- Race norming

THE MANAGEMENT EXPERIENCE

An experiential exercise at the end of each chapter encourages in-depth evaluation and discussion of special topics. Intended to move learning from "seeing" and "listening" to "doing," these exercises can also be used as class assignments.

These exercises include:
- Job search checklist
- What employees want most
- Leadership potential
- Ethics in the trenches

SUMMARIES

Each chapter concludes with a concise summary. By repeating and providing a response to the "Learning Objectives" that open each chapter, summaries reiterate main topics in a logical and thorough manner.

REVIEW AND DISCUSSION QUESTIONS

Every chapter is supplemented with relevant questions to assess student understanding of the main topics examined. Each question calls for an analysis or practical application of what has been learned, thus serving as a mechanism for self-teaching.

KEY TERMS AND GLOSSARY

A four-way glossary helps to identify and define key terms. Each key term is boldfaced and defined in the text where it first appears. The term is also placed in the margin of that page for emphasis and easy study. There is a complete glossary at the end of the text. Additionally, key terms are listed at the end of each chapter, along with page references, as a study tool.

CHAPTER CASES

Cases at the end of each chapter help students learn how to use course material to solve an actual management challenge.

VIDEO CASES

Written cases pertinent to each part are presented at the end of the text and are accompanied by videos. The videos are intended to enhance class discussions by visually profiling a company and illustrating managerial concepts presented in the text. Additional videos coordinated with specific chapters are available for text adopters.

COMPREHENSIVE LEARNING PACKAGE

Management is supported by a comprehensive learning package designed to ensure the lively presentation warranted by this dynamic subject. Materials available to instructors include the following:

INSTRUCTOR'S MANUAL

Co-authored with F. David Alexander of Angelo State University, this guide contains detailed lecture outlines, learning objectives, responses to review and discussion questions, notes for end-of-chapter cases, and additional teaching examples.

COMPUTERIZED INSTRUCTOR'S MANUAL

A disk will be available to text adopters that contains most elements of the *Instructor's Manual*. These elements can be electronically cut and pasted together to create customized lecture outlines.

TEST BANK

The most important part of the teaching package is the *Test Bank*. The *Test Bank* accompanying the third edition was given special attention because test questions must accurately and fairly assess student competence in subject material. Prepared by George Foegen of Metropolitan State College, the *Test Bank* provides approximately 2,500 multiple-choice, true/false, matching, and essay test items. New multiple-choice items based on self-contained mini-cases are a great time-saving substitute for essay questions, combining the comprehensive testing of concepts and applications with the ease of an objective test.

COMPUTERIZED TEST BANK

A *Computerized Test Bank* with versions for IBM, Apple, and Macintosh computers is available free to text adopters. The *Computerized Test Bank* allows instructors to select and edit test items from the printed *Test Bank* as well as add an unlimited number of their own items. Up to 99 versions of each test can be custom printed.

VIDEO INSTRUCTOR'S MANUAL

This manual contains video cases and teaching notes for each chapter and part of the text. It lists the title, running time, teaching objectives, and a detailed outline for each video case. It also provides page references for chapter concepts highlighted in the videos and video warm-ups, as well as answers to both case questions and video recap discussion questions. A multiple-choice test is also available for each video. The manual was developed by William D. Schulte of George Mason University.

TRANSPARENCY MASTERS AND ACETATES

More than 150 transparency masters from text art and 100 all-new color acetates are available to text adopters. Acetates are accompanied by detailed teaching notes that include summaries of key concepts and discussion questions for in-class use.

COMPUTER SIMULATION

This management simulation, written by Eugene Calvasina, James L. Barton, Jr., Ava Honan, Richard Calvasina of Auburn University-Montgomery, and Gerald Calvasina of University of North Carolina-Charlotte, places students in the role of a manager and requires them to make decisions about key operational areas. This is an interactive simulation designed to offer students the opportunity to learn how decisions affect all aspects of an on-going organization.

SUPPLEMENTAL MODULES

Supplemental course modules in the areas of organizational behavior, operations management, and small business/entrepreneurship are available. These are designed to supplement text coverage and to address the needs of schools whose management principles courses emphasize these areas.

STUDY GUIDE

Co-authored with Sally A. Coltrin and Lawrence R. Jauch, this guide contains chapter outlines, learning objectives, key terms and concepts, chapter summaries, and sample true/false, multiple-choice, and essay test items. Answers to the sample test items are given at the end of each chapter, along with page designations in the text for student reference.

THE MANAGERIAL EXPERIENCE: CASES AND EXERCISES, SIXTH EDITION

This companion volume to *Management*, co-authored by Lawrence R. Jauch and Sally A. Coltrin, supplements the study of management principles by using cases and exercises to develop student skills in the areas of leadership, communication, decision making, planning, organization design, dealing with individual and group behavior, staffing, resolving conflict, maintaining control, and implementing change.

INSTRUCTOR'S MANUAL FOR THE MANAGERIAL EXPERIENCE: CASES AND EXERCISES, SIXTH EDITION

This manual contains a cross-referencing grid that indicates where concepts from *The Managerial Experience* are covered in *Management*. A quick glance at the grid shows instructors which chapters in *The Managerial Experience* provide appropriate supplemental materials corresponding to the text. In addition, there are analyses for every case and exercise in *The Managerial Experience*.

CASES AND EXERCISES TO ACCOMPANY *MANAGEMENT*

Two companion volumes, a case book and an exercise book, co-authored with Lawrence R. Jauch and Sally A. Coltrin, supplement *Management,* by providing additional classroom materials. Both follow the organization and content coverage of *Management* to provide a truly integrated perspective. These additional materials help develop student skills in the areas of leadership, communication, decision making, planning, organization design, dealing with individual and group behavior, staffing, resolving conflict, exercising control, and implementing change. An instructor's material is available for these supplements.

CAREER DESIGN EXERCISES

This manual contains career exercises based on the work of John C. Crystal, the man whom Richard N. Bolles credits as the major contributor to *What Color is Your Parachute?*—the best-selling career book of all time. The exercises and the accompanying software program have been praised by career and computer experts, including Joyce Lain Kennedy, careers columnist for the *Los Angeles Times Syndicate, The Wall Street Journal's National Business Employment Weekly,* and *PC Magazine.*

Career Design Exercises will help students to:

- Decide on a major
- Identify their best skills
- Discover what career direction to pursue
- Find out if starting a business may be the appropriate career path
- Determine key preferences for co-workers and working conditions
- Make personal contacts leading to job interviews
- Create custom resumes that will stand out from others
- Handle themselves in a professional manner during an interview
- Locate employers who are eager to hire people with their skills but who do not recruit on campus and do not advertise their job opportunities
- Develop communication skills by organizing their thoughts in writing

- Discover their personal leadership style
- Increase managerial effectiveness and sensitivity to cultural differences

ACKNOWLEDGMENTS

No book, fact or fiction, is ever exclusively the product of the individual whose name appears on its title page. Inevitably, an author is influenced by interactions with others.

The Louisiana State University College of Business Administration has continued to provide a unique setting in which to work. Research support and release time were provided by the Ralph and Kacoo Olinde Distinguished Professorship. Special thanks go to Dean James B. Henry for giving me the autonomy to continue my work. Appreciation is also due Brenda M. Gatlin and Patti J. Gunter for their excellent administrative support. The efforts of Andrew H. Ferguson, John E. Gould, Shelly C. Whittington, Ravindran Adimoolam, Lisa J. Sebastian, Robin M. Landry, and Rebecca G. Long, my graduate assistants over the past four years, were indispensable, especially in the final stages of manuscript preparation.

A special acknowledgment goes to the following people who served as collaborators in their area of expertise: John D. Blair and Grant T. Savage, Texas Tech University (social responsibility and managerial ethics); James A. Buford, Jr., Auburn University (human resource management); Michael J. Savoie, University of New Orleans (quality), Thomas E. Hendrick, Arizona State University and Byron Finch, Miami University (operations management); M. Kris McAlister and Julio C. Rivera, University of Alabama in Birmingham (information systems); and Michael R. Czinkota, Georgetown University and George S. Vozikis, The Citadel (international management).

I am particularly grateful for the suggestions and encouragement of the following people who reviewed all or part of the present edition in manuscript form:

McRae C. Banks
Mississippi State University

Alfred A. Bolton
Averett College

Deb Buerkley
Southwest State University

Stephen C. Bushardt
University of Southern Mississippi

Courtland M. Chaney
Louisiana State University

James G. Combs
Louisiana State University

Michael R. Czinkota
Georgetown University

Hy Finkelstein
Texas Tech University

John Hughes
Texas Tech University

Nabil A. Ibrahim
Augusta College

Thomas E. Jones
Southern Oregon State College

Russell L. Kent
Georgia Southern University

Dorothy P. Moore
The Citadel

Gerald Perselay
Winthrop College

Craig J. Russell
Louisiana State University

William G. Steingruber
University of North Texas

Dana L. Stover
University of Idaho

Herb True
University of Notre Dame and St. Mary's College

Richard A. Wald
Eastern Washington University

Reviewers of previous editions to whom a continuing debt is owed follow:

Robert J. Amann
Florida International University—Bay Vista

Debra A. Arvanites
Villanova University

Larry G. Bailey
San Antonio College

Cynthia M. Beath
University of Minnesota

Dan Benson
Kutztown University of Pennsylvania

William Bliesoth
Mott Community College

Allen C. Bluedorn
University of Missouri—Columbia

Aaron A. Buchko
Michigan State University

James A. Buford, Jr.
Auburn University

Jon L. Bushnell
University of Denver

Richard Choyke
University of Wisconsin—Stevens Point

Arthur L. Darrow
Bowling Green State University

James B. Dilworth
University of Alabama in Birmingham

Mike Farley
Del Mar College

Marvin Hill
Northern Illinois University

Jim Klinger
Villanova University

Arthur La Capria, Jr.
El Paso Community College

William Lindsay
Western Kentucky University

Miller C. Lovett
University of Massachusetts—Boston

Nyrna P. Mandell
California State University—Northridge

James C. McElroy
Iowa State University

Marjorie L. McInerney
University of North Carolina—Wilmington

Edward J. Morrison
University of Colorado—Boulder

Minton O. Newman
Southwest Texas State University

Nikki Paahana
DeVry Institute of Technology—Columbus

Gary J. Parson
Central Washington University

David E. Shepard, Sr.
Virginia Western Community College

Harvey Shore
University of Connecticut

Stanley J. Stough
University of Dayton

Susan Virden
Towson State University

Sanford Weinberg
Drexel University

Patricia A. Wells
Oregon State University

Robert Worthington
Western Texas State University

William Wright
Mt. Hood Community College

Special thanks are due Sally A. Coltrin, University of North Florida, and Lawrence R. Jauch, Northeast Louisiana University, for their work in preparing the companion volumes, the *Study Guide* and *The Managerial Experience: Cases, Exercises, and Readings.* I am also indebted to George Foegen, Metropolitan State, for preparing the *Test Bank*, to William D. Schulte, George Mason University, for preparing the Video Instructor's Manual, to Stephen C. Bushardt, University of Southern Mississippi, for assistance in locating chapter cases, and to F. David Alexander, Angelo State University, for assistance in preparing the accompanying *Instructor's Manual.* It was a privilege to work with them all.

At The Dryden Press, Ruth Rominger, Carla Houx, Traci Keller, Martha Beyerlein, and Karen Shaw were a pleasure to work with on this project. In every instance, they were supportive and professional. Dee Salisbury and Sheila M. Spahn saw *Management* through the various stages of production. Doris Milligan skillfully obtained necessary permissions. Designer Garry Harman applied his creative talent to integrate the text type and graphics, resulting in a visual presentation that captures the dynamic spirit of *Management.* Jan M. Richardson, Carolyn D. Smith, and Carol Cerulli provided invaluable editorial assistance. The copyediting skills of Jim Merk added greatly to the clarity of the text. The work of Debra Lilly, proofreader, and Maggie Jarpey, indexer, is also appreciated, as is the promotion support of Lisé Webb and Rachel Stowe. The efforts of Mary Golgenboom and Doris Milligan, photo researchers, are gratefully acknowledged. The production team at York Graphic Services, Fred Reinholtz and Denise Mathias, deserve a special word of thanks for their exceptional care and accommodation in making many last-minute changes.

Finally, on the home front, Katherine and Tab were again encouraging and helpful in ways that defy description. And my wife, Lynda, once more survived the arduous task of living with the discontent that an unfinished book creates. To my family, expressions of gratitude are long overdue.

Arthur G. Bedeian
Louisiana State University

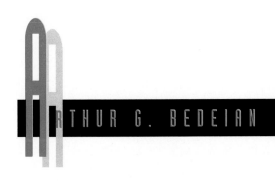

Arthur G. Bedeian, D.B.A., is the Ralph and Kacoo Olinde Distinguished Professor of Management at Louisiana State University, where he specializes in the study of organization design and employee behavior.

A past-president of the Academy of Management, Professor Bedeian has also been president of the Allied Southern Business Association, the Southern Management Association, the Southeastern Institute for Decision Sciences, and the Foundation for Administrative Research. In 1987 he received the Distinguished Scholar Award from the Southern Management Association. He was elected a Fellow of the Academy of Management in 1979 and of the International Academy of Management in 1992.

A former editor of the *Journal of Management,* Professor Bedeian's work has appeared in the *Academy of Management Journal, Journal of Applied Psychology, Journal of Management, Journal of Vocational Behavior, Academy of Management Review, Behavioral Science, Personnel Psychology, Human Relations, Strategic Management Journal,* and *Organizational Behavior and Human Decision Processes.* In addition to a leading principles text, he is the author of *Organization Design: Structure, Strategy, and Environment* (with Raymond F. Zammuto). Both texts have appeared in numerous international and foreign language editions.

Professor Bedeian is an active teacher and consultant. He has taught management, organization theory, organizational behavior, and the development of management thought. The 1991 recipient of the LSU Alumni Association Distinguished Faculty Award, he has also received several outstanding teaching awards. He has been involved in management development and consulting for the Veterans Administration, The Dryden Press, the United States Air Force, and the LSU Executive Program.

TABLE OF CONTENTS

MANAGEMENT

THIRD EDITION

PART
ONE

UNDERSTANDING THE MANAGERIAL TASK

CHAPTER 1

LEARNING OBJECTIVES

Upon completing this chapter, you should be able to:

- Define the term *management*.
- Answer the question, "What is a manager?"
- Identify and describe the five functions of management.
- Explain what is meant by the phrase "the management process."
- Understand the duties associated with different levels of management.
- List the roles that a typical top manager performs.
- Identify the three essential skills used by all managers.
- Know the meaning of the acronym *GEMS*.

At some time or another, many of us dream of being the chief executive officer (CEO) of a large organization—sitting in a paneled office on the top floor of a tall office building, barking orders into a telephone, having dozens of assistants, taking the afternoon off to play golf. But what is it really like to be a CEO, especially a good one?

When Louis V. Gerstner, Jr., took over as CEO of RJR Nabisco in 1990, he discovered that almost all of its senior managers had departed during the capricious reign of his predecessor. In addition, Gerstner knew little about the food and tobacco business, having just come from the presidency of American Express's Travel Management Services. A delicate touch was needed to avoid scaring off the remaining managers and to get operations back on track. Even the seemingly simple question of where and how to meet with division heads required careful thought.

Taking the bull by the horns, Gerstner traveled 150,000 miles during his first year as CEO, visiting plants around the world, touring supermarkets, and talking to workers. He learned of RJR's strong

AN INVITATION TO MANAGEMENT

marketing skills, but to his horror he also learned that RJR had no long-term strategy and that little cooperation existed among its various divisions. Since he believes that brand strength is the key to profitability, he dropped less successful product lines and concentrated on RJR's more profitable brands. And he pushed its food and tobacco divisions to work together on promotions and research.

Gerstner maintains a human touch in his management style. He meets with division heads at their offices once a month, quickly going over RJR's financial performance and then discussing specific operational questions at length. And he periodically gathers about two dozen middle-level and lower-level managers for lunch or dinner to get their impressions on quality, service, and prices.

Gerstner enjoys his work. He had better—he spends 7 days a week at it. But the payoff to RJR has been a 30 percent increase in profits and a 40 percent reduction in its $29.6 billion debt. In this chapter, we invite you to enter the world of management and learn what it really means to be a successful manager.

Source: Patricia Sellers, "Does the CEO Really Matter?," *Fortune* April 22, 1991: 81–82, 86, 90, 94.

This book is about *management*. Rarely, if ever, in human history has an institution emerged as fast as management and proven so indispensable so quickly.[1] Although advantages in raw materials and technology characterized earlier developed economies, it is management that now determines global winners and losers. In the words of Peter F. Drucker, well-known management expert, "In less than 150 years, management has transformed the social and economic fabric of the world's developed countries. It has created a global economy and set new rules for countries that would participate in that economy as equals."[2]

In short, **management**—the process of achieving desired results through efficient utilization of human and material resources—has been the most influential force in modern times. "For," as Drucker adds, "it is management that explains why, for the first time in human history, we can employ large numbers of knowledgeable, skilled people in productive work. No earlier society could do this. Indeed, no earlier society could support more than a handful of such people because, until quite recently, no one knew how to put people with different skills and knowledge together to achieve common goals."[3] What makes this possible is management.

Management.
The process of achieving desired results through efficient utilization of human and material resources.

WHAT ARE MANAGERS?

Good management is a scarce resource. Organizations fail for many reasons—insufficient funds, improper marketing, incompetent product design, and so on. However, they most often fail because of poor management. For this reason, an organization, no matter how potentially valuable, is worth no more than the quality of its management. It has been observed that "[n]o job is more vital to our society than that of the manager. It is the manager who determines whether our social institutions serve us well or whether they squander our talents and resources."[4]

At one time in North America, Europe, and Japan, the world of work was largely composed of individuals working alone, rather than groups of people working together. Farmers produced food for themselves and their families, and, if they were lucky, had a surplus to sell. Potters, silversmiths, tanners, and other craftworkers produced their goods independently. Families who needed homes built them alone or with help from their neighbors. Even government was individualized, consisting of a lord or knight who reigned over a relatively small territory. Sometimes cooperatives were formed to build a road or church or to confront a common enemy, but these lasted only a brief time.

Individualized work patterns still exist in many developing countries. In more developed nations, however, relatively few people continue this pattern. Small farmers and independent carpenters may still work alone, but generally, work is more complex. Goods such as Boeing 747 airplanes, television sets, and heating and air-conditioning systems could not be produced efficiently by a single individual. Services such as electrical power for homes and offices, cable TV, accident insurance, and international investments in currencies and real estate can rarely be performed single handed. The intricacies of producing modern goods and services

4

Even in countries and industries where individuals work largely alone, managers and their organizations make substantial contributions. This Hungarian field worker displays hand-picked ears of Pioneer Hi-Bred International Inc. seed corn.

call for the joint efforts of many people. Seldom does one person possess the necessary money, knowledge, abilities, or other resources to "go it alone." People are needed who can efficiently utilize the human and material resources required to accomplish desired goals. These people are *managers*.

Managers are individuals in organizations who hold positions of authority and make decisions about the allocation of resources. In recent years, the demand for professionally trained managers has increased at an accelerating rate. This demand has come from business firms, health care facilities, educational institutions, philanthropic foundations, government, and the arts. It is reflected in the over 75,000 MBA (Master of Business Administration) degrees granted each year and in the thousands of managers and prospective managers attending management seminars and in-house training programs at an annual cost of some $60 billion.[5]

Manager.
An individual in an organization who holds a position of authority and makes decisions about the allocation of resources.

THE FUNCTIONS OF MANAGEMENT

The owner of a small business is responsible for all aspects of its operation. Thus, a single person, the owner, may hire employees, order inventory, obtain a bank loan, and decide to hold a sale. In contrast, when an organization is large enough to involve many employees and stockholders, it is often difficult to determine who will make certain decisions and accept various responsibilities. In such situations, several questions frequently arise:

1. Who decides what an organization should accomplish? Who decides which societal needs should be served? Who deals with those who provide money, labor, and equipment?

2. Who ensures that employees perform the proper tasks? Who coordinates these tasks? Who is responsible for changing outmoded methods?

3. Who sees to it that individuals needed to perform required tasks are hired, well trained, and rewarded for their work?

4. Who is responsible for seeing that employees work together in harmony and receive adequate support to complete their jobs? Who is charged with seeing that employees find satisfaction in their work?

5. Who is responsible for seeing that organization goals are being achieved efficiently?

Taken together, these questions outline the functions that society, employees, and stockholders expect professional managers to perform. These functions are listed in Table 1.1 and are numerically keyed to the preceding questions. The chapters in which these functions will be discussed are also indicated. A brief description of each function follows below.

Planning is the process of establishing goals and selecting a future course of action for their accomplishment. It includes establishing goals, developing an understanding of the environment in which the goals are to be accomplished, selecting a course of action for accomplishing them, initiating activities necessary to translate plans into action, and evaluating the outcome of that planning.

Organizing is the process of dividing work among groups and individuals and coordinating their activities to accomplish goals. Organizing also involves establishing managerial authority.

Staffing and human resource management is the process of ensuring that competent employees are selected, developed, and rewarded for accomplishing goals.

Leading and interpersonal influence is the process of inducing individuals (peers, superiors, subordinates, and nonsubordinates) or groups to assist willingly and harmoniously in accomplishing goals.

Controlling is the process of ensuring the efficient accomplishment of goals. It is essential for determining how well an organization is performing, whether improvement is needed, where it should occur, how much is needed, and how quickly.

Planning.
The process of establishing goals and selecting a future course of action for their accomplishment.

Organizing.
The process of dividing work among groups and individuals and coordinating their activities to accomplish goals. Organizing also involves establishing managerial authority.

Staffing and human resource management.
The process of ensuring that employees are selected, developed, and rewarded for accomplishing goals.

Leading and interpersonal influence.
The process of inducing individuals (peers, superiors, subordinates, and nonsubordinates) or groups to assist willingly and harmoniously in accomplishing goals.

Controlling.
The process of ensuring the efficient accomplishment of goals.

TABLE 1.1 THE FUNCTIONS OF MANAGEMENT	
Management Function	**Chapter Where Function Is Discussed**
1. Planning the use of resources	5 "Goal Setting and Planning"
	6 "Strategy Formulation and Implementation"
	7 "Managerial Decision Making"
2. Organizing resources	8 "Organization Design"
	9 "Authority and Power"
	10 "Job Design and Self-Managing Teams"
	11 "Organizational Culture and Change"
3. Staffing and human resource management	12 "Human Resource Planning and Staffing"
	13 "Developing Human Resources"
	14 "Managing a Successful Career"

Continued on next page.

Management Function (Continued)	Chapter Where Function Is Discussed (Continued)	
4. Leading and interpersonal influence	15	"Motivating Human Behavior"
	16	"Effective Leadership"
	17	"Group Dynamics and Conflict"
	18	"Effective Communication"
5. Controlling resources	19	"Effective Control"
	20	"Information Systems for Managing"
	21	"Operations Management and Productivity"

THE MANAGEMENT PROCESS

Different management scholars employ varying terms to describe what we have labeled the *functions of management.* For instance, some refer to leading and interpersonal influence as *directing,* while others have labeled it *actuating.* Although there is some disagreement over the preferred language, all agree that the various functions of management are interrelated and are performed by all managers. Collectively, they make up a set of interdependent activities that are commonly termed the **management process.** The pattern of interrelationships that comprise the management process is illustrated in Figure 1.1.

Note that while the functions of management are performed concurrently, there is a logical flow of activities. That is, an organization must first plan in order to determine its goals. Without goals, an organization would drift aimlessly and ultimately perish. Once goals are established, however, managers are in a position to design a supporting structure. They can then select employees to perform required tasks. Next, managers use leadership and interpersonal influence to spur employees to meet goals. Finally, through control, managers determine whether goals are being efficiently achieved.

Management process.

A phrase used to collectively refer to the five functions of management: (1) planning, (2) organizing, (3) staffing and human resource management, (4) leading and interpersonal influence, and (5) controlling.

FIGURE 1.1 THE MANAGEMENT PROCESS

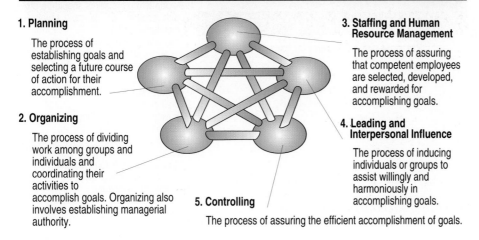

1. Planning

The process of establishing goals and selecting a future course of action for their accomplishment.

2. Organizing

The process of dividing work among groups and individuals and coordinating their activities to accomplish goals. Organizing also involves establishing managerial authority.

3. Staffing and Human Resource Management

The process of assuring that competent employees are selected, developed, and rewarded for accomplishing goals.

4. Leading and Interpersonal Influence

The process of inducing individuals or groups to assist willingly and harmoniously in accomplishing goals.

5. Controlling

The process of assuring the efficient accomplishment of goals.

The functions of management work in a complicated circle, with each function dependent on the other four. In addition, the effect of one function depends on the state of all the others. Sound planning, for example, will not lead to a competitive advantage unless an organization is also well designed. At the same time, advantages in one function can create advantages in others.

Managers who truly understand the management process and manage accordingly will be successful. They will be the kind of managers who build world-class organizations and leave as a legacy not only a great capacity to produce wealth, but a vision for the future.

LEVELS OF MANAGEMENT

Although the term *manager* refers to anyone in an organization who holds a position of authority and makes decisions about the allocation of resources, in most large organizations, managers at different levels perform different activities. Typically, three distinct but overlapping levels can be identified: *first-line managers* at the lowest level, *middle managers,* and then *top managers* at the highest level. As will be discussed in Chapter 9, the middle and top management levels generally are comprised of various additional layers. In any instance, all three levels require a different managerial emphasis, as outlined in Figure 1.2.

FIGURE 1.2 MANAGEMENT ACTIVITIES AT THREE DIFFERENT LEVELS

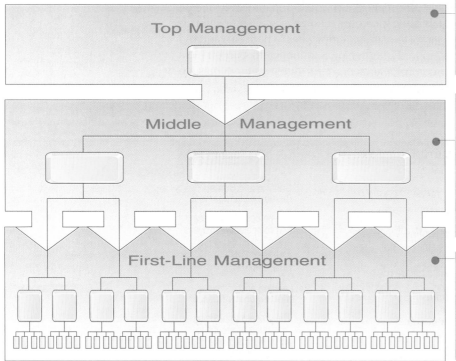

Top Management
- Develop/maintain customer/vendor relations.
- Monitor sales performance and promotional activities.
- Identify developing national/multinational business environment and economic trends.
- Consult on company-wide problems.
- Attend outside meetings as a representative.

Middle Management
- Establish target dates for products or services.
- Estimate resource requirements for operational needs.
- Develop evaluation criteria to measure progress and performance.
- Decide which programs should be provided with resources (for example, employees, materials, funds).
- Translate general directives from superiors (for example, strategic plans) into specific operational plans.

First-Line Management
- Motivate subordinates to change or improve their performance.
- Provide subordinates ongoing performance feedback.
- Take action to resolve performance problems.
- Blend subordinates' goals (for example, career goals) with work requirements.
- Identify ways of improving communications among subordinates.

Source: Based on Allen I. Kraut, Patricia R. Pedigo, D. Douglas McKenna, and Marvin D. Dunnette, "The Role of the Manager: What's Really Important in Different Management Jobs," *Academy of Management Executive* 3 (November 1989): 286–293.

FIRST-LINE MANAGEMENT

First-line managers comprise the largest managerial group in most organizations. They hold various titles: lab supervisor, head nurse, department head, section chief, and so on. First-line managers are exactly what their title suggests—management's first line of contact with labor. As such, they are responsible for directly managing operating (nonmanagerial) employees and resources. It is the first-line manager's job to make sure that the plans developed for an organization by higher management are fulfilled by the employees who actually produce the organization's goods and services. First-line managers are the only managers who do not manage other managers. For this reason, they have been referred to as the "man (or woman) in the middle," caught in a figurative limbo between labor and higher management. No longer master craftworkers, today's first-line managers are now in a strange period of declining power but newfound importance. On one hand, the duties of first-line managers have been curbed by union contracts specifying procedures for grievances, changes in work assignments, and hiring and firing. Government regulations, such as laws on discrimination, have shifted certain decisions from first-line managers to human resource managers. On the other hand, their jobs have grown in importance as first-line managers become increasingly responsible for the complex "factory of the future." Some observers have predicted that no job is going to change more over the next decade than that of first-line management.

A large number of college graduates enter management at the first-line level. In many ways it is an exciting job—it's where the action is. When a first-line manager solves problems and makes decisions, there is immediate feedback, and this can be rewarding. Studies indicate that first-line managers are busy, experience frequent interruptions, and often must shift back and forth between tasks. They spend most of their time with subordinates discussing matters related to product quality and work scheduling. Staffing requirements and issues involving personal relations also occupy a large portion of their day. The following example outlines $11\frac{1}{2}$ minutes of a typical first-line manager's workday. Pat was one of 56 supervisors observed on an automobile assembly line. Note that he had personal contacts with 13 people and tried to solve eight problems in 13 different places, all in only $11\frac{1}{2}$ minutes. His day tends to continue that way.

2:15 p.m.	Pat checks with scheduler S. He looks at the hourly report of the number of cars coming through the body shop.
2:16	He walks over to R (repairer) on the pickup line and checks to see if the earlier repair trouble was corrected.
2:17	He calls over the inspection supervisor to show her a hole in a piece. The inspection supervisor says she will notify the trim department.
2:19	Pat tells the repairer to locate the hole by eye until it comes through all right.
2:19$\frac{1}{2}$	Pat has a drink of water.
2:20	Pat walks over to station 5 and asks his utility man how many operators he still has to relieve.
2:20$\frac{1}{2}$	He moves along the line—stations 5, 6, 7—checking visually on the quality of the work.
2:21	He checks a loose nut on a fixture at station 7. He speaks with the operator.

First-line managers.
Managers responsible for directly managing operating (nonmanagerial) employees and resources. Management's first line of contact with labor.

Santa Fe Pipeline Partners' Area Supervisor Don Rufsteck works in the field with technicians inspecting vapor seals on a tank in Concord, California. Supplying hands-on assistance and direction to employees in field locations is a frequently performed aspect of the first-line supervisor's job.

2:22	The operator at station 3 calls for materials.
2:22$\frac{1}{4}$	Pat tells the operator at subassembly bench E to make up more material.
2:23	He walks over to MH (stockkeeper). He tells the stockkeeper that the line is getting low on hinges. They discuss the number short and agree that there is enough for tomorrow.
2:25	Pat walks from MH to station 1 and makes a visual inspection of the car body to check on the hole discussed earlier at the pickup line.
2:26	Pat sees the supervisor from the preceding section and tells her about the hole.
2:26$\frac{1}{2}$	Pat receives a hand signal from welder W.[6]

MIDDLE MANAGEMENT

Middle managers occupy roles positioned above first-line management and below top management. Typical middle-management titles are plant manager, division head, and operations manager. Above them, top managers determine an organization's form and define its overall character, mission, and direction. Below them, first-line managers oversee the way daily tasks of an organization are performed. Middle managers are charged with integrating the activities of different work groups so they operate in harmony with one another and are better able to cope with the demands made upon them. Middle managers thus manage other

Middle managers. Managers occupying roles positioned above first-line management and below top management.

managers and serve as a link between top management and first-line management. They transfer information and materials among different work groups and coordinate organization activities.

As might be expected, the workday of most middle managers is fairly hectic. They interpret and implement top management directives and forward messages to and from first-line management and lower level employees. Middle managers thus spend their days giving, receiving, or seeking information. They typically spend a lot of time in meetings and on the telephone. They spend the least amount on activities aimed at defining objectives and specifying the ways they should be attained. This is not surprising, given middle management's role. The transmission and receipt of information is vital to coordinate work group activities. It is also important in creating the conditions necessary for implementing top management's plans.

An example of a morning's activities for Katherine Kennon, a typical middle manager, follows. Note how frequently Katherine transmits and receives information to facilitate the activities of various work groups. Also note the time spent in meetings and on the telephone. Finally, note the hectic pace, frequent interruptions, and wide variety of activities in which she is involved.

6:45 a.m.	Katherine and her husband, who heads his own engineering firm, coordinate the home front. He prepares breakfast while she wakes their two children, a 3-year-old son and 6-year-old daughter.
7:02	Before darting for her 20-minute ride into the city via commuter train, Katherine instructs her voice mail to call the house-cleaning service, as well as a gourmet carryout service that will prepare that evening's dinner.
7:14	On the way out, Katherine hurriedly scribbles a note for the children's nanny concerning their day-care and after-school activities.
7:29	On the commuter train to work, Katherine reviews her day's appointments, checks her electronic mail, and reads the latest *Business Week* via her laptop computer.
7:56	Arriving at work, Katherine unpacks her briefcase and gets coffee.
8:05	Together with her administrative assistant, Brock, Katherine goes over her schedule for the day. They informally chat for a few minutes.
8:12	Off to her first scheduled meeting, Katherine is intercepted by a subordinate who wishes to discuss a disagreement with a fellow co-worker.
8:34	Arriving 4 minutes late for her first meeting, Katherine gets coffee. Following a few minutes' banter, she composes herself and begins her presentation.
9:17	Having finished her presentation, Katherine answers questions.
9:30	Meeting adjourns. Katherine stays around until 9:42 to chat. She then hurries back to her office.
9:48	Based on feedback received in response to her presentation, Katherine quickly updates various aspects of a final report.

9:58	Brock reminds Katherine that her second meeting of the day is set for 10:00 a.m. in another building.
10:06	Arriving 6 minutes late, Katherine gets more coffee. She is introduced to representatives of a new supplier. Problems with product quality and on-time delivery are discussed. A followup meeting in 2 weeks is scheduled.
10:32	Upon returning to her office, Katherine finds a subordinate wishing to talk. He alleges possible improper accounting practices. Following a 15-minute conversation and two telephone calls, an apparent misunderstanding is resolved.
10:54	Katherine calls an annoyed customer. "Thank you for letting me know about the problem," she says. "No, that's not the kind of customer service we want to provide. I apologize for it. Won't you give us another opportunity?"
11:04	Brock informs Katherine that her 3 p.m. meeting with her boss has been rescheduled for 2 p.m. She hurriedly assembles her meeting notes and once again goes over the final report she has prepared. Based on feedback received earlier in the day, she quickly uses her personal computer to replot several graphs that will be made into overheads to accompany her report.
11:42	Having missed a weekly manager's lunch set for 11:30 a.m., Katherine grabs a diet soft drink from a vending machine and a piece of fruit from the building cafeteria for lunch. She eats at her desk while sorting through the morning's telephone messages, faxes, and mail.[7]

TOP MANAGEMENT

Top managers determine the form of an organization and define its overall character, mission, and direction. They shape an organization's goals and do what is necessary on the highest levels—from authorizing new facilities and launching research and development projects to acquiring other organizations—to achieve those goals. They provide resources, monitor progress, and make strategic decisions. Perhaps most importantly, they establish the emotional atmosphere that starts at the top of an organization and cascades down. Top managers have job titles such as chairperson of the board, CEO, president, executive vice-president, hospital administrator, or secretary of state. They are the chief officers of an organization.

In performing their duties, top managers fulfill many roles. Henry Mintzberg has identified ten different but highly interrelated roles a typical top manager performs.[8] These roles can be separated into three basic groupings: *interpersonal roles* (figurehead, leader, liaison), *informational roles* (monitor, disseminator, spokesperson), and *decisional roles* (entrepreneur, disturbance handler, resource allocator, negotiator). Table 1.2 presents a summary description of each role, along with various examples.

Interpersonal Roles

The three interpersonal roles (figurehead, leader, and liaison) derive from a top manager's formal authority. First and foremost, top managers are *figureheads*. They serve as organization representatives in all social and legal matters. In many ways, this representation is often symbolic or ceremonial, as when top managers

Top managers.
Managers who determine the form of an organization and define its overall character, mission, and direction.

TABLE 1.2 TEN ROLES PERFORMED BY A TYPICAL TOP MANAGER

Role	Description	Activities
Interpersonal Roles		
Figurehead	Symbolic representative in social and legal matters	Welcomes dignitaries; signs official documents
Leader	Influences hiring, training, and motivating of subordinates	Performs all activities involving subordinates
Liaison	Interacts with peers and other individuals in different organizations to gain favors and knowledge	Processes mail, telephone calls; confers with clients
Informational Roles		
Monitor	Receives and collects information necessary to deal with in-house events and environmental occurrences	Attends professional meetings and trade shows; reads industry periodicals and newsletters
Disseminator	Transmits information *internally* to peers, subordinates, and superiors	Chairs staff meetings; prepares internal reports and memos
Spokesperson	Transmits information *externally* into an organization's environment	Holds press conferences; conducts public interviews; gives speeches to external groups; engages in political lobbying
Decisional Roles		
Entrepreneur	Initiates changes to improve organization performance	Develops new products, original sales promotions, novel pay schemes
Disturbance handler	Deals with unforeseen events or crises	Resolves subordinate conflicts; responds to disgruntled suppliers
Resource allocator	Decides how an organization will expend its resources	Distributes workforce, money, materials, and information
Negotiator	Bargains with individuals, representatives of other organizations	Negotiates labor-management contracts; settles shipping rates; deals with wholesalers; mediates consumer claims

Sources: Henry Mintzberg, *The Nature of Managerial Work* (New York: Harper & Row, 1973) 54–99; Henry Mintzberg, "The Manager's Job: Folklore and Fact," *Harvard Business Review* (July–August 1975): 49–61; Jay W. Lorsch, James P. Baughman, James Reece, and Henry Mintzberg, *Understanding Management* (New York: Harper & Row, 1978) 219–262.

greet and entertain visiting dignitaries, or sign employee retirement letters. President Bush fills this role in his many diplomatic encounters as a representative of the United States. A top manager's *leadership role* entails influencing the activities of subordinates. This involves hiring, training, and motivating employees. As founder, Bill Gates fills a leadership role at Microsoft. He provides a combination of energy, intellect, and vision. Above all, he is known as a "high-horsepower, high-energy" leader. He is personally involved in recruiting new employees and motivating Microsoftians through his famous one-on-one "Bill meetings." In their *liaison role,* top managers interact with peers, as well as individuals in other organizations, to gain favors and knowledge. For instance, in conferring with prospective customers or suppliers, processing mail, answering and making telephone calls, and attending outside meetings, a hospital administrator is acting as a liaison. Xerox CEO Paul Allaire regularly meets with representatives of both large and small organizations to win new accounts. He personally handles several of Xerox's largest accounts, including AT&T, General Motors, 3M, and Honeywell.

Informational Roles

In performing their various interpersonal roles, top managers engage in many interactions that involve the exchange of knowledge (informational roles). As a result, top managers are a focal point for the transmission of both *internal* and *external* information. As *monitors,* top managers collect information that enables them to deal more effectively with events within an organization, as well as with developments in an organization's external environment. For instance, Chicago Mayor Richard M. Daley, Jr., monitors federal and state legislation to determine its impact on local funding, and attends political conventions to keep informed on recent political developments. In their role as *disseminators,* top managers transmit information *internally* to peers, subordinates, and superiors. For instance, at a general faculty meeting, an administrative vice-president might disseminate information about the influence of state appropriations on anticipated salary improvements. As another example, General Motors CEO Robert Stempel regularly holds companywide employee meetings via the company's own private television network. Finally, as a *spokesperson,* a top manager transmits information *externally* into an organization's environment. Thus, when CEOs deliver a speech at an annual trade show, hold a press conference, or give a public interview, they are serving as a spokesperson. Mesa Petroleum CEO T. Boone Pickens makes himself readily available to the press. In addition, as a normal part of his job, he accepts 100 speaking engagements a year.

Apple Computer Inc.'s Chairman John Sculley gives speeches, makes promotional videos, and eagerly comments on how the personal computer industry will change life in the Twenty-first Century.

Decisional Roles

Although maintaining interpersonal relations and receiving and transmitting information are important top management activities, they are not ends in themselves. The unique access of top managers to information, together with their formal authority, place them in a central position to commit an organization to action. Here four decisional roles can be identified. First, in the role of *entrepreneur,* top managers initiate changes to improve organization performance. For example, a vice-president for sales may institute a new marketing campaign to expand a company's product exposure or champion the introduction of new products. Stanley Gault is an example of a classic corporate entrepreneur. At Rubbermaid he completely revamped all product lines, introducing hundreds of new items. A detailed-oriented manager with a strong focus on customer service and bottom-line results, he strung together 41 record quarters of earnings growth. Second, as a *disturbance*

SMART MANAGEMENT "... AND LUCK WALKED IN."

Although managers, like other professionals, prefer to think that their skill alone propelled them into successful careers, luck (good and bad) invariably plays a role in many people's careers. As Aristotle noted over 2,000 years ago in *Nichomachean Ethics,* "all manner of chances" affect a person's prospects in life. Among these chances, of course, are the swiftly changing fortunes of the management world. As one former senior vice-president has mused about luck: "Most people who are successful have had fortuitous breaks. A lot of success is being in the right place when there's an opportunity and you're the easy choice."

Career success is thus often undeniably a matter of luck. It might even be argued that almost all careers are something of a crapshoot. Consider two classic cases.

Case 1: Carter Burgess—Former president of Trans World Airlines (TWA), former president and chairman of American Machine & Foundry (AMF).

In December 1941 Burgess was an Army second lieutenant at Fort Meyer, Virginia. One day as Burgess was passing post headquarters, the post adjutant flagged him down and asked if he had a pressed uniform. Burgess did, and was immediately directed to the Federal Reserve Building in nearby Washington, D.C. Franklin D. Roosevelt and Winston Churchill were meeting there with a number of senior military aides and urgently needed someone to operate a mimeograph and serve tea.

Burgess made such an impression on the high-level military personnel attending the meeting that his army career ignited. When World War II ended, Burgess's military connections led to several middle-management positions, then to a term as Assistant Secretary of Defense, then to TWA, and finally AMF. Burgess frequently wonders how his career would have developed if his uniform had not been pressed.

Case 2: George Weissman—Chief executive of Philip Morris.

Shortly after World War II, Weissman's career was going nowhere. The newspaper where he worked before joining the Navy had offered him his old job back at a paltry $55 a week.

Discouraged, he happened to attend the motion picture, *The Best Years of Our Lives.* Extremely impressed, he sold a glowing review to a press syndicate. Sam Goldwyn of Metro-Goldwyn-Mayer Film Company was delighted by the review, called to tell Weissman so, and arranged to have him hired in the MGM public relations department at an overwhelming $150 a week.

Two years later, Weissman joined the public relations firm of Benjamin Sonnenberg, where he was responsible for the Lever Brothers and Philip Morris accounts. In 1952 he was pirated away by Philip Morris, becoming president in 1967 and chairman from 1978 until his retirement in 1984. By 1983, he was the nation's tenth highest paid executive, with annual compensation totaling $3.7 million.

Sources: Daniel Seligman, "Luck and Careers," *Fortune* November 16, 1981: 60–72; William G. Glanagan, "Choosing a Career—the Agony and the Ecstacy," *Forbes* March 15, 1982: 138–144; Earl C. Gottschalk, Jr., "How the Top Students at Harvard Business Fare 20 Years Later: Most Do Well Financially, But Few Lead Big Firms; The Importance of Luck," *Wall Street Journal* December 20, 1982: 1, 12.

handler, top managers must deal with unforeseen events or crises. Conflicts between subordinates, the loss of an important supplier, or a product recall are all examples of unforeseen disturbances with which top managers might have to deal. Perhaps the best-known example of a CEO fulfilling this role is the widely applauded performance of former Johnson & Johnson CEO James E. Burke, who handled the famous Tylenol crisis involving product tampering. In the role of *resource allocator*, top managers must decide where an organization will expend its resources. Resources include people, money, materials, and information. Each of these can be allocated in a variety of ways. For instance, as President of the United States, Bill Clinton, in conjunction with Congress, must decide whether to allocate more resources to national defense or domestic programs. Finally, as *negotiators*, top managers must bargain with various individuals or representatives of other organizations. Typical examples include a vice-president for industrial relations participating in labor negotiations, or a publisher negotiating royalty rates with an author. Phillips-Van Heusen CEO Bruce T. Klatsky personally negotiates with potential customers. It took 6 months, but he was successful in convincing Dillard Department Stores to stock his company's G. H. Bass shoes.

In a given situation, a top manager may play a number of different roles, which may be at least partially inconsistent. The roles of entrepreneur and disturbance handler are a case in point. The initiation of change (entrepreneur role) is seldom achieved without some form of unforeseen crisis (disturbance-handler role). This dilemma underscores the complexity of the top manager's job and the extraordinary finesse required for top management success.

MANAGEMENT SKILLS

The preceding discussion of the activities performed at different management levels has direct implications concerning the essential skills that managers must possess. Moreover, it has long been realized that the relative importance of these essential skills varies by management level.[9] In general, managers use three different skills—*technical, human,* and *conceptual*. Although these skills are interrelated in practice, they can be considered separately.

Technical skill refers to the knowledge and ability necessary to perform a specific task. Examples are the skills learned by surgeons, musicians, accountants, or engineers. Such skill may be acquired through formal study in professional or vocational schools, on-the-job training, or combinations of academic and internship or apprenticeship programs. Technical skill is the distinguishing feature of job performance for first-line managers. As Figure 1.3 shows, however, its importance diminishes as one moves to higher management levels. This shift in emphasis occurs as managers who are promoted increasingly depend on the technical skills of their subordinates and, in some instances, manage technical skills they have never mastered. The career of General Electric Chairman Jack Welch provides a good illustration of the importance of technical skills at varying management levels.[10] Welch holds both a B.S. (University of Massachusetts) and Ph.D. (University of Illinois) in chemical engineering. Upon graduating in 1959, he took an engineering job in General Electric's Pittsfield, Massachusetts, plastics division. With a flair for the unconventional, he proved a natural manager. By 1963 he had been given profit-and-loss responsibility for an entire product line, forming joint ventures in Japan and the Netherlands. In 1966, he was made a plant manager. Eleven years later, in 1977, he was appointed a senior vice-president for consumer products at the company's headquarters in Fairfield, Connecticut. In 1981, at age 45, he was named General

Technical skill.
The knowledge and ability necessary to perform a specific task.

Managers use a combination of technical, conceptual, and human skills to perform managerial functions. This combination got Square D's PowerLogic power monitoring and control system off to a fast start. Established as a separate venture, once the system was announced and released for production, products were shipped within 12 months.

Electric's chief executive. At each stage in Welch's meteoric career, the importance of his technical skill diminished as he took on larger and larger management roles and became less involved in actual engineering.

Human skill is the ability to work with other people effectively. The other people involved may be subordinates, peers, superiors, clients, and so on. Human skill is a vital part of virtually everything a manager does and, thus, as shown in Figure

Human skill.
The ability to work with other people effectively.

FIGURE 1.3 VARIATIONS IN SKILLS NECESSARY AT DIFFERENT MANAGEMENT LEVELS

First-Line Management	Middle Management	Top Management

Conceptual Skills

Human Skills

Technical Skills

Skill

Management Level

1.3, is equally necessary at all management levels. Although Jack Welch is regarded as one of the world's most ruthless managers and, indeed, some of his actions can seem harsh and antagonistic, those who spend time with him tend to like him. He is characterized by associates as a sensitive person who views the world as tough. Unquestionably smart, he is unpretentious, seldom standing on ceremony. Whatever is said, Welch's career and General Electric's success attest to his ability to work with other people effectively.[11]

Conceptual skill is the ability to see an organization as a whole; it includes recognizing how the various jobs in an organization depend on one another and how a change in any one part affects all the others. Conceptual skill involves visualizing the different parts and levels of an organization in relation to its overall objectives, attending to overall organization structure, and monitoring pertinent environmental variables, including economic and technological forces. This skill is obviously critical for top managers. When it comes to conceptual skills, Jack Welch is considered by many to be America's best CEO.[12] His bold and often controversial leadership style is based on imbuing General Electric with one corporate vision. His 1990 letter to stockholders is legendary. In it, he described his ultimate vision for the company. Rather than a huge, multinational conglomerate comprising 13 disparate businesses, he envisions "a boundaryless company." Such a company would draw together all of General Electric's businesses "by sharing ideas, by finding multiple applications for technological advancements, and by moving people across businesses to provide fresh perspectives." Welch, with his unique blend of technical, human, and conceptual skills, remains the standard to which a great many other CEOs aspire.

All managers must have some minimum technical skill, some minimum human skill, and some minimum conceptual skill, but the required mix of these skills usually varies by management level. This explains in part why outstanding managers at one level sometimes are ineffective at the next highest level. They lack the proper skill mix required for a higher level job. That is, for example, they may be technically competent, but lack adequate human or conceptual skills.

Conceptual skill.
The ability to see an organization as a whole.

Square D's managing director of Asia/Pacific operations meets with top managers representing a joint venture partner. The success of such joint ventures invariably requires a delicate mix of technical, human, and conceptual skills.

The hunt for the global manager is on. From Amsterdam to Yokohama, recruiters are looking for a new breed of multilingual, multifaceted executives who can map strategy for the whole world.

One of the biggest challenges of the 1990s will be overcoming a severe shortage of Euromanagers. The problem is not the attitude of available young executives, who are usually quite willing to move to new countries and cities even on short notice. Rather, it is that few organizations—even those characterizing themselves as global—systematically develop international managers by rotating young executives through a series of foreign assignments. Finding and training the best cross-border managers will be crucial to reaping the benefits of the 1990s. To accomplish this, many organizations have turned to executive search firms when they need somebody immediately and have also started to change their traditional organization structures.

According to headhunters, the best cross-border managers started out with U.S. multinationals. The new marketing manager for Cadbury-Schweppes PLC's European operation is Joost Pabst, a Dutchman recruited from Colgate-Palmolive Co. in New York City. Pabst, based in Barcelona, is charged with creating a single image for Schweppes in Europe—that of a classy but popular soft drink. "What sold me on this job was the chance to manage brands Europewide," says Pabst.

Restructuring and market development efforts are driving the recruiting surge as well. In 1989, Whirlpool's acquisition of a 53 percent share of Philips's appliance business left Whirlpool without a manager to run the new unit. After a three-continent search, Jan Prising, a 21-year veteran of Sweden's Electrolux, was lured to the post by a salary and bonuses that could reach $500,000 a year. He now runs Whirlpool's U.S. operations out of an office overlooking Lake Varese in Italy.

Major changes have also occurred at the Paris headquarters of Alcatel. Says human resource manager Paul Claudell, "We don't want French domination." The joint venture of Cie Générale d'Electricité and ITT Corp. includes CGE's telephone businesses and ITT's European operations. The company is out to win a big share of the emerging pan-European market for telecommunications equipment. Of the 120 top managers in Paris, 60 percent are not French. For example, Alcatel's finance department includes managers from Italy, Sweden, Portugal, Holland, and Belgium, all recruited in the last 2 years. The Swede, Harald Bauer, was recruited from a top finance post at a Swedish trading company to become controller for Alcatel's subsidiaries in Scandinavia and part of France. "Having a Swede in this job definitely improves communications," says Bauer. "The management here is still very French and hierarchical. With the mix of nationalities, that should change quickly."

Experience with other organizations is increasingly prized. Thorn EMI, the British music, software, and appliance rental company, transformed a management group accustomed to lifetime employment into a team of entrepreneurs. From 1983 to 1988, the company replaced about 130 of its 150 managers, at least half through executive search. Today, the average top manager has had three previous jobs, versus none 8 years ago. Given international expansion and the need to assign top managers responsibility for more than one country, there is a desperate need for managers who understand foreign markets.

Sources: Shawn Tully, "The Hunt for the Global Manager," *Fortune* May 21, 1990: 140–144; and Lester B. Korn, "How the Next CEO Will Be Different," *Fortune* May 22, 1989: 157–161.

MANAGEMENT 2000

Although management has made tremendous contributions to the development of today's global economy, its potential contributions for the future are even greater. As we approach the coming millennium (year 2000), countries around the world are committed to economic growth and raising the standard of living of their people through the efficient utilization of human and material resources.

Sound management is central to the success of all such efforts. Managers of the future will confront a workplace that is vastly different from today's. Even though 75 percent of the people who will be working in the year 2000 are already on the job, the workforce in 2000 will be significantly different, reflecting a broader age distribution, greater equality of men and women, more cultural diversity, a greater range of educational levels, a greater role for persons with disabilities, and a greater mix of values and attitudes.[13]

Confronted with such a different workplace, leading organizations throughout the world are concerned now more than ever with good management. By 2000, managers will face a more diverse, quicker market. They will inhabit an international marketplace in which they "will have to know how to operate in an any-time, any-place universe."[14] Instant performance will be expected, and hiding incompetence will be next to impossible.

As the workplace changes and the world comes to resemble more a global village than a set of nation-states with relatively secure and permanent boundaries, organizations will need to develop theories and models of managerial behavior that reflect a multicultural world and workforce. In such a world, economic boundaries will be almost as important as political boundaries and structures, and policies will need to accommodate workforce diversity. This will require an increased tolerance for different ways of doing business, an increased need for adaptability, and an increased need for understanding cultural practices.

The increasingly competitive world marketplace will no doubt place a premium on so-called **GEMS**,[15] that is, **g**lobal **e**mployees, **m**obile and **s**killed. Employees who are multinational, multicultural, multilingual, and multidisciplinary will be in great demand. One challenge that all organizations will face is attracting and retaining such employees. In doing so, they will be heeding the demands for global competition.

Clearly, the world will enter the first decade of the twenty-first century very different from today. One purpose of the following chapters is to prepare aspiring managers for the challenges of tomorrow by providing them with the latest knowledge available, to help ensure their future managerial success.

GEMS.
An acronym for global employees, mobile and skilled.

SUMMARY

The intent of this chapter has been to introduce you to the world and functions of management with the hope you will accept the challenge of a managerial career.

Learning Objective 1. Define the term *management*.
Management may be defined as the process of achieving desired results through efficient utilization of human and material resources.

Learning Objective 2. Answer the question: "What is a manager?"
A manager is an individual in an organization who holds a position of authority and makes decisions about the allocation of resources.

Learning Objective 3. Identify and describe the five functions of management.
The functions of management are:

1. *Planning*—the process of establishing goals and selecting a future course of action for their accomplishment.
2. *Organizing*—the process of dividing work among groups and individuals and coordinating their activities to accomplish goals. Organizing also involves establishing managerial authority.
3. *Staffing and human resource management*—the process of ensuring that competent employees are selected, developed, and rewarded for accomplishing goals.
4. *Leading and interpersonal influence*—the process of inducing individuals (peers, superiors, subordinates, and nonsubordinates) or groups to assist willingly and harmoniously in accomplishing goals.
5. *Controlling*—the process of ensuring the efficient accomplishment of goals.

Learning Objective 4. Explain what is meant by the phrase "the management process."
The phrase "the management process" is used to refer collectively to the five functions of management.

Learning Objective 5. Understand the duties associated with different levels of management.
The duty of first-line management is to influence the way work is performed. The duty of middle management is to integrate the activities of different work groups so they operate in harmony with one another and are better able to cope with the demands made upon them. The duty of top management is to determine the form of an organization and define its overall character, mission, and direction.

Learning Objective 6. List the roles that a typical top manager performs.
A typical top manager performs ten different but highly interrelated roles. These roles can be separated into three basic groupings: interpersonal roles (figurehead, leader, liaison), informational roles (monitor, disseminator, spokesperson), and decisional roles (entrepreneur, disturbance handler, resource allocator, negotiator).

Learning Objective 7. Identify the three essential skills used by all managers.
In general, managers use three essential skills—technical, human, and conceptual.

Learning Objective 8. Know the meaning of the acronym GEMS.
GEMS is an acronym for Global Employees, Mobile and Skilled.

KEY TERMS

conceptual skill 18

controlling 6

first-line managers 9

GEMS 20

human skill 17

leading and interpersonal
  influence 6

management 4

managers 5

management process 7

middle managers 10

organizing 6

planning 6

staffing and human resource
  management 6

technical skills 16

top managers 12

REVIEW AND DISCUSSION QUESTIONS

1. Give your own definition of management. Based on your personal observations, identify four managerial positions and give practical examples of how
   each involves the five functions of management.

2. Assume you are a vice-president of a major *Fortune* 500 company who has
   been asked to address a class of college juniors. What would you tell them
   about the significance of management?

3. You are a first-line manager in a large manufacturing plant. Describe your typical workday. How do you spend most of your time? With whom? What
   changes do you anticipate in your job over the next decade?

4. You have just been promoted from program manager to division director in a
   federal agency. In what ways would you expect your workday to differ as you
   move from first-line to middle management?

5. Many top managers in today's society have achieved almost celebrity status.
   Drawing on your general understanding of the business world, give examples
   of how corporate celebrities such as Lee A. Iacocca (former chairman,
   Chrysler Motors), R. E. "Ted" Turner III (president and chairman, Turner Broad-
   casting System), and Victor K. Kiam II (chairman, Remington Products) perform the ten top management roles identified in this chapter.

6. Describe and compare the technical, human, and conceptual skills required
   for the four managerial positions you identified in response to Question 1.

THE MANAGEMENT EXPERIENCE DO YOU NEED A CAREER COUNSELOR?

Career counseling is the process of helping individuals identify their personal values and uncover their career assets and liabilities. Respond to the items below to determine if you need
a career counselor. For each item, decide which of the following answers best describes you
and how you feel. Place the number in the box to the left of the item for the appropriate response:

1. Always   2. Usually   3. Sometimes   4. Rarely   5. Never

1. ☐ I can identify my best skills.
2. ☐ Lack of ackncwledgment of my abilities makes me try harder.
3. ☐ I participate in a number of activities, both at and away from my work environment.
4. ☐ I investigate new concepts in my field and closely related fields and try to learn all I can about
   them.

Continued on next page.

5. ☐ I am aware of skills that I possess that I haven't yet used.
6. ☐ Negative feedback causes me to slow down or stop participating.
7. ☐ I often become so engrossed in what I am doing that I lose track of time.
8. ☐ I set my goals a little higher than other people do.
9. ☐ I want to improve or build on my skills.
10. ☐ It is difficult for me to put mistakes behind me and go on to new business.
11. ☐ I believe I should be rewarded when I do a good job.
12. ☐ I plan my career and set goals to achieve my plan.
13. ☐ I know I am able to successfully develop new skills.
14. ☐ I question the validity or motivation of most work-related compliments.
15. ☐ When I fail to accomplish an assigned task, I believe my supervisor/manager has the right to reprimand me.
16. ☐ I review my accomplishment of personal goals periodically.

Total your responses: _____

What Your Score Means

16–45   You possess the basic knowledge and habits to succeed. If these are correctly applied, along with a good program of networking, success will follow.

46–58   You possess some knowledge of and ability for career success; however, they are not fully developed. An influential and skilled mentor, along with a good networking program, will provide a solid foundation for success. If no capable and successful guide is at hand, career counseling should be utilized as a substitute. Without career counseling, undue stress as well as a "spinning wheels" syndrome may occur.

59–64   Career counseling recommended. Your skills are insufficient for career success. There is more to being promoted than working harder and being smarter. (And we are not speaking about being manipulative or conniving.) Counseling can provide the necessary answers.

65–80   Definite improvement is required if career success is important. Career counseling is a must.

Source: Strategies for Rewarding Careers, New York; Shirley A. McArthur & Melvin S. Roy, Cofounders.

CASE 1.1   MAKING IT: THE EASY WAY

Richard Smith eased into his chair hoping to find respite from the tension that had become his steady companion. To his disappointment, home offered no sanctuary from unpleasant reality. His bank was in trouble. What a few years ago had been one of the fastest growing banks in the nation now stood on the precipice. He mused on the previous month's events: the anger of the stockholders at their last meeting, the rumors that the directors were looking for a "sacrificial lamb," and the slights received from his colleagues. Even his personal secretary seemed to behave as if his future were a foregone conclusion. He wondered why he had been singled out. Although a supporter of the policy currently under attack, he had not made the final decision. Was he to be made the scapegoat for the bad judgment of others? Was it his fault that the economy had taken an unexpected downturn? As his indignation mounted, he erupted. "They seem to think I manufactured this recession," he shouted. As his composure slowly returned, he continued to brood over his now uncertain future.

Mr. Smith's Career

Mr. Smith started his career in banking as a clerk in an obscure branch of a large regional bank in New England. Although he possessed only a high school education, he was considered very bright and ambitious by his superiors. This was made evident by his rapid promotion to assistant manager of a larger branch.

One of Mr. Smith's traits was the premium he placed on knowing the right people. While assistant manager he had many opportunities to speak with the bank's regional manager. Mr. Smith never failed to take advantage of all such meetings. It was at these times that he was at his charming best with compliments flowing freely. On occasion, the branch manager would be taken aback by the lack of subtlety of this flattery. However, he said nothing to Mr. Smith about it.

It became obvious that Mr. Smith's strategy was successful when, on one visit, the regional manager asked him to be his partner in a golf match with two other officers of the bank. This was the first of many such social meetings with superiors. Mr. Smith made every attempt at these gatherings to be introduced to as many executives of the bank as possible. Almost all grew to like Mr. Smith because of his energy and spontaneous wit. More than one executive referred to him as a "comer" or a "boy with a future." Mr. Smith fully appreciated the value of these contacts, and many later served him in good stead by way of recommendations for promotion.

While assistant manager, Mr. Smith was involved in an incident that might have damaged his otherwise promising career. A new teller, Regina Jones, had come to him asking for the key to the vault. A regular patron, Mrs. Peters, had come to cash a $5,000 check made out to cash. Mrs. Peters was the secretary of a local restaurant owner, Mr. Unger, and frequently drew money from the owner's large account for business purposes. Mrs. Jones matched the signature on the check to the file signature of Mr. Unger. Although they were alike, Mrs. Jones could not cash the check because she was a new teller and therefore had a limited amount of cash in her till. It was then that she approached Mr. Smith to get additional cash from the vault. After checking to see if it truly was the said patron, whom he was familiar with, Mr. Smith gave her the key and resumed his duties.

It was not many days later that the investigation began. The restaurant owner had claimed that the check had been stolen and the signature forged. Since his secretary had disappeared, it was suspected that she had indeed stolen and forged the check and thereafter left town. Insurance investigators soon arrived to question all parties involved. Mrs. Jones explained what had transpired and was confident that her story would be corroborated. Mr. Smith, however, explained that he did not recall Mrs. Jones ever coming to him about the matter. Furthermore, he stated he was unfamiliar with the secretary in question and had previously chided the teller for lack of concern for bank policy. He confided to the investigator, "She's been a problem ever since she got here. I don't know how we've put up with her this long." The investigator interviewed other employees and Mr. Smith's superior, but none could shed light on what had actually occurred. Although the testimony was contradictory, Mr. Smith's superiors believed his explanation. In light of this incident and the unfavorable evaluation it produced, Mrs. Jones's relationship with the bank was terminated at the end of her probationary period.

As he advanced in his career, Mr. Smith often reflected on this incident. Although he felt a certain amount of guilt for his actions, he believed it was the type of decision one had to make to get ahead in a tough competitive world.

Mr. Smith held the position of assistant manager for a relatively brief period before he was again promoted. This time he would be the manager of his own branch. He continued to gain popularity among bank officers throughout this time. Much time was spent mingling with executives who would normally consider it an affront to their sense of protocol to socialize with a low-level manager.

Mr. Smith's rise in the bank was becoming meteoric. After a transfer to another branch, he was given responsibility for a district that included several branches. Within 5 years he held the post of assistant vice-president, and this promotion was followed 4 years later by a vice-president's chair. Throughout his climb up the management pyramid, Mr. Smith had counted on and received the aid and support of his influential friends. Finally, he was nearing the top. It had taken the former clerk a mere 14 years to achieve what he had strived for.

After having held a vice-presidency for 2 years, Mr. Smith was sought after for his views on a proposal being considered by the bank's top management. In recent years, competitors had been expanding more rapidly than Mr. Smith's bank. The change of policy being considered would involve seeking a higher volume of loans even though it might mean accepting a higher degree of risk. The bank's policy had always been to accept only the most creditworthy applicants. Mr. Smith sincerely believed this proposal was the type of measure needed if the bank was to meet the growth rates of competitors. He endorsed the proposal and could be counted on to advocate it when asked at meetings. Through the limited efforts of Mr. Smith and its other backers, a final decision was reached accepting the new strategy.

A few years later, a recession struck the United States. It became apparent that the growth policy had been too risky when many of the bank's customers defaulted on their loans. The easy credit strategy had led to a large volume of shaky loans to poor credit risks. As the recession deepened, the bank's financial position began to deteriorate, and there was speculation from many sources that insolvency was a possibility that could not be ruled out if firm corrective action was not undertaken soon. The price of the bank's stock began a fall that appalled stockholders. On the eve of the annual stockholder's meeting, the board of directors met to discuss the details of the program of corrective action to be outlined to the stockholders. One of the items was the elimination of one or all of the officers most directly responsible for the current crisis. They agreed that executives whose past performance was excellent should not be terminated if this had been their only serious error in judgment. On the other hand, officers without solid records of achievement in their present positions would be given a different sort of consideration. It was felt that this action would appease the stockholders and help to rebuild confidence in the bank.

Problems

1. Is Smith successful?

2. Do you believe that Smith's behavior is typical executive behavior?

3. "If I had to do what Smith did to get ahead, I'd rather not get ahead." Comment.

4. Do the Smiths of the world make their organizations more effective or less effective?

Source: Francis A. Yeandel,
St. Mary's College, Notre Dame,
Indiana.

NOTES

[1] Peter F. Drucker, *Management: Tasks, Responsibilities, Practices* (New York: Harper, 1974) 10; Peter F. Drucker, "Management and the World's Work," *Harvard Business Review* 66 (September–October 1988): 65.

[2] Drucker, "Management and the World's Work," 65.

[3] Ibid.: 66.

[4] Henry Mintzberg, "The Manager's Job: Folklore and Fact," *Harvard Business Review* 53 (July–August 1975): 61.

[5] Nell P. Eurich, *Corporate Classrooms: The Learning Business* (Princeton, NJ: The Carnegie Foundation for the Advancement of Learning, 1985) 7.

[6] Adapted from Robert H. Guest, "Of Time and the Foreman," *Personnel* 32 (May 1956): 480.

[7] Based on John P. Kotter, "What Effective General Managers Really Do," *Harvard Business Review* 60 (November–December 1982): 156–167; Carol Hymowitz, "Day in the Life of Tomorrow's Manager," *Wall Street Journal* March 20, 1989, B1; Patrick Houston, "48 Hours on the Job," *Business Month* 134 (September 1990): 42–49.

[8] Henry Mintzberg, *The Nature of Managerial Work* (New York: Harper & Row, 1973) 54–99.

[9] Robert L. Katz, "Skills of an Effective Administrator," *Harvard Business Review* 33 (January–February 1955): 33–42.

[10] This section draws on Stratford P. Sherman, "The Mind of Jack Welch," *Fortune* March 27, 1989: 38–50.

[11] Ibid.

[12] This section draws on Tracy E. Benson, "America's Best CEO," *Industry Week* December 2, 1991: 28–41.

[13] Nancy J. Perry, "Workers of the Future," *Fortune* (Spring/Summer 1991): 68–72.

[14] Stanley Davis, quoted in Carol Hymowitz, "Day in the Life of Tomorrow's Manager," *Wall Street Journal* March 20, 1989: B1.

[15] "Investing in GEMS," *HR Magazine* 36 (January 1991): 36–37.

CHAPTER 2

LEARNING OBJECTIVES

Upon completing this chapter, you should be able to:

- Describe what is known today as the Industrial Revolution.
- Discuss the milestone most frequently referred to as the beginning of the search for a science of management.
- Recount Frederick W. Taylor's contributions to the scientific-management movement.
- Relate Frank B. and Lillian M. Gilbreth's quest for the "one best way."
- Explain why Henri Fayol is known as the "Father of Modern Management."
- Set forth the advantages and disadvantages of Max Weber's bureaucracy.
- Give an account of the nature and contributions of the Hawthorne Studies.
- Demonstrate an understanding of the systems approach to management.
- Characterize the contingency approach to management.
- Describe the quality improvement movement.

he Great Pyramid of Pharaoh Cheops at Giza rises in breathtaking geometrical symmetry from the edge of the Sahara Desert. More than 4,500 years after it was built, this awesome structure remains one of the great wonders of the world. Architecturally, it is nearly perfect. The southeast corner of the 13-acre tomb is only half an inch higher than the northwest corner. Astronomically, it is also close to exact. Each side is oriented almost precisely in line with true north, south, east, and west. But perhaps more than any other aspect, the managerial skills required to build such a vast monument with primitive tools is what truly staggers the modern mind.

It has been estimated that it took 100,000 men nearly 30 years to build the structure. Among them were architects, astronomers, stone-cutters, masons, surveyors, mortar makers, carpenters, and thousands of slaves who worked 12 hours a day in the broiling Egyptian sun.

During construction, workers quarried, hauled, and set in place 2,300,000 separate blocks, each weighing an average of 2½ tons, at the rate of 36 stones an hour. And all of this was done using only levers, rollers, and vast embankments of soil to reach the top. There were no cranes, steam engines, or even oxen to pull the giant blocks. No wonder several Western experts on ancient Egyptian building methods have flatly stated that the rulers of the Old Kingdom were "the best organizers of human labor the world has ever seen."[1]

THE EVOLUTION OF MANAGEMENT THOUGHT

Early examples of management brilliance are not confined to the Egyptians. Alexander the Great had to be at least as good a manager as a military tactician to achieve his vast empire. The Great Wall of China is a testament to managerial skills as well as engineering prowess. And the founders of the early Roman Catholic Church combined keen managerial abilities with a compelling spiritual message to successfully spread their faith across continents.

But while many of the ideas first proposed by early management greats persist in modern theory and practice, most historians generally date the initial attempts at systematically studying the development of managerial skills to the last two decades of the nineteenth century. This interest paralleled the growing economic and industrial development of the United States and Western Europe as major manufacturing centers. Expanding technology and commerce, paired with advances in transportation and communication, had dramatically increased the scope and complexity of business ventures. For the first time, problems of managing large-scale enterprises became widespread as industrial and commercial undertakings began to replace individual proprietors and partnerships as the usual forms of business. An unprecedented increase in the size of production facilities resulted in problems of waste and inefficiency that never had been encountered. These problems necessitated the formulation and investigation of new concepts for managing work.

This chapter describes the historical development of management theory and practice. A detailed history of management thought would require a separate volume.[2] Hence, the primary focus of this chapter will be on the evolution of management thought since the late 1800s. The discussion will follow the historical sequence shown in Figure 2.1.

Great Pyramid at Giza

FIGURE 2.1   MAJOR MOVEMENTS IN THE EVOLUTION OF MANAGEMENT THOUGHT

PRESCIENTIFIC MANAGEMENT (1776–1886)

THE INDUSTRIAL REVOLUTION

The seeds of the modern industrial corporation—the forerunner of today's *Fortune 500* company—were sown in Great Britain in the late 1700s.[3] At about the time of the American Revolution, another revolution was taking place in the practice and management of work. The **Industrial Revolution,** as we call it today, resulted from a series of events that occurred in a relatively short period of time. It is perhaps best dated with the year 1776, a time that marks the birth of American democracy and publication of Adam Smith's *The Wealth of Nations.*

The Industrial Revolution was a historical milestone often compared to the mastery of fire and the advent of agriculture. It added a massive output potential to the productive power of humans and domestic animals. The basic change was the transfer of work skills from craftworkers to machines. Before the Industrial Revolution, skilled work was performed by craftworkers who, aided by relatively simple tools, produced an entire good, such as a watch, a pair of shoes, or a gun. These workers sold their goods directly to individual consumers. The Industrial Revolution changed this pattern, which had endured for centuries. New inventions—James Watt's steam engine (1765); Richard Arkwright's "water frame" (1769), which automated textile manufacturing; and Edmund Cartwright's power loom (1785), among others—required only an unskilled operator to feed them material and remove finished parts. Eventually, automated machines were developed that made even an operator unnecessary. These new inventions resulted in an enormous increase in productivity and, subsequently, lower prices. As prices dropped, consumption grew. The cycle of modern capitalism was soon underway. The outcome

Industrial Revolution.

A rapid major economic change occurring around 1776, marking the transfer of work skills from craftworkers to machines.

was phenomenal. In the United States, the railroads were the first industry to feel the resulting need for improved management. Between 1860 and 1910, the number of miles of railroad track in use jumped from 30,626 to 266,185—an increase of 769 percent. By 1890 railroads employed some 750,000 workers.

As the railroads moved west, the nation was soon bound coast-to-coast by a web of steel rails and a network of telegraph lines. By 1866 an underwater telegraph cable brought Europe and the United States minutes rather than months apart. These and other developments in transportation and communication opened new world markets and, together with new production processes, prompted further economic growth. Previously, the only large organizations around were the Catholic Church and various national armies. Not surprisingly, the command-and-control structure common to both had become the model for entrepreneurs building transcontinental railroads, steel mills, banks, and oil companies. As industrial and commercial undertakings expanded in order to capitalize upon the new markets and production processes, it became readily evident that their size and complexity required improved managerial methods.

Many of today's industrial giants can trace their origins to this period. In 1873 Andrew Carnegie began what was to become United States Steel (now USX). In 1879 John D. Rockefeller, Sr., established Standard Oil Company. Henry Ford, Sr., formed Ford Motor Company in 1903, and William C. Durant combined Buick, Oldsmobile, and Cadillac with some 20 other automobile companies to form General Motors between 1908 and 1910. As these and other industrial empires developed, the nature of modern management was further changed.

One way to appreciate the tremendous social impact of the shift to industrialism is to consider life before and after the Industrial Revolution. Numerous institutions we today accept as "given" were products of the transition to an industrial economy. Examples include

> The workday with fixed times (instead of working with the sun), not living at work (on the farm or above the store) and the concomitant commuting, urbanization and suburbanization, large corporations into which capital could be pooled to afford expensive machinery, large bureaucracies required to manage these behemoths of industry, and the mass employment and trade unionism they created.[4]

None of these phenomena existed before the Industrial Revolution.

HENRY R. TOWNE: A SECOND MILESTONE

Truly revolutionary ideas often sound surprisingly self-evident a few decades after they are first proposed. We laugh today to think that people once found such ideas as washing one's hands before surgery a major breakthrough. The thought that management was a subject worthy of study was also considered revolutionary in the late 1800s. It was commonly believed by owners and managers of the day that their knowledge was unique to certain tasks and specific industries. In other words, knowledge was to be passed on more through experience and tradition than by formal study.

The man who first challenged this idea was Henry R. Towne, co-founder and president of Yale & Towne Manufacturing Company. In 1886 he presented a paper called "The Engineer as an Economist" at a meeting of the American Society of

Mechanical Engineers (ASME).[5] In the paper he argued that management as a field of study was equal in importance to engineering. He observed that the management of work was often wholly unorganized, had no medium for the exchange of experience, and was without professional associations. He urged the ASME to "remedy" this situation. Towne's paper is the milestone most frequently referred to as the beginning of a search for a science of management.

ASME president in 1889 and 1890, and co-founder of the Chamber of Commerce of the United States, Towne had far-reaching influence. He was unique in possessing a rare combination of engineering ability and managerial capacity. His ASME paper was significant as an appeal for the acknowledgment and nurturing of management as a science. In the years after his presentation, the ASME was a central forum for the discussion of managerial challenges and engineers were the first to search for potential solutions. For this reason, engineering is known as the "mother discipline" of management.

Henry R. Towne

SCIENTIFIC MANAGEMENT (1898–PRESENT)

FREDERICK W. TAYLOR: "FATHER OF SCIENTIFIC MANAGEMENT"

While Towne's presentation is recognized as marking the beginning of the search for a science of management, the birth of **scientific management** is generally credited to Frederick W. Taylor (1856–1915). A native of Germantown, Pennsylvania, Taylor came from a well-to-do family. After receiving a liberal arts education in Europe and the United States, he passed the Harvard University entrance exams with honors. Poor eyesight, however, forced him to abandon further study. Consequently, at the age of 18 he began an apprenticeship as a machinist and pattern maker for the Enterprise Hydraulic Works, a Philadelphia pump manufacturing company. During his second year, he earned $1.50 a week. By his third, he was pocketing $2.50 a week, and by his fourth, he was commanding the princely sum of $3.00 a week. This initiation was not unusual. Upper-class Philadelphians had long been educated in this manner. It was an accepted means for developing elite mechanical engineers. Through his experience, Taylor received not only excellent preparation but also a strong professional orientation.

Throughout history, it was taken as self-evident that workers could produce more only by working harder or longer. As we will see, Taylor did what few people in history had done before, that is, apply scientific principles to the study of work. In doing so, Taylor showed that the real potential for increased output was not "working harder" but "working smarter."

Taylor at Midvale

In 1878, having completed his apprenticeship, Taylor joined the Midvale Steel Company, which specialized in the manufacture of locomotive wheels and railway axles. Because business was poor and skilled labor not in demand, he took a job as a shop laborer. Over the next few years, he rose from time clerk to foreman of a machine shop. Having been a common laborer himself, Taylor quickly realized that output was unnecessarily low. The reason for this was a practice called **soldiering,** whereby workers deliberately worked as slowly as they dare, while at the same time

Scientific management.
An approach to management pioneered by Frederick W. Taylor.

Frederick W. Taylor

Soldiering.
Working slowly while at the same time trying to make it appear that one is working fast.

trying to make their bosses believe they were working fast. The workers feared that if they worked faster, they would complete their jobs and be laid off. Management was unaware of the practice, since no one had ever bothered to find out how much a worker should be able to produce in a day.

At first Taylor tried to increase production the way any foreman of his day would: through force. A bitter struggle between Taylor and his men resulted. After 3 years, Taylor won, but he was quite disillusioned. Consequently, shortly after becoming chief engineer, he sought a new approach that would make the interests of labor and management the same, rather than antagonistic. Taylor was present at Towne's address and had been impressed with his insights regarding management. As an engineer, Taylor saw that a business is a system of human cooperation that will be successful only if all concerned work toward a common goal.[6] To this end, Taylor called for a "mental revolution" where "both sides take their eyes off the division of the surplus . . . and together turn their attention toward increasing the size of the surplus."[7] Thus, as envisioned by Taylor, the concerns of labor and management should be based on a "mutuality of interests." In brief, he advocated a congruency between the goals of employee and employer. In his words: "It is safe to say that no system or scheme of management should be considered which does not in the long run give satisfaction to both employer and employee, which does not make it apparent that their best interests are mutual, and which does not bring about such thorough and hearty cooperation that they can pull together instead of apart."[8]

Taylor set out to develop a system at Midvale that would meet this ideal. He soon concluded that the problems at the plant were due to ignorance on both sides. Management expected and workers were ready to provide "a fair day's work" for "a fair day's pay." Neither side, however, knew what constituted a day's work. Both relied on tradition and vague impressions that led to continuing disputes.

In an effort to resolve this dilemma, Taylor secured permission to conduct a "scientific study of the time required to do various kinds of work."[9] His idea was to replace guesswork and rule-of-thumb with exact knowledge about every step in the production process. As Taylor explained, "In these experiments we were not trying to find the maximum work that a man could do on a short spurt or for a few days, but . . . our endeavor was to learn what really constituted a full day's work for a first-class man; the best day's work that a man could properly do year in and year out, and still thrive."[10] Since **time study** was the heart of this work, the stopwatch quickly became the popular symbol of Taylor's system. With a stopwatch, weight scale, and tape, he literally measured the distances that men and materials traveled. Gradually, he determined that a large share of both effort and materials was needlessly wasted because of improper management. Through changes he recommended, the time needed to perform various jobs was greatly reduced.

As developed by Taylor, these time studies involved two stages: analysis and synthesis. In *analysis*, a job was divided into its elementary movements. Nonessential elements were discarded and the remainder carefully examined to determine the quickest and least wasteful means of performing the job. These elementary motions were then described, recorded, and indexed, along with the percentages required to cover unavoidable delays, minor accidents, and rest. In the second stage, *synthesis*, the elementary movements were combined in the correct sequence to determine the time and the exact method for performing the job. This information was then presented to the relevant employees in the form of a card with written instructions that left little to their discretion.[11]

Time study.

The study of the time necessary to perform a task.

Taylor at Bethlehem Steel

In 1898 Taylor was hired as a consultant by the Bethlehem Iron (later Steel) Company in Bethlehem, Pennsylvania. It was here that the two most famous applications of his new time study took place. They involved loading pig iron and shoveling iron ore.

Bethlehem Steel pig-iron handlers were among the first beneficiaries of Frederick W. Taylor's work-method studies.

The Pig-Iron Handlers One of Taylor's first assignments at Bethlehem was to improve the work methods of 75 pig-iron handlers—a crew of men who loaded 92-pound pigs (iron blocks) onto railroad cars. Taylor was told that these men, who loaded about 12½ long tons (2,240 pounds = a long ton) a day, "were steady workers, but slow and phlegmatic, and that nothing would induce them to work fast." Taylor, very much impressed by the sheer physical drudgery of the work, was challenged. It was the job of each worker to pick up a pig, walk up an inclined plank, and load it on a flat-bottom railroad car. Assisted by mathematician Carl G. Barth, Taylor studied the pig-iron handlers for several days and concluded that with proper, less-fatiguing methods, a first-class worker could load 47–48 long tons per day—about four times the average. At first Taylor and Barth were so surprised at this that they reran their calculations. They discovered what Taylor called the **law of heavy laboring,** meaning that fatigue is cumulative. With a heavy load, a person's muscles tend to deteriorate in a rapid and cumulative fashion. The only remedy is to ensure that the person takes frequent rest periods.

Law of heavy laboring.
Fatigue is cumulative.

To introduce his method, Taylor developed an incentive piece-rate pay system, which would enable first-class workers who met the 47½-long-ton standard to increase their wages from $1.15 a day to $1.85 (1992 equivalent of $1.85 = $21.05). The man Taylor selected for the first test run was a Pennsylvania Dutchman fictitiously called "Schmidt" (his real name was Henry Noll, and he was 27 years old, 5 feet 7 inches tall, and weighed 135 pounds). Taylor challenged Schmidt to be a "high-priced man" who earned $1.85 a day. Schmidt accepted the challenge. He loaded the pigs exactly as instructed, earned $1.85, and illustrated the virtue of Taylor's methods. The net result of introducing Taylor's system at Bethlehem is summarized in Table 2.1.

TABLE 2.1 RELATIVE COST OF PIG-IRON HANDLING BEFORE AND AFTER INTRODUCING TAYLOR'S SYSTEM AT BETHLEHEM STEEL COMPANY, 1899		
	Before	**After**
Long tons loaded per day, per worker	12½	47½
Average wage per day, per worker	$1.15	$1.85
Average labor cost per long ton	9.2¢	3.9¢
Net savings in labor cost per long ton	—	5.3¢

The Optimum Shovel Taylor then went on to tackle the problem of shoveling at Bethlehem—a task that he wryly described as "a great science compared with pig-iron handling." Operation of the three blast furnaces and seven large open-hearth furnaces required a steady intake of raw materials—sand, limestone, coke, rice coal, iron ore, and so forth. Depending on the season, 400–600 men were employed as shovelers in the 2-mile-long and half-mile-wide Bethlehem yard. Taylor noted that the shovelers were organized into work gangs of 50–60 men under the direction of a single foreman. Each owned his own shovel and used it to shovel whatever he was assigned.

Starting with a "first-class" man, Taylor began a study to determine what shovel-load enabled a worker to move the most material in a day. This was established by varying the weight of the load and keeping records of the results. Taylor's analysis revealed that a shovel-load (depending on the shovel and substance shoveled) varied in weight from 3½ to 38 pounds, and that a shovel-load of 21½ pounds yielded the maximum day's work. As a result, instead of permitting workers to use the same shovel regardless of the material they were handling, Taylor designed new shovels so that for each substance being shoveled the load would equal 21½ pounds.

As a consequence of Taylor's findings, a toolroom was established, and every morning the shovelers were given written instructions stating what tools they would need for the day's work. The material handled by each man was measured at day's end, and a bonus was paid depending upon the tonnage handled. As a result of this new system, the number of shovelers was reduced to 140, average output increased from 16 to 59 tons, average daily wages increased from $1.15 to $1.88, and the average labor cost per long ton dropped from 7.2¢ to 3.2¢. These results are summarized in Table 2.2.

TABLE 2.2 RELATIVE COST OF SHOVELING BEFORE AND AFTER INTRODUCING TAYLOR'S SYSTEM AT BETHLEHEM STEEL COMPANY, 1899		
	Before	**After**
Number of shovelers	400–600	140
Long tons shoveled per day, per worker	16	59
Average wage per day, per worker	$1.15	$1.88
Average labor cost per long ton	7.1¢	3.2¢
Net savings in labor cost per long ton	—	4¢

SMART MANAGEMENT   "SPEEDY" TAYLOR

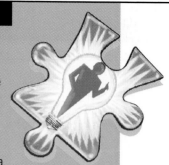

Fred Taylor's ingrained dislike of inefficiency is well known. Less well known is that "Speedy" Taylor, as he was nicknamed by his teammates, applied his zest for efficiency to sports. An accomplished tennis player, he and his brother-in-law, Clarence M. Clark, won the first U.S. Men's National Doubles Championship at Newport, Rhode Island, in 1881. While Taylor's success at tennis was doubtless attributed to his skill, his penchant for improvements was obvious in the spoon-handle racquet he devised and habitually used. Taylor was also known as a golf "fiend." Attacking the golf course with the same scientific vigor with which he attacked other challenges, he designed his own golf clubs. Of particular note was a Y-shaped putter of his own invention. His first love among sports, however, was baseball. He was captain and a starting pitcher on the baseball team at Phillips Exeter Academy. Convinced that the underhand delivery used by pitchers of the day was inefficient, he used the overhand pitch in one of his games. The umpires complained that overhand pitching was not in the rules. He answered that it got results. Taylor's team won the game and baseball was thereafter improved—all because "Speedy" could not tolerate the inefficient underhand motion.

Source: John Dos Passos, *The Big Money* (New York: Harcourt, Brace, 1936), 20.

Taylor's Y-shaped putter

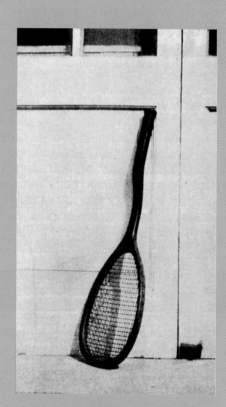

Taylor's spoon-handle racquet

Taylor and the Eastern Rate Case

Although the groundwork of Taylor's system had been laid for several years, it was not until 1910 that it began to receive widespread publicity. At that time, rate hearings were being held to determine if a number of eastern railroads should be allowed to raise their freight charges. Louis D. Brandeis (later a Supreme Court justice), who was counsel for the opposition, coined the term *scientific management* to describe the principles and philosophy of Taylor's work.[12]

It was Brandeis's strategy to prove by expert testimony that the railroads, by adopting the methods of scientific management, could not only considerably reduce their costs but could also increase wages without increasing rates.[13] To this end, Brandeis presented 11 expert witnesses, including Henry R. Towne, Henry L. Gantt, Carl G. Barth, Frank B. Gilbreth, and Harrington Emerson, who testified for almost 3 days. The high point of the hearings was reached with Emerson's testimony that the railroads could save $300 million a year (equivalent to over $11 million a day in today's dollars) through the application of scientific management.[14]

Within 24 hours, scientific management, previously an obscure technology developed by a relatively unknown engineer, became international news. Although Taylor had not testified, most of Brandeis's witnesses acknowledged him as their teacher. Taylor became a national hero overnight. Newspapers and magazines published dozens of articles about his work. This publicity and the publication of Taylor's book, *The Principles of Scientific Management,* in 1911 gave a new impetus to the campaign for efficiency. Within 2 years of publication, it was translated into French, German, Dutch, Swedish, Russian, Italian, Spanish, and Japanese.

Conferences were held and societies formed to study Taylor's work. Taylor's book became known throughout the world, and even Vladimir I. Lenin urged Russian workers to put scientific management into effect to increase production.[15] Indeed, in preparing their first Five-Year Plan during the mid-1920s, the leaders of the former Soviet Union applied scientific management techniques on a national scale in an attempt to revive industrial production.

Watertown and the Congressional Investigation

Not all reactions to the testimony presented in the eastern rate case were positive. Organized labor's response to scientific management was one of intense hostility toward all aspects of time study. Labor leaders characterized Taylor's piece-rate pay system as a return to "sweat shop" exploitation. Since Taylor's more efficient methods often led to layoffs of unnecessary workers, labor feared that widespread adoption of his techniques would lead to loss of jobs. Additionally, organized labor had struggled long and hard to achieve status, and it instinctively assumed that anything new originating in management was for ownership's advantage and labor's disadvantage. Because Taylor firmly believed that his methods were objective, or scientific, he never fully comprehended organized labor's hostility. He tried to counter labor's opposition by stating his support of unions and pointing out that efficient methods such as those he proposed had historically increased employment, not reduced it.

In the summer of 1911 there was a strike at the Watertown (Massachusetts) Arsenal, where scientific management was being introduced by Carl Barth. Trouble erupted when one of Barth's assistants begin stopwatch-timing a group of molders without first, as was Taylor's practice, becoming thoroughly familiar with their work procedures. After the strike ended, workers at the arsenal petitioned Congress to investigate their complaints. Following extended hearings, Congress attached a rider to the 1914–1915 military appropriations bill prohibiting the use of federal funds for "time study with a stopwatch or other time-measuring device." This legislation stayed in effect until 1949. It should be noted that there was never a strike at any factory at which Taylor personally was in charge nor had any workforce operating under his system found it desirable to unionize. Nevertheless, it would be many years before labor and management would share the "mental revolution" that Taylor regarded as the essence of scientific management.

Wizard or Weasel?

Taylor left the Bethlehem Steel Company in 1901 and devoted his remaining life to the promotion of scientific management. His work was, and still remains, revolutionary. In one sense he was a victim of his own success. His ideas aroused much immediate interest and, unfortunately, prompted many imitators who used his name but short-circuited his methods. Undeniably, Taylor was sometimes dogmatic and expressed himself in terms that made him an easy target of contemporary social critics. He once remarked, for example, that the first requirement of a pig-iron handler is that he be so stupid and dull that he resemble an ox, and that an intelligent gorilla, if properly trained, would be better suited to the job. Arguably, his point was intended to illustrate the application of scientific management to menial jobs requiring only physical labor, and to emphasize that there was nothing special about the fact that some men were suited to this kind of job and others were not.[16] But his choice of analogies was less than diplomatic, and such references, understandably, were ill received. On a more sour note, some critics even contend that Taylor falsified his research findings.[17]

The fact remains that the original seed Taylor sowed has spread and multiplied a millionfold. It has spread from the mechanical operations on which he focused at the beginning of his career into activities such as employee selection and training, job design, inventory control, and wage and salary administration. Further, Taylor's efforts began a revolution that enabled industrial workers to earn middle-class wages and achieve middle-class status. Moreover, it is precisely the application of scientific management to the study of work that has enabled many of the world's underdeveloped and poverty-stricken countries—South Korea, for instance, after the Korean conflict—to become world-class competitors within a single generation.

Just as importantly, Taylor's work produced a change in the way managers regarded themselves. The old "rule-of-thumb" and "seat-of-the-pants" images were replaced by "an attitude of questioning, of research, of careful investigation . . . , of seeking for exact knowledge and then shaping action on the discovered facts."[18] Scientific management was to be a tool for greater productivity, greater purchasing power, a higher standard of living. His work struck a responsive chord in a nation intent on achieving economic democracy (mass consumption), through mass production, as well as on conserving its natural resources. Taylor believed that maximum prosperity could result only from maximum productivity and that both poverty and suffering could be diminished by eliminating wasted time and energy.[19] Taylor summarized his work in what have become known as the *four principles of scientific management*. These are listed in Table 2.3 and represent what Taylor conceived to be management's new duties.

Taylor was well aware of the limitations of the scientific knowledge at his disposal. Although he has been severely criticized for ignoring the *human factor*, he

TABLE 2.3 TAYLOR'S FOUR PRINCIPLES OF SCIENTIFIC MANAGEMENT

1. Development of a true science of managing, complete with clearly stated laws, rules, and principles to replace old rule-of-thumb methods.
2. Scientific selection, training, and development of workers; whereas in the past workers were randomly chosen and often untrained.
3. Enthusiastic cooperation with workers to ensure that all work performed is done in accordance with scientific principles.
4. Equal division of tasks and responsibilities between workers and management.

well understood he was dealing with a human problem as well as materials and machines. He readily admitted, "There is another type of scientific investigation . . . which should receive special attention, namely, the accurate study of the motives which influence men."[20] Denouncing Taylor's work for ignoring the intricacies of modern motivation theories is much like attacking Isaac Newton because he failed to invent non-Euclidean geometry or discover the theory of relativity.[21]

In 1915 Taylor went to a hospital in Philadelphia suffering from a nervous breakdown. During his life he had had the habit of winding his watch at exactly 4:30 p.m. On March 21, 1915, the day after his 59th birthday, the attending nurse went to his room at 4:30 p.m. She found him dead with his watch in his hand.[22] The inscription on his tombstone simply reads, "The Father of Scientific Management."

THE GILBRETHS: FINDING THE "ONE BEST WAY"

Frank B. Gilbreth (1868–1924) and his wife Lillian M. (1878–1972) were contemporaries of Fred Taylor and part of the small band of original scientific-management pioneers. Their accomplishments still stand out for their fervor and devotion to a single goal: the elimination of waste and the discovery of the "one best way" of doing work. It was the Gilbreths' contention that of the various ways a particular job could be performed, only one was the best, and it was their job to find it. This ideal became their credo and religion, and they did everything in their power to end the tragedy, as they saw it, of waste going on everywhere. They viewed their quest for the "one best way" as the means by which individuals' personal potential could be maximized with benefit both to themselves and to society.

Although he had passed the entrance exams to the Massachusetts Institute of Technology, young Frank Gilbreth was lured to bricklaying by the impressive pay offered of $3 a day. Gilbreth needed the money and took the job. Trying to learn his new job, he studied how bricklayers worked. He found they performed their task in three ways: They used one set of motions when working deliberately but slowly, a second when working rapidly, and a third when trying to teach their helpers. It was this simple observation that led to the establishment of the first precepts of **motion study.** For, as Gilbreth reasoned, if one set of motions was right, then the other two must be wrong.[23]

Gilbreth was determined to learn to lay bricks the "right" way. At first he was the slowest apprentice on the job, but soon he began developing his own ideas. Designing his own scaffolds and work methods, he cut the motions required to lay a brick from 18 to 6. Within a year he was faster than any of his co-workers. A journeyman was expected to lay 175 bricks an hour. Gilbreth could easily lay 350.

Frank B. Gilbreth

Motion study.
The study of the motions necessary to perform a task.

Several years later, Gilbreth testified before the Interstate Commerce Commission in the eastern rate case. He explained his new science of bricklaying as follows:

> Bricks have been laid the same way for 4,000 years. The first thing a man does is to bend down and pick up a brick. Taylor pointed out that the average brick weighs ten pounds, the average weight of man above his waist is 100 pounds. Instead of bending down and raising this double load, the bricklayer could have an adjustable shelf built so that the bricks would be ready to his hand. A boy could keep these shelves at the right height. When the man gets the brick in his hand, he tests it with his trowel. If anything, this is more stupid than stopping to pick up his material. If the brick is bad he discards it, but in the process it has been carried up perhaps six stories, and must be carted down again. Moreover, it consumes the time of a $5-a-day man when a $6-a-week boy could do the testing on the ground. The next thing the bricklayer does is to turn the brick over to get its face. More waste: more work for the $6 boy. Next what does the bricklayer do? He puts his brick down on the mortar and begins to tap it down with his trowel. What does his tapping do? It gives the brick a little additional weight so it will sink into the mortar. If anything this is more stupid than any of the others. For we know the weight of the brick and it would be a simple matter in industrial physics to have the mortar mixed so that just that weight will press it down into the right layer. And the result? Instead of having eighteen motions in the laying of a brick, we have only six. And the men put on the work to try it lay 2,700 with apparently no more effort than they laid a thousand before.[24]

Nothing Succeeds Like . . .

By 1895 Gilbreth had begun his own construction business in Boston with *speed work* as its motto. He analyzed each job he undertook to eliminate unnecessary motions. In doing so, he devised a system for classifying hand motions into 17 basic divisions called **therbligs** (*Gilbreth* spelled backwards with the *th* transposed).

Before long, Gilbreth's work spread from Maine to New Mexico and from London to Berlin. His reputation for record-setting performances was just as widespread. One of his most famous—and least conventional—practices was to start moving construction materials toward a job site even before a contract was awarded. Then, once the contract was signed, he would startle the public by beginning work within hours. Gilbreth soon became one of the best-known building contractors in the world.

As Gilbreth's ideas gained prominence, they also gained acceptance. Persuaded that a system that was not in writing was unworthy of the name, he set out to put his ideas into book form.[25] Working in conjunction with Lillie, he published *Concrete System* and *Field System* in 1908, and followed with *Bricklaying System* (1909), *Motion Study* (1911), *Fatigue Study* (1916), and *Applied Motion Study* (1917).

As Gilbreth's contacts grew, his interests broadened. Through membership in the ASME, he met Taylor and other leaders of the new scientific-management movement—men like Henry L. Gantt and Harrington Emerson. Gilbreth was one of the few outsiders accepted into the Taylor circle, most members of which were trained by Taylor himself.

And So, into Scientific Management

By 1912 Gilbreth had completely given up the construction business and began devoting full-time efforts to management consulting. With the same single-

Therbligs.
A system for classifying hand motions into 17 basic divisions ("Gilbreth" spelled backwards with the "th" transposed).

minded attention he had given to bricklaying, he now studied the field of scientific management. More and more convinced that "the greatest waste in the world comes from needless, ill-directed, and ineffective motions,"[26] Gilbreth sought new methods of discovering that waste and eliminating it. He was the first person to use motion picture cameras to analyze a worker's motions. In 1915 he put roller skates on messengers in a Montgomery Ward office to reduce their fatigue and increase delivery speed. In another experiment, he observed 150 appendectomies to find the "one best way." In conjunction with Lillie, he authored papers such as "The Application of Scientific Management to the Work of the Nurse," "Motion Study in Surgery," and "Scientific Management in the Hospital." At one point, he even prepared a study of the motions of epileptics. And with the same dedication, he filmed and analyzed the swings of golf champions and baseball players.

Despite the connotations of *speed work,* Gilbreth remained something of an idealist. He went to great lengths to reward workers who had performed well, and he made it a point to develop the skills of those men who worked for him. These efforts were part of his goal of developing employees to their fullest potential. As Gilbreth put it, "We want to find the highest task a man can perform permanently, year after year, and thrive, and be happy. A man wants to do more than get fat; he wants to be happy."[27]

Although Gilbreth had been one of Taylor's most devout disciples, the two became increasingly estranged.[28] This was partially due to problems Gilbreth encountered in applying Taylor's methods, and partially because Gilbreth's innovations made him a competitor with Taylor in the scientific-management movement. Their final break came in 1914 when Gilbreth encountered difficulties implementing the Taylor system at a handkerchief-manufacturing company in New Jersey. Taylor agreed with the company's various charges against Gilbreth and advised his dismissal. In the ensuing years, the Gilbreths went their own way, concentrating their efforts on motion, skill, and fatigue problems.

The First Lady of Management

In his move away from the Taylor system, Gilbreth was increasingly aided by Lillie, who soon became as active a consultant as her husband. She had attended the University of California at Berkeley, majoring in English and modern languages. A Phi Beta Kappa graduate in 1900, she was the first woman to give the university's commencement day address. After receiving an M.A. degree in English literature, she began work toward a Ph.D. degree in psychology. She interrupted her studies in mid-1903 for a trip abroad and, upon arriving in Boston prior to embarking, was introduced to Frank. Shortly after her return from Europe, he proposed marriage and a dozen children, which by his calculations was the most efficient number. Lillie and Frank married in 1904. Lillie completed her Ph.D. degree at Brown University, becoming the first woman in the United States to receive a doctorate in psychology. Her doctoral thesis, one of the first contributions of its kind, was titled "The Psychology of Management." It was published in 1914, but only after she agreed that her name would appear as L. M. Gilbreth and that no publicity would be given to the fact that the author was a woman.[29]

Lillian M. Gilbreth

Lillie fully intended to become a practicing psychologist. However, she soon found she was devoting most of her time to the rearing of her 12 children. The scientific management of the Gilbreth family and their Montclair, New Jersey, home

SMART MANAGEMENT   SCIENTIFIC MANAGEMENT: ALIVE AND WELL IN THE 1990s

Scientific management, Fred Taylor's legacy to the world, is alive and well throughout the corporate world. Indeed, Taylor's search for an answer to the riddle of a fair day's work for a fair day's pay is still a contemporary puzzle. Making every move count is now seen as key to increased efficiency and, thus, competitiveness. Taking their cues from Taylor, the Japanese analyze movements in microseconds and tolerances in fractions of microns. This attention to precision paved the way for computerized manufacturing. In the United States, the spirit of scientific management is perhaps no more evident than at United Parcel Service (UPS).

Every UPS route is timed down to the traffic light. All 62,000 UPS drivers follow a daily routine calibrated to the minute. At regional sorting centers, tasks are meticulously timed. Sorters are expected to load between 500 and 650 packages per hour into delivery vans and unload them almost twice as fast. When drivers leave each day, their superiors usually know within 6 minutes how long pickups and deliveries will take.

As UPS drivers approach each stop, they are trained to shed their seat belt, toot the horn, and cut the engine as they glide to a stop. In one motion, the emergency brake is set and the gearshift placed into first—set for a fast takeoff after delivery. Delivery truck seats have beveled edges for easy dismounting. Drivers are instructed to hold their clipboard under their right arm and packages under the left. Keys, teeth up, are on the middle finger of the right hand. Drivers are allowed one look at each package to memorize the address. They trot to doorways at a prescribed 3 feet per second. Drivers shout "UPS" to announce their presence. Paperwork is completed on the way back to the truck, where a driver's left foot always hits the step first. The routine is always the same.

During a single day, a typical driver will make 145 stops to deliver 246 packages and pick up 70 others. Add 30 seconds on to each stop and the workday suddenly becomes longer by 1 hour and 12 minutes. Multiply that by 62,000 drivers, each with a starting salary of $16 an hour, and the result is a huge wage increase. UPS's mad rush to optimize everything would no doubt make Fred Taylor dance with glee!

Sources: Adapted from Richard B. Chase and David A. Garvin, "The Service Factory," *Harvard Business Review* 67 (July–August 1989): 61–69; Kenneth Labich, "Big Changes at Big Brown," *Fortune*, January 18, 1988, 56–64; Todd Vogel, "Hello, I Must Be Going: On the Road with UPS," *Business Week*, June 4, 1990, 82.

was immortalized in the best-selling books and movies, *Cheaper by the Dozen* and *Bells on Their Toes,* as well as in the later novel, *Time Out for Happiness.*[30]

In 1924 tragedy struck the Gilbreths. Shortly before Frank was to leave to attend the First International Management Congress in Prague, Czechoslovakia, he suffered a heart attack and died while talking to Lillie from a telephone booth at the Montclair railroad station. A family meeting was held, and Lillie decided to fulfill Frank's commitments. She sailed 5 days later and in Prague read the paper he was to have presented, presided at the session he was to have chaired, and was made a member of the Czechoslovakian Masaryk Academy.

Returning to Montclair, Lillie was determined to continue Frank's work. She became president of Gilbreth, Inc., and in the fall of 1924 she joined the faculty at Purdue University as a lecturer. In 1935 she was made a professor of management in the Purdue School of Mechanical Engineering, the first woman to hold such an appointment.

Moving out from under Frank's shadow, Lillie pioneered in the field now known as human resource management. She was keenly interested in the scientific selection, placement, and training of employees. Always progressive in her thinking, she displayed a deep appreciation of the human factor in industry. While much of her work is now taken for granted, it was far in advance of its time. More than 50 years ago, she publicly urged an end to discrimination in both the hiring and retention of workers over 40.[31] Convinced that programs to hire and retain "older" workers were simply "good business," she called for research to measure comparative job performance by age. In the larger public arena, Lillie served under Presidents Hoover, Roosevelt, Eisenhower, Kennedy, and Johnson on committees dealing with civil defense, war production, aging, and rehabilitation of the physically handicapped.

In addition to lecturing throughout the world, Lillie taught at the University of Wisconsin at Madison; Rutgers University at New Brunswick, New Jersey; and Newark College of Engineering. In 1985 she was selected as one of the 100 most important American women of the past 100 years. The recipient of more than 24 honorary degrees, she was the first woman to be named an honorary member of the ASME, as well as the first elected to the National Academy of Engineering.

The Gilbreths were a formidable team. He an engineer and she a psychologist, they pooled their talents in search of the "one best way." Their interests ranged widely. They made contributions to materials handling and work methods, to the study of monotony and fatigue, to the theory of skill transfer, and to modern human resource management. The impact of these contributions continues today. Indeed, the configurations for the crew compartment, crew seats, and instrument panel of the National Aeronautical and Space Administration's Apollo command and service modules were designed using techniques pioneered by Frank and Lillian Gilbreth.

ADMINISTRATIVE MANAGEMENT (1916–PRESENT)

HENRI FAYOL: "FATHER OF MODERN MANAGEMENT"

Henri Fayol (1841–1925) is recognized as the greatest European management pioneer. Although aware of Taylor's theories, he worked independently in France during the same period that scientific management was developing in the United States. Whereas Taylor approached the study of management from the workshop or technical level, Fayol approached it from the viewpoint of upper-level administration. His emphasis on **administrative management** reflected his more than 50 years of experience as an industrial mining executive.

Administrative management.
An approach to management pioneered by Henri Fayol.

Fayol was born near Lyon to an economically lower middle-class family. After training as a mining engineer, he joined the French coal and iron combine, Commentry-Four-chambault.[32] He quickly worked his way up through the ranks to become a manager, general manager, and finally a member of the board of directors until his death in 1925.

Although his training was in engineering, Fayol soon realized that managing an enterprise required skills other than those he had studied. A manager needed to be able to formulate plans, organize plant and equipment, deal with people, and much more. Engineering school had never taught such skills.[33]

In thinking about the problems of a general manager, he concluded that all activities that occur in business undertakings could be divided into six essential groups:

1. Technical (production/manufacturing, adaptation)
2. Commercial (buying, selling, and exchange)
3. Financial (finding and using capital)
4. Security (protection of property and persons)
5. Accounting (stocktaking, balance sheet, costing, statistics)
6. Managerial (planning, organizing, commanding, coordinating, controlling)

Henri Fayol

Fayol held that these six groups of activities are always present in any undertaking—simple or complex, big or small (see Figure 2.2). He noted that the first five were well known, but the sixth—managerial—required further explanation. Fayol was one of the first industrialists to view management as an entity distinct from finance, accounting, marketing, or other business activity. In addition, he is credited with being the first to identify and describe the functions of management (planning, organizing, commanding, coordinating, and controlling) as a process—what we labeled in Chapter 1 (using slightly different terms) the *management process*. Fayol contended that the six groups of activities are interdependent and that it is management's role to ensure the smooth working of all six in order to achieve enterprise goals.

To guide the management process, Fayol formulated 14 principles of management. These are shown in Table 2.4. Recognizing that different situations may require different managerial techniques, he stressed that "there is nothing rigid or absolute in management affairs, it is all a question of proportion. Seldom do we have to apply the same principle twice in identical conditions; allowance must be made for different changing circumstances, for men just as different and changing and for many other variable elements."[34]

FIGURE 2.2 FAYOL'S SIX ESSENTIAL GROUPS OF BUSINESS ACTIVITIES SHOWING THE FIVE FUNCTIONS OF MANAGEMENT

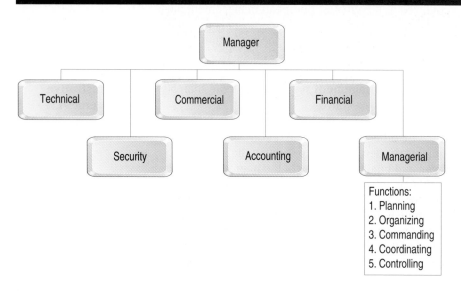

TABLE 2.4 FAYOL'S 14 PRINCIPLES OF MANAGEMENT

1. *Division of Labor.* Work should be divided to permit specialization.
2. *Authority.* Authority and responsibility should be equal.
3. *Discipline.* Discipline is necessary to develop obedience, diligence, energy, and respect.
4. *Unity of Command.* No subordinate should report to more than one superior.
5. *Unity of Direction.* All operations with the same objective should have one manager and one plan.
6. *Subordination of Individual Interest to General Interest.* The interest of one individual or group should not take precedence over the interest of an organization as a whole.
7. *Remuneration.* Rewards for work should be fair.
8. *Centralization.* The proper degree of centralization-decentralization for each undertaking is a matter of proportion.
9. *Scalar Chain.* A clear line of authority should extend from the highest to the lowest level of an organization.
10. *Order.* "A place for everything and everything in its place."
11. *Equity.* Employees should be treated with kindness and justice.
12. *Stability of Tenure of Personnel.* Turnover should be minimized to ensure successful goal accomplishment.
13. *Initiative.* Subordinates should be allowed the freedom to conceive and execute plans in order to develop their capacity to the fullest.
14. *Esprit de Corps.* Harmony and union build organization strength.

Fayol concentrated on the 14 principles he had found most useful in his career as a manager, but he was quick to note that there was nothing sacred about that number, since many other principles could be identified. While many of Fayol's principles are now outdated, we will refer to several such as "unity of command" and "scalar chain" throughout the coming chapters.

Fayol's ideas drew widespread attention after the publication of his paper, "Administration Industrielle et Générale" in 1916. Before long, *Fayolism* became as firmly entrenched in French management thinking as *Taylorism* had become in the United States.[35] In fact, published as a book, his paper soon became known as "a catechism for the chief executive's education."[36] American managers were largely unaware of Fayol's work, however, until it was translated into English in 1930.

The familiar ring of Fayol's ideas suggests how thoroughly they have penetrated current managerial thinking. While many of them may seem relatively self-evident today, they were revolutionary when first advanced. They remain important not only because of his enormous influence on succeeding generations of managers, but also because of the continuing validity of his work. His ideas continue to have a significant impact on managerial thinking. For this reason, Fayol is known as the "Father of Modern Management."

MAX WEBER: BUREAUCRACY AS THE IDEAL

Whereas Taylor's and Fayol's primary attention had been directed toward practical problems of managing for effective goal accomplishment, the concern of Max Weber (1864–1920) was with the more fundamental issue of how organizations are structured. Although Weber (pronounced *Vay-ber*), a German sociologist, published most of his work at the turn of the century, his ideas remained virtually unknown to English-speaking theorists until they began to be translated in the late

1920s.[37] Primarily prescriptive in nature, Weber's writings strike an interesting contrast with the practitioner-oriented recommendations offered by Taylor and Fayol. Weber's major contribution was an outline of the characteristics of what he termed **bureaucracy.**

In reviewing Weber's work, it is important to emphasize four points:

1. Weber did not use the term bureaucracy (that is, government by bureaus) in the disparaging, emotionally tinged sense of red tape, endless lines, and rule-encumbered inefficiency. Rather, he used it as a noncritical label referring to what he regarded as the most modern and efficient method of organizing yet developed. Indeed, what is not often understood is that bureaucracy developed as a reaction against the personal subjugation and cruelty, as well as the capricious and subjective judgments, of earlier administrative systems (such as monarchies and dictatorships) in which the lives and fortunes of all were completely dependent upon the whims of a despot whose only law was his own wish. For this reason, the benefits Weber attributed to bureaucracy can perhaps best be understood when compared to the alternatives it replaced. The world observed by Weber was decidedly unjust. It was dominated by class consciousness and nepotism. To be a military officer or a leader in government or industry presupposed an aristocratic birth. In Weber's view, this was a ridiculous waste of human resources that ran counter to his belief that the working class could produce leaders as well as followers.

2. To Weber, bureaucracy was an ideal that did not exist in reality. Bureaucracy was a standard or model to be used not only in constructing organizations, but also in assessing, through comparison, their relative performance. In this regard his basic model is hypothetical rather than factual. It is not meant to be a working model nor to correspond to reality.

3. Weber's ideal bureaucracy is based on *legal* authority as contrasted with that which rests on either *tradition* (custom) or *charisma* ("the gift of grace"). As developed by Weber, legal authority stems from rules and other controls that govern an organization in the pursuit of specific goals. Managers are given the authority to interpret and enforce these rules and other controls by virtue of their position. Obedience is not owed to a person but to the impersonal authority of an office. Thus, authority adheres to specific positions rather than to individuals. This is necessary if authority is to outlast the tenure of individual officeholders. Familiar examples of legal authority structures are the military, politically elected offices, government bureaus, colleges or universities, and business firms (especially those above a certain size).

4. The need Weber identified for efficient organizing is culture-free. The increasing size of organizations, advanced technology, and modern legal demands combined to make bureaucracy inevitable. Bureaucracy in government has been followed by an increase in the bureaucracy of business corporations, trade unions, churches, service groups, and voluntary associations. Today, all organizations in any culture are bureaucratic to some degree.

Max Weber

Bureaucracy.
A system of management pioneered by Max Weber.

Advantages

Weber identified several essential characteristics of his "ideal" bureaucracy (see Figure 2.3) and believed that certain advantages would accrue to organiza-

FIGURE 2.3 CHARACTERISTICS OF WEBER'S IDEAL BUREAUCRACY

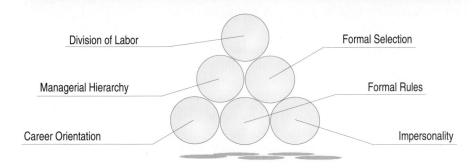

tions that embodied them. These characteristics and sample advantages include:

- *Division of Labor.* Labor is divided so that authority and responsibility are clearly defined.

    Advantage Efficiency will increase through specialization.

- *Managerial Hierarchy.* Offices or positions are organized in a hierarchy of authority.

    Advantage A clear chain of command will develop from the highest to the lowest level of an organization (Fayol's scalar chain principle).

- *Formal Selection.* All employees are selected on the basis of technical qualifications demonstrated by formal examination, education, or training.

    Advantage Employees will be hired and promoted based on merit and expertise.

- *Career Orientation.* Managers are professionals rather than owners of the units they administer. They work for fixed salaries and pursue "careers" within their respective fields.

    Advantage The hiring of "career" professionals will result in a continuity of operations.

- *Formal Rules and Other Controls.* All employees are subject to formal rules and other controls regarding the performance of their duties.

    Advantage Efficiency will increase as formal rules and other controls relating to employee performance are enforced.

- *Impersonality.* Rules and other controls are impersonal and uniformly applied in all cases.

    Advantage When rules and other controls are applied impersonally and uniformly, involvement with personalities and personal preferences is avoided.

Disadvantages

While Weber considered bureaucracy to be the most efficient means of organizing, both his own experience and subsequent research have shown that it often results in certain disadvantages. These include:

- Rules and other controls may take on a significance of their own and, as a consequence, become ends in themselves.

- Extreme devotion to rules and other controls may lead to situations in which past decisions are blindly repeated without appreciation or concern for changed conditions. Such "bureaucratic rigidity" results in managers being compensated for doing what they are told—not for thinking.

- While delegation of authority to lower levels may increase organization effectiveness, it may also encourage an emphasis on subunit rather than overall organization goals, thereby prompting subunit conflict and decreased effectiveness.

- Although rules and other controls are intended to counter worker apathy, they may actually contribute to it by defining unacceptable behavior and, thus, specifying a *minimum* level of acceptable performance. That is, it is possible, once rules have been defined, for employees to remain apathetic, for they now know just how little they can do and still remain secure. This is commonly known as **working to the rules,** since what is not covered by rules is by definition not an employee's responsibility.

Working to the rules.
Performing exactly what is required by prevailing work rules and nothing more.

Despite these and other criticisms, bureaucratic management is a central feature in modern societies. It is thus important to realize that the disadvantages just outlined are not necessarily inherent in bureaucracy per se. As envisioned by Weber, bureaucratic management is both rational and efficient. Gaining its benefits, however, requires learning enough about its characteristics to avoid being controlled by them.

While many of us may feel that we live in a bureaucratic world of baffling rules and other controls, we should not forget that bureaucracy also makes it possible for us to get potable water instantly, place an international telephone call in seconds, and have a package delivered a continent away overnight. Indeed, almost all the benefits we take for granted in today's society—modern medicine, modern science, modern industry—rest upon a bureaucratic foundation.

In sum, Weber's ideas have stood the test of time remarkably well. His pioneering work, like that of Taylor, the Gilbreths, and Fayol, has stimulated a wealth of research into the management process. In this respect, it remains a landmark in the study of management.

HUMAN RELATIONS IN MANAGEMENT (1927–PRESENT)

HAWTHORNE STUDIES

In the 1920s and on into the Great Depression, a group of social scientists led by Australian-born Elton Mayo began to study how employees reacted to performance incentive schemes, job satisfaction, and working conditions. This group of theorists emphasized the human side of management and tended to counterbalance the largely technical engineering emphasis of the scientific-management movement. They believed management should focus primarily on *people.*

One of the most important breakthroughs in the evolution of management thought resulted from a series of studies begun in 1924 at the former Hawthorne (Cicero, Illinois) Works of the Western Electric Company (now AT&T Technologies), manufacturers of equipment for the telephone industry.[38] The studies spanned an 8-year period and dramatically revealed previously unappreciated patterns of employee behavior. Perhaps the most significant feature of the studies was

Elton Mayo

that, for the first time, resources comparable to those normally devoted to research in the physical sciences were directed to a human problem—the dynamic aspects of management. Referred to as the *Hawthorne Studies*, this research had a profound effect upon the so-called **human relations** movement.

The Hawthorne Studies can be divided into three general phases: (1) Illumination Experiments, (2) Relay-Assembly Test Room Experiments, and (3) Bank-Wiring Observation Room Experiment. Each phase grew from the preceding one and added to what had been learned in the others.

Human relations.
An approach to management originating with the Hawthorne Studies.

Phase One: Illumination Experiments (1924–1927)

Initiated in collaboration with the National Research Council of the National Academy of Sciences, Phase One, called the Illumination Experiments, was conducted under the direction of Vannevar Bush, a famed electrical engineer from the Massachusetts Institute of Technology who later developed the analytical systems that led to the modern electronic computer. The original intent of the experiments was to investigate the relationship between variations in work area lighting and employee productivity. It had been hypothesized that as illumination was increased, productivity would increase. The experiments were conducted in several departments employing female coil winders, relay-assemblers, and small-parts inspectors. The researchers systematically varied the level of illumination in each department, fully anticipating worker output to vary directly with light intensity. However, the results showed no such effect. Regardless of whether the lighting was brighter, dimmer, or constant, output increased. As a matter of fact, at one point light intensity was reduced to the equivalent of ordinary moonlight (0.06 footcandles) and output still increased. Other experiments yielded similarly unanticipated and seemingly contradictory results.

Two conclusions were drawn from these findings: (1) illumination was only one of many factors affecting output and (2) no simple cause-and-effect relationship existed between illumination and worker productivity. It was thus recognized that other factors would have to be studied and that better experimental controls were necessary.

The first phase of the Hawthorne Studies, the illumination test room experiments, found that no relationship exists between illumination and worker productivity.

Phase Two: Relay-Assembly Test Room Experiments (1927–1932)

In early 1927 Western Electric asked Elton Mayo, a professor at Harvard University, to try to solve the puzzle presented by Phase One.[39] He was soon joined by his Harvard colleague, Fritz J. Roethlisberger, and research was begun.

The goal of the research team was to determine the effects of working conditions, such as rest breaks and workday length, on employee productivity. This phase of the Hawthorne Studies, known as the Relay-Assembly Test Room Experiments, lasted 5 years. For the purpose of the experiments, six skilled women were selected from a larger group of relay-assemblers. They were average employees whose work consisted of assembling telephone relays. The relays weighed a few ounces, consisted of some 40 parts, and required approximately 1 minute to assemble. Five of the women did the actual assembly work; the sixth kept the others supplied with parts.

Fritz J. Roethlisberger

To control experimental conditions more closely, a test room was constructed. Additionally, careful measurements were made of such factors as blood pressure and vascular skin reaction, as well as general weather conditions and test room temperature and humidity. Every 6 weeks the women were given a complete medical examination by the company physician, since physical health was considered an important variable. Records were kept of the amount of sleep each worker had had the previous night and what food she had eaten. And an observer was placed in the test room throughout the experiments. His job was to record the principal events in the room hour by hour and to create and maintain a friendly atmosphere. The women had no supervisor, as they would have had in a regular department. At most, the observer exercised a quasi-supervisory function.

Throughout the first 2½ years of the experiments, the length and frequency of rest periods and number of hours worked were continually varied. Whenever an experimental change was planned, its purpose was explained to the women and their

The second phase of the Hawthorne Studies, the relay-assembly room, experimented with the relationship between working conditions and worker productivity.

comments requested. Changes that did not meet their approval were abandoned. As in the illumination experiments, the results were startling. Output followed a general upward trend throughout the experiment. This strongly suggested to the researchers that something far more potent than test conditions had influenced productivity.

In seeking an explanation for the marked improvement, Roethlisberger and Mayo slowly began to realize that in addition to the changes they had introduced in experimental conditions, another type of change had taken place. In their attempt to establish the proper conditions for the experiments, they unconsciously had created a change in "human relations." This change distinguished the test room from regular departments in four primary ways:[40]

Supervisory Style. Throughout the Relay-Assembly Test Room Experiments, the women assumed an increasing share of their own supervision. This resulted in a supervisory style that was less restrictive and more friendly. The women were aware they were producing more in the test room than they had in their regular departments, and they said the increase had occurred without any conscious effort on their part. They offered two explanations. First, "it was fun" working in the test room. They enjoyed being the center of attention. Second, the new supervisory style, or more accurately, the absence of the old supervisory style, allowed them to work freely without anxiety. For example, in the test room, the women were allowed to talk with one another, whereas in the regular departments, conversation was not allowed. The observer's efforts to create a friendly atmosphere resulted in the women receiving a great deal of considerate and personal attention. In short, the test room supervision was more thoughtful and less authoritarian than the women had previously experienced, and the atmosphere was freer and less anxiety-provoking.

Control. The change in supervisory style was accompanied by less stringent controls. As noted, the women actually participated in decisions affecting their jobs—a privilege not granted other workers. To begin with, their consent had been sought to take part in the experiments. Furthermore, they were repeatedly asked not to strain but to work "as they felt." Also, they knew that they were taking part in what was considered an important study that could lead to improved working conditions for their fellow employees. Thus, they participated both explicitly and implicitly in making decisions that affected their work lives.

Group Formation. A third factor that distinguished the test room was the social development of the group. For example, when the women went for their second medical examination, someone joked that ice cream should be served. The company did exactly that at the next exam, and the practice was repeated for the duration of the experiments. When one of the women celebrated a birthday, each of the others would bring her a gift and, in return, be offered chocolates. If one of the women felt tired, the others would "carry" her by working faster to compensate for her expected low output. They became friends in the test room and saw one another socially after working hours, attending parties in one another's homes and going to the theater together. In sum, the women became a cohesive group that stressed loyalty and cooperation. The women themselves felt that it was this factor that contributed most to their high output.

Job Satisfaction. Underlying each of the preceding factors was the high esprit de corps that developed within the group. The record of events maintained by the observer indicated that a remarkable shift had occurred in the women's attitudes. They no longer had the feeling they were just a small part of a large department, subject to routine managerial instructions. They felt they were part of something special. This was no doubt a source of satisfaction as the women showed a great deal of pride in being associated with the study. Viewed psychologically, the women had become *ego-involved* in their work.

Phase Three: Bank-Wiring Observation Room Experiment (1931–1932)

The final phase of the Hawthorne Studies has become known as the Bank-Wiring Observation Room Experiment. It grew out of a recognition that individuals in a department or unit are not isolated, but are part of a group with established relationships to one another, to their supervisors, and to their work. It differed from both the Illumination Experiments and Relay-Assembly Test Room Experiments in that it involved no experimental changes. Rather, its purpose was to analyze the spontaneous behavior of a work group in its customary functioning. The research method employed was a combination of observation and interviewing.

The subjects of the experiment were a group of men—nine wiremen, three soldermen, and two inspectors—engaged in assembling terminal banks for use in telephone exchanges. The men were taken out of their regular department and placed in a special test room. With the exception of an observer being present, no change was made in their work conditions. The function of the observer was to keep daily records of significant events, employee conversations, and his own impressions. With the exception of the inspectors, each man was also interviewed on several occasions.

It was clear from early findings that the men constituted a complex social group with well-established norms and a common body of sentiments beyond that formally required by their tasks. They had their own conception of a fair day's work and prevailed as a group upon one another not to exceed this level of output. Employees who exceeded the agreed upon rate were known as "rate-busters." Workers feared that those who could not keep up with the pace of "rate-busters" would be "bawled out." They also were worried that if management adopted such a high out-

Bank wirers were observed and interviewed in the third phase of the Hawthorne Studies.

put as the accepted **bogey** (the daily output expected of each worker), they would find themselves having to work more for the same amount of money. At the same time, the men strongly believed that a person's output should not fall too far below the group norm. If it did, he was known as a "rate-chiseler." Additionally, the men held that a person should never say or do anything that would injure a fellow group member. If he did, he was a "squealer." The men engaged in several practices that violated company policies. For instance, although it was forbidden, the men frequently traded jobs. There also was a great deal of informal helping among workers, which, too, was against company policy. Thus, it was important that no one squeal on a fellow worker. Finally, the men felt that a person should not attempt to maintain social distance. For example, if someone was an inspector, he should not act like one.

The bank-wiring observation group had developed various methods of enforcing its norms. Pressure was executed through subtle forms of ridicule, sarcasm, and **binging,** a practice whereby one worker expressed displeasure with the actions of another by hitting him as hard as possible on the upper arm. Exceeding the group output norm would elicit such chastisement, along with taunts of "Speed King" or "The Slave." The virtue of these practices did not lie in the resulting physical hurt experienced by a worker, but rather in the mental hurt that came from knowing that the group disapproved of his behavior.

In brief, these findings dramatically underscored the significance of informal group relations as a powerful force in the motivation of workers.

Results of Hawthorne Studies

In addition to challenging many prevailing assumptions of the day, the findings of the Hawthorne Studies immeasurably increased our knowledge and understanding of workers and their work.[41] For example,

- It became clear that workers are not motivated solely by money. The importance of personal and social factors in motivation and employee attitudes (toward every aspect of their work) was revealed.

- The importance of individual attitudes in determining employee behavior became undeniable.

- The significance of effective supervision in maintaining employee job satisfaction and productivity became indisputable.

- It became evident that little was known about the character of informal work groups and their influence on employee performance. This influence will be discussed at length in Chapter 17.

Critics note that by current standards the Hawthorne Studies were unscientific; that is, many of the conclusions reached do not necessarily follow from the available evidence.[42] Nevertheless, in their day, they were an intellectual gold mine. For this reason alone, the contributions of the Hawthorne Studies to the growth and development of the human relations approach can hardly be overstated. As though responding to Taylor's plea for a "study of the motives which influence men," the Hawthorne researchers systematically demonstrated the nature and content of the human element. By testing hypothetical assertions about the basis of work rather than allowing their continued acceptance, Mayo and Roethlisberger, with Western Electric's support, pioneered a course of investigation that is still being pursued today.

Bogey.
Daily output expected of a worker.

Binging.
A practice whereby one group member expressed displeasure with the actions of another by hitting him as hard as possible on the upper arm.

MODERN MANAGEMENT

Each of the movements we have discussed has shed light on some aspect of the management process. As one author has observed, a "management theory jungle" arose when each of these movements went its own way and ignored the others.[43] Followers of scientific management emphasized scientific decision making, computer applications, and mathematical models. Human relations enthusiasts (now called behavioral scientists) developed new theories of human behavior. Administrative-management advocates studied managerial work patterns in order to learn the secrets of executive success. But in the past 25 years or so, some management theorists have begun to try to integrate findings of the scientific-management, administrative-management, and human relations movements. Three modern approaches have attempted to integrate these different perspectives. These are the **systems approach,** the **contingency approach,** and the **quality improvement movement.**

SYSTEMS APPROACH

The systems approach has its roots in many disciplines, including biology, psychology, sociology, and information theory. This diversity of origins makes the systems approach truly integrative and provides it with greater explanatory power than that of any of its constituent disciplines alone. A **system** may be defined as a set of interdependent parts that relate in the accomplishment of some purpose. The systems approach views organizations as systems that procure and transform inputs into **outputs** (goods and services), which are subsequently discharged into their external environment. **Inputs,** or what are often termed *factors of production,* may take the form of people, materials, money, or information. For example, a steel mill transforms iron ore and other raw materials into industrial and consumer goods. Colleges and universities transform uneducated students into educated graduates. Hospitals transform sick patients into healthy individuals. Figure 2.4 illustrates this process.

This cycle of inputs, transformations, and outputs must be maintained if an organization is to exist over time. That is to say, an organization can survive only if it is capable of producing some output that can be exchanged for the energy (feedback) necessary to obtain new inputs and also to maintain itself in operating order. In a business setting, the value of the outputs an organization produces is measured by the amount buyers are willing to pay for the goods and services it provides. An

Systems approach.
An approach to management that draws on systems theory.

Contingency approach.
An approach to management that holds it is impossible to specify a single way of managing that works best in all situations.

Quality improvement movement.
An approach to management that integrates quality into every department within an organization in an effort to improve productivity.

System.
A set of interdependent parts that relate in the accomplishment of some purpose.

Outputs.
Goods and services.

Inputs.
People, materials, money, or information.

FIGURE 2.4 BASIC SYSTEMS MODEL

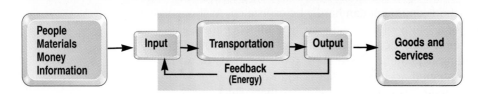

organization is considered profitable if this value exceeds the collective cost of procuring and transforming inputs into outputs. If excess profits exist, they can be held in reserve for hard times or used to finance growth. If an organization cannot achieve a favorable ratio of inputs to outputs, it must receive outside funds to survive. This is why undertakings that do not sell their goods or services (for example, public television, city schools, free museums, nonsubscription libraries) rely on external funding (for example, government and foundation grants) to endure. Table 2.5 illustrates the universal nature of the input→transformation→output cycle.

It is generally emphasized that all organizations are to some degree **open systems** as opposed to **closed systems.** That is, a typical organization (system) depends on other systems for its inputs (money, materials, employees) and thus cannot exist in isolation. It cannot solve a production problem, for example, without

Open (versus closed) system.
A system that depends on other systems for its inputs and thus cannot exist in isolation.

Closed system.
A system that does not depend on other systems for its input.

TABLE 2.5 EXAMPLES OF SYSTEMS			
	Inputs	**Transformation Process**	**Outputs**

General Motors	Steel
	Rubber
	Plastic
	Equipment
	Labor
	Capital
		Fabricate
		Assemble
		Paint
			Automobiles
			Trucks
			Automotive
			    Products
			Diesel Engines
			Turbine Aircraft
			    Engines

Mount Sinai Hospital	Patients Physicians Nurses Equipment Support Staff Insurance Payments Fees	Diagnose Ameliorate Cure Prevent	Healthy People
Folsom Prison	Convicts State/Federal Funds	Therapy Rehabilitation	Productive Citizens

State University	Students
	Faculty
	Support Staff
	Tuition
	Grants
	Contracts
		Teaching
		Research
		Public Service
			Graduates
			Books/
			    Monographs
			Articles/Reports
			Extension
			    Activities

Washington National Cathedral	Communicants Penitents Clergy Tithings	Divine Worship Hymns Prayer Communion	Spiritual Salvation

considering whether other organizations (systems) will ship necessary materials on time or at a mutually acceptable price. Thus, to illustrate, Folger's cannot plan its production of coffee without first considering the willingness of Brazilian exporters to sell coffee beans on demand and at an agreeable price. In addition, an organization (system) sells its outputs (goods or services) to other systems (customers). Thus, if it wishes to survive, the organization must respond to systems that supply it and those, in turn, that it supplies. This highlights the important point that all organizations are dependent for survival on exchange with their environment. That is, they can exist only so long as they are capable of producing some output that can be exchanged in the larger marketplace. When, for example, after a few years of avid interest, teenagers stopped going to video arcades, the video game industry was left with veritable mountains of unsold merchandise. Atari, once an industry leader, suffered huge losses in a short time period. Plants were closed, hundreds of employees laid off, and truckloads of video games buried in a landfill in New Mexico.

As the preceding examples suggest, viewing an organization as an open system forces the realization that all such systems are composed of subsystems that contain their own subsystems. That is, the parts that form an open system may themselves be systems, and their parts may be seen as systems, and so on. For example, the world's economy can be considered a system in which various national economies are subsystems. In turn, each national economy may be viewed as being composed of various industries, each industry of various organizations, and, of course, each organization of various subsystems, such as marketing, accounting, finance, and so forth.[44]

The systems approach does not provide a means for solving all problems. It is, however, useful for viewing the relationships between interdependent parts in terms of how these relationships affect the performance of an overall system. Moreover, it forces managers to ask questions like, "Where do a system's inputs come from?" and "Where do its outputs go?" Such questions highlight the fact that open systems are not comprised of fixed cause-and-effect linkages. Rather, they are characterized by **equifinality,** meaning that the same outputs can be achieved in multiple ways, with different inputs and different transformation processes. In this regard, the systems approach encourages managers to think globally (that is, keeping in mind the whole picture) in searching for and comparing potential courses of action for achieving an organization's goals.

The systems approach also suggests the intriguing thought that if the performance of an organization is a product of the interaction rather than the sum of its parts, it is entirely possible for the action of two or more parts to achieve an effect of which either is individually incapable. The creation of a whole that is greater than the sum of its parts is called **synergy.** This idea is sometimes graphically referred to as "2 + 2 = 5"; that is, the sum of the benefits of an organization's combined operations is more than if they had remained separate.

Synergy explains why the performance of a system as a whole depends more on how its parts relate than on how well each part operates. Indeed, the interdependence of the parts is such that even if each part independently performs as efficiently as possible, the system as a whole may not. The effective management of an organization thus requires management of the interactions of its parts, not their independent actions. Compensation is no more an independent variable than hours of work, working conditions, or quality of supervision. Similarly, the solution

Equifinality.
Achieving the same outputs in multiple ways, with different inputs and different transformation processes.

Synergy.
The creation of a whole that is greater than the sum of its parts.

Reflecting the synergy that can result from combining dedicated employees with quality materials and excellent working conditions, Morrison Knudsen train assemblers have helped capture an 87 percent market share in the transit car industry.

to a production problem will likely have an impact on other parts of an organization. If production experiences an increase in costs per unit and tries to resolve the problem by producing goods in larger batches to achieve greater economies of scale, customer orders may not be shipped on time. As a result, if orders are lost, sales will likely decline (affecting marketing) and profits decrease (affecting finances). Thus, in analyzing a system (organization), simple cause-and-effect reasoning is not applicable. To change one part is to change relationships and thus change the system as a whole.

Finally, the systems approach suggests that the performance of various parts should be evaluated in terms of their contribution to a system's overall goals, not for their individual production or profit. Indeed, some parts may operate at a loss to themselves in order to optimize an overall system. An example of a highly efficient system is a concert orchestra. The musicians do not all play solos. Their role is to support one another.[45] Management's job in such situations is to optimize a system over time, emphasizing the need for individuals, as well as departments, to work together in a cooperative fashion.

CONTINGENCY APPROACH

A second modern approach that has attempted to integrate findings of other perspectives is called the *contingency approach*. Advocates of this approach believe that it is impossible to specify a single way of managing that works best in all situations. Their approach is to spell out conditions of a task (scientific management), managerial job (administrative management), and people (human relations) as parts of a whole management situation (systems emphasis) and integrate them all into an effective solution most appropriate for specific circumstances. Thus, according to contingency theorists, managers should attempt to identify which actions will, in a particular situation, under particular circumstances, and at a particular time, lead to organization success.

The contingency approach recognizes that every organization is unique, existing in a unique environment with unique employees and unique goals. This uniqueness requires that managers analyze the particular circumstances existing in each situation before taking specific actions. What is appropriate in one situation may well be disastrous in another. It should thus be no surprise that the organization design best suited for aircraft production may be inappropriate for building mainframe computers. The contingency approach thus calls for managers to be flexible and to adapt to the situation at hand. Contingency theorists recognize that the world is much too complex for there to be a way of managing that works best in all situations.[46]

Actually, the contingency approach is not really new. Writing over 80 years ago, Taylor stressed "the importance of choosing the general type of management best suited to the *particular* case."[47] Fayol, you will recall, stressed that "there is nothing rigid or absolute in management affairs" and that "allowance must be made for different changing circumstances." Similarly writing in the 1920s, Mary P. Follett spoke of the **law of the situation,** referring to the necessity of acting in accord with the unique requirements inherent in any situation. She noted that such requirements are constantly changing, thus demanding continual efforts to maintain effective work relationships. Commenting specifically on leadership, she observed that "different situations require different kinds of knowledge, and the man possessing the knowledge demanded by a certain situation tends to be in the best managed businesses, and other things being equal, to become the leader at the moment."[48]

Law of the situation.
The necessity of acting in accord with the unique requirements inherent in any situation.

Later chapters will discuss the contingency approach in more detail. It has grown in popularity over the last decade because it recognizes that there is no magical formula for managerial effectiveness, but rather such effectiveness is contingent upon the unique circumstances that prevail in a given situation.

QUALITY IMPROVEMENT MOVEMENT

Improving quality is not a modern idea. It is thousands of years old. Currently, however, there is an avalanche of interest in quality improvement. This interest has resulted in entire industries altering the fundamental way they operate. The ultimate aim of improved quality is total customer satisfaction.[49]

Increasing numbers of organizations worldwide have launched "total quality" initiatives. Such quality programs are aimed at helping organizations in all sectors—manufacturing, service, public—keep pace with surging international competition. This mounting competition has led to a redefinition of quality. More and more organizations have total quality programs that permeate every department, from research to production to sales, in an effort to improve productivity. Industries from banking to insurance to airlines are finding that constant quality improvement is necessary for survival.

Properly executed, quality improvement is a competitive weapon. Motorola has set virtual perfection as its quality goal. Its ultimate aim is to reach the **six-sigma level.** One-sigma means 68 percent of products are acceptable; three-sigma means 99.7 percent. Six-sigma is 99.999997 percent, or 3.4 defects per million parts.

Six-sigma level.
A statistical measure expressing 3.4 defects per million parts.

Someday it may establish an even more amazing goal: a mindboggling 60 defects per billion parts.

Organizations that strive for total quality can achieve a competitive advantage because improved quality means less rework, fewer delays, and better use of management time. This can result in a cost savings of anywhere from 10 percent to 50 percent. Moreover, an almost inevitable consequence is higher customer-retention rates. Research suggests that raising customer retention 2 percent can have the same effect as reducing costs 10 percent.[50]

The list of organizations that have benefitted from quality improvement programs is constantly growing. Swiss chemical producer Ciba-Geigy increased its bottom line a whopping 20 percent of sales by reducing mistakes in product shipments, reducing the amount of business lost because of inventory shortages, and eliminating bad dye batches. Swedish appliance manufacturer Electrolux cut its field-service repairs 40 percent by improving its design methods and other work processes. Its field-service representatives now electronically feed back data to engineers on bad designs and parts. Savin reports that by managing for quality it reduced service expenses some 35 percent. Using a "total quality management" approach, it was able to identify and retrain those 20 percent of its field engineers who were responsible for 80 percent of all customer "callbacks." Similarly, it was able to determine those parts the engineers were most likely to need on a call. By assembling a call kit containing those parts, it was able to significantly reduce time spent shuttling back and forth for spare parts. Now field engineers finish service calls more quickly, leaving time to make more calls.

The reigning demigod of the quality improvement movement is W. Edwards Deming.[51] In his 90s, Deming is the philosophical master of quality and the spiritual leader of Japan, Inc. In 1950, Deming started teaching Japanese managers how to manufacture quality. Japan's metamorphosis from a producer of junk immediately after World War II to a leader in quality is now legend. Today, the Japanese revere Deming as their "Father of Quality Control." He has been awarded Japan's Second Order Medal of the Sacred Treasure. The accompanying award citation says that the Japanese people attribute the rebirth of Japanese industry and its worldwide success to Ed Deming.

Deming has been spreading his gospel about quality control for more than 40 years. Having converted Japan, he is now working on the United States. There is nothing simple about his approach to managing. He promotes a set of guidelines dubbed the "Fourteen Points" (see Table 2.6). He teaches that the more quality you build into anything, the less it costs. Improving quality, Deming says, automatically increases productivity, which, in turn, drives profits up. This chain reaction (see Figure 2.5) was eagerly adopted by Japanese managers as early as 1950. It was not until the late 1970s, however, when Japanese steel, autos, and electronic products began penetrating markets long dominated by U.S. goods, that Deming's ideas were finally heeded at home.

The success of Deming's U.S. efforts is evident in the widespread acceptance of such Japanese ideas as **just-in-time** (JIT) **inventory** and *poka-yoke.* JIT inventory involves having suppliers deliver materials to a factory on the day they are needed, thus eliminating costly inventories. The concept behind poka-yoke is to minimize human error. It is a method for making the workplace mistake-proof. If the parts comprising a car's headlights, for instance, can be assembled in more than one way, promoters of poka-yoke would say change the design.

W. Edwards Deming

Just-in-time (JIT) inventory.
Having suppliers deliver materials to a factory on the day they are needed.

Poka-yoke.
A method for making the workplace mistake-proof.

TABLE 2.6 W. EDWARDS DEMING: A THEORY FOR MANAGEMENT

REQUIREMENTS FOR A BUSINESS WHOSE MANAGEMENT PLANS TO REMAIN COMPETITIVE IN PROVIDING GOODS AND SERVICES THAT WILL HAVE A MARKET.

1. Create constancy of purpose toward improvement of product and service, with the aim to become competitive and to stay in business and to provide jobs.
2. Adopt the new philosophy. We are in a new economic age. Western management must awaken to the challenge, must learn their responsibilities, and take on leadership for change.
3. Cease dependence on inspection to achieve quality. Eliminate the need for inspection on a mass basis by building quality into the product in the first place.
4. End the practice of awarding business on the basis of price tag. Instead, minimize total cost. Move toward a single supplier for any one item, on a long-term relationship of loyalty and trust.
5. Improve constantly and forever the system of production and service, to improve quality and productivity, and thus constantly decrease costs.
6. Institute training on the job.
7. Institute leadership (see point 12). The aim of leadership should be to help people and machines and gadgets to do a better job. Leadership of management is in need of overhaul, as well as leadership of production workers.
8. Drive out fear, so that everyone may work effectively for the company.
9. Break down barriers between departments. People in research, design, sales, and production must work as a team, to foresee problems of production and in use that may be encountered with the product or service.
10. Eliminate slogans, exhortations, and targets for the work force asking for zero defects and new levels of productivity.
11. a. Eliminate work standards (quotas) on the factory floor. Substitute leadership.
    b. Eliminate management by objective. Eliminate management by numbers, numerical goals. Substitute leadership.
12. a. Remove barriers that rob the hourly worker of his right to pride of workmanship. The responsibility of supervisors must be changed from sheer numbers to quality.
    b. Remove barriers that rob people in management and in engineering of their right to pride of workmanship. This means, "inter alia," abolishment of the annual or merit rating and of management by objective, management by the numbers.
13. Institute a vigorous program of education and self-improvement.
14. Put everybody in the company to work to accomplish the transformation. The transformation is everybody's job.

Source: Courtesy of Process Management Institute, Inc.

In an effort to emphasize that quality should be the responsibility of every worker, programs stressing quality improvement have begun worldwide. Perhaps the most well known are Japan's Deming Prize, sponsored by the Union of Japanese Scientists & Engineers, and the U.S. Department of Commerce's Malcolm Baldridge National Quality Award. Other prestigious awards include the Shingo Prize for Excellence for Manufacturing administered by Utah State University and the Japan Prize, a prize for which only former Deming winners are eligible after a 5-year wait. In an effort to spur quality awareness in Europe, the European Foundation for Quality Management presented its first quality award in 1992.

Quality, in its modern conception as an all-encompassing attribute, is a potent competitive weapon. Indeed, managing for quality is unquestionably essential for winning in today's unforgiving global marketplace.

FIGURE 2.5 THE DEMING CHAIN REACTION

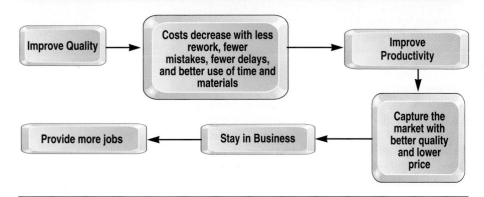

Source: Ross Johnson and William O. Winchell, *Management and Quality* (Milwaukee, Wis.: American Society for Quality Control, 1989), 4.

CLOSE UP: QUALITY THE QUALITY CIRCLE PHENOMENON

An integral aspect of the current quest for competitiveness is a concern for the quality of goods and services. Whether expressed in slogans such as "Quality Is Job One" or "Doing It Right the First Time," a concern for quality has captured the attention of corporate America. Fueled by an admiration for foreign products, as exemplified by Japanese automobiles and consumer electronics, the world has become fascinated by Japanese manufacturing capabilities.

While numerous competing hypotheses have been offered for Japan's industrial success, a leading contender is the use of "quality circles."

Quality circles or QCs can be traced to seminars given to Japanese managers by Dr. W. Edwards Deming following World War II. QCs are voluntary groups of employees who meet together periodically to discuss, analyze, and propose solutions to quality problems. Circle meetings are usually held on enterprise time and premises. It is estimated that in Japan there are over 125,000 circles with some 1.1 million members. Mazda, alone, has 2,147 circles with 16,000 employees involved.

A typical QC has seven to eight members. QC leaders function as group facilitators not as bosses. In addition to providing an opportunity to participate and gain a sense of accomplishment, QCs promote teamwork and build cohesiveness.

Here in the U.S., quality circles have produced impressive results. At a Hospital Corporation of American facility in Atlanta, a QC developed a way to reduce the repeat rate for caesarean deliveries. A QC at Federal Express headquarters in Memphis cut training time from six months to five weeks by devising an easy way to memorize 700 three-letter city codes.

Sources: Adapted from Thomas R. Miller, "The Quality Circle Phenomenon: A Review and Appraisal," *SAM Advanced Management Journal* 54 (Winter 1989): 4–7, 12; Frank Rose, "How Quality Means Service Too," *Fortune* (April 22, 1991): 97–111.

SUMMARY

It is difficult, if not impossible, to understand contemporary management theory and practice without an appreciation of its historical heritage. This chapter has primarily focused on the evolution of management since the late 1800s.

Learning Objective 1. Describe what is known today as the Industrial Revolution.
The so-called Industrial Revolution took place in the latter part of the eighteenth century and continued through the end of the nineteenth century. The basic revolutionizing change was the transfer of work skills from craftworkers to machines. The new manufacturing systems introduced during this period (especially mass production) prompted an enormous increase in productivity and lower prices, and the cycle of modern capitalism was soon underway.

Learning Objective 2. Discuss the milestone most frequently referred to as the beginning of the search for a science of management.
Henry R. Towne's paper "The Engineer as an Economist" is most frequently referred to as the beginning of the search for a science of management. In this paper, Towne argued that the importance of management as a field of study was equal to that of engineering. He noted the almost complete lack of management literature, the virtual absence of a medium for the exchange of managerial ideas and experience, and the total absence of management associations.

Learning Objective 3. Recount Frederick W. Taylor's contributions to the scientific-management movement.
The original seed Taylor sowed has spread and multiplied a millionfold. It has spread from the mechanical operations on which he focused at the beginning of his career into activities such as employee selection and training, job design, inventory control, and wage and salary administration. Just as importantly, Taylor's work produced a change in the way managers regarded themselves. The old "rule-of-thumb" and "seat-of-the-pants" images were replaced by "an attitude of questioning, of research, of careful investigation . . . , of seeking for exact knowledge and then shaping action on the discovered facts."

Learning Objective 4. Relate Frank B. and Lillian M. Gilbreth's quest for the "one best way."
The Gilbreths viewed their quest for the "one best way" as the means by which individuals' personal potential could be maximized with benefit both to themselves and to society. It was their contention that of the various ways a particular job could be performed, only one was the best; and it was their job to find it.

Learning Objective 5. Explain why Henri Fayol is known as the "Father of Modern Management."
Fayol is known as the "Father of Modern Management" in recognition of how extensively his ideas have penetrated current managerial thinking. His ideas remain important not only because of his enormous influence on succeeding generations of managers, but also because of the continuing validity of his work.

Learning Objective 6. Set forth the advantages and disadvantages of Max Weber's bureaucracy.

The advantages of bureaucracy include: (1) a division of labor leads to increased efficiency through specialization, (2) a clear chain of command is developed from the highest to lowest level of an organization (the scalar chain principle), (3) delegation of authority is often necessary for the efficient performance of lower level duties, (4) hiring and promotion are based on merit and expertise, (5) a continuity of operations results from the hiring of "career" professionals, and (6) rules and other controls are applied in such a way as to avoid involvement with personalities and personal preference. The disadvantages of bureaucracy include: (1) rules and other controls may take on a significance of their own and, as a consequence, become ends in themselves; (2) extreme devotion to rules and other controls may lead to situations in which past decisions are blindly repeated without appreciation or concern for changed conditions; (3) delegation of authority may encourage an emphasis on subunit rather than overall enterprise goals, thereby prompting subunit conflict and decreased effectiveness; and (4) rules and other controls may contribute to apathy by defining unacceptable behavior and, thus, specifying a *minimum* level of acceptable performance.

Learning Objective 7. Give an account of the nature and contributions of the Hawthorne Studies.

The Hawthorne Studies spanned an 8-year period in three phases and dramatically revealed previously unappreciated patterns of employee behavior. The phases were: (1) Illumination Experiments (1924–1927); (2) Relay-Assembly Test Room Experiments (1927–1932); and (3) Bank-Wiring Observation Room Experiment (1931–1932). The findings of the studies served to question several then-prevailing assumptions about the nature of workers and their work. For example: (1) it became clear that workers are not motivated solely by money, but that personal and social factors are important in motivation and employee attitudes; (2) the importance of individual attitudes in determining employee behavior became undeniable; (3) the significance of effective supervision in maintaining job satisfaction and productivity became indisputable; and (4) it became evident that little was known about the character of informal work groups and their influence on employee performance.

Learning Objective 8. Demonstrate an understanding of the systems approach to management.

The systems approach views organizations as procuring and transforming inputs (people, materials, money, and information) into outputs that are subsequently discharged into their surrounding environment in the form of goods and services. This cycle is continually repeated. The goods and services provided by an organization are exchanged for the energy (feedback) necessary to secure further required inputs. Thus, an organization can survive only if capable of producing some output that can be exchanged for the resources necessary to obtain new inputs and also to maintain itself in operating order.

Learning Objective 9. Characterize the contingency approach to management.

The contingency approach holds that it is impossible to specify one way of managing that works best in every situation. According to contingency theorists, managers should attempt to identify which actions will, in a particular situation, under particular circumstances, and at a particular time, lead to organization success.

Learning Objective 10. Describe the quality improvement movement.
The quality improvement movement is the application of quality principles to all organization endeavors, including product design, dealings with suppliers, and the elimination of defects.

KEY TERMS

administrative management 41

binging 51

bogey 51

bureaucracy 44

closed system 53

contingency approach 52

equifinality 54

human relations 47

Industrial Revolution 28

inputs 52

just-in-time (JIT) inventory 57

law of heavy laboring 32

law of the situation 56

motion study 37

open system 53

outputs 52

poka-yoke 57

quality improvement movement 52

scientific management 30

six-sigma level 56

soldiering 30

synergy 54

system 52

systems approach 52

therbligs 38

time study 31

working to the rules 46

THE MANAGEMENT EXPERIENCE   THE MANAGEMENT HISTORY CROSSWORD PUZZLE

Across

1. Pioneered motion study
5. Early forum for management ideas
7. "Father of Modern Management"
10. First-class man
13. Steam engine inventor
14. Opposing counsel in eastern rate case
16. 19—, the year of Frank Gilbreth's death
17. Number of children in the Gilbreth family
18. Developed "The Law of the Situation" (first name)
19. Testified railroads could save $1 million a day
20. Systematic restriction of output
21. A favorite sport of Fred Taylor

Down

2. 18th century revolution
3. Mathematician who assisted Fred Taylor
4. Series of studies conducted from 1924 to 1932
6. Led a portion of the studies referenced in #4 above
8. Weighs 92 pounds
9. Item (singular) produced by assembly operators in studies referenced in #4 above
10. Fred Taylor's alma mater
11. "Father of Scientific Management"
12. Author of "The Engineer as an Economist"
15. A modern approach to management (singular)
17. 19—, the year of Fred Taylor's death

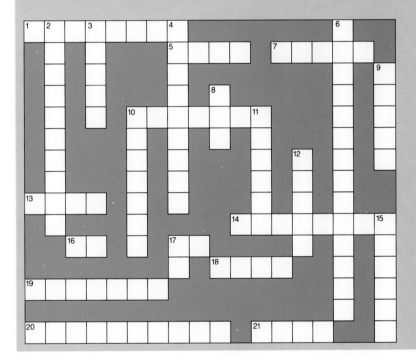

THE MANAGEMENT HISTORY PUZZLE SOLUTION

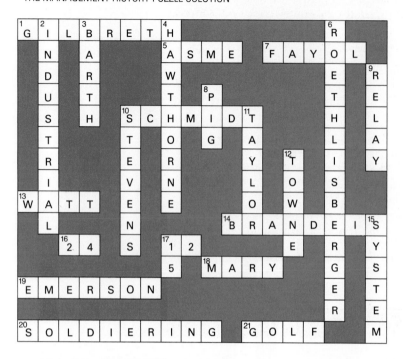

REVIEW AND DISCUSSION QUESTIONS

1. It has been stated that "the past is prologue to the future." With this in mind, why is it difficult, if not impossible, to understand contemporary management theory and practice without knowing its past?

2. A revolution is generally thought of as "a sudden, radical, or complete change." In what ways did the business world of 1776 and shortly thereafter change so that this period is now known as the Industrial Revolution?

3. Why does Henry R. Towne's plea for a recognition of management as an important field of study seem so out-of-date in today's world?

4. The scientific method may be defined as "the systematic pursuit of knowledge involving the recognition and formulation of a problem, the collection of data through observation and experiment, and the formulation and testing of hypotheses." To what extent did Frederick W. Taylor's work (for example, the pig-iron handling and shoveling studies) incorporate these characteristics?

5. The Gilbreths contended that of the various ways a particular job could be performed, only one was the best. Do you agree? If so, why? If not, why not?

6. Fayol's "14 Principles of Management" were based on his 50-plus years of experience as an industrial mining executive. To what extent do his principles apply in other settings (public and nonprofit) and sectors (commercial and service)?

7. Max Weber considered bureaucracy in its pure form to be "capable of obtaining the highest degree of efficiency." Why does this seem to be more the exception than the rule in its present applications? In framing your answer, consider that until recently the Pentagon's specifications for chocolate chip cookies ran to some 20 pages.

8. Assume the role of a first-line supervisor in a large manufacturing firm. Based on your knowledge of the Hawthorne Studies, in what ways do you suppose "human relations" might influence your job?

9. The human body, a system par excellence, is composed of numerous subsystems: skeletal system, circulatory system, muscular system, nervous system, and so on. None of these subsystems, however, can exist alone, and the total system cannot function normally without all its parts. In what way is a business similar?

10. Adherents to the contingency approach believe that it is impossible to prescribe managerial actions that will be effective in every situation. Consequently, they attempt to identify which actions will, in a particular situation, under particular circumstances, and at a particular time, lead to organization success. Recognizing that it would be hard to find a manager who thinks that one way of managing works best in every situation (irrespective of the task, managerial job, and people), what is new about this approach?

CASE 2.1   BATTLING THE BUREAUCRACY

Victoria Martinez is one of the 40,000 students who attend State University. It is the first day of registration for fall courses and Victoria has just left her advisor's office. After a lengthy discussion with her advisor, Victoria has decided to register for Accounting II, Advanced Topics in Human Resource Management, and Management Information Systems.

Victoria walks to the Registration Center and after a 40-minute wait, she turns in her paperwork for her course registration. The administrator indicates that the center's policy has recently changed. Both the advisor's and the department chairperson's signatures are now needed for students to register for advanced courses such as Advanced Topics in Human Resource Management.

Victoria returns to the Business Building and after waiting for the chair to return from teaching class, she obtains her signature and walks back to the Registration Center. After again waiting in line for 40 minutes, Victoria is informed that the human resource class is filled and that she must return to her advisor to discuss other class options. Using a campus telephone, Victoria calls her advisor and schedules an appointment with him for 3:30 p.m. the next day. Her advisor tells her that he just received a memo from the Registration Center informing him of the policy change.

Later that day, Victoria tells her roommate about all the problems she encountered in trying to register for her classes. As they speak, Victoria reviews the letters that have arrived with that day's mail. "Well, Eileen," Victoria tells her roommate, "today wasn't a complete loss. Remember all those forms I filled out to renew my season pass for the home football games? Here's my season pass, delivered right to my door. Guess the bureaucracy works sometimes."

Problems

1. If bureaucratic structures are problematic, why do organizations use such systems?

2. Why did the same bureaucratic process that helped Victoria to easily obtain her season pass for the football games cause her frustration in registering for classes?

3. How is the registration process at your university handled? How could the system be improved?

Source: Case written by Sherry E. Sullivan, Memphis State University.

NOTES

[1] Paraphrased from Desmond Stewart, *The Pyramids and the Sphinx* (New York: Newsweek Book Division, 1971), 37.

[2] For example, see Daniel A. Wren, *The Evolution of Management Thought*, 3d ed. (New York: Wiley, 1987).

[3] The following section is based on Ralph M. Barnes, *Motion and Time Study Design and Measurement of Work*, 7th ed. (New York: Wiley, 1980), 570–571; Alfred D. Chandler, Jr., "Rise and Evolution of Big Business," in *Encyclopedia of American Economic History*, vol. 2, ed. Glenn Porter (New York: Scribner's, 1980), 619–638; and Alfred D. Chandler, Jr., "The American System and Modern Management," in *Yankee Enterprise*, eds. Otto Mays and Robert C. Post (Washington, D.C.: Smithsonian Institution Press, 1981), 153–170.

[4] Lyman W. Porter and Lawrence E. McKibbin, *Management Education and Development: Drift or Thrust into the 21st Century?* (New York: McGraw-Hill, 1988), 24.

[5] Henry R. Towne, "The Engineer as an Economist," *Transactions, American Society of Mechanical Engineers* 7 (1886): 428–432. Also see Harlow S. Person, "The Origin and Nature of Scientific Management," in *Scientific Management in American Industry*, ed. Harlow S. Person (New York: Harper, 1929), 6.

[6] Lyndall F. Urwick, *The Life and Work of Frederick Winslow Taylor* (London: Urwick, Orr & Partners, 1957), 7.

[7] Testimony of Frederick W. Taylor, *Hearings before the Special Committee of the House of Representatives to Investigate the Taylor and Other Systems of Shop Management under Authority of House Resolution 90*, 62nd Cong., 1st sess., October 4, 1911 to February 12, 1912 (Washington, D.C.: Government Printing Office, 1912), 1388.

[8] Frederick W. Taylor, *Shop Management* (New York: Harper, 1903), 21.

[9] Frederick W. Taylor, *The Principles of Scientific Management* (New York: Harper, 1911), 53.

[10] Taylor, *Principles*, 54–55.

[11] Edwin Layton, Jr., *The Revolt of the Engineers* (Cleveland: Case Western University Press, 1971), 137.

[12] Horace B. Drury, *Scientific Management: A History and Criticism* (New York: Columbia University Press, 1922), 38; Henry V. R. Scheel, "Some Recollections of Henry Laurence Gantt," *Journal of Industrial Engineering* 12 (May–June 1961): 221.

[13] Oscar Kraines, "Brandeis and Scientific Management," *Publication of the American Jewish Historical Society* 41 (September 1951): 41–60.

[14] Testimony of Harrington Emerson, U.S. Congress, Senate, *Evidence Taken by the Interstate Commerce Commission in the Matter of Proposed Advances in Freight Rates by Carriers*, 61st Cong., 3d sess., August to December 1910 (Washington: Government Printing Office), S. Doc. 725, Ser. Set 5,908, 2829.

[15] Vladimir I. Lenin, "The Urgent Problems of the Soviet Rule," *Bulletin of the Taylor Society* 4 (June 1919): 35–38. (Reprinted from *Pravda*, April 28, 1918, 3–5.)

[16] Lyndall F. Urwick, "The Truth about 'Schmidt': Reflections of Col. Lyndall F. Urwick," *Working Paper*, series 3, no. 1, Management History Division, Academy of Management, 1978, 8–9, 12.

[17] Charles D. Wrege and Amedeo G. Perroni, "Taylor's Pig-Tale: A Historical Analysis of Frederick W. Taylor's Pig-Iron Experiment," *Academy of Management Journal* 17 (March 1974): 6–27.

[18] Majority Report of Sub-Committee on Administration, "The Present State of the Art of Industrial Management," *Transactions, American Society of Mechanical Engineers* 34 (1912): 1137.

[19] Thomas P. Hughes, *American Genesis: A Century of Invention and Technological Enthusiasm 1870–1970* (New York: Viking, 1989), 199.

[20] Taylor, *Principles of Scientific Management*, 119.

[21] Peter F. Drucker, "The Coming Rediscovery of Scientific Management," *Conference Board Record* 13 (June 1976): 26.

[22] John Dos Passos, *The Big Money* (New York: Harcourt, Brace, 1936), 25.

[23] Lillian M. Gilbreth, *The Quest of the One Best Way* (New York: Society of Industrial Engineers, 1924), 16.

[24] Frank B. Gilbreth quoted in Paul U. Kellogg, "A National Hearing for Scientific Management," *The Survey* (December 3, 1910):411–412.

[25] Gilbreth, *Quest for the One Best Way*, 22.

[26] Frank B. Gilbreth and Lillian M. Gilbreth, "Motion Study and Time Study Instruments of Precision," *Transactions, International Engineering Congress, 1915*, vol. II (San Francisco: 1916), 473.

[27] Frank B. Gilbreth quoted in Milton J. Nadworny, "Frank and Lillian Gilbreth and Industrial Relations," *Journal of Industrial Engineering*, Special Reprint 13 (May 1962): SR–16.

[28] Milton J. Nadworny, "Frederick Taylor and Frank Gilbreth: Competition in Scientific Management," *Business History Review* 31 (Spring 1957): 23–24.

[29] Lillian M. Gilbreth, *The Psychology of Management* (New York: Sturgis & Walton, 1914).

[30] Frank B. Gilbreth, Jr., and Ernestine Gilbreth Carey, *Cheaper by the Dozen* (New York: Thomas Y. Crowell, 1948); Frank B. Gilbreth, Jr., and Ernestine Gilbreth Carey, *Bells on Their Toes* (New York: Crowell, 1950); Frank B. Gilbreth, Jr., *Time Out for Happiness* (New York: Crowell, 1970).

[31] Lillian M. Gilbreth, "Scrapped at Forty," *The Survey* 62 (July 1, 1929): 402–403; Lillian M. Gilbreth, "Hiring and Firing: Shall the Calendar Measure Length of Service?," *Factory and Industrial Management* 79 (February 1930): 310–311.

[32] This and other biographical information was taken from Morris B. Brodie, *Fayol on Administration* (London: Lyon, Grant and Green, 1967); and Donald Reid, *The Miners of Decazeville: A Genealogy of Deindustrialization* (Cambridge: Harvard University Press, 1985).

[33] Norman M. Pearson, "Fayolism as the Necessary Complement to Taylorism," *American Political Science Review* 39 (February 1945): 73.

[34] Henri Fayol, *General and Industrial Management*, trans. Constance Storrs (London: Pitman, 1916/1949), 19.

[35] John D. Breeze and Arthur G. Bedeian, *The Administrative Writings of Henri Fayol: A Bibliographic Investigation*, 2d ed. (Monticello, Ill.: Vance Bibliographies, 1988).

[36] Charles de Freminville, "Henri Fayol: A Great Engineer, A Great Scientist and a Great Management Leader," *Bulletin of the Taylor Society* 12 (February 1927): 304.

[37] Max Weber, *The Theory of Social and Economic Organization*, ed. and trans. Alexander M. Henderson and Talcott Parsons (New York: Oxford University Press, 1922/1947); Max Weber, *The Methodology of the Social Sciences*, ed. and trans. Edward A. Shils and Henry H. Finch (Glencoe, Ill.: Free Press, 1904–1917/1949); and Max Weber, *From Max Weber: Essays in Sociology*, ed. and trans. Hans H. Gerth and C. Wright Mills (New York: Oxford University Press, 1906–1924/1946).

[38] The following section is based on William J. Dickson, "Hawthorne Experiments," in *The Encyclopedia of Management*, 2d ed., ed. Carl Heyel (New York: Van Nostrand Reinhold, 1973), 298–302; George C. Homans, *Fatigue of Workers: Its Relation to Industrial Production* (New York: Reinhold, 1941); Fritz J. Roethlisberger and William J. Dickson, *Management and the Worker* (Cambridge, Mass.: Harvard University Press, 1939); and Urwick and Brech, *The Making of Scientific Management: Vol. 3* (1948).

[39] Lyndall F. Urwick, "Elton Mayo—His Life and Work," in *Papers and Proceedings XIIth International Congress of Scientific Management* (Melbourne: CIOS, 1960), n.p.

[40] Arnold S. Tannenbaum, *Social Psychology of the Work Organization* (Belmont, Calif.: Wadsworth, 1966), 22–24; T. North Whitehead, *The Industrial Worker*, vol. 1 (Cambridge, Mass.: Harvard University Press, 1938), 238–258.

[41] Dickson, "Hawthorne Experiments," 301.

[42] For example, see Richard H. Franke and James D. Kaul, "The Hawthorne Experiments: First Statistical Interpretation," *American Sociological Review* 43 (October 1978): 623–643.

[43] Harold D. Koontz, "The Management Theory Jungle Revisited," *Academy of Management Review* 5(April 1980): 175–187.

[44] Paraphrased from Edley W. Martin, Jr., "The Systems Concept," *Business Horizons* 9 (Spring 1966): 63.

[45] W. Edwards Deming, "A System of Profound Knowledge," *Journal of Private Enterprise* 6 (Fall 1990): 4.

[46] Peter Barnett, "The Contingency Approach—A Positive View," *Graduate Management Research* 5 (Autumn 1990): 7–10.

[47] Taylor, *Shop Management*, 40. (Emphasis added.)

[48] Mary P. Follett, "Some Discrepancies in Leadership Theory and Practice," in *Business Leadership*, ed. Henry C. Metcalf (London: Pitman, 1930), 213.

[49] This section draws on "The Quality Imperative," Bonus Issue, *Business Week*, October 25, 1991, 2–216.

[50] Larry Armstrong and William C. Symonds, "Beyond 'May I Help You?'," Bonus Issue, *Business Week*, October 25, 1991, 102.

[51] Stanley J. Modic, "What Makes Deming Run?," *Industry Week*, June 20, 1988, 84–91; Donald R. Katz, "Coming Home," *Business Month* 132 (October 1988): 56–62; and Lloyd Dobyns, "Ed Deming Wants Big Changes, and He Wants Them Fast," *Smithsonian* 21 (August 1990), 74–82.

CHAPTER 3

991 was an extraordinary year for General Motors, but not the kind of year management had in mind: The company lost $4.5 billion. Recession and a continued reduction in demand for new cars, combined with a higher market share for imports, created a crisis for the corporate giant.

On December 18, 1991, the company announced that it would close either its Willow Run, Michigan, plant or its Arlington, Texas, plant as part of a plan to close 21 facilities to reduce costs and improve quality and production. The choice of which plant to close occupied General Motors chairman Robert Stempel until February 24, 1992, when he decided that the Arlington plant would remain open and by 1993 would be making the cars that were formerly made at Willow Run. Stempel said that his decision was based on the quality of the workers at the Arlington plant, not on the tax incentives offered by Governor Ann Richards of Texas and Mayor Richard Greene of Arlington.

Arlington has a model contract with its workers. The workers are divided into teams. Each team is responsible for a group of jobs, and the jobs are rotated through the team's members so that nobody does the same job day after day. Not only does quality improve be-

MANAGING IN A CHANGING ENVIRONMENT

cause the workers aren't bored, but workers get a better picture of how each job relates to the others. The workers are very open to change, and as a result, they have created the most flexible assembly line at General Motors.

When they learned of the impending decision, local union officials worked with the Arlington plant manager to present their best side to Stempel. They asked the workers to vote on a proposal to go to a 4-day, 40-hour workweek, which was overwhelmingly approved. This allowed for the addition of a future third shift, increasing the potential production of the facility by 50 percent. The workers' willingness to work with management undoubtedly influenced Stempel's decision.

The workers in Arlington are breathing easier now—they know that their houses are safe and that they will be able to send their children to college. But the workers in Willow Run are bitter. They have 18 months to decide what they will do. General Motors expects to add 1,000 workers to the Arlington workforce when the third shift is added, and preference will be given to those employees who have been laid off elsewhere, but by then 11 other plants besides the one at Willow Run will be closed.

In this chapter, we will identify the elements of the business environment. We will see how both management and workers must be able to adapt to change in any of those elements.

Source: Ft. Worth Star-Telegram, February 25, 1992, Michael D. Towle; Mede Nix; Ellen O'Brien and Worth Wren; and Mitchell Schnurman.

Regardless of whether they are public or private, profit oriented or not for profit, large or small, all organizations must consider elements that comprise their environment. In an increasingly dynamic, interdependent, and unpredictable world, virtually all organizations are affected directly and indirectly by what is occurring both domestically and internationally. In Europe, Common Market activities, a unified Germany, democratization of former Eastern Bloc countries, and internal economic difficulties in the Commonwealth of Independent States have created both opportunities and challenges for U.S. organizations. Japan and other Pacific Rim countries continue to be formidable competitors, both in the U.S. and in the international marketplace.

As these developments suggest, to fully understand the challenge of management, one needs to understand the relationship between an organization and its environment. Following the systems approach introduced in Chapter 2, all enterprises must secure inputs (people, materials, money, information) from their surrounding environments and, in turn, be able to exchange the goods and services they provide for the energy necessary to ensure their continued survival. Customers, suppliers, and competitors are but a few of the many elements in an organization's environment that affect this input → transformation → output process. A manager's performance is often dependent on knowing how his or her organization influences and is influenced by its environment. No organization is so powerful and self-contained that it is immune to environmental pressures.

In the broadest sense, an organization's environment is everything external to its boundaries. However, it is useful to think of an organization's environment in two ways: the **general environment,** which affects all organizations, and the **task environment,** which affects the individual organization more directly.

General environment.
All factors external to an organization.

Task environment.
Those elements of the general environment *directly* relevant to an individual organization.

THE GENERAL ENVIRONMENT

The general environment consists of *all* factors external to an organization. These factors represent constraints within which all organizations—businesses, unions, universities, charities—must function. The general environment of a typical organization can be viewed as being made up of different components as depicted in Figure 3.1: governmental, economic, social, technological, and international.

GOVERNMENTAL

Government, at all levels, is an important component of the general environment. The relationship between management and local, state, and federal government has expanded to the point where no U.S. organization or industry is immune from the impact of decisions made in Washington, D.C., or in state or local legislative bodies across the country. It is becoming increasingly apparent that "political advantage" derives from a stable and constructive relationship that makes government and management allies in the battle for global competitiveness.[1]

FIGURE 3.1 GENERAL AND TASK ENVIRONMENTS OF A TYPICAL ORGANIZATION

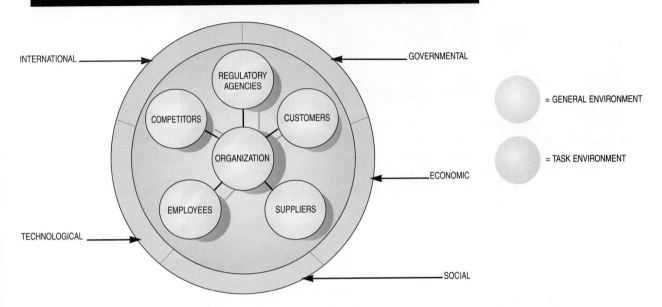

As one commentator has observed, "competing on politics" is part of doing business effectively in today's global economy.[2] The Japanese case is particularly instructive. Japanese businesses have been especially successful in advancing their interests with governments throughout the world. Japan spends more than $100 million a year to hire 1,000 Washington, D.C., lobbyists, lawyers, former government officials, public relations firms, and even former presidents in an effort to influence political decisions. It spends another $300 million every year to influence public opinion and $400 million per year to advance its economic interests, influence U.S. trade policy, and gain market share in the United States for its industries.[3]

The General Agreement on Tariffs and Trade (GATT) and the Omnibus Trade and Competitiveness Act of 1988 reinforce U.S. trade policy. GATT comprises 97 member countries and is the principal multilateral body concerned with international trade. It recognizes the right of governments to levy duties to offset export subsidies or dumping (selling exported goods for "less than fair value"). Together with U.S. trade law, it also permits the President to grant temporary import relief to industries found by the U.S. International Trade Commission to be injured or threatened with injury by import surges. As one option, the President may use trade adjustment assistance to aid workers displaced by imports to retrain or find new jobs. In such cases, GATT also permits foreign governments to demand compensation when their exports are restricted, or they may retaliate by putting restrictions on U.S. exports. The Omnibus Trade and Competitiveness Act (Section 301) mandates federal government action in severe cases of unfair trade and allows U.S. firms to receive protection under antidumping and safeguard provisions of U.S. trade law.

Free-trade advocates argue that such protectionism damages international commerce, suppresses domestic investment, and artificially inflates consumer prices. They note that trade restrictions cost consumers over $70 billion a year. The current quota on sugar imports adds $930 million a year to the $3 billion consumers already spend to protect domestic sugar growers. Similarly, import quotas increase

As the debate over the North American Free Trade Agreement rages, new trade difficulties have arisen from the U.S.-Canada Free Trade Agreement of 1988. The U.S. has accused Canada of subsidizing its lumber exports and gaining an unfair competitive advantage over the U.S. lumber industry. This type of dispute undermines the trading partnership of North American countries that many hope will help the U.S. compete globally with Japan and Europe.

steel prices more than $6.8 billion a year, automobile prices $5.8 billion a year, and clothing and textile imports by at least $27 billion.[4]

In response to these trade barriers, countries such as Japan and Canada, as well as the European Community, have retaliated by restricting the import of many U.S. goods. Japan has continued to restrict imports of textiles, apparel, automobiles, telecommunications equipment, footwear, leather, tobacco products, beef, vegetables, and pharmaceuticals. Canada has passed import barriers on textiles, apparel, automobiles, and leather and nonleather footwear. Similarly, when the United States placed retaliatory duties on pasta imports from the European Community because of duties against U.S. citrus fruits, Europeans counterretaliated with high duties on U.S. lemons and walnuts.[5] Whether the net effect of such tit-for-tat restrictions benefits any of the parties concerned is the subject of much heated debate.

ECONOMIC

Government economic policies at the federal level clearly influence the ability of virtually all organizations to survive and prosper. Over the past half-century, various economists have advocated a variety of government economic programs. Monetarists, for instance, urge the government to make stabilization of money supply a major economic goal. Keynesians, followers of British economist John Maynard Keynes (1883–1946), advocate use of fiscal and monetary methods to increase aggregate demand in slack times and dampen it in peak times.

Most recently, *supply-side* economics has emerged as a third alternative. This newly rediscovered ideology traces back to French economist Jean Baptiste Say (1767–1832). Supply-siders argue that it is not insufficient demand but rather artificial obstacles to trade that cause economic chaos and stunted growth. They contend that there can never be any long-term overproduction (or lack of demand) and cite **Say's Law:** Supply creates its own demand. That is, in a free marketplace, people will use money they are paid for making goods to buy other goods.

Whichever philosophy is "correct," the point remains clear that the impact of government economic policies on management is tremendous. Over the last 125 years or so, the United States has experienced some 30 economic recessions. The

Say's Law.
Supply creates its own demand.

"average" business cycle has lasted slightly more than 4 years. A **business cycle** is defined as a period of economic activity consisting of recession, recovery, growth, and decline, lasting from one *peak* (high point of expansion) or *trough* (minimum point of contraction) to the next. Some cycles have lasted for as little as 28 months, while others have exceeded 100. The intensity of recessions has varied widely. Those that have assumed catastrophic proportions are known as *depressions*. Those that have been hardly noticed are described as *slowdowns*. The ability to predict the duration and intensity of recessions is obviously important to managers, who need some indication of future economic levels before they can make plans. Federal government fiscal and monetary policies are major factors in accurately forecasting general economic activity. Economic forecasting will be discussed further in Enhancement Module 1, "Forecasting: Essential Planning Ingredient."

Although it is easier to think in terms of a national economy, the world trend today is definitely toward a global economy. Economic fluctuations in one country may have an effect in others. Activity in the London and Tokyo stock markets affects Wall Street and vice versa. Thus, both growth and recession are felt worldwide. Organizations that operate multinationally must be aware of the economic conditions in both their parent and host countries.

Business cycle.
A period of economic activity consisting of recession, recovery, growth, and decline, lasting from one peak (high point of expansion) or trough (minimum point of contraction) to the next.

SOCIAL

How a manager deals with an organization's environment is at least partially influenced by whether society views the organization as one pursuing socially acceptable goals in a socially acceptable manner—that is, as legitimate. In other words, society holds a global or summary belief that an organization is proper and worthy of support. Being seen as legitimate facilitates an organization's ability to acquire resources and deflects questions about its rights to provide and competence in providing specific goods and services. Take business corporations as a case in point. In the United States, society's attitude toward business has been cyclical. It has ranged from "The business of this country is business"—when corporate executives were very influential—to "Business is dull, dirty, and beneath the dignity of important people." Today, the roles of the business manager in relating to an organization's environment are generally accepted for the contribution they make to a more productive world. Indeed, as one indication of business's increased legitimacy, the number of television business shows, such as "The Bottom Line" and "Wall Street Week," has expanded as network executives who shunned such programs in the past have become increasingly convinced that they deserve a place in their lineups.

Top-level corporate managers continue to be concerned about society's attitudes toward business. In this regard, **image advertising** has become a major corporate activity. Indeed, close to half of the 800 largest U.S. corporations use advertising to sell ideas as well as products. For example, Philip Morris Cos., the tobacco and consumer-products giant, spent some $60 million on a 2-year television campaign celebrating the 200th anniversary of the Bill of Rights. The campaign did not mention cigarettes or smoking; cigarette ads have been banned from television since 1971. Antismoking advocates, however, immediately took exception at what they saw as Philip Morris's attempt to "purchase innocence by association." While a Philip Morris spokesman denied this claim, he did concede that "If [people] think well of the company through our support of the Bill of Rights, it follows they'll think well of our products."[6]

Image advertising.
Advertising used to sell ideas as well as products.

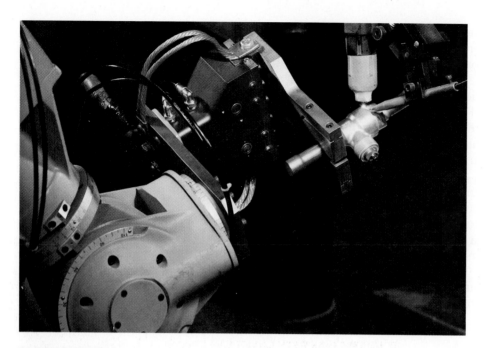

Amcast Industrial Corporation uses this state-of-the-art robotic welding machine to produce welded ball valves for air conditioning and refrigeration systems. Technology has enabled Amcast to design and produce a product that is considered the best in the industry for controlling the escape of refrigerant gases into the environment.

TECHNOLOGICAL

Technology refers to the means by which an organization transforms inputs into outputs. All organizations involve employees in activities that result in the transformation of "things" coming in (for example, labor, knowledge, capital, or raw materials) into "things" going out (either goods or services). Thus, an insurance company has its technology for converting capital, ideas, and labor into insurance services just as an oil company has its technology for converting crude oil and other resource inputs into petroleum products.

Technology is of particular importance because it has been and continues to be the main source of increases in productivity. Despite changes in the means used to motivate people and the variety of incentives that have been offered to stimulate production, the resulting increase has been negligible when compared to that created by technology.

Because of its impact on productivity, technology can either provide a competitive advantage to organizations that can use it effectively or pose a threat to those that lack it. Superior technology, for example, helps Wal-Mart keep operating expenses at 15 percent of sales, far below Kmart's 20 percent. Barcode scanners track inventory as well as ring up customers' purchases. Wal-Mart managers wire merchandise requests to regional warehouses through computer terminals. Warehouse computers are linked via satellite directly with 200 vendors, making deliveries faster and less expensive. As a result of its high-tech point-of-sale and computer distribution systems, Wal-Mart spends 2¢ per dollar shipping as compared to 4¢ per dollar for its competition. Similarly, UPS has increased its productivity installing advanced computer technology. It now provides its drivers with electronic clipboards that include a stylus and a pressure-sensitive receipt pad. The clipboards allow the tracking of shipments and the speeding up of receivables.

The development of technology not only can make goods and services obsolete, but also can create entire new industries and markets. Perhaps the best example is the development of the computer, especially the personal computer, which created an entire industry and innumerable new market opportunities.

Technology.
The means by which an organization transforms inputs into outputs.

INTERNATIONAL

The internationalization of world markets has had profound ramifications for U.S. managers. No longer can they think of their competition simply as the company in the next city or state. However, as world competition intensifies, so do world opportunities. United States manufacturers such as IBM, Gillette, Xerox, Dow Chemical, and Hewlett-Packard sell more of their products abroad than domestically. United States service companies such as McDonald's, American Express, and Citicorp are close behind.

Coca-Cola annually makes more money in both the Far East and Western Europe than at home. Some 70 percent of General Motors' profits are from non-U.S. operations. At the same time, few Americans know that France's Thomson owns the RCA and General Electric names in consumer electronics and that the Netherlands' Philips owns Magnavox, Sylvania, and Philco.

For today's managers competing in a world economy is an accepted fact of life. World trade volume has increased more than twenty-fold in the last three decades from $200 billion to more than $4 trillion. Clearly, the opportunities and threats of world trade are greater today than ever before. Given the significance of the international component of the general environment, Chapter 22 is devoted entirely to various issues posed by international business.

THE TASK ENVIRONMENT

In contrast to the general environment, the task environment consists of those components of the general environment *directly* relevant to an individual organization. A typical organization's task environment (see Figure 3.1 on page 71) includes: customers, suppliers, employees, competitors, and regulatory agencies. Thus, the difference between the general environment and the task environment is that between the broad environment within which all organizations function and the more immediate environment in which an individual organization might operate.

The boundary between an organization's general and task environments, however, should not be viewed as static. Changes in the former will inevitably redefine the latter. In the United States, the October 1987 stock market crash and the 1991 Persian Gulf War are but two examples of events in the general environment that redefined many task environments.

CUSTOMERS

Simply stated, without customers an organization could not exist. Manufacturers need wholesalers, accounting and law firms need clients, hospitals need patients, and educational institutions need students. All organizations rely on customers.

One key to the success of top enterprises—from Frito-Lay to Procter & Gamble, from Domino's Pizza to Disney—is a true customers-first service orientation.[7] Customer service is basic to the IBM creed. It cuddles its customers with a field-service force 25,000 strong. At Neiman-Marcus, where customer service is a fundamental philosophy, Chairman Emeritus Stanley Marcus explains, "It is never a good sale for Neiman-Marcus unless it's a good buy for the customer."[8]

Every year some $5.52 trillion worth of goods and services is produced in the United States. Shops, factories, and offices create an incredible variety of automobiles, health services, clothes, foods, televisions, homes, missiles, machinery, and a

Consumer feedback helps drive the development at many successful companies such as Microsoft, Nintendo, and Hershey Foods. Hershey's consumer relations program plays an important role in keeping the corporation in tune with its customers. Consumers use Hershey's toll-free telephone number to ask questions before preparing a recipe.

million other goods and services aimed at satisfying customer needs. With the advent of the so-called customer service revolution, the line between goods and services is fast eroding.[9] This erosion reflects a new view of the relationship between producer and consumer. As one commentator has observed: "There are no products—only services."[10] The idea is for an organization to think of every product it sells as a service. Thus, realizing that General Motors makes a greater profit from lending its customers money to buy its cars than it makes from producing the cars, one might ask whether it is marketing its goods or its services.

At General Motors and countless other organizations, selling a good is now seen as an opportunity to do something for one's customers. Consider Toyota's Lexus. In partnership with IBM, it maintains a national data bank on every car it has sold. Any dealer from Key West to Tacoma can access the data bank to view a car's maintenance history. Why? Because Lexus realizes that "marketing a product is marketing a service is marketing a product."[11] Stated more directly, Lexus appreciates the importance of a joint product-service focus for building loyal consumer relationships.

Developing loyal consumer relationships requires that an organization understand who its buyers are and what goods and services they need. Clever organizations listen to their customers, realizing that they may be their best collaborators. Customer feedback drives their product development. Thus, top software houses count on user groups or clubs as a source of product ideas and improvements. Nintendo has a telephone hotline, more than 100 game counselors who handle more than 120,000 customer calls a week, and a subscription magazine. Apple, IBM, and Hewlett-Packard depend on their user groups to identify bugs and suggest new product features. In each case, such groups serve as a feedback loop for bringing about change and represent an important aspect of the consumer service revolution, "a shift from monologue to dialogue."[12]

This shift may, in part, be attributed to the emergence of the so-called **consumer movement.** Throughout the world, groups of consumers have joined together to exert pressure on specific firms and even entire industries in an effort to see that the public gets a "fair shake." Pressure from consumer groups has led to tighter scrutiny of food, drugs, and children's clothing, among other products. Major consumer groups include the Consumer Federation of America, the National Consumers League, and the Consumers Union of the United States. Perhaps the best-known representative of this movement is consumer advocate Ralph Nader. Working out of the Center for the Study of Responsive Law, Nader directs a consortium of nonprofit public interest groups, including Public Citizen, to lobby with 50,000 dues-paying members. Nader and his "Raiders" have actively supported such legislative bills as those creating the Occupational Safety and Health Administration, the U.S. Environmental Protection Agency, and the Consumer Product Safety Commission.

Commercial firms, in particular, have responded in several ways to consumer concerns. Procter & Gamble, Whirlpool, Clairol, and other companies have created offices of consumer relations equipped with toll-free 800 telephone numbers. Procter & Gamble receives more than 200,000 calls a year on its 800 number. Such consumer lines not only are helpful for spotting new fads, but also help in marketing new products and in detecting foul-ups before they become major complaints. Other companies have appointed an **ombudsperson** to investigate customer complaints. Of course, groups such as the Better Business Bureau have long been supported by the general business community.

Finally, close attention to product quality is an essential aspect of customer service. The highest quality is consistently maintained at successful companies such as Levi Strauss, American Express, and General Electric. Levi's famous 501 jeans have become such a symbol of quality that a pair hangs in the Smithsonian Institution. American Express has a Quality University that offers courses like "How to Treat the Customer 101." Domino's Pizza pays 10,000 "mystery customers" $60 each to buy 12 pizzas a year at its over 5,000 units and evaluate quality and service. General Electric maintains an information-service center that handles 3 million calls a year. Rubbermaid does such an excellent job of responding to its customers' needs that it even gives refunds on competitors' defective products. By doing so, it hopes to convert an angry consumer into a Rubbermaid customer. In each instance, these companies realize that the payback from these efforts to turn customers into collaborators is worth many times the cost incurred.

SUPPLIERS

Suppliers constitute a second component in a typical organization's task environment. As the systems approach suggests, organizations must respond not only to the customers they supply, but also to the sources from which they receive supplies. The acquisition of inputs thus constitutes a major dependency for most organizations. As an example, the 400-passenger 747–400 contains some 6 million parts that Boeing Aircraft orders from more than 1,500 suppliers.

The relationship between an organization and its suppliers can be characterized as one of mutual benefit. In exchange for their products, suppliers expect to receive a fair price. Discarding their old adversarial ways, more and more organizations and suppliers are working together to reduce costs and upgrade product

Consumer movement.
Groups of consumers joining together to exert pressure on specific firms and even entire industries in an effort to see that the public gets a "fair shake."

Ombudsperson.
Representative who investigates customer complaints.

CLOSE UP: SOCIAL RESPONSIBILITY THE GREENING OF CORPORATE AMERICA

For evidence of how radically business environments can change, one need look no further than the environment itself.

It wasn't long ago that earth issues ranked low on the priority list of corporate America. Companies exploited natural resources without considering the consequences, consumers rarely questioned the ecological impact of products, and environmental legislation was virtually nonexistent. Although some would argue that those statements still hold true today, there is no denying that a metamorphosis has occurred.

Entire companies are now dedicated to selling "ecoproducts" like solar power systems and recycled paper goods. Consumers are buying biodegradable and reusable products. And major pieces of legislation are generating billions of dollars worth of environmental protection work throughout the nation.

This emphasis on environmental responsibility has also created a new set of opportunities for students preparing to enter the business world.

New York University is one of the first schools to offer business students courses in global resource management and green consumerism. Students are also encouraged to take courses in environmental law, science, and even ethics.

At Prescott College in Arizona, students can consult an environmental directory that lists graduate programs, internships, and jobs. In addition, the school has a new program called Common Grounds, which is aimed at improving communication between businesses and environmentalists.

The Rochester Institute of Technology has established a bachelor of science program in environmental management, with a concentration in solid waste. It developed the program with the input of engineers, waste company managers, and government regulators. Students are required to incorporate work-study into the 5-year degree plan, and their final year is spent entirely in the field.

Educators say the opportunities for similar programs are limitless because each industry has its own dynamics. Setting up a plastics recycling program, for example, is different from establishing a nature conservancy or building electric cars.

These new programs also represent a response to needs expressed by students themselves. As one career counselor at the University of Massachusetts explained, students don't want to be a cog in a wheel helping large corporate giants accumulate more money. They want to do something more responsible.

quality, as well as to achieve just-in-time delivery and eliminate inspection and other phases. Some dozen Procter & Gamble representatives attend solely to the needs of Wal-Mart. They have established a just-in-time delivery system for Pampers and Luvs disposable diapers. When inventories for either item run low, a computer submits an order by satellite to a Procter & Gamble factory that then automatically ships more diapers to specific stores. This minimizes Wal-Mart's inventories and the number of times it runs out of disposable diapers.

In today's competitive global environment, suppliers can no longer be played off one another for lower prices. As a Boeing general manager comments, "In the past you negotiated the bejesus out of your suppliers. Today what we're interested in is quality, schedule and cost. The low-cost producer may not get the contract."[13]

When Monsanto Chemical initiated its total quality process, it realized the need to develop a partnership program with its suppliers. Monsanto challenged suppliers to initiate their own quality programs. Sonoco's Fibre Drum Division accepted the challenge, training all the division's employees in a Total Quality System. Sonoco's quality improvement teams began meeting with similar teams from Monsanto, addressing various questions to improve the quality of the customer/supplier relationship. Sonoco Fibre Drum earned a "Preferred" supplier designation from two of Monsanto's manufacturing locations.

Reflecting this sentiment, Motorola (a winner of the U.S. Commerce Department's coveted Malcolm Baldridge National Quality Award) sends design-and manufacturing engineers to suppliers to help with any problems. Motorola, as well as such companies as Procter & Gamble, considers suppliers as partners in their joint destinies.

Realizing that major improvements could be made by working more closely with their suppliers, companies such as Harley-Davidson, A. O. Smith Corporation, Xerox, and Hewlett-Packard have drastically reduced the number of vendors with which they do business. Xerox, for instance, has slashed its number of suppliers from 5,000 to 300. At the same time, these same companies have given their remaining suppliers longer and larger contracts. Harley-Davidson, for example, now signs 3- to 5-year contracts with vendors, compared with 1-year contracts in the past. In some cases, Hewlett-Packard is guaranteeing suppliers they will get 60 percent or more of its requirements for a certain part. These larger volume contracts have, in turn, afforded suppliers economies of scale and the opportunity to automate—both of which reduce costs. From a purchasing company's vantage, working with fewer suppliers increases administrative efficiencies, offers greater flexibility in altering production schedules in response to shifts in demand, and permits a better handle on quality control. The seriousness with which companies regard such benefits is evident in the process many use to select suppliers. General Motors, for instance, sends out inspection teams to rate a supplier's plants. The teams certify suppliers for just-in-time delivery techniques, statistical quality controls, and the ability to handle data electronically, among other attributes. Such efforts do not increase real costs. Rather, they decrease costs by reducing product defects, eliminating excessive field service, and, most importantly, reducing the cost of business lost to competitors. Moreover, when quality increases, productivity usually does, too, since eliminating errors cuts the time necessary to redo work in offices and factories alike.

Some companies, such as National Semiconductor and General Motors, have established supplier councils that meet regularly to discuss common concerns and future plans. Xerox provides its suppliers with computer terminals so that they can access its main computer to develop schedules for parts deliveries. One of Eastman Kodak's suppliers actually runs a Kodak supply room.

Whether an organization is dependent on a few suppliers or many, favorable supplier relations can also lead to improved quality, better shipping arrangements, early warning of major price changes, and advance information about technological or marketplace developments. Thus, managers make an important investment toward organization effectiveness if they develop friendly, professional relations with suppliers in which both will profit.

EMPLOYEES

Employees comprise a third component in a typical task environment. All organizations accomplish their objectives through the actions of their employees. For their part, employees work to meet their own personal, social, and economic needs. As Chapters 15 through 18 explain, it is the responsibility of management to design the leadership and influence processes of an organization in a way that ensures that in all organization activities, employees view their contributions as supportive and consistent with their sense of personal importance. The basic challenge in employee-employer relations is to create a situation in which both parties achieve their goals simultaneously. In such a case, employees are able to satisfy their own needs while fulfilling organization objectives.

Bank of America, Chaparral Steel, Delta Air Lines, Federal Express, Polaroid, and Hallmark Cards are companies known for the quality of their employee relations. Each is a member of a select group of U.S. companies that have either explicit employment guarantee policies or strong implicit traditions that in practice amount to the same. Delta has been known to put pilots temporarily to work loading luggage at their same salary rather than place them on furlough. When its Zap-Mail service failed, Federal Express offered affected employees jobs elsewhere in the company. Similarly, no layoffs occurred after it purchased rival Tiger International's Flying Tiger Cargo line, despite concern that not doing so would hurt earnings. While such traditions as no-layoff policies are expensive, they do pay dividends in terms of a well-motivated, loyal workforce.

If an organization is unionized, employee-employer relations are no less important. Union membership as a percentage of the U.S. workforce peaked in 1954 at 35 percent. Since then it has been slipping, hastened in the 1980s when industrial employment contracted from an economic recession and international competition. Although unions in the United States today barely represent one out of ten private nonagricultural wage and salary workers (13.4 percent) in the over 84.6 million-member private workforce, their national influence and concentration in key industries makes favorable union relations a major managerial priority. Unions can shut down a firm's operations by striking, boycotting its products, or calling upon the National Labor Relations Board to halt certain managerial practices. Thus, if a firm is unionized, it makes sense to maintain a close and congenial relationship with union leaders. Such contacts provide an official channel of communication between labor and management. In addition to the traditional union membership in heavy industry, trucking, and shipping, unionization has recently spread to include government employees, teachers, engineers, retail clerks, university professors, and even graduate students. Some enterprises resist unionization. Others—like John Deere, Jones & Laughlin, and AT&T—pursue cooperation with their unions, believing that they need their active support. Labor-management relations will be dealt with at length in Chapter 13.

COMPETITORS

Competitors comprise a fourth component in a typical organization's task environment. Market competition is the cornerstone of managerial capitalism. To gain competitive advantage, an organization must either provide equal product value but operate more efficiently than its rivals (lower cost) or operate in a unique way that creates greater product value and commands a premium price (differentiation).[14] Organizations that are unable to do either will soon be confronted, as the **law of the marketplace** dictates, with the uncomfortable prospect of either changing their product line or being eliminated. The five forces that shape the degree of market competition operating within an organization's task environment are shown in Figure 3.2. Their combined strength establishes the "ultimate profit potential" of a field or industry by shaping the prices an organization can charge, the costs it must bear, and the investment required to compete.[15]

Law of the marketplace.
Organizations that are unable to compete successfully will soon be confronted with the uncomfortable prospect of either changing their product line or being eliminated.

RIVALRY AMONG EXISTING ORGANIZATIONS

When competing organizations jockey for position, they use tactics like price competition, comparative advertising, and increased customer service or warranties. Rivalry develops because at least one competitor feels marketplace pressure or sees an opportunity to increase its market position. In most industries, market actions by one competitor provoke countermoves by other competitors. Such rivalry may be

FIGURE 3.2 FIVE FORCES THAT SHAPE MARKETPLACE COMPETITION

characterized by phrases like "bitter" or "cutthroat" at one extreme and "polite" or "mannerly" at the other. Competition in the cereal marketplace among Kellogg, General Mills, General Foods, and Quaker is clearly "warlike." Competition in the soft-drink industry between Coca-Cola and Pepsi is almost legendary. The degree of competition in the fast-food industry is well captured in advice offered by Ray Kroc, the legendary founder of McDonald's Corporation. If a competitor is drowning, he said, stick a hose in his mouth.[16]

Competition has good and bad aspects. Good competition can actually improve an organization's position because competitors can stimulate an industry's overall growth by sharing the cost of market development, fighting against substitute products, helping to standardize a new technology, and lending legitimacy to an industry, as Century 21 Real Estate as a national franchiser has done for real-estate brokerage. Competitors can also serve as motivators. A healthy competitor can be a strong impetus for reducing costs, improving goods and services, and keeping pace with technological developments. AT&T, for example, seems to have benefited from the emergence of viable competitors in the telecommunications market.

RELATIVE POWER OF CUSTOMERS
The power of an organization's customers is manifested by forcing down product prices, bargaining for more services and higher quality, or playing organizations off against one another. When such power exists, as when supermarket chains like A&P and Kroger battle each other for the same customers, it may have a negative effect on an organization's bottom line.

RELATIVE POWER OF SUPPLIERS
The power of suppliers is manifested by threatening to raise prices or by reducing the quality of available resources. In the case of increased prices, if an organization is unable to recover such costs in its own pricing, its profitability will suffer accordingly, and the effects of competition will be felt even more directly. With regard to resource quality, in the short run an organization may have no choice but to accept the resources available. In the long run, however, management should make identification of alternative resource outlets a top priority. The competitive advantage of being a dominant customer should be obvious. Companies such as Rolls-Royce, which represents an essential portion of total sales for many suppliers, have been found to receive unusually large levels of credit, whereas minor customers with less power receive normal credit terms. Similarly, major buyers are more likely to be successful in persuading suppliers to submit to rigorous inspection, certification, and education requirements to ensure acceptable quality materials.

THREAT OF NEW ENTRANTS
New organizations in a marketplace generally increase product supply, generally seek to gain market share, and often possess substantial resources. As a consequence of one or more of these factors, market prices will likely be forced down and resource costs inflated. Again, the negative impact this would have on organization profitability and the likely increase in competition are evident. IBM's long-awaited introduction of its original personal computer and its introduction of custom software are two cases in point. Both products resulted in much tougher industry competition.

THREAT OF SUBSTITUTES

The organizations within a marketplace compete not only with one another, but also with other organizations that produce substitute goods or services. Thus, Pizza Hut, Taco Bell, and Kentucky Fried Chicken compete not only with other pizza or taco or chicken restaurants, but with every alternative, from grocery store delis to Mom's Sunday dinner to Burger King.

Likewise, sugar producers compete not only with one another, but also with the manufacturers of high-fructose corn syrup, saccharine, and NutraSweet-artificial sweetener. Substitutes that yield an equal-quality output at a lower price can have a devastating effect on sales and thus result in increased competition. What's more, they may even possess the potential to make an organization's products obsolete. Nylon, for example, has almost totally replaced silk as the fiber in women's stockings. Many observers speculate that olestra, the cholesterol-free artificial fat developed by Procter & Gamble, will have a similar impact on the demand for vegetable oil.

CLOSE UP: INTERNATIONAL MANAGEMENT A GUIDE FOR GLOBETROTTING MANAGERS

With Europe united, the Japanese economic juggernaut racing ahead, and communism crumbled in what was the Eastern Bloc, U.S. industry must compete in an increasingly competitive global market. Companies such as Coca-Cola, Procter & Gamble, and McDonald's have been especially successful in penetrating foreign markets. Coca-Cola claims 650 million individual consumptions of its brand each day. It extracted greater net profits from Japan in 1990 than from the United States. Procter & Gamble boasts of major operations in 46 countries outside the United States. Its brands are sold in nearly 150 countries. The appeal of McDonald's is likewise global and becoming more so. Golden arches beam out from Aurora, Illinois, to Andorra and Malaysia. Worldwide, more people eat at McDonald's each day than live in Australia and New Zealand combined. McDonald's Hamburger University training center resembles the United Nations. It provides simultaneous translations of its 2-week course in 17 languages.

A major part of overseas success is navigating through the thicket of international customs that can ensnare the best-planned business deal:

● Talk business over dinner in France and you'll be seen as an oaf, fair game for some cutting French wit.

● In Saudi Arabia, passing documents with the left hand is the height of poor manners because the left hand is used for bathroom functions.

● Don't send chrysanthemums to a colleague in France. They are a symbol of death.

● Never show the sole of your foot or shoe to an associate in Saudi Arabia. Doing so is very insulting because it implies you feel you can tread upon someone.

● Holding up two fingers will get you a cab quickly in Russia, but think twice before doing so because it means you'll pay double.

● In Korea, contracts are viewed not as binding pacts but as documents to depart from if conditions change.

As is clear from these examples, what's normal from one country to the next can vary quite widely. Learning one's way through the thicket of international customs, however, can make the difference between going abroad and winning or losing an important contract.

Source: Adapted from "Consultants Guide CEOs through Globe's Cultural Thicket," *States-Times* (Baton Rouge), July 31, 1990, 8–A.

REGULATORY AGENCIES

Regulatory agencies are a final component in a typical organization's task environment. The increase in government regulations over the past two decades has been unprecedented. Combined with past legislation, the result has been an extraordinary pattern of regulations that affect almost every aspect of management. As a result, nearly every department or unit of an average organization has a counterpart in one or more federal agencies. Indeed, as Figure 3.3 illustrates, a "shadow" bureaucracy of federal agencies directly matches the structure of a typical industrial corporation.

The scope of regulations enforced by the federal agencies identified in Figure 3.3 ranges broadly, from an organization's activities in input markets (including regulation of employment practices and energy consumption), to conditions in production (including employee safety and health, and environmental pollution), to the nature of outputs (including product safety regulations). The impact of these regulations varies, of course, across industries and companies.[17] A study exploring the impact of regulation on the steel industry identified some 5,600 regulations en-

FIGURE 3.3 A TYPICAL INDUSTRIAL CORPORATION AND ITS FEDERAL GOVERNMENT

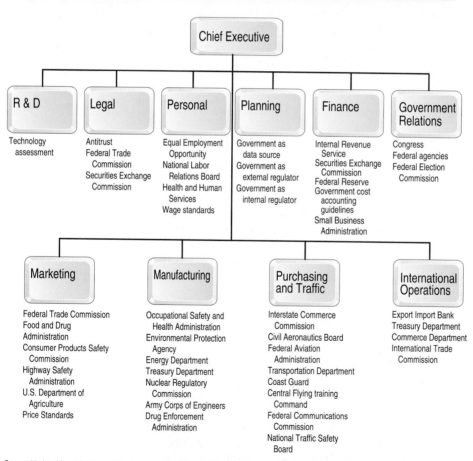

Source: Updated from Murray L Weidenbaum, "Public Policy: No Longer a Spectator Sport for Business", *Journal of Business Strategy* 1 (Summer 1980), 48. Reprinted by permission. Copyright 1980, Warren, Gorham & Lamont, Inc., 210 South Street, Boston, Mass. All rights reserved.

forced by 27 federal agencies. At the individual firm level, Dow Chemical estimates that it spends more than $400 million annually to meet federal regulations. Eli Lilly reports that it fills out more than 27,000 federal forms a year. For the business community as a whole, it has been estimated that the cost of federal regulation (both the expenses of regulatory agencies themselves and the costs they induce in the private sector) exceeds $115 billion annually, or more than $500 a year for every man, woman, and child living in the United States.

For firms that operate in two or more states, federal regulations are only one part of an even larger picture. They must also comply with state and local regulations that vary from region to region. It is estimated that between 150,000 and 200,000 bills are introduced in state legislatures every 2 years, of which some 35,000 actually become law. As a result of widely varying state laws, a firm such as Sterling Drug has to maintain separate inventories and labels for various products and detailed distribution records to ensure that certain items are not distributed to certain states. Says Sterling Drug's director of government affairs, "You think you're serving one master well, and suddenly you're serving a 50-headed hydra."[18] The cost of such service is obviously substantial. As just one example, General Motors reports that it spends $2.2 billion annually complying with different local, state, and federal government regulations.

Recognizing the growth in regulations and their associated cost, President Ronald Reagan ordered a 2-month ban on new regulations shortly after taking office in 1981. Similarly, President George Bush imposed a 90-day ban on new regulation in early 1992 as part of a new economic recovery plan. Both regulatory bans applied to virtually every federal agency and forced each agency to review all its regulations with the intent of either scrapping those that unduly burden business or reducing their costs.

MANAGERIAL RESPONSES

Realizing that no organization or industry is immune to its environment, top-level managers have come to devote more and more attention to environmental issues. Indeed, the necessity for organizations to actively enhance and influence their environment has become increasingly recognized as essential for competing in the global market.

Organizations can pursue many avenues to enhance and influence relations with their environment. The various alternative strategies they may enact in dealing with competitors and customers are discussed in Chapter 6. Likewise, alternate human resource management options in relating to employees are treated in Chapter 12. Four additional avenues that are especially pertinent in the present context are environmental scanning, lobbying, direct political action, and illegal action.

ENVIRONMENTAL SCANNING

One of the biggest advantages an organization can have is early insight into environmental forces and trends. With the internationalization of economic competition and the quickening pace of technical advances, early insight into emerging events can provide the critical advantage in the performance of an organization. Because all sectors of the U.S. economy have become more intimately linked to the global environment, a premium has thus been placed on the capacity to collect, select, assess, and pass on information about forces that affect the general environment.

Environmental scanning is a proactive approach to successfully coping with the forces and trends that affect an organization's environment. It involves monitoring and evaluating environmental changes that others may not have noticed but that may be important. Events that may seem remote and irrelevant when viewed in isolation may signal critical changes when viewed in concert. Perhaps for this reason, studies have repeatedly found a close relationship between organization performance and environmental information gathering. Organizations that pay attention to their environments seem to perform well, while those that ignore or discount the influence of environmental factors often fail.[19] Environmental scanning activities range from informal information gathering to elaborate programs carrying labels such as Competitor Intelligence, Strategic Analysis, and Futures Group. Sears, for example, has a corporate monitoring unit that continuously tracks some 100 publications and research reports to identify potential environmental changes (threats and opportunities). Japan's Mitsubishi Trading Company employs over 60,000 market analysts around the world whose principal job is to gather information about global rivals. Its U.S. intelligence unit includes several hundred employees who occupy two entire floors in a New York City office building.

Other companies may choose not to establish their own internal scanning programs, but to purchase reports prepared by commercial firms such as SRI International (formerly Stanford Research Institute), which publishes *Scan,* or The Futures Group, which publishes *FutureScan.* Many companies subscribe to newspaper-clipping services such as Burrelle's Information Services and International Clipping Bureau. Burrelle's monitors 16,000 newspapers, magazines, and trade journals for 40,000 categories. Still other companies pool and share environmental information through joint programs such as the Trend Analysis Program (TAP) coordinated by the American Council of Life Insurance. Several general sources of environmental information are identified in Table 3.1 along with selected examples of each.

Environmental scanning.
Monitoring and evaluating environmental forces and trends.

Environmental scanning and careful attention to changing political and economic conditions throughout the world has enabled the Coca-Cola Bottling Company to be a forerunner in meeting the needs of new markets in eastern Europe. Here, workers oversee production in one of the thirteen production and distribution centers built by Coca-Cola in eastern Europe by 1991 to serve 17 million new consumers.

TABLE 3.1   SOURCES OF ENVIRONMENTAL INFORMATION

Source	Examples	Comment
Government	Freedom of Information Act Government Contract Administration Patent filings	1974 amendments have led to accelerating use. Examination of a competitor's bids and documentation may reveal competitor's technology and indicate costs and bidding philosophy. Belgium and Italy publish patent applications shortly after they are filed. Some companies (for example, pharmaceutical) patent their mistakes in order to confuse their competitors.
Competitors	Annual reports and 10Ks	Federal Trade Commission and Securities Exchange Commission line of business reporting requirements will render these sources more useful in the future.
	Speeches and public announcements of competitors' officers	Reveal management philosophy, priorities, and self-evaluation systems.
	Products	Systematic analysis of a competitor's products via "reverse engineering" may reveal a competitor's technology and enable a company to monitor changes in the competitor's engineering and assembly operations. Forecasts of a competitor's sales may often be made from observing serial numbers over time.
	Employment ads	May suggest the technical and marketing directions in which a competitor is headed.
	Consultants	For example, if a competitor has retained the Boston Consulting Group, then portfolio management strategies become more likely.
Suppliers	Banks, advertising agencies, public relations firms, and direct mailers and catalogers, as well as hard-goods suppliers	Have a tendency to be more talkative than competitors since the information transmitted may enhance supplier's business. Can be effective sources of information on such items as competitors' equipment installations and on which retail competitors are already carrying certain product lines. Suppliers' biases can usually be recognized.
Customers	Purchasing agents Customer engineers and corporate officers	Generally regarded as self-serving. Low reliability as a source. Valued sources of intelligence. One company taught its salespersons to perform elementary service for customers in order to get the salespersons past purchasing agents and on to more valued sources of intelligence.
Professional Associations and Meetings	Scientific and technical society meetings and management association meetings	Examine competitors' products, research and development, and management approach as revealed in displays, brochures, scientific papers, and speeches.
Company Personnel	Executives, sales force, engineers and scientists, and purchasing agents	Sensitize them to the need for intelligence and train them to recognize and transmit to the proper company location relevant intelligence that comes to their attention.
Other Sources	Consultants, management service companies, and the media	Wide variety of special purpose and syndicated reports available.

Source: Adapted from David B. Montgomery and Charles B. Weinberg, "Toward Strategic Intelligence Systems," *Journal of Marketing* 43 (1979), 46.

Formal scanning activities are typically linked to long-range strategic planning. Evaluation of current events and trends can be quite helpful in determining goods or services to emphasize, markets to penetrate, opportunities to develop, and technologies to exploit. Japanese firms clearly had an early warning about the importance of energy efficiency, McDonnell Douglass used competitor intelligence to best Boeing with its MD91 prop-fan airliner, Motorola got the jump on its Japanese rivals in the European chip market, and Coors sidestepped larger losses in the winecooler business.

The preceding illustrations highlight the importance of environmental scanning in dealing effectively with an organization's environment. Given the strategic significance of environmental changes, effective managers recognize the need for vigilant and formalized scanning programs to monitor environmental forces and trends.

LOBBYING

Organizations lobby indirectly through trade associations (National Association of Manufacturers), professional alliances (American Medical Association), and coordinating groups (Tobacco Institute), and directly through the roles played by their individual managers to gain various economic advantages (including direct cash subsidies, tax credits, rate increases, and rate exemptions) and to protect themselves from unfavorable legislation. Typical of such groups, the Tobacco Institute represents 13 rival companies that join forces when the tobacco industry as a whole is attacked. Member companies such as R. J. Reynolds, Philip Morris, Lorillard, U.S. Tobacco, and American Tobacco providing funding. In addition to its Washington, D.C., headquarters, the institute maintains nine field offices. As a second example, the Business Roundtable has established itself as *the* voice of business in Washington. The 200 big-company CEOs who comprise the Roundtable's membership include CEOs from General Electric, Aetna, and IBM. These and other business executives have seemingly come to the conclusion that politics is too important to be left to politicians.[20]

As incredible as it may seem, some 22,000 special interest bills are debated annually in the halls of Congress and federal regulatory agencies by some 40,000 lobbyists at a cost of over $42 million. Lobbyists were effective in defeating legislation to establish a consumer protection agency and to require businesses to notify former employees who had been exposed to a high risk of disease from toxic chemicals. In a dramatic power display, the 400 staffers of the 13,000-member American Bankers Association were instrumental in defeating legislation requiring a 10-percent withholding of dividend and interest income for tax purposes.

Lobbying by foreign governments in the United States is likewise growing. The case of Japan was mentioned earlier. The power of Japan's American lobbyists is illustrated by the success of their efforts to have light trucks classified as cars for purposes of the prevailing import tariff, which is lower for cars than trucks, and then reclassified as trucks, to satisfy lower fuel efficiency, safety, and emissions requirements, once they were inside the United States. At a cost of $3 million for lobbyists, public relations specialists, and political consultants, the Japanese avoided paying some $500 million per year in import duties.[21]

Because of the vast responsibilities of government employees who may be short on expertise and time, government lobbying has clearly become an essential

SMART MANAGEMENT   SNOOPING TO CONQUER

Every organization has them. Some have only a few. Others have hundreds, if not thousands. They are competitors.

Given the importance of environmental scanning in maintaining an organization's competitive edge, more and more organizations are systematically tracking their competitors. AT&T, Kraft, Motorola, Pfizer, and Combustion Engine are among the growing number of business firms that gather competitive intelligence to help shape their strategic decisions. Motorola, seeking a full-scale effort, hired a former CIA agent to coordinate its competitive intelligence program. Searle Laboratories uses a telephone hotline and electronic mail to speed the delivery of competitive intelligence from its far-flung sales force.

Although most firms don't resort to cloak-and-dagger tactics to gather competitive intelligence, a few can't resist. Kellogg Co. was forced to end an 80-year tradition of cereal–plant tours after two spies from a European competitor toured its Battle Creek, Michigan, plant and stole invaluable manufacturing secrets. Agents from Hitachi of Japan were caught in an elaborate sting operation trying to pay $525,000 to bribe several IBM employees for trade secrets. Avon Products hired Dallas gumshoes to rifle Mary Kay Corp.'s trash in search of competitive intelligence to ward off a $3.5-billion takeover bid. On the international front, electronic eavesdropping is said to be a common form of competitor espionage in many parts of the world. The possibility of government complicity in such matters even exists. Some 70 foreign governments have the ability to monitor communications that multinational corporations transmit into their countries. Indeed, several foreign intelligence services are known to have intercepted satellite transmissions involving telexes, facsimile messages, and telephone calls from U.S. businesses to their overseas representatives. Some do "bag jobs," searching briefcases and luggage left in hotel rooms, photographing anything that looks interesting. Others plant "bugs"—tiny transmitters—in executive offices or recruit nationals working for overseas companies.

Boeing Co. has had technical documents stolen from a Paris hotel room and passed to government-owned Air France. Likewise, IBM-France found a "bug" in its president's office. It was learned that a Frenchman on the IBM staff had connections with French intelligence. A French national working for Texas Instruments in Nice was caught passing technical information to the French government-owned computer firm Cie. des Machines Bull. IBM has had similar information stolen and passed to Bull.

In the Far East, government involvement in competitor intelligence is also a concern. Japanese intelligence agents are noted for intercepting U.S. companies' bid information and using it to allow Japanese competitors to underbid for contractors. Both the Bechtel Group and Caterpillar report being so victimized.

Because foreign governments routinely spy on U.S. corporations, pressure has mounted for U.S. agencies to spy on foreign corporations. In general, a variety of legal and ethical issues are involved. As a consequence, companies such as Caterpillar put all overseas communications in code and use secure phones that scramble conversations. Although no absolute dos and don'ts can be offered, the advice of a noted attorney rings true: "If you do not want to see what you are doing reported in the front page headlines of your local newspaper, do not do it."

Sources: Conference Board News Release #3663, October 14, 1988; Brian Dumaine, "Corporate Spies Snoop to Conquer," *Fortune,* November 7, 1988, 68–76; Wendy Zellner and Bruce Hager, "Dumpster Raids? That's Not Very Ladylike, Avon," *Business Week,* April 1, 1991, 32; and William M. Carley, "As Cold War Fades, Some Nations' Spies Seek Industrial Secrets," *Wall Street Journal,* June 17, 1991, A1, A4.

aspect of "doing business." Indeed, the relationship between certain lobbies and government agencies has become so close that some believe the agencies have been "captured" by the industries over which they serve as watchdogs. For example, allegations have been made in the past that Interstate Commerce Commission decisions were unduly influenced by the motor carrier industry, that Nuclear Regulatory Commission rulings favor the nuclear industry, and that the U.S. Environmental Protection Agency is controlled by environmentalists.[22] Whatever the truth, it is certain that as long as constituencies strive to make their positions known, legislators will have to continue to listen to all sides of important issues.

DIRECT POLITICAL ACTION

A third way in which organizations may attempt to influence their environment is direct political action. Close to 700 companies maintain full government-affairs offices in Washington, D.C. Some 2,500 others have some form of Washington representation. Managers can also be personally active in politics and even run for office. Many well-known politicians were prominent top managers when they were elected. Examples include Senators Robert Kasten, the Wisconsin Republican who was formerly a shoe company executive; Frank Lautenberg, the New Jersey Democrat who co-founded Automatic Data Processing; and Lloyd Bentsen, the Texas Democrat who was formerly an insurance executive. Many state legislators also pursue active managerial careers.

Even managers who do not hold public office can exercise political power by encouraging employees, stockholders, annuitants, and other enterprise constituents to take action. Since these groups are voters, too, companies such as Eaton Corporation, PPG, and Nationwide Insurance have found it very effective to encourage grass-roots programs that generate letters, telegrams, and telephone calls to legislators. Congress receives 300 million pieces of mail each year. Postcards are weighed rather than read or counted. In its lobbying effort to defeat legislation requiring a withholding tax, the American Bankers Association conducted a grass-roots mass-mail campaign that generated some 22 million postcards and letters. In a recent grass-roots effort, the association sent a computer disk to member banks titled "The Congressional Letter Generator." This allowed the banks to pick and mix paragraphs from several model letters, print the result on their stationery, and address it to the appropriate congressmembers and senators.[23]

An additional means of direct corporate political action is the use of *political action committees* (PACs). Although it is generally illegal for corporations and unions to contribute directly to political campaigns, they may form PACs to solicit voluntary political and "in-kind" contributions from employees and stockholders. PACs are restricted to giving $5,000 to a candidate for each election race, although there are no restrictions on the aggregate amount that a PAC can spend independently to advocate the election or defeat of candidates or on other activities, such as staffing phone banks, publicity, and get-out-the-vote drives. There were only 113 PACs in 1972, but the 1971 Federal Election Campaign Act and its 1974 amendments have led to an explosive growth of corporate, labor, and trade/health/membership PACs. By 1990 there were more than 4,100 PACs: 1,795 corporation PACs, 384 labor PACs, 774 trade/health/membership PACs, and 1,062 other PACs (see Figure 3.4). During the 1989–1990 election cycle, PAC contributions totaled about $358.1 million. House and Senate incumbents continued to receive the bulk of PAC

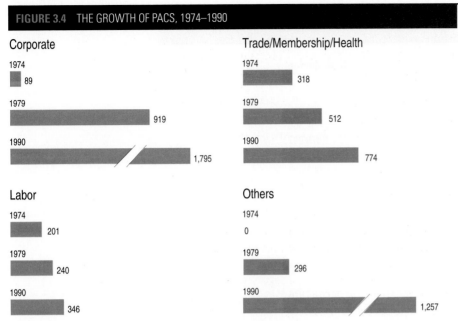

FIGURE 3.4 THE GROWTH OF PACS, 1974–1990

Corporate

1974 — 89
1979 — 919
1990 — 1,795

Trade/Membership/Health

1974 — 318
1979 — 512
1990 — 774

Labor

1974 — 201
1979 — 240
1990 — 346

Others

1974 — 0
1979 — 296
1990 — 1,257

Source: Federal Election Commission press release, January 11, 1991.

contributions, with $98.3 million going to the majority Democrats and $60.8 million to Republicans.

While the direct impact of these contributions cannot be proved, some experts believe they smack of "Congress on the auction block."[24] As one public affairs specialist sees it, "You need a PAC to be a serious player in D.C."[25] Table 3.2 lists the leading corporate, labor, and trade/health/membership PACs, together with their contributions to federal candidates in the 1989 congressional campaign.

ILLEGAL ACTION

A fourth way organizations may attempt to influence their environment is to become involved in various illegal activities. Such activities are typically aimed at sidestepping government legislation and regulation.

Prosecutors have begun to pursue lawbreakers more aggressively in the past few years. New laws and penalties reflect a stiffening in public mood brought on by repeatedly reported stories on insider trading, securities fraud, kickbacks, and corporate income-tax evasion. So-called "white-collar" offenders such as arbitrageur Ivan F. Boesky and junk-bond king Michael R. Milken have received little mercy. Corporate violators have likewise been penalized. Eastern Air Lines (now defunct) pleaded guilty to conspiring to block a federal safety probe and was fined $3.5 million. Chrysler Corporation was fined $7.5 million for allegedly rolling back odometers on more than 60,000 vehicles.

Among the new laws enacted to pursue lawbreakers are the Anti-Trust Amendments Act of 1990, which increases the maximum penalties for price-fixing from $1 million to $10 million, and the Financial Institutions Reform, Recovery, and Enforcement Act of 1989, which increases fines to $1 million and prison sentences to

TABLE 3.2   LEADING PACS AND THEIR CONTRIBUTIONS TO FEDERAL CANDIDATES IN THE 1989 CONGRESSIONAL CAMPAIGN

PAC	Contribution
Corporate	
1. American Telephone & Telegraph	$3,078,219
2. United Parcel Service	1,658,366
3. Federal Express	1,476,937
4. Philip Morris	910,348
5. Waste Management	903,017
6. RJR Nabisco	872,626
7. Union Pacific	731,974
8. Barnett Banks	655,604
9. General Electric	621,083
10. Citicorp	619,798
Labor	
1. Teamsters	$10,564,876
2. National Education Association	4,082,478
3. State, County, and Municipal Employees	3,743,467
4. United Auto Workers	3,287,699
5. Machinists	3,043,777
6. Letter Carriers	2,684,315
7. Communications Workers	2,213,755
8. Carpenters and Joiners	2,131,551
9. Electrical Workers	2,051,998
10. United Transportation Workers	2,009,651
Trade/Health/Membership	
1. National Association of Realtors	$5,417,458
2. American Medical Association	4,707,167
3. Association of Trial Lawyers	3,855,499
4. National Rifle Association	2,536,492
5. Committee to Preserve Social Security and Medicare	2,037,341
6. Association of Life Underwriters	1,978,162
7. League of Conservation	1,922,635
8. Retired Federal Employees	1,881,659
9. Texas Medical Association	1,753,078
10. Automobile Dealers Association	1,633,980

Source: Federal Election Commission press release, March 31, 1991.

20 years for such banking-related crimes as lying to regulators and falsifying credit applications. In short, organizations are expected to operate without acting illegally. It is interesting to note, however, that various managers, when caught in some illegal activity, have maintained that their actions were motivated by an attempt to cope with the extraordinary pressures of their organization's environment.

SUMMARY

Regardless of their nature (public or private, not for profit or economic) or size (large or small), all organizations must consider those elements that comprise their environment. This chapter has explored how organizations relate to those components that comprise their environment.

Learning Objective 1. **Explain why all organizations must take into account the components that comprise their environment.**
All organizations must secure inputs (people, materials, money, information) from their surroundings and, in turn, be able to exchange the goods and services they provide for the energy necessary to ensure their continued survival. No organization is so powerful and self-contained that it is immune to environmental pressures.

Learning Objective 2. **Differentiate between what is meant by the terms "general environment" and "task environment."**
The term "general environment" refers to *all* factors external to an organization. By contrast, the term "task environment" refers to those elements of the general environment *directly* relevant to an individual organization.

Learning Objective 3. **Describe why government, at all levels, is an important component of the general environment.**
Government, at all levels, is an important component of a typical organization's general environment because no organization or industry is immune from the impact of decisions made in Washington, D.C., or in state or local legislative bodies across the country.

Learning Objective 4. **Discuss why the economy is an important component of the general environment.**
The economy is an important component of the general environment because fluctuations in both the national and global economy influence the ability of virtually all organizations to survive and prosper.

Learning Objective 5. **Discuss the significance of society viewing an organization as legitimate.**
The roles enacted by a manager in dealing with an organization's general environment are at least partially influenced by society's view of its legitimacy. For example, in a society where business is valued, corporate managers are encouraged to act as liaisons, spokespersons, and negotiators in relating to an organization's external environment. Conversely, in a society where business is viewed suspiciously, corporate managers will likely be forced into a position of reacting as opposed to initiating action in response to environmental influences.

Learning Objective 6. **Define and understand why technology is an important component of the general environment.**
Technology refers to the means by which an organization transforms inputs into outputs. It is of particular importance because it has been and continues to be the main source of increases in productivity that provide a competitive advantage.

Learning Objective 7. Understand why customers and suppliers are important components of a typical organization's task environment.

An organization can survive only as long as it is able to exchange the goods and services it provides for the resources necessary to obtain new inputs and maintain itself in operating order. Hence, without customers an organization could not exist. Likewise, organizations must respond not only to the customers they supply, but also to the sources from which they receive supplies. The acquisition of inputs thus constitutes a major dependency for most organizations.

Learning Objective 8. Identify the different forces involved in marketplace competition.

The degree of market competition, and thus ultimate profit potential, of an organization's task environment is shaped by five forces: rivalry among existing enterprises, relative power of customers, relative power of suppliers, threat of new entrants, and threat of substitutes.

Learning Objective 9. Grasp the importance of employees as a component of a typical organization's task environment.

Simply stated, all organizations accomplish their goals through the actions of their employees.

Learning Objective 10. Understand why regulatory agencies are an important component of a typical organization's task environment.

Regulatory agencies are an important component in a typical organization's task environment because their regulations affect almost every aspect of management, from an organization's activities in input markets, to conditions in production, to the nature of outputs.

Learning Objective 11. Describe the importance of environmental scanning for an organization attempting to cope successfully with its environment.

As generally practiced, environmental scanning involves monitoring and evaluating events and trends in an organization's environment. In this respect, a close relationship has been repeatedly demonstrated between organization performance and environmental information gathering.

Learning Objective 12. Appreciate the impact of lobbying and direct political action in dealing with environmental issues.

Lobbying and direct political action are two means for organizations to enhance and influence relations with their environment. Trade associations, professional alliances, coordinating groups, and individual managers lobby to gain various economic advantages and protect themselves from unfavorable legislation. Direct political action takes place through the activities of organization government-affairs offices, the personal efforts of managers in politics, the efforts of organization constituents, and the activities of PACs.

KEY TERMS

business cycle 73	general environment 70	ombudsperson 77
consumer movement 77	image advertising 73	Say's Law 72
environmental scanning 86	law of the marketplace 81	task environment 70
		technology 74

REVIEW AND DISCUSSION QUESTIONS

1. Assume the role of an investigative reporter for the television series "60 Minutes." Report a specific situation showing why it is important for a manager to understand how an organization is influenced by its general environment.

2. Identify the major elements or groups in the task environment of a defense contractor whose support would be important to its success.

3. The U.S. Chamber of Commerce predicts that regulatory costs for all businesses will increase 25 percent in the 1990s to $600 billion. What impact do you see this increase having on both small and large businesses in terms of resources and staff necessary to cope with regulatory burdens?

4. Explain how society's attitude toward management at any given point in time would affect you as a manager.

5. Companies such as IBM, Procter & Gamble, Johnson & Johnson, and Coca-Cola are typically ranked among the most admired corporations in the United States. How does the legitimacy that results from a good reputation with customers, suppliers, investors, legislators, job candidates, and so on, spur organization success?

6. One often hears complaints about the impact of government on management. As the owner of a medium-size textile mill, how would you handle government influences affecting the textile industry?

7. Federal standards add some $2,200 to the price and operational cost of a new car. Admittedly, such standards have saved tens of thousands of lives. In your opinion, do the benefits outweigh the costs in this situation? What benefit-cost test did you use in formulating your answer?

8. Suppose you are the proprietor of a small men's (women's) shop located across from the campus of a major state university. What means would you use in relating to your customers?

9. Suppose you are the owner of a pizzeria in your hometown. How would you go about monitoring your competition?

10. How would you characterize the rivalry between competing supermarket chains in your home town? What market actions have been taken recently by one competitor that have provoked counter moves by other competitors?

MANAGEMENT EXPERIENCE   ARE YOU WORLD WISE?

Going Global? Before you buy your plane tickets, test your business-etiquette knowledge (some questions have more than one answer):

1. During business meetings, use first names in:
   a) Great Britain, because everyone is oh so chummy.
   b) Australia, because informality is the rule.
   c) China, because the first name is the surname.
   d) Japan, because the last names are easy to mispronounce.

2. In China, offer expensive gifts to your hosts:
   a) Every time they ask for one.
   b) When you need help getting out of the country.
   c) Never—if they can't reciprocate, they'll lose face.

3. In which country is a business card an object of respect?
   a) Japan: An executive's identity depends on his employer.
   b) Taiwan: It explains a person's rank and status.
   c) France: Especially cards describing a man's mistress.

4. When doing business in Japan, never:
   a) Touch someone.
   b) Leave your chopsticks in the rice.
   c) Take people to pricier restaurants than they took you to.
   d) All of the above.

5. Power breakfasts are inappropriate in all but:
   a) Italy—they like to bring the family along.
   b) Mexico—they don't bother to get to work till 10 a.m. anyway.
   c) United States—we invented them.
   d) France—they're at their most argumentative in the morning.

6. In some countries, colors are key. Which is true?
   a) For Koreans, writing a person's name in red signifies death.
   b) In China and Japan, gifts wrapped in white or black should be presented only at funerals.
   c) Purple suits in Great Britain represent lack of taste.

7. Which of these choices are obscene gestures?
   a) The okay sign in Brazil.
   b) A hearty slap on the back in Switzerland.
   c) Doing anything with the left hand in Saudi Arabia.
   d) Thumb between second and third finger in Japan.

Answers: 1-b, c; 2-c; 3-a, b; 4-d; 5-c; 6-a, b; 7-a, c, d

Source: "Are You World Wise?" *Business Month* 134 (May 1990): 27.

CASE 3.1   LOBBYING IN THE UNITED STATES

Success in the international marketplace often requires more than mere business know-how. A firm also must understand and deal with the intricacies of national politics and laws. In an era of increased business-government interaction, a firm's ability to anticipate, understand, and perhaps even shape government action may be critical for long-term market penetration. To become aware of government policies and to influence the government decision-making process, companies frequently use the assistance of lobbyists. Usually, these lobbyists are well-connected individuals and firms that can provide access to policymakers and legislators.

In the United States, firms have for a long time ensured that their voices are heard in Washington, D.C. Increasingly, foreign countries and companies have participated in this lobbying process as well. Since many government actions are likely to affect international business, numerous lobbyists have been hired to work for foreign firms.

Public attention has particularly focused on the "influence-buying" activities of Japan in the United States. Some believe that Japanese attempts at shaping or influencing U.S. trade policy are inappropriate. For example, Texas Congressman John Bryant claims that his bills, which seek more disclosure of Japanese investment activities in the United States, have repeatedly been rejected due to lobbying efforts by Japanese firms. He believes that as a result of these efforts, the U.S. government is less informed about foreign investment activities than it should be.

Another major concern to many is the fact that former U.S. policymakers often become key lobbyists for Japanese firms. Three former U.S. trade representatives, who were the heads of the government office that develops and executes U.S. international trade negotiations and policy, are now working for Japanese firms. For example, the law firm of Robert Strauss works for Fujitsu; William Brock represents Toyota; and William Eberle works for Nissan. Other examples are former top Nixon aide Leonard Garment, who works for Toshiba, and the former national chairman of the Democratic party, Charles Manatt, who now represents NEC. One Washington insider, Clyde Prestowitz, claims that "about 80 percent of former U.S. high-ranking government officials, and virtually every high-powered political lawyer in Washington, is retained in one way or another by Japanese interests. It is by far the biggest lobby in Washington, and the most well funded." States Pat Choate, author of the book *Agents of Influence:* "It is wrong, I believe, that so many Americans wind up on foreign payrolls, particularly after they have been in high positions in the U.S. government. Americans seem to be available so easily, so cheaply. This demeans us in the eyes of the world. It casts doubt in the minds of our own people about the integrity of our decision-making process."

Many believe that this easy availability of former U.S. trade negotiators to Japanese firms may undermine the U.S. policy process. It is claimed that these individuals may give away secret U.S. trade strategies or help Japanese companies find ways to circumvent existing trade legislation. Frequently cited is the case of a former U.S. negotiator in the automotive sector, who applied for a position with Japanese firms while still holding his position in U.S. government.

Also of major concern are Japanese expenditures aimed at U.S. think tanks and universities. Critics argue that the funding of research projects or the endowment of chairs raises basic ethical questions. They say that Japan's wealth may tempt some of America's elite to accept Japanese funds at the expense of broader U.S. interests.

These views are vigorously disputed by others. For example, William Eberle, one of the former U.S. trade representatives mentioned earlier, maintains that his and other ex–trade officials' influence is greatly exaggerated. He states that he might be able to get the door open, but he doesn't think he has any more influence from the fact that he once held the job of U.S. trade representative. Others are more vocal. In their view, the Japanese funding provided to institutions such as the Reischauer Center of the Johns Hopkins University, or to think tanks like the Brookings Institution and the American Enterprise Institute, has no influence at all on the outcome of research projects. Scholars at these institutions are very upset at having their integrity questioned. States John Makin of the American Enterprise

Institute: "This whole notion that anybody who talks about free trade is being paid off by the Japanese, which is what critics are essentially saying, is schlock."

Problems

1. Should foreign firms be able to represent their interests in Washington, D.C.?

2. Should U.S. ex-policymakers be able to represent such foreign interests? How about domestic interests?

3. Should there be a cooling-off period before ex-policymakers can take on representation of foreign interests? If so, how long should such a period be? Is it fair to impose such an employment restriction burden on former government officials?

4. Do you see the donation of funds by Japanese firms to U.S. think tanks as undermining U.S. interests?

Source: This case was written by Michael R. Czinkota and is based on *America for Sale: Japan's Buy-Out Binge,* Financial News Network; and William J. Holstein, "Japan's Clout in the U.S.," *Business Week,* July 7, 1988, 64–66.

NOTES

[1] David B. Yoffie, "How an Industry Builds Political Advantage," *Harvard Business Review,* 66 (May–June 1988): 82–89.

[2] Rosabeth M. Kanter, "Competing on Politics," *Harvard Business Review* 68 (September–October 1990): 7–8.

[3] Pat Choate, "Political Advantage: Japan's Campaign for America," *Harvard Business Review* 68 (September–October): 87–103.

[4] Michael McFadden, "Protectionism Can't Protect Jobs," *Fortune,* May 11, 1987, 121–126; Carolyn Lochhead, "Hemmed in by U.S. Textile Quotas," *Insight,* October 24, 1988, 34–35; and James Bovard, *The Fair Trade Fraud* (New York: St. Martin's Press, 1991).

[5] Jim Powell, "Super-301: The Economic Equivalent of Civilian Bombing," *Wall Street Journal,* June 30, 1989, A16; and Rahul Jacob, "Export Barriers the U.S. Hates Most," *Fortune,* February 27, 1989, 88–89.

[6] Guy L. Smith quoted in Alix M. Freedman, "Philip Morris to Launch Image Ads," *Wall Street Journal,* November 1, 1989, B1.

[7] Thomas J. Peters and Nancy Austin, *A Passion for Excellence* (New York: Random House, 1985), 37–112.

[8] Mike Sheridan, "Stanley Marcus: Chairman Emeritus, Neiman-Marcus," *Sky* 15 (October 1986): 32.

[9] Rosabeth M. Kanter, "Even Closer to the Customer," *Harvard Business Review* 69 (January–February 1991): 9–10.

[10] Thomas A. Stewart, "There Are No Products—Only Services," *Fortune,* January 14, 1991, 32.

[11] Regis McKenna, "Marketing Is Everything," *Harvard Business Review* 69 (January–February 1991): 76.

[12] Ibid.

[13] James Blue quoted in Marc Beauchamp, "No More Weekend Stands," *Forbes,* September 17, 1990, 191.

[14] Michael E. Porter, *Competitive Strategy: Techniques for Analyzing Industries and Competitors* (New York: Free Press, 1980), 4; and Michael E. Porter, "A Good Competitor Is Not Always a Dead Competitor," *Wall Street Journal,* April 1, 1985, 22.

[15] Michael E. Porter, *The Competitive Advantage of Nations* (New York: Free Press, 1990), 40.

[16] Bill Saporito, "Companies That Compete Best," *Fortune,* May 22, 1989, 44.

[17] Timothy S. Mescon and George S. Vozikis, "Federal Regulation—What Are the Costs?" *Business* 32 (January–March 1982): 33–39.

[18] "State Regulators Rush in Where Washington No Longer Treads," *Business Week,* September 19, 1983, 124.

[19] Richard L. Daft, Juhani Sormunen, and Don Parks, "Chief Executive Scanning, Environmental Characteristics, and Company Performance: An Empirical Study," *Strategic Management Journal* 9 (1988): 123–139.

[20] Robert E. Norton, "Can Business Win in Washington?," *Fortune,* December 3, 1990, 75–84.

[21] Choate, "Political Advantage," 88–89.

[22] Monica Langley, "Friendly Terms: Thrifts' Trade Group and Their Regulators Get Along Just Fine," *Wall Street Journal,* July 16, 1986, 1, 14.

[23] Norton, "Can Business Win in Washington?," 77.

[24] Jeffrey L. Sheler, "Is Congress for Sale?," *U.S. News & World Report,* May 28, 1984, 47–50.

[25] Olga Grkavac quoted in Willie Schatz, "The Name of the Game Is Now Political Action," *Datamation,* January 1, 1987, 41.

CHAPTER 4

LEARNING OBJECTIVES

Upon completing this chapter, you should be able to:

- Identify the two sets of forces that determine an organization's capacity to act with regard to social issues.

- Explain the difference between proactive and reactive behavior with regard to social issues.

- Explain the nature of managerial ethics.

- Cite several criticisms that might be made of the view that a business has responsibilities that extend beyond meeting its legal and economic obligations.

- Recount several criticisms that might be made of the view that a business has only economic and legal obligations.

- State the Iron Law of Responsibility.

- List several social performance guidelines.

- Identify various forces that affect managerial ethics.

ould you have a Central American shaman treat you for a case of flu or respiratory troubles? What if your doctor consulted a shaman when deciding which medicines to prescribe? If Lisa Conte, founding president of Shaman Pharmaceuticals, Inc., succeeds in obtaining a license for her patented drug, SP-303, you could benefit from a shaman's experience while being treated for certain viral diseases.

Tropical rain forests now cover only 2 percent of the earth's surface, but they contain over half of the world's plant species. Only 1 percent of those species have been studied in depth for their useful properties. Screening them for potential new drugs while huge sections of the rain forests are being destroyed is a formidable task, one that most large pharmaceutical firms have given up in favor of laboratory synthesis and testing. Conte's brainstorm was to use a network of ethnobotanical researchers as advisors, bringing in only plants that local shamans have found to have medicinal value. Seventy such plant species were retrieved in the first year, about half of which had potential for producing useful drugs. By comparison, the pharmaceutical firms' method of gathering large numbers of species and then looking at them for possible use has yielded only about 40 useful drugs.

Shaman Pharmaceuticals was founded only 2½ years ago and needs to establish a reliable source of income before its initial financing runs out. Decisions regarding which drugs to license and

MANAGERIAL ETHICS AND SOCIAL RESPONSIBILITY

manufacture therefore are critical. Shaman has chosen to concentrate on SP-303 for very practical reasons. Infectious diseases need treatment for only a few days or weeks, so long-term testing of any potential drug is not required in the licensing process. And if the diseases for which it will be used have no current treatment, a new drug will be licensed even faster. SP-303 is expected to be undergoing human clinical trials only 16 months after being brought into the lab, whereas most drugs take 5–15 years to get that far.

An important question arises when one collects drug material from a disappearing habitat: Will the harvesting of the drug material also contribute to the destruction of the habitat? Fortunately, SP-303 is ideal from a conservationist's viewpoint. Even if the drug generated $1 billion per year in sales, only a very small percentage of the annual growth of the plant material from which it is derived would be required. Moreover, Conte is working out agreements to harvest the plant using local labor. Providing work for local inhabitants will help ease the economic pressures that contribute to rain forest destruction.

Conte's progressive stand on conservation is not simply a personal quirk. Shaman Pharmaceuticals depends heavily on the work of ethnobotanists and the cooperation of conservationists, and Conte would have neither without being conscious of her company's effects on the rain forest. In this chapter, we will explore a variety of situations in which social responsibility plays a major role in an organization's success.

Source: David Riggle, "Pharmaceuticals from the Rainforest," *In Business,* 26–29.

The collaboration of John D. Blair and Grant T. Savage of Texas Tech University in the preparation of this chapter is gratefully acknowledged.

Regardless of whether an organization is domestic or international in scope, its success inevitably depends on its contributions to society. In this chapter, we will examine the extent to which organizations should be held socially responsible for their behavior. Additionally, we will consider the thorny issue of managerial ethics.

We begin by considering society's expectations for the social performance of organizations. After identifying various factors influencing an organization's potential and actual social performance, we will discuss different aspects of social performance, commenting on the belief that organizations have not only economic and legal obligations, but also responsibilities to society that extend beyond these obligations. Next, this chapter offers guidelines for answering the question "What constitutes a socially responsible action?" Then, various forces affecting managerial ethics are examined. Finally, the creation of long-term social responsiveness is addressed.

CHANGING EXPECTATIONS

It has been suggested that modern organizations are less socially responsible than their predecessors. The actual performance of contemporary organizations, how-

---

FIGURE 4.1 RELATIVE SOCIAL PERFORMANCE OF ORGANIZATIONS OVER TIME

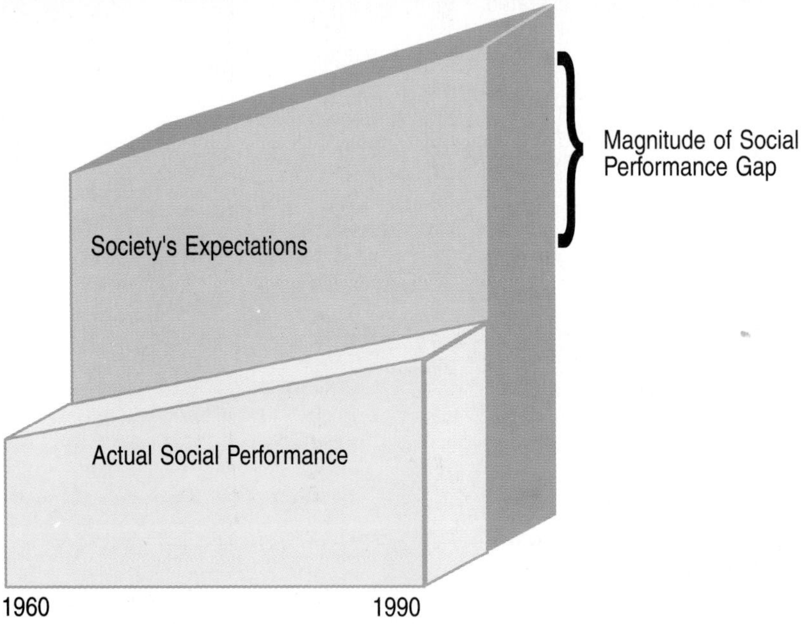

Source: Based on Archie B. Carroll, *Social Responsibility of Management* (Chicago: Science Research Associates, 1984) 5.

ever, must be put into the context of today's society as compared to yesterday's. Even though the social performance of organizations has improved over time, society's expectations have increased at an even greater rate. As a consequence, a wider gap exists today than yesterday between society's expectations and the actual social performance of most organizations. The relative magnitude of this gap is shown in Figure 4.1.

SOCIAL PERFORMANCE

Various factors influence an organization's potential and actual social performance (see Figure 4.2). The two major factors are an organization's current capacity to act and the social responsiveness of its actions. **Current capacity to act** refers to the extent an organization is able to act or react to challenges in its surrounding environment. This capacity is a result of the tension between two sets of forces: those for *change* and those for *stability*. The relative strength of these forces will largely determine the degree to which an organization develops a capacity to perform in a socially responsive manner. An organization's capacity in this regard will set limits

Current capacity to act.

The extent to which an organization can respond to major challenges in its environment, including changing social issues.

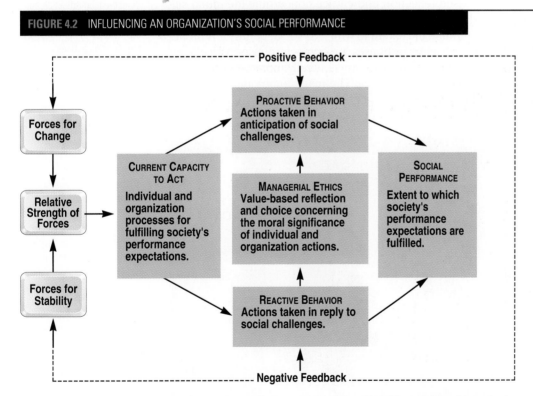

FIGURE 4.2   INFLUENCING AN ORGANIZATION'S SOCIAL PERFORMANCE

Sources: Based on John D. Blair and Carlton J. Whitehead, "Developing Long-Term Adaptability and Innovativeness in the U.S. Army," in *Leadership on the Future Battlefield*, eds. James G. Hunt and John D. Blair (Washington, D.C.: Pergamon-Brassey's, 1985): 251; Edwin M. Epstein, "The Corporate Social Policy Process: Beyond Business Ethics, Corporate Social Responsibility, and Corporate Social Responsiveness," *California Management Review* 29 (Spring 1987): 107; Elizabeth Gatewood and Archie B. Carroll, "The Anatomy of Corporate Social Response: The Rely, Firestone 500, and Pinto Cases," *Business Horizons* 24 (September–October 1981): 9–16.

on its ability not only to identify social issues, but also to recognize the full range of society's expectations with respect to these issues.

Social responsiveness requires developing individual and organization processes for fulfilling society's social performance expectations. The extent to which an organization develops such processes will be reflected in both its proactive and reactive behavior. The former, **proactive behavior,** includes actions taken in anticipation of a social challenge. As such, it involves taking social initiatives to protect the welfare of key constituencies, such as employees, customers, and society in general. A program initiated by Du Pont to buy used Freon and other chlorofluorocarbons (CFCs) is a prime example of proactive behavior. CFCs are used to chill refrigerators and air conditioning units. Released into the air, they deplete the Earth's ozone layer, a section of the atmosphere that screens out harmful sun rays. Du Pont will even buy used CFCs made by its competitors. **Reactive behavior** includes actions taken in reply to social challenges. Typically, such actions involve "doing only what is legally required." Both the tobacco industry's financing of a multimillion-dollar smokers' rights campaign and its continued denial of any connection between smoking and cancer is seen by many critics as examples of reactive behavior. To date, the tobacco industry has done no more than legally required to warn the general public of the danger of its products.

Managerial ethics is an additional factor influencing an organization's social behavior. It involves value-based reflection and choice concerning the moral significance of individual and organization actions. The ethical standards of an organization's managers will determine the extent to which its social behavior is proactive or reactive. In contrast to reactive responses, proactive responses typically go beyond minimum legal requirements, and they are generally more consistent with increasing expectations for social performance. The many forces affecting an organization's managerial ethics are discussed later in the chapter.

Proactive behavior.
Actions taken in anticipation of social challenges.

Reactive behavior.
Actions taken in reply to social challenges.

Managerial ethics.
Valued-based reflection and choice concerning the moral significance of individual and organization actions.

Proactive socially responsible behavior may take the form of large-scale action on the part of an organization or the personal efforts of individual employees. Union Electric clerk Vanita Joerling, shown here with Charles Rabenau and his dog Hans, understands that some customers have unique needs. For over ten years, she has provided special assistance to Mr. Rabenau, whose blindness prevented him from reading his electric bill. Although UE now offers braille billing to its customers, Ms. Joerling continues to pay Mr. Rabenau's bill using checks he writes in advance, a system the two established long ago.

As Figure 4.2 indicates, the nature of the feedback an organization receives about its social performance will also influence the extent to which its social behavior is proactive or reactive. *Positive feedback* strengthens behaviors that lead to favorable social outcomes, and *negative feedback* weakens behaviors that lead to unfavorable social outcomes.

MANAGING SOCIAL CHALLENGES

Much of what has been written about social performance has focused on the various legal and economic requirements confronting a typical organization. There is a growing sense, however, that organizations should do more than satisfy their basic legal and economic obligations. Figure 4.3 builds on this notion.

ECONOMIC AND LEGAL RESPONSIBILITIES

The left side of Figure 4.3 identifies society's basic performance expectations. These relate to the performance of required *economic* and *legal responsibilities.*

In this vein, traditional economic theory has long held that an organization's only duty is to lawfully make as much money for its owners as possible. For instance, Nobel laureate and economist Milton Friedman maintains that the primary goal of a business in a free-enterprise system should be to maximize profits and serve the interests of its owners.[1] Stated more directly, he contends that the business of a business is to make money. Friedman argues that if a business distributes its profits to benefit society, it is, in effect, paying a tax on profits, and only elected or appointed public officials should have the power to tax. Of course, managers should be socially responsible as *individuals,* but with their own money, not someone else's. Those who accept Friedman's position argue that when each business maximizes its profits, the cost of all goods is lowered and the economic well-being of everyone is improved. In defending this argument, they make several points:

1. Money earned as profit does not belong to corporate officials but to an organization's stockholders. Those who direct corporations serve as stockholder agents and have no independent (legal) right to fund social projects without stockholder approval. By funding such projects, they are spending someone else's money, not their own. Further, money spent on such projects lowers the dividend and price of an organization's stock. This denies stockholders the use of their money, which is a rightful return on invested capital.

FIGURE 4.3   DIFFERENT ASPECTS OF SOCIAL PERFORMANCE

Source: Based on Archie B. Carroll, "A Three-Dimensional Conceptual Model of Corporate Social Performance," *Academy of Management Review* 4 (October 1979): 499.

Stockholders have the opportunity to comment on corporate decisions at annual shareholders' meetings. H.J. Heinz Company has a stated mission that includes "advancing the interests of its shareholders through supporting its big brands, pursuing strategic expansion, and fostering internal growth," balanced by a commitment to meet consumers needs through environmentally safe products and production processes.

2. If one organization in an industry spends money on socially responsible projects and its competitors do not, it operates at a relative cost disadvantage. To remain competitive it may have to raise its prices and, consequently, may lose business. If the organization is economically marginal, it may even be forced to close. Thus, by incurring costs for social purposes, an organization may find it more difficult to compete.

3. Insofar as spending money on "social acts" increases prices to all customers or lowers wages of some employees, corporate managers are again spending someone else's money. This is, in effect, "taxation without representation," because the parties involved lose the opportunity to spend the money in question on other goods.

4. Unlike government officials, politicians, and certain specialists, managers generally are not trained or competent at judging which socially desirable projects should be funded. Consequently, many of the activities chosen for support may not result in maximum benefits to society. Indeed, some managers may choose to serve their own narrow interests and not those of society at large.

5. Making managers guardians of the public welfare puts too much power in the hands of the relatively few who direct our nation's corporations. Doing so gives political-social power to those who already possess economic power. A fundamental idea of a democratic society is *pluralism*, that is, a condition in which power is widely distributed among individuals and institutions.

6. If managers are to be responsible for the welfare of society, they should be elected or appointed like public officials. Then business would be a public rather than a private institution. This would mark the downfall of pluralism and the free-enterprise, private property system. Therefore, social responsibility is a move toward socialism.

Xerox's *proactive response* to the environment is reflected in its social service leave program, enabling people like Sarah Lampard (center) to deliver truckloads of food to churches that help feed poverty-stricken families. Every Friday, Lampard drops off food to Pastor Robert Woolfork and his assistant LaShawn Marshal, whose church feeds the working poor in Denver's inner-city. Xerox leave-takers receive full pay and benefits, and get their old or equivalent jobs back when they return. Lampard says that her six-month leave from her job as a Xerox account manager to work for a nonprofit food bank cooperative changed her personal values, prompting her to care less for material things and more about helping others.

ETHICAL AND DISCRETIONARY RESPONSIBILITIES

The right side of Figure 4.3 identifies society's anticipated and desired performance expectations. These relate to the performance of **ethical** and **discretionary responsibilities.** Ethical responsibilities involve anticipated behavior that exceeds legal obligations. Reflecting an even broader expectation, discretionary responsibilities involve proactive behaviors taken to protect the welfare of key constituencies. Those such as consumer advocate Ralph Nader, who argue for recognizing ethical and discretionary responsibilities, hold that businesses have not only economic and legal obligations, but also responsibilities to society that extend beyond these obligations. They contend that a business is responsible not only to its owners, but to its employees, customers, and society in general, as well as other constituencies. Therefore, profit maximization should not, indeed cannot, be the only objective of a business. They further contend that funds diverted to "social acts" in the short run will result in improvements in society that make it easier for a business to survive and enjoy "satisfactory" long-run profits. In defending these contentions, they make several points:

1. Times have changed. People *expect* institutions (including businesses) to be socially responsible. Those that refuse may not survive the wrath of their clients or customers.

2. If businesses are not socially responsible, the public will press for more government regulation. So it makes sense to be socially responsible to prevent further government regulation.

3. In the long run a business's profits will be higher if it is socially responsible. For instance, if a business located in an area of high unemployment does not make an effort to hire members of its surrounding community, it most likely

Ethical responsibilities.
Responsibilities that exceed legal responsibilities on the part of an organization.

Discretionary responsibilities.
Responsibilities that exceed ethical responsibilities and lead to truly proactive actions on the part of an organization.

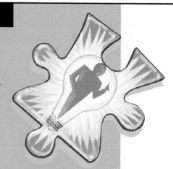

SMART MANAGEMENT   THE CORPORATE ETHICS TEST

To get a sense of how CEOs of major companies would handle specific situations that might involve ethical issues, The Conference Board asked executives at 300 companies worldwide to respond to various hypothetical cases. Compare your ethical choices with those of the executives surveyed on the following case.

Toxic Emission Standards and a "Whistleblower"

Brookfield Corporation operates a plant that conforms fully to local requirements for maximum emission of toxic substances, as established 10 years ago. The facility is inspected annually and toxic emissions have always been and remain well below the acceptable level.

Relying on recently published research, one of the company's quality-control inspectors argues that the cumulative effects of the low level of pollution from the plant entail a possible risk to public health. He says that public officials would agree if they had known of these studies when the original figures were set.

Although there is some support for his views, most of the company's other quality-control inspectors disagree, and the community has not modified its requirements. Changing the manufacturing process would be costly—it would necessitate substantial layoffs, and the plant is the largest single employer in the town.

1.   Brookfield should:

A.   Change the manufacturing process to achieve lower levels of toxic emissions   ☐

B.   Discuss the new data with local health officials, and agree to stricter standards if they determine that the data are persuasive   ☐

C.   Take no action   ☐

The quality-control inspector is not satisfied with the company's decision and feels that it exposes the public to unacceptable risks. He has released company data to the press and his views are liberally quoted in local newspapers. He has worked for the company for 15 years and his personnel record is exemplary.

2.   Brookfield should:

A.   Insist that he resign; if he refuses, he should be fired   ☐

B.   Insist that he accept reassignment as a condition of future employment   ☐

C.   Take no action   ☐

Ethics Survey Results

The results from The Conference Board study for the above case were:

1A.	18	6%	2A.	141	45%
1B.	228	76%	2B.	69	23%
1C.	54	18%	2C.	87	29%

Source: Adapted from Ronald E. Berenbeim, "The Corporate Ethics Test," *Business and Society Review* 63 (Fall 1987): 22–25, 71.

will have fewer customers because many of its potential clients will be without a means of support. Accordingly, it makes sense for a business to be socially responsible over the long run, even if it costs more to do so in the short run.

4. Businesses should become involved in socially responsible projects because they have the financial resources and expertise to do so. Besides, business executives are efficient and can do a better job of improving social conditions than managers of other institutions.

5. Short-run profit maximization must be tempered by social responsibility. A business will not have long-run viability unless its quest for profits is tempered with social responsibility. As one leading management authority has phrased it, there is an *Iron Law of Responsibility*, which states that "in the long run those who do not use power in a manner society considers responsible will tend to lose it."[2]

The *degree* to which an organization should be socially responsive is a complex subject. Too often the question of social responsibility seems to be presented as an either-or situation. Clearly, business must adapt to a changing world. The belief that the marketplace can be remade to reflect simpler times by turning back the clock is pure folly. The demands of today's society are much too complex for yesterday's solutions.

Just as clearly, however, social responsiveness must be tempered by legal constraints and economic limitations. Realistically, business cannot attempt to solve all of society's ills. The nature of the problems involved and their complex causes call for a comprehensive approach beyond the limits of any one institution.

SOCIAL PERFORMANCE GUIDELINES

Although Figure 4.2 identifies different aspects of social performance, it offers little guidance for making socially responsible decisions. No set answer can be given to the question "What constitutes a socially responsible action?" But three criteria can serve as guidelines[3]:

1. Organizations should follow this basic criterion: "Above all, do no harm!" Taken from advice given by the Greek physician Hippocrates (460–377 B.C.), this guideline will ensure responsible as well as legal behavior.

2. Organizations should be accountable for their impact on society and should minimize the negative consequences of their actions. This may include restoring land that has been damaged or air that has been polluted, or financing medical care for employees and consumers whose health has suffered.

3. Organizations, by their actions, should enhance society's long-term welfare. This is a price that organizations should be willing to incur for sharing in society's benefit. It is also "good business." Successful organizations realize that their continued survival depends on a healthy society.

MANAGERIAL ETHICS

As depicted in Figure 4.2, managerial ethics are a factor influencing an organization's social behavior. Managerial ethics involve value-based reflection and choice concerning the moral significance of individual and organization actions. The ethical standards of an organization's managers will determine the extent to which its social behavior is reactive or proactive. The greater the degree to which an organization's behavior is proactive, the more its long-term social responsiveness will be enhanced. Reactive behavior may be sufficient for the moment, but generally it will place an organization in a defensive posture. In this regard, managerial ethics affect an organization's success through the decisions that its managers make. The critical choice is whether managers should simply react by doing that which is legally expected and nothing more or whether they should proactively engage in social initiatives.

FORCES AFFECTING MANAGERIAL ETHICS

What forces influence managerial ethics? Many forces lead managers to behave in ways that are less than ethical, just as there are other forces to behave ethically. Figure 4.4 identifies various forces influencing managerial ethics. As indicated, both external and internal forces affect an organization. Together, they influence a manager's ethical thinking. Ethical thinking, however, does not always translate into ethical behavior, and behavior is the real issue. More than just ethical posturing is required.

External Forces Affecting Managerial Ethics

Figure 4.4 identifies seven external forces influencing managerial ethics:

1. *Family.* One's family is a key determinant of one's ethical standards. In addition, one's family provides pressure to succeed in one's career and earn adequate income. Thus, family forces may not encourage ethical behavior.

2. *Religion.* Religious beliefs may be a powerful influence on one's ethical thinking. However, in a secular society, they often fail to translate into ethical behavior.

FIGURE 4.4 FORCES AFFECTING MANAGERIAL ETHICS

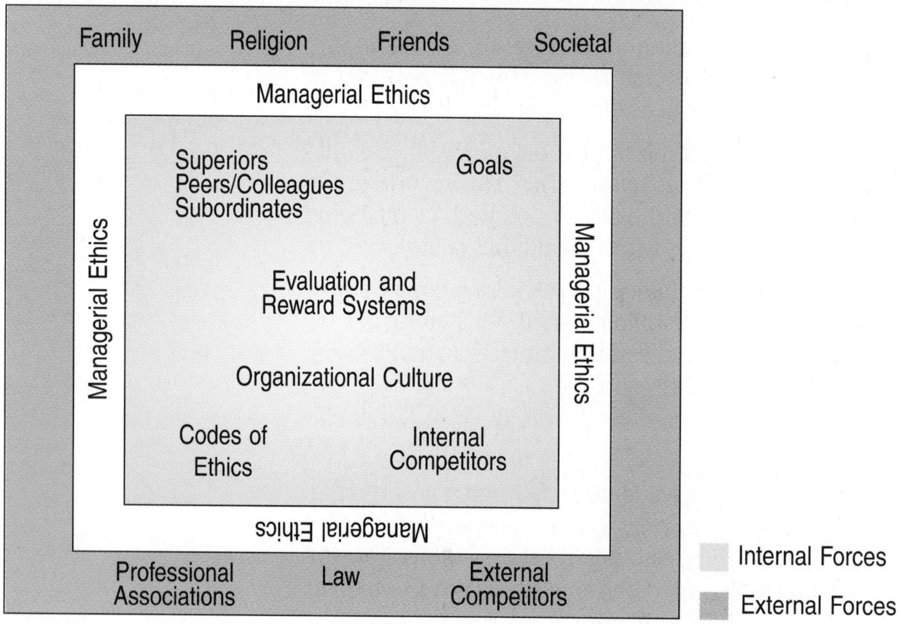

3. *Friends.* Peer groups outside a work setting may help buffer a manager against ethics-related pressures. Those outside an organization, however, may find it easy to condemn a decision if they do not understand the pressures facing a manager who must grapple with its complexities.

4. *Societal culture.* To a large extent, the ethical standards of an organization's managers will be a function of the societal culture in which they are located. For this reason, managerial ethics differ inside and outside of the United States. In some societies, it is necessary to pay commissions to gain business. While such payments would be considered illegal in the United States, they would be seen as quite legitimate in the Middle East. Thus, for example, a firm competing in Turkey would find that paying "baksheesh" is a standard practice that is considered to be neither illegal nor unethical. It should be noted, however, in instances where an American firm does make such payments, it is violating the U.S. Foreign Corrupt Practices Act.

5. *Professional associations.* Many professional associations have developed codes of conduct. Such codes can assist managers by helping to resolve ethical conflicts that arise between employees' professional roles and their work roles.

6. *Law.* The law is essentially the officially compiled customs or practices of a society. Unfortunately, it has two major limitations: (1) it does not incorporate ethical considerations that go beyond mere legal requirements; (2) because law enforcement mechanisms are imperfect, many violators are not caught, prosecuted, convicted, or punished. Although the law helps guide managers with regard to social performance, simply refraining from illegal actions is often judged insufficient.

7. *External competitors.* External competitors are important to an organization. Perceptions of competitors' behaviors will put pressure on an organization's managers to respond in kind. Experience suggests that most people perceive others as generally less ethical than themselves. Therefore, managers may suspect that their competitors are not being fully honest and ethical in their

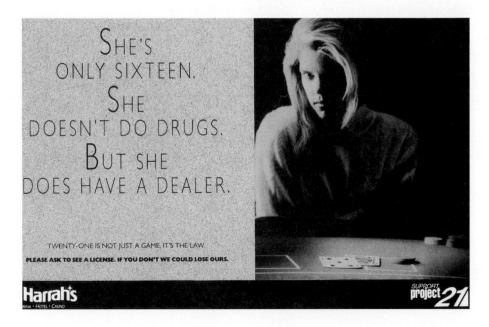

Harrah's Casino Hotels, a division of The Promus Companies, goes beyond the requirements of the law in its role as a leader in fighting underage and compulsive gambling. The company's efforts help to guide its managers in socially responsible performance and have won national recognition.

dealings. Trade groups and personal networks may help allay this fear of unfair competition to some extent. If managers perceive—correctly or incorrectly—that competitors are being unethical, however, they will find themselves confronted with a fundamental question: "If everybody else is doing it, why shouldn't we?"

Internal Forces Affecting Managerial Ethics

Following is a discussion of the eight internal forces affecting managerial ethics, as shown in Figure 4.4.

1. *Superiors*. Ideally, one should be able to look to one's superiors as role models. Unfortunately, from an ethical point of view, they can be models of negative as well as positive behavior. In addition, they may implicitly, or even explicitly, encourage or demand unethical behavior on the part of their subordinates. The simple pressure to succeed, to perform, or to meet production schedules or cost levels may induce subordinates to questionably resolve ethical issues in an organization's interest.

2. *Peers/colleagues*. Peers can be a source of ethical support as well as a source of ethical compromise. One's colleagues are likely to understand the pressures a manager faces but at the same time may be a source of negative peer pressure. This type of pressure may be just as strong among mature managers as it is among teenagers. Ivan F. Boesky and Michael Milken, both of whom have paid multimillion-dollar settlements resulting from their insider stockmarket trading, clearly acted in response to peer pressure. With respect to Milken, he could have left Drexel Burnham Lambert any time he wanted, increased his net worth, and received an even higher percentage of his earnings. However, he didn't. Milken stayed, in part, as a result of pressure from Drexel directors and his fellow brokers, not to mention from his clients. All were dependent on his technical skills for their continued success.

3. *Subordinates*. Managers are highly dependent on their subordinates because they must accomplish their assigned objectives through the efforts of others. In certain instances, subordinates can exert pressure on managers to conceal their ethical shortcomings because such failings may reflect on the managers themselves. This issue most often takes the form of falsified documents and reports to superiors. This "problem hiding," rather than "problem surfacing," interferes with effective management. It also may compromise managers, opening them to subtle forms of blackmail. Instances where subordinates have inflated sales figures come immediately to mind. Managers who are aware of such practices, but fail to correct them because they, in turn, also benefit, subject themselves to future pressure to continue allowing this and other forms of misrepresentation.

4. *Goals*. Goals provide direction for an organization. They also may be a major source of pressure to behave unethically. Consider the Alka-Seltzer commercial in which managers who have achieved ambitious goals are rewarded with even more ambitious goals for the following year. The commercial shows the consumption of the advertised product as the remedy for the "symptoms of stress that come with success." However, the stresses that real-life managers face in trying to achieve difficult goals can lead them into unethical behavior.

5. *Codes of ethics.* It has become increasingly popular for organizations to have their own ethics codes. ITT Corp. has a 16-page "Code of Corporate Conduct" that touches on everything from antitrust issues to fire prevention. Like professional association codes of conduct, ethics codes may buffer an individual from pressures to act unethically. They also may help clarify what behavior is appropriate and what is not.

6. *Evaluation and reward systems.* Organizations that seriously wish to encourage ethical behavior reward it through their evaluation systems. However, they must be careful not to reward one type of behavior when they really want another kind. In other words, if they want people to act ethically, then they need to be sure they are not rewarding them for performance gained unethically.

7. *Internal competitors.* In some ways, competitors within an organization combine the worst of peer group and external competitor influences on managers. Again, perceptions often are skewed in terms of how unethical others are thought to be, so managers may be tempted to "join them, if they can't beat them," and behave unethically themselves.

8. *Organizational culture.* The unique culture possessed by every organization has become of more and more interest to contemporary managers. Organizational culture will be discussed further in Chapter 11. In essence, *organizational culture* refers to the common set of beliefs and expectations shared by members of an organization. Employees learn about an organization's culture both through formal training and through everyday listening and watching. State-of-the-art ethics programs and other similar efforts are no substitute for a true organizational culture stressing ethical behavior. If an organization's culture truly stresses honesty and respect for customers as priorities comparable to growth and profits, employees will follow the lead.

Taking a long-term view, Toyota is proactive in fulfilling social responsibilities. It participates in charitable causes, cultural and sporting events, and supports educational and environmental issues in each of its host nations. Toyota also seeks to make lasting economic contributions to the nations in which it operates by providing stable employment and joint production opportunities, as represented by the Toyota-GM joint venture in California.

LONG-TERM SOCIAL RESPONSIVENESS

Beyond addressing managerial ethics, how do organizations create a long-term social responsiveness? One way is to consider various questions that relate to the framework presented in Figure 4.2. In particular, a consideration of two questions will aid in balancing forces for change and stability so that an organization can design its responses to achieve the greatest effectiveness:

- *How powerful are key forces for change?* In particular, how are social issues in an organization's environment providing an impetus for change? For example, public opinion against smoking is now so strong that advertising campaigns involving cartoon characters such as R. J. Reynolds Tobacco Company's "Old Joe Camel" campaign are being criticized by many different groups for appealing to children and teenagers. Economic and social conditions in both the domestic and the international environment are, of course, also important considerations. These conditions typically determine those issues that will be important not only now but also in the future. Significantly, managers should ask, *"How can an organization deal with these issues to enhance its capacity to respond?"*

- *How powerful are key forces for stability?* Many managers may seek to maintain the status quo because of long-term career aspirations or because of deeply set ways of viewing available possibilities. Of course, not all resistance to change is inappropriate, misguided, or self-interested. There also are real financial constraints and limitations in technology and in the methodologies that can induce and sustain social responsiveness. As recommended above, managers should ask, *"How can an organization deal with these issues to enhance its capacity to respond?"*

When all is said and done, successful managers will be those who are able to anticipate and appropriately respond to social challenges. Doing so will require an organization-wide commitment to proactive, long-term social responsiveness. Such a commitment will be one of the best investments an organization can make to ensure its future survival.

CLOSE-UP: SOCIAL RESPONSIBILITY   MAKING THE WORLD A BETTER PLACE: GOOD FOR BUSINESS

To many companies, social responsibility is secondary to profits. At Body Shop International, profits and social responsibility go hand in hand.

The more than 600 Body Shop stores worldwide are stocked with a wide array of primarily natural products bearing names like Banana Shampoo, Pineapple Facial Wash, and Peppermint Foot Lotion. Recycling is encouraged through discounts for customers who bring back plastic bottles for refills. And use of shopping bags is frowned on because they're likely to end up in a landfill.

The company's social responsiveness doesn't end there. Mixed in among its environmentally correct cosmetic lines is literature promoting a host of other causes. It might be a pamphlet for groups that help save the whales or a membership application for Amnesty International. Body Shop doesn't hesitate to promote what it considers a good cause, even if it means go-

Continued on next page.

ing head to head against its competitors: One of the company's booklets outlines its opposition to animal tests for cosmetics.

The driving force behind all the social activism is Anita Roddick, who opened the first Body Shop store in Brighton, England, in 1976. Some of her conservation efforts began out of necessity. Because she had only 600 bottles when she started out, recycling was a must. And the green decor in the stores? The walls were green in the first shop because it was the only color that covered the damp patches on the walls.

Today, Roddick leaves the day-to-day administration of the company, based in Littlehampton, England, to her husband, Gordon, while she devotes most of her time to marketing and product development. That sometimes means traveling to the Brazilian rain forest to gather oil from nuts harvested by Indians, or visiting one of the three orphanages the company supports in Romania.

Not surprisingly, Roddick considers herself one of Ralph Nader's biggest fans and says that she is convinced that businesses can make the world a better place. And in Body Shop's case, making the world a better place has also been good for business. For one thing, it has generated plenty of free publicity, which is essential because the company shuns paid advertising. And sales have skyrocketed. In 1990, Body Shop's retail sales hit $391 million. Earnings were $21 million, based on wholesale revenues of $197 million. With a social agenda that matches its corporate agenda, Body Shop has given new meaning to the phrase *good corporate citizen*.

Sources: Rahul Jacob, "What Selling Will Be Like in the '90s," *Fortune,* January 13, 1992, 63–64 and Laura Zinn, "Whales, Human Rights, Rain Forests—and the Heady Smell of Profits," *Business Week,* July 15, 1991, 114–115.

SUMMARY

This chapter examined the extent to which organizations should be held socially responsible for their behavior. Additionally, the thorny issue of managerial ethics was considered.

Learning Objective 1. Identify the two sets of forces that determine an organization's capacity to act with regard to social issues.
An organization's capacity to act with regard to social issues is a result of the tension between two sets of forces: those for change and those for stability. The relative strength of these forces will largely determine the degree to which an organization develops a capacity to perform in a socially responsive manner.

Learning Objective 2. Explain the difference between proactive and reactive behavior with regard to social issues.
Proactive behavior includes actions taken in anticipation of a social challenge. As such, it involves "taking social initiatives" to protect the welfare of key constituencies, such as employees, customers, and society in general. In contrast, reactive behavior includes actions taken in response to social challenges. Typically, such actions involve "doing only what is legally required."

Learning Objective 3. Explain the nature of managerial ethics.
Managerial ethics involve value-based reflection and choice concerning the moral significance of individual and organization actions.

Learning Objective 4.   Cite several criticisms that might be made of the view that a business has responsibilities that extend beyond meeting its legal and economic obligations.

Criticisms that might be made of the view that a business has responsibilities that extend beyond meeting its legal and economic obligations include:

1. Those who direct corporations serve as stockholder agents and have no independent (legal) right to fund social projects without stockholder approval.

2. If one organization in an industry spends money on socially responsible projects and its competitors do not, it operates at a relative cost disadvantage.

3. Spending money on "social acts" increases prices to all customers or lowers wages of some employees.

4. Managers generally are not trained or competent at judging which socially desirable projects should be funded.

5. Making managers guardians of the public welfare puts too much power in the hands of the relatively few who direct our nation's corporations.

6. If managers are to be responsible for the welfare of society, they should be elected or appointed like public officials.

Learning Objective 5.   Recount several criticisms that might be made of the view that a business has only economic and legal obligations.

Criticisms that might be made of the view that a business has only economic and legal obligations include:

1. People *expect* institutions (including businesses) to be socially responsible.

2. If businesses are not socially responsible, the public will press for more government regulation.

3. In the long run a business's profits will be higher if it is socially responsible.

4. Businesses should become involved in socially responsible projects because they have the financial resources and expertise to do so.

5. A business will not have long-run viability unless its quest for profit is tempered with social responsibility.

Learning Objective 6.   State the Iron Law of Responsibility.

The Iron Law of Responsibility states that "in the long run those who do not use power in a manner society considers responsible will tend to lose it."

Learning Objective 7.   List several social performance guidelines.

Three social performance guidelines are:

1. Above all, organizations should do no harm.

2. Organizations should be accountable for their impact on society.

3. Organizations, by their actions, should enhance society's long-term welfare.

Learning Objective 8.   Identify various forces that affect managerial ethics.

External forces that affect managerial ethics are family, religion, friends, societal culture, professional associations, law, and external competitors. Internal forces that affect managerial ethics are superiors, peers/colleagues, subordinates, goals, codes of ethics, evaluation and reward systems, internal competitors, and organizational culture.

KEY TERMS

current capacity to act 103

ethical responsibilities 107

proactive behavior 104

discretionary responsibilities 107

managerial ethics 104

reactive behavior 104

REVIEW AND DISCUSSION QUESTIONS

1. Describe a situation where you feel you have not been treated in a responsible manner by an organization that you have been involved with. What actions have you taken?

2. Explain how society's increasingly demanding attitude that management be socially responsive would affect you as the CEO of a large corporation producing children's toys.

3. Explain how this attitude would affect you as the owner and manager of a small service organization, like a bowling alley.

4. Explain how this same attitude would affect you as a manager of professionals in a large, service-oriented business, such as a "Big Six" accounting firm.

5. Imagine that you were chairman of the board of Union Carbide at the time of the Bhopal poison gas leak. How would you have responded to this disaster?

6. The annual General Motors stockholders' meeting is about to start. Put yourself in the role of Roger Smith, former GM chairman and CEO. You are going to be questioned about your decision to pay H. Ross Perot $700 million to quit criticizing your leadership and to resign from GM's board of directors. You will undoubtedly be confronted by a barrage of bare-knuckled questions from outraged stockholders. How are you going to convince them that you and other GM directors behaved ethically and responsibly?

7. Suppose you are the dean of the college of business at your university. Identify the key constituencies with which you have to deal. What social challenges are you likely to encounter? What would you do in each case?

8. Contrast and compare the position that a business only has economic and legal obligations with the view that businesses have additional ethical and discretionary responsibilities. Which do you feel you would favor as a manager?

THE MANAGEMENT EXPERIENCE ETHICS IN THE TRENCHES

The two scenarios below are based on the real experiences of business executives. Analyze both and explain how you would deal with each situation.

Scenario One: The "price" of doing business outside the United States.

It is often said that business ethics differ inside and outside of the United States. In some places, it is necessary to pay commissions to gain business. Is it an "unrealistic American moralism" to prohibit such payments? Or is it moral courage? And if it is moral courage, is it akin to business stupidity? On the other hand, "integrity has no national limitations." Increasingly, firms must deal with this issue because many expanding markets lie outside of America. How would you respond to the following ethical dilemma?

Continued on next page.

I am CEO of an international trading company in Turkey. One state-owned manufacturing company (Company A) in one of the Middle East countries opened a tender for 15,000 tons PVC granule K value 70. Company A makes all its purchases through tenders. For 7 years in that market, my company has never been able to do any business with Company A (though we have sold many bulk materials to other state-owned companies in that market). One of our new managers had a connection with the purchasing manager of Company A, who promised to supply us with all of our competitors' bids if we pay him a 2 percent commission on all of our sales to his company. Our area manager accepted this arrangement. He got the competing bids, made our offer, and we got the tender. I learned of this situation when reviewing our income and expenses chart, which showed the 2 percent commission.

What shall I do given the following: (1) If I refuse to accept the business without any legitimate reasons (presently there are none) my company will be blacklisted in that country—where we get about 20 percent of our gross yearly profit. (2) If I accept the business and do not pay the 2 percent commission, the purchasing manager will make much trouble for us when he receives our shipment. I am sure that he will not release our 5 percent bank guarantee letter about the quality and quantity of the material. (3) If I accept the business and pay the 2 percent commission, it will go against everything I have achieved in the 30 years of my career.

Scenario Two: Disposal of hazardous waste.

While most executives are seemingly unanimous in condemning the dumping of hazardous waste in violation of the law, there are numerous subtle ethical questions that arise in day-to-day business. Is it ethically correct for firms to lobby government with the intention of influencing environmental laws? Is the notion that legal rules provide the proper bounds for ethical activities valid? Any comfort we take in legal rules guiding ethical conduct is dashed by the reality that we face a global economy, and laws vary across nations. Some products banned in America may be legally sold in other countries. Does that make the sale of those products unethical here but ethical elsewhere? It is not possible or wise to define every ethical and unethical activity through law. It is up to all companies and individuals to define their own ethical standards. How would you respond to the following ethical dilemma?

I am currently in a business regulated by the U.S. Environmental Protection Agency. It deals with hazardous waste, not toxic waste, although I guess that various combinations of our wastes could probably be fatal. The question here is that of disposal. The cost of proper disposal is very expensive. How do you dispose of waste, bear the cost, and remain competitive, knowing that your competitors are dumping their waste illegally? You see, I can simply flush the waste, and a city investigator said that I wouldn't have to worry whether some of the waste dumped accidentally because even if everyone dumped everything they had, the city system could handle it. So if the city system can handle it, why should I bear the cost? Why can't I flush it down the tap? The EPA does check the tap every now and then, but it doesn't do so at midnight or 5 a.m. Should I dispose of this waste at a great expense or should I dump it down the drain?

Source: Adapted from John Delaney and Donna Sockell, "Ethics in the Trenches," *Across the Board* 27 (October 1990): 15–26.

CASE 4.1   AMAX AND CRESTED BUTTE, COLORADO

Crested Butte is a former mining town of 1,000 persons who have restored its Victorian buildings. Many of Crested Butte's leaders and townspeople are transplanted—educated former New Yorkers, Californians, and ex-Atlantans. The town is nestled beneath Mt. Emmons in an unspoiled valley almost entirely surrounded by national forest land.

Amax, a company with assets of $3 billion, wishes to develop a $1 billion mine to process molybdenum from the mountain. The world market for molybdenum (*moly* for short) is $7 billion and rising at 7 percent a year. Amax produces half the world's supply of moly, and Mt. Emmons is believed to contain the world's largest deposit. Moly is used to give durability to steel. It also reduces corrosion, helps steel resist severe temperatures, and makes it lighter. In World War II, it was considered the country's most strategic metal, and troops surrounded the moly mines to prevent possible Nazi sabotage. If the mine is built, 2,000 workers will be employed in the construction process, and 1,300 people will be needed to run it later.

The Crested Butte area is now supported by recreation: 1.5 million campers, hikers, anglers, backpackers, and others visit the area every year. Some of the locals believe the mine and its associated waste products—perhaps 200 million to 300 million tons—will ruin the area for recreation. They think a mine also will destroy the wilderness. At present, there is little unemployment. Many locals believe that the doubling of their town's and county's population will bring all the problems of growth they came to "the Butte" to avoid: unemployment, housing cost increases, and drugs.

Amax has faced many challenges from those who oppose the mine, including:

- Bumper stickers against the company
- Shots taken at executives' homes
- Opposition of a paraplegic mayor who received national publicity
- Opposition of the city council
- Attempts of state and county planning boards to prevent or control the mine

Amax has been involved in the following legal activities to try to develop the mine:

- Expenditure of $800,000 to clean a creek that the previous mine owners polluted
- Construction of a $2 million water treatment plant to clear up water pollution further
- Placement of full-page advertisements in local papers and the production of *Moly News*, a monthly newsletter
- Use of unarmed security guards
- Participation in Colorado Review Process, a government planning agency promoting balanced growth of jobs, housing, transportation, sewerage
- Contribution of $100,000 to the county planning commission toward a computerized planning system
- Employment of spokespersons to explain Amax's position
- Tours for 36 town and county officials to see how other mining towns adapted

Still, the locals are fighting the mine.

Problem

You are a spokesperson for Amax. You were in charge of environmental controls during the construction of the most environmentally sound mine in the world. Design a program for improved negotiator and spokesperson roles for Amax.

Source: Roger Williams, "A Tiny Town Battles a Mining Giant," *New York Times Magazine*, March 4, 1979, 17.

NOTES

[1] Milton Friedman, *Capitalism and Freedom* (Chicago: University of Chicago Press, 1963); Milton Friedman, "The Social Responsibility of Business Is to Increase Its Profits," *New York Times Magazine*, September 13, 1970, 33, 122–126.

[2] Keith Davis, "The Meaning and Scope of Responsibility," in *Contemporary Management: Issues and Viewpoints*, ed. Joseph W. McGuire (Englewood Cliffs, N.J.: Prentice-Hall 1974), 631.

[3] Based on Thomas Donaldson, *The Ethics of International Business* (New York: Oxford University Press, 1989), 54.

PART

TWO

PLANNING

CHAPTER 5

LEARNING OBJECTIVES

Upon completing this chapter, you should be able to:

■ Appreciate why organizations plan.

■ Identify the various forms of standing and single-use plans.

■ Comment on the need to balance short- and long-range plans.

■ Explain how short- and long-range plans are interrelated.

■ Answer the question: "How long should a long-range plan be?"

■ Demonstrate an understanding of rolling plans.

■ List some benefits of goals.

■ Name the *key result areas* in which all organizations should establish goals.

■ Explain the central idea behind management by objectives (MBO).

■ Relate the basic assertion underlying goal-setting theory.

■ Outline the five basic steps that comprise the MBO process.

■ Identify the benefits and problems commonly associated with MBO.

ow do you make money selling a product that has been around for 50 years, in an era of constantly changing consumer tastes and preferences? Most companies don't try. Managers plan for the finite lifespan of most products and rely on acquisitions and new products for profits and growth.

General Mills CEO Bruce Atwater is an exception, and his strategy includes a system of goals that may appear to be somewhat unconventional within the food industry. Although Atwater's targets include the goal of realizing 25 percent of his company's total sales through products introduced by General Mills in the last 5 years, the performance of existing brands retains priority.

To ensure the success of the company's established brands, General Mills managers work toward the goal of improving one-third of these products every year. Changes are made in taste, nutrition, texture, packaging, and promotion, but the basics of the business remain constant. The results can be spectacular—50-year-old Cheerios continues to be a leading seller since reaching the industry's number-one spot in 1989, and sales of the 54-year-old Kix brand rose 30 percent in 1990. In 1991, the company's cereal division captured an impressive 29 percent share of the cereal market.

PLANNING AND GOAL SETTING

Brand managers must work hard and think creatively to meet the goals set by Atwater, but his strategy works. General Mill's total U.S. sales volume rose 8 percent in 1991, and net earnings have been rising steadily at the rate of 20 percent per year.

Still, why not simply generate a continuous supply of new products to keep the company growing? Atwater is aware that the expense of new products can erode profits and skim business from existing brands, so he has carefully balanced his company's plans for introducing new products with rejuvenating older ones.

Even within an organization as successful as General Mills, this kind of balance is not always easily maintained. Just as plans and projects compete for company resources, different departments and managers have goals that may compete and conflict. The goals of increasing production speed and efficiency among plant personnel responsible for producing fruit snacks has at times conflicted with the goal of innovating the product through new packaging or in-package prizes. And at one point, after plant personnel had continually vetoed the idea of selling multicolored Fruit Roll-Ups, marketers marched into the plant and threw fruity pieces shaped like Garfield the cat into production lines, which promptly produced crude versions of the desired product. Finally won over, plant managers began producing the product, known as Crazy Color Roll-ups, and Fruit Roll-Up sales began to rise for the first time in 8 years.

General Mills's system of goals may be unconventional, but it is successful. In this chapter, we explore the processes by which managers set goals and develop plans.

Source: Patricia Sellers, "A Boring Brand Can Be Beautiful," *Fortune,* November 18, 1991, 169–170, 174–176.

With this chapter, we begin a three-chapter sequence on the first function of management—planning. Because virtually all organizations operate in a changing environment and face conditions of uncertainty in all but the simplest circumstances, planning is essential. After commenting on the importance of planning, the current chapter examines the scope and application of different types of plans. Next, after we have defined what we mean by goals, we explore the various functions that goals serve. Finally, we will see how the goals of both individuals and organizations can be integrated through the goal-setting approach known as *management by objectives*.

As defined in Chapter 1, **planning** is the process of establishing organization goals and selecting a future course of action for their accomplishment. Its primary purpose is to reduce the risk surrounding future operations. Managers assume a role somewhat akin to fortunetellers in the process, gazing into reams of computer printouts rather than a crystal ball. The goal is to determine what might happen in the future if this or that course of action is adopted.

Planning.
The process of establishing organization goals and selecting a future course of action for their accomplishment.

THE IMPORTANCE OF PLANNING

The importance of planning in an organization's efforts to survive in today's changing environment is undisputed. As one top manager explains, "An enterprise without a plan is like a ship sailing in dense fog without any navigational means whatsoever. The only thing it can possibly be sure about is whether it is afloat or not."[1] Experienced managers know that planning is important for four basic reasons:

1. *Other things being equal, planning helps organizations succeed.* Organizations that emphasize planning have been shown to have higher profits and sales than those that do not. Additionally, organizations that have introduced planning programs have been found to significantly outperform their own past results on measures of success such as return on equity, earnings-per-share growth, and return on investments.[2] By clarifying what is expected in an organization's operations, a plan can help managers to identify early threats and possible opportunities that may exist in an organization's environment. Ideally, threats then can be neutralized and opportunities capitalized on.

    Note that when we say other things being equal, planning can pay off, we are acknowledging that although planning can be beneficial, it does not by itself guarantee success. First, if planning is done badly, it is unlikely to be effective. Second, as we will note in Chapter 6, even the best plans are unlikely to succeed if they are poorly implemented. These two points aside, consider the following example: Two teams of equal ability are scheduled to compete in 2 weeks. Team A scouts its competition, alerts its players to team B's strengths and weaknesses, and prepares a game plan designed to exploit team

B's weaknesses and isolate its strengths. Team B comes to the game with a standard set of plays, assuming that all opponents are alike. Which team do you think will have the best chance of winning?

2. *Planning provides direction and a sense of purpose.* Without plans, organizations are reduced to merely reacting to day-to-day events in their environments. In contrast, by focusing attention on clearly stated goals, a plan helps managers to make decisions for the future within a broader perspective. This shared purpose also enables managers to coordinate and unify their actions. Just as an adequate defense capability is impossible without coordination among the army, navy, and air force, the parts of an organization (marketing, production, finance, and so forth) cannot effectively cooperate without the direction provided by a comprehensive and integrated plan.

Employees also benefit from planning. Once an organization's goals are clearly specified, employees can begin to see how their work contributes to achieving those goals. Then, when well-defined goals are met, employees can share in feeling responsible for an organization's success. In fact, research has shown that these feelings can be further enhanced by encouraging employees to contribute to the planning process. There is evidence that the more employees identify with their work and are involved in planning their own activities, the greater are their feelings of success and satisfaction when goals are achieved. This phenomenon will be discussed further when we consider management by objectives.

3. *Planning helps managers cope with change.* No doubt you have read articles about how fast the world is changing, and how the speed of change is accelerating. There is change in all sectors. We hear about international economic changes every day. The national economy changes, too: A full business cycle ran its course from mid-1990 to 1992. Governments fall and policies change. Social norms and attitudes also change. Consider how attitudes toward the size of cars or the desirability of cigarettes have changed over the last 15 years.

Finally, competitive structures change. Each year about 15 percent of all businesses fail. The number and types of competitors change. Consider the airline industry. Since 1979, when the Airline Deregulation Act took effect, U.S. airlines have been locked in a bruising battle for survival. In 1978, 13 major airlines carried 90 percent of all passengers. Their fares and routes were regulated; their profits regular. Of the 17 new airlines formed between 1979 and 1985 to take advantage of deregulation, 14 no longer exist. Victims include Western Air Lines, Republic Airlines, Frontier Airlines, and PSA, as well as such preregulation giants as Pan American World Airlines, Braniff, and Eastern. Apparently, little support exists in Congress for re-regulation or for government-financed bailouts. The "law of the marketplace," as discussed in Chapter 3, clearly seems to be functioning.

Though whole industries rarely experience such massive upheaval, organizations do tend to rise, stabilize, decline, and even disappear. Managers must cope both with changes in their own organizations and fluctuations in their environment. This is done best through planning. The manager who is able, through planning, to anticipate and prepare for possible future changes has more control than the manager who does not attempt to plan ahead. Effective planning enables a manager to be in a position to affect, rather than simply accept, the future. Although no one can predict the unknown with 100 percent accuracy, experience shows that it is far better to enter the future with some preparation than with none at all.

4. *Planning contributes to the performance of the other managerial functions.* As stressed in Chapter 1, planning sets the stage for the execution of all other managerial functions. In this regard, it is unique, since it involves the establishment of organization goals. This alone gives planning a certain *primacy.* Although the functions of management intermesh in practice, goals must be determined before decisions can be made regarding how best to organize, staff, lead, and control to achieve these goals. Without plans as a guide, all the other managerial functions would be of limited value. However, once goals are determined, managers can then design an organization's structure to ensure their accomplishment. With structure in place, employees can be recruited and selected, and managers can turn their attention to providing effective leadership and developing positive interpersonal relations. Finally, through control, it is determined whether organization goals are being efficiently achieved. This pattern of interrelationships, showing the primacy of planning, is depicted in Figure 5.1.

TYPES OF PLANS

As the preceding section suggests, planning activities differ in nature and scope and in the time period they cover. Consequently, plans can be viewed from a number of different perspectives. From the viewpoint of application, plans can be classified in terms of *functional areas* (for example, marketing plans, production plans, human resource management plans, financial plans, and so forth). Plans may also be classified according to the *period of time* over which they are projected (short versus long range) or with respect to their *frequency of use* (standing versus single use). Since the nature of functional plans is evident, the following discussion examines the character of short- and long-range plans and standing and single-use plans.

FIGURE 5.1 THE PRIMACY OF PLANNING

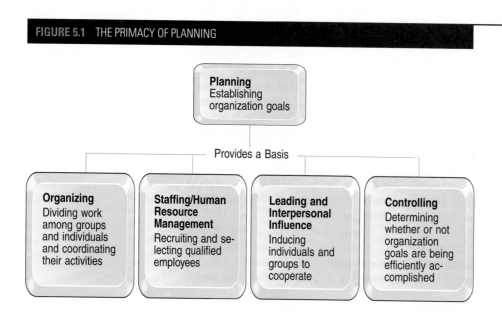

Short- versus Long-Range Planning   One of the more difficult dilemmas virtually all top managers face is the need to balance short- and long-range plans. An organization's long-term performance is established through the cumulative impact of short-range plans. If these short-range plans can be related not only to specific demands of the near term but also to an overall or long-range plan, their internal consistency and cumulative impact will establish a strong and cohesive organization. This is a hallmark of superior management.

In too many instances, American companies have abandoned their future to pursue quick payoffs. Excessive dividends to entice investors, for example, can undermine an organization's long-term success. Corning, Inc., is an object lesson in the benefits of investing time and money in the short term for a long-term payoff. It put 17 years and $100 million into fiber optics before getting a major order. Today, it is a leader in a $600-million-a-year market growing 20 percent annually.

In today's competitive international environment, organizations must overcome the natural bias for the short term. Overemphasis on the longer term, however, is just as inappropriate. Because no established distinction exists between short term and long term, reconciling the conflict inherent in short-range and long-range plans is easier said than done.

In practice, the terms *short range* and *long range* have no precise meaning, but rather express relative periods of time. With the oil industry or electric utilities, it is often necessary to extend plans 20–30 years. Matsushita Electric, the parent company of Panasonic, has a 250-year plan. Forest products companies, such as Potlatch, Georgia-Pacific, and Weyerhaeuser, have reforestation plans that extend well into the next century, which is well explained by the fact that the average lapse of time from sowing of a fir seedling to its harvest at maturity is 99 years. At the other extreme, long-range plans for the manufacturers of children's toys, cosmetics, and packaged foods may extend no more than 6 months to a year. In such volatile industries, where sales levels change suddenly and in considerable magnitude, it is virtually impossible to predict how quickly fads will come and go. Under such circumstances, examples of short-range plans might include a weekly production schedule, a description of supplies to be secured, and a list of employees to be hired.

In sum, short-range and long-range plans are interrelated in at least two respects:

1. Short-range and long-range plans compete for the allocation of resources. Consequently, there can be a dangerous tendency to sacrifice long-term results for short-term gains. An organization may have to decide, for example, whether to use its revenues to mount a lavish advertising campaign to spur sales in the current quarter, or to spend the money on upgrading its manufacturing equipment to improve long-range competitiveness.

2. Short-range plans should be compatible with long-range plans. It is usually difficult, if not impossible, for long-range plans to succeed unless short-range plans are accomplished. Both are important in achieving an organization's objectives.

"How Long Should a Long-Range Plan Be?"   No set answer can be given to the question "How long should a long-range plan be?" But *three* criteria can serve as guidelines.

Long-term planning on the part of Temple-Inland results in the regeneration of thousands of acres of timberland. This assures the availability of timber supplies for future generations. The company-owned acreage is supplemented by timber supplies obtained through long-term lease agreements that extend well beyond the year 2000.

The *first* is to determine how far into the future an organization's fixed commitments extend. Such commitments might include long-term indebtedness and contracts. If an organization is obligated to make mortgage or lease payments over 30 years, for instance, it would seem wise to plan for that period of time.

The *second* criterion is to estimate the degree of uncertainty associated with the future. Without exception, predictive efficiency drops off over time. In some instances, the future may be unpredictable after only a few years. Television executives, for example, would be hard pressed to guess what kinds of programs the public will want 5 years from now. It makes little sense in such cases to develop complex plans covering long periods. While plans could be based on pure intuition or guesswork, their true value would be limited.

The *third* criterion is *lead time*—the time required to bring a new product to market. For example, AT&T can design a new phone in 12 months. It takes 2 years for either Xerox to produce a new copier or Honda to turn out a new car. Planning horizons are strongly influenced by product-development considerations. Although lead time for an album by a new rock group may be only 6 months, many organizations are forced to plan well into the future if their products are ever going to reach market. Thus, Hallmark Card artists work on Christmas cards 2 years in advance, since a single card may pass through 30 different tests before it is finally approved.

Rolling Plans

Given these considerations, planning is often done on a "rolling" basis. Under this system an organization may develop a 5-year plan of future operations, updating on an annual basis. As the current year of a 5-year plan closes, it is extended, or *rolled* forward, to include a "new" fifth year. Such **rolling plans** allow an organization to revise its plans on the basis of new information and to maintain a degree of flexibility in its commitments.

The need for such flexibility is reflected in the comments of a top manager who, in concluding a presentation of a 5-year rolling plan to a board of directors, remarked, "Tomorrow things will start to happen that we were unable to anticipate in the plan, and we had better be prepared to adjust our plans accordingly."[3] Thus, as a general guideline, it is preferable to refrain from formalizing plans until a final commitment is absolutely necessary. Organizations that solidify plans too early run the risk of falling victim to unforeseen events and being "locked in" to a specific course of action. The role of *contingency plans* in identifying alternative courses of action that might be followed if various developments occur (or do not occur) will be discussed in Chapter 6.

Standing Plans

Standing plans, those that can be used again and again, focus on situations that recur repeatedly. They provide ongoing guidance for performing recurring activities and are of particular value in relatively stable operations where similar circumstances are likely to appear frequently. *Policies, procedures,* and *rules* are all forms of standing plans (see Table 5.1).

A **policy** is a general statement that serves to guide decision making. Policies are plans in that they prescribe parameters within which certain decisions are to be made. They set limits on employee actions. Because policies are broad guidelines, they are subject to interpretation; hence, managers must exercise discretion in their application. For example, a policy may state that "preference will be given to hiring veterans." The key here is the word "preference." Note that the extent and degree of preference is unspecified, allowing a measure of managerial latitude.

Other examples of policies are given in Table 5.2. Notice that each example is purposefully broad and provides only a general guideline subject to employer discretion. However, each statement does prescribe parameters for decision making and thus sets limits for the actions of employees. In this respect, policies incorporate two principal advantages:

1. They save time by predeciding future situations likely to recur.
2. They ensure consistency in the manner in which similar situations are decided.

Rolling plans.
Plans of future operations updated on an annual basis.

Standing plans.
Plans that are used again and again, focusing on situations that recur repeatedly.

Policy.
A general statement that serves to guide decision making.

TABLE 5.1 SUMMARY OF STANDING AND SINGLE-USE PLANS		
Type	**Definition**	**Example**
Standing Plans		
1. Policy	A general statement that guides decision making	"Preference will be given to hiring the handicapped."
2. Procedure	A series of related steps to be followed in an established order to achieve a given purpose	Filing for travel expense reimbursement
3. Rule	A statement that either prescribes or prohibits action by specifying what an individual may or may not do in a specific situation	"No eating at work stations"
Single-Use Plans		
1. Budget	A plan that deals with the future allocations and utilization of various resources to different organization activities over a given time	Allocation and utilization of machine hours
2. Program	A plan typically intended to accomplish a specific goal within a fixed time	Space Shuttle Program
3. Project	A subset or component part of a specific program	Manhattan Project

TABLE 5.2   SOME POLICIES FROM ACTUAL COMPANY MANUALS

Customer Service. "It is the policy of this company to provide customers with the finest service possible within limits of sound financial principles." (What are the "limits" of sound finance?)

Employee Benefits. "It is the policy of this company to provide its employees with acceptable working conditions and an adequate living wage." (What is "acceptable" or "adequate"?)

Promotion from within. "It is the policy of this company to promote qualified employees from within company ranks whenever feasible." (What is meant by "qualified" or "feasible"?)

Gifts from Suppliers or Vendors. "It is the policy of this company that no employee shall accept any gift from any supplier or vendor unless it is of nominal value." (What is "nominal"?)

Procedure.
A series of related steps that are to be followed in an established order to achieve a given purpose.

A **procedure** is a series of related steps that are to be followed in a predetermined order to achieve a given purpose. Well-established procedures are often called *standard operating procedures*. Customarily, procedures prescribe exactly what actions are to be taken in a specific situation. Procedures are similar to policies in that both are intended to influence certain decisions. They are different in that policies address themselves to single decisions, while procedures address themselves to a sequence of related decisions. Table 5.3 shows one company's procedure for processing a bill of sale.

TABLE 5.3   ONE COMPANY'S PROCEDURE FOR PROCESSING A BILL OF SALE

Step 1.   Prior to recording, all noncash sales will be forwarded to the credit department for approval.

Step 2.   Following necessary credit approval, all bills of sale will be presented to production scheduling for an estimated product completion date.

Step 3.   Subsequent to production scheduling, all bills of sale will be delivered to the accounting department, where they will be recorded.

Step 4.   Pursuant to their processing in the accounting department, all bills of sale will be filed with the shipping department within 24 hours.

As shown in Table 5.3, a procedure specifies an exact chronological ordering of activities. Compared to policies, procedures leave little room for discretion. By design, they provide a degree of assurance that all similar situations will be handled in a predictable manner. Other circumstances that typically require a step-by-step ordering of actions include hiring, requisitioning office equipment, and filing such forms as travel authorizations and expense vouchers.

Once a procedure becomes routine, a manager is free to concentrate on solving problems that require more thought. Procedures, however, should be reviewed periodically to ensure their continued appropriateness. Unless this is done, standard operating procedures can become simply obsolete practices. Indeed, it has been suggested that "most mistakes are due not to sloppy or indolent employees but to the way they have been told to do their work, procedures that are antiquated, complicated, and redundant."[4]

A **rule** is a standing plan that either prescribes or prohibits action by specifying what an individual may or may not do in a given situation. They are intended to be implemented regardless of the specific individuals involved. As such, rules are different from policies and procedures in that they specify required *personal conduct*. The statements "Safety goggles *must* be worn while working at grinding machines," "No smoking," "Under no conditions will purchase price be refunded after 30 days," "No gambling," and "No drinking or fighting on company premises" are all examples of rules.

Rules are usually accompanied by specifically stated penalties that vary according to the seriousness of an offense and number of previous violations. Unlike policies that guide but do not eliminate discretion, rules leave little room for interpretation. *The only element of choice associated with a rule is whether it applies in a given situation.* For instance, a rule stating that employees must punch their own time cards might be overlooked in case of an emergency or accident. Of the three forms of standing plans discussed, rules are the simplest and most straightforward. They are without question the narrowest in scope and application. The relationship among policies, procedures, and rules is shown in Figure 5.2.

Rule.
A statement that either prescribes or prohibits action by specifying what an individual may or may not do in a given situation.

American Electric Power assisted Mark West Hydrocarbon Co., Inc., with its program to recover and reuse heat. This 800 horsepower heat pump recovers used heat from a distillation tower and uses it to provide process heat to the same tower. Installing the heat pump avoided installing a gas boiler and increasing the size of a cooling tower.

Single-Use Plans

Single-use plans are specifically developed to implement courses of action that are relatively unique and are unlikely to be repeated. The three principal forms of single-use plans are budgets, programs, and projects. (Refer again to Table 5.1.)

A **budget** is a plan that deals with the future allocation and utilization of various resources to different organization activities over a given time period. Budgets are perhaps most frequently thought of in financial terms. However, they also are used to plan the allocation and utilization of labor, raw materials, floor space, machine hours, and so on. In this broader sense, a budget can be thought of as a tool for translating future plans into numerical terms. Budgets also are a method for controlling organization operations, as will be discussed in Chapter 19.

Programs are typically intended to accomplish a specific goal within a fixed time. Their nature and complexity vary widely. They may be as broad and involved as the National Aeronautics and Space Administration's Discovery (Space Shuttle) Program or its Apollo (Man on the Moon) Program, or as focused and inner directed as a program to change an organization's corporate culture.

Budget.
A single-use plan that deals with the future allocation and utilization of various resources for different organization activities over a given period.

Programs.
Single-use plans intended to accomplish a specific goal within a fixed time.

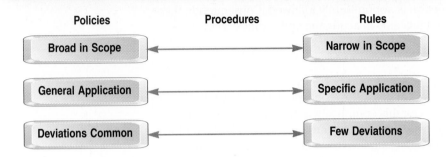

FIGURE 5.2   THE RELATIONSHIP AMONG POLICIES, PROCEDURES, AND RULES

Energy conservation programs, for example, designed to reduce dependence on foreign oil have become popular at many organizations. Depending on the organization, these programs may focus on searching for substitutes, improving a building's insulation, or designing more efficient machines. Other examples might include implementing an equipment expansion program to increase a manufacturing firm's daily output, an electronic data-processing program to computerize a retail outlet's accounting and inventory record-keeping system, an affirmative action program, or a safety program. As these examples suggest, skill is needed to develop meaningful programs for specific situations.

Projects are usually a subset or component part of a specific program. Accordingly, projects often share some of the same characteristics as the overall programs of which they are a part. For example, a project to develop a new or improved product could be part of a total program to increase market penetration.

In general, projects are usually less complex than their supporting programs and are, by definition, narrower in scope. For example, Atlantic Richfield launched a project to expand its deep-water offshore drilling capabilities as part of its program to compensate for the decline in crude oil imports from the Persian Gulf. Perhaps the most famous project in history was the World War II effort to develop an atomic bomb. Established in 1942, the Manhattan Project was but one component of a U.S. Army Corps of Engineers program to unleash the potential of nuclear energy and assist in successfully concluding the war. Project Head Start and the U.S. Navy's Polaris missile/submarine project are other examples of well-known projects.

Projects.
Usually a subset or component of a specific program.

GOALS: THE FOUNDATION OF PLANNING

Goals are objectives. As such, they are those ends that an organization seeks to achieve by its existence and operation. Goals are an essential starting point in planning because, as noted, they provide direction for all other managerial activities.

Effective managers have long recognized that before initiating any course of action, goals should be clearly determined, understood, and stated. This requirement underscores two essential characteristics of goals:

1. Goals are predetermined—stated in advance.
2. Goals describe *future* desired results toward which *present* efforts are directed.

Goals.
Those ends that an organization seeks to achieve by its existence and operation.

At the outset, we should state that although some authors distinguish goals from objectives, in this book they will be considered the same. While differences could be drawn, a clear distinction is not uniformly followed. Consequently, these terms are generally used interchangeably in academic and business circles.

THE BENEFITS OF GOALS

Intelligent planning presupposes clear goals. The concept of goals, however, can be quite complex. The prime reason for this complexity is that goals serve a variety of functions. Consequently, the goals stressed in one instance (social and employee welfare, for example) may not be the same as those emphasized in another (productivity and profit maximization, for example). In fact, they may conflict. Viewed in broad perspective, goals provide several important benefits that vary according to time and circumstance. As illustrated in Figure 5.3, these benefits are as follows.

1. *Guidelines for action.* By describing future desired results, goals serve as guidelines for action, directing and channeling employee efforts. In this way, they provide focus and direction for employees by prescribing what "should be" done. Consequently, goals provide parameters for strategic planning, allocating resources, and identifying new product-development opportunities. They tell employees how and where to direct their strongest efforts. In brief, by identifying what an organization wants to succeed in, goals help it keep on track.

2. *Constraints.* To the extent that goals prescribe what "should be" done, they also serve to prescribe what "should not be" done. An organization that commits itself to certain goals reduces its discretion to pursue other goals. For example, an organization that commits itself to maximizing immediate stockholder dividends, in effect, reduces the amount of financial resources it has available for expanding production or investing in the development of new products. Thus, by their nature, goals also function to constrain employee activities.

3. *Source of legitimacy.* Goals also serve as a source of legitimacy by justifying an organization's activities and, indeed, its very existence to such groups as customers, politicians, employees, stockholders, and society at large. As noted in Chapter 3, legitimacy is a global or summary belief that an organization is proper and worthy of support. The goals that lend legitimacy to hospitals, for example, would include the provision of medical services aimed at curing, ameliorating, and preventing disease. Prisons and mental hospitals gain pub-

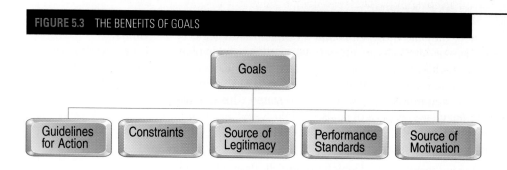

FIGURE 5.3 THE BENEFITS OF GOALS

lic approval by espousing such goals as therapy and rehabilitation, and churches by offering divine worship and spiritual salvation. Imagine how differently we would feel about a hospital if its stated objective was to keep its occupancy rate up by doing as much surgery as possible, or about a church whose avowed objective was to amass funds through the collection plate to finance the opulent lifestyles of its top ministers.

An organization whose goals are deemed legitimate enjoys a greatly enhanced ability to obtain resources and support from its environment. This largely explains the fund-raising success of organizations such as the Girl Scouts, Salvation Army, and United Way. Each has achieved acceptance through the recognized legitimacy of its goals. Three decades ago, the weight-reduction business was seen as a collection of gimmicks engineered by charlatans to take advantage of people in need. Then Weight Watchers International was able to establish the industry's legitimacy by justifying its goals. Currently, massage therapy, dating services, singles bars, and singles-oriented adult education companies are among the many organizations trying to establish the legitimacy of their goals.

4. *Performance standards.* Various elements shape an organization's work environment. Of these elements, the most important are the prevailing performance standards. Broadly speaking, they determine the pace and quality of an organization's efforts. Thus, if an organization's top managers set high standards, other managers will usually follow suit. If the standards that the top managers establish are low, subordinates are not likely to do much better.

Clearly, one of the most important standards top managers set is an organization's goals. The best managers establish goals that force employees to stretch to achieve them. This does not mean arbitrary or unrealistic goals, but rather goals that are demanding and competitive.

5. *Source of motivation.* An organization's goals can also serve as an important source of employee motivation. By presenting a challenge, they tell what characterizes success and prescribe how to achieve or maintain success. Thus, in a very real sense, organization goals are often incentives for employees. This phenomenon is perhaps clearest in organizations that offer their employees awards for achieving specified sales levels. Consider Domino's Pizza. One of its prime goals is to increase sales. Domino's does this with a wide-ranging incentive program. Every manager who tops $10,000 in weekly sales gets a special $70 Hermès brand tie. When a store tops the company's weekly sales record (it now exceeds $60,000), founder Tom Monaghan takes the $16,000 Swiss-made gold watch off his wrist and gives it to the store's manager. Other incentive awards for accomplishing different objectives include trophies, bonuses, trips, outings on Domino's million-dollar yacht, and vacations at its exclusive lodge in northern Michigan. Such victories mean continued success for Domino's and satisfaction for its employees. Employee motivation will be discussed at length in Chapter 15.

These examples, however, should make it clear that by choosing an employer, employees choose a vehicle for achieving their own goals. In this way, they are motivated to help an organization reach its goals because their own success in many ways directly depends on the organization's success.

KEY RESULT AREAS

Many attempts have been made to identify **key result areas** in which all organizations should establish goals. The most widely accepted are those of Peter F. Drucker.[5] It is Drucker's contention that an organization should establish goals in each area vital to its existence. Although principally applicable to profit-oriented organizations, Drucker's eight key result areas (see Figure 5.4 and the following discussion) also are relevant for public-sector and other not-for-profit ventures.

Key result area.
A result area vital to an organization's existence.

MARKET SHARE

Simply stated, every organization should establish goals relative to its competition. Sales figures are meaningless until they are compared against market potential. Thus, Kellogg, which already dominates the U.S. cereal business with 41 percent of the market, has as its long-range goal a towering 50 percent share. Market share also has intrinsic importance in that a business that holds less than a certain share becomes a marginal supplier. The prices it can charge for its products then become dependent on the decisions of its larger competitors. And in a market downturn, it runs the chance of being squeezed out altogether. When competition becomes intense, distributors tend to favor the most popular products. In the soft-drink industry, for instance, every time a bottler loses a fraction of a percentage point of market share, it is likely to lose a little supermarket display space as well, since grocers generally allocate space on the basis of sales per square foot. Furthermore, if a business's market share becomes too low, it may be unable to provide necessary customer service. Moreover, having a substantial market share, as do Eastman Kodak and Gillette, is helpful in establishing brand loyalty, simply because many people are most comfortable buying something that a lot of other people buy. Finally, market share is not just a statistic. Having a high relative market share is typically associated with a low-cost position yielding above-average returns. Thus, market share also involves factories, jobs, and profits. With its market share sliding (from 46 percent in 1980 to below 32 percent in 1990), General Motors has seemingly been in a race to eliminate factories and employees faster than it loses sales. As for the relation between market share and profit, consider that each point of market share Gillette takes from its competitors yields $12 million in profit.

FIGURE 5.4 DRUCKER'S EIGHT KEY RESULT AREAS

Key Result Areas
Market Share
Innovation
Productivity
Physical and Financial Resources
Profitability
Manager Performance and Development
Employee Performance and Attitude
Social Responsibility

Key Results

Market share goals might include:

- Increasing market share from 15 percent to 25 percent within 5 years.
- Increasing military sales by 12 percent over the next 12 months.
- Achieving total sales of 50,000 units per year by 1996.
- Increasing overall company dollar sales by 7 percent annually, and for each product by at least 5 percent annually.

INNOVATION

The message is quite clear in today's technology-driven world: Innovate or evaporate. In their analysis of America's best-run companies, Thomas J. Peters and Robert H. Waterman, Jr., found that excellent companies possess an almost radical preoccupation with innovation.[6] A major case in point is 3M Co., which adds more than 100 new items each year to a catalog that already boasts more than 60,000 products, from Post-it notes to heart-lung machines. An ironclad requirement of 3M's 40-plus divisions is that at least 25 percent of their sales be from products less than 5 years old. This requirement clearly recognizes that 3M's continued existence depends on its ability to develop innovations. Then there is the 15 percent rule, which allows 3M employees to spend up to 15 percent of each work week on anything they wish, as long as it is product related. This practice is called "bootlegging," and its most famous result is the adhesive for Post-its.

Other companies known for their interest in innovation include Johnson & Johnson and General Electric. Both spend between three-quarters of a billion and a billion dollars each year on research and development. At the same time, companies that are known as hotbeds of innovation are also alert to serendipity. An engineer at Raytheon was working with some radar equipment when he noticed that a chocolate bar in his shirt pocket had melted. Intrigued, he bought and prepared some popcorn using the radar equipment. His discovery was eventually transformed into the first microwave oven. The success of Raytheon and other

Playful, life-size sculptures of working people, such as this one by Stephen Hansen, add to the creative culture at Herman Miller, Inc., the innovative office furniture manufacturer. The sculptures add to an internal environment designed to nurture creativity and imagination, which is necessary for innovative furniture design. Herman Miller executives seek participation of all employees in decision making, and employees are urged to try new things and make mistakes.

organizations that always work to develop new products demonstrates one of the oldest marketplace truisms: Consumers flock to true innovations. An organization can never rest on past product successes. A constant flow of new products is needed or customers will be attracted elsewhere.

Innovation goals might include:

- Being the leading contributor to the technology of the plastics industry within 10 years.
- Achieving technological leadership in digital transmission and switching systems for ordering voice communications by a certain year.
- By decade's end, developing a fail-safe means for moving a gene from one living organism to another.

PRODUCTIVITY

Productivity is a measure of an organization's ability to produce more goods/services with fewer inputs (people, materials, money, information) and thus less cost.

Productivity.
A measure of an organization's ability to produce more goods/services with fewer inputs (people, materials, money, information) and thus less cost.

CLOSE UP: INTERNATIONAL MANAGEMENT EUROPE IN AMERICA

Uniroyal tires. Maalox antacid. Carnation evaporated milk. Wisk detergent. Zenith lap-top computers. What do all these familiar products have in common? They are all made by American firms owned or controlled by European companies. Indeed, despite all the uproar about Japanese takeovers in the United States, European companies are the most active in the U.S. economy.

The French are the leading European acquirers of U.S. companies. French deals in 1990 included a merger of Koser, the Pennsylvania-based maker of Maalox and other pharmaceuticals, with Rhône-Poulnec, France's biggest drug manufacturer, and the purchase of Uniroyal-Goodrich by Goupe-Michelin. Groupe Bull, the French electronics company, bought the computer operations of Honeywell and Zenith in 1987 and 1989, respectively.

Elsewhere, Europeans are active in the U.S. publishing, public relations, and advertising sectors. The WPP Group, a British concern, owns the Hill and Knowlton public relations firm and the J. Walter Thompson and Ogilvy Group advertising agencies. The British are also well represented outside the communications area. A sample of British-owned U.S companies includes Pillsbury, Brown and Williamson Tobacco, and British Petroleum America.

Apart from the acquisition binge of recent years, some European companies have been active in the United States for decades. Nestlé, the giant Swiss food company, markets Carnation milk products and chocolate mixes, and candy bars such as Baby Ruth and Butterfinger. Nestlé also sells Mighty Dog canned dog food, Fancy Feast canned cat food, and Stouffer Frozen Foods.

Unilever, a Dutch-British company, has sold the Lever Brothers detergents (including Wisk, Surf, and All) and Dove and Caress soap here for many years. It recently acquired several familiar food brands—Ragù pasta sauces and Boursin cheese—to add to its perennial favorite, Lipton tea. Vaseline Intensive Care and Close-Up toothpaste are also part of the Unilever line.

It appears safe to say that Europe's place in the American economy seems permanent.

Source: Adapted from Steve Dryden, "Europe in America," *Europe* (June 1991): 6–8.

Maintaining a cost advantage while upholding quality is an undisputed formula for marketplace success. Consider that at Ford's Atlanta plant, a new Taurus rolls off the line after 17.6 worker-hours. This is an astounding 50 percent more productive than car production at a typical European plant, which requires about 35 hours. A typical General Motors plant requires about 27 worker-hours, a typical Japanese transplant in the United States requires about 21 hours, and a typical Japanese plant in Japan requires about 17. Ford recognizes that productivity is crucial to its ability to control its destiny. The higher its productivity is, the more flexibility Ford has to cut prices and regain lost market share and, ultimately, profit. Increasing productivity, thereby decreasing costs, is thus one of Ford's or any other management's most important jobs. Productivity goals might include:

- Increasing sales per sales representative from $750,000 to $1 million within the next 18 months.

- Reducing average patient stays within the next year from 5 to 3½ days.

- Processing 30 percent more credit applications each month without adding employees.

- Decreasing labor costs as a proportion of total product costs by 3 percent over the next 6 months.

PHYSICAL AND FINANCIAL RESOURCES

An organization should establish goals for the use of all resources—equipment, buildings, inventory, and funds. Every organization needs both physical and financial resources to produce the goods/services that justify its existence. Goals for

The Neiman-Marcus department store group of General Cinema Corporation has invested more than $300 million to increase square footage and modernize store units. Since 1987, over 50 percent of the company's existing selling space is new or has been remodeled in an effort to meet the goal of improved physical resources.

physical and financial resources should be the result of carefully prepared policies. The costs of using obsolete equipment and patching up old buildings are often hidden. Indeed, such old equipment and buildings may appear very profitable when standard methods of depreciation are used. If they have been written down to zero, they will appear to involve no cost at all. This, of course, is pure fallacy.

Financial resources are generally considered so important that large companies, such as AT&T, have entire departments that attend to nothing else. As part of its effort to keep up to date, 3M has invested $3.2 billion in plant and equipment in the last 5 years.

Physical and financial resource goals might include:

- Increasing plant floor space by 500,000 square feet by 1996.
- Maintaining idle equipment and tools at existing levels of readiness until further notice.
- Increasing monthly cash flow by 6 percent over the next 9 months.
- Maintaining a minimum working capital balance of $1.5 million at all times.

PROFITABILITY

A minimum acceptable objective for **profitability** should be specified. *Note that profit should be interpreted as the gain resulting from an activity and is thus universal to all managerial situations.* Profit need not be thought of only in the narrow sense of money left over after bills are paid. The director of an art gallery may define profit as the increased recognition of the artists he represents, gained by exhibiting in a charity art show. To a university dean, profit may be thought of as the number of new National Merit Scholars on campus.

With respect to the business world, managers should focus on products rather than profits because by doing so the latter will naturally follow. For years there was a saying in Detroit that "General Motors doesn't make cars, it makes money." It was exactly this attitude, hardly peculiar to General Motors, that has made Hondas and Sonys as American as apple pie. Indeed, as Donald E. Petersen, former Ford chairman, has noted, "Managing only for profits is like playing tennis with your eye on the scoreboard, and not on the ball."[7] Stated differently, when organizations focus on their customers and deliver the products that they want, profits will follow.

In this sense, profit is no real measure of the merits of a particular business. A company making $1 million per year may be very profitable, justifying expansion and further investment. On the other hand, a company making $10 million a year may be unprofitable, justifying liquidation. Ultimately, it is not the amount of profit, but the relation of that profit to the real worth of invested capital, that determines whether an activity is worthwhile.

Profitability goals might include:

- Achieving an 18 percent pretax rate of return on investment in the next 3 years.
- Increasing profit from an annual rate of 8 percent to 14 percent in 2 years.
- Increasing annual United Fund contributions by 12 percent.
- Increasing annual student Scholastic Achievement Test scores to the national mean.

Profitability.
The gain resulting from an activity.

MANAGER PERFORMANCE AND DEVELOPMENT

As stressed in Chapter 1, good management is the key to the success of an organization. To accomplish its goals efficiently, an organization principally depends on the quality of its managers. The best organizations know how important it is to attract talented managers, develop them quickly, and keep them challenged and effectively deployed. They link rewards to performance and encourage risk taking. Rather than hire managers that fit a single image, they seek achievers with a variety of styles. Organizations such as Motorola, IBM, Aetna, and Xerox constantly seek to enhance their talent pool in the belief that they never have enough good managers.

Such companies also invest heavily in the continued development of star performers. The knowledge of a manager who graduated in 1970 is nearly obsolete today. Indeed, it has been estimated that the half-life of a management degree is currently 5–10 years, with variations depending on function. That is, half of what is learned today will be technically obsolete within 5–10 years following graduation. Only through continued development can the 1970 graduate have the same capability as one in 1995.

Recognizing this, companies such as Walt Disney Productions, with its Disney U., and McDonald's, with its Hamburger U., invest heavily in training. Every IBM employee, regardless of seniority, spends an estimated 15 days a year in formal training. Bechtel Corporation intentionally takes on small, economically unprofitable projects to provide new managers with on-the-job training.

Goals related to manager performance and development might include:

- Annually sponsoring at least four separate in-house training programs for each level of management.
- Beginning a tuition-reimbursement program for all levels of management by year's end.
- Initiating a "fast-track" top-management training program by the end of 1996.
- Establishing a career counseling office within 2 years to assist every manager in designing a personal career plan.

EMPLOYEE PERFORMANCE AND ATTITUDE

As repeatedly suggested, an organization's employees are its most important asset. Just as with managers, subordinates should receive continuous upgrading of their on-the-job skills to help both employees and organizations pursue new opportunities. By encouraging learning, organizations build innovation and entrepreneurship and, thus, sharpen their competitive edge. Although such learning can take place in high-tech, video-equipped classrooms, it can also involve more traditional educational opportunities such as apprentice programs, job-rotation plans, and lunchtime brown-bag seminar series. Organizations can best protect their future by investing in their employees. As an organization's talent pool deepens, its ability to withstand global competitive pressures becomes more greatly enhanced.

Developing top talent also requires a concern for employee attitudes. In this regard, in their study of America's leading companies, Peters and Waterman found a pervasive theme of *respect for the individual*. These successful companies treat their employees like adults, like partners. This is reflected in the very language the companies use. Employees are called "crew members" rather than personnel at McDonald's, "hosts" at Disney Productions, and "associates" at J.C. Penney. At Delta

Airlines, it's the "Family Feeling." At Hewlett-Packard, it's "the HP Way." Goals related to employee performance and attitude might include:

- Maintaining current levels of employee satisfaction through 1996.
- Establishing an apprenticeship training program by year's end.
- Beginning a lunchtime seminar series within the next 6 months.
- Initiating a General Education Development program over the next 12 months for those employees who did not graduate from high school.

SOCIAL RESPONSIBILITY

The idea of social responsibility supposes that organizations have not only economic and legal obligations, but also certain responsibilities to society. Consistent with our discussion of elements in a typical organization's task environment (Chapter 3), organizations must not only respond to customers, suppliers, employees, and so on, but also to society at large. As noted earlier, whether society views an organization as pursuing socially acceptable goals in a socially acceptable manner is an important consideration if the organization is to be viewed as legitimate (that is, proper and worthy of support). We discussed social responsibility at length in Chapter 4. Goals related to social responsibility might include:

- Hiring and training at least ten handicapped persons every year.
- Sponsoring an annual Junior Olympics for local handicapped children.
- Being a 100-percent contributor to the United Fund.
- Supporting local youth baseball by sponsoring at least two teams.

THREE CONCLUSIONS REGARDING KEY RESULT AREAS

Our discussion of key result areas suggests three conclusions:

1. The view that organizations have one goal (for example, profit) does not reflect the real world. Organizations almost always must pursue multiple goals to

Successful businesses understand that social responsibility goals can be effectively aligned with their goals. Browning Ferris Industries meets the market demand for recycling through the curbside collection of cans, glass, plastics, and newspapers. It also sponsors an in-house office paper recycling effort and allocates the proceeds to charitable causes.

▼

ensure their long-term survival. Market share, innovation, productivity, and so on are all areas that are crucial to an organization's performance and ultimate survival. As one commentator has observed, "In this respect, an enterprise is like a human being. Just as we need a diversity of measures to assess the health and performance of a person, we need a diversity of measures for an enterprise."[8] Organizations are just too complex to be gauged by only a few measures.

2. As a result of multiple goals, virtually all organizations are bound to have competing goals. For example, consider the case of a common pair of goals for a business: increased market share and increased profits. Ordinarily, market share can be increased by decreasing price. The effect of a price decrease on profits, however, would have to be carefully considered. Unless care is taken, these goals could be inconsistent, with one being satisfied only at the expense of the other. For this reason, an organization must be considered as a whole, balancing competing goals.

   Organizations resolve competition among goals, in part, by attending to different goals at different times. Just as a political candidate is likely to resolve competing pressures to "go left" and "go right" by first doing one and then the other, a business is likely to resolve competing goals to "increase market share" and "increase profit" by first doing one and then the other: Differences in the time frames in which goals are to be achieved make this course of action possible. Thus, in the short range, an organization might strive to increase market share while maintaining a long-range goal of increasing profit.

3. Organization goals may serve more than one end. Affirmative action guidelines are a case in point. For many people, increasing the number of women and minority group members in top-management positions undoubtedly serves a social-responsibility goal. To others, it may serve a manager-performance-and-development goal. This realization stresses the point that good managers do not make decisions about goals in a vacuum. In addition to their knowledge, managers need a set of values for their organization, some philosophy, as it were, of goals worth seeking.

MANAGEMENT BY OBJECTIVES

Up to this point we have emphasized establishing overall organization objectives. However, to achieve these objectives, it is important to translate them into objectives for individual employees. In recent years, one approach designed to integrate individual and organization objectives has gained considerable popularity. Known as **management by objectives,** or simply **MBO,** it is perhaps the most widely discussed goal-setting approach in use today.[9]

MBO provides for the meshing of individual and organization objectives. It is based on the belief that joint subordinate-superior participation in translating overall objectives into individual objectives will have a positive influence on employee performance. The central idea behind MBO is that the *mutual* setting and acceptance of objectives will elicit a stronger employee commitment than if a superior unilaterally establishes objectives and imposes them on subordinates. The enhanced commitment by employees who have helped to set personal objectives should, in turn, lead to improved performance. The structure of this belief is outlined in Figure 5.5.

Management by objectives (MBO).
A goal-setting approach based on the belief that joint subordinate-superior participation in translating overall organization objectives into individual objectives will have a positive influence on employee performance.

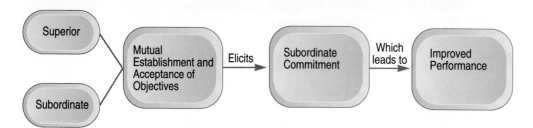

FIGURE 5.5 THE CENTRAL IDEA BEHIND MBO

The fundamental process underlying MBO is goal setting. As developed by Edwin A. Locke, goal-setting theory asserts that an individual's performance is directly regulated by the goals the individual is attempting to achieve.[10] Several hundred studies have shown that specific, challenging yet reachable goals almost invariably lead to higher performance than vague or easy goals: "Increase sales by 10 percent during the next quarter" will improve performance more readily than "Try to improve sales."

Locke points out that for goals to affect performance, there must be commitment to the goals. That is, an individual must be truly trying to attain them. Moreover, goal setting is most effective when feedback allows performance to be tracked in relation to one's goals. Of course, as with any technique, for goal setting to work, the necessary support elements must be in place. Employees must have the neces-

SMART MANAGEMENT MBO THE IACOCCA WAY

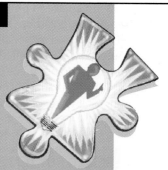

As the accompanying narrative reports, "MBO, like ice cream, comes in 29 flavors." The following excerpt describes how former Chrysler CEO Lee Iacocca, one of the world's best-known managers, has adapted the MBO process for his own purposes.

Over the years, I've regularly asked my key people—and I've had them ask *their* key people, and so on down the line—a few basic questions: "What are your objectives for the next ninety days? What are your plans, your priorities, your hopes? And how do you intend to go about achieving them?"

On the surface, this procedure may seem like little more than a tough-minded way to make employees accountable to their boss. It is that, of course, but it's also much more, because the quarterly review system makes employees accountable to *themselves*. Not only does it force each manager to consider his own goals, but it's also an effective way to remind people not to lose sight of their dreams.

Every three months, each manager sits down with his immediate superior to review the manager's past accomplishments and to chart his goals for the next term. Once there is agreement on these goals, the manager puts them in writing and the supervisor signs off on it. . . . In conversation, you can get away with all kinds of vagueness and nonsense, often without even realizing it. But there's something about putting your thoughts on paper that forces you to get down to specifics. That way, it's harder to deceive yourself—or anybody else.

Source: Lee Iacocca with William Novak, *Iacocca: An Autobiography* (New York: Bantam, 1984), 47.

sary resources and competence to reach or approach established goals. Moreover, situational factors such as low pay and poor working conditions must not inhibit goal attainment. Above all, MBO requires top management support and participation.

MBO programs have reportedly been used with varying degrees of success in more than half the corporations in the United States. Companies such as Du Pont, RCA, General Foods, Wells Fargo, Purex, and General Motors, along with countless others around the world, have used MBO. The accompanying "Smart Management" box describes how MBO was regularly used by former Chrysler CEO Lee Iacocca.

THE MBO PROCESS

Although as one writer suggests, "MBO, like ice cream, comes in 29 flavors,"[11] the typical MBO process is comprised of the following five basic steps as illustrated in Figure 5.6.

Step 1: Discuss job requirements. A superior and subordinate meet to discuss the requirements of the subordinate's job and agree on the relative importance of the subordinate's major duties—the things the subordinate is paid to do. Two-way communication is vital at this point. The superior should tell the subordinate what objectives have been set by top management, explaining what the subordinate's particular work unit is expected to do to help meet those objectives. This step provides an opportunity for the superior and subordinate to better understand one another's priorities and obtain valuable job-related feedback.

Step 2: Develop performance objectives. Here, a subordinate develops potential performance objectives in relation to the major duties and work unit objectives agreed upon in Step 1. Performance objectives should meet at least six criteria. They should be clear and concise, achievable, challenging, measurable, consistent with overall organization objectives, and accompanied by an anticipated completion date. As goal theory research has shown, employees with specific, challenging goals will typically perform better than those with vague or easy goals.

Figure 5.7 shows a typical MBO form for recording objectives. Performance objectives are listed in the first column. The relative importance of each objective is indicated in the second column. An anticipated completion date for each objective is given in the third column. Space is provided in the fourth column for recording the results of an individual's efforts.

FIGURE 5.6 THE MBO PROCESS

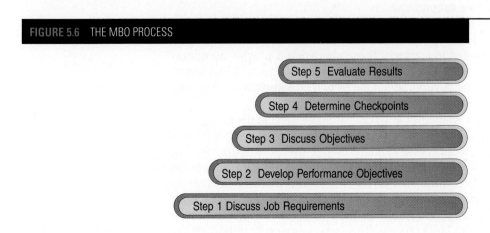

FIGURE 5.7   A TYPICAL MBO FORM FOR RECORDING OBJECTIVES

Performance Objectives

Subordinate's Name _Larry Reed_ Position _Prod Mgr_ Date _7-6-96_

Date Hired _5-7-91_   In Position Since _7-6-96_

Specific Objective	Priority	Completion Date	Results
1. Complete Delta Project	A	5/30	
2. Increase production capacity to 12,000 a month	A	6/1	
3. Increase finished goods inventories to a level 25% of next quarter's planned production	B	3/1	
4. Increase raw material inventories to a level 100% of next quarter's planned usage	B	4/1	
5. Decreased turnover by 10%	A	4/15	
6. Decrease rejected out-put by 3%	B	2/1	
7. Decrease waste and spoilage of raw materials by 6%	A	2/15	

Signature of Subordinate's _Larry Reed_   Date _7-6-96_

Signature of Superior _Ralph J. Teague_ Date _7-6-96_

Step 3: Discuss objectives. During this step, a superior and subordinate meet to discuss the potential performance objectives developed by the subordinate in Step 2. A statement of performance objectives is then *mutually* agreed upon. This, together with a completed and signed MBO form for recording objectives (Step 2), will help minimize angry protests like "I had no idea . . ." or "But it didn't happen that way."

Involvement is a key element at this time. Although a superior should make sure that a subordinate's objectives will contribute to fulfilling an organization's objectives, it is critical that the superior not dictate objectives. To do so would risk a halfhearted commitment to the objectives on the part of the subordinate, who might conclude that MBO is a sham and resentfully view it as "playing games." An imposed objective, no matter how well conceived, is the property of only a superior until personally adopted by a subordinate.

Step 4: Determine checkpoints. Mutually acceptable checkpoints, and standards for monitoring subordinate progress toward accomplishing the agreed upon objectives, should be specified in advance. These checkpoints provide an opportunity to modify objectives rendered unreasonable by either forces within an organization or within its external environment. One or two checkpoints are typically scheduled during a performance period.

Step 5: Evaluate results. A superior and a subordinate meet at the conclusion of an agreed upon performance period to evaluate the results of the subordinate's efforts to accomplish the objectives established in Step 3. The focus of this meeting should be an impartial analysis of subordinate performance. Its tone should be constructive. If there have been problems in reaching objectives, this is the time to discuss them and map plans to resolve them. Employees should also receive positive feedback on objectives achieved. Above all, the meeting should provide a platform for reinitiating the entire MBO process. This step is especially important because research indicates that goal setting without feedback has little long-term effect on performance.

BENEFITS AND PROBLEMS OF MBO

Experience shows that there are both benefits and problems associated with MBO. Given its wide and varied application, it is hardly surprising that MBO has been both praised and criticized. The benefits and problems commonly associated with MBO are listed separately in Table 5.4. Together these lists suggest that, consistent with the contingency approach to management introduced in Chapter 2, the success of MBO is likely to be dependent on a variety of factors specific to a particular situation.

TABLE 5.4 BENEFITS AND PROBLEMS ASSOCIATED WITH MBO

Benefits	Problems
1. Improved communication between superior and subordinate on job content and the relative importance of major duties.	1. Inadequate top management support and participation.
2. Improved utilization of human and material resources.	2. Poorly defined objectives.
3. Improved subordinate development.	3. Inadequate monitoring of progress toward accomplishment of agreed upon objectives.
4. Improved subordinate performance.	4. Inability to modify objectives rendered unreasonable by forces within an organization or within its external environment.
5. Improved criteria for evaluating subordinate performance.	5. Inadequate evaluation of actual accomplishment of agreed upon objectives.
6. Improved overall planning.	6. Overemphasis on paperwork.
	7. Too time consuming.

SUMMARY

This chapter is divided into two principal sections. The first focuses on the importance and benefits of planning, as well as on the scope and application of different types of plans. The second explores the nature of organization goals. As defined, goals are those ends that an organization seeks to achieve by its existence and operation.

Learning Objective 1: Appreciate why organizations plan.
Organizations plan for four basic reasons: planning helps them succeed, it provides direction and a sense of purpose, it helps managers cope with change, and it contributes to the performance of other managerial functions.

Learning Objective 2: Identify the various forms of standing and single-use plans.
The three principal forms of standing plans are policies, procedures, and rules. The three principal forms of single-use plans are budgets, programs, and projects.

Learning Objective 3: **Comment on the need to balance short- and long-range plans.**

An organization's long-term performance is established through the cumulative impact of short-range plans. If these short-range plans can be related not only to specific demands of the near term but also to an overall or long-range plan, their internal consistency and cumulative impact will establish a strong and cohesive organization.

Learning Objective 4: **Explain how short- and long-range plans are interrelated.**

Short- and long-range plans are interrelated in at least two respects: short-range and long-range plans compete for the allocation of resources, and short-range plans should be compatible with long-range plans.

Learning Objective 5: **Answer the question: "How long should a long-range plan be?"**

Although no set answer can be given to the question "How long should a long-range plan be?" three criteria can serve as guidelines: how far into the future an organization's fixed commitments extend, the degree of uncertainty associated with the future, and lead time—the time required to bring a new product to market.

Learning Objective 6: **Demonstrate an understanding of rolling plans.**

A rolling plan is a plan of future operations updated annually. Rolling plans allow an organization to revise its plans on the basis of new information and to maintain a degree of flexibility in its commitments.

Learning Objective 7: **List some benefits of goals.**

Goals serve as guidelines for action, constraints, a source of legitimacy, performance standards, and a source of motivation.

Learning Objective 8: **Name the key result areas in which all organizations should establish goals.**

The eight key result areas are market share, innovation, productivity, physical and financial resources, profitability, manager performance and development, employee performance and attitude, and social responsibility.

Learning Objective 9: **Explain the central idea behind MBO.**

The central idea behind MBO is that the *mutual* setting and acceptance of objectives will elicit a stronger employee commitment than if a superior unilaterally establishes objectives and imposes them on subordinates. The enhanced commitment by employees who have helped to set personal objectives should, in turn, lead to improved performance.

Learning Objective 10: **Relate the basic assertion underlying goal-setting theory.**

Goal-setting theory asserts that an individual's performance is directly regulated by the goals the individual is attempting to achieve. It has been repeatedly shown that specific, challenging yet reachable goals almost invariably lead to higher performance than vague or easy goals.

Learning Objective 11: **Outline the five basic steps that comprise the MBO process.**

The five basic steps that comprise the MBO process are to discuss job requirements, develop performance objectives, discuss objectives, determine checkpoints, and evaluate results.

Learning Objective 12: **Identify the benefits and problems commonly associated with MBO.**
The benefits and problems commonly associated with MBO are listed in Table 5.4.

KEY TERMS

budget 132	planning 124	programs 132
goals 133	policy 129	projects 133
key result area 136	procedure 130	rolling plans 129
management by objectives 143	productivity 138	rule 131
	profitability 140	standing plans 129

REVIEW AND DISCUSSION QUESTIONS

1. What do you imagine the successful CEO of a *Fortune* 500 company would say about the role of planning in the management process?

2. Compare the length of time you would recommend for long-range planning at (a) Milton Bradley, (b) General Electric, (c) Anheuser-Busch, and (d) Standard Oil Co. (Indiana). What are the reasons for differences in the recommended time periods?

3. In his book *Managing*, former ITT chief executive Harold Geneen writes, "I do not believe in long-range planning. No one is wise enough to see five to ten years into the future."[12] Do you agree with Geneen? If so, why? If not, why not?

4. Imagine you are the human resource manager of a medium-size sporting goods company with facilities in seven states. As part of an orientation program for a new group of employees, you have been asked to comment on the company's policies, procedures, and rules. What explanations and examples would you give?

5. As the successful head coach of a nationally recognized university football program, explain what your goals will be for the upcoming season. Of what benefit are these goals to you and your team?

6. Three decades ago, the weight-reduction business was seen as a collection of gimmicks engineered by charlatans to take advantage of people in need. Founded in 1963 by Jean Nidetch, Weight Watchers International (now an H. J. Heinz subsidiary) was able to establish the industry's legitimacy by justifying its goals. Discuss how organizations such as the Girl Scouts, Salvation Army, and United Way have established the legitimacy of their activities.

7. Select any organization you wish as an example and explain the importance of the organization's establishing goals in each of the so-called key result areas.

8. Imagine that you are the CEO of a major chemical company, and cite an example where your company's multiple goals might possibly compete.

9. Imagine that you are the president of a student club that is planning a large party for its graduating seniors. Three members have agreed to be responsible for securing a location for the party, preparing food, and hiring entertainment. Describe how the MBO process might be applied in this situation.

10. Calling on your own experience, relate an instance when specific, challenging goals led to your increased performance.

11. Assume that the firm for which you work has just announced its intention to implement an MBO program, and you strenuously object. What reasons can you give for your opposition?

12. Assume that the firm for which you work has just announced its intention to implement an MBO program, and you heartily approve. What reasons can you give for your support?

THE MANAGEMENT EXPERIENCE ACCOMPLISHING INDIVIDUAL OBJECTIVES: FEAR OF SUCCESS

MBO is a goal-setting approach designed to integrate individual and organization objectives. Yet, many managers achieve only a fraction of their potential. The culprit is often a subconscious fear of success. Each success breeds increased responsibility; each success demands that a person do more. Victims of this "syndrome" experience anxiety from the *anticipated* consequences of success. To determine if your career might be hampered by a fear of succeeding, respond to the following items. Be honest with yourself. Don't "second guess" how a "successful" person might respond. Scoring instructions appear below.

My Attitudes and Feelings

A—Agree   B—In-Between or Don't Know   C—Disagree

1. When things seem to be going really well for me, I get uneasy because I know it won't last. _____

2. Most of the time I find that I measure up to the standards I've set for myself. _____

3. I find it difficult to tell my friends that I excel at something. _____

4. It is important for me to be liked by people with positions of higher status and power than mine. _____

5. When I win a competitive game, I feel a little sorry for the other player. _____

6. When I have to ask others for help, I feel I'm imposing on them. _____

7. Although I may experience occasional difficulty doing so, I generally finish essential projects. _____

8. When I think I've been too forceful in making a point to friends, I get worried that I might have made them feel unfriendly toward me. _____

9. When my peers compliment me on my work, I feel they are being insincere. _____

10. When I complete an important piece of work, I am usually satisfied with the result. _____

11. When engaged in competitive games, I make more mistakes near the end than at the beginning. _____

12. When superiors praise my work, I wonder whether I can live up to their expectations in the future. _____

13. At times, I believe I have gotten as far in my career because of good luck and not because I deserve it. _____

14. It is just as important to win a game as to merely enjoy it. _____

Continued on next page.

15. I often daydream about accomplishing something that no one else has ever accomplished before. _____

16. I like being the center of attention in a social gathering. _____

17. Most of my peers are secretly pleased when I get into trouble. _____

18. I'm pretty skillful at most things I try. _____

19. When I make a decision, I usually stick with it. _____

20. I often get excited when I start working on a new project, but it gets stale rather quickly. _____

21. I often feel let down after completing an important project. _____

22. At times, my accomplishments amaze me because I feel that I rarely put in the effort that I could. _____

23. When I hear about the accomplishments of others, I tend to think how little I myself have accomplished. _____

24. I'm not influenced one way or another by persuasive people. _____

25. When a project seems to be going well, I often get scared that I'll do something to botch it. _____

Scoring Your Answers

Item	Response			Item	Response		
	A	**B**	**C**		**A**	**B**	**C**
1	−1	0	2	14	2	1	−1
2	2	0	−1	15	3	0	−2
3	−1	0	1	16	2	1	−1
4	−1	0	1	17	−1	0	1
5	1	0	−1	18	2	1	−1
6	−2	1	2	19	3	0	−2
7	3	0	−2	20	−2	1	2
8	−2	1	2	21	−1	0	1
9	−1	0	1	22	−1	0	1
10	2	0	−1	23	−2	0	2
11	−2	0	2	24	3	1	−2
12	−2	0	2	25	−1	0	2
13	−2	1	2				

Meaning of Your Score

- A score of 28 to 47 indicates that you have no problem with "fear of success." You are strongly achievement oriented. You like to come up a winner. You are able to make commitments and persevere with your projects until a successful outcome is assured. You take pride in your skills and talents and you have full confidence in yourself. Although you are independent minded and assertive, your relationships with others are trustful and open.

- If you scored 4 to 27, you have a tendency to occasionally pursue unrealistically high standards, and you're not always satisfied with your achievements. You prefer win/win rather than win/lose situations. You're concerned about what others think of you and you want to be liked by everybody. Because of a fluctuating self-esteem, you periodically lapse into self-critical ruminations about your abilities to succeed. You have some

Continued on next page.

trouble making decisions and then sticking with them. Because you have moderate fear of success, you're not fully using your success potential.

- A score of −25 to 3 indicates that you want to win, but frequently lose in the end. You tend to be overly passive and withdrawn and prefer to take the back seat in competitive situations. Because of your excessive need to be liked, you refrain from arguments and contests of will. You lack full self-confidence, and you seldom give yourself the credit you deserve for your accomplishments. Fear of success definitely hampers your accomplishments.

- A score of −36 to −24 means that "fear of success" is a definite problem for you. You're very nonassertive and self-effacing and consider modesty a virtue. You're never satisfied with your achievements and frequently manage to snatch defeat from victory. Doubtful about whether you've any luck at all, you tend to worry about the future most of the time. Because you're too concerned about others' opinions of you, you frequently act like a "doormat," although you don't like it one whit.

Source: Eugene Raudsepp, "Are You Hampered by Fear of Success?" *Supervision* 46 (June 1984), 9–10, 26. Reprinted by permission of *Supervision*. Copyright 1980, 1983, and 1984 by The National Research Bureau, Inc., 424 North Third Street, Burlington, Iowa 52601.

CASE 5.1   KIM DYER AND TRI-STAR, INC.

Kim Dyer, a new buyer's representative for Tri-Star, Inc., had been on the job only 4 months, when one Tuesday morning David Handy, another buyer's representative and her assigned mentor, came into her office and said, "Kim, it's time to submit your goals for the next year. Turn them in next Monday and the boss will send them to corporate headquarters in Knoxville." Handy then walked out of the office.

Dyer had taken the job with Tri-Star, a manufacturer of women's clothing, immediately after graduation from Eastern State University's marketing program. Her day-to-day work consisted of tracking production of 30–40 different lots of women's dresses made in Tri-Star's three plants, as well as distributing the finished products to their major customer, X mart, a major retail corporation. A new set of 30–40 dress lots were created with each of the four fashion seasons.

The buyer's representative job involved keeping the X mart buyer up to date concerning progress of these production lots from raw material to shipping to the various X mart stores and regional distribution centers. Although Kim had little control or power to speed up production or shipments, she still enjoyed her work. She had thought she was getting the hang of it, but now she was confused.

Dyer wondered what this "goal" thing was all about. She felt she hadn't been at Tri-Star long enough to understand her job that well, much less set goals for next year. She hadn't paid much attention to her management classes at Eastern, putting most of her effort into her marketing and distribution classes. Later in the week, on two different occasions, she quizzed Handy on what was expected. Early Friday morning, she finally confessed, "I'm lost, David. I have no idea what the rest of this year will be like, much less next year. I've been through only one seasonal change. How am I supposed to develop goals for next year?"

Handy replied, "Kim, I guess you're right. Here are my goals for last year. I just take the previous year's goals, modify them a little and send them off. You take these and adapt them to fit your line. It really doesn't matter whether your goals are realistic or not. We never see them again, but it's something the bureaucracy at corporate headquarters wants everyone to do."

Problems

1. What was "this goal thing" all about? Was it something like MBO?

2. Given the discussion of this chapter, what is your estimate of corporate headquarters's intentions?

3. Do you believe this program was successfully meeting the expectations of corporate-level management? Why or why not?

4. What should corporate headquarters do to make the process a tool for increasing effectiveness and not just a paper exercise?

Source: William C. Sharbrough, The Citadel.

CASE 5.2 THE RESTAURANT QUESTION

You are Achilles Armenakis. You have just inherited $50,000 (after taxes) from your grandfather. You were graduated from a good business school and have thought of entering the restaurant business because you like it. You would like to move to a warm climate, so you are considering several smaller cities in Florida.

Your present first choice has a population of about 100,000. The city is not contiguous to others. You have heard the population is about one-fourth economically upper class (incomes over $50,000), one-third economically lower class (incomes below $16,000).

At present there are 12 restaurants of the quality you would like to run in this city. Their characteristics are presented in the accompanying table. Four of these restaurants have changed management in the past year. Three others (numbers 2, 7, and 9) previously went bankrupt. You have heard that several of the restaurants are barely managing to continue operation.

You would like to run a very nice, rather expensive restaurant and cocktail bar with a Greek decor. You are wondering if you should go ahead.

Type of Restaurant	Seating Capacity	Liquor License	Years in Business
1. Chinese	100	Yes	4
2. Chinese	75	Yes	1
3. Steak	160	Yes	8
4. Italian	60	Yes	2
5. Steak/seafood	150	No	1
6. Vegetarian	50	No	New
7. German	100	Yes	1
8. General	150	Yes	3
9. General	100	No	1
10. General	125	Yes	2
11. Barbecue	100	Yes	3
12. Mexican	75	Yes	2

Problems

1. What kind of planning should you do before deciding to go ahead on this project in this city?

2. What additional information should you obtain?

3. What goals should you establish?

4. Can a decision like this ever be made on the basis of premises and studies alone?

NOTES

1 Rob Michiels, "Planning: An Effective Management Tool or a Corporate Pastime?" *Journal of Marketing Management*, 2 (Spring 1986): 259.

2 Vasudevan Ramanujam and N. Venkatraman, "Excellence, Planning, and Performance," *Interfaces* 18 (May–June 1988): 23–31; and Brian K. Boyd, "Strategic Planning and Financial Performance: A Meta-Analytic Review," *Journal of Management Studies* 28 (July 1991): 353–374.

3 Quoted in Paul R. Lawrence, "In Defense of Planning As a Rational Approach to Change," *Organizational Strategy and Change*, eds. Johannes M. Pennings and Associates (San Francisco: Jossey-Bass, 1985), 375.

4 Ronald Henkoff, "Make Your Office More Productive," *Fortune*, February 25, 1991, 76.

5 Peter F. Drucker, *The Practice of Management* (New York: Harper, 1954), 62–87.

6 Thomas J. Peters and Robert H. Waterman, Jr., *In Search of Excellence: Lessons from America's Best-Run Companies* (New York: Harper & Row, 1982).

7 Paul Ingrassia, "The Graceful Exit of Ford's Chief," *Wall Street Journal*, March 5, 1990, A10.

8 Peter F. Drucker, "Management and the World's Work," *Harvard Business Review* 66 (September–October 1988): 76.

9 Robert Rodgers and John E. Hunter, "Impact of Management by Objectives on Organizational Productivity," *Journal of Applied Psychology Monograph* 76 (April 1991): 322–336.

10 Edwin A. Locke and Gary P. Latham, *A Theory of Goal Setting and Task Performance* (Englewood Cliffs, NJ: Prentice Hall, 1990).

11 John S. Hodgson, "Management by Objectives—The Experience of a Federal Government Department," *Canadian Public Administration* 16, no. 4 (1973): 423.

12 Harold Geneen, *Managing* (New York: Doubleday, 1984), 88.

CHAPTER 6

LEARNING OBJECTIVES

Upon completing this chapter, you should be able to:

- Explain the importance of strategic planning.
- Demonstrate an understanding of SWOT analysis.
- Define the term "strategic window."
- Identify the three levels of strategic planning.
- Describe the Boston Consulting Group matrix.
- Classify available grand strategies and their subcategories.
- Present Miles and Snow's adaptive strategy typology.
- Identify Porter's three competitive strategies.
- Answer the question, "Why is sound strategy implementation important?"
- Display an understanding of contingency planning.

n the past 10 years, while they have protested against the importation of Japanese cars and computer chips, American businesses have welcomed one Japanese import. This formidable item is not a product but a form of strategic alliance: the *keiretsu*.

Similar to the vast trust companies that were outlawed in the United States in the 1930s, Japanese keiretsu are multicompany alliances with highly centralized control. There are two kinds of keiretsu: horizontal and vertical. The horizontal keiretsu, most similar to the outlawed U.S. trusts, is a group made up of dozens of major companies tied together by friendships among their top managers and stock holdings in one another's companies. The vertical keiretsu is heirarchically structured, with a single large company at the top and varying levels of subordinate companies supplying each other and the master company.

As would be expected, keiretsu have powerful advantages in the marketplace. Intercompany cooperation in research and production helps bring new products to market faster. The stability and security of keiretsu also encourage risk taking and investment in long-term development.

U.S. companies cannot form keiretsu, but they can adopt some features of this approach to exploit its advantages. For example, in

STRATEGY FORMULATION AND IMPLEMENTATION

1979 Ford Motor Company bought a 25 percent share of Mazda, the Japanese auto manufacturer, creating a limited form of horizontal keiretsu. The two companies share information on everything from plant layout and details of auto design to marketing survey techniques. They also engineer or manufacture models for each other and provide assistance when a problem occurs.

The arrangement has benefitted both companies. Ford has profited from Mazda's manufacturing and product development expertise, and Mazda has gained access to Ford's considerable knowledge of international marketing and finance. Both General Motors and Chrysler Corporation have had far less success in their attempts to join forces with Japanese manufacturers.

The success of the Ford-Mazda partnership is based on a seven-point scheme: The partners agreed to keep top management involved, to meet often, to use a matchmaker, to maintain independence, to make each product beneficial for each partner, to appoint a monitor, and to anticipate cultural differences. Although it was not easy to establish the proper working relationship between the two companies, by following these guidelines they have been able to reduce the enormous costs of developing and producing a new car.

In this chapter, we will see many examples of strategies like the Ford-Mazda keiretsu-type arrangement. Careful formulation and implementation of such strategies are essential in an ever-changing and increasingly challenging environment.

Source: Kevin Kelly, Otis Port, James Treece, Gail De George, Zachary Schiller, "Learning From Japan," *Business Week,* January 27, 1992, 52–55; 59–60.

After an organization has established its goals, it knows where it wants to go. Management's task at this point is to develop a strategy to get there. **Strategy,** in the present context, refers to a plan of action that will develop an organization's competitive advantages and compound them.[1] This search is a never-ending process that begins by determining where an organization is and how it will accomplish its goals.

As the preceding chapters suggest, however, all organizations operate in a changing environment, creating uncertainty in all but the simplest circumstances. In Europe, for instance, the implications of the European Economic Community, a unified Germany, the democratization of ex–East Bloc countries, and continuing economic difficulties in the former Soviet Union have created immense uncertainty. Likewise, in the Far East, the so-called Four Dragons—Korea, Hong Kong, Singapore, and Taiwan—continue to be formidable but uncertain influences on the international scene. Facing such a volatile world, how can managers possibly plot strategies to achieve organization goals?

In this chapter, we focus on an organization's continuing relationship with its environment. First, we will define *strategic planning* and discuss its importance. Next, we will outline an approach for assessing an organization's internal strengths and weaknesses in relation to the external opportunities and threats it faces. We will then consider several approaches to strategy formulation. Finally, we will discuss the crucial significance of sound strategy implementation.

Strategy.
A plan of action that will develop an organization's competitive advantages and compound them.

STRATEGIC PLANNING

As we move further into the nineties, it has become increasingly clear that an organization's ability to think and act strategically will determine its continued survival. The most successful organizations will be those that have developed a dynamic marketplace strategy. The concept of **strategic planning** strikes at the very root of this challenge. By focusing on an organization's continuing relationship with its environment, strategic planning allows managers to identify various approaches for achieving specific goals.

Formulating a successful strategic plan is extremely difficult, especially in the face of an unpredictable future. Managers need to ask themselves such questions as:

Strategic planning.
The process of focusing on an organization's continuing relationship with its environment.

- What is our business? What should it be?
- What business should we be in 5 years from now? Ten years?
- Who are our customers? Who should be our customers?
- Should we try to grow in this business or grow primarily in other businesses?

Although answering such straightforward questions may appear simple, experience suggests otherwise. Remember Midway Airlines? Why couldn't IBM become a major competitor in the copy machine field? What led to AT&T's failure in the personal computer market?

In each case, the companies involved failed to address satisfactorily certain fundamental questions. A sound strategic plan helps an organization to attain its goals by:

1. Defining specific markets to be targeted. This definition can be phrased in terms of geography, products to be offered, distribution channels, or pricing policies.
2. Identifying key capabilities necessary to serve targeted markets. These could include ready access, user friendliness, or after-sales service.
3. Outlining a realistic program for developing and maintaining key capabilities.[2] Examples of organizations with successful strategic plans include:

   - G. Heileman Brewing Co., which has become a major force in the beer industry by marketing regional brands (for example, Blatz, Old Style, and Lone Star) for local tastes in competition with the national brands, such as Budweiser and Miller.

   - Motorola, which sees itself as a world leader in wireless communications (for example, wireless local area computer networks and global positioning satellite receivers), and not just a producer of paging devices and mobile telephones.

   - Texas Instruments, which has achieved its goal of "cost leadership" by being the lowest cost, highest quality producer in the industrial-controls business.

   - Federal Express, which has recently expanded overseas in an effort to become "the largest and best transportation company in the world."

ASSESSING STRENGTHS, WEAKNESSES, OPPORTUNITIES, AND THREATS

In formulating a sound strategic plan, an organization must assess its *internal* strengths and weaknesses in relation to the *external* opportunities and threats it faces. By definition, an effective strategy will take advantage of an organization's strengths and opportunities at the same time it minimizes or overcomes weaknesses and threats.

Every organization has both strengths and weaknesses. But unless an organization is fully aware of its strengths, it may not avail itself of opportunities to capitalize on them. Conversely, unless an organization regularly assesses its weaknesses, it may be unprepared to effectively counter unanticipated environmental threats. The assessment of an organization's **s**trengths, **w**eaknesses, **o**pportunities, and **t**hreats is often referred to as **SWOT analysis.**

As noted in Chapter 3, an organization's ability to identify and capitalize on marketplace opportunities and, in turn, respond to external threats will be a function of its environmental scanning proficiency. Each year, General Electric's 13 business heads scan the general environment and prepare five one-page memos identifying possible marketplace opportunities and threats. It took General Electric only 60 days after Hungary sanctioned foreign ownership in state-run companies to acquire 50 percent of Tungsram, the country's leading light bulb manufacturer. Tungsram had been a subject of General Electric's annual memos for years.

SWOT analysis.
The assessment of an organization's internal strengths and weaknesses in relation to its external opportunities and threats.

Amid the commercial bustle of Tokyo, a Motorola two-way communications system helps Footwork International Corporation save delivery time and fuel. The drivers' mobile radio equipment operates on Motorola's Japan Specialized Mobile Radio System, which is among the world's most advanced shared trunked radio systems. Motorola has invested heavily in shared system technology and by 1990 had emerged as a world leader in this market, with systems in the U.S., Japan, China, Germany, and Switzerland.

An untapped opportunity that fits an organization's strengths is known as a **strategic window.** Typically, strategic windows exist for only a short time before they are occupied by alert competitors. The ultimate leaders in many global industries are often among the first to identify an opportunity and respond. For example, Eastman Kodak was the first global competitor in film, Honda in motorcycles, IBM in computers, and Boeing in aircraft. Such early movers typically have the benefit of being the first to establish worldwide distribution networks, which frequently results in reputation, scale, and learning advantages.[3]

Strategic window.
An untapped opportunity that fits an organization's strengths.

The specifics of a SWOT analysis are impossible to detail in the present context. To do so would essentially entail the review of an entire business school curriculum. Table 6.1, however, presents an outline of considerations necessary to assess the attractiveness of a specific industry and position a company within the industry. All considerations may not be significant for a particular company, but the outline suggests a range of factors that should be assessed. A company operating in two or more industries would, of course, perform a separate SWOT analysis for each industry. Because industries, companies, and the environment in which they exist change over time, SWOT analyses must be updated regularly.

LEVELS OF STRATEGIC PLANNING

In those instances where an organization produces one good or service, a single strategic plan is sufficient for specifying the approach it will take in achieving its goals. A great many organizations, however, produce a variety of goods and services, each with its own unique marketplace characteristics. Consider, for instance, a company like Dial Corp., which focuses on three business lines. Its consumer products division sells such household names as Dial soap, Purex laundry detergent, and Brillo steel-wool soap. Its services group includes Premier Cruise Lines, the "official" cruise line of Disney World, and Travelers Express, the leading U.S. issuer of money orders and processor of shared drafts. Finally, Dial's transportation manufacturing group is the nation's leading maker of intercity buses and dominates the parts business.

To respond effectively to the differing opportunities and threats it faces, a company like Dial, which provides multiple goods and services, must formulate a separate strategic plan for each market in which it competes. Dial also has various functional departments, such as finance and marketing, that support its different business units. These likewise require their own strategic plans. As a multiproduct

---

TABLE 6.1 OUTLINE FOR ASSESSING AN ORGANIZATION'S STRENGTHS, WEAKNESSES, OPPORTUNITIES, AND THREATS

Attractiveness of an Industry

A. Demand for goods and/or services
  1. Long-run growth or decline
  2. Stability of demand
  3. Stage in "product life cycle"
B. Supply of goods and/or services of the industry
  1. Industry capacity
  2. Availability of needed resources
  3. Volatility of technology
  4. Social constraints
  5. Government support and regulation
C. Competitive structure
  1. Barriers to mobility
  2. Relative bargaining power
  3. Severity of competition
D. Conclusions
  1. Prospects for volume and profits
  2. Key factors for success in the industry

Position of Company in Its Industry

A. Market position of the company
  1. Relation of company sales to total industry and to leading competitors
  2. Relative appeal of company goods and services
  3. Strength in major markets
B. Supply position of the company
  1. Comparative access to resources
  2. Unique productivity advantages
  3. Research and development strength
C. Special competitive considerations
  1. Relative financial strength
  2. Community and government relations
  3. Ability and values of company managers
D. Conclusions
  Comparative strengths and weaknesses of the company in terms of key success factors identified in "Attractiveness of an Industry" above.

Source: Reproduced from William H. Newman, James P. Logan, and W. Harvey Hegarty, *Strategy: A Multi-Level Integrative Approach*, South-Western Publishing, 1989, pgs. 32, 56, with permission of South-Western Publishing Co. Copyright 1989 by South-Western Publishing Co. All rights reserved.

corporation, Dial must thus develop strategic plans at three levels: *corporate, business unit,* and *functional.* Figure 6.1 shows these three levels as they might apply to Dial.

Corporate-Level Strategic Planning

At the corporate level, strategic planning addresses the question *In what businesses should we compete?* In doing so, it defines the roles that an organization's various businesses will play in achieving its overall goals. Top management's aim at this level should be to integrate the strategies of an organization's different businesses to achieve balanced growth in sales and earnings at an acceptable level of risk. Dial's decision to focus on four business lines is but one example of corporate-level strategic planning. Quaker Oats offers a second example. It competes in a collection of businesses ranging from consumer products (Aunt Jemima and Gatorade) to toys (Fisher-Price) to pet food (Gaines and Ken-L-Ration).

Business-Unit-Level Strategic Planning

At the business-unit level, strategic planning addresses the question *How should we compete in each of our businesses?* Thus, business-unit-level planning involves developing a marketplace strategy for each of an organization's businesses (*or* for organizations that operate a single business). Those units within an organization competing in distinct markets are often referred to as **strategic business units** (SBUs). Formally defined, an SBU is a segment of an organization with a distinct objective, product market, and strategy for dealing with that market. Strategic decisions at this level concern product mix, equipment and facilities, manufacturing technologies, advertising, new products, and so on. Managers at this level should attempt to capitalize on emerging strategic windows by developing strategies tailored to each SBU's capabilities and competitive needs, but yet consistent with overall corporate goals. Thus, Procter & Gamble's corporate-level strategy of relying on research to give birth to superior products it can sell at premium prices is bolstered by its business-unit-level strategy to be the market leader in each of its 39 product categories. With household names like Crest, Ivory, Pert Plus, Pampers, Tide, Secret, Max Factor, Noxzema, Duncan Hines, Crisco, and Folgers, Procter & Gamble is one of the world's leading modern marketers.

Strategic business unit.
A segment of an organization with a distinct objective, product market, and strategy for dealing with that market.

Functional-Level Strategic Planning

At the functional level, strategic planning addresses the question *How do we support each of our SBUs?* It is concerned with devising action plans for the major

FIGURE 6.1   THREE LEVELS OF STRATEGIC PLANNING

functional areas (for example, research and development, production, marketing, human resources, finance) within an organization. These plans must likewise be consistent with and support higher level strategies. At Procter & Gamble, for instance, marketing, finance, research and development, and production all provide a base for gaining market leadership through launching superior products that command premium prices.

In the next several sections, we will examine strategic planning more closely. Because the nature of functional-level plans (for example, marketing plans, production plans, human resource plans, financial plans, and so forth) parallels individual disciplines, we will focus on strategic planning at the corporate- and business-unit levels.

FORMULATING CORPORATE-LEVEL STRATEGIC PLANS

As described earlier, corporate-level strategic planning addresses the question *In what businesses should we compete?* The two most popular approaches to answering this question are *portfolio analysis* and the development of *grand strategies*. These should be viewed as complementary rather than competing approaches. Both can yield valuable information concerning the potential roles that an organization's various businesses may take in pursuing its overall goals. As noted, top management's aim is to integrate the strategies of an organization's different businesses to achieve balanced growth in sales and earnings at an acceptable risk.

Portfolio Analysis

Developed by the Boston Consulting Group, portfolio analysis involves classifying an organization's SBUs along two dimensions: market growth rate and relative market share.[4] The combinations of high and low growth rate and high and low market share result in a 2 × 2 matrix (see Figure 6.2) that classifies an organization's SBUs into one of four distinct categories. The basic concept is that an organization should be managed as a portfolio of businesses, with each business having a strategy appropriate to its capabilities and competitive needs.

FIGURE 6.2   THE BOSTON CONSULTING GROUP GROWTH/SHARE MATRIX

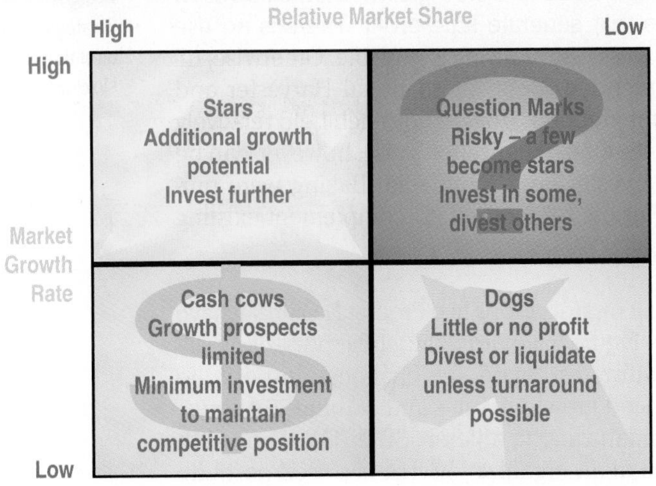

1. **Stars** are SBUs with a relatively large share of a high-growth market. SBUs in this category typically have additional growth potential and merit further investment to maximize long-term profit. The SBUs responsible for successful new medicines like Meavor, a cholesterol cutter from Merck & Co. with annual sales over $600 million, and Prozac, an antidepressant from Eli Lilly & Co. with annual sales close to $700 million, are undisputed stars. Both are dominant players in high-growth markets.

Stars.
Strategic business units with a relatively large share of a high-growth market.

2. **Cash cows** are SBUs with a relatively large share of a slow-growth market. Because cash cows do not require heavy investments in advertising and plant expansion, SBUs in this category typically generate large amounts of cash. The future growth prospects of cash cows are limited, however, so only enough resources to maintain a competitive position should be reinvested. Sara Lee Corp.'s hosiery division is a classic example of a cash cow. Competing in a slow-growth industry, Sara Lee has increased its market share from 35 percent in 1985 to 43 percent. Sara Lee sells L'eggs to drugstore and discount store shoppers, Hanes Silk Reflections and Sheer Elegance to more upscale buyers, and Donna Karan designer hose to the fashion conscious. Just My Size is marketed to large women.

Cash cows.
Strategic business units with a relatively large share of a slow-growth market.

3. **Question marks** are SBUs with a relatively small share of a rapidly growing market. SBUs in this category are risky because they could either become a star or fail. Thus, a decision on whether to invest more resources to gain market share or whether to divest and use available resources elsewhere is not made easily. It may depend on the various forces shaping marketplace competition. These were identified in Chapter 3 as "rivalry among existing organizations," "relative power of customers," "relative power of suppliers," "threat of new entrants," and "threat of substitutes." Procter & Gamble's research labs produce numerous question marks every year. It currently has SBUs with relatively small shares in high-growth markets centered on minoxidil-based baldness remedies and hair-growth products, and synthetic interferon-based cures for the common cold. Whether these SBUs will someday become stars with relatively large shares is certainly Procter & Gamble's hope. At some future point, it will have to decide which question marks merit further investment and which do not.

Question marks.
Strategic business units with a relatively small share of a rapidly growing market.

4. **Dogs** are SBUs with a relatively small share of a slow-growth market. SBUs in this category are poor performers that generate little profit. There is no use wasting resources on such SBUs unless restructuring is possible. Otherwise, divestiture or liquidation is recommended. Both International Harvester and Continental Baking were at one time dubbed "dogs." They each held relatively small shares in small-growth markets. One organization's dog, however, can be another's dream. International Harvester and Continental Baking were purchased by Tenneco and Ralston Purina, respectively, to complement existing product lines.

Dogs.
Strategic business units with a relatively small share of a slow-growth market.

It should be noted that multiproduct organizations like Procter & Gamble have SBUs in more than one quadrant of the Figure 6.2 matrix, thereby representing different relative market shares and growth rates. Again, the challenge in portfolio analysis is to achieve a long-term balanced growth in sales and earnings (at an acceptable level of risk) across all of an organization's different SBUs. F.W. Woolworth & Company provides a classic example of an organization that has used portfolio analysis to meet this challenge. It has followed a strategy of using cash generated

SMART MANAGEMENT   EVERY DOG HAS ITS DAY

As developed by the Boston Consulting Group (BCG), portfolio analysis involves classifying an organization's strategic business units (SBUs) into four distinct categories: question marks, dogs, cash cows, and stars. Although portfolio analysis has become a part of the language of strategic planning, Professor John A. Seeger criticizes such analysis for being an oversimplification.

In the BCG model, dogs are SBUs that have low market shares and whose markets themselves are matured or shrinking; these are components we should discard. The image conveyed by BCG's term is that of a mangy cur slinking off with our picnic hotdogs. Seeger observes, however, that there are other kinds of dogs—warm, loving companions that provide unquestioning loyalty and serve as scouts or watchdogs. These friendly dogs protect our weaker members and occupy the territory so that their wild cousins do not approach our picnic. These dogs can repay handsomely a small investment in dog food and flea powder.

A cash cow is an SBU that dominates its market but whose market is not growing. Because growth cannot logically be expected here, the consultants' advice is to operate the SBU as a cash flow generator. Management should deny requests for new resources from a cash cow and concentrate on milking it for the highest possible returns.

Keeping creativity, innovation, and energy at high levels in an SBU designated a cash cow can be difficult. But Seeger reminds us to take another look at the BCG symbolism. A cow can give more than milk; properly exposed to outside influences and environmental forces, a cow can also give calves. When you already have a cow, the investment needed to produce a calf is incredibly small; without a cow, no amount of investment will do the job. Similarly, the investment needed to produce creative ideas, given a creative workforce, is small. On the farm, even the best producing cows eventually begin to dry up. The farmer's solution to this is to arrange a date between the cow and a bull. After a calf is born, the milk begins flowing again. Isolating the cow from everything but the feed trough and the milking machines only ensures that she will go dry.

Finally, stars in the BCG model are the business units with major shares of growing markets. These are SBUs that need resources and investments to exploit their opportunities. As Seeger points out, however, current market share and market growth rates are insufficient criteria to justify investment.

With proper qualification, the "star" analogy is appropriate. What we know of stars is based on old information. The light we observe has been traveling toward us for eons, and its source may have long since degenerated into a white dwarf or even a black hole, which would absorb any amount of resources we could throw at it without ever permitting any return. Stars, too, take their place in the BCG matrix based on their past performance. Whether they merit additional investment depends on their future potential, not on their past.

No model can safely substitute for analysis and common sense. Models are useful to managers by helping to provide order to the thinking process. But models also bias judgment or substitute for analysis. The BCG model provides a powerful set of descriptors, dangerous in their simplicity because they seem so easy to apply. Seeger reminds us that the dogs may be friendly, the cows may produce more than milk, and the stars may already have burned themselves out. Responsible managers analyze both sides of these images when considering an organization's strategic direction.

Adapted from John A. Seeger, "Reversing the Images of BCG's Growth/Share Matrix," *Strategic Management Journal* 5 (January–March 1984): 93–97.

from its variety stores (cash cow) to fund specialty store stars such as Foot Locker (athletic shoes) and Champs (sporting goods).

Grand Strategies

A second approach for defining an organization's overall strategic direction at the corporate level is to select from among three alternative grand strategies: *growth, stability,* and *retrenchment*. These strategies and their subcategories are shown in Figure 6.3. Selecting a specific grand strategy is a challenge under the best of circumstances; it is especially difficult in today's increasingly competitive global environment. No single strategy is ideal for all circumstances or situations. Top managers are thus often forced to select a blend of strategies to achieve their desired level of long-term balanced growth in sales and earnings.

Growth Strategies A **growth strategy** is used when an organization seeks to expand its relative market share. Reasons for using such a strategy include the following:

Growth strategy.
A grand strategy that involves an organization attempting to expand its relative market share.

1. Growth is necessary for survival in a volatile industry where stability can mean short-term success but long-term death.
2. Many top managers equate growth with effectiveness.
3. Some top managers believe society benefits from growth.
4. Growth organizations are better known, attract more qualified managers, offer greater financial rewards, and provide a means for satisfying the power needs of top managers.
5. As an organization grows, it may be able to achieve economies of scale and overhead.

The five growth strategies shown in Figure 6.3 are *concentration, diversification, horizontal integration, vertical integration,* and *joint venture.*

FIGURE 6.3 GRAND STRATEGIES

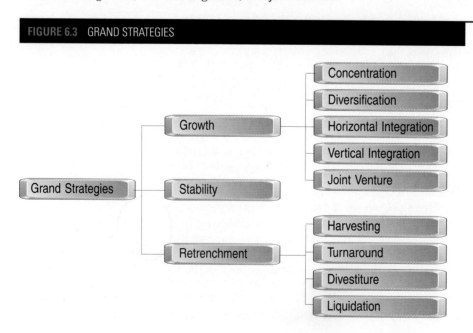

I've got a support group that really helps me out...

It's called "family!" (Thanks!)

You're breaking a habit that's pretty tough! But you're tougher!

We can't choose the people we work with, but sometimes we get lucky and wind up working with someone special...
...the way I did with you.

People say one person can't make a difference in the world. But I know that isn't true...
...because...

Feelings just don't seem to keep for future use. So isn't it nice that they can go straight from you to someone who gets to feel them, too? It all starts with a Just How I Feel card. (And they're just at Hallmark.)

Just how I feel

Hallmark Cards is a classic example of a company whose development of concentration strategy has been spectacularly successful. Hallmark's singular line of "personal expressions" products includes greeting and gift related items for all traditional occasions. Consumers can also choose from Hallmark's selection of "Just How I Feel" cards to express personal messages and feelings not associated with more traditional circumstances such as birthdays, anniversaries, and holidays.

Concentration focuses on increasing the growth of a single product line. Organizations selecting this strategy try to do one thing very well, growing through concentrated expertise and solid marketplace reputation. Organizations that have used this strategy include:

Concentration.
A type of growth strategy that focuses on increasing the growth of a single product line.

- Hallmark Cards, which produces more than 11 million greeting cards in 20 languages daily. Characterizing itself as being in the "social expression business," it also makes more than 1.5 million ribbons and bows, wedding products, and Christmas ornaments each day.

- H. J. Heinz, which continues to expand its over 3,000-item line of grocery staples that runs from its famous ketchup to such powerful brands as Ore-Ida frozen potatoes, Weight Watchers foods, Nine Lives cat food, and Starkist tuna.

- McDonald's, which continues to experiment with its fast-food lineups by test marketing such items as fried chicken, pasta dishes, fish and chips, pizza, and VegiSnaxs, ready-to-eat carrot and celery sticks.

Diversification focuses on affecting an organization's strategic direction by adding new goods and services to its product line. This strategy is frequently used to reduce the risk associated with providing a single product. It is also much used by organizations that believe that their principal product is approaching market saturation or obsolescence. Rather than depend on one product, they diversify

Diversification.
A type of growth strategy that focuses on affecting an organization's strategic direction by adding new goods or services.

through either generating new products internally or entering new fields. A great many organizations have used this strategy, including:

- PepsiCo, which has diversified beyond soft drinks to include Taco Bell, Pizza Hut, Frito-Lay, and Kentucky Fried Chicken.
- Philip Morris, which has diversified beyond tobacco to include Oscar Mayer, Miller Brewing, General Foods, and Kraft.
- General Mills, which has diversified from cereals—Cheerios, Wheaties, Count Chocula—and such established staples as Betty Crocker mixes, Bisquick, and Gold Medal flour into restaurants—Red Lobster and the Olive Garden.

Carried to an extreme, diversification produces what are known as **conglomerates.** In the United States, the largest conglomerate is General Electric. The string of businesses it controls includes Kidder, Peabody & Co. investment bankers, NBC, and RCA. It also produces medical systems and locomotives, as well as advance technology for the aerospace industry. Because it is not a "general electric" company anymore, the words *general electric* no longer appear on the familiar GE logo. Great Britain's largest conglomerate is Grand Metropolitan. Its stable of businesses includes betting shops, liquor stores, pubs, and restaurants in Britain, as well as J&B Scotch, Smirnoff vodka, Gilbey's gin, and Almaden wines. Its crown jewel, however, is Pillsbury Co., with such famous brands as Pillsbury, Green Giant, Van de Kamp's, Jeno's, Burger King, Godfather's Pizza, and Häagen-Dazs.

Horizontal integration, a third growth strategy, involves combining two or more organizations operating at the same stage in the production-marketing chain. As such, it entails the merger of competing organizations through either one competitor acquiring another in exchange for cash or stock, or simply two or more competitors uniting and issuing new stock. Possible motives for horizontal integration include reducing marketplace competition, achieving economies of scale from overlapping product lines, and, in the case of integration through acquisition, entering new markets for the acquiring organization.

Organizations that have used this strategy include:

- British Petroleum, which acquired competitor Standard Oil of Ohio (Sohio).
- Chevron Corp., which acquired competitor Gulf Oil.
- Competitors SmithKline & French Laboratories and Beecham Inc., which merged to form SmithKline Beecham.
- Competitors E. R. Squibb and Bristol-Myers Co., which merged to form Bristol-Myers Squibb.

Vertical integration involves an organization entering one or more additional stages in the production-marketing chain. It is characterized by extension of an organization in two possible directions. **Backward integration** takes place when an organization undertakes to supply some or all of its own inputs. **Forward integration** takes place when an organization undertakes to distribute some or all of its own outputs.

Perhaps the most common reason for vertical integration is that, by broadening its operations to include a larger number of stages in the production-marketing chain, an organization is often able to offset significant uncertainties in the avail-

Conglomerate.
An extremely diversified company.

Horizontal integration.
A grand strategy that involves combining two or more organizations operating at the same stage in the production-marketing chain.

Vertical integration.
A grand strategy that involves an organization entering one or more additional stages in the production-marketing chain.

Backward integration.
When an organization undertakes to supply some or all of its own inputs.

Forward integration.
When an organization undertakes to distribute some or all of its own outputs.

ability of needed resources and in the distribution of its products. Organizations that have used this strategy include:

- Holiday Inns, which integrated backward when it created a supplies division and began producing furniture and distributing items such as cleaning supplies and food to its inns.

- Texaco, which integrated forward from wellhead to refinery to retail service station.

- Seven-Up, which integrated backward when it acquired both its primary flavor supplier and the lemon groves necessary for manufacture of its principal products.

Joint ventures, a final growth strategy, involve an ownership arrangement between two or more organizations that results in the creation of a new managerial entity. They are often used to spread the cost of an undertaking between several organizations or to combine complementary skills. Other reasons include gaining access to local markets or needed technologies, and meeting government requirements for local ownership. Industry research consortia are a form of joint venture that have become increasingly popular in the United States since the National Cooperative Research Act (1984) made cooperative "pre-competitive research" legal. Thus, as long as pricing is not discussed, antitrust laws are no longer violated. Examples of such alliances are the 33-member Semiconductor Research Corporation, whose members include AT&T, General Motors, IBM, and Du Pont, and the Center for Advanced Television Studies, formed by ABC, CBS, NBC, PBS, RCA, and five other companies to improve the quality of television transmission. Other examples of joint ventures include:

Joint venture.
A type of growth strategy that involves an ownership arrangement between two or more organizations that results in the creation of a new managerial entity.

Singapore's newest and most technologically advanced petroleum products storage and distribution facility is the result of a joint venture among Chicago Bridge and Iron Company, GATX Terminals Corporation, and Paktank International B.V. Construction of the $3.3 million barrel terminal relied upon suppliers and sources in 15 nations and employed engineers and construction personnel of over a dozen nationalities.

- New United Motor Manufacturing, Inc., a joint venture of Toyota Motor Co. and General Motors to build four-passenger subcompact cars in Fremont, California, under the Chevrolet Nova/Toyota names. The venture aims to combine General Motors's marketing skills with Toyota's production know-how.

- Inland Steel and Nippon Steel, who joined together to build "the world's most advanced continuous steel mill" at New Carlisle, Indiana. Inland will gain access to Nippon's technology and an injection of low-cost capital. In return, Nippon sidesteps import quotas and will be able to supply Japanese auto plants in the United States.

- Corning, Inc., which has formed 40 joint ventures in the United States and around the world over the past 60 years. Its name is the latter half of Owens-Corning Fiberglass and of Dow Corning. Corning has joint ventures with Siemens of Germany, Ciba of Switzerland, and Samsung of South Korea and has been a partner with Asahi Glass of Japan since 1930. Even its joint ventures have joint ventures: Siecor, the company formed by Corning and Siemens, has formed an alliance with Kaiser Aluminum.

CLOSE UP: INTERNATIONAL MANAGEMENT COMPETE GLOBALLY TO SUCCEED LOCALLY

When a bench chemist accidentally licked his finger some 20 years ago in a G. D. Searle lab and tasted the sweet result of an experiment, there was little reason to suspect that his discovery would lead to development of one of the most profitable and widely used food products in the world. Today, aspartame, or NutraSweet as it has become known by its brand name, is used in over 4,000 products in more than 80 countries.

For the NutraSweet Company, the G. D. Searle division formed around aspartame, the basic premise has always been "compete globally to succeed locally." NutraSweet's strategy is inherently global in scope because of the competitive structure of the food industry and the scale of its opportunities and competitors. Its competitive strategy accepts the interdependence between domestic and international markets. For example, competitive pressure must be applied to European markets not just because of their growth potential, but also to keep competitors off balance within the United States. To serve Coca-Cola, for instance, NutraSweet has located aspartame finishing plants throughout Europe. The lesson for other companies is that they really do not have a competitive strategy these days unless it is global in scope.

Globalization has become more than a catchy slogan. In an increasing number of industries, if a company can't play globally, it probably can't play. It is becoming evident, however, that the key to global success will be "thinking globally but acting locally." Thus, since few can go it alone, companies will be compelled to form alliances with foreign counterparts to exploit global opportunities. U.S. companies entered into over 2,000 alliances in the 1980s with European companies alone. As examples, General Motors teamed up with Sweden's Saab-Scania, Ford with Germany's Volkswagen, and AT&T with Italy's Olivetti. To break into the former Soviet Union, Archer-Daniels-Midland, RJR Nabisco, Johnson & Johnson, Eastman Kodak, Ford, and Chevron formed the American Trade Consortium to negotiate with Moscow.

Sources: Adapted from Joseph E. McCann, "Design Principles for an Innovating Company," *Academy of Management Executive* 5 (May 1991): 76–93; and Louis Kraar, "Your Rivals Can Be Your Allies," *Fortune*, March 27, 1989, 66–76.

Stability Strategies A **stability strategy** is used when an organization seeks to pursue a "steady as it goes" approach to growth. The main focus of this strategy is to achieve a steady, but slow, improvement in performance. Reasons for using a stability strategy include the following:

1. An organization is doing relatively well in a healthy industry.
2. It is a relatively low-risk course of action.
3. It is a relatively easy and comfortable course of action.
4. An organization's top management may unconsciously resist change, preferring the status quo.

Organizations that have used this strategy include:

- Walt Disney Co., which has largely stuck with its theme parks (Disneyland, Disney World, Epcot, Euro Disneyland, and Tokyo Disneyland), network and cable television (the Disney Channel), and films (*Dick Tracy* and *Beauty and the Beast*), generating a good return on investment as sales have steadily grown.
- Gerber Products, which concentrates on a product line that includes 183 varieties of baby foods, juices, and cereals, as well as over 200 other items, such as cribs, strollers, children's apparel, toys, and humidifiers.
- Coors Beer, which has expanded slowly, carefully adding new brands, such as Coors Extra Gold, Coors Cutter, Keystone, and Keystone Light.

Retrenchment Strategies A **retrenchment strategy** is used when an organization seeks to reverse a decline in performance. The main focus of such a strategy is to increase operating efficiencies and improve cash flow. Reasons for using a retrenchment strategy include the following:

1. An organization is doing poorly, or at least its top managers perceive it to be doing poorly.
2. An organization has been unable to meet its objectives using either growth or stability as a grand strategy and is under pressure from stockholders, customers, or others to improve performance.

The four retrenchment strategies shown in Figure 6.3 are *harvesting, turnaround, divestiture,* and *liquidation.*

Harvesting entails minimizing investment in a product line while attempting to maximize short-term profits and cash flow. If necessary, market share may even be sacrificed to generate revenue. Various means can be used for this purpose. Selective price increases is one means; reducing costs without reducing prices is another. Examples of products that have been harvested rather than nourished and defended include:

- Right Guard, which by the end of 1986 had been designated a "hold" brand by the Gillette Company, receiving only maintenance spending and positioned to throw off cash to feed other brands.
- Bee, Bicycle, and Aviator playing cards. Produced by U.S. Playing Card Co., the world's oldest and largest cardmaker, all three brands were treated as cash

Stability strategy.
A grand strategy that is used when an organization seeks to pursue a "steady as it goes" approach to growth.

Retrenchment strategy.
A grand strategy that is used when an organization seeks to reverse a decline in performance.

Harvesting.
A type of retrenchment strategy that entails minimizing investment in a product line while attempting to maximize short-term profits and cash flow.

cows (to use BCG's terminology), being milked for over a decade for their $11-million-a-year cash flow. U.S. Card's newest owner, Jesup & Lamont, has reversed this strategy, realizing the company's strong market franchise and neglected potential for profit.

- Other products that reportedly have been harvested include Lever Brothers' Lifebuoy soap, Textron's Talon zippers, Bristol-Myers-Squibb Ipana toothpaste, Unilever's Lux Beauty Bar, Argo corn starch, and Barbasol shave cream.

Turnaround involves attempting to "restructure" or streamline an organization's operations to reestablish previous performance levels. The main focus of this strategy is to reduce costs and increase revenues. This may involve **downsizing** to eliminate employees and activities that do not directly produce customer value, accelerating collection of accounts receivable, increasing the number of sales per employee, and so on. **Benchmarking** performance to determine how efficient an organization can and should be is another increasingly popular turnaround technique. The idea is for an organization to rate its own practices against the world's best and then emulate those practices. Organizations that have been turned around successfully include the following:

- Levi Strauss Associated, after experiencing a 2-year, $161.7 million plummet in profit, closed 66 factories between 1984 and 1990 and reduced its workforce to 32,000 from 48,000 in 1980. Since then, not only has Levi reclaimed its 1983 profit figures, but by 1989 it had surpassed them by more than $30.3 million.

- A&P, whose 3,500-store empire shrank to only 1,000 stores between 1975 and 1985, is once again one of the United States's strongest supermarket chains. Rebounding from a net loss of $43 million in 1980, A&P had net profits in 1990 of $146.7 million.

- Westinghouse Electric, after experiencing a stall in profits during the mid-1970s, began selling dozens of its operations, including the major appliance group that coined the phrase "You can be sure if it's Westinghouse"; closed inefficient plants; and shed 23,000 employees. By 1983 Westinghouse was outpacing its major rival, General Electric, in return on equity and earning record profits.

Divestiture involves a multiunit organization selling off or divesting one or more of its units. This strategy is a common method for generating cash. Organizations that have used this strategy include:

- General Mills, which divested nearly $3 billion of businesses between 1980 and 1990, including Kenner Parker toys, Izod apparel, and Talbots and Eddie Bauer retailers.

- Mobil Corp., which sold its Montgomery Ward division to General Electric Capital Corp. for $3.8 billion in cash and assumed debt.

- Coca-Cola, which sold its 49 percent interest in Columbia Pictures Entertainment to Sony Corp. for $3.4 billion in cash.

- McDonnell Douglas, which sold 40 percent of its commercial aircraft manufacturing business to a Taiwan partnership.

Turnaround.
A type of retrenchment strategy that attempts to "restructure" or streamline an organization's operations to reestablish previous performance levels.

Downsizing.
Elimination of employees and activities to reduce costs and increase revenues.

Benchmarking.
An organization rating its own practices against the world's best and then emulating those practices.

Divestiture.
A type of retrenchment strategy that involves a multiunit organization selling off or divesting one or more of its units.

Liquidation entails terminating an organization's existence through the sale of its assets. This strategy typically is used only as a last resort, when an organization is unable to resolve its financial difficulties. Organizations that have used this strategy include the following:

- Aldens Inc., a $300-million-a-year general-catalog company that was a subsidiary of Wickes Companies, closed after being unable to locate a buyer for its debt-ridden assets.
- Cowles Communications Inc., which once published *Look* magazine and later owned television stations, liquidated, paying out cash and $48 million in *New York Times* stock.
- Columbia Corp., a $133-million conglomerate, liquidated its assets for an amount per share that exceeded market value.
- W. T. Grant, once an empire boasting 1,100 stores and 75,000 employees, chose to liquidate rather than face bankruptcy.

Because it does imply failure, liquidation generally is chosen as an option only when the alternative is filing for *bankruptcy*. As typically defined, **bankruptcy** is a means whereby an organization that is unable to pay its debts can seek court protection. Under the Federal Bankruptcy Act, an organization can file for bankruptcy in two ways. In a straight bankruptcy, known as Chapter 7, an organization's assets are seized by court-appointed trustees, sold, and the proceeds divided among creditors, with any remaining funds paid to stockholders. The organization ceases to exist. In a Chapter 11 filing, the court protects an organization through such means as stopping interest payments, halting lawsuits, and nullifying contracts to keep it going while its managers devise a plan to repay all or part of its debts. Notable Chapter 11 bankruptcies include R. H. Macy & Co., Bank of New England, Continental Airlines, and Carter Hawley Hale, the west coast retailer.

FORMULATING BUSINESS-UNIT-LEVEL STRATEGIC PLANS

Turning from a corporate-level focus on determining specific businesses in which to compete, this chapter now examines business-unit-level strategic planning, which addresses the question *How should we compete in each of our businesses?* Thus, it involves developing a marketplace strategy for each of an organization's SBUs *or* for organizations that operate a single business. The two best known approaches to business-unit-level strategic planning are Miles and Snow's *adaptive strategy typology* and Porter's *competitive strategies*. As with portfolio analysis and grand strategies, this should not be seen as a case of having to select one approach or the other. Both can yield potentially useful information for capitalizing on emerging strategic windows. Various examples of successful business–unit-level strategies follow.

Miles and Snow's Adaptive Strategy Typology

The major premise of Miles and Snow's **adaptive strategy** typology is that an organization should formulate strategies for each of its SBUs that are congruent with their task environment.[5] A well-crafted strategy, in this sense, will allow each SBU to "adapt" to its unique environmental challenges. Although Miles and Snow

Liquidation.
A type of retrenchment strategy that entails terminating an organization's existence through the sale of its assets.

Bankruptcy.
A means whereby an organization that is unable to pay its debts can seek court protection.

Adaptive strategy.
A type of business-unit-level strategy which holds that an organization should formulate strategies for each of its SBUs that are congruent with their task environment.

recognize that the range of potential strategies is vast, they do suggest that patterns emerge and that four major types can be identified. Success can be achieved with the first three strategies, but the fourth typically results in failure. The four strategies are the *defender,* the *prospector,* the *analyzer,* and the *reactor* (see Figure 6.4).

Defender   Organizations using the **defender strategy** seek stability by emphasizing a limited set of products directed at a narrow market. This strategy is best suited for very stable environments populated by businesses in which internal efficiency and controls can be used to produce reliable goods and services for steady customers. Top managers in defender businesses are typically highly expert in a limited area of operation. Although defenders may employ competitive pricing or high production standards to guard their "turf," they tend to disregard trends and developments outside their narrow market. Over time, successful defenders may be able to carve out and defend specific niches that may seem almost impossible for competitors to penetrate. Well-known examples of defenders include McDonald's in the fast-food industry and Anheuser-Busch in the beer industry. Both are known for their high efficiency and their use of targeted markets, and both aggressively defend their dominant market positions.

Prospector   Users of the **prospector strategy** continually seek market opportunities and regularly experiment with innovations. This strategy is best suited

Defender strategy.
An adaptive strategy that seeks stability by emphasizing a limited set of products directed at a narrow market.

Prospector strategy.
An adaptive strategy that continually seeks market opportunities and regularly experiments with innovations.

FIGURE 6.4   MILES AND SNOW'S ADAPTIVE STRATEGY TYPOLOGY

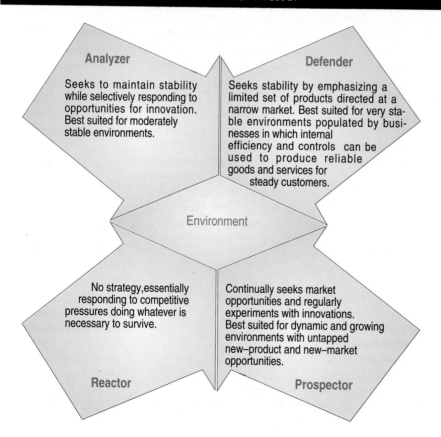

for dynamic and growing environments with untapped new-product and new-market opportunities. Prospectors are often creators of change to which their competitors must respond. Prospectors like Federal Express, originator of the overnight-package business, and Microsoft, led by high-tech star Bill Gates, lead and challenge their industries by not only responding to, but creating environmental trends.

Analyzer Businesses that use the **analyzer strategy** seek to maintain stability while selectively responding to opportunities for innovation. This strategy is best suited for moderately stable environments. Top managers in analyzer businesses watch their competitors closely for new ideas and then rapidly adapt those that appear to be the most promising. Successful analyzers maintain a secure core of traditional customers and products while carefully exploiting new market opportunities. In doing so, analyzers attempt to balance conflicting demands for change and stability. Well-known examples of analyzers include clone makers, such as AST Research and Dell in the personal computer industry, as well as such established companies as Campbell Soup, which maintains its traditional brands like Pepperidge Farm cookies and bread, Swanson frozen foods, Godiva chocolates, Prego spaghetti sauces, and Vlasic pickles, but year in and year out introduces more new products than any other food company. Analyzers generate new product ideas internally, as well as incorporate ideas that work for their competition.

Reactor The **reactor strategy** is no strategy at all. Reactors essentially respond to competitive pressures by doing whatever is necessary to survive. As previously noted, in the long run, this fourth "strategy" typically results in failure and thus is not recommended. The various companies identified in our earlier discussion of liquidation would be prime examples of reactors.

Porter's Competitive Strategies

A second approach to business-unit-level strategic planning has been developed by Michael Porter.[6] Based on extensive research, Porter has identified three strategies that can be used to give an organization (*or* SBU) a "competitive advantage." The three strategies are *cost leadership*, *differentiation*, and *focus* (see Figure 6.5).

Cost Leadership A **cost leadership strategy** involves aggressively pursuing operating efficiencies so that an organization is the low-cost producer in its industry. Cost leadership requires efficient facilities, tight cost and overhead controls, and cost minimization in areas such as research and development, service, sales, advertising, and so on. Lower costs enable an organization to gain a competitive edge by offering lower prices and yielding profits that are above industry averages because of higher profit margins and larger sales volumes. Businesses that have successfully used this strategy include K mart, Timex, Motel 6, BIC pens, and Gallo wines.

Differentiation A **differentiation strategy** involves attempting to develop goods or services that are perceived *industrywide* as being unique. Differentiation can take many forms: high quality (L. L. Bean in outdoor sporting specialties), extraordinary service (Nordstrom's in retailing), innovative design (Gulfstream in business jets), technological capability (Hewlett-Packard in laser printers), or unusually positive brand image (Mercedes in automobiles). Successful differentiation

Analyzer strategy.
A type of adaptive strategy that seeks to maintain stability while selectively responding to opportunities for innovation.

Reactor strategy.
A type of adaptive strategy that entails responding to competitive pressures by doing whatever is necessary to survive.

Cost leadership strategy.
A competitive strategy that involves aggressively pursuing operating efficiencies so that an organization is the low-cost producer in its industry.

Differentiation strategy.
A competitive strategy that involves attempting to develop goods or services that are perceived industrywide as unique.

FIGURE 6.5 PORTER'S COMPETITIVE STRATEGIES

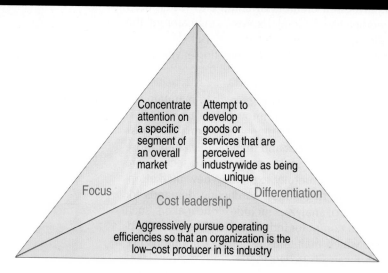

enables an organization to justify a premium price that exceeds the cost of differentiating. While price cannot be ignored, it is not as important as perceived uniqueness.

Focus A **focus strategy** involves an organization concentrating its attention on a specific segment of an overall market. The segment may be a particular customer group (teenagers), a certain geographical region (the northeast), or a specialized product line (running shoes). The objective is to serve the needs of a selected segment more effectively or efficiently than competitors who attempt to serve an entire market. In doing so, an organization may use either a cost leadership or differentiation strategy or both. Businesses that have successfully used this strategy include Athletic Attic, Toys 'R Us, and Oxmoor House, publisher of *Southern Living* magazine.

The major implication of Porter's competitive strategies approach to business-unit-level strategic planning is that every organization needs some form of competitive advantage if it is to succeed. In this respect, an awareness of Porter's three competitive strategies is useful in developing strategies tailored to an organization's (*or* SBU's) capabilities and competitive needs, yet consistent with overall corporate goals.

Focus strategy.
A competitive strategy that involves an organization concentrating its attention on a specific segment of an overall market.

STRATEGY IMPLEMENTATION

Although skilled strategy formulation is essential for an organization's long-term success, no less essential is skilled strategy implementation. A well-conceived strategy is no better than the actions taken to make it a reality. For this reason, managers must make detailed provisions for implementing selected strategies. A well-conceived plan is one that is *implementable*, so implementation must be considered *during* strategy formulation. Managers must look ahead and ask, "Is this strategy workable? Can we make it happen?" If the answer to either question is "No" or "Only at an unacceptable risk," then strategy formulation must continue.[7]

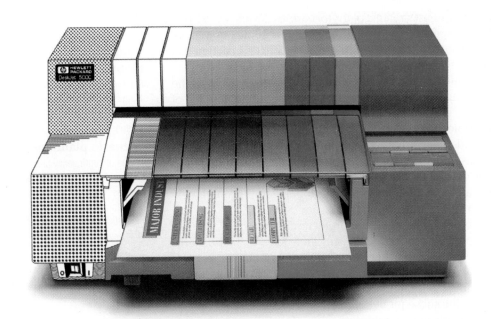

Hewlett–Packard's development of a differentiation strategy has taken the form of technological leadership. The company's advances in technology have made HP's laser printers highly desirable products in a market where technological capability and innovation are prized by consumers.

Creating an Energy

Various obstacles to implementation will invariably exist in most situations. Limited resources, vested interests, and time constraints are but a few of the situational specifics likely to be encountered. Crafting a strategic plan that can be implemented is perhaps most important, however, for creating an energy for the plan in the people who will implement it. Building bases of support among vice-presidents, division managers, and others is crucial for successful strategy implementation.

Thus, as noted by two well-known management authorities, "one of the most effective aids to implementation is to involve people early on in the development and debate of strategic options."[8] Nordson Corp., a developer and manufacturer of industrial application equipment, is one company that recognizes the wisdom of this advice. "Everyone all the way down the organization is included in the planning process," explains Nordson vice-president Sam Dawson. "Routinely in our operating strategic plan we have sales and service people involved from the beginning—lab people, engineers, marketing—people who typically would never sit in those meetings. You really form a consensus stemming from some of that planning that goes on, and you structure everything around it."[9]

At Nordson, strategic planning is a line job, not a staff function. In effect, the people who develop its strategic plan implement it. This practice recognizes that, because of their frequent contact with customers and the marketplace, lower level managers often possess strategy-relevant information that is not necessarily known by top managers. Although it may be impossible to obtain universal agreement on an organization's proper strategic direction, broad-based employee input will improve the quality of choices, raise critical implementation issues, and make those involved feel at least partly responsible for a strategy's success.

Contingency Plans

Given the unpredictable future, good managers know that strategic planning is a process, not necessarily a blueprint for all further action. Prudent managers will be prepared for adjustments in strategy as conditions warrant. Such midcourse corrections require flexibility to adjust strategic plans for various developments that cannot be predicted but that experience indicates may occur at some future time. Thus, **contingency planning** involves identifying alternative courses of action that might be followed if various developments occur.

Perhaps the best-known method for sketching rough alternative visions of the future and constructing contingency plans that would readily adapt to any one of them is known as **scenario planning.**[10] Scenario planners examine "critical uncertainties," such as possible shifts in consumer demographics to heavier government regulation to expanded environmentalism, and then propose ways for an organization to meet its goals under whatever developments occur.

Royal Dutch/Shell has developed two 20-year scenarios. The first, titled "Sustainable World," postulates an increased concern over global warming and an expanded emphasis on conservation, emissions controls, and recycling. The second, called "Mercantilist World," predicts an increase in protectionism, a worldwide economic slump, and a deemphasis on environmentalism. Shell believes that scenario planning has helped its managers to be better prepared than its competitors in reacting to unforeseen events.

The difficulty of predicting the future is obvious. Few planners foresaw either the fall of the Berlin Wall and the subsequent transformation of Eastern Europe, or the Persian Gulf War. This suggests that in conjuring up the future and the accompanying strategic plans, managers will have to continue to depend, to some degree, on such intangible factors as experience, instinct, guesswork, and luck.

Contingency planning.
Planning that involves identifying alternative courses of action that might be followed if various developments occur.

Scenario planning.
A type of contingency plan that examines "critical uncertainties" and then proposes ways for an organization to meet its goals under whatever developments occur.

SUMMARY

This chapter is divided into four principal sections. The first discussed the importance of strategic planning. The second dealt with assessing an organization's internal strengths and weaknesses in relation to the external opportunities and threats it faced. The third considered several approaches to strategy formulation. Finally, the fourth discussed the significance of sound strategy implementation.

Learning Objective 1: **Explain the importance of strategic planning.**
Strategic planning focuses on an organization's long-term relationship with its environment. An organization's ability to think and act strategically will determine its long-term survival.

Learning Objective 2: **Demonstrate an understanding of SWOT analysis.**
SWOT analysis is the assessment of an organization's **s**trengths, **w**eaknesses, **o**pportunities, and **t**hreats.

Learning Objective 3: **Define the term "strategic window."**
A "strategic window" is an untapped opportunity that fits an organization's strength.

Learning Objective 4: **Identify the three levels of strategic planning.**
The three levels of strategic planning are corporate, business unit, and functional.

Learning Objective 5: **Describe the Boston Consulting Group matrix.**
The BCG's portfolio analysis involves classifying an organization's strategic business units (SBUs) along two dimensions: market growth rate and relative market share. The combinations of high and low market growth rate and high and low market share result in a 2×2 matrix (see Figure 6.2) that classifies an organization's SBUs into one of four distinct categories: stars, cash cows, question marks, or dogs. The basic concept is that an organization should be managed as a portfolio of busi-

nesses, with each SBU having a strategy appropriate to its capabilities and competitive needs.

Learning Objective 6: Classify available grand strategies and their subcategories.
In general, three grand strategies with subcategories can be identified: (1) growth, which includes concentration, diversification, horizontal integration, vertical integration, and joint venture; (2) stability; and (3) retrenchment, which includes harvesting, turnaround, divestiture, and liquidation.

Learning Objective 7: Present Miles and Snow's adaptive strategy typology.
The major premise of Miles and Snow's adaptive strategy typology is that an organization should formulate strategies for each of its businesses that are congruent with their task environment, thereby allowing them to "adapt" to their unique environmental challenges. Miles and Snow identify four major adaptive strategies: the defender, the prospector, the analyzer, and the reactor. Success can be achieved in the first three strategies, but the fourth typically results in failure.

Learning Objective 8: Identify Porter's three competitive strategies.
The three strategies identified by Porter that can be used to give an organization (or SBU) a "strategic advantage" are differentiation, cost leadership, and focus.

Learning Objective 9: Answer the question, "Why is sound strategy implementation important?"
Sound strategy implementation is important because a well-conceived strategy is no better than the actions taken to make it a reality.

Learning Objective 10: Display an understanding of contingency planning.
Prudent managers will be prepared for adjustments in strategy as conditions warrant. Such midcourse corrections require flexibility to adjust strategic plans for various developments that cannot be predicted but that experience indicates may occur at some future time. Thus, contingency planning involves identifying alternative courses of action that might be followed if various developments occur.

KEY TERMS

adaptive strategy 171	divestiture 170	reactor strategy 173
analyzer strategy 173	dogs 162	retrenchment strategy 169
backward integration 166	downsizing 170	scenario planning 176
bankruptcy 171	focus strategy 174	stability strategy 169
benchmarking 170	forward integration 166	stars 162
cash cows 162	growth strategy 164	strategic business unit 160
concentration 165	harvesting 169	strategic planning 156
conglomerate 166	horizontal integration 166	strategic window 158
contingency planning 176	joint venture 167	strategy 156
cost leadership strategy 173	liquidation 171	SWOT analysis 157
defender strategy 172	prospector strategy 172	turnaround 170
differentiation strategy 173	question marks 162	vertical integration 166
diversification 165		

THE MANAGEMENT EXPERIENCE STRATEGIC CHOICES: SPINNING GOLD FROM STRAW?

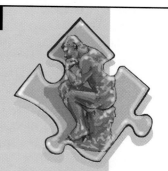

Selecting an appropriate strategic plan requires the ability to process information intelligently, that is, the ability to filter out irrelevant information and condense relevant information. To do so, a manager must learn to recognize and use those variables affecting the success of the strategic choices that must be made in a given task environment. Even the best managers cannot spin gold from straw, but good managers must be able to recognize what is gold and what is straw. Test your ability to distinguish gold from straw by processing the information required to make the following two strategic choices.

SAFE VENTURE

As manager of the Bee Safe Company, whose motto, needless to say, is "Better Bee Safe than be sorry," you have been doing quite nicely manufacturing high-quality, precision-crafted safes. You have been infuriated, however, by the fact that you manufacture 600 pounds of high-quality safe, but reap the same profit as the manufacturer who supplies you with the five pounds of electronic lock that is installed in the door of your safe. The obvious solution is to break into the lock business, and fortunately you have a reasonable supply of capital to finance such an investment. The critical decision is how great a commitment you should make. Is it better to:

A) Play it safe and stick to what you know best, putting your excess cash in the bank?

B) Purchase a small lock manufacturer and equip some of your safes with the lock to see whether this is a workable idea?

C) Find a major manufacturer who can supply all your needs and purchase it, lock, stock, and barrel?

Solutions

A) **2 points**   No one would be surprised by a conservative move from a manufacturer of safes, and there is certainly nothing wrong with making a sensible decision. However, most companies try to grow, and sticking your money in a bank is not the way to do it. Sometimes, if you don't make dust, you eat dust.

B) **5 points**   A sequenced entry is the ideal way to enter a new business. Theoretically, this is a natural merger, which will increase your profits, but theory and practice are often quite different. If this works, you will be in an excellent position to lock up added profits; if it fails, the minimum amount of damage will have been done. An alternative would be some form of quasi integration, in which you make an alliance with a lock manufacturer.

C) **1 point**   On the surface, it seems like a good idea, but it could turn out badly. When purchasing a new business, there are always risks of which a buyer is unaware, and sequenced entry enables the entrant to be in a better position to judge the risks, rewards, and probability of success than an irreversible all-out plunge. Flexible decisions are rarely heavily penalized.

The Bottom Line

A sequenced entry into a new business allows for a more accurate estimation of risks and rewards without assuming unnecessary risk. Frequently, when you go for broke, you go broke.

Continued on next page.

CASH COW

Several years ago, the conglomerate of which you are the head went into a feeding frenzy, during which it bought up a lot of companies doing an assortment of things. On reviewing this year's balance sheet, you were amazed to see that the small yogurt company that was one of your acquisitions has become the country's largest frozen yogurt chain and is making money hand over fist! It's win a few, lose a few, however; some of the other acquisitions that your conglomerate made aren't doing quite as well. You are a little worried that, although many people are putting toppings on their frozen yogurt, the market for frozen yogurt may be doing some topping of its own. Meanwhile, you have an excess of money from your yogurt operations, and what are you going to do with it? Should you:

A) Stick with a good thing and plow the money from selling frozen yogurt back into more frozen yogurt?

B) Use the money to expand capacity in one of your acquisitions that has a small share of a fast-growing market?

C) Use the money to improve the picture of one of your acquisitions that is not doing that well?

Solutions

A) **0 points**   On the surface, it's certainly appealing to continue to back a winner. However, capacity expansion in an industry that appears to have topped out is fraught with peril; if you end up producing too much frozen yogurt at a time when the American taste swings back to ice cream, you may end up in the ignominious position of having turned a winner into a loser. More likely, since the demand has topped out, any expansion on your part can lead to overcapacity, price cuts, and reduced profitability, unless you can somehow take market share away from your competitors.

B) **5 points**   The classic move in this situation is to milk the money that the cash cow is producing and use it to fund capacity expansion in a fast-growing industry. While there is very rarely a sure thing in the capacity-expansion game, it is a lot easier to expand capacity into an increasing demand than into a steady or possibly declining one.

C) **−2 points**   One of the classic investment traps in any integrated business entity is to try to help out the weaker acquisition when it shows no potential. Capital and expertise previously invested are sunk costs and are therefore irrelevant to the problem at hand.

The Bottom Line

The major portion of expansion capital, as well as the best managers in the company, should be focused on the most promising areas because the company's growth is not going to come from the problem areas and losing divisions. It does no good to beat a dead horse.

Source: Adapted from James D. Stein, Herbert L. Stone, and Charles V. Harlow, "Decision-Making: The (Very) Short Course," *Across the Board* 28 (January-February 1991): 28.

REVIEW AND DISCUSSION QUESTIONS

1. It has been repeatedly recognized that the only constant in the equation for the future is change. Likewise, it is recognized that planning is a process that is always evolving. With these two observations in mind, comment on the position that a strategic plan may indeed be a simple snapshot, valuable in many ways, but nonetheless a picture fixed in time.

2. Imagining that you are a potential investor, perform a brief SWOT analysis on a business (for example, McDonald's, Baskin-Robbins, or Pizza Hut) in your local community.

3. Assume that you have been asked to address the local Society for Advancement of Management on formulating a corporate-level strategic plan. Briefly summarize your remarks concerning the Boston Consulting Group matrix.

4. As a Wall Street market analyst, you need to familiarize yourself with the grand strategies of major competitors in various industries. Speaking to a client, how would you describe the grand strategies of the following companies: CBS, Exxon, General Motors, and IBM?

5. How do you think an expert on Miles and Snow's adaptive strategy typology would comment on the following two quotes?[11]

   - "In business, the competition will bite you if you keep running; if you stand still, they will swallow you" (William Knudsen).

   - "The business system is blessed with a built-in corrective, namely, that one executive's mistakes become his competitor's assets" (Leo Cherne).

6. Based on your own marketplace experience, identify five companies (and the goods/services they produce) that follow Porter's differentiation strategy. In each case, describe the form (for example, quality, service, brand image) that the differentiation takes.

7. As the registrar for your university or college, you have just been informed that you are in charge of implementing a plan to switch from a quarter to a semester (or vice versa) schedule. Describe how you would "create an energy" for implementing this plan.

8. Develop a contingency plan for the next 20 years of your life.

CASE 6.1 WAL-MART'S SUCCESS STORY

While most organizations struggled to survive in the early 1980s, Wal-Mart enjoyed tremendous sales and earnings increases. It is perennially ranked by *Fortune* magazine among America's most admired corporations. Some of the considerations that qualified the company for this distinction were its profitability in difficult times, careful financing, smart leadership, and clearly defined direction. This direction involves a carefully conceived strategy to seize a major market from competitors in the merchandise discount field. Wal-Mart continues to implement this plan by opening 150 stores each year and maintaining competitive price levels.

HISTORY

Over 25 years ago, Sam Walton, his wife, Helen, and his brother, Bud, worked together to create the most successful Ben Franklin franchise in the country. Theirs was a 16-store operation with its own buying office and a Ben Franklin warehouse. The entrepreneurs coordinated their advertising and marketing, and their business grew and succeeded. However, Sam Walton recognized a developing trend that foreshadowed the end of the variety store's popularity. More and more giant supermarkets and discount operations appeared each year, stifling the already struggling variety store business.

As Walton expected, a discounter soon opened a store in a town where he operated a variety outlet. When the Texas-based chain Gibson's moved into Fayetteville, Arkansas, Walton realized that he needed a new strategy to stay in business. After searching the country for new ideas, Walton decided to start his own discount business and to operate in small towns. Sam and Bud, who is now a senior vice-president of Wal-Mart Stores Inc., opened the first Wal-Mart Discount City in Rogers, Arkansas, in 1962. Bentonville, also in Arkansas, is currently the company's home base.

Walton was graduated from the University of Missouri in 1940 and worked for J. C. Penney briefly before World War II. He embraced James Cash Penney's idea that customers as well as personnel should know the owner's philosophies. Walton and his fellow Wal-Mart executives expressed their belief in God and never attempted to hide their conviction that everyone should believe in God. Also, as did Penney, Walton referred to his company's employees at all levels as associates.

Walton's formula for success resembled Penney's: Set up business in small towns and offer quality merchandise at low prices. Wal-Mart consistently undersells competition and most of its stores operate in towns with populations averaging 15,000. The company's success is unprecedented since more business exists in these communities than anyone had anticipated.

Wal-Mart now counts 1,720 discount outlets in its empire. Management in each store tailors product offerings to the individual community it serves. If an item does not sell well in one store, there is no reason to believe it will fail in another location. In contrast, Wal-Mart's principal rival, the K mart chain, offers primarily identical merchandise in its over 2,000 stores.

SALES STRATEGY

Wal-Mart's strategy of deep discounting and selling big in small-town stores has made it the fastest growing major retailer in the country. It regularly posts nearly 27 percent annual sales gains, while comparable stores average around 10 percent. The company opens three new stores each week, and sales continue to increase almost three times as fast as the industry average. Sales totaled $40.1 billion in 1991. Wal-Mart is the nation's largest discounter. K mart's 1991 sales were $30.4 billion. Wal-Mart's profits have soared an average of 37 percent a year since 1975.

MERCHANDISING STRATEGY

Wal-Mart's merchandising strategy is to keep as many items as possible on its shelves at all times. Merchandise is displayed in plastic bins and on metal shelves with signs declaring "Buy Now and Save." The typical Wal-mart store has 54,000 square feet of floor space, which is literally stacked to the ceiling with more than 30,000 items. New stores average 100,000 square feet. On average, prices are 7–8 percent lower than those of competing stores. Management emphasizes branded hard-goods items, which account for two-thirds of the company's sales. Wal-Mart has also extended its soft-goods line in the fashion clothing area. In most stores, the clothing departments are carpeted and there is more emphasis on attractive displays than in the hard-goods line.

Like most discounters, Wal-Mart fills the aisles in each store with tables displaying sales items backed by heavy promotion. However, every Wal-Mart sales table generates twice as much revenue as the competition's. The company's overall sales per square foot is $263 compared with the $100 per square foot industry average.

DISTRIBUTION STRATEGY

Recognizing the vital importance of distribution. Sam Walton approached the problem with a different outlook than did his competitors. While other retailers built warehouses to serve existing outlets, Walton had one large warehouse to serve a 400-mile radius. To be successful in small towns, the company needed the same inexpensive and efficient delivery of counterparts in large cities. Walton's method of achieving this was to open stores in clusters, thereby pooling advertising and distribution overhead. Also, using this strategy meant buying in volume at more attractive prices.

Wal-Mart's distribution operations are highly automated. Managers wire merchandise requests to a warehouse through computer terminals. The warehouse will then either ship the merchandise immediately, or place a reorder. Wal-Mart computers are linked directly with 200 vendors, making deliveries even faster. The company spends 2 cents per dollar shipping as compared to 4 cents per dollar for the competition. Wal-Mart owns a fleet of truck-trailers that can deliver merchandise to any store within 36–48 hours after it wires the order. After delivering goods, the trucks quite often pick up new merchandise from manufacturers on the way back to the distribution center. Wal-Mart's back-haul rate averages over 60 percent, another cost-cutting method.

MANAGERIAL STYLE

Top Wal-Mart executives each visit almost a dozen stores every week. They discuss merchandise and promotions with each store's staff, exchange ideas with managers, and help them to solve problems. On Friday, they return to headquarters to attend merchandise meetings and listen to plans for weekly and monthly sales budgets and promotional programs.

EMPLOYEE RELATIONS

In addition to sharing in the company's profits, Wal-Mart's over 365,000 "associates" earn bonuses for reducing shoplifting or suggesting merchandising ideas. Wal-Mart's executives enjoy breakfast at the company's expense each Saturday at 7:30 a.m. Wal-Mart's store managers receive bonuses of up to 10 percent of their unit's pretax profits. The company encourages employee stock purchases and contributes to a profit-sharing plan for associates.

INVENTORY CONTROL

Lost or stolen merchandise costs most retailers 2 percent of every sales dollar. Wal-Mart rewards the staff with 50 percent of the savings over the average loss in the last 3 years. Average loss from shrinkage is 1.3 percent.

NEW STRATEGIES

Wal-Mart is testing its ability to handle larger stores in bigger cities. The company built a store in Spring-field, Missouri, which is 50 percent larger than the company's average store. Springfield's population is 150,000, and the store is showing regular sales and profit increases. Although this is a good indication that the Wal-Mart plan may work in more populous areas, it is clearly not a guarantee of success in all larger market areas.

Another strategy for Wal-Mart will be to introduce even smaller stores in communities with 5,000 or fewer people. However, this possibility is still in the speculation stage, and it may be several years before Wal-Mart tests its methods in these smaller market areas.

Wal-Mart can also expand by taking over failing chains and "Waltonizing" them. In July 1981 Wal-Mart bought Kuhn's Big-K Stores, consisting of one warehouse and 92 outlets. Wal-Mart assumed $19 million in debt and issued $7.5 million worth of preferred stock. Now Kuhn's has a new management team and is beginning to show comfortable profits. The same thing happened after Wal-Mart's only other acquisition, the 1977 purchase of Mohr Value Stores.

Sam Walton passed away on April 5, 1992. Everyone from investors to analysts to associates wondered if Wal-Mart would survive the loss of its beloved founder. To many people, Sam Walton and Wal-Mart Stores Inc. were one and the same. Walton, however, was very instrumental in building a strong organization that would survive him. He ensured a smooth transition and bright future for Wal-Mart in 1988 when he turned over day-to-day operations and the title of chief executive officer to Wal-Mart president David Glass. Glass has been able to carry on the Walton tradition, developing one of the best management teams in the retail business. At his death, Walton was succeeded as Wal-Mart chairman by his son Rob.

CONCLUSION

Wal-Mart stock is currently selling at 36.2 times earnings, an incredible figure in this market. Its 5-year return on equity is over 35 percent. In 1991, *Fortune* called Walton the nation's richest man, with a personal fortune estimated as high as $21.1 billion, so he has done well for himself while leading his company to ever-increasing sales and profits. Part of

Wal-Mart's formula for success involves keeping its investors happy and its associates motivated.

Wal-Mart's corporate executives have no plans to slow the current pace of adding 150 stores each year. They have mapped out an ambitious future for a company that faces stiffer competition as it moves into larger market areas.

Problems

1. What are Wal-Mart's long-range goals, and what assumptions are the company's executives making about the environment in which these goals are to be accomplished?

2. A sound strategic plan should define the specific market segments to be served. Describe these segments for Wal-Mart in terms of

   - Geography

   - Goods offered

   - Intended customers

   - Distribution channels

   - Pricing policies

3. What capabilities does Wal-Mart possess that allow it to effectively serve its target market?

4. What makes Wal-Mart's distribution system so special?

5. Name some of Wal-Mart's current strengths and weaknesses. Describe the firm's identity, distinctive competence, and market niche.

6. What is Wal-Mart's grand strategy, and how has the company implemented its plans?

7. What major contingencies must Wal-Mart consider as it moves into different market areas?

Source: Walter E. Greene, Pan American University.

CASE 6.2 — THE IMPACT OF FAULTY STRATEGY

In the early 1980s, General Signal Corporation was a successful manufacturer of industrial and electrical control systems, supplying them to firms producing capital goods. Because of the maturity of that business and a resulting desire to diversify its operations, General Signal decided to enter into the relatively new, high-tech business of semiconductor production equipment manufacturing. By 1985 the diversification was well under way through the acquisition of established semiconductor equipment manufacturers, among them GCA, an industry leader, rather than by starting its own operations. During the mid-1980s, General Signal spent $240 million in acquiring high-tech companies in its diversification efforts.

Unfortunately, General Signal's move into semiconductor equipment manufacturing happened just as several large Japanese corporations, among them Nikon and Canon, entered into the business. With their huge cash reserves, technical capabilities, and distribution systems, these Japanese competitors were able to establish a dominant 80 per-

cent market share by 1990, reducing General Signal's GCA division to the position of bit player with a 4 percent share. This, coupled with a recessionary decline in its core industrial and electrical control businesses, has resulted in substantial losses and a withdrawal from much of its high-tech diversification with a sale of over $200 million in assets and a 20 percent reduction in its workforce. In addition, a new CEO has been hired, further asset sales are expected, the company is bound by $395 million in debt created by a 1988 stock buyback, and some operation have been discontinued and written off.

The new CEO has chosen to emphasize its process control businesses, expecting them to contribute 80 percent of total sales in 1992 compared with 59 percent in 1987. Furthermore, he has initiated programs to force division presidents to improve profits and efficiency, he has required companywide training in inventory control, he has ordered a cutting of administrative costs, and he has indicated that subsidiary businesses that fail to earn a 20 percent return on assets will be sold off. Unfortunately, GCA is highly unlikely to meet that goal and is even less likely to find a buyer. Therefore, the centerpiece of its diversification into high-tech operations may very well have to be shut down and written off.

Problems

1. What might SWOT analysis have revealed to decision makers at General Signal, and how could it have benefitted?

2. Is the failure of diversification at General Signal the result of poor strategic planning or poor strategy implementation?

3. What new decisions have resulted from the failure of General Signal's original decision to diversify? Could contingency planning have benefitted General Signal?

4. What chance for recovery does General Signal now have?

Source: Aubrey R. Fowler, Youngstown State University, based on "Can General Signal Escape Its High-Tech Hell?" *Business Week,* March 18, 1991, 94–96.

NOTES

[1] Bruce D. Henderson, "The Origin of Strategy," *Harvard Business Review* 67 (November–December 1989): 141.

[2] Milton Lauenstein, "The Strategy Audit," *Journal of Business Strategy* 4 (Winter 1984): 89.

[3] Michael E. Porter, *The Competitive Advantage of Nations* (New York: Macmillan, 1990), 64–65.

[4] Barry Hedley, "Strategy and the 'Business Portfolio,'" *Long Range Planning* 10 (February 1977): 9–15.

[5] Raymond E. Miles and Charles C. Snow, *Organizational Strategy, Structure, and Process* (New York: McGraw-Hill, 1978).

[6] Michael E. Porter, *Competitive Strategy: Techniques for Analyzing Industries and Competitors* (New York: Macmillan, 1980).

[7] Donald C. Hambrick and Albert A. Cannella, Jr., "Strategy Implementation as Substance and Selling," *Academy of Management Executive* 3 (November 1989): 278.

[8] Ibid., 282.

[9] Quoted in Tracy E. Benson, "Empowered Employees Sharpen the Edge," *Industry Week*, February 19, 1990, 14.

[10] Anne B. Fisher, "Is Long-Range Planning Worth It?" *Fortune*, April 23, 1990, 281–284, and Ronald Henkoff, "How to Plan for 1995," *Fortune*, December 31, 1990, 70–79.

[11] James Charlton, ed., *The Executive's Quotation Book* (New York: St. Martin's Press, 1983), 72.

ENHANCEMENT MODULE 1

FORECASTING: ESSENTIAL PLANNING INGREDIENT

When asked what he or she would like most to have in the world, the manager who responded, "I'd like a copy of next Thursday's newspaper," expressed a universal wish. Who wouldn't like to know the future? Who wouldn't like to know what's going to happen in the next year or the next five? Managers are no exception. Effective managers spend a great deal of time and energy attempting to forecast the future. Forecasts are the foundation on which plans are based. Once organization goals have been established, developing a forecast about the future environment in which they are to be accomplished is essential. Unfolding environmental conditions almost inevitably influence goals, forcing modifications in both current and anticipated activities. Clearly, the better an organization's ability to forecast environmental conditions, the more likely its success.

Simply defined, a **forecast** is a prediction of future events. As such, forecasts provide a basis for predicting the environment in which organization goals are to be accomplished. As a manager, you will encounter various forecasts. In general, they will be of three types: economic forecasts, technological forecasts, and sales forecasts. A brief description of each is presented in Table EM1.1.

ECONOMIC FORECASTING

Ever try to find a summer job, only to be told that the economy is tight and that few employers are hiring extra help? One needn't be a strategic planner at a *Fortune* 500 company to experience the effects of economic cycles. As even the most casual observer of the economy is surely aware, economic progress seldom moves in a smooth pattern. Rather, it reflects successive periods of decline and advancement. Perhaps the most commonly used measure for gauging a nation's economic progress is the gross domestic product (GDP). As defined by the Department of Commerce, GDP represents "the total market value of a nation's output of goods and services."

Accurately forecasting turning points in the nation's economy is essential for predicting economic conditions in an organization's industry and in the organization itself. When making planning decisions, managers need to know if the economy will be expanding or contracting over a particular time period. Although they may be unable to predict such changes precisely, they can seek the flexibility necessary to survive economic fluctuations.

TABLE EM1.1   THREE TYPES OF FORECASTS

1. **Economic forecast**—a prediction of conditions in an area's (region, nation, or world) economy.
2. **Technological forecast**—a prediction of developments in technology.
3. **Sales forecast**—a prediction of demand for goods or services.

ECONOMIC INDICATORS

Because the ability to forecast economic turning points is so important, special attention has been given to predicting when these turns are likely to occur. Accordingly, what are known as **economic indicators** have been developed. These are traditionally grouped into three major categories: *leading, roughly coincident,* and *lagging*. A sample listing of commonly used indicators is shown in Table EM1.2. Each month the Department of Commerce Bureau of Economic Analysis publishes 300 economic indicators in its *Business Conditions Digest*. The general theoretical framework underlying the use of these indicators was developed by the National Bureau of Economic Research.

Leading Indicators

As our economy is structured, certain activities frequently foreshadow changes in overall economic conditions. They are, in a way of speaking, signals of things to come. These activities are known as **leading indicators.** For the most part, they foretell future production and employment. Examples include new orders for durable goods, especially machinery and other equipment; contracts for the construction of new plants; and average number of hours worked. For example, the Department of Commerce may report that orders for durable goods (generally considered to be those products intended to last more than 3 years) dropped 3.5 percent in a given month. If such a pattern continues for several months, it may indicate a decline in the economy. Leading indicators give insights into questions

TABLE EM1.2 COMMONLY USED ECONOMIC INDICATORS		
Leading Indicators	**Roughly Coincident Indicators**	**Lagging Indicators**
Liabilities of business failures	Employment in nonagricultural establishments	Personal income, value
Standard and Poor's index of 500 common stock prices	Unemployment	Sales by retail stores, value
New orders, durable goods, value	Corporate profits after taxes	Consumer installment debt, value
New building permits, private housing units, number	Manufacturing and trade sales, value	Bank rates on business loans
Commercial and industrial building contracts, floor space	Value of goods output in 1972 dollars	Manufacturing and trade inventories, book value
Average workweek, manufacturing	Industrial production index	
Industrial materials index, 13 commodities	Gross domestic product, value	
	Wholesale price index, industrial commodities	

such as: How many more months will the economy advance? In what month will the economy begin to decline? In addition to forecasting turning points in the economy, leading indicators are also helpful in assessing the magnitude of advancing or declining economic activity.

To avoid reliance on a single indicator, composites of indexes of many leading indicators are usually constructed. Perhaps the most widely followed "index of leading indicators" is released monthly by the Department of Commerce. It is based on 11 forward-looking components and has long been used as a signal of future economic activity 6–9 months in advance. Three consecutive declines in the index are considered a fairly good, but not infallible, sign of an upcoming *recession*. A **recession** is generally defined as two consecutive quarters with a decline in GDP.

Roughly Coincident Indicators

Indicators that primarily relate to present overall economic conditions are called **roughly coincident indicators.** They reflect what is happening in various sectors of the economy and thus aid in predicting the economy's future direction. Examples include total industrial production, unemployment, corporate profits, and manufacturing and trade sales. If a large number of roughly coincident indicators appear to be changing direction, this is taken as evidence that a turn has *already* occurred in the economy.

If, for example, the Bureau of Labor Statistics reports that the unemployment rate has dropped from 7.4 percent in the previous month to 7.2 percent in the current month, and the Department of Commerce reports a rise in corporate profits and an upturn in industrial production, indications would be strong for economic growth.

Lagging Indicators

In contrast to activities that foreshadow changes in overall economic conditions, there are others that *follow* overall economic activity. These are known as **lagging indicators.** Although lagging indicators reach their turning points after a turn in overall economic activity, they help to confirm (or refute) what leading and roughly coincident indicators have been suggesting. Thus, if changes are observed in lagging variables, it becomes fairly certain that a turning point has occurred and that trends in leading and roughly coincident indicators are not the result of statistical aberrations. Lagging indicators are frequently used for comparative purposes with data from past years. Examples of laggers include consumer debt, bank interest rates, inventories of finished goods, and retail sales.

ECONOMETRIC MODELS

Although such indicators can provide clues to future economic conditions, they are frequently difficult to interpret. In one recent month, for example, the unemployment rate was down in service industries but stable in manufacturing; factory orders declined 2.5 percent, while sales of new single-family homes increased 2.1 percent; third-quarter corporate profits fell 7 percent, but personal income rose 3.9 percent. How is a manager supposed to decipher such confusing crosscurrents?

Given the complexity inherent in accurate economic forecasting, some organizations contract with private consulting firms to develop so-called **econometric models** of the economy. These models use mathematical equations to describe interrelationships among various economic sectors. The largest econometric modeling firms are Chase Econometrics Associates (Chase Manhattan Bank) and Wharton Econometric Forecasting Associates. Some larger corporations (for example, General Electric and Ford) have constructed their own econometric models. Wharton Econometric currently has available a medium-sized model of the economy for use on a personal computer. It forecasts more than 100 economic factors 2 years into the future through the solution of 250 mathematical equations.

Econometric models rest on well-documented theoretical foundations. Nevertheless, they are only abstract generalizations of reality. Their inherent weakness is that they rely on past data and relationships to predict the future. Consequently, they are upset by an increasing number of exogenous shocks—the 1991 Persian Gulf war, for example—that no model could have predicted. The nation's economy is a complex open system with a great many interrelations. As a result, prediction is exceedingly difficult.

TECHNOLOGICAL FORECASTING

As complex as economic forecasting may be, it is relatively well understood compared with predicting changes in technology. The rapid pace of technological change and the importance of new goods and services to an organization's continued success have prompted a growing number of organizations to invest in technological forecasting. Such forecasting is generally concerned with the long term. Motorola, for example, uses 10-year technology forecasts as the basis for its 5-year strategic plans. Technology forecasts ask questions such as: When will such maladies as heart disease, Alzheimer's, multiple sclerosis, and leukemia be defeated? What will be the impact of technological developments such as recombinant DNA (gene-splicing), voice-controlled computers, or a superplane that can race with rockets? When will there be two-way communication with extraterrestrials? Technological forecasting is clearly related to long-range planning and is invaluable for identifying new markets and predicting the decline of current markets. Its purpose is to identify new technologies and forecast their future implications for changes in established organization practices and relationships.

TECHNOLOGICAL FORECASTING: TWO APPROACHES

There are two basic approaches to technological forecasting: exploratory forecasting and normative forecasting. Successful products can come from both approaches.

Exploratory forecasting projects future technological capabilities on the basis of current performance and past progress. It starts from an existing knowledge base and proceeds to the future on the assumption of logical technological progress. This progression is depicted in Figure EM1.1. For example, when Louise Brown, the first test-tube baby, was born in 1978, future-oriented hospitals and research facilities could begin planning for the day when in vitro fertilization (IVF) clinics would be relatively commonplace. They also may have thought beyond what is already called "old-fashioned IVF" (in which a woman's ovum is removed,

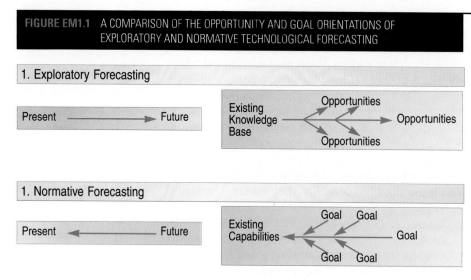

FIGURE EM1.1 A COMPARISON OF THE OPPORTUNITY AND GOAL ORIENTATIONS OF EXPLORATORY AND NORMATIVE TECHNOLOGICAL FORECASTING

fertilized with her husband's sperm, and then placed in her uterus) to possible variations on the process—mixing and matching donors' and recipients' sperm and eggs, and using surrogate mothers, to name a few that have already come to pass. The medical breakthrough has led to all sorts of opportunities—from IVF clinics, to drugs that stimulate hormones, to health insurance plans that cover the formidable expense of such treatment, to attorneys that specialize in arguing the complicated legal questions raised by such cases. Future opportunities seem innumerable.

Exploratory forecasts typically provide specific predictions of what technological breakthroughs can be expected and when they are most likely to occur. Often they are stated in terms of probability estimates, such as, "There is a 0.75 probability that an AIDS vaccine will be developed by the year 2000." In this respect, exploratory forecasting is clearly opportunity oriented.

Normative forecasting, in contrast to exploratory forecasting, considers what future technological innovations would be desirable and works backward to existing capabilities. It starts with a goal for some future date and then assesses present capabilities to determine what technological developments will be necessary for goal attainment. This process is also depicted in Figure EM1.1. U.S. Environmental Protection Agency automobile emission regulations are a classic example of normative forecasting. Car manufacturers were presented with allowable carbon monoxide standards and future dates for their enforcement. Working with existing technology, the manufacturers are responsible for developing emission systems capable of meeting these requirements. As distinct from exploratory forecasting, normative forecasting is clearly goal oriented.

Exploratory and normative forecasts should be linked. The former, with its opportunity orientation, focuses on "what can be developed." The latter, with its goal orientation, focuses on "what needs to be developed." Both perspectives are undeniably necessary for providing sound technological forecasts.

SALES FORECASTING

Of the various types of forecasts you will encounter as a manager, sales forecasts are clearly the most fundamental. Since future demand must be predicted to estimate necessary resource inputs, sales forecasting is the key to all internal planning. Among other things, sales forecasts are the basis for projecting production requirements, needed raw materials, required capital, and necessary employee skills. Although we will continue to use the term **sales forecasting,** we should point out that the process is useful not only to organizations that actually *sell* something, but also to those that are not profit oriented. For example, universities must be able to forecast how many applicants will accept their invitation to enroll, so as to plan dormitory and classroom needs. Museums need to project whether admission fees, donations, and gift shop receipts will cover costs for the coming year, and cities must determine whether tax revenues will be enough to pay for police, fire, sewage, and other services. Forecast sales, in whatever form, comprise the revenue side of an organization's income statement. Thus, based on anticipated demand, an organization can determine what it can afford to spend on raw materials, capital, labor, and marketing to yield a desired profit, or to stay within its budget.

Sales forecasts may be classified in several different ways. However, there are actually only three information bases for forecasting sales: *what people say they will do, what people are doing,* and *what people have done.*[1] These information bases, together with the techniques on which they rely, are listed in Table EM1.3 and described in the following paragraphs.

WHAT PEOPLE SAY THEY WILL DO

Surveys of Buyers' Intentions

A sales forecast is essentially a prediction of buyer behavior under a given set of circumstances. This suggests that one source of useful information concerning future purchases would be buyers themselves. Mail questionnaires, telephone interviews, or personal interviews may be employed as survey techniques to acquire estimates of future buyer intentions. Government and commercial surveys, such as the Department of Commerce's *Consumer Sentiment Index,* Sales & Marketing Management's *Survey of Buying Power,* The Conference Board's *Survey of Consumer Attitudes and Buying Plans,* and the University of Michigan Survey Research Center's *Surveys of Consumer Attitudes,* may also be helpful in forecasting sales.

Since the demand for most goods and services extends to a population much too large to contact directly, sampling procedures are typically used to select a representative cross-section of buyers. In this respect, the accuracy of buyer surveys depends on the proper identification and sampling of potential buyers who are representative of a larger consumer segment. In an effort to define buyer needs and intentions, Kroger Co. conducts more than 250,000 interview surveys a year.

TABLE EM1.3 INFORMATION BASES AND TECHNIQUES FOR FORECASTING SALES		
What People Say They Will Do	**What People Are Doing**	**What People Have Done**
Surveys of buyers' intentions	Test marketing	Time-series analysis
Composite of sales force opinions		Statistical demand analysis
Jury of executive opinion		
Expert opinion		

It should be realized that buyer expectations are not commitments to buy. Also, some buyers, especially those in wholesaling and retailing, may find it difficult to accurately forecast future needs since these are likely to be dependent on uncontrollable factors, such as competitors' actions and consumer preferences. For example, Schwinn Bicycle Co. both underestimated the demand for its traditional two-wheelers and overestimated the demand for lighter, sleeker high-tech bicycles. In other cases, buyers may not wish to confide future intentions, seeing such requests as an invasion of privacy.

Composite of Sales Force Opinion

An organization's sales force can be an excellent source of information concerning future sales. Sales representatives are in fairly constant contact with buyers and have knowledge of buyer needs. They thus may be able to offer insights into developing market trends and predicting future sales. Table EM1.4 illustrates a questionnaire used by one company to survey its sales force concerning future buyer demand.

Sales force estimates are typically combined to form a total sales forecast. Few organizations, however, use such estimates without some adjustment. Sales representatives are not always unbiased, especially if they believe that their estimates will be used to determine future sales quotas. If this is the case, they are likely to offer low forecasts so that they can easily beat their quotas. Furthermore, sales representatives may be unaware of larger economic developments or future organization marketing plans that may influence buyer demand. Finally, some may not have the ability, motivation, or time necessary to prepare accurate forecasts.

Jury of Executive Opinion

This technique consists of combining the opinions of top executives concerning future sales of goods and services. Typically, executives from areas such as marketing, production, finance, purchasing, and staff operations are brought together to form a pool of diversified experience and opinion. Ideally, they are provided with current market information. One advantage of this technique is that it is relatively quick and straightforward. Moreover, it is capable of integrating judgmental factors and experience. This may be especially important in situations where only limited information is available.

TABLE EM1.4   SALES FORCE BUYER DEMAND QUESTIONNAIRE

Date: September 1, 1992
Name of Sales Representative: John Fleetwood
Territory Number: 25
Directions: This form contains dollar sale figures for your territory over the last 2 years, and expected sales for this year. You are asked to estimate dollar sales for next year. Please return this questionnaire to headquarters within 14 days.

1. Dollar sales in your territory 2 years ago were $1.4 million.
2. Dollar sales in your territory last year were $1.52 million.
3. Expected dollar sales in your territory this year are $1.60 million.
4. Considering the status of your present customers, upcoming promotion and pricing programs, and anticipated reactions, what is your best estimate of dollar sales in your territory next year?

Juries of executive opinion, however, are susceptible to several of the same biases as composites of sales force opinion. Executives may not have the necessary insight to develop accurate forecasts. Furthermore, this technique is largely based on opinions, not facts. When market information is supplied, executives may interpret it according to their preconceived notions concerning the future. At General Electric, for example, planners concluded that small appliances were the wave of the future based on data that indicated families and houses were shrinking. Because top management had little contact with homebuilders and retailers, they did not realize that kitchens were not shrinking and that working women wanted big refrigerators to save on trips to the supermarket. As a result, General Electric wasted a lot of time designing smaller appliances.

Nevertheless, past events have often shown that executive hunches and experienced guesses can be of significant value.

Expert Opinion

A fourth technique of sales forecasting based on *what people say* involves relying on the judgments of noted specialists. Some organizations hire outside experts, such as private consultants or university professors; purchase market information packages from commercial firms, such as Predicasts, Inc., and Dun & Bradstreet; or hire market research companies, such as Data Corporation, Dataquest, or Strategic, Inc., to forecast sales. In addition, Department of Commerce publications such as *U.S. Industrial Outlook* are helpful.

It is not unusual for a firm to subscribe to three or four market information packages from each of five or six sources. The total bill in such cases could be well over $500,000 annually. Regarding market research companies, it is estimated that their annual client billings total some $100 million.[2] Private consultants and university professors typically charge consulting fees that range from several hundred to several thousand dollars a day. A partial list of various experts and types of organizations they could possibly serve is presented in Table EM1.5.

TABLE EM1.5 A PARTIAL LISTING OF EXPERTS AND ORGANIZATIONS THEY COULD POSSIBLY SERVE

Expert	Organization
1. Architects	Producers and distributors of building materials
2. Book reviewers	Publishing houses
3. Construction engineers	Producers and distributors of building materials
4. County agents	Producers and distributors of seeds, fertilizers, and feed
5. Home economists	Food processors
6. Medical researchers	Producers of ingredients for prescription and proprietary drugs
7. Physicians	Pharmaceutical houses
8. Public school administrators	Textbook suppliers
9. Retail store buyers	Producers of apparel
10. Trade association officers	The industry within which an organization operates

Source: Based on Charles W. Gross and Robin T. Peterson, *Business Forecasting*, 2d ed. (Boston: Houghton Mifflin, 1983), 35–36.

WHAT PEOPLE ARE DOING

Test Marketing

Test marketing is frequently used as a sales forecasting technique in the case of new goods or services. Its aim is to predict adoption—the percent of buyers who will accept a product as "their brand" and continue to use it over time. Test marketing involves establishing one or more proving grounds to gauge how a product will sell under actual conditions. In the case of multiple test sites, the effect of price differences, alternative advertising themes, and sales promotion campaigns can be compared. The primary advantage of test marketing is obviously the realism it provides by measuring what people do (in buying products) rather than what they say they will do (as in a survey). If a product does not meet sales expectations in test markets, it can be reformulated or abandoned. Products such as Rejoice (liquid soap), Pace (gel toothpaste), Fling (disposable, detergent-filled dishcloths), and Solo (fabric softener) are examples of test offerings discontinued by Procter & Gamble after they failed to capture enough of a market share to warrant continued production. Companies such as Procter & Gamble, General Foods, and General Mills weed out approximately 50 percent of their pilot products through test marketing. Just the same, two out of three new-product entries still fail.[3]

The disadvantages of test marketing must also be considered. Test marketing can be time consuming, expensive, and impractical for all but low-priced goods, such as beauty products, detergents, and snack foods. It is not unusual for a sales test to last 2 years. Pampers disposable diapers took 9 years to go national after entering its first test market. A certain minimum time is required for a product to be purchased initially and then repurchased, thus establishing some form of purchasing pattern. A complete marketing test, including research, media costs, production, and packaging, can easily cost $1 million. General Electric invested $20 million in facilities to support an extended test of Ultem, an extraordinarily heat-resistant specialty plastic for use in manufacturing computer circuit boards.

Just as an accurate survey of buyers' intentions depends on a carefully chosen sample, so too a reliable test market study depends on selection of a representative site. To forecast the national sales of a pilot product requires a town that mirrors, as nearly as possible, the demographics and buying patterns of the nation. For years, Peoria, Illinois, was considered ideal for this, since it so closely duplicated the national average in income and age mixture that it was almost a United States in miniature. But recent high unemployment, coupled with the diminished impact of local television advertising as Peorians increasingly turned their dials to Chicago stations, has caused Peoria to be struck from the list of desirable test markets. Newer favorites are Cedar Rapids and Des Moines, Iowa; Cincinnati; Omaha; Portland, Oregon; South Bend, Indiana; Springfield, Illinois; and Syracuse.

A final disadvantage is that test marketing can aid competitors. It is said that major packaged-goods companies live in fear that their competitors will become aware of a pilot product while it is being tested and beat them to the marketplace. For instance, when Campbell's Soup took its time test-marketing Prego spaghetti sauce, rival Ragú reached the marketplace first with a nearly identical product. In some instances, competitors may not stop at espionage. Sabotage is also a risk. Competitors may cut their prices, double their couponing, and even give samples away, stealing potential buyers from a test marketer. For example, it is reported that when General Mills test marketed Speak, an unsuccessful premium-priced dog food, General Foods slashed the price of its Gainesburgers.

WHAT PEOPLE HAVE DONE

Time-Series Analysis

This technique forecasts future sales by analyzing the pattern of past sales. It rests on the assumption that the future will be a continuation of the past. Time-series analysis requires knowledge of simple arithmetic. Provided that past sales figures are available, it can be performed quickly and inexpensively.

Following the time-series technique, if sales were X last year, and have been increasing at Y percent for the past several years, the sales forecast for next year would be $X + XY$. Using actual figures, assume sales were 1,000 units last year and have been growing at an average rate of 10 percent for the past few years. The sales forecast for next year would be $1,000 + (1,000 \times 0.10) = 1,100$ units. Figure EM1.2 illustrates how this pattern of sales would appear over time.

Forecasters have found it useful to distinguish four main types of sales patterns: trend, seasonal, cyclical, and random. A *trend pattern* exists when there is a long-run pattern of growth or decline in sales. The sales pattern in Figure EM1.2 reflects an upward trend over several years. A *seasonal pattern* exists when sales fluctuate according to some seasonal factor. For example, the sale of swimwear is greater in the spring than the fall. A *cyclical pattern* is similar to a seasonal pattern, but generally the length of a single cycle is longer than 1 year. Housing starts, sales of durable goods (such as washers and dryers), and hog sales each reflect a fairly constant cyclical pattern. Finally, a *random pattern* exists when sales fluctuate in an erratic manner and reflect no consistency. In such cases, sales variations cannot be explained by the other main types of patterns. In the very short run, randomness is the most important pattern influencing sales. As the time horizon lengthens, seasonality increases in importance, followed by trend. Over the very long run, seasonality becomes less important, and trend and cyclical patterns are of major importance.[4]

FIGURE EM1.2   TIME-SERIES ANALYSIS FOR ANNUAL SALES

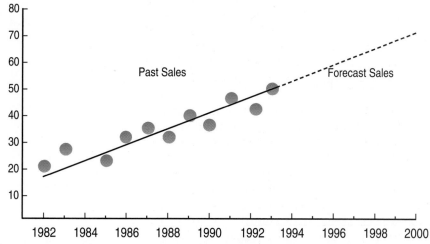

Annual Sales
(in Millions of units)

 Indicates actual sales

Statistical Demand Analysis

In contrast to time-series analysis, which treats past and future sales as a function of time, statistical demand analysis involves forecasting sales (for example, baby food) on the basis of those factors thought to significantly affect sales (for example, live births). Thus, given that the demand for baby food is related to the birthrate, baby food sales can be forecast relative to the number of live births. Such a relationship is shown in Figure EM1.3.

Ideally, an attempt is made to link demand to factors that move in advance of sales. For example, on the basis of factors such as disposable personal income, relative price, unemployment, inventory of autos, and available consumer credit, it is possible to forecast automobile sales. Examples of firms that use statistical demand analysis to forecast sales include:

- American Can Company, which forecasts beer-can sales on the basis of disposable personal income, number of drinking establishments per thousand persons, and age distribution of the population.

- RCA, which forecasts television, radio, and compact disc player sales on the basis of more than 300 economic variables.

- Armour & Company, which forecasts cattle sales on the basis of range-grass conditions and steer-corn price ratios.

- Whirlpool, which forecasts refrigerator sales based on the scrappage of old units, number of wired homes, disposable personal income per household, available consumer credit, and the price index of household furnishings.

These relationships may at first glance seem complex. However, much of the data on which they are based is readily available in the *Statistical Abstract of the United States,* published by the Department of Commerce; in the *Survey of Current*

FIGURE EM1.3 THE RELATIONSHIP OF BABY FOOD SALES TO NUMBER OF LIVE BIRTHS

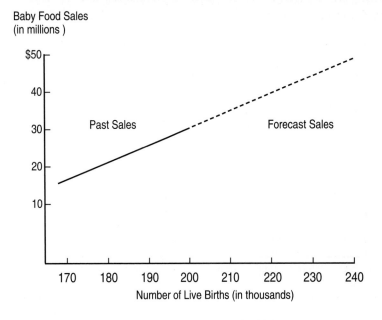

TABLE EM1.6	ADVANTAGES AND DISADVANTAGES OF DIFFERENT SALES FORECASTING TECHNIQUES		
Information Base/Technique	**Advantages**	**Disadvantages**

What People Say They Will Do

- **Surveys of buyers' intentions**

  Advantages:
  1. Government and commercial surveys of buyers' intentions are available.
  2. Sampling procedures can be used to select a representative cross-section of buyers.

  Disadvantages:
  1. Buyer intentions are not commitments to buy.
  2. Buyers may find it difficult to forecast future needs.
  3. Some buyers may not wish to confide future intentions.

- **Composite of sales force opinion**

  Advantages:
  1. Sales representatives are in fairly constant contact with buyers and frequently have knowledge of buyer needs.
  2. Sales representatives may be able to offer insights into developing market trends.

  Disadvantages:
  1. Sales representatives are not always unbiased.
  2. Sales representatives may be unaware of larger economic developments or future marketing plans.
  3. Sales representatives may not have the ability, motivation, or time necessary to prepare accurate forecasts.

- **Jury of executive opinion**

  Advantages:
  1. Relatively quick and straightforward.
  2. Capable of integrating judgmental factors and experience.

  Disadvantages:
  1. Executives may not have the necessary insight to develop accurate forecasts.
  2. Largely based on opinions, not facts.

- **Expert opinion**

  Advantages:
  1. A range of viewpoints can be considered.
  2. Can be used in situations where historical information is not available.

  Disadvantages:
  1. Can be relatively expensive.
  2. Often based more on opinions than facts.

What People Are Doing

- **Test marketing**

  Advantages:
  1. Useful in determining the best pricing strategy, advertising themes, and sales promotion.
  2. If a good/service does not meet sales expectations in test markets, it can be reformulated or abandoned.

  Disadvantages:
  1. Can be expensive.
  2. Can be time consuming.
  3. Impractical for all but low-priced goods/services.
  4. Difficulty of selecting an appropriate test-market site.
  5. Can aid competitors.

What People Have Done

- **Time-series analysis**

  Advantages:
  1. Relatively simple.
  2. Can be performed relatively quickly and inexpensively if historical information is available.
  3. Permits identification of different types of sales patterns—trend, seasonal, cyclical, and random.

  Disadvantages:
  1. Underlying assumption that the future will be a continuation of the past.
  2. Expense of collecting historical information if unavailable.

- **Statistical demand analysis**

  Advantages:
  1. Relatively straightforward.
  2. Can be performed relatively quickly and inexpensively if factors affecting sales can be easily identified and measured.

  Disadvantages:
  1. Inappropriate for some goods/services.
  2. Factors affecting sales may not be easily identifiable and measurable.

Business, also published by the Department of Commerce; and through newsletters issued by the leading Federal Reserve banks.

As should be apparent, each of the sales forecasting techniques discussed has advantages and disadvantages. For this reason, rarely will one be sufficient. In practice, it is common for several to be used together. Results obtained from different techniques may then be used to cross-check one another and further improve sales forecasts. The advantages and disadvantages of the various techniques discussed are summarized in Table EM1.6.

THE SUPERIOR FORECASTING SYSTEM

The preceding description of the various types of forecasts you are likely to encounter as a manager is plainly an oversimplification. Its primary aim has been to familiarize you with basic existing practices. Bluntly stated, forecasting is not simple. No single forecasting technique is appropriate in all cases. Experience suggests that no matter what forecasting technique is used, it probably can be improved upon. Problems are bound to be encountered and, particularly at first, mistakes made. Like anything else, however, forecasting becomes more accurate with practice.

Forecasters are far from infallible. Nevertheless, forecasting remains indispensable for developing planning premises about the expected environment in which objectives are to be accomplished. To aid in your future planning responsibilities, Table EM1.7 presents a list of characteristics that experience indicates are hallmarks of a superior forecasting system.

TABLE EM1.7   HALLMARKS OF A SUPERIOR FORECASTING SYSTEM

1. It encourages an open-minded weighing and testing of alternatives.
2. Its predictive power and cost are well matched to its purposes.
3. Its input data are appropriate, consistent, and reliable, and they are protected from contamination and misuse.
4. Its procedures discourage aimless intervention and tinkering, while encouraging the adjustment of first approximations in light of new data.
5. It has adequate provisions for tracking, updating, and self-correction.
6. Its users are alert to the possibilities of forecast error, they understand its underlying assumptions, they are familiar with and accept its methodology, and their own contribution and involvement at critical points are assured.

Source: Adapted from David L. Hurwood, Elliott S. Grossman, and Earl L. Bailey, *Sales Forecasting* (New York: Conference Board, 1978), iii.

NOTES

[1] Edward M. Tauber, "Forecasting Sales Prior to Test Market," *Journal of Marketing* 44 (January 1977): 80–84.

2 Jon Zonderman, "Forecasts from Teacups?" *Datamation,* May 1, 1984, 28–32.

3 "Marketing: The New Priority," *Business Week,* November 21, 1983, 102.

4 Spyros Makridakis and Steven C. Wheelwright, "Forecasting: Issues & Challenges for Marketing Management," *Journal of Marketing* 41 (October 1977), 30.

CHAPTER 7

LEARNING OBJECTIVES

Upon completing this chapter, you should be able to:

- Distinguish between programmed and nonprogrammed decisions.

- Specify the three conditions under which managers make decisions.

- Explain the concepts of bounded rationality and satisficing.

- Define what is meant by a heuristic and give three examples.

- List the six steps in rational decision making.

- Identify three sources of information leading to problem recognition.

- Detail the advantages and disadvantages of group decision making.

- Recognize the symptoms of groupthink and identify ways it can be prevented.

- Describe brainstorming, nominal grouping, and the Delphi technique.

- Explain probability analysis, queuing theory, linear programming, and simulation.

he phrase *back to the drawing board* has come into widespread use to refer to the need to start over again when a design turns out to be too costly to produce. A Japanese cost management system avoids this problem, and U.S. companies might do well to imitate it.

In the United States and Europe, a product generally is designed first, and then its cost is calculated by a company's accountants on the basis of overhead, labor, and materials expenses. If the cost is deemed to be too high relative to projected sales, the design is re-engineered. Because most of a product's cost is already fixed by its design process, a major redesign is generally necessary to reduce expenses significantly. Seldom it seems does anyone address the question of what the product *should* cost or ask whether it helps sell other items in a company's products in the line. Every product is expected to stand on its own.

In Japan a system called target costing is used. A design team sets a target cost based on a price that it believes potential buyers will be willing to pay. Then that cost is allocated among a product's various components, and the expense for each component is further subdivided into design/engineering, sales/marketing, and manu-

MANAGERIAL DECISION MAKING

facturing expenses. Expense estimates are made by "cost engineers" with experience designing and producing the components involved. Scrapping a design is not a problem because only preliminary work has been done before total cost is calculated. In addition, because design teams interact, expense allocations are balanced to ensure that product quality is not affected and that final products meet the targeted costs.

Target costing allows a company to design products that may not be very profitable but will introduce potential customers to its product line. Thus, Sony developed a ministereo system that was smaller than the systems it had been selling to college students. Sony's marketers expected the minisystem to open up a new market among slightly older adults who were cramped for space and might later buy a larger system, but they didn't expect that this market would be very large or that the product would be profitable on its own. To their surprise, the new system, called the Pixy, quickly became the industry standard for the dormitory crowd. Shortly after the Pixy was introduced into the United States, it began to take over markets where customers wanted a small system, either as a second system for their bedrooms or offices or as an addition to a TV/VCR system; it also appealed to people with small apartments (an increasing portion of the population).

The differences between the Japanese and American approaches to product design show that the process used to reach a decision may be just as important as the decision itself. In this chapter, we will explore several techniques for effective decision making.

Sources: Ford S. Worthy, "Japan's Smart Secret Weapon," *Fortune,* August 12, 1991, 72–75 and Mark Harrington, "Smaller is Better in Mini-Audio," *HFD—The Weekly Home Furnishings Newspaper,* August 6, 1990, 92.

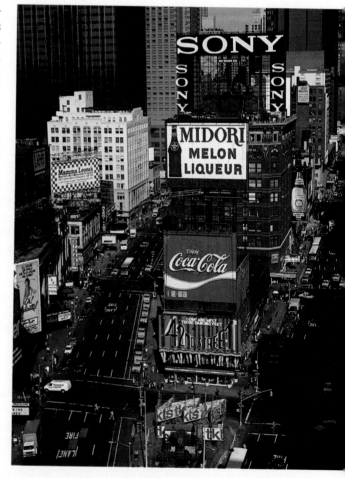

Decision making is a central aspect of the managerial role. Hundreds of decisions are made daily at all levels in a busy organization. Should raw materials be ordered from one vendor or another? Is now a good time to enter into a joint-venture agreement, or is it better to wait? Should operations be expanded or contracted? Regardless of its goals, an organization's long-term survival depends on its managers' decision-making skills.

Because all planning involves decision making, we will explore the decision-making process as we continue our discussion of the planning function. Bear in mind, however, that although decision making is closely linked to the planning function, it is a fundamental aspect of the entire management process.

The present chapter begins by defining and distinguishing between two types of decisions. Next, it describes the various conditions under which decisions are made. After summarizing two decision-making models—the rational and the behavioral—it identifies the six steps in rational decision making. It then discusses group decision making and concludes by reviewing various quantitative tools for decision making.

TYPES OF DECISIONS

A **decision** is a choice made between two or more alternatives. For example, choosing to buy new equipment now rather than later is a decision. Needless to say, proficiency in decision making calls for diagnostic skills and keen judgment. From a career perspective, managers advance largely based on their proficiency in decision making.

Effective managers make various kinds of decisions. In general, these decisions are either **programmed decisions** or **nonprogrammed decisions.**[1] Rather than being distinct categories, however, these types represent a whole continuum with highly programmed decisions at one end and highly unprogrammed decisions at the other.

Decisions are programmed to the extent that they are repetitive and routine. Consequently, for some decisions a definite method for obtaining a solution can be established so that the decisions do not have to be treated anew each time they occur. Examples of programmed decisions include pricing standard customer orders, determining billing dates, and reordering office supplies.

Decisions are nonprogrammed to the extent that they are novel and ill structured. Because nonprogrammed decisions have never occurred before or because they are too complex and elusive, there can be no established methods for handling them. Examples of nonprogrammed decisions include moving into a new market; investing in a new, unproven technology; and changing strategic direction. Obviously, the most difficult managerial situations involve nonprogrammed decisions.

Decision.
A choice made between two or more alternatives.

Programmed decision.
A decision that is repetitive and routine and for which a definite method for its solution can be established so that it does not have to be treated anew each time it occurs.

Nonprogrammed decision.
A decision that is novel and ill structured and for which there can be no established methods for handling it because it has never occurred before or because it is too complex and elusive.

DECISION-MAKING CONDITIONS

Just as there are different types of decisions, the conditions under which decisions occur also vary. In a free-enterprise system, managers make decisions under conditions of *certainty, risk,* and *uncertainty* (Figure 7.1). Each condition will be discussed in turn.

CERTAINTY

A decision is made under conditions of **certainty** when the available alternatives and the benefits (or costs) associated with each are known. In such situations, there is perfect knowledge about available alternatives and their consequences. No element of chance intervenes between an alternative and its outcome. Exact outcomes are known in advance with complete (100 percent) certainty. Alternative 1 will lead to Outcome A, Alternative 2 will lead to Outcome B, and so on. Under such conditions, a manager is faced simply with identifying the consequences of available alternatives and selecting the outcome with the greatest benefit.

As one would expect, managers rarely make decisions under these conditions, because rarely is the future known with perfect reliability. Indeed, it is difficult to think of examples of all but the most trivial managerial decisions that are made under such conditions. One illustration often cited as a decision made under at least near certainty is the purchase of U.S. savings bonds. Barring the fall of the federal government, $1,000 invested in a savings bond for 1 year at 10 percent will yield $100 in interest. It should still be realized, however, that despite the unlikeliness of the government defaulting on its obligations, the possibility still exists. This simply reinforces the point that very few outcomes are "a sure thing."

RISK

A decision is made under conditions of risk when the available alternatives, the likelihood of their occurrence, and the potential benefits (or costs) associated with it are known. Decisions under conditions of risk are perhaps the most common. Alternatives are already known, but their outcomes are in doubt. As an illustration, a gambler who bets on number 6 for a single roll of a fair die has a one-sixth probability of winning, in that there is only one chance in six of rolling a 6. While the alternatives are clear, the outcome is doubtful. Thus, a condition of risk exists.

Certainty.
Decision-making condition in which the available alternatives and the benefits (or costs) associated with each are known.

FIGURE 7.1   DECISION-MAKING CONDITIONS AND LEVEL OF CERTAINTY

Certainty	Risk	Uncertainty
All alternatives known	All alternatives known	All alternatives unknown
Each alternative leads to a certain outcome	Likelihood of alternatives known	Likelihood of alternatives unknown
Decision is a sure thing	Outcome associated with each alternative known	Outcome associated with each alternative unknown
	Decision is a "gamble"	Decision requires "guts"
Complete Certainty	Level of Certainty	Complete Uncertainty

In business, "gambling" is not a popular term, but "risk taking" is. In today's volatile business environment, risk taking has become a virtue. Volatility provides opportunities for profit because the risk-to-reward ratio is higher in volatile environments, where there typically is less competition, than in stable environments. If a business is not nimble enough to adapt to a new risk profile, it can be sunk by its own inflexibility. Indeed, as Gap president Millard Drexler says, "You can't run a business without taking risks."[2] Examples of risk-taking businesses include:

- Sony, which paid a total of $5.6 billion for Columbia Pictures and CBS/Records Group to create a giant consumer-electronics firm with a vast library of music and movies that could spur the sales of VCRs, videotapes, and CD players.

- Hollywood studios such as Paramount and Warner Bros., which invest an average of $20.1 million to produce and $6.6 million to promote a movie when only three or four out of any 10 are likely to be profitable and one will only break even.

- Gillette, still reeling from four hostile takeover bids and a resulting $1-billion long-term debt, which has taken a "bet-the-company" gamble on its new Sensor razor. With development costs totalling $200 million, and a $175-million advertising budget, Gillette is risking an amount equal to 18 months of profits. Each point of market share Sensor takes from competitors will yield $12 million in profit.

Making bold decisions such as these is a way of life at many organizations. Risk taking, for instance, is considered de rigueur at PepsiCo, which is proud that its emphasis on risk taking has set its managers apart from those of many other companies. As one analyst has observed, "[PepsiCo] simply doesn't allow them to not take risks."[3] PepsiCo understands that, in the business world, not taking risks is often the riskiest course of all.

A high degree of risk taking is inherent in the business of movie-making. Hollywood studios frequently seek to capitalize on the success of popular movies by producing sequels and realizing further gains through video sales. Millions of dollars must be invested in producing and promoting even sequels to popular movies, such as Warner's *Batman Returns*, which was rumored to be the most expensive movie of 1992.

UNCERTAINTY

A decision is made under conditions of uncertainty when the available alternatives, the likelihood of their occurrence, or their potential outcomes are unknown. Decisions made under conditions of uncertainty are unquestionably the most difficult. In such situations, a manager has no knowledge on which to even base an estimate of the likelihood of various outcomes. Decisions under uncertainty generally occur in cases where no historical data are available from which to infer probabilities or in instances that are so novel and complex it is impossible to make comparative judgments. Although managerial intelligence and competence are widely available, the ability to deal with uncertainty is rare. For this reason, decisions under conditions of uncertainty are often those that make or break careers and companies. As described in the business press, these are the decisions that "challenge conventional wisdom—sometimes even laugh at it."[4] Such decisions are likely to be the only kind that can catapult an organization toward dramatic new success.

Perhaps the most common occasions for decisions under conditions of uncertainty are those involving the introduction of new technology or new markets. Examples of "gutsy" decisions made under uncertainty include:

- The Texas Instruments decision to bet $50 million annually on the development of artificial intelligence technology. High-tech enthusiasts forecast a $4.2-billion artificial intelligence market by the early 1990s. However, the possibility remains that in its race to market, Texas Instruments could lose out to rivals.

- Eastman Kodak's decision to pioneer in the new field of electronic photography. Its new Photo CD decks play 35-mm negatives and slides, which are recorded on compact disks for viewing on home TV sets. The decks also double as regular CD players. Photo CD decks have superior picture quality, require no special camera, and will not make existing cameras obsolete.

- Xerox Corp.'s decision to invest more than 10 years and $750 million in the new field of electronic document processing. Based on digital scanning technology, Xerox's DocuTech Production Publisher is its most important new product since the plain-paper copier was introduced. DocuTech has the ability to electronically compose and color print countless documents, such as catalogs, annual reports, and product brochures.

DECISION-MAKING MODELS

Ideally, managerial decisions should be completely rational, that is, fully objective and logical. In actuality, however, frequently this is not the case. As the preceding discussion suggests, managers often must make decisions based on incomplete knowledge. It should come as no surprise to find that the results of those decisions may range from wild success to total disaster. This contrast between the "ideal" and the "actual" is reflected in what have become known as the "rational" and "behavioral" models of decision making.

THE RATIONAL MODEL

The **rational model** of decision making is grounded in traditional economic theory. It portrays managers as completely rational decision makers who invariably

Rational model.
A decision-making model that focuses on how managers should behave.

TABLE 7.1 RATIONAL AND BEHAVIORAL MODELS OF DECISION MAKING	
According to the rational model decision makers have . . .	According to the behavioral model decision makers have . . . .
1. . . . perfect knowledge of available alternatives	1. . . . imperfect knowledge of available alternatives
2. . . . perfect knowledge of the consequences of available alternatives	2. . . . imperfect knowledge of the consequences of available alternatives
3. . . . the necessary ability to objectively evaluate the consequences of available alternatives	3. . . . limited ability to evaluate the consequences of available alternatives
4. . . . a well-ordered and stable set of preferences	4. . . . a poorly ordered and unstable set of preferences
. . . and make optimum decisions.	. . . and make satisficing decisions.

seek to maximize benefits. For the most part, it credits managers with the ability to instantly formulate and solve problems of great complexity. In doing so, it assumes that they possess the following characteristics (see Table 7.1):

1. Perfect knowledge of available alternatives.

2. Perfect knowledge of the consequences of available alternatives.

3. The necessary ability to objectively evaluate the consequences of available alternatives.

4. A well-ordered and stable set of preferences.

As suggested, these assumptions flow from two basic traditional economic principles: managers seek to maximize expected benefits (or minimize costs), and managers are completely rational. Given its emphasis, the rational model is considered to be prescriptive—that is, it specifies how managers *should* make decisions. In this respect, it represents an unattainable ideal. In real life, managers seldom make decisions under the conditions of certainty described by traditional economic theory.

THE BEHAVIORAL MODEL

The validity of the rational model was first questioned by Nobel laureate Herbert A. Simon.[5] Initially focusing on the process by which managers identify and evaluate alternatives, Simon advanced the view that managerial decisions, far from being completely rational, are bounded by the limited mental capacity and emotions of the individuals involved, as well as by environmental factors over which they may have no control. This situation he described is one of **bounded rationality.** It reflects not only the limited capability of the human mind and emotions to grasp the full complexity of managerial decisions, but also the uncertainty of future events with which organizations must cope. Given that organizations exist in highly complex environments in which many possible alternatives and their consequences may remain unknown, all intendedly rational behavior is inherently bounded.

Bounded rationality.

A situation that reflects not only the limited capability of the human mind and emotions to grasp the full complexity of managerial decisions, but also the uncertainty of future events with which organizations must cope.

American Restaurants Corporation used the *rational model* of decision making when expanding the eleven-unit chain of Hudson's Grill of America, Inc. restaurants. Top management decided that the concept of an automobile grille seemingly bursting into a dining area could be franchised nationally. This decision was based on surveys of consumer preferences for upscale fast food and 1950s nostalgia.

As this suggests, *optimum decisions* (meaning "best possible" decisions) are almost never made—except perhaps by chance. Even if it were possible to acquire perfect knowledge of all alternatives and their consequences, it is doubtful, given the limitations of human beings as processors of information, that an adequate evaluation could be made. In response to this dilemma, Simon believes that humans typically reduce the complexity they confront by constructing a simplified model of the real situation that encompasses only the information they feel equipped to handle. Thus, only a limited number of alternatives and a limited range of consequences are considered.

Simon further believes that once managers have identified a limited set of alternatives, they typically deviate from the demands of rationality by selecting the first alternative deemed "satisfactory" or "good enough," rather than searching for the optimum choice. That is, rather than examine all possible alternatives and attempt to rank them according to a well-ordered and stable set of preferences, they conduct a sequential search and settle for the first that satisfies some predetermined **aspiration level**—a subjectively defined performance goal that is a product of past organization goals, past organization performance, and past performance of comparable organizations. Thus, choices are influenced more by the order in which alternatives are examined than by the preexistence of clear guidelines for ensuring that the optimum choice is selected.

As a shorthand label for this process, Simon uses the Scottish word **satisficing** (satisfying). Examples of satisficing criteria include "share of market" versus "total market," "adequate profit" versus "maximum profit," and "fair price" versus "best price." Thus, satisficing is evident in a business whose managers are willing to hold to a decision alternative that results in a 25 percent return on investment even if they are aware that there *may* be other alternatives that *might* raise profits still higher.

An example of satisficing on a more personal level occurs when a person seeks a job. To make a completely rational decision, that is, to select the best alternative,

Aspiration level.
A subjectively defined performance goal.

Satisficing.
Settling for an alternative deemed "satisfactory" rather than searching for the optimum choice.

an individual would have to investigate all the available jobs in the world. Thus, instead of searching for the "optimum" employment opportunity, the individual will settle for the first job judged "good enough."

For practical purposes (for example, purchasing a car or selecting a source of raw materials), it is important that satisficing not be seen as irrational. Given the limitations of human information processing, the cost of searching for alternatives, and the uncertainty of future events, satisficing is actually quite sensible, suggesting two important implications[6]:

1. Although there is only one optimum solution to most problems, there are likely several equally good satisficing solutions. For example, two managers may evaluate alternatives in a different order. If they each stop when they find an alternative that is "good enough," they could easily find themselves disagreeing about what should be done. This will likely mean that a final decision will have to be made on some other basis than the logic of the problem itself. Such factors as seniority, persuasiveness, and politics then come into play—something that would not happen if decisions were made on purely rational grounds.

2. Optimizing and satisficing are fundamentally complementary. To a manager, performance that meets or exceeds a level of aspiration is success, and performance that falls short is failure. If a manager's level of aspiration tends to rise after success (or drop after failure), this resetting will often edge in on an optimum solution. Thus, managers do not necessarily have to be permanently satisfied with the first acceptable alternative that pops into their minds. For example, suppose you are in charge of a small manufacturing plant and have to make a decision as to how much the plant will produce. If you set production targets too low, the plant will have idle capacity, sales will be lost, and profitability will suffer. On the other hand, if you try to produce too much, machine maintenance may be neglected, people will work too hard (and perhaps get sick or injured), and so on. Finding the optimal balance is clearly a very tricky decision.[7]

Simon's view of decision making has come to be called the **behavioral model** (see Table 7.1). On balance, Simon rejects the basic traditional economic principles mentioned earlier. Whereas economists have typically focused on how managers *should* behave, Simon has focused on how they *do* behave. He posits that organizations do not merely seek to maximize expected benefits and that managers are not completely rational. The Simon concept of bounded rationality replaces the idea of the so-called "economic decision maker" with the more realistic "managerial decision maker."

Behavioral model.
A decision-making model that focuses on how managers actually behave.

OTHER PSYCHOLOGICAL PROCESSES

Beyond bounded rationality and satisficing, there are other common psychological processes that influence decision making. These psychological processes are often referred to as **heuristics:** intuitive or unconscious methods of structuring, understanding, and solving problems. The difficulty with heuristics, however, is that they tend to produce biases in judgment—biases that decision makers do not always recognize. Three heuristics show up repeatedly in making judgments: representativeness, availability, and anchoring and adjustment.[8]

Heuristics.
Intuitive or unconscious methods of structuring, understanding, and solving problems.

Representativeness

The representativeness heuristic reflects the tendency for people to assess the likelihood of an occurrence by matching it with a preexisting category. The psychological process underlying this heuristic involves examining the essential characteristics of an occurrence, then comparing these characteristics with those of a known category to see if the occurrence is representative of the category. In this respect, representativeness is a form of stereotyping that leads one to ignore useful information. For example, a human resource manager may rely on stereotypes of racial, ethnic, or sexual groups to assess a job applicant's likely performance. In truth, however, each applicant should be assessed as a distinct individual, not as the representative of a stereotyped group.

Availability

The availability heuristic reflects the tendency for people to judge the likelihood of an occurrence by the ease with which information concerning the occurrence is recalled. Frequent events are accordingly given a higher probability of occurring because they are easier to recall than infrequent events. Yet, the availability heuristic can lead to poor decisions because many other factors can influence recall. Certainly, frequent events are readily available, but so are emotional events, highly publicized events, and recent events. Thus, a marketing manager recently responsible for a product failure may overestimate the likelihood that future new products will also fail. The important point is to be sure that the occurrence being recalled is the same as the occurrence that is being forecast.

Anchoring and Adjustment

The anchoring and adjustment heuristic involves setting an initial value (anchor) and then making adjustments to the value in arriving at a final decision. The anchor takes on psychological importance because it forms a threshold that helps define the limits of a decision. For example, budget allocations are routinely calculated by taking the previous year's allocation as a natural starting point (anchor) from which to make adjustments in the face of additional information. Unfortunately, such adjustments typically have been found to be insufficient because they tend to obscure relevant criteria for establishing a "true" starting value based on actual need.

The anchoring and adjustment heuristic is also evident in situations in which decision makers select a course of action and become so committed to it that they fail to see the shortcomings of that course of action. For example, a manager may resist changing a decision whose results are hopelessly contrary to expectations and, instead, commit additional resources to its continued execution. This "decision pathology" has been variously labeled "the escalation of commitment," "the sunk cost effect," "the psychology of entrapment," and the "too-much-invested-to-quit syndrome." This prevalent situation can be readily seen in declining investments, troubled marriages, and faltering careers. In each instance, there is the difficult decision between continuing to pursue an initial course of action and seeking a new alternative. Research suggests that if decision makers feel personally responsible for a losing course of action, they will quite often commit more time, money, or effort in an attempt to turn the situation around and demonstrate the wisdom of their original choice. Indeed, it has been shown that once investors commit a significant sum of money to a project, they will allocate more resources to the project if they receive feedback that the project is failing than if it is succeeding.[9]

Representativeness, availability, and anchoring and adjustment are powerful psychological processes influencing decision making. Effective managers are aware of the biases these processes create. To overcome representativeness, they consciously examine their views for stereotypic thinking. To overcome availability, they rely on hard data rather than personal memory. Finally, they confront anchoring and adjustment by examining alternative anchors when making decisions.

STEPS IN RATIONAL DECISION MAKING

Although managers seldom have total control over the factors that determine the success of their decisions, they can exert substantial control over the process that they use to make decisions by following the six steps illustrated in Figure 7.2. These steps can be applied to both individual and group decisions.

STEP 1: RECOGNIZE A PROBLEM OR OPPORTUNITY

The first step in decision making is recognizing that a problem or opportunity exists. This, however, is often easier said than done. In the complex environments in which most organizations operate, it is not always clear whether a decision situation represents a problem or an opportunity.

A **problem** typically is defined as a discrepancy between an existing and desired state of affairs. It is generally acknowledged that a problem cannot be efficiently solved unless it is precisely identified. Three sources of information help decision makers recognize problems[10]:

Problem.
A discrepancy between an existing and desired state of affairs.

1. *Historical data.* When an organization's or unit's performance declines relative to past performance. For example, October sales are down 15 percent from September sales.

2. *Planned data.* When an organization or unit fails to meet planned goals. For example, actual sales are less than projected sales.

3. *Criticism.* When outsiders note problems or when performance compares unfavorably to that of other similar organizations. For example, when customers identify problems with product quality or when competitors increase market share at an organization's expense.

No set rules exist to help identify problems precisely. The process invariably involves, however, carefully searching for relevant and important information about a problem rather than a blind search for all the facts. The object is to isolate the problem by excluding all that is superficial and irrelevant.

The recognition of opportunities typically involves identifying possibilities that exist in an organization's environment. Opportunities may be recognized in many

FIGURE 7.2   SIX STEPS IN RATIONAL DECISION MAKING

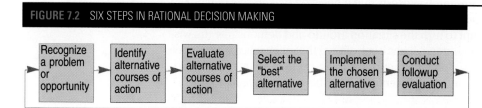

3M Corporation is famous for its history of recognizing opportunities and producing commercially successful products through innovation. Scotch tape was formerly an industrial fastener used within a relatively narrow market until a 3M sales manager invented the desktop dispenser; Post-it notes were developed by a 3M designer looking for a better way to mark pages in his church hymnal.

ways. Procter & Gamble reports that customers using its 800 number are a major source of product-improvement ideas. Levi Strauss got the idea for faded jeans from Bloomingdale's, which was buying Levis and bleaching them. 3M's Scotch Tape didn't take off until a sales manager created a desktop dispenser for what had been a narrow-use industrial fastener. The Big Mac was invented by a McDonald's franchisee in Pittsburgh and the Egg McMuffin by one in California.

Companies such as IBM, Fujitsu, Intel, and Northern Telecom have product-development centers whose sole purpose is to generate product opportunities. Post-it Notes were developed by a 3M product-development engineer in search of a better way to mark passages in his church hymnal during services. ScotchGard fabric protector was discovered when a 3M research chemist spilled a test chemical on her tennis shoes while working. Curious as to its effect, she experimented and found that the treated shoes repelled water and dirt. Perhaps the most famous product-development center is AT&T's Bell Laboratories. With its seven Nobel laureates and nearly 20,000 patents, it has long been a leader in perceiving product opportunities and establishing related objectives.

STEP 2: IDENTIFY ALTERNATIVE COURSES OF ACTION

After a problem or an opportunity has been recognized, the second step is to identify alternative courses of action. Remember, given bounded rationality, it is impossible for a manager to know all available alternatives. However, a systematic effort should be made to identify as many as possible. This is not just an exercise in managerial game playing. The quality of any decision cannot be better than the quality of the "best" known alternative.

The number of available alternatives identified is ordinarily limited by certain constraints. Principal among these are time and money. Rarely do managers have enough time or money to identify, let alone evaluate, an unlimited number of alternatives. Indeed, there may be times when doing something immediately may be more important than taking an otherwise better action at a later date. Consequently, managers must often balance time and expense against identification of additional alternatives.

Identifying a reasonable number of alternatives is usually no problem. Occasionally, however, identifying "good" alternatives can be a challenge requiring a measure of **creativity,** which involves using knowledge and imagination to generate new ideas. Effective managers use all their capacities and often seek both individual and group involvement at this step in decision making. Various ways for stimulating creativity are discussed in a following section titled "Techniques for Improving Group Decision Making."

Creativity.
Using knowledge and imagination to generate new ideas.

STEP 3: EVALUATE ALTERNATIVE COURSES OF ACTION

Having identified a "reasonable" number of alternatives, the third step is to evaluate the alternatives. Each alternative should be evaluated in terms of its strengths and weaknesses, benefits and costs, advantages and disadvantages. Because each alternative is likely to have both positive and negative features, most evaluations involve a balancing of anticipated consequences. Needless to say, such assessments should be as systematic as possible.

The evaluation of alternatives may be intuitive or it may use a more scientific approach. More than likely, it will be a combination of both. Whatever the basis for evaluation, the more systematic the evaluation, the more likely its result will be accurate and complete. Various ways for evaluating alternatives are discussed in a following section titled "Quantitative Tools for Decision Making."

STEP 4: SELECT THE "BEST" ALTERNATIVE

After alternatives have been identified and evaluated, the next step is to select the "best" alternative. Of course, if none of the alternatives is deemed acceptable, a manager should return to Step 2 and attempt to identify additional courses of action.

Theoretically, if Steps 2 and 3—identifying and evaluating alternatives—have been properly handled, selecting a course of action should be easy. The best alternative will be obvious. In practice, however, selecting an alternative is more often a matter of judgment.

In this respect, the actual selection of an alternative often must be made in light of multiple and conflicting requirements. Indeed, the quality of a decision may well have to be balanced against its acceptability. The interrelated nature of actions and outcomes often necessitates certain trade-offs. Resource constraints and political considerations, for example, may prevent managers from using what is otherwise deemed the best alternative. Sound judgment becomes even more important at this point in the decision-making process than at any previous step. Observes former Kraft CEO John M. Richman: "The decisions that are made at or near

Employee involvement and management commitment are evident at TRW Thompson Products in St. Catherines, Ontario, Canada. For one full year before the implementation of a new robotics program, employees learned about robotics through lectures, videotapes, films, and brochures. Employee teams were set up to install the robots, helping to foster a sense of ownership that has been a key factor in the program's success.

the top of a company . . . are not necessarily 'right' or 'wrong.' Most are very judgmental. You get ten CEOs in a room and present them with some of the issues that are facing any one of them and you'll get at least five different opinions."[11] This is where talent and experience come into play.

STEP 5: IMPLEMENT THE CHOSEN ALTERNATIVE

After an alternative has been selected, appropriate actions must be taken to ensure that it is properly implemented. Implementation, the fifth step, is crucial to a decision's success. Indeed, it is considered by some to be the key to effective decision making. The best alternative is worthless if it is improperly implemented—and proper implementation requires managerial skills.

Because no alternative is better than the actions taken to make it a reality, managers must make detailed provisions for implementing an alternative as soon as it is selected. All those who will be involved must be informed, and appropriate resources must be allocated. Again, let us emphasize, sound implementation is every bit as important as selecting an alternative from among available courses of action. Perhaps the largest pitfalls to successful implementation are:

1. *Managers resisting decisions because they do not understand them.* If decisions are to be properly implemented, they must be explained in such a way that they are understood by all relevant parties. Those concerned must understand not only the logic behind a decision, but also what they are supposed to do. This means developing performance standards, establishing reporting relationships, and determining appropriate deadlines for the performance of various

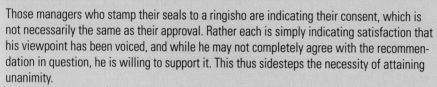

While decisions in a typical U.S. business commonly incorporate both individual and group approaches, well over 90 percent of all large Japanese companies follow a decision-making system known as *ringi*. The system is used to build consensus around major decisions. A *ringisho*, or buck slip, presenting pertinent facts and a recommendation is circulated among managers who are expected to study the proposal and register their agreement by affixing their seals to it. If a manager is unsure regarding a proposal, he will typically have an opportunity in the numerous meetings called to discuss the proposal to voice his reservations. However, once a consensus has been reached concerning a decision, further objection will likely offend the Japanese preference for group action. If a consensus is favorable, the ringisho will ultimately reach a firm's president, and when he affixes his seal, the proposal is officially adopted.

Those managers who stamp their seals to a ringisho are indicating their consent, which is not necessarily the same as their approval. Rather each is simply indicating satisfaction that his viewpoint has been voiced, and while he may not completely agree with the recommendation in question, he is willing to support it. This thus sidesteps the necessity of attaining unanimity.

The quality of the resulting decisions is claimed to be high, since managers at all levels— perhaps 20 or more—participate. Consensus refines a decision, ensuring that those it affects fully understand its rationale and implications. It also creates commitment of all parties involved to a chosen solution.

The ringi process should not be confused with "participative management," the practice of having superiors and subordinates cooperate that has been widely adopted in the West. Rather, it is an effort to reach consensus through closely coordinating the activities of each area affected by an issue.

Decision by consensus is not without its costs. It is a slow and difficult process. The inherent pressure for smooth relationships can result in important issues failing to get a full airing. Managers who object to a recommendation may remain silent simply to appease one or another faction. Thus, at its best, the ringi process taps the expertise of various managers and tempers factional conflicts. At its worst, however, it encourages politicking and compromise.

activities. The pitfall posed by a lack of managerial understanding was perhaps best summarized by the executive who observed, "Most managers would rather live with a problem they can't solve than use a solution they don't know."[12]

2. *Managers resisting decisions because they have not been sold on them.* If all relevant managers have participated in selecting an alternative, they are more likely to accept it. An intensive effort should be made to encourage questions, observations, and challenges in advance of a final decision. The likelihood of effective implementation will be increased greatly if all those concerned not only understand a decision, but also feel they are partly responsible for its success.

In reviewing these pitfalls, it is clear that implementation is an ongoing challenge. Experience suggests that the following five factors will help promote successful implementation.[13]

1. *Communicate, communicate, communicate.* Two-way communication that permits and solicits questions from affected employees should be abundant. It should include clear explanations of the new duties that need to be performed and who should perform them.

2. *Start with a good idea.* No amount of time and effort spent on implementation can rescue a decision that is not sound to begin with.

3. *Obtain employee commitment and involvement.* To avoid resistance, involve affected employees right from the start of problem identification. Involvement and commitment should be developed and maintained throughout the implementation process.

4. *Provide sufficient resources.* Four resources are particularly important: money, personnel, technical expertise (or knowledge), and time.

5. *Develop an implementation plan.* Prepare an action plan detailing who is to do what and when it is to be accomplished.

STEP 6: CONDUCT FOLLOWUP EVALUATION

Once implemented, a decision should be evaluated. This final step is critical to decision success. It should take place at all managerial levels, from top managers to first-line supervisors. Without exception, once a decision has been set into motion, evaluation is necessary to provide feedback on its outcome. Adjustments are invariably needed to ensure that actual results compare favorably with hoped-for results.

With evaluation, the feedback loop shown in Figure 7.2 is closed. The soundness of a decision can be evaluated against its results. As necessary, modifications can be made and further alternatives identified and evaluated.

Evaluation enables managers to learn from experience and thus increase their capacity for making future decisions. No matter how thoroughly an organization has moved through the steps in decision making, variations are bound to occur. To regard any decision as static is the surest road to organization failure. There may be times when perceived opportunities do not materialize, goals are unrealistic, or the selected means of implementation are inappropriate.

Much can be gained from analyzing the aftermath of such situations. Managers should not feel guilty when unforeseen conditions or events require corrective action. Such action should be considered a normal and predictable managerial activity. At its inception, a decision should be viewed as the very best course of action available. However, it also should be seen as an opportunity for learning new knowledge to improve future decisions.

GROUP DECISION MAKING

Groups are often used to make decisions. Committees, special councils, and task teams are all examples of groups that are frequently involved in decision making. Whether groups make better decisions than individuals working alone has been a topic of extended discussion. We've all heard that "two heads are better than one." We also have heard that "too many cooks spoil the broth." Given the conflicting nature of these observations, let's review the advantages and disadvantages of group decision making (see Table 7.2).

TABLE 7.2 ADVANTAGES AND DISADVANTAGES OF GROUP DECISION MAKING

Advantages

1. Acceptance by those affected is increased.
2. Coordination is easier.
3. Communication is easier.
4. Greater number of alternatives can be considered.
5. More information can be processed.

Disadvantages

1. Group decisions take longer to reach than individual decisions.
2. Groups can be indecisive.
3. Groups can compromise.
4. Groups can be dominated.
5. Groups can play games.
6. Groups can fall victim to "groupthink."

ADVANTAGES

Advocates of group decision making cite the following advantages:

1. *Acceptance by those affected is increased.* Decisions made by a group are often more readily accepted by its members. This, of course, makes implementation much easier.

2. *Coordination is easier.* When decisions are made by a group, the amount of co-ordination necessary to bring the decisions into play is reduced.

3. *Communication is easier.* When decisions are made by a group, the amount of communication necessary to implement the decisions is reduced.

4. *Greater number of alternatives can be considered.* Since "several heads are better than one," a greater number of alternatives are generated by a group than by individuals operating alone.

5. *More information can be processed.* Because several individuals are involved, more information can be brought to bear on a decision.

DISADVANTAGES

Critics of group decision making cite the following disadvantages:

1. *Group decisions take longer to reach than individual decisions.* Groups are slower to arrive at decisions than individuals acting alone.

2. *Groups can be indecisive.* A group may be unable to reach a decision as a result of disagreement among its members.

3. *Groups can compromise.* It has been argued that, because groups place a premium on compromise, they may generate mediocre decisions. Mediocrity often results when an individual's thinking is brought into line with the average quality of a group's thinking. This has been called the **leveling effect.**

4. *Groups can be dominated.* When a group is comprised of individuals of different ranks and status, low-status individuals fearing criticism of their ideas are

Leveling effect.
When individual thinking is brought into line with the average quality of a group's thinking.

likely to feel inhibited. Consequently, the highest status individual may be able to influence a group so that it selects his or her choices.

5. *Groups can play games.* Members may use a group to enhance their self-images by playing off factions and trying to win "points."

6. *Groups can fall victim to "groupthink."* When group norms become extremely internalized, **groupthink** may occur. This phenomenon occurs in situations where the drive to achieve consensus among group members becomes so powerful that it overrides independent, realistic appraisals of alternative actions. In these situations, criticism is suppressed, and conflicting opinions are either unvoiced or inadequately considered. (See the accompanying "Smart Management" box for more on groupthink.)

Groupthink.
A phenomenon that occurs in situations where the drive to achieve consensus among group members becomes so powerful that it overrides independent, realistic appraisals of alternative actions.

INDIVIDUAL VS. GROUP DECISION MAKING

Given the preceding advantages and disadvantages, it would appear that group decision making is appropriate in some situations but less so in others. To illustrate the contingent nature of individual versus group decision making, Table 7.3 summarizes the situational factors supportive of each. As it indicates, when certain factors are present, individuals are likely to be superior at decision making; when others are present, groups are likely to be superior.

TABLE 7.3 INDIVIDUAL VERSUS GROUP DECISION MAKING

Situational Factors Supportive of Individual Decision Making	Situational Factors Supportive of Group Decision Making
1. Time is short.	1. Creativity is needed.
2. The decision is relatively unimportant to the group.	2. Data for the solution rest within the group.
3. A manager has all the data needed to make the decision.	3. Acceptance of a solution by group members is important.
4. One or two group members are likely to dominate the discussion.	4. Understanding of a solution by group members is important.
5. Destructive conflict is likely to erupt among group members.	5. The problem is complex or requires a broad range of knowledge for solution.
6. People feel that they attend too many meetings and that they don't need to be involved, or they feel pessimistic about the value of group meetings.	6. A manager wants subordinates to feel part of a democratic process or wants to build their confidence.
7. The relevant decision-making data are confidential and cannot be shared with all group members.	7. More risk taking in considering solutions is needed.
8. Group members aren't capable or qualified to decide.	8. Better group-member understanding of each other is desirable.
9. A manager is dominant or intimidates group members.	9. The group as a whole is ultimately responsible for the decision.
10. The decision doesn't directly affect the group.	10. A manager wants feedback on the validity of her or his ideas.

Source: Adapted with permission from Lyle Sussman and Samuel D. Deep, *COMEX: The Communication Experience in Human Relations* (Cincinnati: South-Western, 1984), 120.

SMART MANAGEMENT   GROUPTHINK: ITS SYMPTOMS AND PREVENTION

In *Groupthink: Psychological Studies of Policy Decisions and Fiascoes,* 2d ed., psychologist Irving L. Janis contended that certain common processes by which groups develop and maintain consensus can undermine the quality of group decision making. Janis defined *groupthink* as "a mode of thinking that people engage in when they are deeply involved in a cohesive ingroup, when the members' strivings for unanimity override their motivation to realistically appraise alternative courses of action."

Groupthink exists in a group to the degree that these eight symptoms are present:

1. Illusions of the group as invulnerable.
2. Rationalization of data that refute basic assumptions.
3. Unquestioned belief in the group's inherent morality.
4. Stereotyped views of competitors as evil, weak, and stupid.
5. Direct pressure on deviates to conform.
6. Self-censorship by members.
7. A shared illusion of unanimity.
8. Emergence of self-appointed "mindguards" to protect the group from negative data.

Janis ties several well-known historical blunders to groupthink. These include the decision to launch the Bay of Pigs invasion of Cuba, the decision not to fly reconnaissance missions north of Hawaii just before the Japanese attack on Pearl Harbor, the decision to invade North Korea during the Korean conflict, and the decision to bomb North Vietnam during the Vietnam War. Adding to Janis's list, more recent examples include the decision to launch the space shuttle *Challenger* and the Iran-contra affair.

Although most managers have probably experienced groupthink at one time or another, it is not inherent in all group decisions and can be avoided. Janis offered the following guidelines for preventing groupthink:

- Group leaders should encourage open expression of objections and doubts.
- Higher status group members should initially adopt an impartial stance.
- Duplicate groups should be established to work on the same problem.
- Group members should discuss issues with outsiders and report back their reactions.
- Outside experts should be invited periodically to meet with the group.
- At least one group member should be assigned the role of devil's advocate.
- Scenarios of competitors' possible intentions should be developed.
- The group should divide into subgroups for surveying alternative courses of action.
- A "second chance" meeting should be held after a preliminary consensus is achieved to retest the consensus.

Source: Irving L. Janis, *Groupthink: Psychological Studies of Policy Decisions and Fiascoes,* 2d ed. (Boston: Houghton Mifflin, 1982); revised form *Victims of Groupthink: A Psychological Study of Foreign Decisions and Fiascoes,* 1972.

TECHNIQUES FOR IMPROVING GROUP DECISION MAKING

To overcome the disadvantages and to capitalize on the advantages of group decision making, various ways of making group decision making more creative have been suggested. The most useful are brainstorming, nominal grouping, and the Delphi technique.

BRAINSTORMING

Developed by Alexander F. Osborn, a principal of the New York advertising agency Batten, Barton, Durstine & Osborn, **brainstorming** remains one of the most effective techniques for identifying creative alternatives.[14] Osborn coined the term to mean using the *brain* to creatively *storm* a problem.

The sole concern of brainstorming is idea generation, not idea evaluation. A group of six to eight members is presented with a problem and asked to identify as many potential solutions as possible. Group members may not be from the same organization. Brainstorming is based on the premise that when people interact in an unrestrained setting, they will generate creative ideas, because as one person generates one idea, it will serve to stimulate the thinking of others and produce a second and third idea, and so forth. This interchange is supposedly contagious, creating an atmosphere of free discussion and spontaneous thought. The object is to generate as many ideas as possible in the belief that the greater the number of ideas, the greater the likelihood of an outstanding one being among them. The four rules governing brainstorming sessions are listed in Table 7.4.

Brainstorming.
A creativity technique that involves the identification of alternatives by individuals interacting spontaneously in an unrestrained setting.

Brainstorming is a frequently employed technique that allows group participants to voice a variety of ideas in a creative, spontaneous atmosphere. In this picture, Ford of Canada Customer Assistance employees Alan St. Pierre, Marc Testani, Veronique Kendrick, and manager Tony Russell listen to Valerie Hartleib during a brainstorming session dealing with ideas to improve customer service.

TABLE 7.4   THE FOUR RULES OF BRAINSTORMING

1. *Criticism is prohibited.* Judgment of ideas must be withheld until all ideas have been generated. (It is believed that criticism inhibits the free flow of ideas and group creativity.)
2. *"Freewheeling" is welcome.* The wilder and further out the idea the better. It is easier to "tame down" than to "think up" ideas.
3. *Quantity is wanted.* The greater the number of ideas, the greater the likelihood of an outstanding solution.
4. *Combination and improvement are sought.* In addition to contributing ideas of their own, members are encouraged to suggest how the ideas of others can be improved, or how two or more ideas can be combined into still another idea.

Brainstorming sessions usually last from 30 minutes to an hour. At least 2 days before a session, group members are given a one-page summary of the problem they are to consider. The summary includes background information and examples of the kinds of ideas desired. A 1-hour session is likely to generate 50–150 ideas. Typically, most will be impractical, but a few will merit serious consideration. Brainstorming has been used with encouraging results in the field of advertising, all branches of the armed forces, and various federal, state, and local agencies.

NOMINAL GROUPING

The **nominal grouping technique** was developed by André Delbecq and Andrew Van de Ven.[15] This technique differs from brainstorming in two important ways:

1. It does not rely on the free association of ideas.
2. It purposely attempts to *restrict* verbal interaction.

It is from this latter point that the nominal grouping technique derives its name; it is a group "in name only."

This technique is particularly useful in situations where individual ideas need to be tapped, but where a group consensus is desired. It generally follows a highly structured procedure involving five steps:

- *Step 1.* Seven to 10 individuals of varying backgrounds and training are brought together as a group and familiarized with a problem such as, "What alternatives are available for increasing sales?"
- *Step 2.* Working silently and alone, each group member is asked to prepare a list of ideas in response to the problem.
- *Step 3.* After a period of 10–15 minutes, members share their ideas, one at a time, in a round-robin manner. A facilitator records the ideas on a flip chart for all to see. The round-robin process continues until all ideas are presented and recorded.
- *Step 4.* A period of structured interaction follows in which members openly discuss and evaluate each recorded idea. At this point, ideas may be reworded, combined, deleted, or added.
- *Step 5.* Each group member votes by privately ranking the recorded ideas in order of assessed importance. Following a brief discussion of the vote's outcome, a

Nominal grouping technique.

A five-step technique useful in situations where individual ideas need to be tapped, but where a group consensus is desired.

final secret ballot is conducted. The group's preference is the arithmetic total of the ranked votes. This concludes the meeting.

The nominal grouping technique has been used successfully in a wide variety of organizations. Its principal benefit is that it minimizes the inhibiting effects of group interaction in the initial identification of alternative solutions. Additionally, by requiring that group members generate their own ideas rather than hitchhike on the ideas of others, this technique is proactive rather than reactive. Furthermore, the use of a round-robin recording procedure allows risk-inclined members to state risky solutions early, making it easier for less secure members to engage in similar disclosure. This technique, however, also has limitations. Like brainstorming, it can be time consuming and therefore costly. Additionally, it is subject to the leveling effect. Because of the arithmetic nature of the selection process, an alternative can be selected that has received only a moderate ranking from a majority of group members.

DELPHI TECHNIQUE

The **Delphi technique** was developed by Norman Dalkey and Olaf Helmer at the RAND Corporation to overcome the undesirable effects of group interactions while retaining the positive effects of interactive group judgments.[16] This technique gets its name from Delphi, a place that was famous before the time of Christ as the seat of the most important temple of the Greek god Apollo. Kings and other powerful rulers from all over the ancient world came to Delphi to consult with Apollo through his priestesses, or oracles, who they believed could foretell the future.

In a typical Delphi session, a panel of experts is formed to study a particular question, such as when a new technological process will gain widespread acceptance or what new developments will take place in a given industry. Rather than meeting physically to debate the question, the panelists are kept apart so that their judgments will not be influenced by social pressure or by other psychological aspects of group behavior such as undue persuasion, an unwillingness to abandon publicly expressed opinions, and the bandwagon effect of majority opinion. Panelists are asked to answer a carefully designed questionnaire that seeks their opinions about certain future events. After an initial round of responses is collected, a coordinator prepares a summary of panelists' views. The summary is then fed back to the panel in the form of a second questionnaire. With this information in hand, panelists are asked to reevaluate their earlier predictions and make a second forecast of the events being considered. This round-robin procedure continues until a consensus exists or until further rounds fail to yield new results. The Delphi technique essentially assumes that, as repeated forecasts are conducted, the range of responses will narrow, and a valid consensus will emerge. Experience indicates that there are both advantages and disadvantages associated with the Delphi technique. A list of these is presented in Table 7.5.

Delphi technique.
A creativity technique intended to overcome the undesired effects of group interactions while retaining the positive effects of interactive group judgments.

QUANTITATIVE TOOLS FOR DECISION MAKING

Still another way for managers to improve their decision-making skills, especially in evaluating alternatives, is by using various quantitative decision tools. Although a variety of quantitative tools exist, four are used most often: probability analysis, queuing theory, linear programming, and simulation (see Table 7.6).

TABLE 7.5 ADVANTAGES AND DISADVANTAGES OF THE DELPHI TECHNIQUE

Advantages

1. It eliminates the need to have face-to-face meetings.
2. It reduces the influence of psychological factors, such as undue persuasion, the unwillingness to abandon publicly expressed opinions, and the bandwagon effect of majority opinion.
3. It provides panelists with time to carefully and thoroughly consider their responses.
4. It avoids interpersonal problems, such as power struggles and leadership rivalries.
5. It can be used when the panelists involved are not in close proximity.

Disadvantages

1. The quality of results is only as good as the quality of panelists.
2. It is very dependent on the ability of a coordinator to develop questionnaires that will elicit the information being sought.
3. It does not entirely eliminate the influence of psychological factors because a tendency may still exist for some panelists to concur with the majority.
4. It can be extremely time consuming; several days or weeks may lapse between rounds.
5. Panelists interest and motivation may diminish if too much time passes between rounds.

PROBABILITY ANALYSIS

Probability analysis is used under conditions of risk or uncertainty. The term *probability* refers to the estimated likelihood, expressed as a percentage, that an outcome will occur. If we believe a particular outcome will occur 65 times out of 100, we say its probability of occurring is 65 percent, or 0.65. Probabilities range in value from 0.00 (no likelihood of occurrence) to 1.00 (certain occurrence). Moreover, probabilities may be either objective or subjective. When probabilities are known (such as in the case of a fair coin), or when they are based on historical data, they are labeled *objective probabilities*. Probabilities based on intuition, "gut feeling," or simple "guesstimates" are termed *subjective probabilities*. The actuarial tables compiled by insurance companies are good examples of objective probabilities. Based on historical data, these tables can predict that less than 1 percent of all males under 20 will die before age 25, or that once you pass age 65 your chances of reaching 75 are one in two. But any prediction a hopeful marketing manager might make about the chances of success for an advertising campaign would have to be labeled

Probability analysis.

A quantitative tool used under conditions of risk or uncertainty.

TABLE 7.6 QUANTITATIVE TOOLS FOR DECISION MAKING

1. *Probability analysis*—a quantitative tool for evaluating alternative courses of action under conditions of risk or uncertainty.
2. *Queuing theory*—a quantitative tool for determining the optimal balance between the cost of increasing service and the amount of time individuals, machines, or materials must wait to be serviced.
3. *Linear programming*—a quantitative tool for optimally allocating limited resources among multiple uses to maximize benefits or minimize losses.
4. *Simulation*—a quantitative tool for imitating a set of real conditions so that the likely outcomes of alternative courses of action can be compared.

a subjective probability because historical data on which to base such a prediction generally do not exist.

There are two complementary approaches to using probability analysis: payoff matrices and decision trees. Both are among the most helpful quantitative tools available to a manager. A **payoff matrix** is a tool for calculating the benefits or costs likely to result from alternative courses of action. An illustration is given in Table 7.7.

Imagine that you plan to sell dictionaries door-to-door during the summer holidays. After considerable thought, you estimate that there is a 0.60 probability of selling 500 dictionaries and a 0.40 probability of selling 1,000 dictionaries. You can purchase either 500 or 1,000 dictionaries for $2 each. The anticipated selling price is $10 a dictionary, yielding a profit of $8 a volume sold. Of course, you lose the $2 purchase price on each dictionary that is not sold. Which alternative is most likely to yield the highest *expected value?* The payoff matrix in Table 7.7 provides an answer. Looking first at the alternative of buying 500 dictionaries, we see that by multiplying our potential income (Column 3) by the estimated probabilities (Column 2), the result is an expected value of $4,000. Repeating these calculations for buying 1,000 dictionaries indicates an expected value of $5,000. As a rational decision maker, you would obviously select the alternative with the highest overall expected monetary value.

A **decision tree** is a visual display of the same analysis involved in preparing a payoff matrix. Indeed, the previous dictionary problem can be structured in decision-tree form, as shown in Figure 7.3. True to its name, a decision tree graphically displays each alternative course of action like the branch of a tree. Note that the

Payoff matrix.
A tool for calculating the benefits or costs likely to result from alternative courses of action.

Decision tree.
A visual display of the benefits or costs likely to result from alternative courses of action.

TABLE 7.7	EXAMPLE OF A PAYOFF MATRIX				

		Alternative Courses of Action			
		Buy 500 Dictionaries		**Buy 1,000 Dictionaries**	
(1) Possible outcomes	(2) Estimated probability of occurrence	(3) Potential income (500 dictionaries sold × $8)	(4) Expected value [(2) × (3)]	(5) Potential income (dictionaries sold × $8 *less* dictionaries not sold × $2 *purchase price*)	(6) Expected value [(2) × (5)]
Sell 500 dictionaries	0.60	$4,000	$2,400	$3,000	$1,800
Sell 1,000 dictionaries	0.40	$4,000ᵃ	$1,600	$8,000	$3,200
Overall expected monetary value			$4,000		$5,000ᵇ

ᵃ Only 500 dictionaries can be sold because only 500 were purchased.

ᵇ Best alternative.

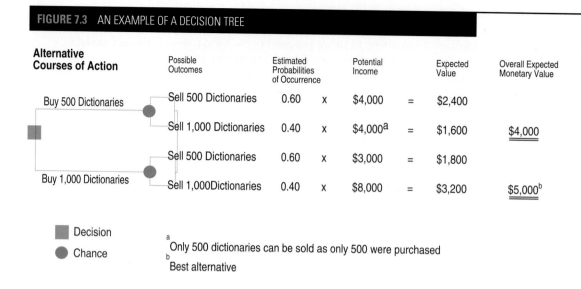

FIGURE 7.3 AN EXAMPLE OF A DECISION TREE

Alternative Courses of Action	Possible Outcomes	Estimated Probabilities of Occurrence	Potential Income	Expected Value	Overall Expected Monetary Value
Buy 500 Dictionaries	Sell 500 Dictionaries	0.60 x	$4,000 =	$2,400	
	Sell 1,000 Dictionaries	0.40 x	$4,000[a] =	$1,600	$4,000
	Sell 500 Dictionaries	0.60 x	$3,000 =	$1,800	
Buy 1,000 Dictionaries	Sell 1,000 Dictionaries	0.40 x	$8,000 =	$3,200	$5,000[b]

■ Decision
● Chance

[a] Only 500 dictionaries can be sold as only 500 were purchased
[b] Best alternative

overall expected value resulting from each alternative course of action is computed just as in the payoff matrix (Table 7.7). Like a payoff matrix, a decision tree requires assigning an estimated probability of occurrence to each possible outcome. Similarly, multiplying the potential income associated with each possible outcome by its estimated probability of occurrence yields an expected value. The overall expected monetary value for each alternative is obtained by adding the expected values associated with its possible outcomes.

Decision trees offer two major benefits. First, they are particularly useful for complex decisions involving a series of chance events over time. By forcing managers to identify alternative courses of action, estimate the probability of their occurrence, and calculate their expected value, decision trees make it possible to understand the true likelihood of different consequences. Second, decision trees serve to highlight the interdependence of events that are likely to occur over a given time period.

QUEUING THEORY

Queuing theory is a quantitative tool for analyzing the costs of waiting lines. Its objective is to achieve an optimal balance between the cost of increasing service and the amount of time individuals, machines, or materials must wait for service. A typical queuing problem exists where units (for example, trucks, customers, materials) arrive at service points, are processed, and then are forwarded or depart. If the service points are not designed to efficiently process the units, then a waiting line may develop. Not only are there costs associated with allowing a waiting line, there are costs associated with increasing service to prevent such lines. Thus, the problem is to determine the best balance between the cost of upgrading service and the amount of time users of a service must wait in line.

Consider, for example, the problem of providing check-in service at an airline reservations counter. A customer waiting in line is potentially a lost customer. If every check-in lane were staffed continually, few customers would have to wait in line, but labor costs would be very high. On the other hand, if only one check-in lane were staffed, even when many people are waiting, there would surely be fran-

Queuing theory.
A quantitative tool for analyzing the costs of waiting lines.

tic passengers, missed planes, and an eventual loss of business to other airlines. While the labor costs of maintaining only one check-in lane would be low, the subsequent loss in sales would quickly outweigh the initial savings. Neither extreme is acceptable. In such situations, queuing theory can be used to identify an optimal solution for maximizing service while minimizing costs.

Other applications of queuing include:

- Determining the optimal number of loading docks and forklifts to service delivery trucks.
- Determining the optimal number of highway toll booths to avoid traffic jams.
- Determining the optimal number of bank tellers to reduce the number of customers awaiting service.
- Determining the optimal number of airport gates and runways to speed passenger arrivals and departures.
- Determining the optimal number of gas pumps for a service station to avoid excessive waiting lines.

As the preceding list suggests, queuing applications are very commonplace. Consequently, queuing theory represents a very important and useful quantitative tool.

LINEAR PROGRAMMING

Of all the quantitative tools identified in Table 7.6, **linear programming** is perhaps the most frequently and extensively used. Virtually all managers face the problem of how best to allocate limited resources among competing uses to maximize benefits or minimize losses. The resources in question may be money, raw materials, equipment, buildings, and people.

Linear programming is commonly used in manufacturing to achieve the most profitable product mix, given limited materials, floor space, and labor. For example, oil refineries use this tool to determine the most profitable blend of ingredients for gasoline and other petroleum products. Animal-feed manufacturers use linear programming to determine what combination of grains will provide the minimum required nutrients at the lowest cost. It has also proved helpful in arriving at the least costly method of routing materials from shipping to receiving points, in determining the adequacy of alternative power sources, and in menu planning so as to minimize cost and maximize nutrition.

The so-called "traveling salesman" problem is a classic linear programming application. The problem is to determine the shortest, or least costly, route for a salesperson to travel to visit a set list of cities. The salesperson must visit each city only once, never retrace any steps, and return to the starting city. Linear programming is capable of determining which route is the shortest or least costly to follow. Similarly, this tool has been used in determining optimal routes and schedules for airline flights, tankers, and school buses. It has also been likewise applied to drilling circuit boards in the electronics industry, where 17,000 different spots are involved, and to fabricating integrated circuits involving as many as 1.2 million "locations."

As with queuing theory, linear programming applications are numerous and varied. Because of its broad applicability, it is one of the most widely used quantitative tools. Indeed, of all the quantitative tools available, perhaps linear programming has the greatest utility to practicing managers.

Linear programming.
A quantitative tool used for optionally allocating limited resources among competing uses to maximize benefits or minimize losses.

SIMULATION

Perhaps the most complex quantitative tool, **simulation** involves the use of several different methods, all with the common objective of imitating a set of real conditions so that the likely outcomes of alternative courses of action can be compared. These methods involve constructing and testing a model of a real-world phenomenon. Simulation is particularly useful for complex problems where it is too costly or impossible to work with real-life pilot studies or full-scale applications. In this way, a manager can rapidly compare the outcomes of different alternatives under various conditions.

Airplane models tested in a wind tunnel, scaled-down automobile models, war games, mock space mission exercises, and flight simulators are all simulation applications. Simulation can also be used with mathematical models to predict probable outcomes of pricing and investment decisions, proposed inventory control systems, assembly-line scheduling routines, alternative design specifications, and alternative competitive strategies. At conglomerate Allied-Signal, personal computers are used to run business simulations to let managers launch experiments in product design, test advertising strategies, and even fail—without suffering the consequences. Such simulations try to reproduce the human frailties and unexpected events that complicate the business world. In a typical simulation, just as managers have perfected a strategy they think will work, the supporting software flashes news of unexpected events like an accident or a supplier price increase.

Computer simulations are available for mimicking new factories, partial modernizations of older ones, computer and telecommunication networks, even roads and intersections.

Simulation.
A quantitative tool for imitating a set of real conditions so that the likely outcomes of alternative courses of action can be compared.

At Ford's Engineering Computer Center in Dearborn, Michigan, this electronic equivalent of a full-size sedan just hit a "wall" at 31 mph. After analysis, any needed structural or restraint-system improvements are programmed into the simulation for more tests. Later, actual prototypes will be built and crash-tested to confirm the safety performance data generated by the simulator.

Simulation can save time and money, not to mention managers' careers. It brings more information to those who use it, allowing them to make better decisions. Simulation's place among quantitative tools is secure because it is proving to be indispensable in today's fast-changing world.

CONCLUDING REMARKS

Quantitative tools are an invaluable aid for evaluating alternatives. They, however, do not and cannot replace the need for managers to think and make independent judgments. Thus, they should be viewed as a supplement rather than a replacement for less systematic forms of decision making. As their name suggests, they require hard data, so for many problems, obtaining quantitative solutions may be impossible. Situations involving social, cultural, political, and behavioral factors can seldom be accurately quantified. Thus, the very important point emerges that decisions are only as good as the data on which they are based.

SUMMARY

This chapter explores the nature of decision making. In doing so, it focuses on the importance of decision making as a central aspect of the managerial role, noting that an organization's long-term survival depends on its managers' decision-making skills.

Learning Objective 1: Distinguish between programmed and nonprogrammed decisions.
Decisions are programmed to the extent that they are repetitive and routine. Consequently, for some decisions a definite method of obtaining a solution can be established so that the decisions do not have to be treated anew each time they occur. Decisions are nonprogrammed to the extent that they are ill structured. Because nonprogrammed decisions have never occurred before or because they are too complex and elusive, there is no established method for handling them.

Learning Objective 2: Specify the three conditions under which managers make decisions.
In a free-enterprise system, managers make decisions under conditions of certainty, risk, and uncertainty.

Learning Objective 3: Explain the concepts of bounded rationality and satisficing.
Bounded rationality refers to the view that managerial decisions, far from being completely rational, are bounded by the limited mental capacity and emotions of the individuals involved, as well as by environmental factors over which they may have no control. Satisficing refers to the decision process in which, rather than examining all possible alternatives and attempting to rank them according to a well-ordered and stable set of preferences, managers settle for the first alternative that is judged "good enough."

Learning Objective 4: Define what is meant by a heuristic and give three examples.

A heuristic is an intuitive or unconscious method for structuring, understanding, and solving problems. Three heuristics show up repeatedly in making judgments: representativeness, availability, and anchoring and adjustment.

Learning Objective 5: List the six steps in rational decision making.

The six steps in rational decision making are to recognize a problem or opportunity, identify alternative courses of action, evaluate alternative courses of action, select the "best" alternative, implement the chosen alternative, and conduct a followup evaluation.

Learning Objective 6: Identify three sources of information leading to problem recognition.

Three sources of information leading to problem recognition are historical data, planned data, and criticism.

Learning Objective 7: Detail the advantages and disadvantages of group decision making.

The advantages and disadvantages of group decision making are detailed in Table 7.2.

Learning Objective 8: Recognize the symptoms of groupthink and identify ways it can be prevented.

The symptoms of groupthink and measures for its prevention are given in the "Smart Management" box titled "Groupthink: Its Symptoms and Prevention."

Learning Objective 9: Describe brainstorming, nominal grouping, and the Delphi technique.

Brainstorming is a creativity technique that involves the identification of alternatives by individuals spontaneously interacting in an unrestrained setting. Nominal grouping is a creativity technique that involves the identification of alternatives through a highly structured procedure that purposely attempts to *restrict* interaction. The Delphi technique is a creativity technique intended to overcome the undesirable effects of group interactions while retaining the positive effects of interactive group judgments.

Learning Objective 10: Explain probability analysis, queuing theory, linear programming, and simulation.

Probability analysis is a quantitative tool for evaluating alternative courses of action under conditions of risk and uncertainty. Queuing theory is a quantitative tool for determining the optimal balance between the cost of increasing service and the amount of time individuals, machines, or materials must wait for service. Linear programming is a quantitative tool used for optimally allocating limited resources among competing uses to maximize benefits or minimize losses. Simulation is a quantitative tool for imitating a set of real conditions so that the likely outcomes of alternative courses of action can be compared.

KEY TERMS

aspiration level 207

behavioral model 208

bounded rationality 206

brainstorming 219

certainty 203

creativity 212

decision 202

decision tree 223

Delphi technique 221

groupthink 217

heuristics 208

leveling effect 216

linear programming 225

nominal grouping technique 220

nonprogrammed decision 202

payoff matrix 223

probability analysis 222

problem 210

programmed decision 202

queuing theory 224

rational model 205

satisficing 207

simulation 226

REVIEW AND DISCUSSION QUESTIONS

1. You have just returned from an open lecture given by the College of Business's executive-in-residence, a CEO for a major oil company. During her address, she quoted author John McDonald: "The business executive is by profession a decision maker. Uncertainty is his opponent. Overcoming it is his mission."[17] Explain what McDonald meant.

2. Imagine that you are the last of 400 students remaining at the final exam for this course. You have one item to complete within 5 minutes. The item reads, "Give an example of a decision made under each of three conditions: certainty, risk, and uncertainty." How would you respond?

3. Assume that you are on a dinner date. You and a companion have just completed a delicious meal at one of San Francisco's finest restaurants. The conversation has turned to conditions in the world today. Your companion insists that if he (she) were "King (Queen) for a Day," he'd (she'd) make nothing but rational decisions. What would your response be to this assertion?

4. You are representing your school in this year's College Bowl. The category for the next question is "Decision Making." As the moderator is halfway through reading the question, you sound your buzzer, indicating that you know the answer. For 15 points and the national championship, "Distinguish between the rational and behavioral models of decision making."

5. One disadvantage of group decision making that is often cited is known as the *leveling effect.* That is, in group situations people often compromise; consequently, individual thinking is brought into line with the average quality of a group's thinking. In commenting on this dilemma, Swiss psychologist Carl G. Jung wrote: "When a hundred clever heads join a group, one big nincompoop is the result, because every individual is trammeled by the otherness of the others."[18] Do you agree? If so, why? If not, why not?

6. In his book *Victims of Groupthink,* Irving L. Janis stated that he uses the term *groupthink* as "a quick and easy way to refer to a mode of thinking that people

engage in when they are deeply involved in a cohesive in-group, when the members' strivings for unanimity override their motivation to realistically appraise alternative courses of action." He goes on to explain that groupthink is a "term of the same order as the words in the newspeak vocabulary George Orwell presents in his dismaying *1984*—a vocabulary with terms such as 'doublethink' and 'crimethink.'"[19] By being placed with these Orwellian words, the word *groupthink* takes on an offensive connotation. Bearing this in mind, recount from either your personal experience or knowledge of history, an instance of groupthink.

7. Calling on your personal experience, cite examples of when brainstorming, nominal grouping, or the Delphi technique would have been appropriate for identifying alternative courses of action.

8. There is an instructive probability question that has become known as the "Birthday Problem." Among 24 people chosen at random, it might seem difficult to estimate the probability that two of them have the same birthday. Contrary to intuition, however, the probability is slightly greater than 0.50 and rises rapidly if the number of randomly chosen people is increased. The probability that two among 50 people will have the same birthday is about 0.98. How can this be explained? Test the "Birthday Problem" in your class.

9. Construct a payoff matrix or decision to aid in the solution of a major decision you are facing.

10. Assume you are a principal in a major management consulting firm, quite familiar with different quantitative tools for decision making. Cite several examples where linear programming, queuing theory, and simulation could be applied in your local community.

THE MANAGEMENT EXPERIENCE CHECK YOUR DECISION-MAKING SKILLS

When you face problems, do you usually try to act promptly, or do you delay as long as possible? When pressed for a decision, do you often act too hastily, or do you seem to function best when under pressure? Do you believe in consulting others, or do you consider it a sign of weakness? Do you often agonize both before and after making important decisions, or do you deal with such decisions calmly with no subsequent brooding?

The ability to make decisions sensibly, calmly, and with reasonable speed is helpful in any walk of life, and especially so for managers. One sure way to distinguish between good and inadequate managers is by the way they cope with decision making. Effective and reasonably prompt decision making is important to win the respect of one's superiors and subordinates.

To learn how well you deal with decision making, answer the following questions:

1. Do you often try to avoid or delay making important decisions and even hope that problems will go away?   Yes _____   No _____

2. When required to make a decision fairly promptly, do you become flustered and fail to function at your best?   Yes _____   No _____

3. Would you consider it demeaning to consult your subordinates regarding a problem with which they have experience?   Yes _____   No _____

Continued on next page.

4. In deciding a complicated problem where strong arguments exist for either side, would you trust your "gut reaction"? Yes _____ No _____

5. Do you often wish that you didn't have to make any decisions? Yes _____ No _____

6. When faced with a serious decision, are your sleep and appetite usually adversely affected? Yes _____ No _____

7. Do you secretly dislike making decisions because you lack self-confidence? Yes _____ No _____

8. Are you uneasy even when required to make unimportant decisions? Yes _____ No _____

9. Would you fire a friend if his continued employment was against the welfare of the organization in which you held a high position? Yes _____ No _____

10. When baffled by a problem within your jurisdiction, would you try to fob it off to others? Yes _____ No _____

11. At home, do you participate in all or most of the important decisions? Yes _____ No _____

12. Are you usually edgy both before and after making important decisions? Yes _____ No _____

Scoring: The most desirable response earns 4 points, the least desirable, 1 point. Give yourself 4 points for "yes" responses and 1 point for "no" responses to items 4, 9, and 11. Give yourself 4 points for "no" responses and 1 point for "yes" responses to 1, 2, 3, 5, 6, 7, 8, 10, and 12.

A score ranging from 42 to 48 is above average to excellent and suggests a strong capacity for decision making. A score of 30 to 40 is average, while a score of 27 or lower is below average.

Source: Adapted from Walter Duckat, "Check Your Decisionmaking Skills," *Supervision* 41 (February 1979): 3. Reprinted by permission of *Supervision.* Copyright 1979 by The National Research Bureau, Inc., P.O. Box 1, Burlington, Iowa 52601.

CASE 7.1   WHO SHOULD DIE WHEN NOT ALL CAN LIVE?

You are among 30 survivors of a shipwreck crowded into a lifeboat designed for no more than two dozen adults. In the boat with you are two others from the ship's crew, three married couples (one with a baby), three children whose parents went down with the ship, three elderly men and women, six other women, and the rest men, three of whom were very severely injured during the wreck. Already many of the 30 are seasick and most are terrified. It is a dark night, and the weather continues to worsen. The boat is already shipping water at the gunwales; if the sea gets any rougher, the boat is sure to swamp and sink. It looks as if the only hope for any to survive is for five or six persons to get out of the boat, leaving the rest to bail and row in the hope that dawn will bring a slackening wind and chance of rescue.

As senior surviving ship's officer, and an experienced seaman, you are looked to for leadership. Having decided that the boat *must* lighten its human load, you ask for volunteers to jump overboard and take their chances in the icy waves. No one responds, even though all sense the danger to the overcrowded boat. You are not surprised at their response, and you quickly review the alternative methods of deciding who shall be the unlucky half dozen.

Voting or a contest of some sort, which might do well enough in another situation, you immediately discard as unworkable here. One method that occurs to you is drawing straws—that seems fair enough—except that it, too, may be infeasible in the situation. Then you think of a different sort of random selection process, such as designating every fifth person as an unlucky one. You also consider throwing out the last six people who got into the boat, whoever they turn out to be (*you* are not among them). The thought crosses your mind to calculate the utilities of all possible combinations of 24 survivors and throw overboard the six whose utility is the lowest, but this seems too time consuming and conjectural under the circumstances. Yet another thought suddenly occurs to you: Perhaps you and the other crewmen have a duty to the passengers to given them safe voyage, and so the three of you must be among the six to abandon the boat however the other three are determined! You are also tempted to dismiss all these vexing ethical considerations and simply grab the weakest and nearest to you and, with the help of other able-bodied men, throw them overboard as quickly as possible and get it over with. You do not have much time to weigh these alternative methods of decision making—perhaps no more than a few minutes, to judge by the waves and wind, before panic or disaster overtakes all of you.

Problem

What method of decision should you choose and why? Who goes overboard and who stays?

Source: This case was inspired by *United States v. Holmes,* Circuit Court, Eastern District of Pennsylvania, 1842, 26 Federal Cases 360, #15,383. Hill/*Making Decisions,* © 1978. Addison-Wesley, Reading, Mass., 207–208.

NOTES

[1] Herbert A. Simon, *The Shape of Automation for Men and Management* (New York: Harper & Row, 1965), 58–59.

[2] Quoted in Susan Caminiti, "How the Gap Keeps Ahead of the Pack," *Fortune,* February 12, 1990, 129.

[3] Gary Stibel quoted in "PepsiCo's Fast Track," *Business Month* 129 (June 1987): 50.

[4] Charles R. Day, Jr., "The Year's Gutsiest Decisions," *Industry Week,* February 23, 1987, 26.

[5] Herbert A. Simon, *Administrative Behavior: A Study of Decision-Making Processes in Administrative Organization,* 3d ed. (New York: Free Press, 1976).

[6] The following discussion draws on Terry Connolly, *Scientists, Engineers, and Organization* (Monterey, Calif.: Brooks-Cole, 1983), 22–24.

[7] Ibid., 23–24.

[8] Ronald N. Taylor, *Behavioral Decision Making* (Glenview, Ill.: Scott, Foresman, 1984), 139–141.

[9] Barry M. Staw and Jerry Ross, "Understanding Behavior in Escalation Situations," *Science* (October 13, 1989): 216–219.

[10] William F. Pounds, "The Process of Problem Finding," *Industrial Management Review* 11 (Fall 1969): 1–19.

[11] Quoted in Neesa Sweet, "John M. Richman: Chairman & CEO, Dart & Kraft, Inc.," *Sky* 14 (October 1985): 64.

[12] Francis F. Bradshaw quoted in Louis T. Rader, "Roadblocks to Progress in the Management Sciences and Operations Research," *Management Science* 11 (February 1965): C-2.

[13] Adapted from Larry D. Alexander, "Successfully Implementing Strategic Decisions," *Long Range Planning* 18 (June 1985): 96–97.

[14] Alexander F. Osborn, *Applied Imagination: Principles and Procedures for Creative Problem-Solving,* 3d ed. (New York: Scribner, 1963).

[15] André L. Delbecq and Andrew H. Van de Ven, "A Group Process Model for Problem Identification and Program Planning," *Journal of Applied Behavioral Science* 7 (1971): 466–492; and André L. Delbecq, Andrew H. Van de Ven, and David H. Gustafson, *Group Decision Making Techniques in Program Planning* (Glenview, Ill.: Scott, Foresman, 1974).

[16] Norman Dalkey and Olaf Helmer, "An Experimental Application of the Delphi Method to the Use of Experts," *Management Science* 9 (April 1963), 458–467; Olaf Helmer, *Social Technology* (New York: Basic Books, 1966); and Olaf Helmer, *Looking Forward: A Guide to Future Research* (Beverly Hills, Calif.: Sage, 1983).

[17] Quoted in *The Macmillan Book of Business and Economic Quotations,* ed. Michael Jackman (New York: Macmillan, 1984), 127.

[18] Hans A. Illing, "C.G. Jung on the Present Trends in Group Psychotherapy," *Human Relations* 10 (February 1957): 80.

[19] Irving L. Janis, *Victims of Groupthink: A Psychological Study of Foreign-Policy Decisions and Fiascoes,* 2d ed. (Boston: Houghton-Mifflin, 1986), 9.

PART

THREE

ORGANIZING

CHAPTER 8

LEARNING OBJECTIVES

Upon completing this chapter, you should be able to:

■ Identify different forms of departmentalization.

■ Clarify what is meant by *chain of command*.

■ Define the term *unity of command*.

■ Explain the inverse relationship between span of control and number of management layers.

■ List the various factors that influence the appropriateness of a manager's span of control.

■ Discuss how technology influences organization design.

Within any large or medium-size organization, a parallel informal organization also operates. It consists of the alliances people form and the power each person has to influence others, and it is this organization that actually gets work done. Many business experts feel that the power of informal organizations will be tapped more effectively in companies of the future.

The *adaptive organization,* as the experts term it, will be able to change its structure easily to meet specific goals. Projects will be managed by teams whose members' expertise crosses traditional functional or departmental lines. A team may even include individuals from outside a company, perhaps someone from a supplier's engineering department or a customer's operations department.

This more flexible structure is designed to unleash the creative and innovative spirit lurking in employees and to improve responsiveness to suppliers and customers, as well as overall efficiency. It is also intended to give employees more job satisfaction and reduce the need for managers to supervise many details of a company's operations.

ORGANIZATION DESIGN

Whenever a company's structure changes, its employees must make an extra effort to adjust; thus, it is expected that managers in an adaptive organization will spend much of their time helping others deal with changes and smoothing out new work relationships. They will spend more time acting as cheerleaders and hand-holders and less time setting task parameters. And because the traditional ladder to top management will have fewer rungs, some incentives must be provided to convince employees to move laterally.

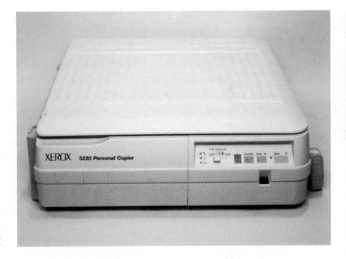

Will it work? Nobody knows how far this approach can go, but many companies are heading in that direction now. Take the case of Xerox. A few years ago, as part of its goal of focusing on customer satisfaction, Xerox prided itself on shipping copiers to its customers faster than the competition. Yet customer satisfaction wasn't as high as Xerox's managers would have liked. They discovered that customers didn't really care how fast their copiers were delivered, but they did want to know when the machines would arrive and be installed, and they wanted the copiers to be operational. Xerox discovered that it had no way of providing this assurance.

CEO Paul Allaire assigned an experienced middle manager to the problem, and the manager chose team members from a number of different departments. They worked together to develop and implement a tracking system that follows each copier through distribution and generates the correct paperwork. Customer satisfaction rose from 70 percent to 90 percent.

Although the adaptive organization may be the structure of the future for some companies, an already developed structure may prove right for others. In this chapter, we will discuss how companies can develop the structure that is right for them.

Source: Brian Dumaine, "The Bureaucracy Busters," *Fortune,* June 17, 1991, 36–50.

It has long been recognized that a single organization structure cannot be effective in all situations. Because no two organizations have the same people or resources, a structure suitable to one organization may well prove ineffective in another. One structure will not fit all.

Moreover, organizations must continually adapt to meet competition in this country and abroad. Consequently, their structures must be modified periodically. Management expert Tom Peters estimates that a full 50 percent of organization problems come from inappropriate organization structure.[1]

The importance of proper structure in achieving organization goals cannot be overestimated. It has been said that during the 1990s, a kind of structural Darwinism will be taking place in U.S. industry.[2] Organizations that do not fine-tune their structures to meet the onslaught of global competition will face extinction. Sound structure is a prerequisite for organization effectiveness.

As defined in Chapter 1, organizing is the process of dividing work among groups and individuals and coordinating their activities to accomplish goals. As a result of organizing, activities are segmented or departmentalized, and connections are established within and among departments according to some logical pattern. It is this patterning that is known as **organization structure.** The creation or modification of an organization's structure is called **organization design.**

The present chapter begins by discussing various organization design alternatives, highlighting their relative advantages and disadvantages. After explaining what is meant by *chain of command* and *unity of command,* it then considers a fundamental question that must be addressed by all organizations: "How many employees can effectively report *directly* to a single manager?" As we shall see, the answer is related to the number of layers of management between an organization's chief executive and first-line supervisors. Finally, this chapter explores the influence of technology on organization design.

Organization structure.
Segmented or departmentalized activities and connections established within and among departments according to some logical pattern.

Organization design.
The creation or modification of an organization's structure.

DESIGN ALTERNATIVES

Whatever an organization's goals, its structure should facilitate the most effective and efficient use of available resources. Because adaptation is a key to competitive survival, the "right" structure for an organization is determined by numerous factors. For this reason, selecting an organization structure might best be described as an evolutionary, trial-and-error process. For example, in its earliest days, Digital Equipment Corporation had little structure at all; engineers were free to create and run their own programs. Later, Digital organized around its major computer lines, with a top manager in charge of each product as though it were a separate business. Today, Digital is organized with top managers in charge of major functions like engineering, marketing, accounting, and so on. Such tinkering has proven phenomenally successful, placing Digital among the world's most competitive organizations.

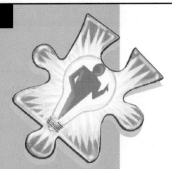

SMART MANAGEMENT ORGANIZATION CHARTS: A PRIMER

An **organization chart** is simply a diagram of all the positions in an organization and their formal relationships to one another. The immediate value of organization charts is that they illustrate an organization's overall shape or configuration in a readily comprehensible manner. As indicated in Figure 8.1, an organization chart shows:

1. The hierarchical structure that is typical of most organizations
2. The number of management layers
3. Degrees of authority, status, and compensation (indicated by a position's location in relation to other positions)
4. How an organization's activities are departmentalized (for example, by function, by product, by territory, and so on)
5. The work being done in each position (indicated by the labels in the boxes)
6. Interaction of equals (indicated by the horizontal connecting lines)
7. Relations between superiors and subordinates—who reports to whom (that is, the chain of command)
8. How many subordinates report *directly* to each manager (that is, the span of control)
9. Career pathways—routes to the top
10. Formal channels of communication (indicated by the connecting lines)

An organization chart does not show:

1. The ongoing dynamics of workplace behavior—organization charts are static
2. Interactions between people who have no official reporting relationship (that is, the *informal organization*)
3. Personal preferences and coalitions
4. Informal communication channels (that is, the *grapevine*)
5. Interference by outsiders

Although the range of possible organization design alternatives is vast, there are only six primary approaches to organizing: functional, product, territorial, customer, matrix, and network. These are conventionally referred to as bases or forms of *departmentalization*. The relative advantages and disadvantages of each must be considered closely before the design best suited for achieving an organization's goals can be selected. Most often, these six are adapted to fit the specific character and needs of an organization.

FUNCTIONAL DEPARTMENTALIZATION

Functional departmentalization was developed at the turn of this century in response to the increasing size and complexity of business undertakings. A functionally structured organization groups its activities into separate units or departments, each of which undertakes a distinctive function—production/operations, marketing, finance/accounting, engineering, and so on. Figure 8.1 presents a view of how these functional departments could be grouped. Functional departmentalization is the most common approach to organizing, with adherents ranging from Ford Motor Co. to small, independently owned businesses.

Organization chart.
A diagram of all the positions in an organization and their formal relationships to one another.

Functional departmentalization.
A method for organizing activities into separate units or departments, each of which undertakes a distinctive function—production/operations, marketing, finance/accounting, engineering, and so on.

FIGURE 8.1   FUNCTIONAL DEPARTMENTALIZATION

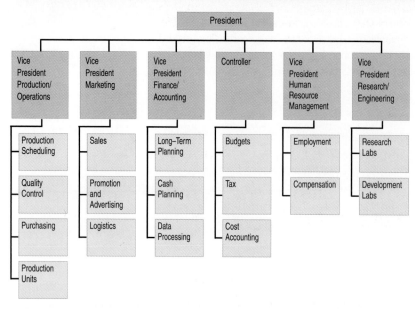

Advantages

Emphasizes individual specialized functions within units
Results in efficient use of resources
Provides simple communication and decision network
Facilitates measurement of functional output and
  results
Simplifies training of functional specialists
Gives status to major functional areas
Preserves strategic control at top
  management level

Disadvantages

Makes coordination among functional areas more difficult
Fosters parochial emphasis on department goals
Can significantly increase coordination costs among
  departments
Makes change difficult because employees identify with
  specialist groups
Limits preparation of broadly trained managers
Encourages interdepartmental rivalry and conflict
May lower client satisfaction

As might be expected, the principal strength of functional departmentalization is its emphasis on individual functions within specialized units. With organization growth, there is a multiplication of employees performing the same function and an ever-increasing refinement of specialized skills. The result is a gain in economies of scale and overhead resulting from the combination of otherwise underutilized, scattered, and duplicated facilities and personnel into one functional department. For instance, once all engineers are organized into a central engineering department, it is possible to more efficiently use their skills. Functional departmentalization is particularly effective when an organization mass produces standardized items, such as washers, ovens, refrigerators, and televisions, to sell from on-hand stock. Among other advantages, it:

- Provides a simple communication and decision network.
- Facilitates measurement of functional outputs and results.
- Simplifies training of functional specialists.
- Gives status to major functional areas.
- Preserves strategic control at the top management level.

The major shortcoming of functional departmentalization is that the larger the number of departments, the more difficult it becomes to coordinate among specialties. Under such circumstances, interdepartmental cooperation may fail. This problem in turn fosters a narrow emphasis on department objectives and decreased emphasis on broader organization goals. A classic example is General Motors's finance department, whose decisions led to Cadillacs that looked like Pontiacs that looked like Chevrolets. The finance department got what it wanted—cars that were cheaper to build—but marketing could not sell them.

Other disadvantages of functional departmentalization include:

- Cost of coordination among departments can be high.
- Employee identification with specialist groups makes change difficult.
- Preparation of broadly trained managers is limited.
- Interdepartmental rivalry and conflict are encouraged.
- Client satisfaction with service can be lower than that obtained with other methods of departmentalization.

PRODUCT DEPARTMENTALIZATION

As an organization grows and functional departments become larger and more unwieldy, making coordination a problem, **product departmentalization** often becomes necessary. Organizing activities along product lines was pioneered by E. I. du Pont de Nemours & Company and General Motors in the 1920s. As both companies grew, they encountered two major structural problems: their size hampered them from quickly responding to their competition, and they found it more and more difficult to efficiently coordinate an increasing number of specialized skills. Their response was to reorganize their departments by product rather than function.

With product departmentalization, each major product line is administered through a separate and semiautonomous division. Each division operates as a minicompany,

Product departmentalization. A method of organizing activities into separate units or departments according to product line.

Apple Computer is organized along product lines in order to get new products to market quickly and maintain market leadership. QuickTime, pictured here, is a new Apple product that will allow any Macintosh with a color monitor to become a vehicle to adding sound, video, and animation to documents. QuickTime and other Apple products of this type have wide potential for use in education and entertainment.

with its own departments for production, marketing, finance, and so on. The result is a structure that is responsive to competition and that efficiently coordinates an increasing number of specialized skills. To this end, specialists of different types are grouped together to perform all the duties necessary to produce an individual good or service. For example, 3M (which sells over 60,000 products) is organized into four autonomous product divisions: Industrial and Electronic, Information and Imaging Technologies, Life Sciences, and Commercial and Consumer. Each does its own research and development, production, and marketing. A majority of the world's largest corporations are structured according to product departmentalization. Examples include Quaker Oats, Kimberly-Clark, RCA, Du Pont, and Westinghouse Electric. An organization chart for an insurance firm organized along product lines is shown in Figure 8.2.

As Figure 8.2 indicates, each separate division (for example, life insurance, health insurance, and so forth) in a firm departmentalized by product is a replica of an individual, functionally structured organization. A major difference between product and functional departmentalization is in how each division can be assessed. In a functional structure, divisions can be assessed either as an **expense center,** whose criterion of control is service provided, or as a **revenue center,** whose criterion of control is revenue generated. By contrast, in a product firm, divisions can be evaluated as **profit centers** since they have identifiable cash flows comprised of both revenues and expenses. Moreover, product departmentalization is better able to accommodate growth than its functional counterpart. New de-

Expense center.
A unit whose criterion of control is service provided.

Revenue center.
A unit whose criterion of control is revenue generated.

Profit center.
A unit whose criterion of control is net profit.

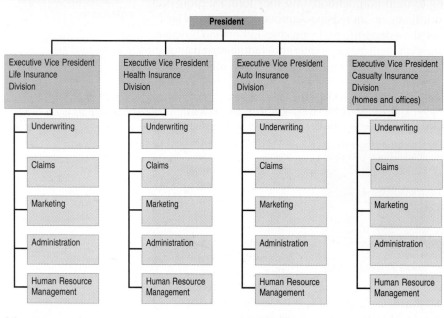

FIGURE 8.2   PRODUCT DEPARTMENTALIZATION

Advantages
Evaluates departments as autonomous profit centers
Accommodates growth
Facilitates coordination among functions for rapid response
Adds flexibility to an organization's structure
Focuses on client need
Develops broadly trained managers

Disadvantages
Increases coordination problems among specialized product areas
Leads to decreased communication among functional specialists
Contributes to a duplication of services in each division
Fosters parochial emphasis on product objectives

partments can be added on a self-contained basis having a similar relationship to headquarters as do existing departments.

Additional benefits of product departmentalization are:

- It facilitates coordination between functions for rapid response.
- It focuses on client needs and thus leads to greater customer service and satisfaction.
- It develops broadly trained managers.

The major disadvantages associated with product departmentalization stem from maintaining coordination across product areas. In particular, decreased communication between product departments can be a problem. Consider Campbell Soup Co. Its products include not only soups, but such household names as Swanson frozen foods and Pepperidge Farm baked goods. In the 1980s, managers in these product departments seldom communicated. Interdepartmental coordination became so poor that the soup company ran a promotion with Nabisco crackers even though Pepperidge Farm made a competing product.

Other coordination problems can result from unclearly delineated responsibilities. In such situations, departments may even find that they are unwittingly competing with each other. Although this may spur innovation and aggressiveness, it can lead to confused customers. Hewlett-Packard, for instance, at one time had at least three autonomous departments marketing different—and incompatible—computers aimed at the same customers. The fact that the products were being sold competitively against one another led to marketing confusion and costly duplication. The managers involved were making decisions in the best interests of their individual products, but this clearly did not coincide with what was best for Hewlett-Packard.

TERRITORIAL DEPARTMENTALIZATION

Also known as *geographic, area,* or *regional departmentalization,* **territorial departmentalization** is especially appropriate for large organizations whose activities are physically dispersed. Territorial departmentalization organizes activities based on geographic location. Boundaries are determined by distance, natural, legal, political, and cultural considerations. Its principal advantages are that it allows units operating in different regions to better sense changes in market needs and thus provide specialized local services; encourages logistic efficiency, locating units according to regional resource sources or markets and so obtaining reduced transportation, communication, and storage costs; and lessens exchange rate risks, political risks, risks of supply interruption, and other risks that result from performing all activities in one location. Government regulations can also be a powerful reason for dispersing activities. Tariffs, tax credits, surcharges, and the like, as well as nationalistic purchasing requirements, can encourage or discourage investment in overseas markets. For these reasons, territorial departmentalization is particularly popular not only among organizations that are geographically dispersed within a country, but also among those that operate in several countries with different legal, political, or cultural environments. A classic illustration would be Coca-Cola, which operates in more than 160 nations. The sun never sets on its empire. The Coke logo appears at bullfights in Spain, camel races in Australia, and sheep-shearing contests in New Zealand. In South Korea, baseball fans have a Coke

Territorial departmentalization.
A method for organizing activities according to geographic location.

and a squid. As a further example, consider McDonald's. In Brazil, McDonald's serves a soft drink made from guaraná, an Amazonian berry. In Malaysia, Singapore, and Thailand, it serves milk shakes flavored with durian, a foul-smelling (to non-Asian noses) Southeast Asian fruit. In Japan, you can order a Teriyaki McBurger. Both Coca-Cola and McDonald's have semiautonomous territorial offices to meet market needs, as well as encourage logistic efficiency.

Achieving coordination among local units can be a formidable challenge, especially for organizations operating in several nations. Orchestrating the efforts of local units on a global level is often complicated by language and cultural differences. Another difficulty is aligning the interests of local units with those of an organization as a whole. This can be especially tricky if the governments of the different countries in which an organization operates have, for instance, a trade dispute. Digital Equipment faced such a challenge when the United States fought Brazil's policy of limiting imports of American computer products and refused to recognize foreign technology rights. Digital, which manufactures in both the

FIGURE 8.3 TERRITORIAL DEPARTMENTALIZATION

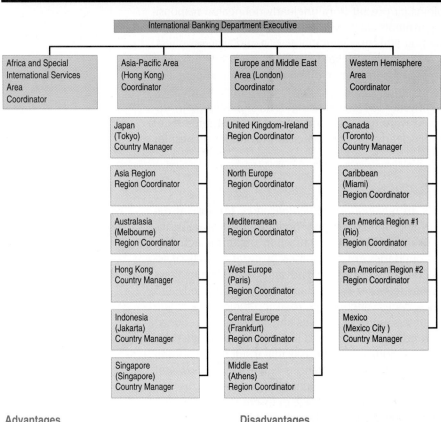

Advantages

Allows units to adapt to local circumstances
Takes advantage of local legal, political, and cultural
  differences
Encourages logistic efficiency
Lessens risk of performing all activities in one location
Provides territories as a training ground for general managers

Disadvantages

Requires a large number of general managers
Leads to possible duplication of staff services
Hinders top management's control of local operations
May create conflict between local unit and overall
  organization interests

United States and Brazil, had to negotiate a settlement that guaranteed it continued access to Brazil's markets while satisfying U.S. government concerns. Thus, despite some anxious moments, Digital was able to align the interests of its local Brazilian manufacturing units with those of the corporation as a whole.

Organizations that are territorially departmentalized within the United States include the Federal Reserve Board, Internal Revenue Service, and the U.S. Postal Service. Massey-Ferguson, Singer, NEC, ITT, Matsushita, and Unilever are among numerous international companies that are territorially departmentalized. An organization chart for the International Banking Department of a commercial lending bank is shown in Figure 8.3.

CLOSE UP: INTERNATIONAL MANAGEMENT   THINKING GLOBALLY, ACTING LOCALLY: BULL'S 10-STEP GUIDE TO GLOBAL SUCCESS

Success in today's merciless global business climate requires nothing less than a global perspective. Parochial attitudes have to go. In a global company, competing alternatives will exist about where to market a product, where to obtain the resources for it, and how to design it. Only those management teams that see the world as a global business can make decisions in a company's best interest. This requires both the understanding that good ideas can happen anywhere in the world and the ability to find and develop them quickly. Bull HN Information Systems, Inc., the North American arm of France's Groupe Bull, believes that structuring its company with the following characteristics as guidelines is critical to its success in the 1990s—and beyond.

1. *View the world as one market.* Regard boundaries as low—or nonexistent. Develop products for the world. Decentralize profit centers.

2. *Pool your resources.* Regard worldwide resources, including human resources, as one. Bring research and development together from around the globe. Manufacture where it gives you an advantage. Sell worldwide.

3. *Flatten organization structures.* Encourage innovation and information sharing. Create multidisciplinary teams that mix cultures as well as skills.

4. *Empower local management.* Give them decision-making authority, enabling them to respond quickly to local customers' needs.

5. *Recruit internationally.* Open senior ranks to foreign employees. Make the board of directors as international as possible.

6. *Use communications to change attitudes.* Bring people together. Hold regular international meetings so that ideas and perspectives can be shared.

7. *Become culturally sensitive.* Speak the language of your customers.

8. *Form strategic partnerships.* In markets you can't penetrate alone, ally yourself with local distribution and sales channels and technical-development firms.

9. *Think in 5-, 10-, and 20-year time frames.* Be prepared to accept projects with low returns on equity with a view to longer term competitive gains.

10. *Know who you are.* Prepare a clear mission statement—and distribute it internally and externally.

Source: Adapted from John S. McClenahen, "Not Fun in the Sun," *Industry Week* (October 15, 1990): 22–24. Reprinted with permission from *Industry Week*. Copyright, Penton Publishing, Inc., Cleveland, Ohio.

CUSTOMER DEPARTMENTALIZATION

A fourth popular approach for organizing activities is **customer departmentalization.** This approach is often selected when an organization's clients have very different needs, and the organization seeks to cater to their specific requirements. Commercial banks, for instance, have different departments for various types of customers—airlines, manufacturing companies, stockbrokers, consumers, and so on. A university, to cite another example, may offer on-campus and extension courses, day and night classes, and undergraduate and graduate classes, all designed to meet the specific needs of the various customers it hopes to serve. Departmentalization by customer (retail, government, and industrial) is shown in Figure 8.4.

While customer departmentalization facilitates responsiveness to customer needs, it is not without disadvantages. Given the diverse nature of the client groups served, establishing consistent and uniform company-wide practices is quite difficult. As a consequence, pressure often develops for special treatment of various buyers. Such preferential consideration may not be merited. An additional drawback emerges when customer groups develop at an unequal pace. During periods of recession, for example, banks may find that the number of new construction loans to be processed is so low that maintaining a staff for a separate department to serve that segment is uneconomical. However, during expansion, that same segment may grow at such a rapid pace that managing staffing and arranging facilities to meet the demand become a problem. Either instance will likely result in the underutilization of facilities and personnel.

Customer departmentalization. A method for organizing activities according to customer needs.

FIGURE 8.4 CUSTOMER DEPARTMENTALIZATION

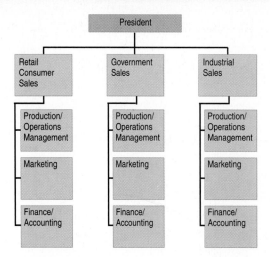

Advantages
Increases responsiveness to customer needs
Ties performance to requirements of key market segments

Disadvantages
Hinders establishment of uniform companywide practices
Increases pressure for special treatment of various buyers
May cause customer groups to develop at unequal paces, leading to underutilization of resources

MATRIX DEPARTMENTALIZATION

A fifth approach for organizing that has received serious attention in the past few years is **matrix departmentalization.** This approach was developed by TRW Inc. cofounder Simon Ramo when available forms of departmentalization proved inadequate for managing complex technological developments in the aerospace industry and in rapidly emerging joint military-industrial ventures. Such undertakings as the Atlas, Titan, Thor, and Minuteman defense missile projects were so complex that it was impossible to make a single manager responsible for their execution. It became necessary not only to coordinate large numbers of people, materials, and facilities internally, but also to coordinate these activities with those of outside contractors. Managers had to figure out how to coordinate such diverse activities as research, engineering, testing, and production over an extended period in a cost-beneficial manner. To complicate matters further, technological developments cut across standard functional boundaries. What was needed was a structure for blending the technical know-how of different disciplines. Available alternatives for organizing could not accomplish the required undertaking. The structure that resulted to meet this need was matrix departmentalization.

This approach for organizing activities attempts to cross product departmentalization with functional departmentalization to get the best (and avoid the worst) of each. The distinguishing feature of matrix departmentalization is that functional and product or project lines of authority are overlaid to form a grid, or matrix. As a consequence, many employees belong to two groups simultaneously, a functional or specialist group, and a product or project group. They report to two or more superiors—a permanent boss in a functional department and one or more temporary bosses (called *project managers*) who direct various projects. This arrangement eliminates duplication of overhead costs since basic activities, such as engineering, purchasing, and human resource management, are provided by an organization's

Matrix departmentalization. A method for organizing activities that crosses product departmentalization with functional departmentalization.

The Aerospace Corporation is a private, nonprofit company that provides engineering and support services for United States military launch and space systems. Defense-related organizations such as Aerospace frequently employ matrix departmentalization to transfer the experience of highly specialized technical personnel from one project to another. In this picture, Aerospace employees Wanda Austin, Lorraine Urquhart, Rob Tang, and Brian Kimsey discuss design details of the Defense Satellite Communications System with Major Mark Fechtel of the U.S. Air Force.

▼

customary functional departments. Employees report to project managers regarding project objectives and to their respective functional managers regarding technical-specialist objectives. Thus, project managers and functional managers have separate but complementary responsibilities. Functional managers are responsible for developing and deploying, in the form of skilled personnel, a technical resource. Project managers are responsible for project completion.

A typical matrix structure is illustrated in Figure 8.5. As indicated, Universal Aerospace Company (a hypothetical organization) is divided into functional departments (such as research and development, engineering, and production), as well as project groups based on unique product needs. Note how the authority of project managers runs horizontally, while the authority of functional managers runs vertically. Consequently, an engineer, for example, may report to several bosses at the same time. For Project Manager A, she might be charged with designing navigation systems. For Project Manager B, she might be responsible for testing the strength of component parts. All the while, as a member of the engineering department, she would continue reporting to the manager of that department.

FIGURE 8.5 MATRIX DEPARTMENTALIZATION: UNIVERSAL AEROSPACE COMPANY

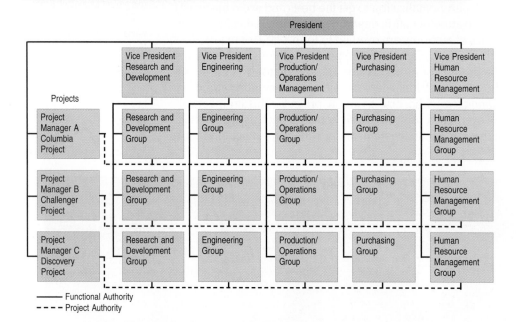

——— Functional Authority
– – – Project Authority

Advantages

Adapts to fluctuating work loads
Contributes to a high rate of innovation
Makes it possible to respond to several market segments simultaneously
Establishes one person as focal point for all matters pertaining to an individual project
Permits maximum use of limited pool of functional specialists
Makes specialized functional assistance equally available to all projects
Provides a home base for functional specialists between projects
Provides excellent training for running a diversified organization

Disadvantages

Places a premium on teamwork
Leads to interpersonal and command conflict with existence of two separate operating systems
Creates power struggles among project managers and functional area heads
Slows down decision making
Promotes a narrow viewpoint

While matrix departmentalization was once thought to be applicable only to high-technology undertakings, it has been adopted by health care agencies, electronics firms, construction companies, banks, and a variety of other profit and not-for-profit organizations. Its users include General Electric, ITT, NCR, Lockheed Aircraft, Johnson Wax, Shell Oil, Monsanto Chemical, and Equitable Life Insurance.

Matrix departmentalization is an especially flexible and responsive approach to grouping activities. It is particularly suited to fluctuating work loads and has the advantage of allowing an organization to respond simultaneously to various market segments that may be critical for its success. As projects are completed, they are simply disbanded, and project members return to their respective functional departments for reassignment.

An additional advantage of matrix departmentalization is that the interdisciplinary nature of project teams contributes to a high rate of new product innovation.[3] If project teams are able to maintain autonomy while retaining access to the functional resources of a larger organization, they can incorporate the behavioral and structural advantages of a small firm with all the benefits of big firm support. Moreover, it is not uncommon for project leaders to become "product champions," acting as entrepreneurs, to confront and reduce obstacles in the way of a project's success.

Other benefits associated with matrix departmentalization are:

- It establishes one person (a project manager) as focal point for all matters pertaining to an individual project.
- It makes possible the maximum use of a limited pool of functional specialists.
- It makes specialized functional assistance equally available to all projects.
- It provides a home base for functional specialists as ongoing projects are completed.
- Successful experience in operating under a matrix provides a manager with excellent training for running a diversified organization in which complex and conflicting interests must be balanced.

Although matrix departmentalization offers many advantages, it also has drawbacks. Chief among these is that the existence of two separate operating systems (project-oriented control flowing horizontally, and functionally oriented control flowing vertically) within a single organization introduces the serious possibility of command conflict, particularly where authority intersects. While in theory, matrix departmentalization calls for the appointment of a project manager to act as a central coordinator for all work related to a specific project, in reality, the authority of project managers often amounts to little more than mere persuasiveness. The potential detrimental effects of such a situation are understandably great. Experience suggests it is most efficient (and less stressful) for employees to report to only one superior. This principle is referred to as *unity of command* and will be discussed later in this chapter.

While matrix advocates admit that difficulties can arise from such a conflict-prone structure, they argue that in truly complex undertakings, unity of command is impractical. Despite their disclaimer, however, a detailed study of organizations using matrix departmentalization found that the matrix form of dual command is more vulnerable not only to anarchy, but also to "pathologies" such as power struggles, indecision, and "groupitis."[4] In particular, the study reported that matrix departmentalization promotes a narrow viewpoint associated with a specific project and a failure to adopt company-wide objectives. Because of such difficulties, companies like Dow Chemical and Citibank, once leading adherents of matrix departmentalization, have abandoned it.

Obviously, matrix departmentalization should not be adopted indiscriminately. It is generally recommended that it be considered only in the following situations[5]:

1. When complex, short-run products are an organization's principal output.
2. When a complicated product design calls for both innovation and timely completion.
3. When several kinds of sophisticated skills are needed in designing, building, and testing a product—skills that need constant updating and development.
4. When a rapidly changing marketplace calls for significant changes in products, perhaps even between the time they are conceived and the time they are delivered.

NETWORK DEPARTMENTALIZATION

The emergence of the so-called **network departmentalization** is the newest approach to departmentalization.[6] Like its predecessors, it is another in a series of responses to changing market conditions. In management jargon, organizations designed according to this approach are "vertically disaggregated," meaning that they temporarily tie together the resources required to achieve specific tasks. In doing so, they serve as assemblers and distributors for components or entire products made by other organizations.

A typical organization designed according to a network structure maintains a small central headquarters and contracts with other organizations to perform manufacturing, distribution, marketing, and other services needed for sales. Take Lewis Galoob Toys, Inc., as an example. It is hardly a corporation at all. Indeed, it has been called a "hollow corporation." Just 100 employees run the entire show. Galoob's products are designed and engineered by outside specialists based on ideas submitted by independent investors and entertainment companies. Product manufacturing and packaging is done by a dozen contractors in Hong Kong who subcontract work to factories in China. Product distribution is handled by commissioned manufacturers's representatives. Rather than collect its own accounts, Galoob sells its receivables to Commercial Credit Corp. The Galoob "network" is connected to its central headquarters electronically, with all coordination taking place via phones, facsimile machines, and telexes.

An illustration of a hypothetical network structure is shown in Figure 8.6. An increasing number of organizations, such as Nike, Esprit, Liz Claiborne, Schwinn Bicycle, and Ocean Pacific Sunwear, are similarly structured. Each contracts outside for the complementary services needed to create its products. In doing so, they employ modern communication technology to coordinate suppliers and customers around the world.

The primary advantage of network structures is that they are flexible, able to adapt quickly to new markets and new technologies. With no need to invest in fixed assets, they need less capital than would otherwise be necessary. Likewise, overhead expenses are generally less because network structures do not support multi-

Network departmentalization. A method for organizing that temporarily ties together resources required to achieve specific tasks.

FIGURE 8.6   NETWORK DEPARTMENTALIZATION

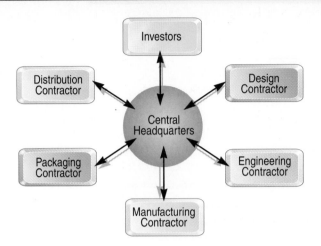

Advantages
Adapts quickly to new markets and technologies
Requires less capital
Has lower overhead expenses
Uses lowest cost labor

Disadvantages
Results in less control over operations
Allows contractors to become rivals
Allows contractors to become unreliable
Results in lack of product security

ple management layers or large staff units. Finally, rather than having to maintain a standing work force, they are able to search worldwide for the lowest cost.

By their very nature, however, network structures have less control over operations. As a consequence, even slight misunderstandings can result in product misspecifications. A second disadvantage is that organizations designed as networks are particularly vulnerable to competition from their manufacturing contractors. Seiko Instruments & Electronics, which originally made only computer display terminals for Tektronix, now markets its own comparable, lower priced model. A further disadvantage relates to the reliability of contractors. If a contractor fails to deliver or goes out of business, an entire network could fail. Finally, it is especially difficult, if not impossible, to closely guard innovations that are developed, designed, and manufactured by multiple contractors that may be located thousands of miles from a central headquarters.

MIXED DEPARTMENTALIZATION

Organizations designed according to any of the approaches we have reviewed may also contain subgroupings based on other forms of departmentalization. In larger organizations, such mixed departmentalization is quite common. For example, although General Motors is organized primarily along product lines—Buick, Oldsmobile, Cadillac; Chevrolet, Pontiac, General Motors-Canada; and truck and bus—within each division, departments are structured functionally: production, distribution, finance, and so on. Further, within functional areas, such as distribution, departments are structured according to geographic regions. This example is depicted in Figure 8.7. Mixed departmentalization typically is used to combine the advantages and minimize the disadvantages of contrasting design alternatives. This

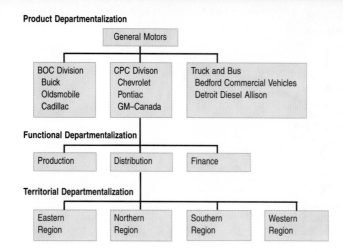

FIGURE 8.7   MIXED DEPARTMENTALIZATION

further highlights the fact that no single organization design is ideal for all situations. Managers often are confronted with the need to mix design alternatives to accommodate situational requirements.

CHAIN OF COMMAND

With an organization's various activities divided among departments, coordination becomes necessary for integrating individual and work group efforts so as to efficiently achieve overall goals. Such coordination is most commonly achieved through a systematic ordering of positions and duties that defines a managerial hierarchy. This ordering is commonly termed a *scalar chain* (to use Fayol's term) or, even more frequently, a **chain of command.**

Since ancient times, it has been recognized that the only way to structure unified working systems involving hundreds, thousands, and even tens of thousands of employees is through a chain of command. The resulting pyramidal form is found in every nation and in every company, union, and club that exceeds a certain minimal size.[7] A chain of command exists whenever one individual is made subordinate to another. Figure 8.8 depicts the chain of command in a hypothetical manufacturing company.

In addition to defining different degrees of authority, and thus individual discretion, a chain of command routes directives and other information up and down the levels within an organization. Moreover, a chain of command is a basis for compensation, as well as status. Further, the various links comprising a chain of command tend to define career pathways within an organization, from lower to higher positions. To the extent that upward mobility is possible, the promise of "promotion" up a chain of command is a primary inducement for high performance.

At the same time, the pyramidal hierarchy that results from making some managers senior to others does have inherent drawbacks, especially when the top is relatively far from the base. Pyramids emphasize power, promote insecurity, hobble interaction, and, as we'll discuss in a moment, distort communications. Despite these drawbacks, pyramids have nevertheless persisted, being the only way to co-

Chain of command.

A systematic ordering of positions and duties that define a managerial hierachy.

FIGURE 8.8   A CHAIN OF COMMAND

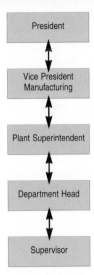

ordinate the efforts of large numbers of people and to hold them accountable for performing assigned work.

Actual chains of command vary widely. General Motors has 22 layers between its chief executive office and plan floor. Ford Motor Co. has 17, General Electric five, Toyota four, and Apple Computer three.

UNITY OF COMMAND

Implicit in the chain of command is a basic feature of organizing: one subordinate, one boss. If the efforts of subordinates are to be coordinated, it seems necessary that they be subject to the direct command of only one superior. In this respect, **unity of command** supplements an organization's chain of command by clarifying areas of responsibility and establishing exactly who reports to whom. Thus, there should be no question about who is responsible for different organization activities, or who gives orders and who carries them out. The truth of the matter is, however, unity of command is violated in varying degrees in almost every organization. For instance, nurses often receive orders from their nurse supervisors, as well as physicians. As noted earlier, it has been especially undermined by the emergence of matrix departmentalization.

Unity of command.
The notion that no subordinate should report to more than one superior.

SPAN OF CONTROL

Whereas chain of command and unity of command relate to the vertical structure of an organization, **span of control** relates to its horizontal structure. Just as a growing organization will ultimately reach a point at which it is impossible for one person to handle all the work, there is a limit to the number of subordinates that a manager can effectively supervise. The actual number of subordinates that report *directly* to a manager is termed *span of control*.

Span of control.
The actual number of subordinates that report *directly* to a manager.

SPANS AND LAYERS

An inverse relationship generally exists between span of control and number of management layers in an organization. That is, if an organization has *wide* spans, it will be *flat,* with few layers of management. Conversely, if an organization has *narrow* spans, it will be *tall,* with many management layers. This inverse relationship is shown in Figure 8.9. Both Company A and B have 64 operative employees. In Company A, each supervisor's span of control covers four subordinates, and four department heads report to the president. Further, there are a total of 21 managers, arranged in three management layers. In contrast, in Company B, each of the eight supervisors exercises control over eight subordinates, within two management layers. In this case, by increasing the span of control from four to eight, one layer of management is eliminated, thereby reducing the total number of managers from 21 to nine. Seldom, of course, are spans uniform throughout an organization or are management layers uniform for each department. Nevertheless, despite differences, there is a basic inverse relationship between spans and layers.

COMMUNICATION

The impact of increased spans and fewer layers of management is generally noticeable in several ways. First, the distance between the top and bottom of an organization affects communication. Experience shows that the greater the number of management layers a message must pass through, the longer it will take to reach its destination and the less likely it is to be accurate. In effect, successive layers of management often act as communication filters that distort the transmission of information. The fatal launch of the space shuttle *Challenger* is at least partially attributed to a chain of command in which the flow of information up and down was as flawed as the synthetic rubber O-rings that were supposed to seal the joints between the stacked sections of its booster rockets.

FIGURE 8.9   SPANS OF CONTROL

Company A: Tall structure caused by narrow spans of control for 64 operative employees
(Spans of control: 4; Management layers: 3)

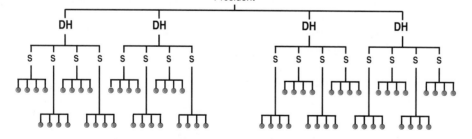

Company B: Flat structure caused by wide spans of control for 64 operative employees
(Spans of control: 8; Management layers: 2)

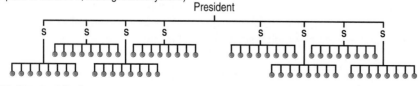

DH = Department Head
S   = Supervisor

It is often suggested that the best way to free up internal communication is to get rid of excessive management layers. This remedy, however, also has its drawbacks. By eliminating management layers, an organization generally is forced to increase its spans, thereby making superior-subordinate communication more difficult at remaining layers. In such situations, if spans become too broad, communications will ultimately break down as a consequence of managers not having enough "air time" to talk with their subordinates.

MANAGERIAL CONTROL

The distance between the top and bottom of an organization also affects control. It is often assumed that the narrower the span, the tighter the managerial control, and the wider the span, the looser the managerial control. This assumption, however, is only partially correct. Although narrow spans typically allow managers to exercise tighter control over subordinates, they loosen overall control by increasing the number of management layers, and thereby extending the distance from the top to the bottom of an organization. Conversely, while decreasing management layers reduces the distance between the top and bottom of an organization, the resulting increase in spans lessens control at each layer.

DOWNSIZING AND SALARY SAVINGS

For the most part, management experts predict that future organizations will have wider spans and looser overall managerial control, with fewer layers of management between top and bottom. This prediction is based on a continuation of a trend that has seen millions of managerial jobs "surplused" in the downsizing of once-mighty corporate giants. IBM alone has eliminated 40,000 jobs. Others paring down include Citicorp, General Motors, Sears, and Texas Instruments.

The result of increasing spans of control and reducing layers of management is payroll savings totaling hundreds of millions of dollars. Assuming an average manager's salary plus employee benefits is $60,000, the cost of the 11 additional managers in Figure 8.9's Company A is $660,000 a year. Mercury Marine, for example, eliminated one entire level of management, some 200 people, and saved $6 million a year.

Sears was among the first of many large organizations that initiated permanent downsizing in the late 1980s. Sometimes known as "right-sizing," downsizing is an effort to make organizations leaner and more flexible.

Employee Empowerment

A key element in the move to create flatter structures with fewer managers is **employee empowerment,** that is, greater authority for employees at lower levels. The aim is not only to eliminate costly managers, but to increase motivation and productivity by unleashing employee talent. As will be discussed in the following two chapters, empowering employees can have a major impact on an organization's ability to compete successfully.

Employee empowerment.
The pushing of authority down to lower organization levels.

THE DOWN SIDE

Unfortunately, downsizing is also likely to change how employees will be promoted and, thus, rewarded. With fewer rungs on the promotion ladder, there will be fewer opportunities for advancement. This can ultimately lead to a form of "career plateauing" known as **career gridlock**—a problem created by an organization's structure that leaves little chance for employees to move up. With more people chasing higher level positions than there are rungs on the shrunken career ladders, promotions will be slower (and pay raises less frequent) as employees spend more time at lower rungs. More lateral career opportunities, which are not designed around promotions and salary increases but nevertheless enable employees to grow, will be needed. This will require redefining what is meant by a successful career, as well as different kinds of rewards and recognitions.

Career gridlock.
A problem created by an organization's structure that leaves little chance for employees to move up.

With fewer promotions to offer as a result of downsizing, RJR Nabisco encourages employees to accept lateral moves. To make such sideway moves more acceptable, Nabisco has added a few tiers to each of its salary ranges, increasing the chances that the moves can bring pay raises rather than pay cuts. Some employees who are reluctant to accept lateral moves have chosen to leave Nabisco.

With fewer layers and fewer managers, survivors in leaner and flatter structures also may have to bear a heavier work load. It appears, however, that too often organizations seek to flatten their structures by jettisoning layers (and jobs) without analyzing what tasks are critical. After jobs are cut, the remaining employees are supposed to rebalance the work load among themselves. If this cannot be done, employees are likely to find themselves overloaded or, worse, unable to function.[8] So now, in addition to being worried about whether they are going to lose their job in the advent of any future downsizing, they also have to worry about performing their job.

OPTIMAL SPANS

The preceding dilemmas naturally give rise to the question of whether there is an optimal, or ideal, span of control. Research clearly indicates that while a limit exists to the number of subordinates a manager can effectively supervise, there is no optimal span that applies in all situations.[9] President Bush's span of control is 65, while Apple Computer CEO John Sculley's is 15. At Japan's Fanuc Ltd., the world's largest manufacturer of numerical control systems for machine tools, some 60 subordinates report directly to President Seiuenon Inaba. Thus, as we might expect from our study of the contingency approach to management, the appropriate span for a given situation depends on several factors. Ten factors of particular significance in determining whether a manager's span should be wide (many subordinates) or narrow (few subordinates) are summarized in Table 8.1.

TABLE 8.1 MAJOR FACTORS INFLUENCING SPAN OF CONTROL

1. *Manager's personality.* If managers share a strong need for power, they may prefer a wider span of control. Personality may partially explain why some managers develop reputations as "empire builders" and attempt to increase their spans to match their ambitions and egos. On the other hand, some managers feel threatened because they cannot oversee every detail as easily when they are supervising, say, 12 people as when they are supervising five or six. Such "extra-hands-on" managers typically would prefer a narrower span of control.

2. *Manager's capabilities.* An experienced, well-trained, and knowledgeable manager should be able to handle a relatively wider span than a less capable manager.

3. *Subordinates' capabilities.* Experienced, well-trained, and knowledgeable subordinates should be able to resolve difficulties for themselves or with one another, thereby reducing their need for supervision and increasing their superior's possible span.

4. *Fatigue tolerance.* Physical and mental fatigue may limit a manager's capacity for control. There are only so many hours in a day and only so many things that can be done at once. The greater the physical or mental demands of a job, the narrower the appropriate span of control.

5. *Activity level.* The pace and pattern of work in a shipyard, an investment house, and a university differ in many respects. Moreover, similar differences will exist most likely between units (for example, production compared to marketing) within the same organization. Thus, the more active the pace and pattern of a manager's work, the narrower the appropriate span of control.

6. *Nonsupervisory activities.* The more time spent on nonsupervisory activities such as long-range planning and outside assignments, the less time a manager has for subordinates and the narrower the appropriate span of control.

7. *Similarity of activities supervised.* It is usually easier to supervise two similar rather than two dissimilar job assignments. Fewer unique problems are likely to arise, and standard instructions are possible. Thus, less supervision will be necessary, and a wider span of control will be possible.

8. *Complexity of work.* Simple job assignments are usually easier to supervise than complex ones. The problems that arise are generally less demanding and take less time to solve. Thus, less supervision will be necessary, and a wider span of control will be possible.

9. *Available assistance.* The more a manager receives help from subordinates and staff units, or has available high-speed telecommunications capabilities such as electronic mail or a satellite communication network, the wider the appropriate span of control will be.

10. *Location.* If subordinates are physically dispersed, a manager will need to spend more time traveling and communicating. Thus, the appropriate span of control will be narrower.

TECHNOLOGY AND ORGANIZATION DESIGN

Finally, our discussion would not be complete without noting the influence of technology on organization design. The pioneering work in this area was performed by Joan Woodward, who set out to determine if such basic components of design as the number of managerial levels and span of control have universal applicability.[10] Her findings challenged the notion that there is a universal "best way" to design an organization. Instead, she concluded that different technologies impose different kinds of demands on organizations, and that these demands must be met through an appropriate design.

Woodward studied the design and performance of 100 British manufacturing firms. She found no relationship between their success and their design. Only when she classified the firms according to their dominant technology did such a relationship become evident. She identified three distinctive types of technology:

1. **Unit production,** where either one or a small number of finished goods are manufactured according to customer specification. Examples include cus-

Unit production.

A production system in which either one or a small number of finished goods are manufactured according to customer specifications.

Just after NCNB began downsizing, Jack Karson, left banking in order to buy into a wholesale fish company. He's starting at the bottom, at the company's West Palm Beach plant. By America's conventional social standards, handling fish may be a step down from handling loan requests, but as a part owner, Karson believes he'll have more control of his own destiny.

tom-made accessories, specialty glass products, custom-tailored clothing, special-order printing, prototype electronic components, locomotives, lunar modules, and special-order machine tools. The earliest factories were organized along the lines of unit production.

2. **Mass production,** where large batches of standard products are manufactured in assembly-line fashion by combining component parts in a specified manner. Examples include automobile and television assembly lines, bakeries, mechanized textile mills, and modern tobacco-processing plants. Mass production requires standardization, and this is usually achieved through specialization of jobs, a topic in Chapter 10.

3. **Continuous-process production,** where raw materials are transformed into finished products using a production system in which the composition of raw materials is changed. Production is characteristically maintained at a set level, and lot sizes are generally large. Examples include the manufacturing of petroleum products, gases, chemicals, and pharmaceuticals. In such production systems, both skill and labor are built into machines, which perform one or more changes on raw materials taken in at one end and turned out at the other end as various finished products.

Mass production.
A production system in which large batches of standard products are manufactured in assembly-line fashion by combining component parts in a specified manner.

Continuous-process production.
A production system in which raw materials are transferred into finished products using a modern system in which the composition of raw materials is changed.

Using this scheme, Woodward found that organizations with similar technologies tended to have similar designs. Unit-production technologies were associated with flat structures (resulting from few managerial levels), a small proportion of managerial employees, relatively few policies, and medium spans of control for first-line supervisors. Mass-production technologies were associated with the widest spans of supervisory control, the sharpest distinction between line and staff units (discussed in Chapter 9), and the largest number of policies. Continuous-process-production technologies were characterized by tall structures (resulting from many

TABLE 8.2 WOODWARD'S FINDINGS ON TECHNOLOGY AND ORGANIZATION DESIGN			
	Design Component		
Technology Type	**Median Number of Managerial Levels**	**Mean Supervisory Span of Control**	**Ratio of Managers to Other Employees**
Unit production	3	24	1:23
Mass production	4	48	1:26
Continuous-process production	6	14	1:8

managerial levels), the narrowest spans of supervisory control, and the greatest proportion of managerial employees. These findings are summarized in Table 8.2.

Thus, Woodward's findings suggest that technology is a major factor influencing effective organization design. Of particular importance is the conclusion that organization success is directly related to a proper fit between technology and organization design. Within each technology type (unit, mass, continuous process), there was a marked tendency for the most successful organizations to be similarly designed. This suggests that although there seems to be no universal "best way" to design an organization, the type of technology involved is important in determining the most appropriate design.

SUMMARY

The present chapter first discussed various approaches to organizing, highlighting their relative advantages and disadvantages. After explaining what is meant by *chain of command* and *unity of command,* it then considered a fundamental question that must be addressed by all organizations: "How many employees can effectively report *directly* to a single manager?"

Learning Objective 1:   Identify different forms of departmentalization.
There are numerous forms of departmentalization. Six of the most popular are functional, product, territorial, customer, matrix, and network.

Learning Objective 2:   Clarify what is meant by *chain of command*.
The term *chain of command* refers to the systematic ordering of positions and duties defining a managerial hierarchy.

Learning Objective 3:   Define the term *unity of command*.
Simply stated, *unity of command* means that no subordinate should be subject to the direct command of more than one superior.

Learning Objective 4:   Explain the inverse relationship between span of control and number of management layers.
Other things being equal, if an organization has *wide* spans, it will be *flat* in appearance, with few layers of management. Conversely, if an organization has *narrow* spans, it will be *tall,* with many management layers.

Learning Objective 5:   List the various factors that influence the appropriateness of a manager's span of control.
The factors that influence the appropriateness of a manager's span of control are listed in Table 8.1.

Learning Objective 6:   Discuss how technology influences organization design.

Based on the findings of Joan Woodward, technology influences organization design in at least three ways: (1) the number of managerial levels tends to increase as technology varies from unit to mass to continuous-process production; (2) the span of control for first-line supervisors tends to vary in relation to technology, increasing from unit to mass production and then decreasing from mass to continuous-process production; and (3) the proportion of managers to other employees tends to increase as technology varies from unit to mass to continuous-process production. Of particular importance is Woodward's conclusion that organization success is directly related to a proper fit between technology and organization design.

KEY TERMS

career gridlock 256

chain of command 252

continuous-process production 258

customer departmentalization 246

employee empowerment 256

expense center 242

functional departmentalization 239

mass production 258

matrix departmentalization 247

network departmentalization 250

organization chart 239

organization design 238

organization structure 238

profit center 242

product departmentalization 241

revenue center 242

span of control 253

territorial departmentalization 243

unit production 257

unity of command 253

THE MANAGEMENT EXPERIENCE   FUNCTIONAL VERSUS PRODUCT DEPARTMENTALIZATION

A basic decision confronting every organization is how to organize. The various forms of departmentalization reviewed have both advantages and disadvantages. Such differences have consequences that are not always immediately evident. Consider the following comparison of functional and product departmentalization.

Assume a manufacturing firm performs three primary operations—A, B, and C. Further, assume that one volume of output requires one each of A, B, and C. Under these circumstances, the firm could be departmentalized either by function or product:

- *Functional departmentalization.* Following a functional structure, the firm could be organized as three functional departments, one department having all three A operations, another all three B operations, and the third, all three C operations. Such a structure could be diagrammed as follows ("S" indicating first-line supervisor and "M" plant manager):

Functional Departmentalization

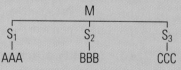

- *Product departmentalization.* Following a product form, the firm could be organized as three product departments, with each operation (A, B, and C) represented in each department. Such a structure could be diagrammed as follows:

Product Departmentalization

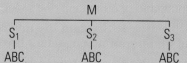

Respond to these items:

1. In which structure is the job of supervisor more difficult?

Continued on next page.

Answer: Product. Supervisors must deal with all three operations (A, B, and C) rather than just one.

2. In which structure are supervisors more qualified for promotion to plant manager?

   Answer: Product. Supervisors have experience in dealing with all three operations (A, B, and C) rather than being specialists in just one.

3. Which structure contains a deeper division of labor at the operative level?

   Answer: Neither. At the operative level, the division of labor is identical. Both structures contain three A, three B, and three C operations.

4. In which structure is conflict between departments likely to be greater?

   Answer: Functional. To be resolved, conflicts between different operations (for example, A and C) require the interaction of two supervisors. In the product form, conflicts between different operations can be resolved within the department in which they occur.

5. Which structure allows a better measure of each supervisor's performance?

   Answer: Product. Since S_1, S_2, and S_3 are each involved in a similar activity, a comparison of their performance is quite simple.

6. In which structure is the number of qualified candidates for promotion to first-line supervisor greater?

   Answer: Product. All nine operative employees have experience working in a department that produces a complete good. Other things being the same, each would be equally qualified for promotion to any of the three supervisory positions. By contrast, in the functional form, there are only three qualified candidates for each supervisory position. Operative employee experience is limited to a single operation (A, B, or C).

7. In which structure will output be most affected by the shutdown of a department?

   Answer: Functional. Given that a complete good requires one unit each of A, B, and C, the shutdown of any department will result in a complete cessation of output. By contrast, in the product form, the shutdown of a department will result in only a one-third reduction in output since each department is relatively autonomous. Thus, a failure in one product department is limited in its effect to that department. A failure in one functional department affects the whole firm and may destroy the effectiveness of all the work being done.

REVIEW AND DISCUSSION QUESTIONS

1. You are the founder of a company. You've watched it grow from a "one-person shop" to an organization with some 50 employees. In the beginning, you personally knew each employee, the name of each employee's spouse, and where each lived. Today, you know the names of only the few remaining "old-timers" like yourself. Tired of making all the decisions yourself, you've been thinking about redesigning the company. What advantages and disadvantages would such a change offer?

2. As a management consultant with McKinsey and Company, you are currently working with several clients. One is an international farm equipment company. A second is a regional retailer. A third is a family-owned mattress manufacturer. What form of departmentalization would you recommend for each? Why?

3. You've just returned from an interview with a major aerospace supplier that is seeking to recruit new project managers. Given what you know about matrix departmentalization, how do you feel about accepting such a position?

4. Assume you have just given a guest lecture on matrix departmentalization at the U.S. Army War College. During your presentation, you commented that "matrix departmentalization attempts to cross product departmentalization

with functional departmentalization to get the best (and avoid the worst) of each." In the ensuing question-and-answer session, you've been asked to more fully explain what you mean. What do you mean?

5. Calling upon your personal experience as a student of management, give several examples of chains of command.

6. With the increasingly competitive economic environment, organizations around the globe have been busy eliminating layers of management, reducing administrative staff, and pushing decisions down to lower managerial levels. The result of this downsizing is not just lower administrative costs but more autonomy for employees at almost every level. Reflecting this trend, Nucor Corp. CEO Ken Iverson says, "I'm a firm believer both in having the fewest number of managerial levels and in delegating authority to the lowest level possible."[11] Do you share Iverson's twin belief? If so, why? If not, why not?

7. Fantasize that it is 25 years from today. You are the CEO of a *Fortune* 500 company and have recently been contemplating a corporate reorganization. What factors can you identify that would influence the appropriateness of your span of control?

8. In describing the challenge of managing, Professor Kenneth D. MacKenzie has observed that effectively designing an organization is "similar to repairing and/or improving a truck while it is being driven along an interstate."[12] Comment on Professor MacKenzie's metaphor, being sure to emphasize the dynamics of design.

CASE 8.1 RESTRUCTURING FOR IMPROVED DECISION MAKING

IBM has long dominated the computer business, particularly production of mainframes, and has been a leading example of a highly successful American company in an increasingly competitive international economy. With its success it has developed a centralized, bureaucratic structure, an unwillingness to share ownership in any of its business subsidiaries, and a corporate policy of not laying off employees.

In spite of its reputation and financial strength, IBM is facing increasing challenges in the marketplace and in its operations. As a result of these challenges, IBM reduced its workforce from 407,000 to 353,000 between 1986 and late 1991, and it plans an additional reduction to 325,000 by late 1992. Because of the no-layoff policy, these reductions have and will be accomplished through normal attrition and early retirement programs. In addition to changing the size of its workforce, IBM is making

structural changes intended to increase organizational flexibility and streamline decision making. The cost of the restructuring and workforce reductions will exceed $7 billion.

The restructuring will lead to a reduction in some of its manufacturing operations and substantially greater independence for its various business units. In addition, there will be a greater emphasis on effective employee performance and less tolerance for poor performance, along with a greater willingness to engage in business as a partner with other owners rather than require 100 percent ownership of all of its businesses. Early examples of this policy change include working agreements with Toshiba and Apple Computer, two of IBM's biggest competitors in personal computers.

The restructuring is planned to proceed slowly, at least in the near future, but will involve such immediate changes as having separate business units produce individual rather than combined financial statements and allowing business units greater flexibility in how they market their products or services, instead of requiring all units to use the primary IBM sales force. In general, the restructuring will allow for greater independence in organizational decision making and will allow individual business units much greater input in planning their own business activities without having to rely on, or explicitly follow, corporate decisions. This will place decision authority closer to IBM's various business activities and should allow it to respond more effectively to market conditions. Furthermore, by decentralizing decision making, fewer levels of approval will be needed, allowing IBM to implement decisions more quickly.

Source: Aubrey R. Fowler, Youngstown State University, based on John Boyne, et al., "IBM: As Market and Technology Change, Can Big Blue Remake Its Culture?" *Business Week*, June 17, 1991, 25–32; and Paul Carroll,

"IBM Plans $3 Billion Change and about 20,000 Job Cuts," *Wall Street Journal*, November 27, 1991, A3.

Problems

1. Is IBM representative of the structural Darwinism mentioned in this chapter? Other than the demands of global competition, what reasons do organizations frequently have for deciding to restructure?

2. Do you agree that the move away from a centralized, bureaucratic structure will improve decision making at IBM?

3. What is likely to happen to spans of control at IBM?

4. What are some of the anticipated effects of the proposed downsizing on employees who will remain with IBM? How will managers be affected?

NOTES

[1] Tom Peters, "Biting the Systems and Structures Bullet," *Baton Rouge Business Report* 9 (December 1990): 66.

[2] John S. McClenahen, "Flexible Structures to Absorb the Shock," *Industry Week*, April 18, 1988, 41.

[3] Harvey F. Kolodny, "Matrix Organization Designs and New Product Success," *Research Management* 23 (September 1980): 29–33.

[4] Stanley M. Davis and Paul R. Lawrence, *Matrix* (Reading, Mass.: Addison-Wesley, 1977), 129–144; and Stanley M. Davis and Paul R. Lawrence, "Problems of Matrix Organization," *Harvard Business Review* 56 (May–June 1978): 131–142.

[5] Adapted from Sherman K. Grinnel and Howard P. Apple, "When Two Bosses Are Better Than One," *Machine Design*, January 9, 1975, 86.

[6] This section draws on John W. Wilson and Judith H. Dobrzynski, "And Now, the Post-Industrial Corporation," *Business Week*, March 3, 1986, 64–71, and Raymond E. Miles and Charles C.

Snow, "Organizations: New Concepts for New Forms," *California Management Review* 28 (Spring 1986): 62–73.

[7] Elliott Jacques, "In Praise of Hierarchy," *Harvard Business Review* 68 (January–February 1990): 129.

[8] Carol Hymowitz, "When Firms Slash Middle Management, Those Spared Often Bear a Heavy Load," *Wall Street Journal*, April 5, 1990, B1, B5.

[9] David D. Van Fleet and Arthur G. Bedeian, "A History of the Span of Management," *Academy of Management Review* 2 (April 1977): 356–372.

[10] Joan Woodward, *Industrial Organization: Theory and Practice* (London: Oxford University Press, 1965), 35–40.

[11] John Grossman, "Ken Iverson: Simply the Best," *American Way*, August 1, 1987, 24.

[12] Kenneth D. MacKenzie, "Designing the Adaptive Organization," in *Creating the Competitive Edge through Human Resources Application*, eds. Richard J. Niehaus and Karl F. Price (New York: Plenum, 1988): 64.

CHAPTER 9

LEARNING OBJECTIVES

Upon completing this chapter, you should be able to:

- Differentiate between authority and power.
- Describe the classical and acceptance views of authority.
- Explain Barnard's so-called "zone of acceptance."
- Identify five basic types of power.
- Explain the difference between line and staff authority.
- Describe functional authority.
- Explain what is meant by *employee empowerment*.
- Recognize the importance of parity of authority and responsibility.
- Appreciate why some managers resist delegating authority.
- Understand why some subordinates resist accepting delegation.
- Identify the different types of task interdependence that can exist between work units.
- Specify the different types of coordination likely to exist in a typical organization.

ou hear a lot these days about people working out and feeling much better afterward. General Electric has been giving its managers a similar experience, but instead of shedding pounds, they are shedding some of their decision-making power.

Work-Out is one of three techniques aimed at removing the "boss element" at the company. Similar to a New England town meeting, a Work-Out is a work forum whose participants are chosen from all ranks and functions within a GE subdivision. An agenda (typically starting with a request for ideas about ways to reduce paperwork or eliminate unnecessary meetings and then evolving into other topics) is outlined by the group's boss, who then leaves. Guided by an outside facilitator, the group divides into teams to consider each item on the agenda. The teams wrestle with ideas for a day and a half; then the boss returns and each team presents its complaints and recommendations. The boss can say "yes" or "no" or set a date to hear further information and appoint a team to gather it.

When the plant services group from GE Aircraft Engines met for a Work-Out, the members fired 108 proposals at their boss in as many minutes. He approved all but eight, and the resulting changes saved the company $200,000. This also helped gain the confidence of the members, who now know that the Work-Out program really is intended to give them more say in the company's continued success.

A second technique, called Best Practices, involves selecting for analysis a number of other companies whose productivity growth is deemed superior to GE's. The analysts screen out competitors, com-

AUTHORITY AND POWER

panies whose operations are vastly different from GE's, and companies that are unwilling to interact with GE. When this technique was used in 1990 and 1991, the companies selected included AMP (an electrical manufacturer), Ford Motor, Hewlett-Packard, and Xerox. The analysis disclosed a common practice among the selected companies: They focused more on interdepartmental interactions than on the performance of each individual department. This showed GE which aspects of its structure needed to be examined, and the information gained became part of a course for managers given at GE's Management Development Institute.

Process Mapping, a third technique, involves employees, managers, suppliers, and customers all working together to make a detailed flowchart showing every step in a production process, from initial order to delivery. Generating such a chart is much more difficult than it sounds, and it often reveals large gaps or inefficiencies. Camco, the Canadian subsidiary of GE Appliances, combined this technique with the Work-Out and Best Practices approaches to achieve a 50 percent reduction in the time required to respond to a change in consumer demand.

All three of these techniques involve shifting decision making—and hence power—away from top management levels. In this chapter, we will discuss authority and power and how they are distributed throughout an organization. As noted in Chapter 8, authority relationships exist among managers and subordinates at each level in an organization's chain of command. In this respect, authority may be viewed as the cement that holds the various levels of an organization together. As typically defined, **authority** is the right to perform or command. It is a fundamental aspect of organization life.

Source: Adapted from Thomas A. Stewart, "GE Keeps Those Ideas Coming," *Fortune*, August 12, 1991; 41–44, 48–49.

The present chapter explores the nature of authority. Specifically, it focuses on (1) sources of authority (who grants whom authority), (2) the relationship between authority and power, (3) different types of authority (line, staff, and functional), (4) delegation (and decentralization) of authority, and (5) different types of coordination.

Authority resides in positions rather than in people. Managers acquire authority by virtue of the rank or title associated with their position, not their personal characteristics. The military expression "You salute the uniform, not the man (or woman)" illustrates this concept. An officer's rank carries with it certain inherent rights regardless of his or her personal attributes. A classic example that further illustrates this point is the transfer of authority involved in the inauguration of a new U.S. president. When a president steps down, he relinquishes his authority. The authority that he once held remains in the office of president and its new incumbent.

Authority.
The right to perform or command.

SOURCES OF AUTHORITY: TWO VIEWS

There are two principal views regarding the source of authority. The classical view holds that authority passes from the "top down." In contrast, the acceptance view contends that authority flows from the "bottom up" (see Figure 9.1). Both views have merit.

CLASSICAL THEORY OF AUTHORITY

According to the **classical view of authority,** managers derive their authority from the right of private property.[1] In the United States, this right is guaranteed in the Constitution. This guarantee gives owners the right to manage their affairs as

Classical view of authority.
Managers derive their authority from the right of private property.

FIGURE 9.1 TWO VIEWS OF AUTHORITY

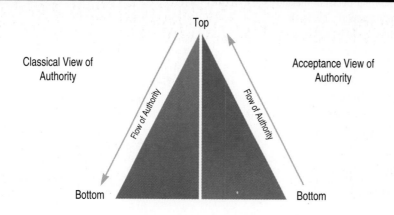

they see fit, as long as they do not violate the rights of others. In most large organizations, owners transfer their ownership rights to a board of directors, which, in turn, may appoint a president (or CEO) to manage an organization's day-to-day operation. Likewise, the president may appoint a vice-president and so on until all of an organization's managers possess some formal authority. This "top down" transfer of authority is depicted in Figure 9.2.

In the United States, employees, in agreeing to abide by the Constitution, acknowledge the rights of owners to manage their property within generally prescribed legal limits. By entering into an employment contract, subordinates acknowledge the authority of owners and managers and accept a duty to obey.

ACCEPTANCE THEORY OF AUTHORITY

The **acceptance theory of authority** was popularized by AT&T executive Chester I. Barnard. It contends that authority stems from below because subordinates can always reject a directive. It is only by accepting an order that a subordinate affirms the right of a manager to issue the order.[2]

According to Barnard, subordinates will accept orders given by their superiors provided that the orders meet four conditions. These conditions define what is acceptable to a subordinate and, thus, create a **zone of acceptance** within which authority may be exercised.[3] A subordinate will accept an order and comply with authority under the following four conditions:

1. The subordinate understands the order.
2. The subordinate believes the order is consistent with organization goals.
3. The subordinate believes the order is compatible with his or her personal interests.
4. The subordinate is mentally and physically able to comply with the order.

Effective managers make certain that their orders clearly fall within their subordinates' zones of acceptance. Otherwise, they can expect that their orders will be met with resistance, if not open hostility.

AN ASSESSMENT

Authority is both allocated from above and acknowledged from below. The acceptance view of authority clearly recognizes that a manager can govern effectively

Acceptance theory of authority.
Authority stems from below because subordinates can always reject a directive.

Zone of acceptance.
A conditional range within which subordinates will accept their superiors' orders.

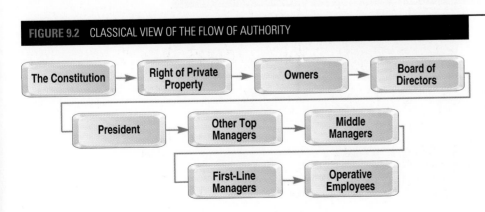

FIGURE 9.2 CLASSICAL VIEW OF THE FLOW OF AUTHORITY

only with the consent of those being governed. Managers are, however, granted authority from above and consequently possess power to impose sanctions on recalcitrant subordinates to achieve organization goals. This condition stresses the high degree of interdependence common to most superior-subordinate relationships. Not only do subordinates depend on those above them to satisfy their personal needs, but managers depend on all those below them to achieve both their own and organization goals. Managers who approach their job by overestimating their own importance and underestimating that of their subordinates are asking for trouble. As a dramatic illustration of this point, consider the following anecdote:[4]

> An agent of the Textile Workers Union of America likes to tell the story of the occasion when a new manager appeared in the mill where he was working. The manager came into the weave room the day he arrived. He walked directly over to the agent and said, "Are you Belloc?" The agent acknowledged that he was. The manager said, "I am the new manager here. When I manage a mill, I run it. Do you understand?" The agent nodded, and then waved his hand. The workers, intently watching this encounter, shut down every loom in the room immediately. The agent turned to the manager and said, "All right, go ahead and run it."

POWER

The terms *authority* and *power* are quite frequently confused. Authority, as noted, is the right to perform or command. **Power** is the capacity to influence others. All managers have power by virtue of the positions they occupy. Power, however, does not necessarily derive from authority. Stated differently, people with authority have power; not all people with power, however, have authority. Thus, as commander in chief of the armed forces, the President has both authority and power, but an armed robber can be said to have power but no authority. In a more common example, a great many executive secretaries have tremendous power (but no authority) in screening who gets past their desks or is scheduled for appointments with their bosses.

John R. P. French and Bertram Raven have identified five basic types of power (see Figure 9.3).[5] The first three types—*reward, coercive,* and *legitimate*—generally

Power.
The capacity to influence others.

FIGURE 9.3   FIVE TYPES OF POWER

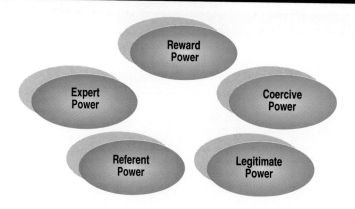

Managers and workers can gain greater power in their job as a result of building expertise over a period of years. 3M Brazil's longest-serving employee, Jose dos Santos Carneiro, is a master of tape coating machinery. Carneiro learned his craft by watching equipment work and once repaired a system that had confounded technicians for weeks. He has perfected his skills during a 40-year career that began in 1951. Today, he is the supervisor of tape coaters.

are associated with a manager's position. The higher a manager's rank, the more of this power he or she has. The final two—*referent* and *expert*—are part of the person, not the position, so they can exist anywhere in an organization.

Reward power is based on a manager's ability to provide various kinds of rewards for complying with orders. Rewards under a manager's control typically include salary increases, promotions, favorable job assignments, praise, and recognition.

Coercive power is based on a manager's ability to punish for not complying with orders. Coercion may take the form of verbal reprimands, disciplinary layoffs, fines, demotions, and threatened termination.

Legitimate power is based strictly on an individual's position in a managerial hierarchy. The higher a manager is in a chain of command, the greater his or her legitimate power. Generals have more power than privates, and presidents more than vice-presidents. An individual's legitimate power and formal authority are one and the same.

Referent power attaches to specific managers because people admire them, want to be like them, or are impressed by their integrity, charisma, or charm. For example, popular, highly respected managers will have referent power if subordinates identify with or admire them. This may even involve a subordinate emulating an admired manager (dressing like her, playing the same sports, driving the same brand car, and so on). Referent power can also operate among peers. For example, admired colleagues may be able to sway their peers to vote a specific way in department meetings.

Reward power. Power based on a manager's ability to provide various kinds of rewards for complying with orders.

Coercive power. Power based on a manager's ability to punish for not complying with orders.

Legitimate power. Power based on an individual's position in a managerial hierarchy.

Referent power. Power that attaches to specific managers because people admire them, want to be like them, or are impressed by their integrity, charisma, or charm.

SMART MANAGEMENT MANAGING FORMER CO-WORKERS

After the glow is off that big promotion, managing former co-workers can be like cutting diamonds. Proper judgment and sensitivity will yield jewels, but mishandling can turn working relationships to dust.

Most colleagues will be happy about your promotion. But the reactions of others can range from jealousy and envy all the way to outright sabotage. In coping with the situation, it pays to keep a few rules in mind.

Some new managers feel the urge to crack the whip in an effort to bludgeon legitimacy and recognition from subordinates. A more conciliatory approach might be to circulate a memo outlining new managerial responsibilities. Formal acknowledgment from above makes it easier for former co-workers to make a formal acknowledgment of their own.

Management consultants agree that the next move should be a group discussion regarding the promotion and what the future holds. A look toward common goals and methods of achieving them will go a long way toward diffusing tension.

Critiquing the job performance of former co-workers is one of the most delicate tasks of a new manager, but here the rules are the same for friends as they are for employees. Personal judgments are out. Direct confrontations are generally a bad idea. Criticism should come in the form of constructive feedback and be based on specific problems. It should always be directed at a person's productive or counterproductive behavior, not the person.

Doing away with old habits can become a bone of contention, particularly if a newly promoted manager was once an eager cohort. Pastimes such as grousing about company policy, holding occasional goof-off sessions, or using company phones to call friends in distant cities are no longer options. Along with the position of manager comes the responsibility of supporting a company's policies. And the key to heading off any hostility that the sudden about-face might cause is to openly admit past indiscretions while resolving to make necessary changes.

Ultimately, a new manager must determine what degree of familiarity is best for both himself and his former co-workers. The managerial role creates a wall of authority and brings about inevitable changes in friendships. How a manager copes with these changes will determine whether the relationships that emerge are cooperative or combative.

Source: Jim Harmon, "How to Manage Your Former Co-workers," *Young Executive*, Spring 1992, 42–43.

Expert power is based on possessing valued knowledge or special skills. A manager who possesses such knowledge or skills has power over others who do not. A manager's power is enhanced by knowing work schedules and assignments before subordinates. A manager who knows how to deal with a difficult customer likewise has expert power. Similarly, managers who have the right answers to subordinates' questions and are organized to provide support wield expert power. In a very real sense "knowledge is power."

Power should be accepted as a natural part of a manager's position. Although better managers more likely rely on personal sources of power (referent and expert), the typical manager's ability to function effectively will be the result of some blend of the five basic types of power. Thus, managers should recognize and develop their power to enhance their effectiveness, as well as that of their subordinates.

Expert power.
Power based on possessing valued knowledge or special skills.

TYPES OF AUTHORITY

Three main types of authority exist within a typical organization: line authority, staff authority, and functional authority. Each type exists to enable managers to perform their different duties.

LINE AND STAFF AUTHORITY

In most large organizations, a distinction is made between line units and staff units. **Line units** are those that contribute *directly* to accomplishing an organization's goals. Thus, production, marketing, and finance are considered the major line units in a manufacturing firm because they contribute directly to achieving the objectives of producing and selling goods at a profit. Similarly, infantry, artillery, and armor are line units in an army because they contribute directly to achieving the objectives of meeting and defeating an enemy. Managers who work in line units have **line authority,** which is authority that follows an organization's direct chain of command, starting with its board of directors and extending down through intervening layers to first-line management.

    Staff units are those that contribute *indirectly* to accomplishing an organization's goals. Managers working in staff units have **staff authority** in that they provide advice and expertise to assist line units in achieving their goals. Any number of staff units can exist. For example, in the previously mentioned manufacturing firm, labor relations, accounting, logistics, administrative services, management information systems, research and development, public relations, and legal affairs would be considered staff units because they provide advice and expertise to assist line units. In the army, ordnance, intelligence, medical corps, and quartermaster are staff units because they also provide similar services to infantry, artillery, and armor units. Note that in most companies auditing would be regarded as a staff unit. However, in a public accounting firm, auditing is clearly a line unit. One way of determining whether a unit is line or staff is to ask, "Does this unit contribute *directly* to achieving an organization's goals?" If the answer is "yes," it is line. If the answer is "no," it is staff.

    In organization charts, staff units traditionally are positioned to the right of line units. Because staff units provide advice and expertise, but have no general authority over line units, they are customarily indicated on organization charts by a broken line. This shows that they fall outside an organization's direct chain of command. Line units are so called because they are on "the line of authority" from an organization's president. Staff units are so called because they provide support much like a shepherd's staff. Figure 9.4 depicts both line and staff units.

    As organizations grow in scope and complexity, a point is generally reached when it becomes necessary to seek the assistance of specialized staff. It is a rare top manager who is able to juggle the many demands of a large organization simultaneously. Emergence of staff units represents another aspect of a seemingly irresistible trend toward a greater and greater division of labor in a society becoming ever more complex.

FUNCTIONAL AUTHORITY

Functional authority broadens the concept of staff authority. It enables staff managers to exercise limited line authority over other units in matters related directly to staff expertise. Such authority typically covers only specific activities. For instance,

---

Line unit.
A unit that contributes directly to accomplishing an organization's goals.

Line authority.
Authority that follows an organization's direct chain of command.

Staff unit.
A unit that contributes indirectly to accomplishing an organization's goals.

Staff authority.
Authority to provide advice and expertise to assist line units in achieving their goals.

Functional authority.
An arrangement that enables staff managers to exercise limited line authority over other units in matters related directly to staff expertise.

a staff manager may have functional authority to request that line managers prepare certain financial reports in a specific manner by a certain date. Alternatively, staff managers might also be granted functional authority over their counterparts at lower organization levels. Thus, a vice-president for human resources located at a manufacturing firm's home office is likely to have not only functional authority to require that line managers comply with federal employment regulations, but also functional authority over the activities of human resource specialists at the local plant level.

LINE-STAFF CONFLICT

Despite good intentions, line-staff relationships often generate problems for all parties involved. As viewed by the typical line unit manager, common problems include the following:[6]

- *Staff is pushy.* Staff offers advice to line managers without being requested to do so.

- *Staff interferes.* Staff bypasses line managers and gives advice to lower level subordinates.

- *Staff causes conflict.* When several staff managers are involved in solving a problem, their advice often conflicts or may even be contradictory.

- *Staff will not help.* In some cases, line managers may want staff managers to make decisions in their area of expertise. Staff, however, will usually avoid doing this for fear of infringing on the line managers' "responsibility" to handle a situation.

- *Staff takes credit for results.* Staff managers are credit grabbers—unless things go wrong.

Conversely, staff managers often feel they are experts and that line unit managers should heed their advice more often than they do. This view may result from any one of the following line responses to staff advice:

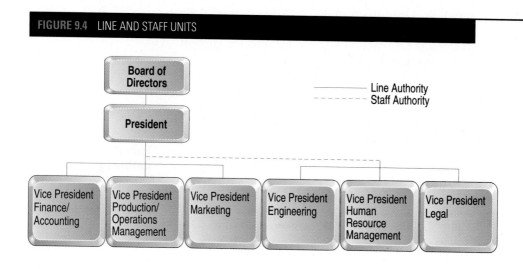

FIGURE 9.4   LINE AND STAFF UNITS

CLOSE-UP: SOCIAL RESPONSIBILITY   THE CHALLENGE OF COMMUNITY RELATIONS

Bob Stephens was faced with one of the biggest challenges of his life when he was unexpectedly put in charge of his company's emergency disaster relief program.

As director of human resources for Solid State Circuits Inc., Stephens had years of experience dealing with people. But nothing could have prepared him for the task of handling an angry community endangered by a toxic chemical leak at his company's industrial plant.

The nightmare began on August 10, 1985, when chlorine used by Solid State to etch printed circuit boards began seeping out of a one-ton storage tank at the plant in Springfield, Missouri. When initial attempts to plug the leak proved futile, the police began evacuating residents of the surrounding area. Before it was all over, 3,000 people were forced to leave their homes.

No one was injured during the six-hour debacle, but it left the community up in arms. They had opposed the plant's presence from the beginning. Now they wanted compensation for their inconvenience and any resulting drop in property values.

With its back against the wall, Solid State decided to mobilize a company-wide community relations campaign. Since Solid State President Thomas Kawaski considered Stephens the best man for the job, he gave him full authority to do whatever was necessary to turn the tide of public opinion.

Stephens started out by appearing on public television with his most vocal opponent, Chuck Puskus, president of the local property owners association. Stephens was forthcoming with information, responding to most questions on the spot and writing down those he could not answer.

Stephens then followed up his words with action. He made sure Solid State removed the one-ton chlorine tanks and put several smaller ones in its place. The Department of Labor was asked to voluntarily conduct inspections of the plant. And local residents were given permission to go on tours of the facility.

Today, plant workers and property owners are on a first-name basis. The homeowners' newly formed Environmental Concerns Committee meets regularly with the company's safety manager and other key personnel. They also play softball together, go on picnics and even cosponsor blood drives.

Solid State has continued its own solo efforts to make sure it is prepared in the future. At least one person on every shift is participating in Red Cross disaster training and the company has inspected the neighborhood to identify people who will need special help during an emergency.

Now that the worst is behind him, Stephens has this advice for companies trying to improve community relations: Don't wait for disaster to strike. Get top managers involved in the community, share information, explain corporate actions, and develop trust through familiarity. That's how Solid State transformed a crisis into a model community relationship.

Source: Adapted from Keith Denton, "Improving Community Relations," Small Business Reports August 1990: 33–41.

- The "Rejection Approach"—Line managers reject staff advice outright.

- The "Bottom Drawer Approach"—Line managers "file" staff advice after sending a memorandum praising it.

- The "Political Support Approach"—Line managers defend their interests against staff advice by mobilizing support from colleagues or superiors.

- The "Pick-It-to-Death Approach"—Line managers find as many errors in staff work as possible and use these to indicate that staff advice is ill conceived.

- The "Future Play"—Line managers agree with staff's analyses but argue that, because the assumptions on which they are based are unrealistic, the staff advice is unsound.

- The "Avoidance Technique"—Line managers simply avoid staff managers by scheduling conflicting appointments or using similar evasive tactics.

Many of the above actions are the product of an inherent conflict between line and staff. Their different perspectives are often as much a consequence of different training and roles as of separate career paths. Wise line managers use staff managers well, expecting them to make positive contributions, not to nitpick. Strong staff managers provide innovative problem solutions and are open in their interactions with line. It is simply not enough to say that staff should provide advice and expertise to line managers. Line and staff need to respect one another for the contributions they make to an organization's success. A common method to encourage such respect is to rotate managers through both line and staff units when possible, allowing line managers to work staff positions (and vice versa), to learn more about the others' job.

DELEGATION, ACCOUNTABILITY, AND RESPONSIBILITY

Delegation is the process by which authority passes from one organization level to another. Managers seemingly always have more duties than time to carry them out. By delegating authority, they extend their reach, thereby achieving greater output. Indeed, the diversity of some organizations makes delegation inevitable. As Allen F. Jacobson, 3M chairman and CEO, maintains, "You have to be a delegator in a company that has the complications of 3M. We've got four kinds of diversity: 60,000 or more products; 100 different technologies; markets—we sell to more SIC (Standard Industrial Classification) codes than anyone in the country; and geography (we operate in 52 countries). You can't do that without delegation and without a management system that is good at delegation."[7]

It is important to realize that by delegating authority, managers do not reduce their own *accountability.* That is, they remain accountable for their own actions and those of their subordinates. Thus, managers can hold their subordinates responsible for doing a certain job, but this by no means diminishes their accountability to their own superiors. They can no more divorce themselves from this liability than they can excuse themselves from blame for a subordinate's failure or take full credit for a subordinate's success.

At the same time, neither managers nor subordinates can legitimately be held responsible for things they cannot control. For this reason, traditional management theory (dating back to Fayol) holds that for effective delegation to take place, au-

Delegation.
The process by which authority passes from one organization level to another.

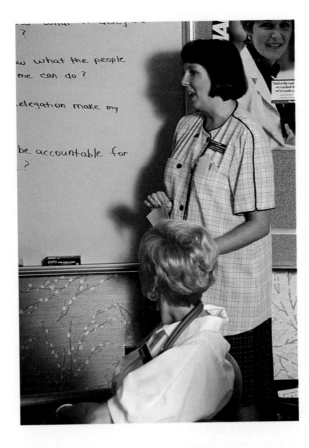

At Humana, a nursing practice model has been developed in an attempt to achieve an optimum level of patient care. The practice model identifies how a nurse's time is spent and how time management can be improved. Nurses are taught how to delegate tasks to staff units as a way to manage the wide range of activities and services a nurse is expected to provide.

thority must be made equal to responsibility. This condition is known as **parity of authority and responsibility.** Simply stated, no one should be expected to shoulder responsibility without being provided commensurate authority. As Firestone Tire & Rubber CEO John Nevin points out, "If you want to drive a person crazy, the easiest way to do it is to give him a deep sense of responsibility and no authority."[8]

In reality, managers often confront situations in which their responsibility exceeds their authority. For instance, to achieve their assigned goals, virtually all managers must interact with units over which they have no direct control. In such situations, a gap exists between the amount of authority they have been delegated and the responsibility with which they have been charged. Successful managers are those who are able to bridge such responsibility-authority gaps. Experience suggests that, in doing so, they generally tend to rely more heavily on personal sources of power (referent and expert) than their less successful counterparts.

Parity of authority and responsibility. No one should be expected to shoulder responsibility without commensurate authority.

DECENTRALIZATION AND EMPLOYEE EMPOWERMENT

An organization is considered **centralized** to the degree that authority is not delegated, but concentrated at higher managerial levels. In contrast, to the degree that authority is delegated, an organization is considered **decentralized.** The terms *centralization* and *decentralization* are meaningful only in a relative sense. An organization could not operate on a completely decentralized basis, since all au-

Centralized/ decentralized. Terms denoting the degree to which authority is delegated in an organization.

thority to make decisions would rest at the lowest managerial level, and it would lack the coordination essential to operating efficiently. Nor could an organization, other than perhaps a very small and simple firm, be completely centralized, since all authority would be reserved for top management, and it would lack the needed flexibility to get a variety of jobs done.

In most large organizations, especially multinational companies, the trend is toward decentralization. It is important to note, however, that size and geography do not necessarily dictate decentralization. It is entirely possible to have either a centralized company with sites all over the world, or a decentralized company in one place. This aside, decentralization does typically become more necessary as a company gets bigger.

The trend toward decentralization closely parallels the move to greater *employee empowerment,* as introduced in Chapter 8. Pushing authority to lower levels in an organization can result in an environment of freedom and experimentation. By encouraging employees at all levels to accept responsibility, to unleash their full potential, and, most important, to think and innovate, employee empowerment can help maintain the entrepreneurial spirit that made an organization successful in the first place. As a case in point, employee empowerment has kept Johnson & Johnson one of the world's most successful companies. It has prospered from products as common as the everyday Band-Aid to medical breakthroughs as exotic as Orthoclon OKT3, a monoclonal antibody that keeps the body from rejecting a transplanted kidney. The company's secret is no secret. It has created a highly decentralized structure that gives managers the freedom to succeed.

As suggested, Johnson & Johnson is not the only organization pushing authority down to lower levels. Aluminum Co. of America (Alcoa) recognizes it cannot succeed unless it grants its employees added authority. In the past, decisions suffered for months while five management layers scrutinized every detail. Now, because Alcoa has eliminated four managerial levels and given the presidents of each of its 25 businesses authority to spend up to $5 million without prior approval, most decisions are made within hours.

The benefits of decentralization and employee empowerment are clear. Nevertheless, the extent of decentralization appropriate for individual organizations will vary according to the unique requirements inherent in any situation. There is no single correct formula. Moreover, decentralization also has drawbacks. The relative advantages of both centralization and decentralization are listed in Table 9.1.

RESISTANCE TO DELEGATION

Delegating authority can be one of the most difficult aspects of any job. Properly executed, however, delegation can benefit both managers and their subordinates. Nonetheless, some managers are as reluctant to delegate authority as some subordinates are to accept it. The reasons managers and subordinates give for their resistance vary widely.

MANAGER RESISTANCE

For some, the transformation from doer to delegator is extremely traumatic, even impossible. Managers give a host of reasons why they do not delegate. They may

TABLE 9.1   ADVANTAGES OF CENTRALIZATION AND DECENTRALIZATION

Centralization

1. A greater uniformity in decisions is possible.
2. Top-level managers are more aware of future organization plans and thus more likely to make decisions in an organization's best interests.
3. It requires fewer skilled (and higher paid) managers.
4. It requires less extensive planning and reporting procedures.

Decentralization

1. Lower level managerial problems can be dealt with on the spot.
2. It provides lower level managers with an opportunity to develop their decision-making skills.
3. The motivation of lower level managers is greater when they are entrusted to make decisions rather than always following orders issued at a higher level.
4. It spreads an organization's work load and allows top-level managers more time for strategic planning.

feel that they lack experienced or trained subordinates to whom authority can be safely delegated. Paradoxically, although a manager may fear that untrained or inexperienced subordinates will make mistakes, the same manager may feel threatened if a subordinate handles a task well.

Other managers resist delegation believing that they are irreplaceable, being the only ones capable of correctly doing a task. In trying to dispel this myth, Richardo Semler, president of Semco S/A, Brazil's largest marine and food-process-

A quality team examines fabric samples at Spring Industries' Lyman Dyeing and Finishing Plant. This team is part of Spring Industries' quality process. The company believes that by empowering employees to suggest changes, create solutions to problems, and seek opportunities to improve quality, not only will product quality improve, but employees will feel greater satisfaction and pride as their ideas are implemented.

ing machinery manufacturer, tells such managers, "The truth is, you *are* replaceable, as everyone will discover within a week of your funeral."[9]

Then, too, some managers resist delegation for fear of losing control. Former FBI chief J. Edgar Hoover was one such manager. He insisted on approving every decision, even going so far as to dictate the width of margins in agency memos. The results of such micromanagement are obvious from an anecdote told by PepsiCo CEO Wayne Calloway:[10]

> One day Hoover received [a memo] whose margins were too small. In big red letters he scrawled an angry warning across the top: "Watch the borders!" The next morning his frightened assistants transferred 200 FBI agents to Canada and Mexico.

Table 9.2 lists some of the more popular reasons managers give for not delegating.

SUBORDINATE RESISTANCE

A major reason why some managers may find it difficult to delegate is that subordinates do not want to accept delegation. A manager will most commonly encounter resistance of this kind when subordinates:

- Have not received proper job information.
- Have not been trained properly.
- Lack self-confidence and fear personal failure.
- Have not been provided proper equipment or tools.
- Are uncertain there is anything to gain by accepting authority.
- Find it easier to let the manager make all the decisions.

To overcome such resistance, managers need to be sure that subordinates possess the necessary knowledge, skills, and abilities; obtain the proper equipment or tools; and have sufficient incentives for taking on an assignment.

TABLE 9.2 EXCUSES MANAGERS GIVE FOR NOT DELEGATING

1. My employees lack the training and experience.
2. It takes more time to explain than to do the job myself.
3. A mistake by an employee could be costly.
4. My position enables me to get quicker action.
5. My employees are specialists, and they lack the overall knowledge that many decisions require.
6. My employees are already too busy.
7. No one else can do it right.
8. I'm concerned about lack of control over employee performance when I delegate.
9. I like keeping busy and making my own decisions.
10. I'm afraid of being "shown up" by my employees.

Source: Based on Robert B. Nelson, *Delegation: The Power of Letting Go* (Glenview, Ill.: Scott, Foresman, 1988) 28.

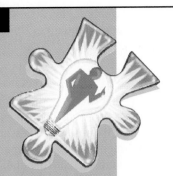

SMART MANAGEMENT   THE ART OF DELEGATING AUTHORITY

Bob Crawford has found a fail-safe formula for learning how to delegate authority: He spends about half his time away from his office.

As CEO of Brook Furniture Rental, based in Arlington Heights, Illinois, Crawford oversees 40 showrooms in four states. In his view, it's virtually impossible to effectively manage 450 employees, including 55 outside salespeople, by telephone or through the mail. So he takes to the road instead, visiting showrooms, going on calls with salespeople, and attending conventions and chamber of commerce meetings.

Crawford says he believes face-to-face encounters give him two major advantages: a unique insight he couldn't get from second-hand reports, and the opportunity to personally teach and coach employees. In the process, he also has learned the art of delegating authority.

The only way Crawford can keep up his hectic travel schedule is if his office can do without him while he's away. So he hires and trains strong team members who can handle responsibility on their own.

Crawford also takes his philosophy of delegation on the road with him. For example, he never goes on a call with a salesperson alone. Because Crawford's goal is to be a facilitator and initiator, he brings along the salesperson's boss, or boss's boss. That helps ensure that someone besides Crawford will be in charge of a followup.

Traveling in groups is not designed to steal the thunder from salespeople. Crawford usually organizes the sales calls so that his subordinates take the lead. Having only one person in charge helps avoid the confusion that can develop from having too many people talking at once. Crawford does, however, occasionally jump in with a question or two of his own.

Customers aren't the only ones who provide Crawford with feedback. He also takes time to listen to his own employees. Crawford considers conversation with employees in the field a forum for conducting industry research, and he typically dedicates 4 hours per contact to give each person enough time to speak candidly.

Although some executives might balk at the idea of spending so much time in the field, Crawford believes his rental furniture company has grown and prospered precisely because he spends 50 percent of his time away from his office. He says his extended travels have given him the ability to temper reported facts with his own feelings for the marketplace. And he adds that the proof is in the numbers. In the 10 years since he bought Brook, revenues have grown from $800,000 to $50 million.

Crawford has a message for managers who say there's too much going on to leave their office for long periods of time: There *is* too much going on—out in the field.

Source: Leslie Brokaw, "Road Warriors," *Inc.* 14 (March 1992): 44–52.

COORDINATION

As soon as authority is delegated and thus passes from one organization level to another, coordination becomes necessary. **Coordination** may be defined as the process of integrating various individual and work group activities to efficiently achieve a common goal. The need for coordination between tasks can differ significantly. However, even in the simplest organization—a Boy Scout patrol, a sailboat crew—activities must be coordinated to achieve a common purpose.

Coordination.
The process of integrating various individual and work group activities to efficiently achieve a common goal.

In general, the degree of coordination required between tasks depends on their interdependence. Three types of task interdependence are typical: *pooled interdependence, sequential interdependence,* and *reciprocal interdependence.*[11]

POOLED INTERDEPENDENCE

To say that two work units are interdependent does not mean that they are *directly* dependent on the activities of one another. The advertising department at a Neiman-Marcus store is essentially independent from the shipping and receiving department. Yet, they are interdependent in the sense that each is part of the same organization. Failure of either could threaten the entire company and thus other departments. A situation in which each work unit renders a discrete contribution to an organization and is, in turn, supported by the organization is referred to as **pooled interdependence.** The degree of coordination required between units is minimal. Such a situation is depicted in Figure 9.5 (Panel A).

SEQUENTIAL INTERDEPENDENCE

The opposite of pooled interdependence is labeled **sequential interdependence.** In such situations, the outputs from one work unit are the inputs for a following work unit. The second unit is directly dependent upon the first finishing its work so that it can begin its assigned task. In other words, there is a direct, one-way interdependence. Take the example of a brewery as shown in Figure 9.5 (Panel B). A direct one-way interdependence exists between units. Hence, greater coordination is required in sequential than in pooled interdependence.

RECIPROCAL INTERDEPENDENCE

Reciprocal interdependence occurs when outputs from one work unit may serve as inputs for another *and* vice versa. In other words, there is a two-way interdependence. As shown in Figure 9.5 (Panel C), the maintenance and operations units of an airline provide an illustration of reciprocal interdependence. The output

Pooled interdependence.
A situation in which work units render a discrete contribution to an organization and, in turn, are supported by the organization.

Sequential interdependence.
A situation in which the outputs from one work unit are the inputs for a following work unit.

Reciprocal interdependence.
A situation in which outputs from one work unit serve as inputs for another and vice versa.

FIGURE 9.5 TYPES OF TASK INTERDEPENDENCE

A. Pool Interdependence

Work Unit A (Advertising) → Organization (Neiman-Marcus) → Work Unit B (Shipping and Receiving)

B. Sequential Interdependence

Purchase and Transportation of Raw Materials → Brewing → Bottling → Distribution

C. Reciprocal Interdependence

Input → Airplane Maintenance → Output → Airplane Operations → Output
Input

of the maintenance unit is input for the operations unit in the form of a serviceable aircraft. In turn, the byproduct (or output) of operations is an input for maintenance, in the form of an aircraft needing service. Obviously, this close interdependence necessitates a high degree of coordination since problems in either will be quickly felt by the other unit.

TYPES OF COORDINATION

Given different types of task interdependence, different forms of coordination would be expected. In addition to the chain of command, which, as described in Chapter 8, serves to define different degrees of authority and route directives and other information up and down the levels of an organization, there are four other

In Alcoa's smelting plant in Massena, NY, materials from the Rodding Department move sequentially to an area known as the Potroom for the next step of the production process. Workers from both departments formed a quality team to solve problems experienced by the Potroom with materials received from the Rodding Department. Here, smelting electrode superintendent Liz Fessenden and rodding servicer Bob Doran check the results of the new system developed by the quality team to reduce the "burnoff" problem. Group coordination helped reduce burnoffs by 96 percent per month.

basic types of coordination: informal coordination, programmed coordination, liaison coordination, and group coordination.

Informal Coordination

A great deal of coordination within an organization comes about voluntarily. Since it is impossible to anticipate everything, all organizations must rely on *informal coordination* to some degree.

Informal coordination includes those spontaneous gestures (often taken for granted) that lubricate an organization's social processes but are not directly part of task performance. Examples include helping co-workers with problems, accepting orders without a fuss, and accommodating the job-related requests of colleagues in other work units. For informal cooperation to develop, employees must:

1. Know and understand their own goals and those of their work unit
2. Have a clear understanding of what their jobs require
3. Identify with an organization and be willing to assist in achieving its goals

With regard to this last point, strong organization identification is often found in churches, charities, art foundations, and sometimes in business firms and government agencies, especially in crises like wars, disasters, and economic disruptions. A "let's pull together to get us through" attitude often develops at such times. Identification is often a result of careful employee selection and orientation and is usually strongest in employees who have undergone a lengthy training process (for example, clergy, nurses, and elite military groups, such as the Green Berets).

Informal coordination is helpful in all instances of interdependence. As organizations grow larger, however, informal coordination generally needs to be supplemented with other forms of coordination.

Programmed Coordination

As an organization becomes more complex, the importance of *programmed coordination* also increases. This involves establishing routines that channel work unit activities into paths consistent with an organization's overall goals. Ways of handling repetitive problems are often specified in an organization's standing plans, policies, procedures, and rules. Programmed coordination is found in organizations of all sizes. It is particularly useful in situations of pooled or sequential interdependence.

Liaison Coordination

Informal and programmed coordination are not always totally effective. Work units may interpret established routines differently than intended. In large organizations where such problems of coordination between work units are common, it is not unusual for separate *liaison* positions to be established for resolving disputes. For example, the House and Senate minority leaders serve the President as liaisons with Congress. Customer coordinators and ombudsmen similarly serve as liaisons. The former take care of major accounts, investigating and resolving complaints. The latter investigate employee, student, or consumer complaints and help achieve equitable settlements. The use of liaisons can be expensive, and their authority is often quite limited. The frustration that can result under such circumstances is understandably great. Consequently, liaisons are often used sparingly. However, they can be effective when time is crucial and expense is unimportant.

Group Coordination

Just as it is occasionally necessary to use a liaison to facilitate coordination between work units, situations occur when coordination is best achieved by having work group representatives formally meet. *Coordinating committees* are perhaps the best known means for this purpose. Representatives from different work units meet to resolve disputes and coordinate their activities. Joint House of Representatives and Senate congressional committees that meet to "hammer out" differences in proposed legislation are an example of *group coordination*. Such coordination is particularly useful in situations of sequential or reciprocal interdependence.

SUMMARY

This chapter has explored the nature of authority. It focused on (1) sources of authority (who grants whom authority), (2) the relationship between authority and power, (3) different types of authority (line, staff, and functional), (4) delegation (and decentralization) of authority, and (5) different types of coordination.

Learning Objective 1: Differentiate between authority and power.
Authority is the right to perform or command. Power is the capacity to influence others. People with authority have power; not all people with power, however, have authority.

Learning Objective 2: Describe the classical and acceptance views of authority.
There are two principal views regarding the source of authority. The classical view holds that authority passes from the "top down." In contrast, the acceptance view contends that authority flows from the "bottom up."

Learning Objective 3: Explain Barnard's so-called "zone of acceptance."
Barnard's so-called "zone of acceptance" is a conditional range within which subordinates will accept their superior's orders.

Learning Objective 4: Identify five basic types of power.
The five basic types of power are: reward power, coercive power, legitimate power, referent power, and expert power.

Learning Objective 5: Explain the difference between line and staff authority.
Line authority is authority that follows an organization's direct chain of command, starting with its board of directors and extending down through intervening layers to first-line management. Staff authority is authority to provide advice and expertise to assist line units in achieving their goals.

Learning Objective 6: Describe functional authority.
Functional authority is an arrangement that enables staff managers to exercise limited line authority over other units in matters related directly to staff expertise.

Learning Objective 7: Explain what is meant by employee empowerment.
Employee empowerment is the pushing of authority down to lower organization levels.

Learning Objective 8: **Recognize the importance of parity of authority and responsibility.**
Neither managers nor subordinates can legitimately be held responsible for things they cannot control. For this reason, traditional management theory holds that for effective delegation to take place, authority must equal responsibility.

Learning Objective 9: **Appreciate why some managers resist delegating authority.**
Managers give a host of reasons why they do not delegate. Table 9.2 lists some of the more popular reasons.

Learning Objective 10: **Understand why some subordinates resist accepting delegation.**
Subordinates commonly resist accepting delegation when they (1) have not received proper job information, (2) have not been trained properly, (3) lack self-confidence and fear personal failure, (4) have not been provided proper equipment or tools, (5) are uncertain there is anything to gain by accepting authority, and (6) find it easier to let their superior make all the decisions.

Learning Objective 11: **Identify the different types of task interdependence that can exist between work units.**
The three types of internal interdependence between work units are pooled, sequential, and reciprocal.

Learning Objective 12: **Specify the different types of coordination likely to exist in a typical organization.**
In addition to the chain of command, the different types of coordination likely to exist in a typical organization are informal coordination, programmed coordination, liaison coordination, and group coordination.

KEY TERMS

acceptance theory of authority 267

authority 266

centralized/decentralized 275

classical view of authority 266

coercive power 269

coordination 279

delegation 274

expert power 270

functional authority 271

legitimate power 269

line authority 271

line unit 271

parity of authority and responsibility 275

pooled interdependence 280

power 268

reciprocal interdependence 280

referent power 269

reward power 269

sequential interdependence 280

staff authority 271

staff unit 271

zone of acceptance 267

THE MANAGEMENT EXPERIENCE   HOW WELL DO YOU DELEGATE?

You can get a good idea of whether you are delegating as much as you should by responding to the following items. Answer as accurately and frankly as possible.

How to Test Your Delegation Habits

	Strongly Agree				Strongly Disagree
1. I'd delegate more, but the jobs I delegate never seem to get done the way I want them to be done.	5	4	3	2	1
2. I don't feel I have the time to delegate properly.	5	4	3	2	1
3. I carefully check on subordinates' work without letting them know I'm doing it, so I can correct their mistakes if necessary before they cause too many problems.	5	4	3	2	1
4. I delegate the whole job—giving the opportunity for the subordinate to complete it without any of my involvement. Then I review the end result.	5	4	3	2	1
5. When I have given clear instructions and the task isn't done right, I get upset.	5	4	3	2	1
6. I feel the staff lacks the commitment that I have. So any task I delegate won't get done as well as I'd do it.	5	4	3	2	1
7. I'd delegate more, but I feel I can do the task better than the person I might delegate it to.	5	4	3	2	1
8. I'd delegate more, but if the individual I delegate the task to does an incompetent job, I'll be severely criticized.	5	4	3	2	1
9. If I were to delegate a task, my job wouldn't be nearly as much fun.	5	4	3	2	1
10. When I delegate a task, I often find that the outcome is such that I end up doing the task over again myself.	5	4	3	2	1
11. I have not really found that delegation saves any time.	5	4	3	2	1
12. I delegate a task clearly and concisely, explaining exactly how it should be accomplished.	5	4	3	2	1
13. I can't delegate as much as I'd like to because my subordinates lack the necessary experience.	5	4	3	2	1
14. I feel that when I delegate I lose control.	5	4	3	2	1
15. I would delegate more but I'm pretty much a perfectionist.	5	4	3	2	1
16. I work longer hours than I should.	5	4	3	2	1
17. I can give subordinates the routine tasks, but I feel I must keep nonroutine tasks myself.	5	4	3	2	1
18. My own boss expects me to keep very close to all details of my job.	5	4	3	2	1

Total score

Scoring: 90–72, Ineffective delegation; 71–54, Delegation habits need substantial improvement; 53–36, You still have room to improve; 35–18, Superior delegation.

Source: Reprinted by permission of the publisher from Theodore J. Krein, "How to Improve Delegation Habits," *Management Review* 71 (May 1982), 59, © 1982. American Management Association, New York. All rights reserved.

REVIEW AND DISCUSSION QUESTIONS

1. Recognizing that authority is both allocated from above and acknowledged from below, reconcile the classical and acceptance views of authority.

2. Typical U.S. workers would likely find it unacceptable if their supervisors gave them orders about where they should live. Explain why this might be so in terms of Barnard's "zone of acceptance."

3. The first three types of power identified by French and Raven—reward, coercive, and legitimate—are associated with a manager's position. The higher a manager's rank, the more of this power he or she has. Referent and expert power are part of the person, not the position, so they can exist anywhere in an organization—a crackerjack engineer or a secretary who's the only one who really understands a company's filing system. Drawing on your past experience, give examples of each type of power being wielded.

4. In 1597, Francis Bacon observed, "Knowledge is power." What did he mean? Give examples to support your answer.

5. Line-staff conflict occurs for many reasons. Reflect on the following timeworn adages: "Staff should be on tap, not top," and "Staff should sell, not tell."

6. Malcolm Forbes, the late publisher of *Forbes* magazine, has been quoted as saying, "Those who enjoy responsibility usually get it; those who merely like exercising authority usually lose it."[12] Comment.

7. Explain why delegation of authority should not be confused with the relinquishing of accountability.

8. The Union Pacific Railroad operates 23,000 miles of rail in 19 states. It has 2,800 locomotives, 84,000 freight cars, and 30,000 employees. Reflecting on these statistics, comment on why decentralization typically becomes more necessary as a company gets bigger.

9. Despite repeated attempts, you've been unable to persuade a supervisor in a department under your direction to delegate authority. As a result, the supervisor is always working overtime, and the department is invariably a production bottleneck. What can you do to convince the supervisor of the benefits of effective delegation?

10. Explain how delegation can be made a basic ingredient of a subordinate development program by providing learning opportunities.

CASE 9.1 "ALL CHIEFS AND NO INDIANS"

Kennon Industries is a medium-size manufacturer of business equipment and supplies. Located in Wilton, Iowa, it has grown fast in recent years, although profit margins have not kept pace with increases in sales and employment.

Kennon Industries's president, Ann Fletcher, was brought in from a larger company when the previous president retired and the board felt that an outsider was needed to rejuvenate the company, especially in terms of profitability. When Fletcher asked about some other success indicators, she found that absenteeism and turnover were up, quality was down, and customer relations were poor.

The number of problems Fletcher faced was large. The company's financial record had been weakening, and production costs were increasing

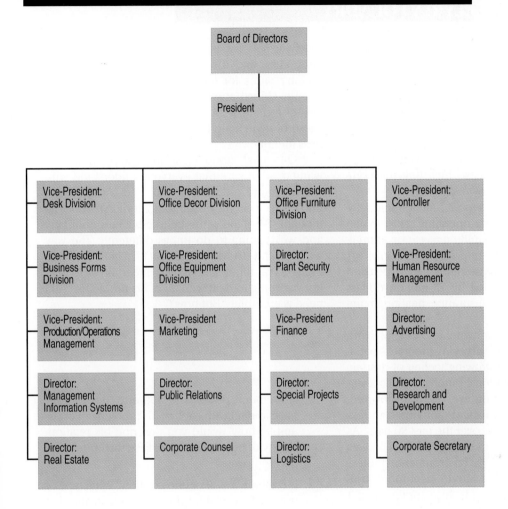

relative to past performance. Fletcher knew she could not run the company the way her predecessor, Noel Lincoln, had. Lincoln had built up the company for the widow of the founder, Ed Upton, after Upton died. Essentially a salesman, he had let the company take care of itself. "Just get enough orders—that's what keeps a company going," he believed.

Fletcher looked at the organization chart that Lincoln had left her (see Case Exhibit 1) and was not sure she could live with a large span of control. Fletcher felt that this was the time to centralize some of the decisions that had been left to drift. Yet she knew she could not make all the key decisions herself (nor did she desire to). She began to think about what she should do to make the company easier to handle, yet not overly centralized.

Problems

You are a consultant hired by Fletcher.

1. Recommend a better organization structure to deal with the firm's problems.

2. Recommend an appropriate span of control for Fletcher.

3. Justify your recommendations.

CASE 9.2 ELYRIA FOUNDRY

Elyria Foundry is an 85-year-old iron foundry located in a blue-collar town some 30 miles from Cleveland, Ohio. Originally started as a job shop for the area's heavy manufacturing companies, the company still turns out large compression valves for industrial air conditioners, engine frames, and pump housings. In 1980 Elyria Foundry posted sales in excess of $16 million and employed over 350 workers. The demand was so high that the company didn't even have its own sales force.

In 1982 sales slumped to $7.7 million annually. In August 1983 the plant was operating at just 15 percent of capacity, losing $3 million a year on annualized sales of $4 million, and employed only 107 people. Additional expenses included a pension plan that was underfunded by $3 million dollars and monthly charges for insurance, heating, maintenance, and security.

Gregg Foster, the new owner and CEO of Elyria Foundry, sat in his office, surveying the stacks of paper on his desk. With a growing feeling of despair, he realized what he had just purchased. His leveraged net worth, including everything he owned, borrowed, or had as collateral, amounted to less than the company's losses over the past 90 days. As if these problems were not enough, the union was threatening to strike, the U.S. Environmental Protection Agency might require him to meet more stringent and expensive standards, his suppliers might require cash up front rather than deal on a credit basis, and his payroll was full of expensive perks such as 5 weeks' vacation a year. "How am I going to deal with all of these people?" he wondered. "I can't force my suppliers to give me credit, and I can't move the EPA. I can control payroll, but the union might strike."

Next, Foster's thoughts turned to his staff: 38 professionals who were holdovers from the previous management. These employees, in addition to receiving salaries, also had the benefit of six company cars, and the company itself owned three country clubs for employee use. "They are good people, skilled at what they do, but they are sterile—corporate people," he thought. "There is no sense of ownership about them. We have no business identity."

One goal stood clear in Foster's mind: He wanted to be sure that everyone understood who was in charge and what he expected. "As of today, I don't care what they used to do. It didn't work," he thought. "As of today, this becomes a new company and we're going to do things differently. The way we're going to do them isn't negotiable." His thoughts rambled, and he was uncertain as to how he was going to deal with all of his problems. "All I need is credibility. But how?"

Source: John B. White, University of Alabama at Birmingham, based on Robert A. Mamis, "Man of Iron," *Inc.* January 1992: 56–59.

Problems

1. How much power and authority does Foster have to deal with each of his problems? For example, how would you describe his relationship with his suppliers, the EPA, the union, and his employees?

2. Is Foster in a staff or line position? What type of power do you think he will exert in the first months of his ownership? How about later?

3. Assume for the moment that Foster manages to deliver his speech about how things are going to be different. What position of power (that is, reward, coercive, legitimate, referent, or expert) do you think he should use in his speech?

4. Is Barnard's acceptance theory of authority applicable to Foster's problems? If so, how? If not, what theory would you apply?

NOTES

[1] Cyril J. McDonnell, "The Source of Managerial Authority," *Political Science Quarterly* 67 (December 1952): 573–588.

[2] Chester I. Barnard, *The Functions of the Executive* (Cambridge: Harvard University Press, 1938), 161–184.

[3] Herbert A. Simon, *Administrative Behavior,* 3rd ed. (New York: Macmillan, 1976), 12.

[4] Douglas McGregor, *The Human Side of Enterprise* (New York: McGraw-Hill, 1960), 23.

5 John R. P. French, Jr., and Bertram Raven, "The Bases of Social Power," in Dorwin Cartwright (ed.), *Studies in Social Power* (Ann Arbor: Institute for Social Research, University of Michigan, 1959), 150–165.

6 William F. Whyte, *Organizational Behavior: Theory and Application* (Homewood, Ill.: Irwin, 1969), 409.

7 Quoted in Russell Shaw, "Allen F. Jacobson: Chairman & CEO, 3M," *Sky* 18 (September 1989): 56.

8 Quoted in Thomas A. Stewart, "New Ways to Exercise Power," *Fortune*, November 6, 1989, 64.

9 Richardo Semler, "Managing without Managers," *Harvard Business Review* 67 (September–October 1989): 80.

10 Quoted in Patricia Sellers, "Pepsi Keeps on Going After No. 1," *Fortune*, March 11, 1991, 68.

11 James D. Thompson, *Organizations in Action* (New York: McGraw-Hill, 1967), 54–56.

12 Quoted in "Thoughts on the Business Life," *Forbes*, June 25, 1990, 340.

CHAPTER 10

LEARNING OBJECTIVES

Upon completing this chapter, you should be able to:

- Distinguish between job specialization and person specialization.
- List the advantages and disadvantages of job specialization.
- Distinguish between job enlargement (horizontal loading) and job enrichment (vertical loading).
- Identify different core dimensions that can be modified to enrich jobs.
- Enumerate various methods for implementing job enrichment.
- Discuss self-managing teams.
- Identify various preconditions and constraints on job-design efforts.

n October 4, 1991, while negotiations for a new labor contract were under way, auto workers at General Motors's Saturn plant in Spring Hill, Tennessee, staged a demonstration, wearing black-and-orange armbands and participating in a work slowdown. Were they looking for higher pay, shorter hours, or more fringe benefits? No—they were protesting management's pressure to increase production at the expense of quality.

When General Motors started up the Saturn plant in 1983, its major goal was to produce high-quality small cars that would compete with Japanese imports. The cars were well designed: Flexible materials were used for doors, fenders, and quarter panels to reduce the possibility of damage; dipsticks were color coded and made more accessible; and the cars boast a glove compartment that doesn't spill its contents when opened. While attractive styling and peppy response have contributed to the Saturn's success, it is the well-engineered and well-built details that have allowed dealers to sell the new cars at list price.

JOB DESIGN AND SELF-MANAGING TEAMS

The car itself isn't the only aspect of Saturn that was well designed. Environmentally safer water-based paints, just-in-time inventory control methods, and new worker involvement in decision-making processes were all part of the plan. As a matter of fact, assembly workers were consulted when the car was still in the design stage.

Implementing all these ideas has not been easy, and in the first year, production lagged far behind initial goals—hence the pressure from top management for higher production and the resulting worker revolt. The workers contended that more time was needed to smooth out the new system. Because of the unusual relationship between labor and management at Saturn, both sides won: Production goals were lowered and the 20 percent of the workers' pay that was to be tied to production goals was paid anyway; meanwhile, the workers redoubled their efforts to bring the plant up to capacity and voted to extend the 4-day workweek to 5 days. The Saturn plant was operating at 85 percent of capacity by the first quarter of 1992.

The Saturn plant incorporates many different jobs, and the unique way in which those jobs have been designed contributes in large part to the quality of its cars. In this chapter, we will investigate job-design considerations and how they affect an organization's success and employee job satisfaction.

Source: Adapted from David Woodruff, "At Saturn, What Workers Want Is...Fewer Defects," *Business Week*, December 2, 1991, 117–118.

In recent years, efforts have been made throughout North America and Western Europe to "humanize work" and give employees "a voice that matters." These efforts have been prompted by a feeling among top-level managers that organizations in general have only begun to tap maximum employee potential. The current generation of employees brings more abilities, higher expectations, and a greater desire for self-responsibility to the workplace than at any other time in history. As a consequence, various programs for workplace reform and employee empowerment have emerged. They bear labels such as *quality of work life, employee involvement,* or, more generally, *job design.*

The so-called "job design movement" rests on the premise that effective performance and authentic workplace satisfaction flow mainly from job content. Thus, the practice of **job design** is concerned with designing the content of jobs to enhance feelings of achievement, worthwhile accomplishment, and other intrinsic outcomes.

Job design.
Designing the content of jobs to enhance intrinsic outcomes.

In this chapter, we will examine the nature of job design. We will first explore *specialization,* distinguishing between the specialization of jobs and the specialization of people. We will then consider *job enlargement* and *job enrichment,* two concepts associated with the job-design movement. Next, we will identify five "core dimensions" that can be modified to enrich jobs. Finally, after commenting on self-managing teams, we will note various preconditions and constraints on job-design efforts.

SPECIALIZATION

As recounted in Chapter 2, an important aspect of the Industrial Revolution was the transfer of work skills from craftworkers to machines. Paralleling this transfer was a shift from craft jobs to specialized jobs. A degree of confusion can be avoided at the outset of our discussion by distinguishing between **job specialization** and **person specialization.**[1] The first refers to the narrowing of activities to simple, repetitive routines. The individuals who perform such tasks acquire little power because virtually anyone can perform them, often with little or no training. Classic examples of extreme job specialization include tightening bolts on an assembly line or stuffing pimentos into olives. Person specialization, on the other hand, involves individuals with a high degree of training, such as medicine, law, accounting, engineering, and management. Such specialists have power because their ability makes other people dependent on them. By virtue of their power, they can influence the satisfaction they receive from others. Consequently, their fate is not entirely beyond their own control.

Job specialization.
The narrowing of activities to simple, repetitive routines.

Person specialization.
Individuals with a high degree of training who have power because their ability makes other people dependent on them.

Job specialization is illustrated in Figure 10.1 on page 294. As shown, a completed assignment requires the assembling, testing, and packaging of a single unit. With job specialization, the assignment is separated into three jobs, each performed by a different specialist. In a furniture company, for example, a manager may have four options for manufacturing wooden chairs:

Rolls-Royce has an unsurpassed reputation for the luxury and quality of its products. The degree of handcraftsmanship found in every Rolls-Royce motor car is unique within the automobile industry. Rolls-Royce employees are highly skilled and work in jobs designed to facilitate a lengthy and painstaking production process.

1. Each employee makes an entire chair.

2. Each makes a major subpart (seats, arms, legs).

3. Each makes one complete part (chair backs).

4. Each performs a few operations on one subpart (such as running a lathe to turn spindles).

Alternative 4 is a classic example of job specialization. Managers who select job specialization as a job-design alternative typically do so in anticipation of certain benefits. These include:

- Less skilled (and lower paid) employees can be hired because of simple job assignments.

- Jobs can be mastered in less time, thus reducing training costs.

- Constant repetition leads to heightened expertise, which increases productivity.

- More opportunities are provided for utilizing the primary talents of individual employees.

- Work is performed more quickly because employees do not lose time shifting from one activity to another.

- Dependence on particular employees or special skills is minimized because, for all practical purposes, employees are interchangeable.

FIGURE 10.1 JOB SPECIALIZATION

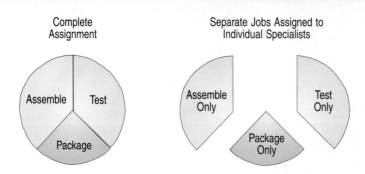

These benefits allow Honda to assemble 875 cars each working day. Rolls-Royce, on the other hand, requires 6 months to build a car that can cost as much as $225,000. Indeed, Honda makes as many cars in an afternoon as Rolls-Royce does in a year.

Despite the economic attractiveness of these benefits, increased criticism has led to demands for less fragmented and more challenging jobs. Critics charge that job specialization impedes employee performance by breeding discontent and resistance, which are expressed through workplace carelessness and indifference, absenteeism and turnover, and sabotage and strikes. "Monday cars" from Detroit assembly lines and even violence are potent reminders of how employees have rebelled through the years against mundane work. Consider the American Motors Jeep plant in Toledo, where 5,400 assembly-line workers produce 750 cars per day. Several years ago, tension built to a point where a group of workers began sabotaging the assembly line, bashing Jeeps with welding tools. The line was intermittently shut down over the next week with a resulting cost in lost wages of more than $1 million. More recently, 15 percent of the plant's second shift failed to report for work one Friday, forcing Jeep to shut the plant and send the other 85 percent of the employees home, without pay. As this example attests, several disadvantages are associated with job specialization that managers must consciously balance against the aforementioned benefits. These disadvantages include:

- Diminished motivation
- Poor-quality output
- Diminished job satisfaction
- High turnover
- High absenteeism
- Sabotage and strikes

JOB ENLARGEMENT

Job enlargement is one of the earliest concepts associated with the job-design movement. A job is enlarged when an employee carries out a wider range of activities of approximately the same skill level. For example, in Figure 10.2 (Panel A), Job 1 consists of five activities. To enlarge its range, four activities could be added, two from the preceding job and two from the following job. Job enlargement, therefore, has been referred to as *horizontal loading*. It serves to increase the number and va-

Job enlargement.
Extending a job's range so that the number and variety of different activities an employee performs is increased. (Also known as horizontal loading.)

CLOSE UP: QUALITY "QUALITY IS JOB #1"

What goes around comes around, or so the saying goes. The 1980s was a period of increased competition and perilous change for blue-collar manufacturing workers. The lucky ones merely experienced major upheaval in their job responsibilities and place of work. The less fortunate received pink slips.

Increasing global competition and the recession of the early 1990s brought about the need for similar measures among white-collar workers. The streamlining techniques originally tested on the factory floor will now help to redesign operational methods at upper ranks, with the primary objective being improved productivity.

Companies of all kinds are now stressing two concepts: quality and customer service. Practically speaking, this means minimizing errors, eliminating excessive inspections and approvals, and delegating whenever possible. It also means concentrating only on input that adds value for customers.

After observing several Japanese companies, among them Hitachi and Toyota, a senior IBM manager concluded that the company's Rochester, Minnesota, minicomputer plant had roughly 20 percent too many indirect laborers—engineers, accountants, managers—who didn't actually add value to tangible products. He immediately set about boosting the productivity of these employees, turning their emphasis away from the actual nuts and bolts of manufacturing and toward product design, development, integration, and support—the jobs they were hired to do.

Pitfalls have materialized along the path toward increased productivity, often because the process sometimes involves a total overhaul of how things are done. Managers who scrupulously economized entire factory structures balked at applying the same measures to themselves and their own staffs.

Interestingly, although the first impulse might be to cut back on clerical help, that was not always the best move. A Georgia economist found over the course of a 6-year study that such action often resulted in managers' spending as much as one-fifth of their time on completing clerical tasks. Another executive who analyzed the relation between work force levels and overall financial performance concluded that companies with the most clerks per manager or professional tend to have the highest profits.

Wholesale computerization doesn't seem to hold the answer either, or at least not all of it. Lengthy studies have shown that marginally productive companies often spent far more money on sophisticated information systems than highly productive ones. The consensus seems to be that automating inefficient ways of doing things won't necessarily improve efficiency. Mistakes usually aren't related to incompetence on the part of employees, but rather to the way they have been instructed to do their work. Systematic procedures that are antiquated, redundant, or overly complicated must first be identified and eliminated, before new technology can be introduced to provide measurable benefits in productivity.

Making offices more productive is an imperative of the 1990s, and companies are learning new ways to increase output among white-collar workers. Product quality and customer service are getting new emphasis. Busywork is on the way out. And automated information systems, once seen as saviors, are now considered only a complementary part of overall office job design.

Source: Adapted from Ronald Henkoff, "Make Your Office More Productive," *Fortune,* February 25, 1991, 73–76, 78, 80, 84.

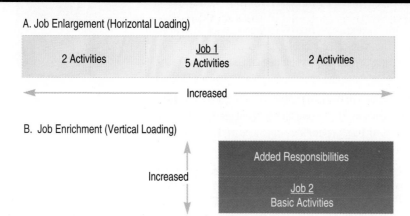

FIGURE 10.2 JOB ENLARGEMENT AND JOB ENRICHMENT

A. Job Enlargement (Horizontal Loading)

riety of activities performed. Examples include a traveling salesperson who is given an additional territory to cover, a secretary who is assigned work from a second manager, and an assembly-line worker who bolts on car bumpers as well as wheels. The underlying assumption in each case is that an expanded job will be more interesting because it is more varied.

JOB ENRICHMENT

Job enrichment is a second way in which jobs may be enhanced. It involves extending a job's depth so that employee control is increased. For example, in Figure 10.2 (Panel B), Job 2 consists of certain basic activities. To extend its depth, employee control could be expanded by adding new responsibilities, such as ordering materials or verifying quality. Job enrichment, therefore, has been referred to as *vertical loading*. For example, a supervisor with the traditional duties of filling production quotas, meeting delivery deadlines, achieving quality levels, and controlling costs could be given responsibility for helping cut the time required to get a new product on line; implementing a new, computerized customer order tracking system; and devising a materials handling system that reduces costs below current levels. Job enrichment encourages employers to give as much responsibility to their employees as possible.

CORE DIMENSIONS

Most job-enrichment applications draw on the work of J. Richard Hackman and Greg R. Oldham.[2] They have identified five job characteristics, termed *core dimensions,* that can be modified to enrich jobs. The basic idea is that the more a job contains these core dimensions, the more likely it is to provide employees with feelings of satisfaction and motivation. Higher quality performance and lower absenteeism and turnover should also be more likely. Accordingly, Hackman and Oldham suggest that managers determine the quantity and quality of the different core dimensions present in the jobs they supervise. These core dimensions are:

1. *Skill variety.* Jobs entailing several activities, each requiring a different set of skills, are said to be high in **skill variety** and are typically viewed as chal-

Job enrichment.
Extending a job's depth so that employee control is increased. (Also known as vertical loading.)

Skill variety.
The extent to which a job requires employees to perform a wide number of activities.

lenging, since they allow employees to perform a wide range of skills. In addition to providing more challenge, such variety allows increased freedom and creativity. However, it also requires more education, training, and experience.

As an illustration of high skill variety, consider one assembly station at the General Motors Buick plant in Lansing, Michigan. Working together as a team, three assemblers put together a Buick Reatta's dashboard, install its steering assembly, and hook up its various electronically operated hardware—stereo, digital instrument panel, door locks, antenna, ignition, and lights. Before the Reatta moves to the next station, the assemblers run the hardware through a series of computerized checks. All three assemblers switch positions daily and thus have to master dozens of tasks involving numerous skills.

2. *Task identity*. **Task identity** refers to the extent to which a job allows employees to perform a "whole" piece of work and to clearly identify the outcome of their effort. Specialized jobs are low in task identity because employees perform only a small segment of an entire job. This rarely provides a sense of accomplishment because the employees never have a picture of the whole. Designing jobs so that employees perform a job from beginning to end increases task identity.

Consider the job of a dressmaker. This job could be designed so that one group of dressmakers cuts patterns, another assembles them, a third sews them, and a fourth inspects the finished garments. Conversely, individual dressmakers could be allowed to cut, assemble, sew, and inspect completed dresses. The latter would constitute a "whole" job, with the dressmakers not only using a variety of skills, but being able to clearly identify the results of their individual efforts. Ford Motor Co.'s Aston Martin Lagonda auto works in England provides a second example of task identity. Each engine is handmade and autographed by a single craftsman. It takes 16 weeks to complete a car.

3. *Task significance*. The extent to which a job has a substantial impact on the lives of others is referred to as its **task significance.** The impact may be local or worldwide. Feeling that they have accomplished something significant in life is important to many employees.

At Apple Computer, for example, many employees speak with pride of their pioneering work in introducing the first personal computer, realizing that

Task identity.
The extent to which a job allows employees to perform a "whole" piece of work and to clearly identify the outcome of their efforts.

Task significance.
The extent to which a job has a substantial impact on the lives of others.

U.S. Shoe uses job enlargement to increase employee motivation and satisfaction. Modular work areas have been created as part of U.S. Shoe's quick-response manufacturing techniques. Greater quality and flexibility are achieved by cross-training employees to perform two or three shoe-making steps instead of only one as in traditional production lines. Employees are also given training in communication skills and group dynamics to enhance the satisfaction and motivational impact of working in modular teams.

they had an important part in making history and changing the world. Likewise, the fact that Bristol-Myers-Squibb spends more on cancer research than any other pharmaceutical company makes its employees feel part of something significant.

4. *Autonomy.* The extent to which employees are free to act—to schedule their own activities, decide procedures, and select required equipment—is referred to as **autonomy.** Some companies, for example, allow employees to decide what to do, when to do it, and how to do it, as long as the necessary work is completed within a set time and within cost and quality limits. This way, the employees control their own job pace, tool usage, and other factors. On the other hand, some jobs are highly programmed. A sales representative, for example, might be told when to start work, which customers to call, what sales pitch to use, and what answers to give to common customer questions.

Autonomy.
The extent to which employees are free to act.

Autonomy can empower managers to feel like owners rather than rabble who have to ask permission at every step. This is important in retaining the very best and brightest who will not accept a short leash. It can also tap their entrepreneurial impulses. At one time, Du Pont manager Kurt M. Landgraf found the hassle of initiating a new project daunting. Proposals had to undergo four separate reviews. Recognizing the negative impact of this practice, Du Pont now rewards its best and brightest managers with more autonomy. When Landgraf recently wanted $5 million to start a new generic-drug venture, he needed approval from only one manager above him.[3]

Autonomy is also important at the operative level. On Toyota's assembly line, each employee serves as a quality-control inspector for the process just

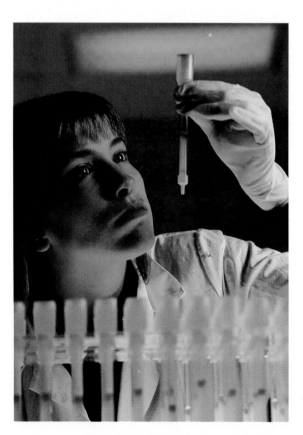

Bristol-Myers-Squibb employees can take pride in their company's efforts to combat cancer and heart disease. Here, a cardiovascular researcher at the company's Princeton, New Jersey, facility uses ion exchange columns to test a new compound that may lower cholesterol and save many lives. Employees of socially responsible companies such as Bristol-Myers-Squibb know that their work is important to society as well as to their companies.

before his. If a part is not installed properly, he can reject it by pulling a rope to alert his supervisor. If the problem is not fixed by the next unit, he is free to stop the line by tugging the rope a second time. As is the case with managers, such autonomy can empower operative employees to feel like owners, too.

5. *Performance feedback.* **Performance feedback** refers to the extent to which employees are provided with information about how well they are doing their jobs. It may come from a job itself, co-workers, immediate supervisors, clients, or perhaps subordinates. Other possible sources include performance appraisals, awards and promotions, and even personal evaluations of one's own feelings and ideas.

> To facilitate performance feedback, operative employees at Procter & Gamble's Duncan Hines cake factory in Jackson, Tennessee, are given letters from customers who have had baking problems. The employees are responsible for calling the letter writers and figuring out what caused their problems. Tektronix goes one step further. Attached to every oscilloscope it sells is a card listing the names of the employees who built it, along with a toll-free telephone number where they can be reached. Every day several calls are received from customers. The employees and their managers meet daily to discuss these calls and the possible need for further follow-up.

Figure 10.3 contrasts the profile of a specialized job (an auto assembler's) with that of an enriched job (a research scientist's), according to the core dimensions identified by Hackman and Oldham. Although there are admittedly large individual differences in how various employees react to the five core dimensions, try predicting how you would respond to these two jobs.

APPROACHES TO JOB ENRICHMENT

Numerous approaches have attempted to capitalize on the work of Hackman and Oldham in an effort to tap maximum employee potential and increase employee empowerment. *Flextime, compressed workweeks, job rotation,* and *job sharing* are four examples of such efforts.

Performance feedback.

The extent to which employees are provided with information about how well they are doing their jobs.

FIGURE 10.3 CONTRASTING CORE-DIMENSION PROFILES FOR AN AUTO ASSEMBLER AND A RESEARCH SCIENTIST

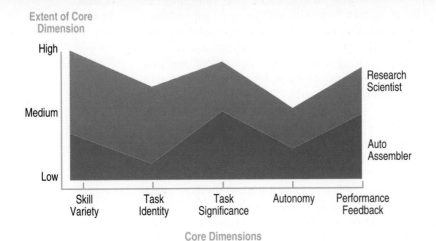

Flextime is an attempt to increase autonomy by allowing employees to determine their own work schedules. It allows employees, within certain limits, to vary their arrival and departure times to and from work. Typically, during a so-called *core time* (for example, 9:00–10:00 a.m. and 1:00–3:00 p.m.), everyone is expected to be at work. During the remaining hours (flexible time), employees can choose their own schedule, as long as they work an 8-hour day.

The so-called **compressed workweek** is another form of innovative scheduling intended to increase autonomy by allowing employees more control over their workday. A typical compressed schedule involves a shortened workweek in which employees work more than 8 hours a day. For instance, employees may work either four 10-hour or three 12-hour days. The work schedules of different employees typically are staggered so that an organization is open 5 or 6 days a week. Some organizations, however, simply shut down for the balance of each week.

Job rotation is a third form of job enrichment. It consists of periodically shifting employees from one job to another to increase skill variety and task identity. Job rotation can also be used as a training method to increase employee knowledge, skills, and abilities. It will be discussed further in this regard in Chapter 13, "Human Resource Development."

Job sharing represents an additional form of job enrichment intended to increase employee autonomy. It involves one job being shared by two or more people. For example, one person might work from 8:00 a.m. until noon, with another working from 1:00 p.m. until 5:00 p.m. Job sharing allows an organization to use the talents of more than one person in a given job. It also can be used to attract employees who may not be available on a full-time basis, such as retirees with special skills or parents who wish to spend more time with their families than is possible when working full time. Job sharing can likewise be a way to accommodate the needs of physically impaired employees.

SELF-MANAGING TEAMS

Examples of successful job-enrichment applications abound. In broad terms, these applications represent an effort to fulfill organization requirements, as well as the personal needs of individual employees. An increasing number of job enrichment applications involve **self-managing teams**—that is, groups of employees who have the day-to-day responsibility for managing themselves and the work they do. The teams are self-managing in the sense that they work with minimal supervision; make decisions about who performs which tasks on a given day; and set their own production and, often, profit goals. In addition, these teams often are also responsible for maintaining product quality, ordering materials and equipment, meeting customers, developing and monitoring their own budgets, hiring and terminating team members, and even poring over financial records.

By pushing decision making down in the ranks, self-managing teams not only represent an application of job enrichment, but also another move toward greater employee empowerment. It is hoped that such empowerment will increase motivation and productivity by unleashing employee talent and, thus, improve an organization's ability to compete.

Self-managing teams typically consist of five to 12 multiskilled members who rotate jobs and produce an entire product. Members are cross-trained to perform all of the jobs that fall within a team's work area. This makes it possible for team members to fill in for one another and respond quickly to changes in models and

Flextime.
Allowing employees, within certain limits, to determine their own work schedules.

Compressed workweek.
A shortened workweek in which employees work more than 8 hours a day.

Job rotation.
Periodically shifting employees from one job to another to increase skill variety and task identity.

Job sharing.
One job being shared by two or more people.

Self-managing teams.
A group of employees who have the day-to-day responsibility for managing themselves and the work they do.

At Whirlpool's Oxford, Mississippi, division, employees are encouraged to take greater control of their jobs by becoming more involved in the facility's daily operation. Hourly workers take an active part in screening, interviewing, training, and sometimes dismissing coworkers.

production runs. Moreover, because members understand an entire production process, they are more adept at diagnosing defects. Experts estimate that this flexibility and its resulting benefits can result in a 30–50 percent increase in productivity.[4]

Team members are given incentives to learn. At companies like Motorola and Northern Telecom, employees receive pay raises for each new skill they master. An employee at Lake Superior Paper can reach a top salary by mastering 14 different skills. Promotions and pay at Lake Superior are determined by team members who evaluate one another's performance.

Beyond its beneficial effect on productivity, developing a range of skills can make work more satisfying, increasing feelings of dignity and self-worth. In this respect, as employees have been encouraged to use their brains, as well as their bodies, enormous stores of hidden energy and talent have been unleashed. A multiskilled team at General Motors figured out how to reduce from 52 to 30 the number of parts in the rear floor of Oldsmobiles and Cadillacs. This, in turn, reduced the number of required stamping dies from 93 to 38 and the number of presses needed from 93 to 10. The result was a $52 million savings.

Self-managing teams represent a fundamental change in how jobs are designed. Their advocates contend that to deny people responsibility for all aspects of their jobs is to lose much of their potential impact. At the same time, the investment required to build and maintain effective teams should not be underestimated. Moreover, apart from the dollars and cents involved, building an effective team can take years and, perhaps, may never be accomplished. Teams require constant monitoring and, in many cases, renewing. Some never gel, the only solution being to disband them and start all over again. The dynamics of group development are discussed further in Chapter 17, "Group Dynamics and Conflict."

VOLVO: AN EXAMPLE

Perhaps the most well-known example of a job-enrichment application involving self-managing teams is Volvo's new Uddevalla plant, where eight teams of seven to

SMART MANAGEMENT　TELEWORK: A NEW WAY OF WORKING

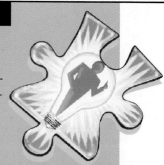

Telework, a rapidly developing, wide-ranging phenomenon, has redrawn the traditional boundaries of work. This phenomenon, also known as "telecommuting," originally referred to on- or off-line electronic work performed at home by employees using information or communication technologies. Its meaning has more recently evolved to include work involving satellite centers geographically removed from a central headquarters, but remaining in constant electronic communication; work performed at neighborhood centers shared by different users and belonging to various organizations or self-employed entrepreneurs; and work performed by employees who travel and use electronic communication facilities to link up with their headquarters and to access electronic mail, data banks, and so forth.

Advantages of telework include the following:

1. *Productivity increases.* The consensus is that large productivity gains result from telework. These gains are attributed to the lack of interruptions and to improved concentration, increased motivation and job satisfaction, higher dedication and morale, and a higher energy level resulting from the elimination of the wasted time and frustration of commuting.

2. *Recruitment and retention.* Telework permits the retention of employees considering withdrawal from work, such as women after maternity leave and senior employees nearing retirement. It can also tap new labor sources among the home-bound and in economically depressed areas, especially where specific skills are in short supply. Finally, it is attractive to employees who are searching for better places to live or for alternative family, leisure, and work arrangements.

3. *Rural development.* Telework can be used to create employment opportunities in rural and isolated areas and thus help reduce regional imbalances. This idea was sparked by public initiatives to provide services not previously available in remote areas. The Commission of the European Communities has highlighted the potential of telework "to reduce the social and economic gap between urban and rural, central and peripheral regions."

4. *Reduced commuting time.* The reduction or elimination of time spent commuting is typically among the main reasons cited for choosing telework. For society, telework means reduced pollution and reduced traffic congestion.

5. *Flexible scheduling.* For many, telework's flexibility is a key factor in their search for practical ways to reconcile their family responsibilities or styles of life with earning an income. In many cases, an added incentive is the significant reduction in time spent commuting. Teleworkers also often enjoy relative autonomy and the possibility of concentrating harder and being more productive away from office distractions.

Certain drawbacks are also associated with telework, however. Most notably, it may lower teleworkers' pay, reduce their benefits, and affect their health. Computer professionals performing telework typically earn less than on-site workers performing similar activities. Additionally, overtime compensation, which can make up a large proportion of a computer professional's salary, is not usually paid to teleworkers. Further, teleworkers often are denied benefits because they are frequently classified as self-employed or independent contractors. Finally, telework can affect the physical and psychological well-being of the individuals involved. Regarding the former, adequate levels of safety and health protection for teleworkers may be jeopardized by difficulties in carrying out inspections. The access of public authorities to private homes may be limited. Regarding psychological well-being, by separating em-

Continued on next page.

ployees from their co-workers, telework can generate feelings of isolation and stress and have an adverse impact on their morale.

Sources: Adapted from Vittorio Di Martino and Linda Wirth, "Telework: A New Way of Working and Living," *International Labour Review* 129 (5), 1990: 529–554; Edward Segal, "How to Commute in Your Bathrobe," *Wall Street Journal*, July 1, 1991, A10; and Meghan O'Leary, "Home Sweet Office," *CIO* 4 (July 1991): 30–40.

10 members routinely assemble entire cars from chassis to windshields. Each team assembles four cars per shift. Members are cross-trained to handle all assembly jobs. The teams largely supervise themselves, handling production scheduling, maintaining product quality, hiring new members, and performing other duties normally reserved for supervisors.

The Uddevalla plant has no assembly lines. Rather, at each work station a car body is mounted on a "tilt," rotisserie-like device which raises, lowers, or rotates the prepainted car body while team members install the components to complete the vehicle. Each assembly stage takes an hour or more, with components such as pre-assembled engines, transmissions, suspensions, and dashboards being delivered from a central warehouse by a computer-guided parts carrier which follows magnetic strips buried in the plant's floors. Uddevalla's self-managing teams are designed to provide their members with skill variety, task identity, and autonomy, while building high-quality cars. Only time will tell, however, if Volvo's approach to building cars will spread. Skeptics wonder if it will ever match the productivity and cost-effectiveness of reasonably efficient U.S. and Japanese assembly lines. At present, it takes 50 hours for each team to assemble a car at Uddevalla, compared to 25 hours at Volvo's "traditional" assembly line plant in Ghent, Belgium. If Volvo's approach does, however, increase productivity and cost-effectiveness over the long term, the world's automobile industry could be revolutionized.

JOB ENRICHMENT: PRECONDITIONS AND CONSTRAINTS

The effectiveness of different approaches to job-design content will depend on the situation and prevailing circumstances. Thus, even though job enrichment has enjoyed a great deal of publicity, it has not always led to favorable results. A variety of preconditions and constraints have been identified as influencing its successful application:

1. *Employee readiness*. The percentage of employees who favor job enrichment is unknown. Given an opportunity to exercise more skill variety, autonomy, and so on, employees respond differently. In this respect, employees seek to satisfy different needs through their work, ranging from the most basic need for a paycheck, to a desire for recognition and personal growth. Some employees resent the change to enriched jobs with their new pressures; others welcome it. Many quit rather than accept more responsibility and, in the case of self-managing teams, movement from job to job. Even some team members at Volvo's Uddevalla plant have had trouble coping with increased freedom and in taking over managerial duties, reporting friction and disagreements.

2. *Job complexity*. In general, the less complex a job, the less suited it is for job enrichment and, especially, self-managing teams. The team concept makes sense only if a job entails a high degree of dependency among several people. The idea is that, by combining their talents, team members can handle new

situations quickly and effectively. Thus, it is pointless in jobs with simple repetitive tasks. This explains why self-managing teams are mushrooming in the auto, chemical, paper, and electronics industries with their complex manufacturing processes. They are also gaining a foothold at banks, insurance firms, and other companies that provide specialized financial services. However, they have not yet caught on in less complicated service industries where teamwork is rare.

3. *Union cooperation.* The job-design movement has divided organized labor. In many instances, unions are seemingly torn between a desire to support efforts to enhance competitiveness and, hence, increase job security and a reluctance to encourage their members to identify too closely with management goals. Much of the opposition comes from a deep-rooted suspicion of management motives. Members of the United Automobile Workers (UAW) union who oppose cooperation go under the name "New Directions." They insist that job-design programs are a management ploy to increase output without sharing the gains resulting from increased productivity. Further, they charge that self-managing teams are little more than union-busting devices that foster "management by stress," speeded-up assembly lines, and the pitting of employees against each other.

   Despite such allegations, an increasing number of job-design programs are being undertaken in tandem by labor and management. The United Steelworkers, the UAW, the International Union of Electrical Workers, and the Communication Workers of America have signed national agreements with their respective managements calling for the development of job-design projects. As suggested by the opening chapter vignette, there's probably no more innovative partnership than at the General Motors Saturn plant in Spring Hill, Tennessee. The UAW has a seat on the plant's governing board. Saturn's plant manager and UAW coordinator have offices in the same suite. All major decisions—including picking dealers, an advertising agency, suppliers, and equipment—are made by consensus. Teams interview and hire co-workers. Everyone is salaried. Pay for operative employees begins at 80 percent of the UAW-General Motors scale, with the balance contingent on meeting productivity and other targets.

4. *Management support.* Experience has repeatedly demonstrated that the initial success and long-term survival of job-enrichment programs largely depend on sustained management support.[5] If negative management attitudes surface, they will likely be interpreted as a lack of support. Unfortunately, the introduction of self-managing teams, in particular, can prompt such disenchantment and lead to the early demise of even the best-conceived programs. This disenchantment is often rooted in changes to the traditional manager's role that accompany the redesign of subordinates' jobs. At the same time that operative employees are being given more autonomy, their immediate superiors are being stripped of traditional responsibilities. As a consequence, they may likely sense a steady erosion of authority and power. Thus, while operative employees are experiencing a broadening of their jobs, their managers—unless corrective action is taken—experience a narrowing of theirs. Instead of being active, involved participants, managers can feel rejected, threatened, and excluded.[6] Understandably, their first concern typically has to do with job security. A second area of common concern is job definition. Often, it is unclear

what managers are expected to do. A third frequent concern is the additional work that is initially generated by the introduction of a job-design program. The outcome in too many instances is all too predictable: Seeing nothing in the program for themselves, managers fall into a pattern of resistance.[7] The irony is that unless a job-design program moves up an organization, it will likely collapse. To avoid this, job-design programs must actively involve managers and help them readjust to new roles. In switching to self-managing teams, Eastman Kodak was able to eliminate three layers of management. The role of those who remained was redefined. They are now called "advisers." Their new role involves counseling and assisting, but not directing, team members. Some of the activities in which they might be involved include:[8]

- Training team members in their newly designed jobs, then counseling them about work-related problems and career opportunities
- Helping team members set performance goals
- Providing increased open communication; sharing team member concerns with higher management, both upward and downward; and sharing with team members information about ongoing and future organization activities
- Developing and testing new innovations with team members
- Coordinating the evolution of the overall job-enrichment program

SUMMARY

The present chapter examined the nature of job design. It first explored *specialization,* distinguishing between the specialization of jobs and the specialization of people. It then considered *job enlargement* and *job enrichment,* two concepts associated with the job-design movement. Next, it identified five "core dimensions" that can be modified to enrich jobs. Finally, after commenting on self-managed teams, it noted various preconditions and constraints on job-design efforts.

Learning Objective 1: Distinguish between job specialization and person specialization.
Job specialization refers to the narrowing of activities to simple and repetitive routines. *Person specialization* involves individuals with a high degree of training who have power because their ability makes other people dependent on them.

Learning Objective 2: List the advantages and disadvantages of job specialization.
The advantages of job specialization include (1) less skilled (and lower paid) employees can be hired because of simple job assignments; (2) jobs can be learned in less time, thus reducing training costs; (3) constant repetition leads to heightened expertise, which increases productivity; (4) more opportunities are provided for utilizing the primary talents of individual employees; (5) work is performed more quickly since employees do not lose time shifting from one activity to another; and (6) dependence on particular employees or special skills is minimized.

The disadvantages of job specialization include (1) diminished motivation, (2) poor-quality output, (3) diminished job satisfaction, (4) high turnover, (5) high absenteeism, and (6) sabotage and strikes.

Learning Objective 3: Distinguish between job enlargement (horizontal loading) and job enrichment (vertical loading).

Job enlargement, or horizontal loading, involves extending the *scope,* or *range,* of a job so that the number of different activities an employee performs is increased. Job enrichment, or vertical loading, involves extending the *depth* of a job so that employee discretion or control over a job is increased.

Learning Objective 4: Identify different core dimensions that can be modified to enrich jobs.

The five so-called core dimensions that can be modified to enrich jobs are skill variety, task identity, task significance, autonomy, and performance feedback.

Learning Objective 5: Enumerate various methods for implementing job enrichment.

Methods for implementing job enrichment include (1) combining several jobs into a larger job, requiring a broader range of skills; (2) giving employees a "whole" piece of work so they can accomplish a meaningful task; (3) allowing employees to deal directly with consumers, suppliers, and peers performing related jobs; (4) allowing employees more responsibility for quality control and self-determination of work procedures; and (5) providing open communication channels so that employees can monitor and self-correct their work behavior.

Learning Objective 6: Discuss self-managing teams.

Self-managing teams are groups of employees who have the day-to-day responsibility for managing themselves and the work they do.

Learning Objective 7: Identify various preconditions and constraints on job-design efforts.

Four preconditions and constraints on job-design efforts were identified: employee readiness, job complexity, union cooperation, and management support.

KEY TERMS

autonomy 298	job enrichment 296	person specialization 292
compressed workweek 300	job rotation 300	self-managing teams 300
flextime 300	job sharing 300	skill variety 296
job design 292	job specialization 292	task identity 297
job enlargement 294	performance feedback 299	task significance 297

THE MANAGEMENT EXPERIENCE WHAT DOES IT TAKE TO IMPROVE THE QUALITY OF WORK LIFE?

The expanded role of employees in workplace activities is part of a general upheaval in traditional labor-management relations. This upheaval is aimed at "humanizing work" and increasing the "quality of work life." The question remains, however, "What contributes to a high quality of work life?" Working alone, complete the following instrument by indicating the five dimensions that you believe are the most important and the five dimensions that you believe are the least important in contributing to a high quality of work life. After you have completed the instrument, your instructor will lead a discussion to determine the degree of agreement among class members.

Continued on next page.

Quality of Work Life Dimensions

Dimensions	Most Important	Moderately Important	Least Important
1 *Employee commitment:* feelings of loyalty: a commitment to and concern for the future of the organization.			
2 *Absence of developing apathy:* a measure of employee concern and ambition regarding their work.			
3 *On-the-job development and utilization:* opportunity for the employee to learn and apply skills and abilities in a meaningful and challenging way.			
4 *Employee involvement and influence:* the extent to which employees feel involved in decision making.			
5 *Advancement based on merit:* the extent to which management is interested in the progress of individuals and rewards people on the basis of ability, performance, and experience.			
6 *Career goal progress:* making progress in the achievement of career objectives and the belief that there are opportunities for further progress.			
7 *Relations with supervisor:* the working relationship with one's supervisor as reflected in fairness, honesty, and mutual respect.			
8 *Work group relations:* the way employees in a work group provide mutual support and encouragement.			
9 *Respect for the individual:* the feeling of being treated as an adult, with respect and dignity.			
10 *Confidence in management:* belief that management is aware of and concerned about employee problems and interests.			
11 *Physical working environment:* conditions affecting employees' health, comfort, and convenience.			
12 *Economic well-being:* receiving adequate financial rewards and having income protection.			
13 *Employee state of mind:* whether the employee feels upset or depressed while at work.			
14 *Absence of undue job stress:* the relative absence of excessive work demands and pressures that might interfere with doing the job well.			
15 *Impact on personal life:* the spillover effect of the job on employees' personal lives.			
16 *Union-management relations:* the extent to which the union and management recognize mutual goals and are working together.			

Source: Adapted from Ernest C. Miller, "Measuring the Quality of Work Life in General Motors . . . An Interview with Howard C. Carlson," *Personnel* 55 (November–December 1978): 21–26.

REVIEW AND DISCUSSION QUESTIONS

1. The economist Joseph Schumpeter liked to say, "Mass production means that a shop girl can have silk stockings as well as a queen."[9] Comment on the changes mass production has wrought in our society.

2. Management expert Peter F. Drucker contends, "Truly knowledgeable people tend toward overspecialization, whatever their field . . . because there is always so much more to know."[10] Explain what Drucker means.

3. A typical General Motors assembly plant can produce more than 100 cars an hour. By comparison, as noted earlier in this chapter, it can take up to 6 months to build a Rolls-Royce, a car that can cost as much as $225,000. With this in mind, comment on the advantages and disadvantages of specialized jobs.

4. Imagine that as a distinguished graduate of your college or university, you have just completed an address at the annual honors banquet. The title of your address was "Work Revolution in U.S. Industry." In making your comments, you noted that "job enrichment is a move back toward craft jobs." You have been asked by a newspaper reporter to explain what you meant by this statement. Respond.

5. Imagine you have just turned to the first question of your midterm exam in this course. It reads, "To illustrate your understanding of job enrichment, contrast the jobs of drill press operator and physician with regard to their core dimensions—that is, skill variety, task identity, task significance, autonomy, and performance feedback." How would you respond?

6. Calling upon personal experience, select a specialized job with which you are familiar and redesign it so that it is enlarged.

7. Consider the job you selected in Question 6 and redesign it so that it is enriched.

8. Assume that you have been promoted to the position of plant manager at a unionized automobile assembly facility in the Midwest. In your weekend MBA classes you've recently been discussing the design of jobs at the Volvo Uddevalla plant in Sweden. What factors might you consider before introducing such changes in an attempt to increase plant productivity?

9. You are writing a report on job design to present to your boss. She specifically has requested to know under what circumstances job enrichment is likely to be effective. How will you answer her question?

10. It has been said, "If you have a job without any aggravations you don't have a job."[11] Do you agree? Why? Why not?

CASE 10.1   "THE BEAT GOES ON"

The workday is only a half-hour old and Tab Talbot's head already aches. He grabs another housing assembly with his right hand. He transfers it to his left hand and turns it so the black-and-white cog is on the left-hand side.

By day's end, the 19 year old has handled so many housing assemblies that his hands are swollen and his eyes feel ready to fall out of their sockets. At night, when he closes his eyes to sleep, he often sees cam shafts and screws whirling through the air.

By day's end, the 19 year old has handled so Talbot is a thermostat assembler at Mouledoux

Medical Manufacturing. It is a job with a name succinctly describing its nature and one little changed over the past 50 years. By August 15, when Talbot returns to college, he will have assembled 24,000 thermostats, enough so he will be able to assemble them in his sleep.

"You have to be a psycho, a subhumanoid, or a college student out for the money to do this," says Ashton Vidrenne, Talbot's co-worker. Vidrenne pauses and gets a far-away look in his eyes: "It's like the gulag," he says.

Talbot remembers his first day on the job. His supervisor escorted him to his work bench and outlined the following assembly procedure:

1. Pick up a housing assembly with your right hand and transfer it to your left. Turn it so the black-and-white cog is on the left-hand side facing you.
2. Turn large exposed gear with index finger of left hand until dividing line between black and white on cog dial runs up and down with *black on left* and *white on right*.
3. Pick up time wheel with right hand while you hold big gear in place with left to maintain black-white dial setting.
4. Assemble time wheel to housing assembly, time face out, with 6 p.m. mark on time wheel aligned to mark on housing.
5. Pick up one cam shaft screw with right hand. While doing this, turn over your left hand, which is holding housing assembly, so that the assembly's back side is facing you.
6. Insert cam shaft screw into cam shaft hole with right hand.
7. Use both hands to place and seat housing assembly upside down in holding fixture.

8. Pick up two self-tapping screws, one in each hand.
9. Insert screws into two small holes in bearing plate.
10. Grasp screwdriver with right hand and tighten screws.
11. Remove housing assembly from holding fixture with left hand while you dispose of the screwdriver with your right.
12. Place completed housing assembly on bench at left with left hand so that the next employee can pick up the assembly, while you pick up another with your right hand.

Assemblers say their worst enemy is the tedium of long days at their work benches. Some try to pass the time by counting the countless stream of thermostats; others attach notes, including vulgar ones, to thermostats and send them down to product inspectors who are their friends.

"That job lobotomizes some people. We had one kid—really bright, articulate. After 2 weeks, he no longer spoke in complete sentences," says Talbot.

Problems

1. As you review the 12-step procedure for assembling a thermostat, think how you would feel repeating each step 50 times an hour, 400 times a day, 2,000 times a week, 100,000 times a year until you reach retirement age.
2. Is Talbot's situation an example of job specialization or person specialization?
3. Suggest ways to enrich the jobs of Talbot and his fellow factory workers.

Sources: Based on Frank Pieper, *Modular Management and Human Leadership* (Minneapolis: Methods Press, 1958), 69–70; and Ken Wells, "Is a Year of College Worth a Summer on the Slim Line?" *Wall Street Journal*, August 27, 1990, A1, A12.

NOTES

[1] Victor A. Thompson, *Modern Organization: A General Theory* (New York: Knopf, 1961), 25–33.

[2] J. Richard Hackman and Greg R. Oldham, *Work Redesign* (Reading, Mass.: Addison-Wesley, 1980).

[3] Joseph Weber, "Farewell Fast Track," *Business Week*, December 10, 1990, 194.

[4] Patrick Houston, "Timmberrr!" *Business Month* 112 (December 1989): 54; and John Hoerr, "The Payoff from Teamwork," *Business Week*, July 10, 1989, 57.

[5] Greg R. Oldham and J. Richard Hackman, "Work Design in the Organizational Context," *Research in Organizational Behavior* 2 (1980): 271.

[6] Michael A. Verespej, "Don't Forget Supervisors," *Industry Week*, May 7, 1990, 29–33.

[7] Janice A. Klein, "Why Supervisors Resist Employee Involvement," *Harvard Business Review* 62 (September–October 1984): 87–95.

[8] Oldham and Hackman, "Work Design," 272.

[9] Quoted in "The Quest for Quality," *Royal Bank Letter* 69 (November–December 1988): 2.

[10] Peter F. Drucker, "The Coming of the New Organization," *Harvard Business Review* 66 (January–February 1988): 46.

[11] Malcolm Forbes quoted in "Thoughts on the Business Life," *Forbes*, April 30, 1990, 460.

CHAPTER 11

LEARNING OBJECTIVES

Upon completing this chapter, you should be able to:

- Define *organizational culture*.
- Name four elements of culture.
- Identify the three phases required for successful change.
- Explain why people resist change.
- Describe force-field analysis.
- Discuss tactics for overcoming resistance to change.
- List the four major methods that an organization may use to introduce change.
- Describe various organization development techniques.

When a company is controlled by a single family over a long period, it may become highly resistant to change and lose its competitive advantage. An exception is Corning, Inc., which is currently run by James R. Houghton, great-great-grandson of the founder. Houghton has instituted difficult and far-reaching changes in Corning's organizational culture.

Quality control was an early target. In 1983 Houghton announced a total-quality program. At first no one was impressed by the announcement, but Houghton meant what he said. He appointed a director of quality and sent every employee to a 2-day quality seminar. Specific quality goals were announced and reiterated in open meetings at all Corning locations. And when a new plant was constructed for the production of molten-metal filters, Corning employees were allowed to design it. In doing so, they made some rather interesting departures from conventional layout and job structuring, such as including a production line that allows an entire team to work within earshot of one another and a system in which employees rotate through jobs

ORGANIZATIONAL CULTURE AND CHANGE

weekly and earn higher pay for each new skill they learn. The result of these changes was a dramatic reduction in the rate of defects—from 10,000 parts per million to only three per million.

Houghton also saw the need for greater diversity in Corning's workforce. Although it had tried to attract black and female managers, Corning could not keep them—they often left after completing their training. In 1987 Houghton established two teams to address this issue. Promotion and compensation practices were investigated; networks of mentors were established to advise new hires; even life in the outside community was affected—a Corning team encouraged local stores to increase minority employment and persuaded the local cable-TV operator to offer the Black Entertainment Television channel. The result of these efforts was lower attrition and increased minority participation in top management. Efforts will soon be expanded to include Asian and Hispanic employees.

Houghton's actions show how an inspired, committed manager can bring about change in an organization's culture. For Corning, the changes have had tangible results: They have increased its earnings while simultaneously raising product quality and employee satisfaction.

Source: Keith H. Hammonds, "Corning's Class Act—How Jamie Houghton Reinvented the Company," *Business Week*, May 13, 1991, 68–71, 122.

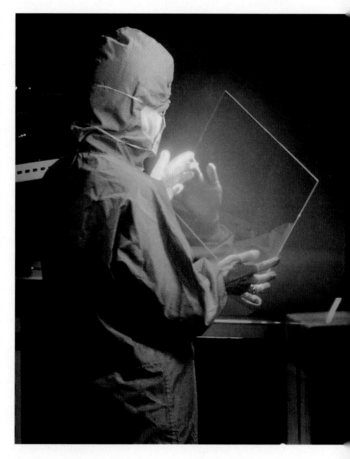

With the internationalization of economic competition and the quickening of technological advances, change is a universal and inevitable aspect of all organizations. Thus, more than ever, organizations are having change thrust upon them. To stay competitive, they are being forced to improve quality, increase speed, and adopt a customer orientation. They have no choice. Competitors are smarter and quicker. Product life cycles are continually shrinking. Markets seemingly emerge and disappear in a flash.

In today's world, change is a universal aspect of all organizations. The organizations that will do better now and in the future are those that can manage and adapt to change. The challenge is to take charge of change. One company that has accepted this challenge is Quad/Graphics, a half-billion-dollar-revenue printing firm. Boasts its chairman, Harry Quadracci, "We eat change for breakfast."[1] Seeing change as necessary for survival, and recognizing that change is more acceptable when it is understood than when it is not, Quad/Graphics requires each of its employees to spend a day each week in the classroom—a "day a week, forever," as Quadracci puts it.

Farsighted managers, such as Harry Quadracci, are excited by change. They encourage change to happen so that they can be the first to take advantage of it. Such managers recognize that although change can threaten an organization's survival, it can also offer unprecedented opportunities for growth. Indeed, some organizations seek out rapidly changing markets for this very reason. This explains, for example, Canadian-based Northern Telecom's move into Japan in advance of the privatization of Nippon Telegraph & Telephone. As a consequence of the changing market and the opportunities it presented, Northern was able to land a 7-year, $250-million contract to supply NTT with digital switching machines.

This chapter describes how to manage change successfully. We begin by commenting on the forces for change that exist both within organizations and within their surrounding environment. We then review the relationship between change and organizational culture. Next, we examine change as a multiphase process that occurs over time. Then, we consider various reasons people resist change and suggest several tactics for overcoming this resistance. Finally, we identify four methods for introducing change.

FORCES FOR CHANGE

Forces for change exist both within organizations and within their surrounding environment. Consequently, change results from both internal and external forces. An organization's success depends on its ability to anticipate change and to alter its capabilities to meet new demands.

INTERNAL FORCES

Internal forces for change arise from the challenge of creating an organization structure capable of remaining current and viable in the face of unprecedented demands. Paradoxically, an organization's success depends on its ability to maintain stability while managing change. Both change without order and order without change are equally crippling.

Thus, new employees must be hired while older employees retire, new products must be introduced while established products are discontinued, and new markets must be exploited while old ones are abandoned. These and countless other actions create internal forces for change. Each must be introduced in a manner that is not only consistent with an organization's goals, but acceptable to those affected.

EXTERNAL FORCES

External forces creating the need for change derive from an organization's general and task environments. For example, in an increasingly dynamic, interdependent, and unpredictable world, virtually all organizations are affected by both domestic and international events. Political decisions made in Washington, D.C., together with those made in London, Paris, Rome, and Tokyo, among other world capitals, have a direct influence on global marketplace competition. Similarly, fluctuations in the world's leading economies have worldwide repercussions. Activity on the London and Tokyo stock markets affects Wall Street and vice versa.

Rapid technological developments, both domestic and international in origin, continue to outpace the ability of many organizations to absorb them. Goods and services, even entire markets, seem to vanish overnight. Competition for consumers is now conducted on a global scale. Organization workforces span the globe, cutting across all nationalities and ethnic boundaries. The concept of a global village is a reality. The expanding environment of worldwide economic connections has created unprecedented opportunities for organizations that are willing to change and grow.

CULTURE AND CHANGE

With the internationalization of competition moving full speed ahead, the changes that many organizations are being forced to make simply to survive—improving quality, increasing speed, adopting a customer orientation—are so fundamental that they involve transforming an organization's very essence, which means its *culture*. As typically defined, **organizational culture** refers to the common set of beliefs and expectations shared by members of an organization. As such, culture is a complex and pervasive part of any mature workplace.

British Petroleum (BP) is but one example of the numerous organizations that are undergoing cultural change to stay competitive. Taking over as chairman and CEO of BP in 1988, Robert Horton found a bureaucratic jungle. Endless committee meetings and unanswered memos were routine.

Determined to change BP's culture from one of endless debates to one of instant action, Horton eliminated 80 of 86 corporate committees, reduced headquarters staff from 2,400 to 1,400, and empowered lower level employees by pushing spending authority down into the ranks. To encourage a free flow of information at all hierarchical levels, he required that all employees attend workshops to discuss change. Significant, lasting change in an organization as sprawling and complex as BP can take 5–10 years. Horton's goal of transforming BP's culture so

Organizational culture.
The common set of beliefs and expectations shared by members of an organization.

British Petroleum employees review details of a deal in the company's London oil trading room. BP has attempted to establish an organizational culture that enables it to respond quickly and flexibly to the business environment of the future. Employee involvement, assisted by an open style of management, is fundamental to the company's goals for cultural change.

that it is quicker and smarter than its opposition has already enhanced its competitiveness.

An organization's culture is determined by numerous elements (see Figure 11.1). Principal among these are its *values, heroes, symbols,* and *legends.*[2]

VALUES

Values are an organization's beliefs about what is good or bad, desirable or undesirable. They are the foundation of any culture, defining its fundamental character. In outstanding organizations, values are deeply felt and reinforced. They are passed on by the actions of key managers. At IBM, the three most fundamental values are respect for the individual, unparalleled customer service, and the pursuit of superiority in all that the company undertakes.

Values provide a sense of common direction. They serve as guidelines for day-to-day employee behavior. Thus, employees at 3M are constantly reminded of the company's 11th commandment: "Thou shall not kill a new product idea." Similarly, "hosts" at Disney Productions are repeatedly confronted with founder Walt Disney's guiding philosophy: "There is no cynicism in me and none is allowed in our work." Judging by the success of both 3M and Disney Productions, values can clearly be a powerful influence on what employees actually do. Shaping and enhancing values is thus an important job for all managers.

Values.
An organization's beliefs about what is good or bad, desirable or undesirable.

FIGURE 11.1   FOUR ELEMENTS OF ORGANIZATIONAL CULTURE

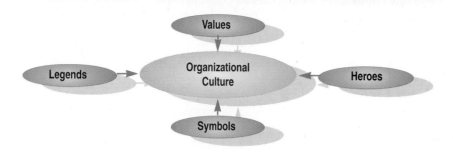

HEROES

An organization's values are primarily reinforced by its lead players—its **heroes.** These may be the founders or CEOs of organizations, but they also may be individuals who personify an organization's highest ideals. Thus, although Will Durant and General Motors, John D. Rockefeller and Standard Oil, and Mary Kay Ash and Mary Kay Cosmetics are part of U.S. folklore, so are countless other, less well known, outstanding employees. Joe McClosky, a veteran IBM sales representative, is an acknowledged company hero. McClosky is a 30-year member of IBM's highly honored Hundred Percent Club. Only those who have consistently met their sales quotas are eligible for membership. At innovation-driven Sikorsky Aircraft, the heroes are inventors. Employees who have been awarded patents are each presented with a special name tag emblazoned with a U.S. Patent Office logo. The name tags convey a clear message. Simply stated, "Look at these people. Be like them. It pays."

By acknowledging outstanding employees as heroes, organizations thus create role models for others to follow. As role models, heroes personify an organization's values and reinforce its desired culture. In doing so, they epitomize an organization's desired strength.

Heroes.
An organization's lead players.

SYMBOLS

Symbols are nothing more than objects or events that convey meaning. The power of symbols in establishing culture should not be underestimated. Plaques, pins, and slogans are symbols that convey what is important in an organization. One company awards outstanding performance with "Attaboy" plaques, five of which qualify an employee for a "Gotcha" tribute, personally signed by its CEO. TGI Friday's awards brass, silver, and gold stars for meritorious service. The U.S. Army similarly uses various insignia, such as medals, badges, and patches, to denote

Symbols.
Objects or events that convey meaning.

Pacific Bell account manager Kathy Madlem has repeatedly won her company's top sales awards for her outstanding service to client company Apple Computer, Inc. Ms. Madlem and a Pacific Bell technical team designed and installed one of the largest private fiber optic networks in Pacific Bell history, which connects Apple's office buildings in Cupertino, California.

CLOSE-UP: DIVERSITY   MANAGING DIVERSITY

One of the greatest changes to sweep corporate America this century undoubtedly is the move toward racial equality in the workplace. Companies, both large and small, have taken major steps toward integration by putting a strong emphasis on minority hiring. As a result, the U.S. workforce has undergone a revolutionary transformation.

Women have made the greatest gains and now account for about 45 percent of the labor market. The number of black employees is up 50 percent since 1966—a significant increase even taking into account the growth in the black population. And although their progress has been less dramatic, Hispanics and Asians have taken big strides as well.

But so-called affirmative action plans have not come without resistance. The plans' biggest critics are white employees who claim to be penalized by the preferential treatment given to minorities. Their accusations grow even louder during hard economic times, when there are fewer jobs to go around. Conversely, many minority employees complain that affirmative action does not go far enough because it does not lead to a much-needed transformation in white-dominated corporate cultures. Once on the job, some minority employees say they are met with indifference or outright hostility. And the few who do make it to the top said they often feel isolated.

The highest level of satisfaction among both white and minority employees has occurred in companies where management looked for ways to make affirmative action an integral part of the corporate environment. In some cases, that has meant setting up minority support groups, or sponsoring seminars where employees could air their grievances. In other cases, employees have had to be taught how to adapt to the changing culture. Here are some of the more innovative approaches taken by major corporations:

- The Avon Corp. established an in-house, race-based network to serve as an advocacy group, social club, and self-help organization all rolled into one. The Black Professionals Association, Avon Hispanic Network, and Avon Asian Network also encourage minority recruiting and career development.

- The DuPont Corp. tackled the race issue head on by encouraging workers to confront their often unspoken biases in 5-day workshops. The company also sponsored all-expenses-paid conferences where black managers could discuss how the African-American culture could improve the company's bottom line.

- When massive defense cutbacks led to huge layoffs at Hughes Aircraft Corp., the Los Angeles-based company opted to take a long-term view of minority hiring. It appointed a vice-president for cultural diversity and charged him with getting minorities into top jobs. The company also invested in an internship program that brought minority students and professors to work with company scientists.

- Executives at the Monsanto Corp. discovered that simply hiring minorities was not enough to change its deeply ingrained white, male-dominated culture. While the company was bringing minorities in, just as many were trying to get out. To put a stop to the exodus, Monsanto began conducting detailed exit interviews and used the results in diversity training workshops.

Source: James Ellis, "Monsanto's New Challenge: Keeping Minority Workers," *Business Week*, July 8, 1991, 60–61 and Howard Gleckman, Tim Smart, Paula Dwyer, Troy Segal, and Joseph Weber, "Race in the Workplace," *Business Week*, July 8, 1991, 50–53, 56, 58, 60–63.

outstanding accomplishments. Slogans likewise stress what an organization values. Accordingly, General Electric is associated with "Progress is our most important product" and Avis with "We try harder."

Symbols can be used to convey and promote an organization's values and, thus, reinforce its culture. They can create a sense of identity for those in an organization, making employees feel special. Finally, symbols can deepen an organization's culture by facilitating individual commitment to collective goals, such as excellence in service or customer satisfaction.

LEGENDS

A **legend** is a story about an actual event or person. Often embellished with fictional details, legends help preserve an organization's culture by imparting values to new employees. Thus, the story is told of Hewlett-Packard co-founder Bill Hewlett finding a lab stockroom door padlocked one Saturday. He cut the lock and left a note saying, "Don't ever lock this door again. Thanks, Bill." This story has been repeated thousands of times over the years and has come to personify "the HP Way," with its emphasis on creativity.

Similar stories are told at leading organizations throughout the world. In addition to providing guidelines for employees, they tell a great deal about what it takes to get ahead in an organization. At Nordstrom, Inc., for instance, customer responsiveness is a key to career success. The extent to which Nordstrom will go to ensure customer satisfaction is indicated in a story about a customer who received a refund on a set of tires. Nordstrom doesn't sell tires.

Legends.
Stories about a true event or person.

SMART MANAGEMENT CORPORATION TRIBES: FOUR GENERIC CULTURES

Culture is a major component affecting organization performance and behavior. The principal determinants of an organization's culture are its *values, heroes, symbols*, and *legends*. According to Terrence E. Deal and Allan A. Kennedy, authors of *Corporate Cultures*, these elements shape four generic cultures:

- *Macho/Tough Guy.* A world of individualists who thrive on high risks, intense pressure, and quick feedback. The most grueling of all cultures, it prevails in the construction, cosmetics, advertising, and entertainment industries.

- *Work Hard/Play Hard.* A world of fun and action where employees take few risks. Activity is everything. Computer firms (Intel), direct personal sales in the home (Mary Kay Cosmetics), mass-consumer-sales companies (Frito-Lay), and office-equipment manufacturers (Xerox) characterize this culture.

- *Bet-Your-Company.* A world of high risks, slow feedback, and big stakes. Investing in the future is the main focus of this culture, which is known for deliberateness. Oil concerns (Mobil), aerospace companies (Boeing Aircraft), and diversified chemical/energy firms (Du Pont) typify this culture.

- *Process.* A world of little or no feedback where the emphasis is on *how* things are done rather than *what* is done. Bureaucracy is another name for this culture when processes get out of control. Technical perfection is the value base in such circumstances. Insurance companies (Chubb), accounting firms (Price Waterhouse), and banks (Chase Manhattan) exemplify this culture.

Source: Terrence E. Deal and Allan A. Kennedy, *Corporate Cultures: The Rites and Rituals of Corporate Life* (Reading, Mass.: Addison-Wesley, 1982, 107–127.

CHANGE AS A PROCESS

The creation of a new culture may well be the most difficult pursuit any manager can undertake. As noted, such fundamental change can take years to accomplish. For this reason, change should best be viewed as a multiphase process, not as an event. The famous psychologist Kurt Lewin suggested that successful change requires moving through three phases: *unfreezing, changing,* and *refreezing* (see Figure 11.2).[3] Implicit in this process is the recognition that merely introducing change does not ensure its establishment.

Unfreezing. This phase involves recognizing a need for change. It occurs when a situation is recognized as being deficient or inadequate in some way. Crises are especially likely to stimulate unfreezing. Loss of a key client, a dramatic drop in market share, or an unexpected decline in profits are examples of such crises.

Changing. This phase involves modifying old ways so new behavior patterns can be introduced. Changes can range from minor to major. A new recruiting program might involve a small number of people and be fairly easy to implement. Conversely, major changes might involve installing new equipment or implementing a new performance appraisal scheme.

Refreezing. This phase involves establishing new behavior patterns. It is frequently accomplished through new training programs, revised policies, updated procedures, and other support mechanisms that reinforce new behavior. Evaluation is also a key element in this final phase. Unforeseen problems can be resolved, and positive feedback can be used to further enhance desired outcomes.

Polaroid Corporation represents an example of an organization currently undergoing change. For decades, it was one of the world's most innovative companies. Over time, however, without breakthrough products to replace its instant-camera monopoly, its revenues stagnated. Currently, Polaroid is undergoing a dramatic overhaul as it attempts to unfreeze its old ways and adopt new changes. It has not yet decided whether it should embrace incremental change, such as that represented by quality improvement programs, or strive for revolutionary change involving a dramatic technological innovation. In either case, Polaroid hopes that its culture, by creating shared beliefs and expectations, will provide the common understanding necessary to link employees together in its efforts to "refreeze," that is, to establish new behavior patterns.

RESISTANCE TO CHANGE

As the preceding discussion suggests, behavior patterns often are firmly frozen in place and may require unfreezing before change can occur. In this respect, change

FIGURE 11.2 LEWIN'S THREE-PHASE CHANGE PROCESS

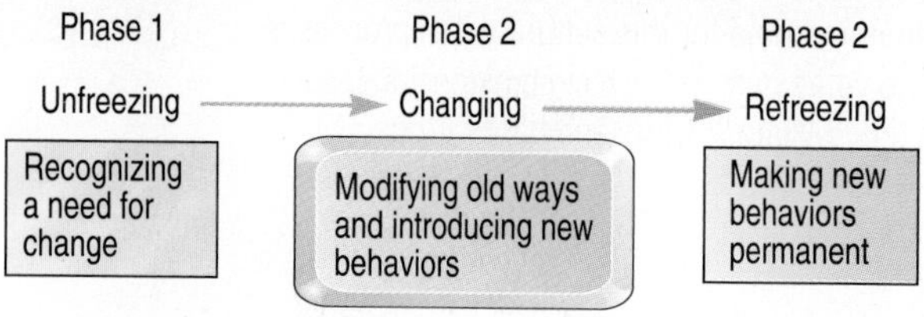

Phase 1 — Unfreezing → Phase 2 — Changing → Phase 2 — Refreezing

- Unfreezing: Recognizing a need for change
- Changing: Modifying old ways and introducing new behaviors
- Refreezing: Making new behaviors permanent

is rarely received without protest. Indeed, resistance to change is a natural human reaction. Reasons for this are varied and often difficult to determine. Whether soundly based or not, however, resistance should always be considered an important signal for further inquiry.

Managers are often unfamiliar with even the most basic reasons that resistance might occur. The following is an abbreviated discussion of four of the most common reasons (see Figure 11.3).[4] To fully describe any one of them would require a discussion of far greater depth than we can reasonably attempt here.

THREATENED SELF-INTEREST

Virtually all organization members can be expected to behave in ways that will maximize those goals that they personally consider most important. Consequently, individuals (and groups) are likely to resist proposals for change if they believe they stand to lose something of value as a result. In such circumstances, the individuals involved will usually focus on their own self-interest, and only incidentally on an organization's overall good. A sample listing of personal goals that, when threatened, will almost inevitably provoke resistance would include:[5]

1. *Power.* Authority and control over organization resources.
2. *Money.* Increases in income or income substitutes.
3. *Prestige.* Respect and approval from those responsible for funding, determining promotions, hiring, and firing.
4. *Convenience.* Avoidance of conditions that will require additional personal efforts.
5. *Job security.* Protection against loss of position.
6. *Professional competence.* Respect from peers for knowledge, technical proficiency, or professionally ethical behavior.

At Boeing Aircraft, the construction of a state-of-the-art sheet metal fabrication center clearly threatened the self-interest of all involved. The new factory nearly halved the previous facility's 2,600-person workforce. Employee opposition was stemmed by taking several steps. First, all those affected were presented with

FIGURE 11.3   FOUR REASONS FOR RESISTANCE TO CHANGE

Boeing's need to modernize in order to strengthen its competitive position. Next, employees were involved in designing the new center. Finally, Boeing provided training for displaced workers to qualify them for new positions within the company.

LACK OF UNDERSTANDING AND TRUST

People also tend to resist when they do not understand the intended purpose of a planned change. Such a predicament is most likely to occur when there is a lack of trust between the parties involved in initiating and those involved in adopting a proposed modification. Distrust and suspicion often result in widespread rumors and distorted information. This makes effective communication difficult and poses a real problem in instituting change. The new owners of Reading Industries, for example, resorted to putting out periodic "rumor-control" memos when employees' fears about a plant closing threatened to become too disruptive. Sometimes even this tactic didn't work, since employees had seen too many changes in management to trust the word of the latest owners. Having been buffeted by constant change and forced to make innumerable concessions to each group of owners, they had become angry, cynical, and distrustful. Their unhappiness often expressed itself in high absenteeism, endless complaints, and a resistance to changes intended to increase productivity.

It is important to note that people do not resist change per se, only the uncertainties that change can bring. Such resistance is easier to prevent than to remove once it has developed. Therefore, it is important to tell employees in advance why a change is being made and how it will affect them.

DIFFERENT ASSESSMENTS

Resistance to change frequently occurs when organization members differ in their evaluation of a change's likely costs and benefits. Such evaluations obviously depend on what these individuals think a proposed change will mean for themselves and also for their organization. Take the example of hospitals. Hospital managers, finding themselves caught in the squeeze between legislation that imposes a ceiling on Medicare reimbursements and the increased reluctance of private insurers to foot the tab for staggering medical costs, have begun to seek ways of trimming expenses. But physicians worry that patients' welfare will be jeopardized as hospitals push to become more cost effective. As a former American Medical Association president remarked of the cost-control programs, "It's treating the patient as if he were a number—the 62-year-old cardiac in 4B who's been here for 18 days, when the average stay should be 13 days."[6] The challenge in such cases is to bring these differing assessments into line, so that each party understands the concerns and constraints motivating the other.

Differing assessments of the effectiveness of proposed changes often occur when information concerning a change is not widely disseminated. Consequently, organization members may possess different degrees of information about the change and arrive at different assessments. We should point out that opposition to change is not always bad. Change initiators are not infallible. Constructive opposition, mounted by knowledgeable parties, may save an organization from the unproductive, or even disastrous, consequences of an ill-conceived change.

FEAR OF THE UNKNOWN

Finally, people may resist change because of personal concerns about their ability to be effective after a change. The unknown consequences of change may present a psychological threat to the self-esteem of many individuals. While research confirms that personal anxieties are to be expected in the face of change, there are individuals who let their anxieties go beyond the norm and will oppose a new plan or idea even when they recognize its soundness. These are people with an excessively low tolerance for change. They may be afraid they will be unable to develop the skills and behavior demanded by a new position or by the unfamiliar circumstances associated with a reorganization. Can I do it? How will I do it? Do I have the ability to learn a new way? These and other concerns may produce active resistance to change without ever being stated out loud.

For example, a person who receives a significantly more important job as a result of a promotion will probably be very happy. But it is just as possible for that person also to feel uneasy and to resist giving up the comfort of a previous position. A new and very different job will require new and different behavior, new and different relationships, and the loss of some satisfactory activities and relationships. If the changes are significant, and the individual's fear of the unknown is high, the person might begin to actively resist the change for reasons not consciously understood.

QUESTIONS TO ASK WHEN CONTEMPLATING CHANGE

As we suggested, these are just a few of the reasons that change might be resisted. No doubt, there are innumerable others. They will vary in importance from situation to situation. Realizing this, managers might do well to ask themselves the following questions when contemplating a change:

1. What are the consequences of implementing or not implementing the proposed change?
2. Has the process for change and its effect on individuals been clearly explained?
3. How much resistance will the proposed change generate?
4. In what form will resistance show itself?
5. What is the level of trust between the parties involved?
6. Do all parties involved have the information necessary to understand the reasons for the proposed change and benefits that will result?
7. Have real incentives been provided for accepting the proposed change?

OVERCOMING RESISTANCE TO CHANGE

Managers can use several tactics for dealing with resistance to change.[7] Four of these tactics are shown in Figure 11.4 and will be discussed. Choice of a tactic will, of course, depend on the combination of factors present in each individual situation. In visualizing different situations, it may be helpful to identify the contrasting forces at play. Developed by Kurt Lewin, **force-field analysis** depicts an existing situation (the status quo) as an equilibrium locked between two opposing forces—driving and restraining (see Figure 11.5).[8] **Driving forces** direct behavior away

Force-field analysis.
A depiction of the status quo as an equilibrium locked between two opposing forces—driving and restraining.

Driving forces.
Forces that direct behavior away from the status quo and facilitate change.

FIGURE 11.4 HOW TO DEAL WITH RESISTANCE TO CHANGE

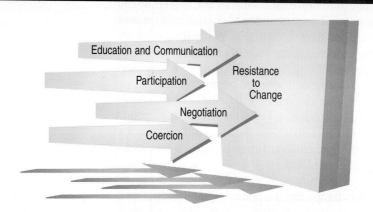

from the status quo and facilitate change. **Restraining forces** direct behavior toward the status quo and hinder change. Thus, managers contemplating change should identify both sets of forces and attempt to weaken the restraining forces and strengthen the driving forces. Force-field analysis is particularly helpful in identifying the forces that can and cannot be altered. After completing the analysis, managers can avoid wasted effort by directing their attention to enacting tactics to influence those forces over which they have some control.

Restraining forces.
Forces that direct behavior toward the status quo and hinder change.

EDUCATION AND COMMUNICATION

Change initiators often possess information about a situation that is not readily available to other organization members. By sharing this knowledge, they may be able to counter opposition to proposed changes. This tactic—education and communication—assumes that organization members share common objectives and that resistance can be overcome by training people to recognize the existence of problem areas and, hence, the necessity for change. Furthermore, it assumes that resistance is based largely on misinformation or poor communication. This tactic, therefore, involves securing relevant facts, eliminating misunderstandings attributable to incorrect or incomplete information, and resolving different viewpoints through discussion.

Depending on the nature of the change, this tactic may involve mass media educational campaigns, one-on-one discussions, memos, group presentations, and reports. To be successful, such education and communication programs must always be unquestionably and firmly grounded in mutual trust and credibility.

FIGURE 11.5 LEWIN'S FORCE-FIELD ANALYSIS

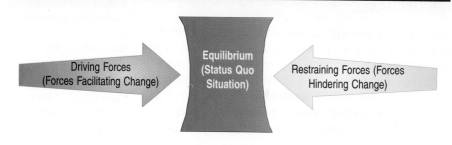

Goulds Pumps Incorporated is dedicated to developing an organizational culture that will help it maintain its competitive advantage. In 1991, Goulds opened the Goulds Pump Institute in Seneca Falls, New York. The institute's curriculum supports the developmental needs of all employees, including courses in quality management, information systems, presentation skills, negotiation skills, time and project management, selling, technical skills, and other areas of self improvement. Here, Institute Director Jeryl Mitchell discusses the curriculum with her staff.

PARTICIPATION

Perhaps the most effective way to reduce anticipated opposition and to engender commitment to a proposed change is to involve potential resisters in its planning and implementation. Participation gives employees a way to express their fears about proposed changes and to use their specialized skills to help in planning. As Mary Kay Ash, founder of Mary Kay Cosmetics, advises, "People will support that which they help to create."[9] Evidence for the wisdom of Ash's advice is readily available. When Allstate Insurance undertook a reorganization, it formed employee "growth teams," representing all departments and employees, to participate in the rejuggling. Acting on their suggestions, Allstate relocated many of its 40,000 employees, stripping away an entire managerial level. Allstate attributes the success of its reorganization to this employee participation.

As a tactic for overcoming resistance to change, participation involves open communication and the exchange of perspectives on the part of all parties involved. Such interaction rests on the assumption that all parties are rational, possess the required expertise to contribute meaningfully, and are willing to act in good faith. It is generally accepted that although participation necessarily lengthens the actual change process, it shortens the implementation process and aids in its success.

NEGOTIATION

Another tactic for dealing with resistance to change involves conferring and bargaining—negotiating—to reach an agreement regarding a proposed change.

Because bargaining implies reciprocity, this tactic suggests that a change initiator is willing to tailor a change to meet the needs and interests of active or potential resisters. Negotiated agreements are particularly appropriate in situations where some individual or group will clearly lose out in a change and has considerable power to resist. However, while negotiating with those affected may succeed temporarily in quelling resistance, it often signals the beginning of a continuing relationship based on give and take. After it becomes known that an initiator of change is willing to modify a stance to avoid resistance, the way is open for continued bargaining and even blackmail.

COERCION

Use of coercion assumes that the principal opposing parties are operating from relatively fixed positions. When efforts at reaching consensus are abandoned, at least temporarily, there may be an effort to compel acceptance of a change by means of orders accompanied by virulent arguments, as well as threatened firings, transfers, and loss of promotion possibilities. For obvious reasons, coercion is used sparingly.

In this respect, as former General Motors chairman Roger B. Smith observed in connection with the reorganization of the company's North American car operations: "You can't push people to do what we're trying to do. And you can't drag them. If they don't want to do something—and if they aren't dedicated to doing it—the human being . . . has a marvelous capacity for screwing things up. And he feels justified in doing it too. He just says, 'I don't believe in it. I'm not going to do it.'"[10]

Perkin-Elmer, world-wide producer of analytical instrumentation systems, believes that its employees have the knowledge and expertise required to generate fundamental and lasting changes within the company's culture. In December of 1990, CEO Gaynor Kelley issued the Perkin-Elmer Call to Action to all employees, emphasizing the need for new ideas, fresh approaches, and a commitment to high levels of excellence. Kelley's Call to Action was accompanied by a set of guiding principles for action and achievement, and has been translated into a Plan of Action program to implement improvement and innovation. Here Kelley conducts a Plan of Action meeting with key executives.

METHODS OF INTRODUCING CHANGE	
Method	**Examples**
1. Task	Job enrichment, job enlargement
2. Structure	Modified bases of departmentalization, authority delegation, spans of control, managerial levels
3. Technology	New equipment, new computer-support systems, new tools, new forms of automation
4. People	Survey feedback, process consultation, team building, intergroup interventions, Grid OD.

METHODS OF INTRODUCING CHANGE

As we saw in our opening discussion of Corning, initial changes of one type often create a need for further changes of another type. The four major methods of introducing change are task change, structural change, technological change, and people change (see Figure 11.6):

1. *Task change* involves the redesign of jobs using the methods described in Chapter 10. Principal among these are job enrichment and job enlargement. Because of their ease of implementation, task changes are among the most frequently used methods for introducing change.

2. *Structural change* involves modifying any of the basic components of structure discussed in Chapters 8 and 9. Included would be modified bases of departmentalization, authority delegation, spans of control, and managerial levels.

FIGURE 11.6 METHODS OF INTRODUCING CHANGE

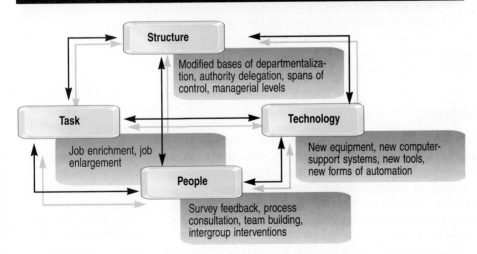

Source: Based on Harold J. Leavitt, "Applied Organization Change in Industry: Structural, Technical, and Human Approaches," *New Perspectives in Organizational Research,* ed. William W. Cooper, Harold J. Leavitt, and Maynard W. Shelly II (New York: Wiley, 1964), 56.

3. *Technological change* involves modifying means whereby an organization transforms inputs into outputs. Examples would include introducing new equipment, new computer-support systems, new tools, or new forms of automation, such as robots.

4. *People change* involves modifying the way employees think and act. Above all, the process of change is essentially a process of altering the relationships of employees with one another and with their jobs. Among the many "people" approaches for introducing change are survey feedback, process consultation, team building, intergroup interventions, and Grid OD. Since these techniques are so important, we will discuss them separately in the following section.

A key point illustrated by Figure 11.6 is the interrelated nature of the four methods for introducing change. Indeed, change cannot be introduced using one method without causing implications for the others. For example, changes in technology are almost inevitably accompanied by task changes. In turn, changes in task and technology usually produce changes in structure. Likewise, changes in task, technology, and structure typically require changes in people. This point is well underscored by H. Ross Perot, a former General Motors director, in commenting on the problems the company has encountered in its high-tech drive to build "factories of the future." Perot warns, "GM cannot become a world-class and cost-competitive company simply by throwing technology and money at its problems."[11] He argues that fundamental changes in people, their jobs, and General Motors's tradition-bound structure, which is said to fight change the way fluoride fights tooth decay, will be required.

Practical people have long recognized the extreme difficulties involved in changing complex systems, for it is difficult to foresee all the consequences. Some of these consequences may be intended, but others may not. Consider the hospital that installed a computerized scheduling system for its nurses in an effort to give them greater working-hour flexibility and thus reduce turnover. An unanticipated result of the new scheduling system was that nurses' awareness of their marketability increased, leading some to seek jobs elsewhere. While the system was still judged a success, it clearly illustrates how a change in one area (technology) can have an unintended consequence in another (people). Identifying potential unintended consequences is essential for successful organization performance. In this sense, the incredible complexity of change may be a cliche, but it is a fact.

ORGANIZATION DEVELOPMENT

Although **organization development (OD)** has been defined in many ways and applied in different fashions by various people, it is generally viewed as a long-range program that focuses on changing employee attitudes and behavior, thereby improving organization performance. Simply stated, its intent is to discover symptoms of ineffective performance and to correct their underlying human causes. These symptoms could be excessive turnover, low productivity, dysfunctional group conflict, high absenteeism, and so forth.

Organization development (OD).
A long-range program that focuses on changing employee attitudes and behavior, thereby improving organization performance.

OD ASSUMPTIONS

OD incorporates a set of underlying assumptions concerning the nature of people and work. These assumptions exert a powerful influence on both the process and content of OD programs. The first is that most employees desire personal growth and enhancement. Another is that most employees are capable of making a greater contribution to their work than they are permitted. Still another OD assumption is that managers cannot possibly perform all their duties at all times. Thus, some form of collaboration between managers and their subordinates is desirable to take advantage of subordinates' greater potential contributions and to allow subordinates increased personal growth and enhancement.

OD TECHNIQUES

To implement OD, *change agents* (as OD practitioners are known) use a variety of techniques. Some of the more frequently used techniques are described in the following paragraphs. These techniques should not be considered mutually exclusive, but complementary. Their suitability will vary from situation to situation.

Survey Feedback

This technique consists of conducting a survey of employee attitudes regarding matters such as decision-making practices, extent of communication, and motivational conditions. Survey results are fed back to employees for analysis and interpretation so that necessary changes can be designed by the employees themselves. Changes might include restructuring committees, reallocating work, or altering communication patterns.

Survey feedback.
An OD technique in which survey results are fed back to employees for analysis and interpretation so that necessary changes can be designed by the employees themselves.

The Timken Company, headquartered in Canton, Ohio, is an international manufacturer of highly engineered bearings and alloy steels. The company's goals include the strengthening of its human resources in the '90s through education and training. As a result, employees such as David Ayers, tool grinder, seek out new ways to serve customers and increase productivity. Timken employees are credited with making a greater contribution to their company and their jobs than ever before, and enjoy personal growth through participation in nearly every facet of the company's decisions.

Process Consultation

This OD technique involves analyzing managerial and work group activities. Rather than offering "expert advice," a change agent using process consultation helps employees to understand and act upon *process events* in their work environment. Process events considered to be the most crucial for effective organization performance include communication, employee roles, problem solving, group norms, leadership, and intergroup relations.

Team Building

Team building combines survey feedback and process consultation. Its objective is to build cohesive and successful work groups. Specific team-building activities include clarifying employee roles, reducing conflict, improving interpersonal relations between group members, and improving problem-solving skills.

Intergroup Intervention

Whereas team building is designed to resolve issues of concern to a single work group, intergroup interventions are aimed at improving the effectiveness of two or more interdependent groups. By giving such groups an opportunity to discuss their relations with one another, intergroup interventions are intended to provide them with an insight into how they are seen by others.

Grid OD

In comparison to the previously described OD techniques, which are typically custom tailored to a specific organization, a variety of "packaged" OD techniques also exist. They consist of standardized materials and activities that are usually copyrighted and available only through licensed individuals. Among the most widely known is the *Leadership Grid* ® developed by Robert R. Blake and Anne Adams McCanse[12].

The concept of the Leadership Grid rests on the belief that there are two key interlocking dimensions found in all organizations: concern for production and concern for people. *Concern for production* emphasizes getting results or accomplishing a mission. *Concern for people* emphasizes developing mature and healthy relations among work group members. The grid provides a means for assessing managerial styles and then training managers to move toward a maximum concern for both production and people.

As shown in Figure 11.7, the horizontal axis represents the concern-for-production dimension, while the vertical axis represents the concern-for-people dimension. Each axis is on a scale of 1 to 9 points, with 1 reflecting minimum concern and 9 reflecting maximum concern. The dimensions are viewed as being interdependent. It is impossible to describe a managerial style on one dimension without concurrently describing it on the other, because they interact at every point. This interdependence is designated by a comma (,) in the following discussion.

Although there are 81 possible combinations (9 × 9), five styles stand out clearly and will be the focus of our discussion. As can be seen from the grid, the lower right-hand corner represents the "authority-compliance" style (9,1). Here, output outweighs everything. People are viewed solely with regard to their contribution to production and are not allowed to interfere with efficiency. At the opposite corner of the grid, the top left, is the 1,9 style. Known as "country club management," this style views production as incidental to maintaining a comfortable work

Process consultation.
An OD technique in which a change agent helps employees to understand and act upon process events in their work environment.

Team building.
An OD technique that combines survey feedback and process consultation to build cohesive and successful work groups.

Intergroup intervention.
An OD technique aimed at improving the effectiveness of two or more interdependent groups by allowing them an opportunity to discuss relations with one another.

Grid OD.
A copyrighted OD technique based on the *Leadership Grid.* ®

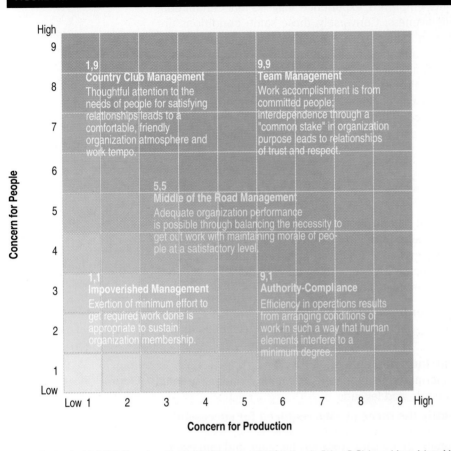

FIGURE 11.7 THE LEADERSHIP GRID

Source: The Leadership Grid ® Figure from *Leadership Dilemmas—Grid Solutions,* by Robert R. Blake and Anne Adams Mc-Canse. Houston: Gulf Publishing Company, P. 29. Copyright © 1991, by Scientific Methods, Inc. Reproduced by permission of the owners.

tempo. The 1,9 manager believes that with good fellowship and harmony, production will take care of itself.

The "impoverished management" style (1,1), shown in the lower left corner, deemphasizes concern for production, doing just enough to get by. This manager also disregards the importance of people, ignoring human relationships. In the center of the grid is the 5, 5 style known as "Middle of the Road Management." The 5, 5 manager is a compromiser, an individual who balances concern for people with concern for productivity.

The upper right corner (9,9) is the position in which maximum concern for production is integrated with maximum concern for people. This is the rarest manager. The 9,9 manager believes that results will be best when managers and subordinates have a "common stake" in organization objectives. The 9,9 position represents "team management." Production proceeds from an integration of task and human requirements. The 9,9 manager is considered by OD advocates to be the most effective of all. The notion of one best managerial style, of course, stands in opposition to contemporary contingency theory.

CONDITIONS FOR OD EFFECTIVENESS

Regardless of the OD techniques employed, experience suggests that certain conditions contribute to OD effectiveness. Conversely, these same conditions are generally found to be absent from ineffective OD programs.[13] The first is that key employees realize that certain organization problems must be solved. Another is that top management lend its commitment and support to a search for solutions. Still another condition for OD effectiveness is that change agents be honest and live up to whatever they profess. For instance, if they call for openness, they should display this trait themselves. A final condition is that change agents keep everyone informed about what is happening and why, so as to minimize fears and suspicions about an OD program's objectives.

SUMMARY

Change is a universal aspect of all organizations. This chapter has discussed the relationship between organizational culture and change, examined change as a multiphase process that occurs over time, considered various reasons why people resist change, suggested several tactics for overcoming this resistance, and identified four different methods for introducing change.

Learning Objective 1: **Define *organizational culture.***
Organizational culture refers to the common set of beliefs and expectations shared by members of an organization.

Learning Objective 2: **Name four elements of culture.**
An organization's culture is determined by numerous elements. Principal among these are its values, heroes, symbols, and legends.

Learning Objective 3: **Identify the three phases required for successful change.**
The phases required for successful change are freezing, changing, and refreezing.

Learning Objective 4: **Explain why people resist change.**
People resist change for many reasons. The four most common are threatened self-interest, lack of understanding and trust, different assessments, and fear of the unknown.

Learning Objective 5: **Describe force-field analysis.**
Force-field analysis is a means for depicting the status quo as an equilibrium locked between two opposing forces—driving and restraining.

Learning Objective 6: **Discuss tactics for overcoming resistance to change.**
The chapter discussed four methods for overcoming resistance to change: education and communication, participation, negotiation, and coercion.

Learning Objective 7: **List the four major methods an organization may use to introduce change.**
Four major methods for introducing change are task change, structural change, technological change, and people change.

Learning Objective 8: **Describe various organization development techniques.**
The chapter describes five OD techniques: survey feedback, process consultation, team building, intergroup interventions, and Grid OD.

KEY TERMS

driving forces 321

force-field analysis 321

Grid OD 328

heroes 315

intergroup intervention 328

legends 317

organization development (OD) 326

organizational culture 313

process consultation 328

restraining forces 322

survey feedback 327

symbols 315

team building 328

values 314

REVIEW AND DISCUSSION QUESTIONS

1. After reading the following opinion, explain how organizational survival in today's competitive environment is shark-ism. "Consider the shark," says Irwin Federman, founder of Monolithic Memories, a major Silicon Valley semi-conductor company.

   > The shark has been around for 15,000 years. And do you know why? It's because the shark adapts, constantly moves, never sleeps. It's the ultimately flexible animal, with no bones, only cartilage. And the shark keeps renewing its weapons, discarding its old teeth, new teeth continually moving forward. It is ever-vigilant, the shark, always on the prowl, able to adjust to changing circumstances like a rise in the water temperature or an ice age. Whatever happens, the shark survives.[14]

2. A noted management authority has stated that the same properties that enable organizations to survive and keep on course under changing conditions also make them resistant to change in general. Given your reading of Chapter 11, explain this statement.

3. Comment on the following quote: "Consider how hard it is to change yourself and you'll understand what little chance you have of trying to change others."[15]

4. As a seasoned manager with some 40 years of service, you've experienced both the good and the bad. Reflecting on your career, you've repeatedly observed that the old saying "Human nature resists change" is only partially true. People do welcome some changes. What advice would you offer new managers for introducing changes that are welcome?

5. Conduct a force-field analysis showing the forces for and against your changing your college major.

6. You are commander of the U.S. Pacific Fleet. You've just received an order to further integrate female personnel in all aspects of sea duty. You anticipate varying degrees of resistance on the part of both male and female personnel, as well as their spouses. What tactics would you use to deal with this resistance to change?

7. You are the well-known author of a best-selling book titled *Successful Change*. Moments ago you completed a telephone conversation with a representative of a large corporation pleading for advice on successfully implementing a company-wide reorganization. What advice did you offer?

8. Being a successful manager, you realize that change cannot be introduced without potential unintended side effects. Your department is in the process of changing to a computerized production system. What task, structural, and people difficulties might you anticipate?

9. Thomas J. Peters, author of the best-selling book *Thriving on Chaos*, reasons that "if the word 'excellence' is to be applicable in the future, it requires whole-

sale redefinition." In this respect, he suggests that "Excellent firms don't believe in excellence—only in constant improvement and constant change."[16] Comment on Peters's suggestion.

10. Modern management has been described as a baseball game in which both the ball and the bases are in motion. "As soon as the ball is hit, the defending players can pick up the base bags and move them to anywhere in fair territory. The offensive players never know in advance where they must run to be safe."[17] This metaphor highlights the terrific pace of change in today's world—not only in the structure of an organization, but in its supporting environment. Recognizing that change is the status quo, further develop this metaphor.

THE MANAGEMENT EXPERIENCE SELF-ASSESSMENT OF MANAGERIAL STYLE

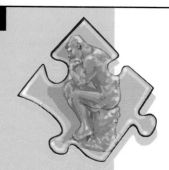

A major challenge facing virtually all managers is how to solve their people-production problems. Grid OD provides managers with an opportunity to evaluate their managerial style and identify alternative ways of managing for increased organization effectiveness. To assess your own managerial style, respond to the following items according to how you would likely behave if you were a manager. Each item describes an aspect of managerial behavior. Circle whether you would probably behave in the way described: always (A), frequently (F), occasionally (O), seldom (S), or never (N).

If I were a work group manager,

1. I would act as group spokesperson.   A   F   O   S   N

2. I would allow group members complete freedom in their work.   A   F   O   S   N

3. I would encourage the use of uniform procedures.   A   F   O   S   N

4. I would permit group members to use their own judgment in solving problems.   A   F   O   S   N

5. I would needle group members for greater effort.   A   F   O   S   N

6. I would let group members perform their jobs the way they think best.   A   F   O   S   N

7. I would keep the work moving at a rapid pace.   A   F   O   S   N

8. I would settle conflicts when they occur in the group.   A   F   O   S   N

9. I would decide what should be done and how it should be done.   A   F   O   S   N

10. I would turn group members loose on a job and let them go to it.   A   F   O   S   N

Continued on next page.

11. I would be reluctant to allow group members any freedom of action.	A	F	O	S	N
12. I would assign group members to particular jobs.	A	F	O	S	N
13. I would push for increased production.	A	F	O	S	N
14. I would be willing to make changes.	A	F	O	S	N
15. I would schedule the work to be done.	A	F	O	S	N
16. I would persuade others that my ideas are to their advantage.	A	F	O	S	N
17. I would refuse to explain my actions.	A	F	O	S	N
18. I would permit the group to set its own pace.	A	F	O	S	N

Scoring

1. Count the number of A (always) or F (frequently) responses for the odd questions (1, 3, 5, 7, 9, 11, 13, 15, 17). This is your *concern-for-production* score.

2. Count the number of A (always) or F (frequently) responses for the even questions (2, 4, 6, 8, 10, 12, 14, 16, 18). This is your *concern-for-people* score.

Source: Adapted from Thomas J. Sergiovanni, Richard Metzcus, and Larry Burden, "Toward a Particularistic Approach to Leadership Style: Some Findings," *American Educational Research Journal* 6 (January 1969), 62–79. © 1969, American Educational Research Association, Washington, D.C. Reprinted with permission.

CASE 11.1   HOSPITAL DEPARTMENTAL CONSOLIDATION

Janet Johns is the administrator of Suburban Memorial Hospital, a 275-bed hospital in an economically upper class suburb of a western state. Johns recently asked the new assistant administrator, Sam Donalds, to investigate whether consolidation of the EKG, Pulmonary Function, and Cardio-Pulmonary Rehabilitation Departments would result in a significant savings to the hospital.

Background

The three departments do basically the same types of patient tests. As medicine has progressed, there has been a movement away from static (at rest) testing to dynamic (in motion) testing. Dynamic testing is used in the EKG Department for heart tests, in the Pulmonary Function Department for lung tests, and in the Cardio-Pulmonary Rehabilitation Department for both heart and lung tests.

At present there is a duplication of services and equipment among the three departments at Suburban Memorial. In addition, three separate technicians are employed as well as three different part-time physicians who work on a percentage basis, according to the volume of work.

The EKG and Pulmonary Function Departments make a significant contribution to Suburban's revenue. The contribution margin of Pulmonary Function has been 80 percent (for every $100 earned, the hospital spends only $20 to earn it), and that of EKG has been 60 percent.

Revenues for each department are shown in the following table:

Department	Annual Revenue	Contribution Margin
EKG	$360,000	60%
Pulmonary function	520,000	80%
Cardio-pulmonary (new department, less than 1 year)	80,000	Unknown

Total annual revenue of Suburban Memorial is $32.2 million, and net income is $2.6 million. Donalds has calculated that a departmental consolidation could initially save the hospital $200,000 by selling duplicated equipment. In addition, the annual savings would amount to:

$ 88,000	personnel costs (fewer technicians needed)
30,000	ordering and supplies reduction (no duplication, less ordering)
200,000	reduced physician fees (only one physician would be needed)
32,000	plant and facilities (can lease out space not needed after consolidation)
$350,000	

Therefore, the annual savings would be $350,000, in addition to the initial $200,000 received from the sale of equipment.

Physicians

Dr. Bartl, head of Pulmonary Function, is responsible for 80 percent of pulmonary admissions to the hospital and about 4.7 percent of total admissions. He is an extremely popular physician, attracting respiratory cases from well outside the normal service area of Suburban Memorial.

Dr. Neumann, head of EKG, controls 20 percent of the hospital's cardiac/internal medicine cases. Overall, she admits about 30 percent of the hospital's patients.

Finally, the head of the new Cardio-Pulmonary Rehabilitation Department, Dr. Hermann, controls 100 percent of those cases, which at this point represent a negligible percentage of the hospital's total patient revenue.

All three physicians have more or less equal support from the medical staff.

Johns is wondering what to do about the physicians *if* she decides to go through with the consolidation. One of the three physicians would have to be chosen (with a new reimbursement contract) to head this new department, or perhaps a new salaried physician could be brought in. The combined workload would still be less than full time.

However, Johns sees several problems with either of those two alternatives. First of all, the physicians who would be "excluded" from this new department might become resentful and start admitting their out-of-service-area patients to other hospitals. Johns and Donalds have estimated a 25 percent probability that the three physicians would do so, which would mean a possible loss to the hospital of 15 percent of these physicians' admissions.

Johns has asked Donalds to prepare a report of the situation, including his recommendations, which will be discussed at the next management council meeting.

Problems

1. If you were Sam Donalds, what would you recommend? Prepare the type of report Janet Johns has asked for, as if it were going to be presented to Suburban Memorial's management council.

2. Assuming the council votes for consolidation, prepare another report outlining your recommended strategy to minimize alienation and maximize cooperation.

Source: Dorothy M. Hai, University of Wisconsin, La Crosse, and Richard C. Housley, Arizona State University, Tempe.

NOTES

[1] Quoted in Tom Peters, "Prometheus Barely Bound," *Academy of Management Executive* 4 (November 1990): 79.

[2] The following discussion largely draws on Terrence E. Deal and Allan A. Kennedy, *Corporate Cultures: The Rites and Rituals*

of Corporate Life (Reading, Mass.: Addison-Wesley, 1982) and James C. Collins and Jerry I. Porras, "Organizational Vision and Visionary Organizations," *California Management Review* 33 (Fall 1991): 30–52.

[3] Kurt Lewin, *Field Theory in Social Science* (ed.), Dorwin Cartwright (New York: Harper, 1951), 228–229.

[4] John P. Kotter and Leonard A. Schlesinger, "Choosing Strategies for Change," *Harvard Business Review* 57 (March–April 1979): 106–114.

[5] Rino J. Patti, "Organizational Resistance and Change: The View from Below," *Social Service Review* 48 (September 1974): 371–372.

[6] William Y. Rial quoted in "The Upheaval in Health Care," *Business Week,* July 25, 1983, 48.

[7] Kotter and Schlesinger, "Choosing Strategies for Change," 109–112.

[8] Lewin, *Field Theory,* 256–269.

[9] Mary Kay Ash, *Mary Kay on People Management* (New York: Warner Books, 1984), 73.

[10] "Roger Smith Takes on GM's Critics," *Fortune,* August 18, 1986, 27.

[11] Quoted in Doron P. Levin, "In a High-Tech Drive, GM Falls Below Rivals in Auto Profit Margins," *Wall Street Journal,* July 22, 1986, 1.

[12] Robert R. Blake and Jane S. Mouton, *The Managerial Grid III: The Key to Leadership Excellence* (Houston: Gulf Publishing, 1985).

[13] Kenneth N. Wexley and Gary A. Yukl, *Organizational Behavior and Personnel Psychology,* rev. ed. (Homewood, Ill.: Irwin, 1984), 327–328.

[14] Quoted in David L. Kirp and Douglas Rice, "Fast Forward—Styles of California Management," *Harvard Business Review* 66 (January–February 1988): 75.

[15] Jacob M. Braude quoted in "Thoughts on the Business of Life," *Forbes,* February 17, 1992, 188.

[16] Thomas J. Peters, "Facing Up to the Need for a Management Revolution," *California Management Review* 30 (Winter 1988): 8.

[17] "Changes in Management," *Royal Bank Letter* 69 (January–February 1988): 1.

P A R T

F O U R

STAFFING AND HUMAN RESOURCE MANAGEMENT

CHAPTER 12

LEARNING OBJECTIVES

Upon completing this chapter, you should be able to:

- Explain how human resource planning contributes to achieving organization goals.
- Describe a replacement chart.
- State the purpose of a skills inventory.
- Specify the most common job-analysis methods.
- Explain what is meant by a *job description*.
- State the purpose of job specifications.
- Describe various sources from which job applicants can be recruited.
- Delineate the basic steps in a typical selection decision.
- Describe a bona fide occupational qualification.
- Distinguish between a structured and an unstructured interview.
- Describe an ability test.
- Describe a work sample test.

ince its inception 25 years ago, the European Economic Community (EEC) has been gradually reducing barriers to international economic cooperation. Formerly, anyone who wished to work in one of the member countries but was not a native of that country had to apply for a work permit, which, if it was approved, would typically take 3 months to obtain. This requirement has been dropped in 1992. As a result, employees of multinational companies have a much easier time crossing national boundaries.

The change is expected to affect mainly white-collar employees because blue-collar employees are less inclined to move to another country unless economic conditions at home are bad. At first, the greatest effects will be felt by experienced managers and specialists, who are already internationally mobile. In time, professionals such as engineers and architects will also be able to obtain international certification. But in the long run, recent college graduates who have the flexibility to learn new languages and adapt easily to new environments will have an advantage. A company will be able to move these employees freely

HUMAN RESOURCE PLANNING AND STAFFING

throughout the EEC as they mature and gain experience. Such training is essential for top-level managers in a multinational or global company.

Increased flexibility in the deployment of employees will affect the structure and composition of the companies involved. For example, for many years, British Petroleum has sent managers to other countries. These managers ran local operations but were still oriented toward London. Some of the tenets of BP's restructuring programme, known as Project 1990, help meet the challenges of the changing EEC environment. To meet the challenges of the changing EEC environment, British Petroleum is implementing its Project 90. While BP retains its corporate centre in London, the company has recently set up a headquarters for its European region in Brussels. The composition of the management staff has changed from predominantly British to European. Career planning is evolving so that soon many of the company's managers within a given country will be promoted to positions outside of that country. Training in European languages other than English is being encouraged.

Planning for the recruitment and development of managerial talent abroad is a key element of the human resource planning and staffing function. In this chapter, we will discover how organizations ensure the continuing availability of qualified employees.

Source: Barry Louis Rubin, "Europeans Value Diversity," *HR Magazine* 36 (January 1991): 37–41, 78.

The collaboration of James A. Buford, Jr., Auburn University, in the preparation of this chapter is gratefully acknowledged.

As defined in Chapter 1, staffing and human resource management is the process of ensuring that competent employees are selected, developed, and rewarded for achieving organization goals. Sound staffing and human resource management benefits both an organization and its employees. From an organization's perspective, it not only ensures the effective utilization of employee talents, but sustains a supply of well-trained employees. From an employee's perspective, it serves to increase workplace satisfaction and make organization membership personally and socially desirable. The shift in nomenclature from *personnel*, which implies strictly employee hiring, to *human resources*, which views employees as dynamic assets, reflects an appreciation of both perspectives.

This is the first of three chapters that explores the staffing and human resource management function in detail. The current chapter is devoted to human resource planning and staffing. It discusses the importance of securing an adequate human resource mix so that an organization can achieve its goals. Chapter 13 continues this discussion by examining the need to continually develop human resources through appropriate orientation, performance appraisal, training, and so forth. Finally, Chapter 14 considers how to manage a successful career.

HUMAN RESOURCE PLANNING

Human resource planning is the process of providing an adequate mix of employees for achieving organization goals. It includes forecasting employee skill needs, comparing them to the present skill base, and determining the appropriate human resource actions. As diagrammed in Figure 12.1, human resource planning should follow (or at least coincide with) an organization's strategic plan. Depending on an organization's overall strategic direction—growth, stability, retrenchment—its human resource requirements could vary dramatically. Although not shown in Figure 12.1, potential influences, such as technological changes and government regulatory requirements originating in an organization's external environment, also should be considered.

After skill needs have been forecast and compared to an organization's present skill base, managers must typically make several decisions. Figure 12.1 shows these decisions and suggests alternative actions in response to each. When an organization's forecast skill needs exactly match its present employee skill base, no actions are necessary. An exact match is rare, however. The result is usually a forecast surplus of some skills and a shortage of others.

Several alternatives exist for reducing a surplus should it develop as a consequence of inaccurate past skill forecasts, a change in overall strategic direction, an economic downturn, or any other reason. These alternatives range from retraining to encouraging early retirements to initiating layoffs or even terminations. In situations where a shortage exists, a manager's options range from scheduling overtime to recruiting new employees, transferring existing employees, using subcontractors, or retraining current employees to perform new jobs. In either case—surplus or shortage—it would not be unusual to pursue several alternatives simultaneously.

Human resource planning.
The process of providing an adequate mix of employees for achieving organization goals.

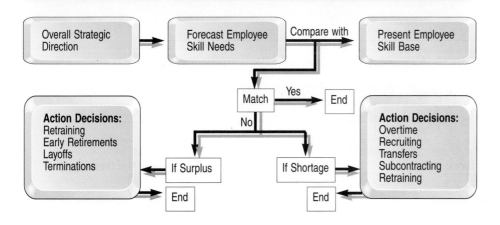

FIGURE 12.1 HUMAN RESOURCE PLANNING PROCESS

Polaroid has undertaken an innovative program in an effort to ensure that its present workforce is equipped to handle its future skill needs. Although many companies send employees to outside job-related skill courses, Polaroid broadcasts courses into various work sites from MIT, Harvard, and Northeastern. It even has a satellite relay from the National Technological University—a consortium of 38 institutions—to offer advanced degrees. As an incentive, Polaroid gives a raise to any employee who masters a needed skill.

FORECASTING SKILL NEEDS

Ideally, employment planning should be a continuous activity involving unit managers and representatives from an organization's human resource management department. A key element in such planning is the preparation of a **replacement chart,** indicating the various positions in an organization, the jobholders and their present performance, and the readiness of different candidates for promotion into each position. A sample replacement chart is shown in Figure 12.2. The age of each employee is shown on the chart only as an indication of likely retirement eligibility. Indeed, the Age Discrimination in Employment Act of 1967 prohibits age-based discrimination in the hiring, promoting, and terminating of persons over 40 years old. The act is enforced by the Equal Employment Opportunity Commission.

A replacement chart enables a unit manager or human resource manager to get an overall view of the promotability and performance of current employees, as well as the potential effects of losses from retirements, resignations, and other causes. In this respect, replacement charts help expose the likely ramifications of such losses. In addition, the domino effect of individual promotions is also revealed, because attention is drawn to filling resulting vacancies. Likewise, any potential difficulties are exposed. The best candidate for one position may be the only candidate for another position likely to be vacant in 6 months. At the least, such **succession planning** can help lessen the impact of the sudden or unexpected loss of an employee. On a more positive note, replacement charts can also be used to spot **position blockage,** that is, to spotlight employees who have not been promoted for, say, 2 years or more because the positions above them are filled. Position blockage has become increasingly common because of the flattening of downsized organizations (see Chapter 8).

Replacement chart.
A chart indicating the various positions in an organization, the jobholders and their present performance, and the readiness of different candidates for promotion into each position.

Succession planning.
The identification of likely candidates for future vacant positions.

Position blockage.
Employees not being promoted because the positions above them are filled.

FIGURE 12.2 EXAMPLE OF A REPLACEMENT CHART

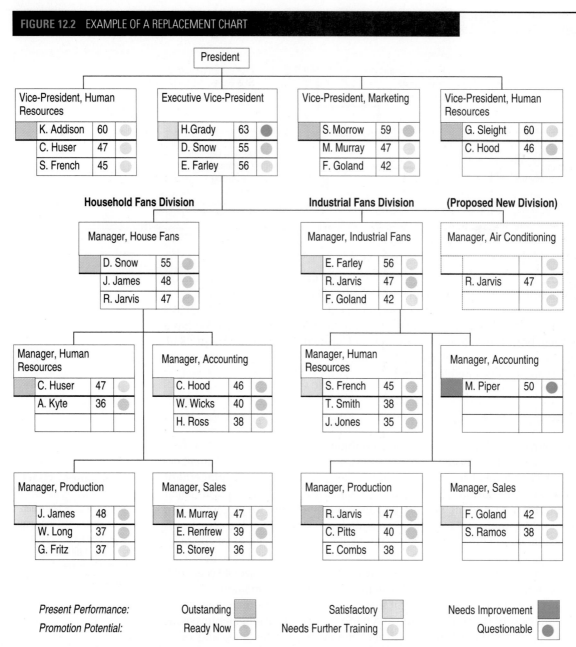

Present Performance: Outstanding / Satisfactory / Needs Improvement
Promotion Potential: Ready Now / Needs Further Training / Questionable

Source: Adapted from Walter S. Wikstrom, "Developing Managerial Competence: Changing Concepts, Emerging Practices," *Studies in Personnel Policy* 189 (New York: National Industrial Conference Board, 1964), 99. Reprinted with permission.

Companies such as Emerson Electric and Johnson & Johnson also use replacement charts to plot the career paths of high-potential managers—or High Ps, as they are called—those slated for rapid promotions. IBM maintains a computerized employee replacement table listing 6,000 High Ps for filling its top 1,500 positions. Emerson maintains a human resource command room in which the names, photographs, current positions, expertise, and experience of its top 700 managers are displayed on magnetic boards. If an experienced manager is needed for an assignment at either IBM or Emerson, a qualified candidate can likely be found in a matter of minutes.

ASSESSING CURRENT SKILLS

When it is clear what an organization's future employee skill needs will be, the organization may then proceed to catalog its current employee skill base. This is generally done with a **skills inventory,** which, in its simplest form, is a list of an organization's employees that includes information on various characteristics and skills they possess. The purpose of a skills inventory is to determine as specifically as possible the talents, education, training, and skills of an organization's employees. Skills inventories range in sophistication from manually compiled forms and index cards to computerized employee-tracking systems.

A skills inventory recognizes that the value of an organization includes its employees' know-how. Although this knowledge may not be included on an organization's balance sheet, the ability to maximize employee talent distinguishes winners from losers. As an example, consider Apple Computer. It has a skills inventory called *Spider* that allows a manager assembling a project team to instantly call up the skill profiles of employees who work anywhere from Tuscaloosa to Timbuktu. Using video conferencing, the manager can even interview the candidate in living color. This ability not only enables Apple to efficiently utilize employee know-how, but contributes to workplace satisfaction through the fullest realization of employee talents.

IBM maintains one of the most comprehensive skills inventories. It contains information on the skills of some 100,000 employees located worldwide. Using the inventory, IBM can quickly locate, for example, all managers with 5 years of finance experience who have supervised more than 15 subordinates, speak Italian, and are skilled in advanced graphics.

Skills inventory.
A list containing information on various characteristics and skills possessed by an organization's employees.

JOB ANALYSIS

Although skills inventories are important for establishing what individual employees can do, the specific requirements of the jobs within an organization must also be established. The process of collecting and studying information pertaining to a job is known as **job analysis.** Through job analysis, information is typically collected to answer the following questions:

1. What tasks are performed?
2. What knowledge, skills, and abilities are required?
3. What physical activities are required?
4. Under what environmental conditions is a job performed?

Although many different methods of job analysis are possible, all focus on collecting information from a source—for example, by observing and interviewing employees or by having them report similar information on a questionnaire. The most common job-analysis methods include:

1. Interviewing jobholders, superiors, and others qualified to provide job-related information.
2. Observing jobholders perform their work.

Job analysis.
The process of collecting and studying information pertaining to a job.

3. Evaluating questionnaires completed by jobholders, superiors, and others qualified to provide job-related information.

4. Evaluating activity logs kept by jobholders.

More often than not, several of these methods are used in conjunction with one another. Each has its strengths and weaknesses. For instance, the effectiveness of *interviews* depends on the ability of an interviewer to ask appropriate questions and the ability of interviewees to provide meaningful responses. The *observation method* allows in-depth analysis, but its accuracy depends on the validity of a job analyst's perceptions. *Questionnaires* are relatively easy and inexpensive but subject to jobholder bias. Finally, while *activity logs* can be comprehensive, they can also be quite bothersome to busy jobholders.

After it is collected and studied, the information from a job analysis is used in preparing a **job description.** A job description lists the important duties to be performed on a job. **Job specifications** should also be developed. Linked to job duties, these focus on the knowledge, skills, and abilities, as well as physical characteristics, experience, and other qualifications, necessary for successful job performance. Table 12.1 provides a job description for a human resource manager's job, and the job specifications for the same position are described in Table 12.2.

When determining job specifications, special caution should be taken to ensure that they truly are required for successful job performance. For example, a college degree should not be required for a job unless it has never been performed effectively by a person without one or unless it is unthinkable that a nongraduate

Job description.
A list of important duties to be performed on a job.

Job specifications.
The knowledge, skills, and abilities, as well as physical characteristics, experience, and other qualifications, necessary for successful job performance.

TABLE 12.1 A JOB DESCRIPTION FOR A HUMAN RESOURCE MANAGER

General Description

Performs responsible administrative work managing human resource activities of a large state agency or institution. Reports to top manager. Work involves responsibility for the planning and administration of a human resource program that includes recruitment, examination, selection, evaluation, appointment, promotion, transfer, and dismissal of employees, as well as maintenance of a system of communication for disseminating necessary information to employees. Works under general supervision, exercising initiative and independent judgment in performing assigned tasks.

Examples of Work Performed

1. Participates in overall planning and policy making to provide effective and uniform human resource services.
2. Communicates policy by bulletin, meetings, and personal contact.
3. Interviews applicants, evaluates qualifications, and classifies applications.
4. Recruits and screens applicants to fill vacancies and reviews applications of qualified persons.
5. Confers with supervisors on human resource matters, including placement problems, retention or release of probationary employees, transfers, demotions, and dismissals of permanent employees.
6. Supervises administration of selection tests.
7. Initiates training and development activities.
8. Establishes effective performance appraisal, compensation, and employee benefits systems.
9. Maintains employee files.
10. Supervises a group of employees directly and through subordinates.
11. Performs related work as assigned.

TABLE 12.2 JOB SPECIFICATIONS FOR A HUMAN RESOURCE MANAGER

General Qualification Requirements

Experience and Training
Should have experience and training in human resource management. Four years of prior experience is a minimum.

Education
Graduation from a 4-year college or university, with courses in human resource management.

Knowledge, Skills, and Abilities
Considerable knowledge of principles and practices of human resource management, including labor relations legislation, employee selection and assignment, performance appraisal, training and development, compensation, and employee benefits.

could competently perform the job. Similarly, lengthy experience requirements (for example, 10 years) should not be listed unless no one with less experience could possibly perform the job successfully. Unnecessary job specifications that can be shown to favor certain candidates and eliminate others could be in violation of federal "fair employment" laws.

FAIR EMPLOYMENT

The term **fair employment** refers to nondiscriminatory employment practices, that is, those practices basing selection, pay, promotion, and other conditions of employment on job requirements, not on gender, race, age, or other non-job-related factors. In the past, managers were able to make human resource decisions

Fair employment.
Nondiscriminatory employment practices.

A voice-activated computer enables Tony Norris, a quadriplegic, to prepare budgets and plans for apparel in the Sears, Roebuck and Company Merchandise Group at company headquarters in Chicago. Technological tools like voice-activated computers, voice synthesizers, and character recognition systems allow employers to tap an underused human resource, physically impaired workers.

with little concern for legal requirements. Today, however, legal regulations extend to virtually all human resource activities. Whereas the first fair employment laws were passed immediately following the Civil War, the most important comprehensive federal legislation aimed at securing equal employment opportunity has been a series of laws and regulations beginning in the early 1960s (see Table 12.3). The most comprehensive of these is Title VII of the Civil Rights Act, passed in 1964 and variously amended, most recently in 1991. Title VII prohibits discrimination on the basis of race, color, national origin, religion, or gender in all aspects of employment and by all employers with 15 or more employees. It is administered by the U.S. Equal Employment Opportunity Commission, an independent federal agency.

An effect of Title VII was the establishment of specific groups identified by race, color, national origin, religion, or gender who are "protected" from unfair employment practices. Any action that limits, segregates, or classifies **protected group** members in any way so as to deprive them of employment opportunities is illegal. The concept of protected groups was extended by the Age Discrimination in Employment Act (1967) to people over age 40 and by both the Vocational Rehabilitation Act (1974) and Americans with Disabilities Act (1990) to the mentally and physically impaired. With respect to the latter, discrimination is prohibited against qualified individuals with disabilities, defined as persons who can with "reasonable accommodation" perform the "essential functions" of a particular job.

Protected group.
Specific groups identified by race, color, national origin, religion, gender, age, or impairment who are "protected" from unfair employment practices by the 1964 Civil Rights Act.

TABLE 12.3 MAJOR FEDERAL FAIR EMPLOYMENT LAWS AND REGULATIONS

Law/Regulation	Provision
Equal Pay Act, 1963	Prohibits gender-based differences in pay for substantially equal work
Civil Rights Act, 1964 (amended in 1972, 1977, 1978, 1991)	Prohibits discrimination based on race, color, religion, gender, or national origin
Executive Orders 11246 and 11375, 1965	Prohibit discrimination based on race, color, religion, gender, national origin, physical impairment, or veteran's status by federal contractors and subcontractors
Age Discrimination in Employment Act, 1967 (amended in 1974, 1978, 1986)	Prohibits age discrimination against individuals over age 40, as well as forced retirement because of age
Vocational Rehabilitation Act, 1973 (amended in 1974, 1976, 1978)	Prohibits discrimination based on mental or physical impairment by federal agencies, contractors, and subcontractors
Vietnam Era Veterans Readjustment Act, 1974	Prohibits discrimination against disabled veterans and Vietnam veterans by federal agencies, contractors, and subcontractors
Pregnancy Discrimination Act, 1978	Requires employers who provide benefits for other disabilities arising off the job to provide them also for pregnancy
Americans with Disabilities Act, 1990	Prohibits discrimination based on mental or physical impairment by private employers

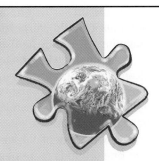

CLOSE UP: INTERNATIONAL MANAGEMENT THE TRANSFORMATION OF JAPANESE HUMAN RESOURCE PRACTICES

Throughout the 1980s, the popular business press and academics challenged the human resource (HR) practices used by U.S. employers. Frequently, Japanese HR practices were held up as an alternative to emulate. But Cornell University professor Vladimir Pucik says that Japanese HR practices are themselves facing challenges.

For instance, the winds of change are weakening the commitment of many Japanese employers to lifetime employment. Pucik observes that the present surplus of aging middle managers is forcing greater use of transfers, limits on the amount of time a person can stay in a position, and "voluntary" retirement. But as young professionals see employers backing away from commitments to their fathers, the next generation may want to take greater personal control over their careers and change employers. Because there is currently a shortage of Japanese male graduates in professional and managerial fields, employers are facing more severe competition to attract a new generation of "lifetimers" at the same time that they are trying to loosen their bonds with older managers.

Pucik recounts that during his first visit to Japan 20 years ago, there was nearly universal agreement among human resource managers that existing compensation systems based on seniority would be substantially modified, with more weight given to performance and ability. But today's age-related wage differences are only slightly smaller than they were 20 years ago. Does this mean that Japanese organizations are not meritocratic? Pucik says that they are but that Japanese employers reward managers through career path differentiation, not through compensation. First, the limited influence of an external labor market dampens the need for market-sensitive compensation. Second, a narrow salary range among an age cohort fosters the sense that all managers are part of a winning team. Pucik says that an examination of managerial salary distribution by age in a typical U.S. firm would show most managers bunched at lower levels, with a relatively large differential between the highest paid executive and the majority of managers. The effect of such a system is to make apparent the returns associated with outstanding performance, in order to reward high performers and motivate others. But Japanese employers feel that such a differential would label lower paid managers as losers. Rather than motivate behavior, a large pay gap between the majority and the highest performers is believed to be divisive. It would make it difficult for managers to feel they are all part of the team and thus would undercut the traditionally strong cohesion.

Pucik sees the greatest challenge to Japanese HR practice as the ever-increasing process of globalization and the accompanying need for global managers. Without work experience in headquarters in Japan, non-Japanese managers will find it difficult to assume executive responsibility in their home countries. Pucik asserts that Japanese language and culture training is necessary to permit non-Japanese employees to operate effectively within the Japanese managerial culture. A truly global company searches for managerial talent and secures advancement opportunities regardless of where an employee is hired. As in the United States, developing and fully utilizing such global managers may be the greatest challenge facing Japanese employers today.

Source: Adapted from "Revolution or Evolution: The Transformation of Japanese Personnel Practices," *On Center* (Center for Advanced Human Resource Studies, Cornell University), No. 2 (1991): 9, 11.

The standard for determining if a reasonable accommodation can be made is whether it would cause "undue hardship" to an employer. Establishing the exact meanings of "undue hardship" and "essential functions" is left to the federal courts.

As presently interpreted, discrimination against a protected group can occur if employment practices involve or result in either **disparate treatment** or **disparate impact.** Disparate treatment consists of using race, color, national origin, religion, gender, or disability as a basis for treating people unequally (for example, refusing to hire minorities or women for certain types of jobs). Disparate impact occurs when an identical standard is equally applied to all applicants or employees, but one group is more negatively affected than another. For example, if a height standard is equally applied to all applicants, Hispanics and Asians are more negatively affected than whites, and women more than men. Disparate impact thus focuses on the *effect* of employment practices rather than the *causes*. It need not be motivated by ill will or bias. Although disparate treatment can involve either protected groups or individual group members, disparate impact always involves groups.

Both disparate treatment and disparate impact can be used by complainants as a basis for a prima facie (meaning presumed) case of discrimination. Charges of discrimination may be filed with the Equal Employment Opportunity Commission by individuals either on their own behalf or on that of a similarly "affected class," or by others on behalf of such persons. Where conciliation is unsuccessful, the commission can litigate against an employer. In such cases, an employer would have to demonstrate that the allegedly discriminatory employment practice is, in the words of the Civil Rights Act of 1991, "job related for the position in question and consistent with business necessity." The 1991 Civil Rights Act does not define "job related" or "business necessity." Clarifying these terms is left to the federal courts.

Although much has been said about the complexity of fair employment laws and regulations, most organizations today see them as an integral part of their normal operations. Indeed, fair employment has over the past 20–30 years become the norm and has been firmly established in law as national policy. It should be noted that there are state and local laws, as well as constitutional elements, that likewise regulate employment.

Disparate impact.
The result of an employment practice that appears fair, but has an adverse effect on protected group members.

Disparate treatment.
Using race, color, national origin, religion, or gender as a basis for treating people unequally in employment practices.

SEXUAL HARASSMENT

In 1980 the Equal Employment Opportunity Commission amended its existing Guidelines on Discrimination Because of Sex to specifically include sexual harassment. As defined by the commission, sexual harassment is virtually any verbal or physical conduct of a sexual nature that makes submission an implicit or explicit term or condition of employment, that is used as a basis for employment decisions, and that substantially interferes with an employee's performance or creates a "hostile work environment." Under the 1991 Civil Rights Act, if employees claim harassment was intentional, they can get a jury trial.

It is important for organizations to understand that they are responsible for the behavior of their employees. They should act to prevent sexual harassment by developing and communicating a strict policy prohibiting such behavior, providing special training for all organization members, establishing a procedure to investigate complaints, and taking appropriate disciplinary action against offenders.

A recruiter for Walgreen's meets with pharmacy students at Purdue University. Like many companies, one of Walgreen's external recruiting sources is college campuses. Walgreen Company is the largest employer of Purdue pharmacy graduates, hiring more than one quarter of the 1991 class.

RECRUITING

Developing a legal and effective human resource program is a formidable but essential task. With respect to our discussion of human resource planning, the goals of hiring competent employees and staying safely within the law are not mutually exclusive. Nondiscriminatory employment practices will usually result in hiring a more competent workforce. With this in mind, if human resource planning suggests the likelihood of a skill shortage, one alternative is to recruit.

Recruiting is the process of attracting job applicants who have the talents necessary to achieve an organization's goals. Job applicants can be recruited from many sources. A typical organization will find it necessary to utilize both *internal* and *external sources* to attract a sufficient pool of qualified applicants. Table 12.4 lists the most common internal and external recruitment sources.

As Table 12.4 indicates, an organization making use of internal sources might use its skills inventory to locate potential job applicants from among its current employees. It might also ask its present employees to encourage qualified friends to apply. Security Pacific Corporation has an employee referral program, called The Superscout program. All its retirees, regular full-time, part-time, and temporary employees are eligible to participate. Everyone who makes a qualified referral is entered in a quarterly drawing for $500. The person who made the referral for the applicant who is hired receives a cash award ranging up to $1,500.

Job posting is a third internal source. Job openings may be posted on bulletin boards and listed in in-house publications. This gives current employees the opportunity to apply for openings first, before they are advertised externally, and also helps organizations meet equal employment opportunity commitments. Security Pacific lists all job openings in its employee newsletter, *Career Opps.* Tandem Computers posts job openings company-wide using its internal electronic mail system. Job posting not only indicates an organization's commitment to internal promotion, but also can help employees to identify career paths, help them to clarify

Recruiting.
The process of attracting job applicants who have knowledge, skills, and abilities needed to achieve an organization's goals.

Job posting.
The posting of job openings on bulletin boards and in organization publications.

TABLE 12.4 RECRUITMENT SOURCES BY JOB APPLICANT TYPE			
Source	**Blue Collar**	**White Collar**	**Managerial, Technical, and Professional**
Internal			
Skills inventories	X	X	X
Present employees' friends	X	X	X
Job posting	X	X	
External			
Walk-ins	X	X	
Agencies			
Temporary help agencies		X	
Private employment agencies		X	
Public employment agencies	X	X	
Search firms ("headhunters")			X
Educational institutions			
High schools	X	X	
Vocational/technical schools	X	X	X
Colleges and universities			X
Other			
Union hiring halls	X		
Professional associations			X
Military services	X	X	X
Former employees	X	X	X
Want ads	X	X	X
Suppliers	X	X	X

career goals, and encourage superiors to talk to subordinates about their career progress.

External sources for recruiting include employment agencies, educational institutions, professional associations, the military services, and former employees. People who walk in and fill out applications or respond to want ads are also a major external source of job applicants. Finally, it should be noted that some union contracts restrict recruiting to union hiring halls. In such cases, recruiting is turned over to union officials who are legally required to refer both union and nonunion members for employment in a nondiscriminatory manner.

As Table 12.4 also indicates, the types of job applicants likely to be recruited by different recruitment sources vary. Blue-collar workers, for instance, are seldom recruited from private employment agencies. White-collar workers are unlikely to be hired through union halls. Finally, managerial, technical, and professional employees are the only one of the three types of employees shown to likely be placed by search firms, sometimes known as "headhunters."

SELECTION

Selection involves making decisions about people. When several people apply for a job opening, an organization must decide who is the most qualified. As with recruiting, care must be taken to ensure that all aspects of the selection process meet fair employment requirements. Selection practices that involve treating protected groups unequally can provide grounds for charges of disparate treatment. Examples of such practices include:

- Making exceptions regarding application deadlines, interview schedules, and documentation required for certain job applicants.
- Communicating news on job openings only to selected people or groups.
- Writing job specifications to favor certain job applicants.
- Coaching certain job applicants on desirable responses to interview questions or employment tests.

When these or similar practices work to the disadvantage of protected groups, there is likely to be a strong presumption that discrimination occurred. To avoid legal challenge, it is thus important to make selection decisions in a consistent manner and to treat all applicants fairly.

Although smaller employers may take an informal approach to selection, larger ones typically rely on an established process to identify the most qualified job applicants. This process might best be viewed as a series of steps or "hurdles" through which applicants progress. At each step, some are screened from further consideration. Figure 12.3 illustrates the various steps in a typical selection decision.

To reduce the time and expense of using all the steps indicated, many employers perform Steps 4 and 5 at about the same time. Generally speaking, however, the more important a job, the more likely each step will be used. Almost all employers use the preliminary screening interview, application blank, and employment interview. A relatively small number of employers use tests to screen applicants. Background/reference checks are used for some jobs.

STEP 1: PREAPPLICATION SCREENING

For some jobs, prospective job candidates often simply walk into an organization's employment office. In such cases, a human resource specialist will typically spend

FIGURE 12.3 STEPS IN A TYPICAL SELECTION DECISION

Step 6: Selection Decision
Step 5: Reference Checks/Letters of Recommendation
Step 4: Employment Tests
Step 3: Employment Interview
Step 2: Application Blank
Step1: Preapplication Screening

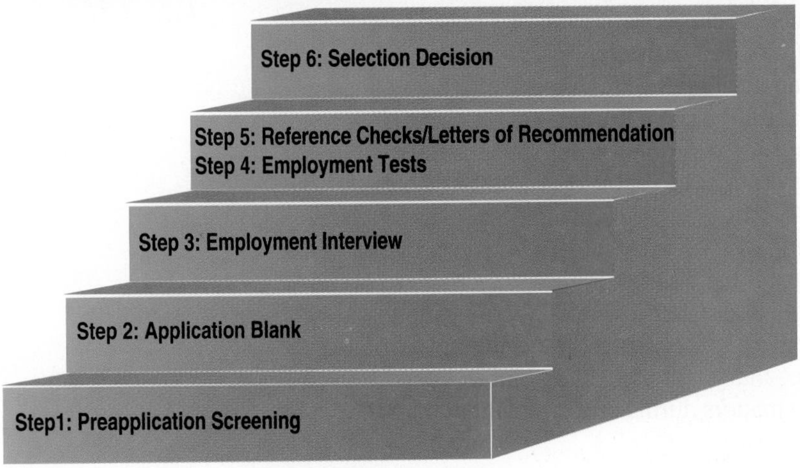

a few minutes with such individuals, conducting a preapplication screening. The intent is to weed out those who do not meet employment requirements. This thereby reduces the time and expense associated with the further consideration of unqualified individuals. Only those individuals who meet established criteria are asked to complete an application blank (Step 2). In some smaller organizations, if a walk-in appears to be a promising job candidate, preliminary screening may progress directly to an employment interview (Step 3).

STEP 2: APPLICATION BLANK

Job applicants who pass the preliminary screening are next typically asked to complete an application blank. A completed application form is a dated record of an applicant's interest in a position. Additionally, it serves as a profile of the applicant for classification, further screening, and record keeping. If the applicant is subsequently hired, the information contained in an application blank becomes a permanent part of the person's work record.

An integral part of most selection processes, application blanks must adhere to all federal and state fair employment provisions. Exceptions are allowed only when a **bona fide occupational qualification (BFOQ)** is involved. Thus, questions about race, color, age, gender, national origin, religion, and mental or physical handicaps are unfair unless they are job related. For instance, a church-affiliated school might legitimately inquire into applicants' religious denominations, but not their birthplaces. The BFOQ defense is most often used when it is necessary to select applicants on the basis of gender. It would be permissible, for example, to specify that a woman be hired for the position of jail matron. But a BFOQ cannot be used to justify beliefs that result in gender-segregated job classifications, such as "women do not have the strength to be equipment operators" or "men are not suited for secretarial jobs." The BFOQ defense has been used, however, to justify excluding applicants on the basis of race for the sake of believability (for example, actors in stage roles or servers in specialty restaurants).

The Equal Employment Opportunity Commission does require employers to gather information on applicant race, color, age, gender, national origin, religion, and disability for use in computing and reporting appropriate statistics. This information may be collected using a detachable or separate form indicating that it will be used solely for equal employment opportunity purposes and will be kept separate from other application materials. Because employment decisions can be based only on job-related factors, information of this type should be kept separate so that hiring decisions cannot be inappropriately influenced. Although collecting this information may seem paradoxical in view of the preceding discussion, not having the information on record is not a legally defensible excuse for failing to satisfy Equal Employment Opportunity Commission reporting requirements.

Properly used, application blanks can be an effective aid in selection. However, one cautionary note should be made. Their usefulness is largely dependent on the accuracy of data furnished by job candidates. In their eagerness to obtain work, some applicants may be tempted to stretch the truth concerning matters such as past experience, responsibilities, salary, and reasons for leaving a previous job. For this reason, many human resource managers make it a point to query promising applicants further regarding these matters during an employment interview.

Bona fide occupational qualification (BFOQ).

A permissible job-related exception to the fair employment requirement that all human resource decisions be made without regard to race, color, age, gender, national origin, religion, and mental or physical impairment.

STEP 3: EMPLOYMENT INTERVIEW

An employment interview is part of almost every selection process. Indeed, most studies indicate the interview is the *most important step* in selection. The reason for this is that an employment interview may be the only way an organization can gather information about such things as an applicant's communication skills, personal traits, and mannerisms. At Toronto-based Four Seasons Hotels, job applicants undergo up to five rigorous interviews to sort out those with a friendly nature and a sense of teamwork. Disneyland interviews applicants in groups of three to observe how they interact: Do they show respect, for example, by being attentive when others speak?

An interview also presents an opportunity for both an organization and job applicant to "sell" themselves to one another and to establish their mutual expectations. For such expectations to be accurately established, however, it is essential that employment interviews be as realistic as possible. From an employer's perspective, unless care is taken, interviews may create unrealistic expectations in new employees. When such expectations clash with actual job requirements, disillusionment and feelings of being misled are likely to develop. A lack of job commitment and early turnover are a common result.[1] To prevent this, applicants should be told negative as well as positive aspects of a position, so that those who view the negative aspects as unacceptable can remove themselves from further consideration.

At Apple Computer, as many as 15 interviews may take place to ensure that job applicants understand the company's high performance expectations. At the New York investment banking house of Morgan Stanley, managing directors and their spouses may take promising job applicants and their spouses to dinner as part of the interviewing process. At that time, they discuss the often arduous demands of

An employment interview is often the most important step in a selection decision. To successfully interview an applicant an interviewer must be familiar with the job to be filled, prepare questions that elicit pertinent information, and listen carefully to answers.

the job with the couple. In that way, applicants and their spouses can get a realistic idea of how the job may affect their lives.

As is the case with application blanks, it is illegal in an employment interview to make decisions based on race, color, national origin, religion, gender, or disability unless these factors can be shown to be job related. Although it is not technically illegal to ask for such information, it is almost certainly illegal to use the information in making selection decisions. Likewise, other personal inquiries that are not clearly job related should be avoided. For example, an interviewer probably should not ask a woman about her marital plans, birth control, or plans for childbearing. If a job requires extensive overnight travel, an interviewer might legitimately ask whether any factors in an applicant's life might prohibit such travel. Otherwise, for a typical 9-to-5 job, such an inquiry would likely be inadvisable.

Table 12.5 on page 356 contains guidelines for preemployment inquiries. The guidelines, although not exhaustive, illustrate the care that must be exercised to avoid the appearance, as well as the actual fact, of discrimination.

In general, there are two principal types of employment interviews: structured and unstructured. The type of interview that should be used depends on the kind of information desired and the purposes to be served. Both types are used by a wide assortment of organizations. AT&T uses both types. Structured interviews, however, are more typically used for entry-level positions, whereas interviews for middle-level and upper-level positions usually involve some combination of structured and unstructured questioning.

In a **structured interview,** an interviewer asks each job applicant a set of predetermined questions. This type of interview is frequently conducted by an interviewer who uses a standard form for recording responses.

A prime advantage of structured interviews emerges when more than one interviewer is screening applicants. In such instances, structured interviews are more likely to provide consistent (and thus reliable) information from the various interviewers. A second advantage is that, provided specific interview questions are drawn from an accurate job analysis, structured interviews are also more likely to be valid. These advantages, however, must be weighed against the limited flexibility structured interviews offer. The structured interview format restricts adaptation to unusual circumstances or unusual interviewees. It is equally constraining to applicants, who may not be afforded the opportunity to demonstrate their job knowledge, communication skills, and so forth.

In an **unstructured interview,** there are no predetermined questions or prearranged sequence of topics for discussion. Consequently, unstructured interviews are by design highly flexible. Interviewers are free to probe into those areas seeming to merit further investigation and to adapt their approach to the prevailing situation, as well as to a changing stream of job applicants.

Spontaneity characterizes this type of interview. Its direction is largely determined by a job applicant's answers. To be effective, an unstructured interview requires a highly skilled interviewer. Experience shows that, if properly conducted, an unstructured interview can lead to significant job-related insights. However, the fact that its results are more difficult to replicate—and thus verify—cannot be denied.

STEP 4: EMPLOYMENT TESTS

Some organizations use employment tests to gather additional information on which to base their selection decisions. The primary intent of such tests is to aid in

Structured interview.
A job interview in which an applicant is asked a predetermined set of questions.

Unstructured interview.
A job interview in which there are no predetermined questions or prearranged sequence of topics for discussion.

predicting an applicant's future job performance. An organization's human resource management department usually is charged with seeing that these tests are properly administered and professionally evaluated.

Of the many types of test available, *ability tests* and *work sample tests* are the most common. The former are almost always "pencil and paper" instruments that include psychological, vocational interest, and cognitive skill tests. Retailers and banks have long used psychological tests to exclude applicants who might steal or use drugs on the job. As the U.S. economy has become more dependent on cognitive (as opposed to physical) skills, the importance of cognitive ability for job performance has been especially enhanced.

Work sample tests require that applicants perform activities that closely approximate those they will actually perform on a job. Test performance is taken to reflect likely performance in an actual job situation. Examples of work sample tests would include asking applicants for a mechanic's job to repair a gearbox or applicants for a motor grader operator to grade an area to specifications established by reference stakes.

Several cautions are in order with regard to both ability tests and work sample tests. Both can be misused. To be legally defensible, ability tests must be shown to be highly *valid* with low disparate impact. **Validity** reflects the relation between test results and actual job performance. Thus, we would expect job applicants who score high on a clerical knowledge test to perform well as secretaries, and those who score low to perform poorly. If this prediction holds true, then the test is valid; it measures what it was intended to measure.

Validity.
The relation between test results and actual job performance.

Companies use occupational proficiency tests and results from professional licensing examinations to help predict which applicants are likely to be productive employees. The Psychological Corporation is the world's largest for-profit publisher of these educational and psychological tests.

TABLE 12.5 GUIDE FOR APPROPRIATE PREEMPLOYMENT INQUIRIES

Subject	Fair Preemployment Inquiries	Unfair Preemployment Inquiries
Age	Inquiries as to birth date and proof of true age.	Any inquiry that implies a preference for persons under 40 years of age.
Arrests	None. (Law enforcement agencies are exempt from this rule.)	All inquiries relating to arrests.
Citizenship	Whether applicant is prevented from lawfully becoming employed in this country because of visa or immigration status. Whether applicant can provide proof of citizenship, visa, or alien registration number after being hired.	Whether applicant is a citizen. Requirement before hiring that applicant present birth certificate or naturalization or baptismal record. Any inquiry into citizenship that would tend to divulge applicant's lineage, ancestry, national origin, descent, or birthplace.
Convictions	Inquiries concerning specified convictions that relate reasonably to fitness to perform the particular job(s) being applied for, *provided* that such inquiries are limited to convictions for which the date of conviction or prison release, whichever is more recent, is within 7 years of the date of the job application.	Any inquiry that does not meet the requirements for fair pre-employment inquiries.
Credit rating	None.	Any inquiries concerning credit rating, charge accounts, or automobile ownership.
Disability	None.	Any inquiries relative to current or past medical history.
Family	Whether applicant can meet specified work schedules or has activities, commitments, or responsibilities that may prevent him or her from meeting work attendance requirements.	Specific inquiries concerning spouse, spouse's employment or salary, children, child-care arrangements, or dependents.
Height and weight	Inquiries as to ability to perform actual job requirements. Being of a certain height or weight will not be considered to be a job requirement unless the employer can show that no employee with the ineligible height or weight could do the work.	Any inquiry not based on actual job requirements.
Marital status (see also Name and Family)	None.	( ) Mr. ( ) Miss ( ) Mrs. ( ) Ms. Whether the applicant is married, single, divorced, separated, engaged, widowed, and so on.

Subject	Fair Preemployment Inquiries	Unfair Preemployment Inquiries
TABLE 12.5 *continued*		
Memberships	Inquiry into memberships, excluding any organization the name or character of which indicates the race, color, creed, gender, marital status, religion, or national origin or ancestry of its members.	Requirement that applicant list all clubs, societies, lodges, and the like to which he or she belongs.
Military	Inquiries concerning education, training, or work experiences in U.S. armed forces.	Type or condition of military discharge. Applicant's experience in other than U.S. armed forces. Request for discharge papers.
Name	Whether applicant has worked for the host organization or a competitor under a different name and, if so, what name. Name under which applicant is known to references if different from present name.	Inquiry into original name if it has been changed by court order or marriage. Inquiries about a name that would divulge marital status, lineage, ancestry, national origin, or descent.
National origin	Inquiries into applicant's ability to read, write, and speak foreign languages, when such inquiries are based on job requirements.	Inquiries into applicant's lineage, ancestry, national origin, descent, birthplace, or mother tongue. National origin of applicant's parents or spouse.
Photographs	May be requested *after* hiring for identification purposes.	Request that applicant submit a photograph at any time before hiring.
Pregnancy (see also Disability)	Inquiries as to duration of stay on job or anticipated absences that are made to males and females alike.	All questions as to pregnancy and medical history concerning pregnancy and related matters.
Race or color	None.	Any inquiry concerning race or color of skin, hair, eyes, and so on.
Relatives	Names of applicant's relatives already employed by the host organization or by any competitor.	Names and addresses of any relative other than those listed as proper.
Religion or creed	None.	Inquiries concerning applicant's religious denomination, religious affiliations, church, parish, pastor, or religious holidays observed.
Residence	Inquiries about address to the extent needed to facilitate contacting the applicant.	Names and relationships of persons with whom applicant resides. Whether applicant owns or rents own home.
Gender	None.	Any inquiry.

Source: Updated and adapted from Washington State Human Rights Commission, *Employment Regulations,* vol. 2 (Seattle: Washington State Human Rights Commission, 1982), 4–6.

SMART MANAGEMENT NORMIN' STORMIN': RACE-NORMING

Race-norming is the practice of adjusting scores on job-placement tests to account for race. The test scores of black and Hispanic job seekers are graded only against those of other blacks or Hispanics who have taken the test. Their scores are then ranked by percentile using one of three scales: one for blacks, one for Hispanics, and one for whites and others.

As a result, scores of blacks and Hispanics are generally boosted. Minority candidates for jobs may end up with higher percentile scores than some whites or Asian Americans who actually outperformed them according to the raw, unadjusted results. Thus, if a white, a black, and a Hispanic each earned a raw score of 300 on a test for bus drivers, the three would be assigned different scores. For example, the black might be given an 83 (meaning the 83rd percentile of all black applicants), the Hispanic a 67, and the white a 45, making it appear that the black applicant scored almost twice as high as the white applicant.

Until race-norming was outlawed by the 1991 Civil Rights Act, some 34 state employment agencies and private employers, such as Texas Instruments and Philip Morris, made racial adjustments of job seekers' test scores. State agencies used the General Aptitude Test Battery (GATB), an ability test developed by the U.S. Department of Labor. The GATB is a standardized test of cognitive ability in such areas as arithmetic, reasoning, and vocabulary. When controversy erupted over race-norming, the Labor Department suspended use of the GATB. In 1989 the National Academy of Sciences reported that the GATB was not biased against blacks: It accurately predicted job performance using scores before they were adjusted for race.

Civil rights advocates who supported race-norming said that the GATB was culturally biased toward whites, although Asians did so well that they were scored as though they were white. Critics claim that two main groups were hurt by race-norming: the applicants whose scores were artificially made to appear lower and the many hard-working, able minorities for whom such treatment was unwanted and who resented the implication of inferiority that comes with racial preferences. Critics further contended that rather than using distorted test data, a better answer lies in improving basic educational performance so that more people can meet objective standards that apply to all. The Labor Department is spending $6 million to conduct "extensive research" to improve the GATB. It still considers the GATB to be a valid test but believes that it "shouldn't be the sole means of referrals and shouldn't be used to the exclusion of such other factors as experience and education."

Sources: Timothy Noah, "Job Tests Scored on Racial Curve Stir Controversy," *Wall Street Journal*, May 26, 1991, B1, B8; Peter A. Brown, "Normin' Stormin'," *New Republic*, April 29, 1991, 12–14; William M. Welch, "Adjusting Job Test Scores by Race Looms as Latest Civil Rights Fight," (Baton Rouge) *Morning Advocate*, May 6, 1991, 7A.

Disparate impact—when an identical standard is applied to all applicants, but one group is more negatively affected than another—is a special concern in using ability tests. The widespread use of cognitive ability tests, for example, is hindered by the fact that some minorities achieve lower scores on average than whites. Thus, their use results in disparate impact.

Underutilization of minorities—that is, having a percentage of minority employment lower than the percentage of minority members in a labor market—can lead to a prima facie charge of illegal discrimination. In such instances, an ability test that disproportionately screens out protected group members will be judged illegal unless it can be shown to be job related. Table 12.6 gives examples of employment test items that have been judged to have unequal consequences for various protected groups.

Although work sample tests are inherently valid, they must also be shown to be job related to avoid legal difficulties. Consider a standard 5-minute typewriting test designed to measure the skill to type 60 words per minute with 95 percent accuracy. If a job requires typing internal documents only occasionally, the test would be inappropriate. Similarly, if a job requires a person to type highly technical material with numerous equations, then the test would not measure the needed skills. It again would be inappropriate, being unrelated to the job.

STEP 5: REFERENCE CHECKS/LETTERS OF RECOMMENDATION

Virtually all organizations require applicants to submit references—names of people for whom an applicant has worked—or letters of recommendation. Use of

---

TABLE 12.6   QUESTIONABLE EMPLOYMENT TEST ITEMS

What follows is a sampling of employment test items that have been considered invasive, irrelevant, or discriminatory. In some cases, the items have been removed following court orders or the efforts of advocacy groups. Other items continue to appear on tests but remain the subject of controversy. The collection was put together by Robert Schaeffer, public education director for the National Center for Fair & Open Testing.

Item 1: I have often wished I were a girl (Or if you are a girl) I have never been sorry that I am a girl. (True or False)

Item 2: I like mechanics magazines. (True or False)

Item 3: Everything is turning out just like the prophets of the Bible said it would. (True or False)

Answers: 1. False for men, true for women. **2.** True, if you hope to appear manly and macho. **3.** False, if you don't want to appear to be a religious fanatic.

Explanation: These questions are taken from the Minnesota Multiphasic Personality Inventory. The Boston Police Department uses the MMPI in preemployment screening and, according to Schaeffer, these three items were among those that the department dropped following lengthy protest by gay activists and the B'nai B'rith Anti-Defamation League.

Item 4: Sanitation trucks are painted mainly to:
  A. prevent rusting
  B. beautify the trucks
  C. kill germs on the inside
  D. advertise the Department of Sanitation
  E. increase the cost of operation

Item 5: Air pressure is measured by a:
  A. barometer
  B. photometer
  C. humidifier
  D. thermometer
  E. rain gauge

Answers: 4. A. **5.** A.

Explanation: Taken from previous editions of the written examination for New York City sanitation workers. Of these two items, Schaeffer asks: "What is the demonstrated connection between being able to answer questions such as these and driving a truck or loading garbage?"

Source: Adapted from Justin Martin, "Workplace Testing: Why Can't We Get It Right?" *Across the Board* 27 (December 1990): 32–39.

reference checks and letters of recommendation is based on the idea that the best predictor of future performance is past performance. This logic suggests that by gaining insight into an applicant's past behavior, the probability of a sound selection decision will be increased.

For references or letters of recommendation to be useful, they must meet certain conditions:

1. The person preparing them must know an applicant's past performance and be competent to assess it.
2. This person must also be able to effectively communicate the assessment.
3. This person must be truthful.

If job applicants choose their references or arrange for their own letters of recommendation, the first two conditions may not be met. With regard to the third, more and more people are reluctant to express (either in written form or orally) their true assessment of an applicant's performance for fear their remarks may not be held in confidence. In several instances, job applicants have sued their former employers for libel, slander, or defamation of character, based on statements made to a prospective employer. In one case, $25 million in punitive damages was awarded from John Hancock to a former employee as settlement in a reference related lawsuit.

Fear of such suits has prompted many employers to refuse to say anything about a former (or current) employee—even if they have something nice to say—except "name, rank, and serial number." This practice has had an adverse effect on the screening of job applicants, causing some employers to make hiring blunders and even face negligent hiring suits. In one case, a car rental agency had to pay $75,000 in damages to a customer who was repeatedly assaulted with "judo chops" by an employee. The court reasoned that the employer had failed to appropriately secure background information about the employee's emotional stability.

To counter such suits, some employers are turning to nontraditional sources to find information on job applicants. For a fee, data vendors such as Equifax, Fidelifacts Metropolitan New York, and Apscreen will comb various data bases and provide summaries that describe an applicant's credit record, criminal and driving histories, workers' compensation claims, and more. One major problem, however, is that some of the preemployment information gathered may not be legal to use in making selection decisions. Reference checking is legally viewed as a type of employment test, and information sought must be job related. Moreover, information standards should be uniformly applied. If a background item is cause for eliminating a job applicant, the same should be true for all other applicants. Finally, reference checks should be documented to prove, if necessary, that selection decisions were based on job-related information.

STEP 6: SELECTION DECISION

Since the selection process can be time consuming and expensive—and more importantly, long lasting in its consequences—employers are naturally eager to minimize the chance of an unwise selection decision. Yet, few managerial decisions are so difficult to make. Indeed, management professor Peter F. Drucker contends that, by and large, employers make poor selection decisions. He estimates that their batting average is no better than .333, reasoning that "one-third of such decisions turn out right; one-third are minimally effective; and one-third are outright failures."[2]

The burden of an unwise selection decision is obvious when one considers the enormous cost of hiring the wrong person. The typical hiring cost is estimated to run from 25 percent to 33 percent of a person's first-year salary. This covers expenses such as those for advertising, searching, traveling, and relocating. Training expenses and 12 months' lost salary would boost the cost even higher. Other costs are impossible to estimate. These would include a sour employment relationship, discontentment among other employees, a loss of operational continuity, and, perhaps the biggest cost, lost opportunity.[3]

With assurances that all aspects of the selection process have been fair and therefore nondiscriminatory, the resulting job candidates can be compared and a final hiring decision rendered. Usually an organization's human resource management department will recommend two or three candidates as the most qualified. They will then be interviewed by the unit in which a job opening exists. This final screening ensures that candidate expectations about a job are accurate. It also allows both unit members and candidates to pose any unanswered questions. The final decision concerning the candidate actually hired should be made by the unit members because they will be responsible for training and developing the new employee. After a decision has been reached, it can then be forwarded to the human resource management department, which will formally extend a job offer.

Note that before passage of the 1990 Americans with Disabilities Act, some organizations required a medical evaluation *before* making a final selection decision. The act specifically prohibits the use of preemployment medical exams. Such exams can now be given only *after* a job candidate has been offered employment— and only if all new employees are required to take them. The results from an exam can be used only if they reveal a condition that would prevent a new employee from performing the "essential functions" of a particular job and if "reasonable accommodations" cannot be made for the condition without causing "undue hardship" to an employer. Thus, a history of heart disease, for example, would be insufficient cause for not retaining a new employee unless it could be shown that it would prevent performance of essential job functions and, also, would be an undue hardship for an employer to make reasonable accommodations.

One foreseeable consequence of passage of the act is that it will increase the potential for wrongful-hiring lawsuits if employees who have mental problems or who are potentially unstable because of mental stress are hired. Another concern is its impact on health-care costs. With these costs rising, many employers are increasing their efforts to control medical expenses. This includes hiring only nonsmokers, for instance, as is the policy of the Cable News Network and the City of North Miami. Until political opposition became too great, the City of Athens, Georgia, screened applicants based on their cholesterol scores. Such policies raise questions of privacy, biology, and fairness. Colorado, Oregon, North Dakota, and Nevada have passed privacy laws forbidding employment discrimination based on virtually any off-duty behavior (for example, smoking and alcohol consumption) that is legal. Another 19 states prohibit employers from penalizing off-the-job smokers in any way. Evidence does indicate, however, that healthy employees not only save their employers thousands of dollars in medical costs, but also are absent less frequently and are thus more productive.[4] Whether policies pertaining to health habits are "lifestyle discrimination" or legitimate employer concerns is seemingly a matter of opinion.

Another contemporary issue that has become increasingly controversial is the status of new (and old) employees with respect to acquired immune deficiency syndrome (AIDS). The Supreme Court has held that a contagious disease should be considered a disability and, thus, persons thereby disabled are protected from discrimination if otherwise qualified.

SUMMARY

This chapter was devoted to human resource planning and staffing. It discusses the importance of securing an adequate mix of employees so that an organization can achieve its goals.

Learning Objective 1: Explain how human resource planning contributes to achieving organization goals.
Human resource planning contributes to achieving organization goals by forecasting employee skill needs, comparing them to the present employee skill base, and determining appropriate human resource actions.

Learning Objective 2: Describe a replacement chart.
A replacement chart indicates the various positions in an organization, the jobholders and their present performance, and the readiness of different candidates for promotion into each position.

Learning Objective 3: State the purpose of a skills inventory.
The purpose of a skills inventory is to determine as specifically as possible the talents, education, training, and skills of an organization's employees.

Learning Objective 4: Specify the most common job-analysis methods.
The most common job-analysis methods are interviewing jobholders, superiors, and others qualified to provide job-related information; observing jobholders perform their work; evaluating questionnaires completed by jobholders, superiors, and others qualified to provide job-related information; and evaluating activity logs kept by jobholders.

Learning Objective 5: Explain what is meant by a *job description*.
A job description is a list of important duties to be performed on a job.

Learning Objective 6: State the purpose of job specifications.
The purpose of job specifications is to clarify the knowledge, skills, and abilities, as well as other qualifications, necessary for successful job performance.

Learning Objective 7: Describe various sources from which job applicants can be recruited.
Table 12.4 indicates various sources from which an organization can recruit blue-collar, white-collar, and mechanical/technical/professional job applicants.

Learning Objective 8: Delineate the basic steps in a typical selection decision.
The basic steps in a typical selection decision are preapplication screening, application blank, employment interview, employment tests, reference checks/letters of recommendation, and selection decision. Few employers use all six steps, for they can be time consuming and expensive. To partially overcome this problem, Steps 4 and 5 may be performed at about the same time.

Learning Objective 9: Describe a bona fide occupational qualification.
A bona fide occupational qualification is a permissible job-related exception to the fair employment requirement that all human resource decisions be made without

regard to race, color, age, gender, national origin, religion, or mental or physical impairment.

Learning Objective 10: **Distinguish between a structured and an unstructured interview.**
In a structured interview, an interviewer asks each job applicant a set of predetermined questions. In an unstructured interview, there are no predetermined questions or prearranged sequence of topics for discussion.

Learning Objective 11: **Describe an ability test.**
An ability test is almost always a "pencil and paper" instrument, such as a psychological, vocational interest, or cognitive skill test.

Learning Objective 12: **Describe a work sample test.**
A work sample test requires that applicants perform activities that closely approximate those they will actually perform on a job. Test performance is taken to reflect likely performance in an actual job situation.

KEY TERMS

bona fide occupational
  qualification (BFOQ) 352

disparate impact 348

disparate treatment 348

fair employment 345

human resource planning
  340

job analysis 343

job description 344

job posting 349

job specifications 344

position blockage 341

protected group 346

recruiting 349

replacement chart 341

skills inventory 343

structured interview 354

succession planning 341

unstructured interview
  354

validity 355

THE MANAGEMENT EXPERIENCE HOW MUCH DO I KNOW ABOUT SEXUAL HARASSMENT?

A True or False Test for Employees

	T	F
1. If I just ignore unwanted sexual attention, it will usually stop.	☐	☐
2. If I don't mean to sexually harass another employee, there's no way my behavior can be perceived by him or her as sexually harassing.	☐	☐
3. Some employees don't complain about unwanted sexual attention from another worker because they don't want to get that person in trouble.	☐	☐
4. If I make sexual comments to someone and that person doesn't ask me to stop, then I guess my behavior is welcome.	☐	☐
5. To avoid sexually harassing a woman who comes to work in a traditionally male workplace, the men simply should not haze her.	☐	☐
6. A sexual harasser may be told by a court to pay part of a judgment to the employee he or she harassed.	☐	☐
7. A sexually harassed man does not have the same legal rights as a woman who is sexually harassed.	☐	☐
8. About 90% of all sexual harassment in today's workplace is done by males to females.	☐	☐
9. Sexually suggestive pictures or objects in a workplace don't create a liability unless someone complains.	☐	☐
10. Telling someone to stop his or her unwanted sexual behavior usually doesn't do any good.	☐	☐

Answers: 1) False. 2) False. 3) True. 4) False. 5) False. 6) True. 7) False. 8) True. 9) False. 10) False.

A Test for Managers

	T	F
1. Men in male-dominated workplaces usually have to change their behavior when a woman begins working there.	☐	☐
2. An employer is not liable for the sexual harassment of one of its employees unless that employee loses specific job benefits or is fired.	☐	☐
3. A court can require a sexual harasser to pay part of the judgment to the employee he or she has sexually harassed.	☐	☐
4. A supervisor can be liable for sexual harassment committed by one of his or her employees against another.	☐	☐
5. An employer can be liable for the sexually harassing behavior of management personnel even if it is unaware of that behavior and has a policy forbidding it.	☐	☐
6. It is appropriate for a supervisor, when initially receiving a sexual-harassment complaint, to determine if the alleged recipient overreacted or misunderstood the alleged harasser.	☐	☐
7. When a supervisor is talking with an employee about an allegation of sexual harassment against him or her, it is best to ease into the allegation instead of being direct.	☐	☐
8. Sexually suggestive visuals or objects in a workplace don't create a liability unless an employee complains about them and management allows them to remain.	☐	☐
9. The lack of sexual-harassment complaints is a good indication that sexual harassment is not occurring.	☐	☐
10. It is appropriate for a supervisor to tell an employee to handle unwelcome sexual behavior if he or she thinks that the employee is misunderstanding the behavior.	☐	☐
11. The *intent* behind employee A's sexual behavior is more important than the *impact* of that behavior on employee B when determining if sexual harassment has occurred.	☐	☐

Answers: 1) False. 2) False. 3) True. 4) True. 5) True. 6) False. 7) False. 8) False. 9) False. 10) False. 11) False.

Source: Brian S. Moskal, "Sexual Harassment: An Update," *Industry Week*, November 18, 1991, 40. Reprinted with permission from *Industry Week*. Copyright, Penton Publishing, Inc., Cleveland, Ohio.

REVIEW AND DISCUSSION QUESTIONS

1. Thomas J. Neff, president of Spencer Stuart, an international executive search and consulting firm, has offered the following advice for becoming an organization with executive staying power. After reading Neff's advice, offer your own observations on this subject.

   > Hire good people to begin with; identify the ones to be kept as early in their careers as possible; design individual development programs for them, including above-standard pay; keep in close communication with them—and their spouses; let them know they're special; give them as much opportunity and latitude as they can handle; anticipate their restlessness by having fresh challenges always on deck.[5]

2. As a future manager, explain the importance of proper job analysis.

3. Based on your years of experience as a student, prepare a sample job description for the job of college professor.

4. Again based on your years of experience as a student, develop the job specifications for the job description prepared in response to the preceding item.

5. Complete a skills inventory listing as specifically as possible your talents, education, training, and skills.

6. Assume that you are the manager of an electrical engineering department in a large public utility. You have just completed a forecast of the department's human resource needs. The forecast indicates a likely future shortage of college-trained engineers. How will you recruit job applicants to meet this shortfall?

7. Again assume that you are the manager in Question 6. Briefly describe the selection procedure you will use to identify acceptable job applicants.

8. Identify some of the costs associated with hiring the wrong person.

9. The National Organization for Women maintains, "Neither sex has a monopoly on jobs with two exceptions: wet nurses and sperm donors." Comment.

10. Cite examples of various ability tests and work sample tests you have taken.

CASE 12.1   ALBERTA MOBILE HOMES LTD.

Alberta Mobile Homes Ltd. (AMH) is a small manufacturer of mobile and modular homes located in Calgary, Alberta, Canada. It has about 250 employees. Alice Butkus, AMH president, recently attended a seminar on human resource management in Calgary conducted by Professor Warren Simpson of the University of Calgary's business school. After the session was over, Butkus approached Simpson and asked him if he'd be willing to come to her company and provide consulting help for several human resource management problems.

"Sure, I'd be delighted," replied Simpson. A few days later, he went to meet with Butkus.

Butkus introduced the situation this way: "Look, Warren, we seem to be having problems with our promotion and performance-appraisal systems. Let me describe two incidents that have come up just in the last 2 months. We're in a growth industry. We've doubled our workforce in the last year and a half. This means we need to move some people up, but we are having the darnedest time with it.

"Recently, George Drester, the head of our plant, came to see me. He said he'd been wrestling with this problem for months. He'd promoted Jay Gilbreth to supervisor about 6 months ago. Jay was good at his job before, but he's not a good supervisor.

His employees don't like or respect him. Jay himself seems aware of the situation. George is wondering what he can do about Jay.

"Then there's the case of Ed Bankhead, the head of marketing. He needs to recommend someone for promotion to sales manager. I've been asking him to do so for weeks, and no recommendation yet. See what you can do about it, will you?"

With this send-off, Simpson went to meet Bankhead. After some preliminaries, he came to the point. "Look, Ed, I'm here to see about establishing some policies about promotion. Frankly, Alice gave you as a case in point. She's wanting to know what you've done about the sales manager's job."

Bankhead shifted around in his chair. He then described in some detail the people he was thinking about:

1. *James Prior.* Ten years of experience in construction sales, lots of personality, no supervisory experience, high school graduate.

2. *Helen Cortney.* Four years of sales experience for AMH, the best salesperson of the bunch, college degree in business, no supervisory experience, very quiet, almost introverted.

3. *Matt Dotler.* Older, 12 years of experience selling, 5 of it for AMH, outgoing personality. He supervised two employees with his previous company.

"Frankly, Warren," Bankhead said, "I'm leaning toward Helen. I figure the best salesperson is bound to make the best sales manager. But I really don't have a lot of facts and figures to back up my choice. How should I go about this, anyway?"

Simpson said he would make a recommendation on this shortly. Next he visited Drester. "What am I going to do about Jay?" asked Drester. "He's not cutting it."

Simpson pressed Drester and asked him how he "knew" that Gilbreth's employees didn't like or respect him. He quickly determined that these were just Drester's general impressions, not based on any objective evidence. He also learned that Drester had not tried to discuss the issue with Gilbreth or tried to counsel or help him.

Problems

You are Professor Simpson. Write a report detailing your recommendations to Butkus, copies of which will go to Drester and Bankhead. The report should include recommendations on:

1. How to decide on a sales manager and, if possible, whom Bankhead should recommend.

2. What to do about Drester and Gilbreth.

3. Recommendations for improving promotion, appraisal, and counseling at AMH.

CASE 12.2 MODER AIRCRAFT, INC.

Moder is a medium-size company that supplies subassemblies for major aircraft firms. It ships its parts to all the major airframe manufacturers, as well as to firms that make executive aircraft and similar products. Its president is Jason Fleming.

Recently, Fleming has seen many articles about equal employment opportunity for women and minority groups. He wondered how his company would be evaluated on this issue. So he asked the personnel vice-president to prepare a report on Moder's employees. Exhibit 1 is that report.

After looking the report over, Fleming called the personnel vice-president, Elling Takover, into his office. The following is an excerpt from their discussion.

Fleming: "El, tell me the truth. If a government guy came in here, what'd happen?"

Takover: "We'd be in trouble, boss."

Fleming: "It's not like we discriminated. We hired minorities long before others did. But most of our managers are engineers or ex-engineers. How many female engineers are there? Black engineers?"

Takover: "I'm not sure that'd cut much ice. We really have an EEO problem, I think. Maybe we haven't been as socially responsible as we thought."

Problem

Takover is asked by Fleming to recommend some preventive action. You are Takover. What do you recommend?

EXHIBIT 1 MODER AIRCRAFT, INC., EMPLOYEE ANALYSIS

Level of Employees	Employees by Gender			Employees by Ethnic Group					
	Male	Female	Total	White	Black	Hispanic American	American Indian	Asian-Pacific Islander	Total
Top management	100%	0%	100%	100%	0%	0%	0%	0%	100%
Middle management	99	1	100	99	0.5	0.5	0	0	100
Technical	93	7	100	97	1.5	1.5	0	0	100
Supervisory	89	11	100	94	2.0	4.0	0	0	100
Clerical	1	99	100	79	11.0	10.0	0	0	100
Operative	92	8	100	61	28.0	11.0	0	0	100

NOTES

[1] John P. Wanous, *Organizational Entry: Recruitment, Selection, and Socialization of Newcomers* (Reading, Mass.: Addison-Wesley, 1980), 37–44.

[2] Peter F. Drucker, "How To Make People Decisions," *Harvard Business Review* 63 (July–August 1985): 22.

[3] James Barham, "Hiring Mr. Wrong," *Industry Week*, March 7, 1988, 34.

[4] Peter Shinkle, "Women's Health Becoming New Corporate Focus," (Baton Rouge) *Morning Advocate*, December 13, 1991, 5D.

[5] Thomas J. Neff, "How to Keep the Headhunters at Bay," *Wall Street Journal*, May 13, 1985, 22.

LEARNING OBJECTIVES

Upon completing this chapter, you should be able to:

- List several purposes that effective orientation serves.

- Identify several different approaches to training.

- Outline the purposes that sound performance appraisal serves.

- Identify various performance appraisal techniques.

- Recount different sources of rater error.

- Present guidelines for preparing and conducting an appraisal interview.

- Comment on the legal aspects of performance appraisal.

- Explain the importance of a well-conceived compensation program.

- List means, other than salary, by which employees may be compensated.

- Specify the minimum requirements of a well-publicized and unambiguous disciplinary process.

- Describe different types of unions and their jurisdictions.

- Depict a typical grievance procedure.

s a result of the increasing mechanization of labor and the shift toward a service economy, organizations are having difficulty recruiting new employees with sufficient education for the jobs available. Even existing employees are often limited in their ability to deal with new aspects of their jobs. To avoid discharging these loyal and often highly motivated individuals, and to help raise the educational quality of new hires, many companies are getting into the education business. The CIGNA Insurance Group is one such company.

CIGNA has its headquarters in Philadelphia, Pennsylvania, and recruits many of its entry-level employees from that city. Many insurance companies have taught professional insurance courses in the past, but CIGNA's current programs have a wider scope. Its Neighborhood School Partnership Program spends $500,000 a year to help students in five schools in one south Philadelphia neighborhood. Its Office Professional Staffing and Training Program hires recent graduates of Philadelphia and Hartford high schools and gives them 10 weeks of off-site business ed-

DEVELOPING HUMAN RESOURCES

ucation and several months of on-the-job training before placing them in permanent positions. To motivate current employees to earn a Bachelor's or even a graduate degree, CIGNA will pay their tuition if they attend the nearby University of Pennsylvania.

It is too soon to know how well CIGNA's program will pay off in the long run. Marriott Corp. knows already that its education program is getting excellent results. The hotel operator has a general employee turnover rate of 105 percent per year, which means that it is, in effect, training new workers to work elsewhere. Marriott has found, however, that it pays to train potential employees who are physically or mentally impaired. Although this group is harder to train initially, the extra effort pays off in an annual turnover rate of only 8 percent.

Education is a powerful tool for tailoring new employees to available jobs and retraining existing employees as needs change. In this chapter, we will discuss education along with other aspects of human resource development.

Source: Nancy J. Perry, "The Workers of the Future," *Fortune Special Issue—The New American Century,* Spring/Summer 1991, 68–72; Robert G. Knowles, "Education Helps Employees Reach Full Potential," *National Underwriter,* October 21, 1991, 11–12.

The collaboration of James A. Buford, Jr., Auburn University, in the preparation of this chapter is gratefully acknowledged.

For an organization to survive and prosper, it must be able not only to identify and select qualified employees, but also to develop and retain them. Thus, an effective human resource effort may begin when a new employee is first hired, but it must continue throughout the employee's tenure with an organization. The present chapter examines the need for an organization to continually develop its human resources. The specific human resource development activities to be discussed are orientation, training, performance appraisal, compensation, discipline, and labor relations.

ORIENTATION

Orientation is the process that introduces new employees to their new work environment. Experts generally agree that a premium orientation process is critically important for establishing a "healthy" work attitude among new employees because it not only gives them their first impression of how an organization operates, but sets the tone for their entire stay.

Effectively performed, orientation serves several purposes. First, a systematic approach to orientation carries the clear message that new employees are valued. It says that an organization is willing to invest in them long before a return is realized. The feeling of being valued can engender more loyalty than a paycheck can buy.

Second, orientation can reduce startup costs that invariably occur when an employee is first hired. New employees are generally unfamiliar with the specifics of their jobs, how an organization functions, and whom to see on different matters. Thus, at least for a while, new employees are less efficient than their experienced peers, and additional costs may be incurred as a result.

Third, orientation can also reduce the amount of anxiety and hazing that new employees experience. *Anxiety* in this case means fear of job failure. This is a normal fear resulting from new employees' anxiousness about their ability to perform as expected. Such anxiety can be made worse by hazing, experienced in some form by virtually all new employees before they are deemed "acceptable" by their peers. Hazing serves to teach new members their place in a work group's pecking order and to test—either overtly or covertly—new members' skills. Typically, the more tightly knit a work group is, the longer the initiation period. Examples of hazing include the following:

- Hospital orderlies may be asked to find a new fallopian tube.
- Factory workers may find their tools glued to a table.
- Lawyers may be assigned to research a case that doesn't exist.
- Trainees may be sent to fetch nonexistent items, such as pigeon's milk, elbow grease, striped paint, a left-handed monkey wrench, or a can of cold steam.

Orientation.
The process that introduces new employees to their new work environment.

The common message delivered by hazing is clear: While you may be accomplished in many respects, you are in kindergarten as far as what you know about this organization. In this respect, hazing should not be confused with harassment. Whereas the goal of hazing is inclusion, the intent of harassment is exclusion.

In organizations where it occurs, hazing is best dealt with by a grin-and-bear-it attitude. Indeed, new employees who aren't hazed might actually consider themselves disadvantaged in that they may never get an opportunity to prove themselves. Whatever the situation, effective orientation alerts new employees to hazing and minimizes anxiety.

Fourth, orientation can help reduce new employee turnover. If new employees judge themselves as unvalued, and therefore experience negative feelings, they may seek to deal with these feelings by quitting. Turnover is typically high during the "break-in" period. As noted, a new employee's first few months on a job are critical for establishing a healthy work attitude. By helping new employees to establish realistic job expectations, and as a first step introducing them to an organization's culture—a process known as *socialization* and discussed in Chapter 17—effective orientation can greatly reduce costly turnover.

Fifth, orientation can save time for superiors and peers. Poorly oriented employees may need frequent help in performing the work for which they were hired. The most likely sources of assistance are superiors and peers. By helping new employees "learn the ropes," effective orientation can save everyone time.

The nature and design of orientation programs vary among organizations. Table 13.1 lists the general information customarily presented in a typical orientation program. At IBM, new managers receive 80 hours of orientation. Above all, they are steeped in the three-point IBM philosophy: *one*, give the best service of any company in the world; *two*, strive for superior performance; and *three*—the most important point—respect the individual.

TRAINING

Training is the process of developing an individual's knowledge, skills, and abilities so as to improve present and future organization performance. As employees face the challenge of learning new skills to maintain their proficiency or become qualified for promotion, the importance of training becomes evident. Virtually all large and medium-size organizations offer some form of training, if only informally. It is estimated that U.S. corporations spend some $60 billion annually for training programs involving some 8 million employees and 15 billion work hours. Training, however, should be viewed as an investment rather than an expense. The payoff is improved product quality, productivity, and profits.

Companies such as General Motors, IBM, and Intel Corporation have extensive training programs. Indeed, General Motors calls itself "the country's largest privately funded educational institution." It invests $1 billion a year in training in areas ranging from literacy skills to robotics. IBM spends $900 million a year—more than the annual budget of Harvard University—to train employees in everything from salesmanship to public speaking. On a typical day, 18,000 employees of IBM receive training. At Intel, 2–4 percent of an employee's time is spent in classroom training. Intel has a "university catalog" that lists some 50 classes. Courses range from proper telephone etiquette to strategic planning.

Training.
The process of developing knowledge, skills, and abilities so as to improve present and future performance.

TABLE 13.1 INFORMATION COVERED IN A TYPICAL ORIENTATION PROGRAM

Overview

Goods/services and customers served
Steps in getting goods/services to customers
Scope of organization activities
Structure and relationship of organization and its branches
Chain of command
Information on key managers
Community relations, expectations, and activities

Key Policies and Procedures

Compensation

Employee Benefits

Holidays and vacations (for example, patriotic, religious, birthday)
Other employee services

Safety and Accident Prevention

Occupational Safety and Health Act requirements (review of key sections)

Employee and Union Relations

Bringing things on and removing things from organization grounds

Physical Facilities

Restricted areas

Economic Factors

Costs of absenteeism, lateness, and accidents

Source: Adapted from Walter D. St. John, "The Complete Employee Orientation Program," *Personnel Journal* 59 (May 1980): 376–377.

For these and other companies, training is a matter of survival in competing against a better educated Japanese workforce. Companies such as General Motors, IBM, and Intel realize that, as never before, people are the key to the performance and competitiveness of U.S. companies. In an age of robots, mainframe computers, and image-processing systems, advanced knowledge, high skills, and enhanced abilities are required to replace yesterday's blue-collar laborer.

In response to the demands of today's high-tech automated workplace, Goodyear, Eastman Chemical, and Hewlett-Packard conduct literacy training and remedial classes in basic math and science to enable their employees to learn new technical skills. Motorola spends over $60 million a year teaching new technical skills to all 100,000 of its employees, from its chairman to the newest caretaker. Much of this training takes place at its Motorola University. Other companies with their own training centers include McDonald's and Mrs. Fields Cookies. Both suc-

Employees of Armenian Nursing Home in Jamaica Plains, Massachusetts attend company-sponsored classes after work and receive half their regular wages for the time they spend in class. Courses include English as a second language; basic reading, writing, and arithmetic; a program leading to a high school diploma; and a program leading to practical nursing certification. The company has found that educational programs help increase employee professionalism and productivity.

ceed globally on the basis of their well-trained employees. McDonald's Hamburger University provides technical training in 17 languages. Mrs. Fields Candy Factory and Cookie College prepares technically trained store managers for its over 700 outlets, including stores in Hong Kong, Japan, Australia, Canada, and England.

Companies without their own in-house training facilities commonly sponsor employee attendance at professional conferences and university management development programs. The nonprofit American Management Association annually holds some 5,000 1- to 3-day conferences on a vast array of technical and nontechnical topics ranging from total quality control to computerized information systems to strategic planning. Prices typically start at $500 for a 2-day conference, not including living and traveling expenses. By comparison, the 11-week Harvard Business School Advanced Management Program for senior managers runs $31,000. Rather than pick off-the-rack courses, some organizations arrange with universities to offer tailor-made programs to selected employees. These can cost as much as $15,000 a day, plus room and board.

Perhaps still the most common approach to training is also probably the oldest. **On-the-job training** consists of assigning a new employee to an experienced supervisor or senior co-worker. Typically, the supervisor or co-worker is told to "break in this trainee" or "teach Bob your job." The trainee is expected to learn by observing the supervisor or co-worker and working with the actual equipment and materials that will be used once the training is completed. At Intel, some 200 hours of on-the-job training are required to learn how to operate an ion implanter. The advantages are that no special facilities are required and trainees are immediately engaged in productive work. However, if the training is improperly handled, the expense of damaged machinery, wasted materials, dissatisfied customers, and poorly trained employees can be high. To avoid such problems, trainers must be carefully chosen and rewarded for doing a good job.

An increasingly popular approach to training is associated with the job enrichment movement and self-managed teams. **Job rotation** consists of periodically shifting employees from one job to another to increase skill variety and task

On-the-job training.
Assigning a trainee to an experienced supervisor or senior co-worker for training.

Job rotation.
Periodically shifting employees from one job to another for training.

CLOSE UP: INTERNATIONAL MANAGEMENT   SOCIAL GUIDELINES FOR HOSTING FOREIGN BUSINESS VISITORS

With business going global, understanding foreign protocol has become important not only for those who travel abroad but also for those who host foreign executives here in the United States.

The task is easier than you might think, according to such experts as corporate consultant Letitia Baldrige and the Business Council for International Understanding. Here are some of their pointers:

- Learn a few words or phrases in your guest's language—even just "hello" or "thank you."

- Brief yourself on basic information about your visitor's country—such as who the political leaders are and what religion is practiced there.

- Meet your visitor's plane if possible—or send a representative (preferably one who speaks the language).

- Provide a flexible printed schedule for your guest and his or her spouse.

- Go slow on personal topics, particularly politics, until you know your guest better.

- Present—or later send—a gift, such as a briefcase or a book, if your visitor is a guest speaker at a program.

- Take your guest sightseeing, remembering that what's common to you may be very unusual to a visitor.

As Baldrige notes, it's the subtle touches, such as sending photos of the visit, that might have the most lasting impact.

Source: "Easy Traveler: Social Guidelines for Hosting Foreign Business Visitors," *Travel and Entertainment* 7 (April 1990): 4.

identity. The advantages of job rotation include:

- *Flexible assignments.* Employees learn other jobs so they can cover for one another during vacations or illness.

- *Employee development.* Employees acquire additional knowledge, skills, and abilities, thus creating a larger pool of qualified candidates for promotion.

- *Easier staffing.* Jobs that require extensive physical exertion or exposure to disagreeable working conditions may be difficult to staff. Rotation allows employees to "share" such jobs.

- *Less boredom.* Jobs that require a narrow range of skills can easily become boring. As noted in Chapter 10, boredom can lead to low employee motivation, low-quality performance, low job satisfaction, high turnover, and high absenteeism. Rotation provides skill variety and offsets boredom.

As is true with on-the-job training, the effectiveness of job rotation depends on competent and interested trainers. Job rotation is used extensively by companies such as General Motors. For example, at the Cadillac engine plant in Livonia, Michigan, production employees are encouraged to learn all the jobs in their section,

Each year Tenneco's Apprentice School of Newport News Shipbuilding receives nearly 1,000 applications to fill 300 openings to work on ships like the Los Angeles-class submarine. Apprenticeships are a small but growing educational program in the U.S. Companies offering some form of apprenticeship include Textron, Hilti A.G., Baker Oil Tools, and American Airlines.

giving management flexibility in making assignments and filling in during vacation periods. Employees are paid according to the skills they acquire, giving them an incentive to learn new ones.

Many other training approaches are available. These include use of apprenticeship programs, computer-assisted instruction, videodisc systems, and equipment simulators. The American Airlines jet cockpit simulator in Dallas trains pilots how to react to situations such as engine flameout on takeoff. Pilots in training can see what they would see through the windows on a flight from Dallas to San Francisco in the daytime, at night, in fog, or on a rainy day. Whatever approaches are selected, it is in an organization's best interests to maintain a well-trained workforce.

PERFORMANCE APPRAISAL

Over 90 percent of all U.S. organizations employ some form of *performance appraisal*.[1] Formally defined, **performance appraisal,** sometimes called *review*, is the process of determining the extent to which an employee is performing a job effectively.

In most organizations, employees are appraised yearly, on the anniversary of their hiring. New employees—considered to be on probation—typically receive more frequent appraisals.

A sound performance appraisal system serves a number of purposes.[2]

- It provides employees with feedback so that they will know how well they are performing.

- It develops valid data for pay (salary and bonus) and promotion decisions.

- It helps managers make discharge and retention decisions and provides a means of warning subordinates about unsatisfactory performance.

- It helps managers counsel subordinates so that they will improve their performance and develop their future potential.

Performance appraisal.
The process of determining the extent to which an employee is performing a job effectively.

- It develops commitment to an organization by identifying career opportunities and encouraging career planning.

- It motivates employees through recognition and support.

- It strengthens manager-subordinate relations.

- It provides input to the human resource planning process, as discussed in the preceding chapter.

Although performance appraisal can take many forms, including peer appraisal, self-appraisal, and appraisal by outsiders, the following discussion focuses on the appraisal of subordinates (ratees) by their managers (raters).

PERFORMANCE APPRAISAL TECHNIQUES

As one might expect, there are numerous performance appraisal techniques. All have advantages and disadvantages. The four most commonly used techniques involve graphic rating scales, essay appraisals, comparative methods, and behaviorally anchored rating scales. In general, these techniques are applicable to both operative employees and all levels of management. Each is discussed below.

Graphic Rating Scales

Graphic rating scales are the oldest and, no doubt, most commonly used performance appraisal technique. They require a manager to appraise a subordinate's performance on a variety of specific factors, using a scale that ranges from "outstanding" to "unsatisfactory." An example of a typical graphic rating scale is given in Figure 13.1. Particular importance, however, is attached to the "overall summary score," which makes it possible to compare large numbers of ratings. This overall score is determined by totaling the scores given to specific factors. To make the score more useful, the manager is also required to justify the appraisal and to identify suggestions for improvement in space provided for written comments. These comments provide a more rounded picture of a subordinate's performance than a numerical rating alone and may be useful for counseling subordinates in areas needing further development.

Graphic rating scales are relatively simple to develop, easy to understand, and less time consuming to administer than other techniques. They possess several limitations, however:

- They assume that each of the factors being rated is of equal importance. In some positions, though, job knowledge, for example, may clearly be more important than relations with others. One way to avoid this limitation is to weight individual factors in accordance with their importance to overall job performance. Using job analysis, it is possible to weight factors on an appropriate basis, such as amount of time spent, frequency of performance, or relative importance.

- They assume that the factors are "additive," that is, that strength in one area (for example, dependability) is capable of offsetting a weakness in another (for example, initiative). The fallacy of this belief should be obvious. Indeed, when a manager uses the form in Figure 13.1, a subordinate could be judged outstanding on the first five factors and unsatisfactory on the last five and still receive an average rating.

Graphic rating scale.

A scale that requires a manager to appraise a subordinate's performance on a variety of specific factors.

- They assume a clarity in standards. However, unless all raters agree on the underlying meaning of terms such as "below average" and "outstanding," their ratings cannot be compared. "Below average" to one rater may mean "average" to another.

- They place an excessive emphasis on traits such as leadership ability, initiative, attitude, and dependability. Such factors are highly subjective and difficult to define. They would also be difficult to defend in a legal proceeding stemming from a disputed performance appraisal. Where does one draw the line, for example, between initiative and aggressiveness? Moreover, it is unrealistic to expect subordinates to make a real change in their traits, as if they were changing overcoats.

- They are subject to various rater errors, including *halo, recency, central tendency, rater pattern,* and *stereotyping* errors, which will be discussed further in this chapter.

FIGURE 13.1   A GRAPHIC RATING SCALE

Performance Appraisal Form

Employee's Name _____ Position _____ Date _____

Date Hired _____ In Position Since_____

Using the following scale, rate the employee's performance over the period specified above.

5 = Outstanding; 4 = Above Average; 3 = Average; 2 = Below Average; 1 = Unsatisfactory

Job Knowledge
Shows clear understanding of facts pertinent to the job.   _____

Attitude
Tries to do more than expected and takes more than average interest in the job.   _____

Dependability
Conscientious, thorough, accurate, reliable with respect to attendance,   _____
lunch periods, reliefs, and so on.

Quantity of Work
Thoroughness, neatness, and accuracy of work.   _____

Quality of Work
Volume of acceptable work under normal conditions.   _____

Initiative
Earnestness in seeking increased responsibilities, self-starting, unafraid to   _____
proceed alone.

Cooperation
Ability and willingness to work with peers, superiors, and subordinates toward   _____
common goals.

Personal Qualities
Personality, appearance, sociability, integrity.   _____

continued

FIGURE 13.1 *continued*

Leadership Ability
Accepts leadership responsibilities and excels at motivating others.   _____

Relations with Others
Obliging and easy to get along with.   _____

Overall Summary Score

Outstanding: 45 – 50; Above Average: 35 – 44; Average: 25 – 34; Below
Average: 16 – 24; Unsatisfactory: 10 – 15   _____

Identify three performance factors that need improvement

What might this employee do to improve his or her job performance?

General Comments

Signature and title of rater _____
Signature of employee_____Date_____
Employee Comments

Approved by_____
Important: this appraisal must be discussed with the employee and his or her signature
must be secured for rating to be valid.

Essay Appraisals

An **essay appraisal** is a written commentary of a subordinate's performance.
It is typically prepared by a subordinate's immediate superior, who is asked to describe such things as strengths, weaknesses, and potential, as well as offer suggestions for improving performance. A portion of an essay appraisal form is given in Figure 13.2.

This technique assumes that an honest expression from a superior knowledgeable about a subordinate's performance is just as accurate as more quantitative alternatives. Indeed, essay appraisals can provide detailed performance feedback, but they have several drawbacks. They are inherently unstandardized, making performance comparisons across subordinates difficult, if not impossible. Moreover, a subordinate's rating may depend more on a manager's writing skills than on the subordinate's performance. Finally, essay appraisals are highly subjective, time consuming, and impractical for large groups.

Essay appraisal.
A written commentary of a
subordinate's performance.

FIGURE 13.2 PORTION OF AN ESSAY APPRAISAL FORM

Make a clear and concise statement describing the employee's performance on each of the factors below.

Productivity: Volume of work and major accomplishments.

_____

Accuracy: Meeting quality standards.

_____

Coordination: Planning and organizing work and supervising employees.

_____

Comparative Methods

Comparative methods compare subordinates with one another rather than to abstract standards. Using this technique, a manager is asked to rank subordinates from first to last in terms of their performance. Figure 13.3 illustrates how the actual ranking normally involves first identifying the best and worst performers, then selecting the next best and next worst, and alternating back and forth until all subordinates are ranked.

In an alternative procedure, called the **paired-comparison method,** all subordinates are compared one at a time with each other, with a final performance ranking determined by the number of pairings in which an individual is rated the better performer. A performance ranking using the paired-comparison method is illustrated in Figure 13.4.

In a second alternative procedure, called the **forced-distribution method,** managers are required to assign their subordinates to performance categories. The

Comparative method.

A performance appraisal technique that compares subordinates with one another rather than using abstract standards.

Paired-comparison method.

A procedure in which all subordinates are compared one at a time with each other, with a final performance ranking determined by the number of pairings in which an individual is rated the better performer.

FIGURE 13.3 PERFORMANCE RATING USING ALTERNATION RANKING METHOD

Consider the employees in your unit in terms of overall job performance. Select the best employee and put his/her name in column A, Line #1. Then select the worst employee and put his/her name in column B, line 20. Continue this process until the names of all employees have been listed.

Column a (Best)

1. Warren Clark
2. Sandra Burton
3. James Strawn
4. Deborah Stinson
5. William Buford
6. _____
7. _____
8. _____
9. _____
10. _____

Column B (Worst)

11. _____
12. _____
13. _____
14. _____
15. _____
16. Wilson Fowler
17. Sylvia Watt
18. Heather Larkin
19. Robert Lee
20. John McCord

Note: The more similar to each other employees are in terms of job performance, the more difficult ranking becomes. Alternation ranking, as shown above, continually removes extreme performers from a rating group.
Ranking is simplified because, as the choices become harder, the group becomes smaller.

key feature of this procedure is that the percentage of employees to be assigned to each category is predetermined (thus "forced" on a manager). The underlying logic here is that employee performance is distributed "normally." This is somewhat analogous to an instructor's "grading on the curve," resulting in a few A's and F's, slightly more B's and D's, and a large number of C's. An example of a rating by forced distribution is shown in Figure 13.5.

Applications of the forced-distribution method vary. At General Motors, only 10 percent can earn a top rating. Only 8 percent can at IBM. At PepsiCo, managers are divided into four categories. The top group gets promoted. Those at the bottom are terminated. Critics object to such arbitrariness, contending that all comparative methods assume that there is a certain proportion of good, fair, and poor performers in every group. Many work groups are too small (fewer than 30–50 members) for this to be probable. Moreover, if misused, the results of comparative methods can be meaningless and, because someone must be last, damaging to morale. To

Forced distribution method.

A procedure that requires managers to assign their subordinates to predetermined performance categories.

FIGURE 13.4 PERFORMANCE RATING BY PAIRED-COMPARISON METHOD

Persons Rated	As compared to:										SCORE	RANK
	SB	WB	WC	WF	HL	RL	JM	DS	JS	SW		
Sandra Burton		X		X	X	X	X	X	X	X	8	2
William Buford				X	X	X	X			X	5	5
Wanda Clark	X	X		X	X	X	X	X	X	X	9	1
Wilson Fowler				X	X	X				X	4	6
Heather Larkin							X	X			2	8
Robert Lee							X				1	9
John McCord											0	10
Deborah Stinson		X		X	X	X				X	6	4
James Strawn		X		X	X	X		X		X	7	3
Sylvia Watt				X	X						3	7

Note: X means that a person's performance is better than the person with whom he/she was paired. For example, Clark's performance is better than all others. Lee's is only better than McCord's.

illustrate how comparative methods can distort reality, consider that there is a slowest runner on the U.S. Olympic gold-medal relay team and a fastest runner among 45- to 55-year-old finishers in a local "fun run." To consider the latter a better performer than the former is ludicrous. Finally, if subordinates are compared on the basis of subjective factors, comparative methods are no more likely to provide valid performance ratings than any other technique.

Behaviorally Anchored Rating Scales

Behaviorally anchored rating scales represent an attempt to replace the subjectivity inherent in other appraisal techniques. Accordingly, these scales are illustrated by specific behaviors that are related, or "anchored," to varying levels of performance. An example of one scale, or set of behaviors, from a behaviorally anchored rating scale developed to assess one dimension of a supervisor's performance is shown in Figure 13.6. Here, a supervisor being appraised can be allocated points ranging from 1 through 7 for "resolving employee problems," depending on where his superior places him relative to the various anchors.

Because these scales are based on extensive job analysis, they can be made highly job related and, thus, less subjective, but they do have several limitations. The most glaring problem, to refer back to our example, is that many more behaviors describe performance under the dimension of "resolving employee problems" than the seven provided on the scale in Figure 13.6. Further, a manager might observe both "good" and "bad" performance on the same dimension. For example, a supervisor who "calms down frustrated employees" (6 points) might also "cover up drinking on the job" (2 points). Finally, developing behaviorally anchored rating scales can be extremely time consuming and expensive, especially in situations involving a wide variety of jobs, each with numerous and distinct performance dimensions.

SOURCES OF RATER ERROR

Several sources of rater error are common to virtually all performance appraisal techniques. Some can be controlled by rater training. However, no performance

Behaviorally anchored rating scales.
A performance appraisal technique in which specific behaviors are related to varying levels of performance.

FIGURE 13.5 PERFORMANCE RATING BY FORCED-DISTRIBUTION METHOD

Instructions: Assign the employees in your unit to the appropriate categories using the following distribution as a guide:

Outstanding (10%)	Above Average (20%)	Average (40%)	Below Average (20%)	Unsatisfactory (10%)
W. Clark	S. Burton	D. Stinson	H. Larkin	J. McCord
_____	J. Strawn	W. Buford	R. Lee	_____
	_____	W. Fowler	_____	
		S. Watt		
		_____		
		_____		
		_____		
		_____		

Note: The forced-distribution method takes various forms. In the example shown here, five categories are used to approximate the bell-shaped curve of the "normal" distribution. A similar result is obtained when raters are instructed to place an equal number of employees in four quartiles. The second and third quartiles are then combined into an "average" category containing 50 percent of the employees rated. Still another variation is to divide employees evenly into upper, middle and lower thirds. The key feature of the forced-distribution method is that the number of employees assigned to each category is predetermined; thus "forced" on a rater.

appraisal system can be made totally error free. Some of the most frequent rater errors are described in the following paragraphs.

Halo error is the tendency to generalize about all of a person's characteristics based on knowledge of one or a few characteristics. If, for example, a manager has a high opinion of a subordinate's performance on one factor, such as "cooperation," this may color her view of the subordinate's performance on all other factors. Bad relations between a manager and a subordinate can have the opposite effect, producing unfair low ratings. In either case, the manager's appraisal is based on a general impression of the subordinate as a person rather than on specific performance factors. Clearly specifying performance dimensions and training raters are the best ways to overcome halo error.

Recency error is the tendency for managers to remember events that occurred most recently rather than consider a subordinate's performance over an entire appraisal period. Thus, a subordinate may have made a major contribution early in an appraisal period, but if it is not properly recorded, it may be overlooked at appraisal time. Subordinates also contribute to recency error by becoming more concerned with improved job performance as appraisal time approaches. One way

Halo error.
The tendency to generalize about all of a person's characteristics based on knowledge of one or a few characteristics.

Recency error.
The tendency for managers to remember events that occurred most recently rather than considering a subordinate's performance over time.

FIGURE 13.6   A BEHAVIORALLY ANCHORED RATING SCALE

Performance Dimension: Resolving Employee Problems

Assisting employees in coping with on- and off-the-job stress and related problems by recognizing early signs, counseling employees, taking other corrective actions, and/or making appropriate referrals.

Extremely Outstanding Performance	7~	You can expert this supervisor to recognize and deal effectively with the symptoms of excessive employee stress.
Good Performance	6~	You can expect this supervisor to calm down frustrated employees.
Fairly Good Performance	5~	You can expect this supervisor to use discretion when employees confide in him/her about personal matters.
Acceptable Performance	4~	You can expect this supervisor to be flexible in rearranging work assignments for troubled employees.
Fairly Poor Performance	3~	You can expect this supervisor to refer most employees with problems to the Human Resource Management Department.
Poor Performance	2~	You can expect this supervisor to cover for an employee who drinks on the job.
Extremely Poor Performance	1~	You can expect this supervisor to ridicule an employee who cannot adjust to a new work procedure.

---

to overcome recency error is to maintain accurate records on subordinate performance.

Central tendency error is the tendency to steer away from assigning extreme performance ratings. Managers subject to central tendency error avoid the "outstanding" category as well as the "unsatisfactory" category and assign virtually all ratings around the "average" or midpoint range. Consequently, all subordinates are judged "average" on nearly all performance dimensions even though some may perform better than others. One reason central tendency occurs is that a manager may fear having to explain either very good or very poor ratings. To overcome this error, managers must be made to realize that most people have stronger and weaker areas of performance and that appraisals must make this distinction.

Rater pattern error is the tendency toward either excessive leniency or strictness in assigning performance ratings. As every student is aware, there is a big difference between hard and easy graders. In an organization, this difference may surface in situations where a manager is reluctant to give low ratings for fear of

Central tendency error.
The tendency to steer away from assigning extreme performance ratings.

Rater pattern error.
The tendency toward either excessive leniency or strictness in assigning performance ratings.

antagonizing subordinates, or perhaps for fear that low ratings will reflect negatively on the manager's own ability. Someone may ask, "If your subordinate's performance is so poor, why haven't you done something about it?" Moreover, the knowledge that they will likely have to confront potentially hostile subordinates in an appraisal interview, as is the case in most organizations, tends to inhibit managers from rating as honestly as they should when a subordinate's performance is below par. Rater pattern error is especially troublesome when appraisals conducted by different managers are compared. Perhaps the only way to overcome this error is through rater training and counseling.

Stereotyping is the tendency to attribute characteristics to a person based on certain observable traits, such as race, gender, or appearance. This bias may be reflected in a subordinate's performance appraisal. For example, a manager may attribute "hotheadedness" to all subordinates with red hair or "untrustworthiness" to anyone with a foreign accent. The effects of stereotyping can be reduced by making managers aware that they have this tendency. Appropriate training programs are one way to bring personal biases to a manager's attention.

Stereotyping.
The tendency to attribute characteristics to a person based on certain observable traits, such as race, gender, or appearance.

APPRAISAL FEEDBACK INTERVIEWS

After a manager has finished assessing a subordinate, an appraisal feedback interview should be conducted to discuss the subordinate's performance. Such interviews can be particularly trying because appraisal, more clearly than almost any other activity, represents a manager's use of power. In addition, because appraisals are inherently judgmental, all too often, appraisal interviews are confrontational, with emotions running high on both "sides." Outbursts of temper, hurt feelings, sarcasm, and resentfulness are common. For the appraisal feedback interview to be effective, the manager must know how to handle anger and other uncomfortable emotions. Managers who are reluctant to judge a subordinate's performance, however, should bear in mind that their job is to critique not the subordinate but the behavior of the subordinate.

Table 13.2 presents guidelines for preparing and conducting an appraisal interview.

Performance appraisal is an excellent opportunity for communication between managers and employees. However, some managers find it difficult to provide negative feedback during a performance appraisal interview. In this role-play sequence designed to build supervisory skills for employees of Varian Associates Inc., managers practice performance appraisal interviewing. Managers take turns in roles of manager and subordinate. They learn to assess performance accurately and give the positive and negative feedback necessary for their subordinates' continued development.

| TABLE 13.2   GUIDELINES FOR PREPARING AND CONDUCTING AN APPRAISAL INTERVIEW |

Preparing for the Appraisal Interview

1. Hold a group discussion with subordinates to be evaluated and describe the factors on which they will be appraised.
2. Discuss your subordinates with your superior and with several of your peers.
3. Clarify any differences in language between the formal written appraisal and the appraisal interview.
4. If you are angry with a subordinate, talk about it before, not during, the appraisal interview.
5. Be aware of your own biases in judging other people.
6. Review the subordinate's compensation history before the appraisal interview.
7. If the subordinate has previously received a number of negative appraisals, be prepared to take action.

Conducting the Appraisal Interview

1. Focus on the subordinate's strengths.
2. Remember that strengths and weaknesses usually spring from the same characteristics.
3. Admit that your judgment is subjective.
4. Make it clear that the responsibility for development lies with the subordinate, not with you.
5. Be specific when citing examples.

Source: Adapted from John Cowan, "A Human Factors Approach to Appraisals," *Personnel* 52 (November–December 1975): 50–55.

Because appraisal requires that managers act as both judges and counselors, it is generally recommended that *administrative feedback*, such as a salary decision, be communicated at a separate session from *developmental feedback*.[3] As suggested, a person being judged is likely to be defensive. For counseling to be effective, an employee must be open to advice. A performance appraisal interview in which a pay cut, for example, is communicated may not provide a climate favorable for achieving developmental purposes.

The importance attached to appraisal interviews is highlighted by the fact that subordinates are generally asked to sign and date their appraisal form. In doing so, a subordinate is not indicating that he necessarily agrees with an appraisal form's content, but simply that he has seen the form and an appraisal interview actually took place.

LEGAL ASPECTS OF PERFORMANCE APPRAISAL

Many employee lawsuits are a result of inadequate performance appraisal. In general, four types of human resource actions stemming from performance appraisals may trigger an employee lawsuit:[4]

- Demotion
- Failure to promote
- Layoff
- Discharge

CLOSE UP: DIVERSITY   WHERE THERE'S A WILL THERE'S A WAY

In 1972 IBM Corp. broke new ground by setting up a computer training program for people with a reputation for being "unemployable." The outcome? Nearly 85 percent of its graduates have gone on to well-paying jobs in their field.

The initiative is called "Computer Programmer Training for Severely Disabled Persons"—CPT for short—and it has shattered myths about the employability of people with physical disabilities.

In launching the program, IBM executives reasoned that because computer programming required mental rather than physical skills, even people with severe mobility impairments could learn to program. Time has proved them right.

CPT started out with IBM providing technical consultants to local rehabilitation agencies. In 1987 it also began supplying the necessary computer equipment in a move that significantly cut startup costs. Today CPT has expanded to 50 cities, with hundreds of local employers serving on the advisory boards of its training centers. In fact, only a small percentage of CPT graduates have taken jobs with IBM. Most have selected other companies, proving that CPT has universal appeal.

Following IBM's lead, more and more companies are beginning to recognize the contributions disabled employees can make.

The Marriott Corp. has created a nonprofit foundation aimed specifically at promoting employment of the disabled through a program called Bridges. Last year, the school-to-work employment program produced jobs for 270 people with some 70 different employers. Marriott set the example: Its hotels and restaurants currently employ about 8,000 people with disabilities.

The American Express Co. has also developed a training program designed to help companies recruit and hire workers with disabilities. Known as "Giving Us the Tools," it is operated in conjunction with the National Center for Disability Services.

Despite the efforts of these companies and many others, there is still room for growth. Of the approximately 13 million disabled people of working age, fewer than 25 percent are currently employed. And the majority of those who do have jobs work only part time.

Perhaps the main reason for the high unemployment figures is employers' skepticism as to whether disabled people can do the work. One employer that has been measuring the job performance of its disabled workers for more than three decades is the Du Pont Co. Results of its 1990 survey show that 90 percent of its disabled workers ranked either average or above in overall job performance. Data from the U.S. Office of Vocational Rehabilitation show that 95 percent or more of disabled employees have the same or lower rates of absenteeism, job turnover, and work-related accidents as nondisabled employees, and that their productivity is at least as high in most cases.

But numbers don't tell the whole story. Employers have found that people with physical and mental impairments make productive employees and bring a unique perspective to the workplace. The key is to focus on their abilities instead of their disabilities.

Source: Kevin R. Hopkins and Susan L. Nestleroth, "Willing and Able," *Business Week* (Special advertising section), October 28, 1991, 1–34; 61–98.

Designing a legally defensible performance appraisal system that is executed in a professional manner can minimize legal liability. As with other employment practices, performance appraisal can carry legal consequences if either *disparate treatment* or *disparate impact* occurs.

Disparate treatment—using race, color, national origin, religion, gender, or disability as a basis for treating employees unequally—is a frequent cause of unfair performance appraisal complaints. It, however, is perhaps the most obvious and easily avoided legal risk of performance appraisal. Examples of disparate treatment include the following:

- A black and a white employee receive different ratings when there is no observable difference in their job performance.
- Male employees receive day-to-day counseling to improve their performance ratings. Female employees do not.
- Written procedures providing for a hearing are followed only when white male employees are discharged for poor performance. Blacks and females do not receive the same protection.

Such incidents can form the basis for a prima facie case of discrimination. Under current law, it is not necessary for a complainant to provide evidence of "evil intent." All that is required is to establish the fact that a practice was carried out inconsistently between individuals or groups. An employer is then legally required to provide a "legitimate, nondiscriminatory reason" for not treating all employees in a consistent and equal manner.

Disparate impact—when an identical standard is applied equally to all employees, but one group is more negatively affected than another—is typically less obvious than disparate treatment. In the case of performance appraisals, disparate impact would be evidenced where:

- An analysis reveals that blacks receive significantly lower performance ratings than whites.
- Performance ratings lead to differential promotions for males and females.
- Performance ratings led to pay disparities between blacks and whites.

As with disparate treatment, disparate impact can form the basis for a prima facie case of discrimination. In such instances an employer, as discussed in Chapter 12, must then provide evidence to the Equal Employment Opportunity Commission that a practice is job related or face legal action.

COMPENSATION

To obtain (and retain) a high-performing workforce, an organization must develop a well-conceived compensation program. In general, there are three basic compensation strategies:

- *Above market.* Organizations that follow this strategy provide employees better than average compensation. The assumption behind this strategy is that "you get what you pay for." These organizations believe that providing above-market compensation will enable them to attract and retain the best employees. Delta Air Lines, Steelcase, Inc., and Mars, Inc. are each well known for paying higher than average salaries and thus attracting the best employees.

- *At market.* This is perhaps the most frequently followed compensation strategy. It sets compensation at the prevailing market rate. The goal is simply to provide the compensation necessary to be competitive.

- *Below market.* This strategy is followed by organizations that compensate at the minimum rate required to hire just enough employees to remain in operation. It might be used because this is all an organization can afford and still remain solvent. Or, an organization could be attempting to maximize short-run profits. Whatever the reason, its implications for the long-term maintenance and retention of a qualified workforce are clearly unfavorable.

Within these strategies, managers have two tasks. First, they must undertake job analysis to ensure that jobs are paid in accordance with their internal worth to an organization. How, for example, should the pay for an accounting manager compare to that of an accountant? Jobs that are similar in content and responsibility should be compensated similarly, just as dissimilar jobs should be compensated differently. Second, managers must ensure that pay differences among employees doing the same or similar work reflect differences in work-related contributions. The best managers realize that compensation is a means to an end, not an end in itself. Thus, they link rewards to performance.

The creation of a benefit program completes the job of compensation management.

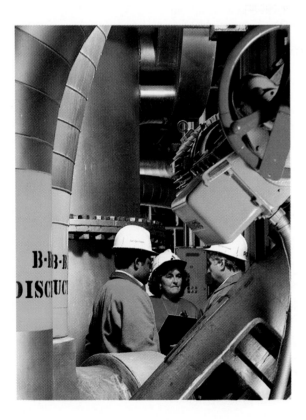

The manager of Georgia Power's Bowen Plant discusses operations with two workers. An incentive pay plan that emphasizes pay-for-performance has been instituted at Georgia Power and all the companies of its parent, The Southern Company. Under this plan employee compensation is tied to achieving specific corporate, organizational, and individual goals.

BENEFIT PROGRAMS

Most organizations offer various **benefits** to aid in retaining employees. The U.S. Chamber of Commerce estimates that the cost of employee benefits averages almost 38 cents per payroll dollar. These benefits are noncash forms of compensation that employees customarily receive in addition to a salary. Table 13.3 lists various common benefits.

Recently, so-called **cafeteria benefit plans** have become quite popular. Generally, the plans give employees a specific dollar value of benefit "credits" based on their position or years of service. The credits can be spent on a menu of benefit options. Employees can reduce one benefit—cutting vacation time, for instance—and use the additional credits to boost another benefit or increase their pay. Cafeteria plans are in effect at companies such as Mellon Bank, PepsiCo, Quaker Oats, American Can, and Morgan Stanley.

BONUSES

Compensation received in addition to one's regular salary is a **bonus.** Bonuses are customarily tied to some measure of organization returns or profits. Such

Benefits.
Noncash forms of compensation that employees customarily receive in addition to a salary.

Cafeteria benefit plan.
A plan that allows employees to choose from a menu of benefit options.

Bonus.
Compensation received in addition to one's regular salary.

TABLE 13.3 COMMON EMPLOYEE BENEFITS

Accidental death, dismemberment insurance	Outside medical services
Birthdays (vacation)	Paid attendance at professional and other outside meetings
Commissions	Parental leave
Day-care centers	Parking facilities
Deferred compensation plan	Pension
Dental and eye care insurance	Personal accident insurance
Disability insurance	Personal counseling
Discount on organization products	Personal credit cards
Education costs	Physical examinations
Educational activities (time off)	Political activities (time off)
Elder care	Private office
Free checking account	Professional activities
Free or subsidized lunches	Professional memberships
Group automobile insurance	Profit sharing
Group homeowners' insurance	Psychiatric services
Group life insurance	Retirement gratuity
Health insurance	Savings plans
Holidays (extra)	Severance pay
Home health care	Shorter or flexible workweek
Hospital-surgical-medical insurance	Sickness and accident insurance
Incentive growth fund	Social Security
Interest-free loans	Social service sabbaticals
Layoff pay	Split-life insurance
Legal, estate-planning, and other professional assistance	State disability plans
Long-term disability benefits	Stock-option plans (qualified, nonqualified, tandem)
Matching educational donations	Survivors' benefits
Medical assistance	Tax assistance
Nursing home care	Vacations

additional employee compensation serves as an incentive for improved individual performance. Bonus programs enable an organization to attract and retain well-qualified employees without jeopardizing its underlying salary structure. Rather than paying a high salary at a flat rate, employees are offered the opportunity to earn a bonus. In this way, compensation earned for outstanding performance in one year does not become a continuing salary obligation.

PERQUISITES

Known as *perks*, **perquisites** are extra, noncash forms of compensation. Typical examples include "car services," expense accounts, extra life insurance, supplemental pension programs, club memberships, guaranteed attendance at annual conventions, personal investment counseling, personal legal advice, security protection, low-interest or no-interest loans, and apartments for top managers. Table 13.4 lists some of the more prevalent perks on a continuum according to use.

Perquisites.
An extra, noncash form of compensation.

DISCIPLINE

Simply defined, **discipline** is action taken against an employee for violating work rules. Many managers are uncomfortable as disciplinarians, even though they are aware that discipline may be necessary occasionally for maintaining organization performance.

Discipline.
Action taken against an employee for violating work rules.

One of a manager's biggest challenges is to encourage self-discipline among subordinates. Indeed, self-discipline is the best discipline. Once subordinates understand that self-discipline is expected of them, they will more likely perform satisfactorily. Yet, the possibility of having to use discipline always exists.

Effective discipline requires a well-publicized and unambiguous disciplinary procedure. At a minimum, such a procedure should include the following four steps.

Step 1 involves establishing rules stipulating the behavior required of all employees. These rules should specify what an individual may or may not do in a given situation, and each rule should be categorized as *major* or *minor*. A sample listing of major and minor offenses appears in Table 13.5.

TABLE 13.4 A CONTINUUM OF PERQUISITES			
Most Common ◄──────────────────────────────► **Least Common**			
Better appointed office (choice of office furnishings)	Airline VIP lounge	Company plane (personal use)	Car phone
	Extra vacation		In-town apartment
	Financial counseling	Executive dining room	Legal counseling
Company car	Tax preparation	Home-security system	Low-interest loans
Company plane (business)	First-class air travel	Personal-liability insurance	Sabbatical leaves
	Liberal expense account		Tickets for theater and sporting events
Medical exam	Club memberships	Spouse travel	Dependent tuition reimbursement
Business travel insurance		Chauffeur	

Source: Based on W. Gordon Binns, Jr., and Gregory E. Lau, "Executive Compensation," in *AMA Management Handbook,* 2d ed., ed. William K. Fallon (New York: AMACOM, 1983), 7/57; and "Popular Perks," *Wall Street Journal,* April 18, 1990, R25.

TABLE 13.5 EXAMPLES OF MAJOR AND MINOR DISCIPLINARY OFFENSES	
Disciplinary Offenses	
Major	**Minor**
Possessing an illegal/ intoxicating substance	Leaving work without permission
	Gambling
Possessing a weapon	Using profane or abusive language
Fighting	Committing safety violations
Theft/dishonesty	Horseplay/troublemaking
Sabotage	Excessive tardiness
Sleeping on the job	Excessive absenteeism

Step 2 involves communicating rules to all employees. Unless employees are aware of rules, they cannot be expected to follow them. Experience suggests that if employees participate in establishing rules, they will be more likely to observe them. Employees also must be convinced that the rules are fair for discipline to be accepted.

Step 3 involves assessing employee conduct. Rule violations should receive attention when they are observed. Additionally, an attempt should be made to determine the underlying cause of an offense. Employees should be given full opportunity to present their side of the story to determine if mitigating circumstances are present.

Step 4 involves exercising actual discipline. Major offenses may require immediate disciplinary action, including discharge. Minor offenses are customarily handled using a *progressive discipline* scheme that traces back to management pioneer Lillian Gilbreth. The scheme imposes increasingly stern penalties for repeated offenses: *first* offense prompts an oral warning; *second* offense, a written warning; *third* offense, suspension without pay; *fourth* offense, discharge. The oral and written warnings are intended to inform employees of rule violations and notify them that a repeat offense will lead to more serious consequences. Suspension without pay—typically from 1 day to 2 weeks—is a forewarning of the economic results of discharge. It provides a final opportunity for an employee to comply with work rules.

Experts advise that in imposing discipline, managers should be guided by the "hot stove rule."[5] The *first* element is that discipline should be immediate, just as the pain from a hot stove is immediate to whoever touches it. *Second,* discipline should be consistent: anytime someone brushes up against the stove, he'll get burned. *Finally,* hot stoves are impersonal, and discipline should be, too. Managers should not lose their temper or single out an employee because of race, creed, color, gender, or age. Rather, they should calmly explain the rule violation and the resultant penalty.

If various warnings and penalties do not resolve a disciplinary problem, discharge may be the only alternative. Employers, however, may encounter legal liability when they attempt to discharge an employee. Representations made in employee handbooks, policy manuals, initial-offer letters, and even oral agreements can be construed as implied contracts that are binding in some states. If a contract is found to exist, an employee has a legal claim if its terms are not

SMART MANAGEMENT   WELLNESS WORKS: SHAPING UP FOR LESS

The average U.S. company spends an amount equal to 25 percent of its profits on employee health care. Desperate to control rising health-care costs, a growing number of companies are waking up to the benefits of work site wellness. Johnson & Johnson (J&J) estimates that its "Live for Life" program saves it an average of $378 per employee in reduced absenteeism, greater productivity, and savings on health-care benefits. With 35,000 employees in the United States and 5,000 in Western Europe, that translates into over $15 million in savings. For small businesses, which frequently measure profits in thousands—not millions—of dollars, the net effect of an employee wellness program can mean the difference between profit and loss.

Experts generally agree that a successful wellness campaign begins with a health-risk appraisal of a company's workforce. A thorough review of prior health insurance claims can help discern patterns that might be addressed effectively through health promotion. All employees who enter the J&J wellness program complete a 190-page health profile, which includes questions about smoking, alcohol and drug use, eating habits, level of physical activity, dental habits, driving habits, medical care and history, and what stress factors an employee may be contending with. A computer analysis then offers employees suggestions on how to improve their health.

J&J has 35 fitness centers nationwide, which usually include an indoor track, an aerobics work out area, rowing machines, cycles, weight equipment, Nautilus machines, and Stairmasters. It also maps outdoor jogging or running trails for employees.

The wellness program even goes beyond treadmills and exercise bikes. J&J promotes the consumption of heart-healthy foods in its employee cafeterias. Signs list the caloric and fat intake of menu items. It also offers programs on issues such as stress management, smoking cessation, weight reduction and control, and drug and alcohol control.

Other companies, like Adolph Coors, even include family members in their wellness programs. Coors's comprehensive approach to wellness includes on-site cardiac and orthopedic rehabilitation programs, as well as on-site mammography and blood-pressure screening, employee and family counseling, and prenatal and postnatal education.

Some companies, like the Bank of Delaware, have taken to paying employees for good health habits. By not smoking, agreeing to wear seat belts, and attending health promotion workshops, employees net an extra $72 a year. They can earn $144 a year by getting a fitness evaluation and following a prescribed exercise plan. The notion behind "Wellness Money" is that a healthy employee is not only a cheaper employee—saving an employer thousands of dollars in medical costs—but also more productive. A growing number of companies, such as U-Haul and Southern California Edison, are offering similar incentives. Some programs have been extended to include incentives in other areas, such as cholesterol counts, blood pressure, and weight.

Sources: Adapted from Shari Caudron, "Wellness Works," *Industry Week*, February 4, 1991, 22–24; Michael A. Verespej, "A Ticket to Better Health," *Industry Week*, February 4, 1991, 24–25; and Ted Moncreiff, "Wellness Programs: Shaping Up for Less," *CFO* 7 (March 1991): 52–54.

followed. A common breach of contract involves employers failing to follow their own specified discharge procedure. Even when a specified procedure is followed, arbitrary, capricious, or malicious acts may be seen by the courts as violations of an implied covenant of "good faith and fair dealing."

To reduce their risk of a wrongful-discharge suit, some employers have gone so far as to eliminate employee handbooks for fear that they will be construed as granting contractual rights to employees. A few, such as Sears, Roebuck, have gone a step further and require prospective employees to sign disclaimers that clearly state that no employer statements are to be considered a binding contract between employer and employee.

In a further innovative move to avoid litigation, employers such as Polaroid, Federal Express, Northrop Corporation, and Citicorp have each established a "company court" to hear complaints from disgruntled employees and ex-employees. By ensuring due process, such courts can reduce lawsuits, improve public relations, keep out unions, and increase employee commitment.

LABOR RELATIONS

In most organizations, human resource activities such as recruiting, selecting, training, and appraising employee performance are the sole responsibility of management. However, when employees are organized into a labor union, management's freedom to act independently is constrained.

A **union** is a group of employees who join together to bargain to improve their wages, benefits, work hours, and conditions. Union membership as a percentage

Union.
A group of employees who join together to bargain to improve their wages, benefits, work hours, and conditions.

When unionized Greyhound bus drivers went on strike, company executives immediately hired nonunion, permanent replacements. Some buses became snipers' targets, causing injury to several passengers. The union disavowed the shootings, but the incidents generated bad publicity for the union cause.

of the U.S. workforce peaked in 1954 at 35 percent. Since then it has been slipping, hastened in the 1980s, when industrial employment contracted from an economic recession and international competition. Today, unions represent slightly more than one out of ten private nonagricultural wage and salary workers (13.4 percent) in the over 84.6-million-member private workforce.

Employees typically join unions to collectively bargain for higher wages and better working conditions. Unionism is also generally seen as a means for receiving fair treatment on the job and acquiring more meaningful work because it allows employees to challenge an employer's actions. Union contracts with rules defining equitable procedures for discipline, promotions, safety matters, or training are considered ways to eliminate poor managerial practices. Furthermore, joining a union provides employees security in knowing that they cannot be discharged without just cause. For others, unionization may represent a last alternative when employers refuse to correct unsafe working conditions or act with favoritism toward certain employees.

Unions are classified as being either *craft, industrial,* or *general.* **Craft unions** organize employees only in particular occupations or skills. Craft unions include the United Brotherhood of Carpenters and Joiners, International Union of Bricklayers, and International Brotherhood of Painters. **Industrial unions** organize employees along industry lines regardless of occupation or skill. The United Automobile Workers is an industrial union, as are the United Steelworkers, Rubber Workers, and the International Ladies Garment Workers. Each of these unions may attempt to organize all of the clerical, production, maintenance, or shipping employees at a single location within their respective industries. Classifying labor unions as either industrial or craft, however, is not always possible. Some, namely the Teamsters, are classified as **general unions** since they organize employees in any industry, occupation, or skill.

Employee associations are another important element of U.S. labor. They usually represent employees in the public sector (federal, state, or local government). Frequently, they negotiate for professional employees (such as engineers, lawyers, or professors) having special demands and bargaining objectives. The National Education Association, which represents classroom teachers, the American Nurses Association, and the California State Employees Association are examples of large employee associations. Although some labor authorities treat unions and employee associations separately because of the constituents they serve, the distinction between the two is often blurred, since both have common goals and use similar techniques to advance member needs.

Collective bargaining is the process by which labor and management establish and administer conditions under which employees will work. The outcomes of bargaining are contained in a labor contract, which normally is negotiated every 3 years. As with any legal document, both sides must follow the contract or face various penalties.

When contract disputes are not settled successfully, employees sometimes strike. When strikes do occur, the parties may try to resolve the dispute by **mediation,** a process in which an outside, neutral person assists in reaching a settlement. A mediator does not dictate final contract terms. Rather, through persuasion, offering alternative solutions to troublesome issues, and skillful communication, a mediator helps the parties to reach accord on their own terms. Mediators working for the Federal Mediation and Conciliation Service or state agencies are an important part of collective bargaining when bargaining deadlocks occur.

Craft union.
A union that organizes employees only in particular occupations or skills.

Industrial union.
A union that organizes workers along industry lines regardless of skill or occupation.

General union.
A union that organizes employees in any industry, occupation, or skill.

Employee associations.
Groups that represent employees in the public sector (federal, state, or local government) and negotiate for professional employees (such as engineers, lawyers, and professors).

Collective bargaining.
The process by which labor and management establish and administer conditions under which employees will work.

Mediation.
The process in which an outside, neutral person assists in reaching a settlement.

GRIEVANCE PROCEDURE

Although collective bargaining is often discussed as simply negotiating a labor contract, it also involves resolving employee concerns or grievances arising during the life of a contract.

A **grievance** is an employee charge alleging a labor contract violation. Grievances are distinguished from employee complaints that are not contract violations. Typically, a labor contract will define exactly what a grievance is and list areas expressly excluded from grievances.

Virtually all labor contracts include some form of grievance procedure. The method for solving employee grievances varies among contracts, depending upon the size and structure of the parties concerned and upon their needs. A typical procedure will contain three to five appeal steps to be followed within specified time limits. Figure 13.7 illustrates a five-step grievance procedure. The procedure operates as described in the following paragraphs.

Step 1 When employees believe they have been unfairly treated or their contract has been violated, they discuss the problem with their immediate supervisor. Experience suggests that better relationships are developed when employees and

Grievance.
An employee charge alleging a labor contract violation.

FIGURE 13.7 A FIVE-STEP GRIEVANCE PROCEDURE

Step	Management	Union	Form	Management Answer	Union Appeal
	Arbitration				
Fifth			Written	20 days	20 days
	Industrial Relations Manager	Grievance Committee			
Fourth			Written	10 days	10 days
	Division Manager	Chief Steward			
Third			Written	5 days	5 days
	Immediate Supervisor	Shop Steward			
Second			Written	5 days	5 days
	Immediate Supervisor	Grievant			
First			Oral	Immediate	Immediate
	Issue in Dispute				

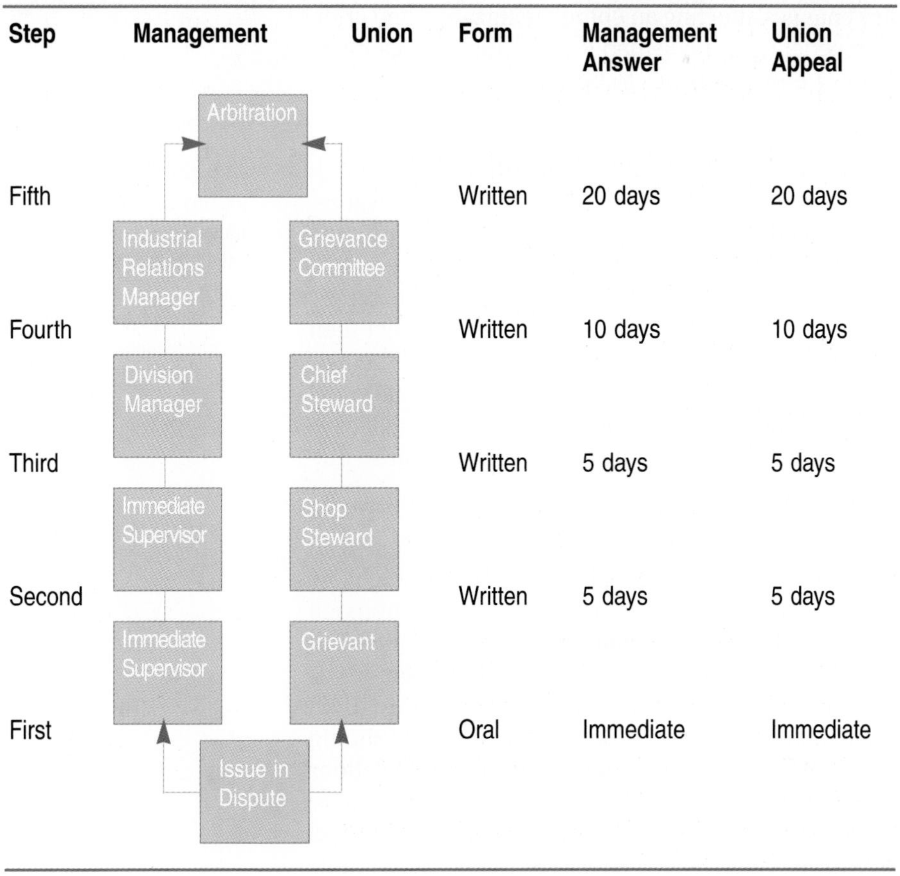

managers first discuss grievances alone without union intervention. Involving a union steward tends to formalize a grievance and create a "we-them" attitude. If a grievance is not resolved at this level, it is appealed to Step 2.

Step 2 The grievance is now put into writing. Using a grievance form, employees will describe the nature of their grievance, the contract provision violated, and the remedy sought. The form will be signed by the employees and presented to management. A formal meeting is scheduled between the relevant shop steward and manager to discuss the grievance; the grievants may or may not be present. If the grievance is settled, the procedure ends here. If a solution is not reached, management has 5 days to respond and the union has 5 days to appeal management's decision to Step 3.

Step 3 At this level those individuals initially involved at Steps 1 and 2 are replaced by higher union and management officials. A new perspective will be obtained. In some grievances, higher management levels are needed to settle a grievance because only they have the necessary authority to resolve a dispute. Again, if no solution is found, management has 5 days to respond and the union has 5 days to appeal management's decision.

Step 4 This step involves a meeting between the union's grievance committee and the organization's human resource or industrial relations manager. Because of their importance, certain issues do not lend themselves to resolution at lower steps. For example, policy changes affecting an entire organization and grievance solutions that establish precedent can be settled only by top management. Some grievance procedures allow important issues to be submitted directly to an advanced step.

Step 5 Almost all grievance procedures end with **arbitration,** which entails selecting a neutral third party (an arbitrator) to render a decision on a grievance. Arbitration decisions are final and binding, and the parties must comply with the arbitrator's award. Arbitration hearings are rather formal undertakings resembling court procedures. It is common for labor and management to be represented by lawyers, although, typically, those individuals involved at Step 4 will present their own case. Since both sides risk receiving an adverse decision, labor and management typically use arbitration only as a last resort to resolving contractual problems. Practitioners often refer to arbitration as the "cornerstone" of the collective bargaining process, since this procedure brings finality to problems that arise during the duration of the agreement.

Arbitration.
The final step in the union grievance procedure. A neutral third party is selected to render a final and binding decision on a grievance between labor and management.

Given the opportunity, managers would typically prefer not to deal with unions. Following unionization, however, management is obligated to negotiate with a union over employment concerns. How labor and management approach their relationship as they adjust to collective bargaining will affect the quality of their interactions and the outcomes reached. Responsible labor relations is founded on a spirit of cooperation gained through mutual honesty and trust. Both labor and management have legitimate rights and motives that each side should respect. These ends can be achieved only when labor-management relations are based on joint understanding. Such understanding is evident in the increasing number of job design programs undertaken in tandem by labor and management. As discussed in Chapter 10, the United Steelworkers, the United Automobile

Workers, the International Union of Electrical Workers, and the Communication Workers of America have all signed national agreements with their respective managements calling for more cooperation to enhance competitiveness and, hence, increase job security.

SUMMARY

This chapter examined the need to continually develop human resources so as to maximize the efficient use of employee talents. The specific human resource development activities discussed were orientation, training, performance appraisal, compensation, discipline, and labor relations.

Learning Objective 1: List several purposes that effective orientation serves.
Effective orientation serves at least four purposes: it carries the message that new employees are valued, it reduces startup costs that invariably occur when an employee is new, it reduces the amount of anxiety and hazing new employees experience, and it saves time for superiors and peers.

Learning Objective 2: Identify several different approaches to training.
There are numerous different approaches to training, including on-the-job training, job rotation, use of company-owned training centers, company-sponsored attendance at conferences and university management programs, apprenticeship programs, computer-assisted instruction, and use of videodisc systems.

Learning Objective 3: Outline the purposes that sound performance appraisal serves.
A sound performance-appraisal system serves the following purposes: (1) It provides employees with feedback so that they know how well they are performing. (2) It develops valid data for pay (salary and bonus) and promotion decisions. (3) It helps managers make discharge and retention decisions and provides a means for them to warn subordinates about unsatisfactory performance. (4) It helps managers counsel subordinates so they will improve their performance and develop their potential. (5) It develops commitment to an organization by identifying career opportunities and encouraging career planning. (6) It motivates employees through recognition and support. (7) It strengthens manager-subordinate relations. (8) It provides input to the human resource planning process.

Learning Objective 4: Identify various performance appraisal techniques.
The most commonly used performance-appraisal techniques involve graphic rating scales, essay appraisals, comparative methods, and behaviorally anchored rating scales.

Learning Objective 5: Recount different sources of rater error.
The most frequent sources of rater error are halo, recency, central tendency, rater pattern, and stereotyping.

Learning Objective 6: Present guidelines for preparing and conducting an appraisal interview.
Guidelines for preparing and conducting an appraisal interview are presented in Table 13.2.

Learning Objective 7: Comment on the legal aspects of performance appraisal.

Designing a legally defensible performance appraisal system that is executed in a professional manner can minimize legal liability. Performance appraisal can particularly carry legal consequences if disparate treatment or disparate impact occurs.

Learning Objective 8: Explain the importance of a well-conceived compensation program.

A well-conceived compensation program is important for obtaining (and retaining) a high-performing workforce.

Learning Objective 9: List means, other than salary, by which employees may be compensated.

In addition to a salary, employees may be compensated with benefit programs, bonuses, and perquisites.

Learning Objective 10: Specify the minimum requirements of a well-publicized and unambiguous disciplinary process.

At a minimum, a well-publicized and unambiguous disciplinary process should include four steps: establish rules stipulating the personal conduct required of all employees, communicate these rules to all employees, assess employee conduct, and exercise actual discipline.

Learning Objective 11: Describe different types of unions and their jurisdictions.

Craft unions organize employees only in particular occupations or skills. Industrial unions organize employees along industry lines regardless of occupation or skill. General unions organize employees in any industry, occupation, or skill. Employee associations are groups usually representing employees in the public sector (federal, state, or local government).

Learning Objective 12: Depict a typical grievance procedure.

When employees or union officials believe a labor contract has been violated, they may file a grievance. A typical five-step grievance procedure is illustrated in Figure 13.7.

KEY TERMS

arbitration 396

behaviorally anchored
   rating scales 381

benefits 389

bonus 389

cafeteria benefit plan 389

central tendency error 383

collective bargaining 394

comparative method 379

craft union 394

discipline 390

employee associations 394

essay appraisal 378

forced distribution method
   380

general union 394

graphic rating scale 376

grievance 395

halo error 382

industrial union 394

job rotation 373

mediation 394

on-the-job training 373

orientation 370

paired-comparison method
   379

performance appraisal 375

perquisites 390

rater pattern error 383

recency error 382

stereotyping 384

training 371

union 393

REVIEW AND DISCUSSION QUESTIONS

1. Hazing is a common rite. Based on personal experience, cite several examples of hazing with which you are familiar.

2. Looking toward the next several decades, what training do you expect to need to maintain your proficiency, as well as to qualify for continued promotion?

3. As a successful manager who recognizes the importance of a sound performance-appraisal system, what guidelines would you follow in preparing and conducting a performance-appraisal interview?

4. Imagine you are a management consultant. You've just finished interviewing the eighth member of a General Motors research team. He was disturbed by General Motors's requirement that no more than 10 percent of any work group can be given a top performance rating. He explained:

   > Evidently there is an effort to fit everyone within a work group to a bell-shaped curve so that raises can be doled out and not go over the salary budget. But as a scientist, I know that a bell curve should be applied only when a population is large enough, and most work groups are small. As a result, my work could be outstanding, but if one other person in my group was outstanding, I could be denied such a rating.[6]

   How would you respond?

5. Many managers express a distaste for performance appraisal because of a reluctance to "play God" in evaluating their subordinates. Comment on the notion that in performance appraisal their job is to critique a subordinate's behavior, not the subordinate.

6. Cafeteria benefit plans are becoming an increasingly popular means of compensation. Design such a plan to meet your anticipated needs as a new college graduate. Be sure to consider benefits such as health insurance, professional memberships, and vacations.

7. Imagine that you have been on your first job as a welding department supervisor for 2 months. Moments ago you had to intervene in a fistfight between two subordinates. John, the one who started the fight, has a long, unblemished work record. Inquiring into the cause of the fight, you learned that yesterday John's wife filed suit for a divorce. How would you discipline John in this situation? What problems might you expect if you decide to discharge John?

8. The chapter notes that discharge is a final alternative and can cause serious problems. Former ITT chief executive Harold Geneen, however, contends that it can also be a constructive management action. After reading the following quote, comment on Geneen's contention.

   > It is the duty of the leader to recognize the person who isn't doing his job and get rid of him. It may take a bit of time before the laggard's excuses, glib talk, or lies catch up with him. But the alert leader will recognize the clues and will move forcefully as soon as he learns the facts. And when he does, he will earn the respect of all the others who are hardworking and who have long resented the freeloader in their ranks. In one sense, firing people can be a constructive role of management. It clears the air and improves the climate.[7]

9. Common wisdom is that the top two items on the list of "hardest things for a manager to do" are discharge an employee and conduct an appraisal review—but not necessarily in that order. Why do you suppose this is true?

10. After class, a fellow student makes the comment that unions are bad and that a manager should fight unions at every turn, making life miserable for union officials. Do you agree? What are several likely outcomes of implementing this attitude?

MANAGEMENT EXPERIENCE BEHAVIORALLY ANCHORED RATING SCALES IN ACTION

The accompanying discussion notes that behaviorally anchored rating scales represent an attempt to replace the subjectivity inherent in other appraisal techniques. It also notes that developing such a scale can be extremely time consuming. To engender a feel for the effort involved in developing a behaviorally anchored rating scale, follow the four steps below to create one that assesses one dimension of a college instructor's performance. A sample scale is provided as a guide.

Step 1. Generate a list of five to ten performance dimensions for the position of college instructor. Such dimensions might include relationships with students, ability to present course material, interest in course, reasonableness of workload, and fairness of testing and grading.

Step 2. Select one performance dimension and develop a list of ten to 15 examples that indicate both effective and ineffective behavior.

Step 3. Rate each of the examples according to the scale used in the accompanying example.

REASONABLENESS OF THE WORKLOAD

This dimension refers to the amount of work (reading, homework problems, class and lab work, papers, tests, and so on) assigned by the professor. It includes such things as clearly specifying assignments and due dates, scheduling the work evenly throughout the quarter, and keeping the workload appropriate to the credit-hour value of the course.

Best Possible	This professor could be expected to discontinue or reduce homework assignments around midterms and finals so that his students would have more time to study.
	This professor could be expected to distribute the workload evenly across the term.
	This professor could be expected to assign reasonable amounts of homework every other day.
	This professor could be expected to assign homework a few times a week but not every day.
	This professor could be expected to assign a four- to five-page typewritten paper and specify the format and style in which it is to be written.
Exactly	This professor could be expected to assign about 50 pages of reading per week.
Neutral	This professor could be expected to require a term paper, oral presentation, and weekly tests.
	This professor could be expected to require a lot of memorization for his class.
	This professor could be expected sometimes to assign two chapters for one night's assignment.
	This professor could be expected to surprise her students with an extra assignment toward the end of the term.
Worst Possible	This professor could be expected twice to assign five-page papers 2 days before they are due.

Continued on next page.

Step 4. Prepare the behaviorally anchored rating scale for the particular performance dimension under consideration.

Answer these questions:

1. What advantages does this scale offer ratees and raters?

2. Explain how the four-step process for developing a behaviorally anchored rating scale can be helpful to both ratees and raters.

Sources: William I. Sauser, Jr., "A Comparative Evaluation of the Effects of Rater Participation and Rater Training on Characteristics of Employee Performance Appraisal Ratings and Related Mediating Variables." Ph.D. diss., Georgia Institute of Technology, Atlanta, 1978; and William I. Sauser, Jr., Kenneth L. Evans, Cecilia H. Champion, "Two-Hundred-and-Fifty Scaled Incidents of College Classroom Teaching Behavior" (ED 174394), *Resources in Education,* 1980, *15*(1):30.

CASE 13.1   **CHALLENGE**

Delaware Community College is a small state-supported school situated in a quiet, rural area just south of the state capital. Chartered in 1911, it has become an integral part of the community, with programs aimed primarily at preparing students to enter 4-year colleges and universities, although a few are 2-year paraprofessional programs. Like most schools, Delaware uses a traditional A, B, C, D, F grading system. Karen Mayes, an instructor at Delaware, was soon to find herself seriously questioning this time-honored tradition.

Mayes took her teaching seriously, working hard to balance the demands of her doctoral studies at the university with her teaching duties at the community college. In the classroom, she was "relationship oriented," trying to involve the students in active discussions of the material. The students seemed to respond well.

Today she had taught her Introduction to Management class. The class became energetic, and she got caught up in their enthusiasm. The cause of the excitement was a case study about grading and the problems it caused at a particular university. The case was complicated because the class had been subjected to three different teachers during a term. Predictably, these teachers had different styles and different expectations.

The class discussion quickly became a discussion of grading at Delaware Community. Here, too, many teachers at the college had different styles. Some lectured exclusively; others, like Mayes, lectured and led class debate; others relied almost entirely upon class participation. Professors used different testing methods—objective tests, essay tests, or both. Nevertheless, despite these varied inputs, practically all teachers used the traditional grading system, and in the opinion of the class members, it left a lot to be desired.

"Grades, grades, grades, why do we need them anyway?" Leroy Mark asked.

"You don't like them because you can't get good ones—that's why you complain," Pamela Johnson said.

"It's not that at all; they just aren't fair. They don't measure what I've learned. You mean to tell me that when I can answer questions well in class, but not on some test, I should only get graded for my test answers? That's not fair!" Mark retorted.

"That's true, Leroy's got a point. Plus, we know teachers use the old A, B, C scale. Somebody's got to get the D's and F's. But what happens if the whole class is pretty smart?"

"Well, why don't they give all A's and B's? Then nobody's hurt," Richard Green suggested.

Peggy Vandero chimed, "Now that idea I like!"

And so the discussion raged, back and forth, back and forth. Alternatives were suggested and rejected. Even when the bell rang, the discussion went on; no one in the class moved! Finally, Mayes stopped them. But now, reflecting on what she'd suggested, she was beginning to wonder if she'd let things go too far.

"I hate to interrupt this lively discussion, but the bell's rung, and there's another class coming in," Mayes said. "To summarize, I hear you saying that there are a number of grading systems being used, including our traditional A, B, C, D, F system. Furthermore, you believe the traditional system is unfair and does not always reflect the quality of your work. Here today you've discussed some alternatives, including pass-fail and blanket grades, yet these appear to have faults as well. Let me make a proposition. I challenge you to put your money where your mouth is. We're only in the second week of class and if *you* can come up with a grading system that meets the dual criteria of being fair and reflecting the quality of work done, I'll implement it. You have from now until Friday to prepare your proposals either individually or in groups. During Friday's class, the proposals can be presented and voted on, and the one deemed most acceptable will be instituted."

Problems

1. Grading, of course, is a form of performance

appraisal with which all students can readily identify. What are some of the more common types of grading systems?

2. What factors influence the grade a student may be assigned?

3. How might the grades and grading systems used affect people *after* graduation?

4. Does the problem go beyond/ just grading? What are the social implications of coping with varying grading systems? How does it affect equity in the university environment?

5. If a university changes its grading system from an A, B, C, D, F scale to pass-fail, what might be some of the behavioral implications?

Source: This case used with permission of the authors, George E. Stevens, University of Central Florida, Orlando, and R. Penny Marquette, University of Akron, Akron, Ohio.

CASE 13.2 "YOU'VE COME A LONG WAY, HONEY"

Many women applaud the strict laws and recent judicial decisions cracking down on sexual harassment in the workplace. But not all women share this view. Sarah J. McCarthy, a Pittsburgh restauranteur, says that, "as a feminist I am outraged by attempts to turn flirting into a federal crime."

McCarthy owns a restaurant/bar that her husband and son help manage. In addition to many waitresses, she employs some 20 young men whose role models, she says, "range from Axl Rose to John Belushi." They work hard in a hot kitchen at a fast-paced, high-stress job. They often use salty language, and they have been overheard telling off-color jokes. They often flirt with the waitresses, ask them for dates, and habitually call them "honey." McCarthy claims that this behavior does not create a hostile or offensive work environment, however. Quite the contrary. She says that it is done in the spirit of fun and that it creates a relaxed, informal atmosphere that relieves tension and fosters teamwork.

Now McCarthy is frightened. She could be forced to pay up to $100,000 in punitive damages

and court costs if one of her employees is offended. Recent judicial decisions make it clear that employers are financially liable unless they take steps to prevent sexual harassment from taking place and respond effectively if allegations are made. Whether or not one agrees with McCarthy that laws and litigation have gone too far, one thing is sure: To protect themselves from financial liability, employers must develop and implement well thought out policies, rules, and procedures concerning sexual harassment.

Problems

1. Write a sexual harassment policy statement for McCarthy's business.

2. Develop a set of rules in support of the policy.

3. Develop a set of procedures for implementing the policy and enforcing the rules.

Source: Brooks E. Smith and John C. Burch, University of Southern Mississippi—Gulf Coast, Long Beach, Mississippi, based on "Cultural Fascism," *Forbes*, December 9, 1991, 16.

NOTES

[1] Clinton O. Longenecker and Dennis A. Gioia, "Ethical Dilemmas in Performance Appraisal Revisited," *Journal of Business Ethics* 9 (December 1990): 961.

[2] Adapted from Michael Beer, "Performance Appraisal: Dilemmas and Possibilities," *Organizational Dynamics* 9 (Winter 1981): 25.

[3] Herbert H. Meyer, "A Solution to the Performance Appraisal Feedback Enigma," *Academy of Management Executive* 5 (February 1991): 68–76.

[4] Patricia S. Eyres, "Assessment: Legally Defensible Performance Appraisal Systems," *Personnel Journal* (July 1989): 58–62.

[5] George Strauss and Leonard R. Sayles, *Personnel: The Human Problems of Management*, 4th ed. (Englewood Cliffs, N.J.: Prentice-Hall, 1980), 221–229.

[6] Adapted from Saul W. Gellerman and William G. Hodgson, "Cyanamid's New Take on Performance Appraisal," *Harvard Business Review* (May–June 1988): 37.

[7] Harold S. Geneen, "The Art of Leadership," *The Best of Business* 6 (Fall 1984): 10.

CHAPTER 14

LEARNING OBJECTIVES

Upon completing this chapter, you should be able to:

- List the steps in developing a career plan.
- Explain what is meant by *networking*.
- Know what is meant by *mentoring*.
- Outline guidelines for playing "success chess."
- Recognize the pressures faced by new managers.
- Describe the impact of job-related stress.
- Appreciate the challenges faced by dual-career couples.
- Answer the question, "What is midlife crisis like?"

n Mondays, Tuesdays, and Thursdays, Anne Brown is part of a high-powered Wall Street group that sells securities to big institutional investors. On Wednesdays and every other Friday, her life is a little more down to earth: She stays at home in Greenwich, Connecticut, with her two children.

Brown is part of a growing number of employees on the so-called "mommy track," women who want to have a career and raise a family—and who are willing to make the sacrifices necessary to do both. Thanks to progressive companies that are willing to design flexible work schedules, more employees now are getting that choice.

Nontraditional hours, job sharing, leaves of absence, and part-time work are among the options open to workers struggling to juggle families and careers. And it's not just small companies that have managed to find ways to get around the rigidity of the 8-to-5 routine. Flexibility is being offered by corporate giants like American Express, IBM, Levi Strauss, NationsBank, and PepsiCo.

Although altruism may seem to be the primary motive, the reality is that flexibility sometimes is the only way to keep good people on the payroll. When Aetna Corp. noticed a high drop-out rate among employees who had to choose between keeping their job and staying home with a new baby, it began offering 6-month unpaid leaves and encouraged managers to offer their employees part-time work after the leave expired. As a result, the rate of attrition among female employees was cut in half, to 12 percent.

But qualifying for flex-time is only the first of many hurdles that pioneering employees have to overcome when they choose not to

MANAGING A SUCCESSFUL CAREER

conform to the standard 40-hour workweek. For starters, co-workers may view a flexible schedule as tantamount to slacking off. And subordinates may resist putting in a full-time effort for someone they consider a part-time boss. When everyone doesn't abide by the same rules, it also raises concerns about fairness. But the reality is that not everyone is willing to accept the pay cut that comes with working fewer hours.

The best way to quiet critics is with results. Individuals who have such arrangements say that the treatment they receive gives them more incentive to work even harder. They also learn how to manage their time better by delegating responsibility to subordinates and planning ahead. More often than not, the dedication pays off.

At Lotus Development, nine teams of employees who were the first to participate in the company's job-sharing plans ranked among the top performers in the annual merit-raise appraisals. And sometimes those who return to full-time jobs continue their climb up the management ladder.

For the most part, men are still reluctant to take advantage of the new flexibility for fear that they may lose face. But there nevertheless are major benefits for companies that give employees the freedom to choose. More women stay on the job, and the workplace moves one step closer to being both more humane and more efficient.

In this chapter, we will explore some of the rewards and pitfalls associated with careers. We will discuss alternatives for developing a career strategy and discover various means by which work life can be made more enjoyable and productive.

Source: Alan Deutschman, "Pioneers of the New Balance," *Fortune,* May 20, 1991, 60, 62, 64, 68.

What does it take to land that first good job? How does one then parlay that position into a managerial career? In this chapter we will discuss these questions and others that relate to the various rewards, challenges, and crises that affect most managers' careers.

A **career** is a sequence of job-related experiences that spans a person's work life. To build a successful career, it is important to know how an organization develops an effective managerial team. This knowledge is important whether your career objectives are economically oriented, or whether you look to your career to satisfy personal fulfillment needs. Bearing this in mind, let's first consider how to get a job that matches your career plan. Understand that finding the right job—especially the right first job—is a skill that can be learned.

Although some employers do contract with private employment agencies, or "headhunters," to recruit on their behalf, and some job hunters do list themselves with such agencies, the following comments are aimed principally at those seeking employment on their own or working through either a university placement center or state employment service, neither of which would charge a fee to employers or prospective employees.

Career.

A sequence of work-related experiences that span a person's work life.

CAREER PLANNING

Developing a career plan is similar in some ways to developing a marketing plan for a new product. To get hired, you must prove to potential buyers that the "product" you are offering possesses the qualifications the customer seeks . . . and that it comes neatly and attractively packaged. A tall order? Maybe so. But consider this: The effort you invest in marketing yourself should be at least equal to the energy you would put into making a $2 million sale. Why? Because the chances are good that you will earn at least $2 million before you retire.

Just as a successful marketing strategy doesn't stop once an advertising campaign is decided upon, so too should career planning continue even after you have secured that first right job. To advance in that career, you should set goals and determine a strategy for achieving them. Although career planning is far from a science, both research and experience show that if you have a plan, you will be better able to capitalize upon the opportunities that you encounter. In doing so, remember the following career-planning axioms:

1. You, and you alone, must assume primary responsibility for developing a sound career plan.

2. With a well-developed plan, you have a much better chance for a successful career.

3. Career planning does not guarantee success, but it will enable you to have some control over your environment, rather than being its helpless victim.

4. Implementing a career plan requires self-confidence and personal commitment.

Career planning is a multistep process involving many ongoing activities. Figure 14.1 illustrates the necessary steps.

STEP 1: TAKE CHARGE

Career planning is a self-directed process. Rather than waiting for opportunity to knock, you should take charge. When new employees enter an organization, they are placed not only in a job, but also in an opportunity structure that defines future prospects. A leading executive search adviser estimates that "maybe one out of ten people" has a clear career plan. The rest, he says, "end up tearing themselves up inside, looking for answers on what they want to be and whether they can make it."[1] The result of such poor career planning may be what one human resource manager has termed "a crisis of personal power" that could lead to heart attacks, high blood pressure, and doubts about one's success in life. Careful career planning can help you avoid this trauma. Always remember, no one has your own best interests more in mind than you.

STEP 2: EXAMINE YOUR CAREER ASPIRATIONS

Perhaps the most difficult yet essential step in career planning is to gain an insight into yourself. Deciding what you value will help you to understand your career aspirations. Table 14.1 presents 20 questions to help you know yourself and your career aspirations better. Look these over. Be honest with yourself.

FIGURE 14.1 STEPS IN DEVELOPING A CAREER PLAN

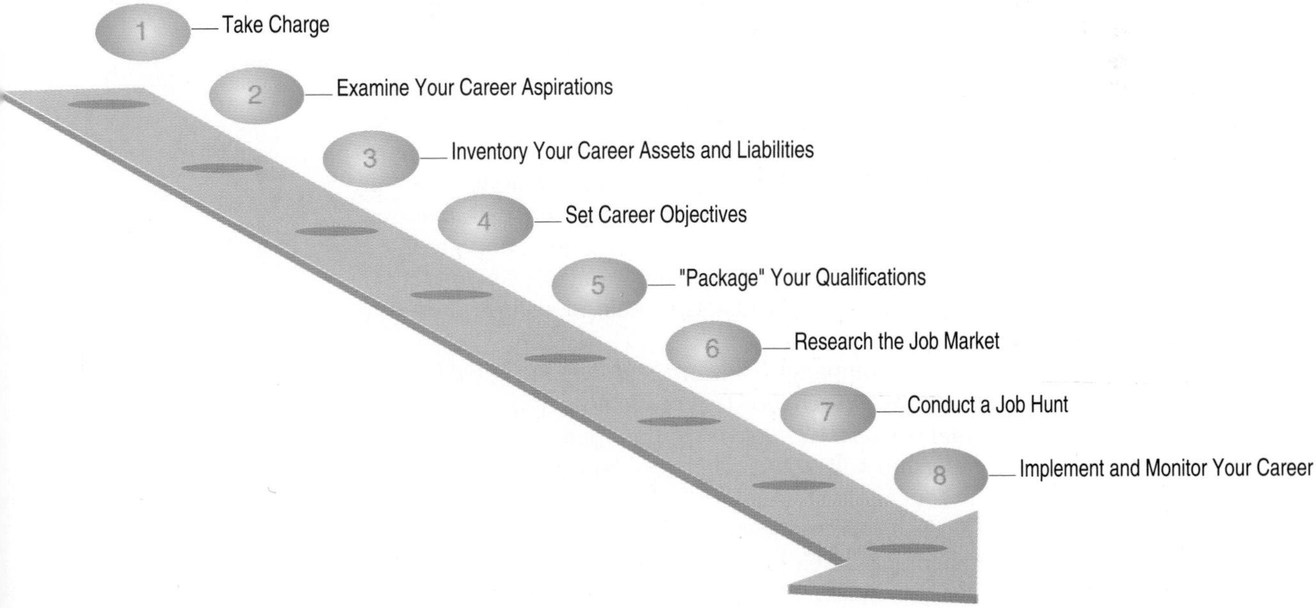

1 — Take Charge
2 — Examine Your Career Aspirations
3 — Inventory Your Career Assets and Liabilities
4 — Set Career Objectives
5 — "Package" Your Qualifications
6 — Research the Job Market
7 — Conduct a Job Hunt
8 — Implement and Monitor Your Career

TABLE 14.1 20 QUESTIONS TO HELP YOU KNOW YOURSELF AND YOUR CAREER ASPIRATIONS

Self-analysis is an indispensable part of career development. Here is a set of questions developed by organization recruiters over the years to help you know yourself and your career aspirations better. They are
also, by the way, questions that an aggressive recruiter is likely to ask you during an unguarded moment in
an interview. Try them on yourself and be frank; don't try to kid yourself. Review these questions about
once every 3 months. They will help you keep an inventory of your career assets and liabilities.

1. Do I work better in a large or small group?
2. How important is geographic location to me? To my family?
3. Am I a loner, or do I work better as a member of a group?
4. Am I more comfortable following than leading?
5. Do I analyze better than I execute?
6. Am I an innovator?
7. Do I work more successfully under pressure?
8. Am I a good planner?
9. Am I a good listener?
10. Do I think well on my feet?
11. Do I express myself well orally? In writing?
12. What characteristics do I admire in others?
13. Which function of my job do I perform most effectively?
14. Which do I perform least effectively?
15. What do I enjoy doing most?
16. In the last 6 months, what accomplishment has most satisfied me?
    Which has been the most difficult?
17. What have I done to correct my shortcomings?
18. What level of responsibility do I aspire to in 5 years?
19. What should I be earning then?
20. How will I achieve these levels?

Source: Robert S. Ankerson, "Marketing a 'New Product,'" *MBA Magazine* 9 (October 1975): 28.

STEP 3: INVENTORY YOUR CAREER ASSETS AND LIABILITIES

Everyone has marketable talents—qualifications developed in previous jobs, while
performing volunteer work, or in pursuing hobbies. One way to identify your qualifications is to think of your six most satisfying accomplishments. These are things
you enjoyed, were proud of, and did well. Write each accomplishment across the
top of a separate sheet of paper and list the various actions you took that contributed to your success. Now identify the qualifications you used, and prepare a
list of the things you have done or skills you possess that would set you apart from
others. You can use these comparative advantages to help in selling yourself to
prospective employers.

   As an illustration, your list of comparative advantages might include *education*
(grades, courses, and knowledge), *experience* (variety, relevance, amount, skills,
and abilities), *personality and personal characteristics* (interpersonal skills, consci-
entious/ambitious, and leadership skills), and *contacts* (business people, bankers,
and professors). Regarding education, more than 50 years of research has yielded
absolutely no correlation between academic success and career success. Attending an elite university is undeniably a helpful first step up the career ladder. However, a person's level of success in school apparently has little bearing on that
person's level of success during the next 40 years.[2]

It may also be helpful to assess your liabilities. Do you panic when you must speak to a group? Are you less assertive than you think you should be? Are you at a loss when it comes to assembling a career-appropriate wardrobe? By facing your weaknesses, you have taken the first step toward remedying them. One way to turn those weaknesses into strengths is to attend adult education classes, seminars, or workshops that address the areas you have targeted for improvement.

STEP 4: SET CAREER OBJECTIVES

Ever since you were small, people probably have been asking you, "What do you want to be when you grow up?" Well, the moment of truth is finally here. What will it be—a firefighter or a nurse? A figure skater or a stockbroker? Once you graduate, you finally will be in a position to begin turning some of those fantasies into realities.

Before launching a job search, you should have a clear idea of what you want. Reviewing your inventory of career assets and liabilities should help to crystallize where you might begin your search. But it also is helpful to consider where you would like your search to end. One way of doing this is to jot down your loftiest ambitions. If all your dreams came true, what would you like to be? President of United Airlines? Head buyer at Bloomingdale's? The next John D. Rockefeller? Don't be afraid to be ambitious, daring, outrageous. Nobody need see this list but you.

Once you have settled on an ultimate goal, begin to work backwards. What positions might you have to hold before reaching the top? One way of envisioning the steps necessary to fulfill your career aspirations is to map them on a chart or graph. In preparing the graph, you may want to establish milestones that will let you know if you are on track and on schedule. If you are just beginning your career, for example, a milestone on your graph might be "division manager by age 32." Some sources suggest developing four or five alternate graphs. The thought required for their preparation will encourage you to investigate optional paths for achieving your career objectives. A sample career graph with two alternative paths is presented in Figure 14.2.

Eventually you should be able to identify an entry-level position that would set you on the path you have chosen. Given the examples we have mentioned, that

FIGURE 14.2 CAREER GRAPH WITH TWO ALTERNATIVE RETAIL CAREER PATHS

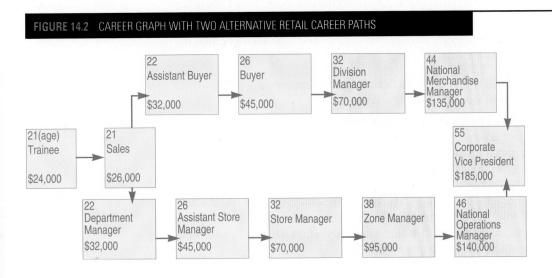

might be an assistant buyer's job at a local department store or a position as a management trainee with an airline. In any given field, there are beginning jobs available to freshly minted graduates who can demonstrate enthusiasm and interest.

STEP 5: "PACKAGE" YOUR QUALIFICATIONS

Now that you have identified the kind of job you are seeking, you must aggressively pursue it using all the skills and contacts you have acquired. You may wish to prepare a cover letter and résumé highlighting your strengths. Before you begin, consider the following:[3]

- A personally addressed cover letter that is one page long and no more than three short paragraphs or less is generally preferred. If you don't know whom you are targeting, call the employer in question and get the person's name. Triple-check the spelling.

- When things are equal between job applicants, qualities such as training and experience and a well-crafted cover letter and résumé can determine who gets interviewed and who doesn't. Microsoft reviews some 12,000 cover letters and résumés a year before selecting some 7,500 job applicants for face-to-face interviews.

- One-half of all résumés are never read because they are disorganized, too long, or too messy. Condense your accomplishments to one or two type-written pages, and then have three people proofread it. It must be letter-perfect, neatly formatted, and on high-quality, neutral-colored paper. An example of a good résumé is presented in Table 14.2. As evident from this example, a résumé should:[4]

1. Invite reading by virtue of its clear layout, top-quality printing, and relevant, concise content, free of extraneous information.
2. Start sentences with action verbs, such as *organized, managed,* and *designed* rather than wordier openings ("I was the person responsible for . . .").
3. Highlight those accomplishments related to future work.
4. Be free of spelling, punctuation, and grammatical errors.
5. Speak the reader's language by using the vocabulary of the industry being targeted.
6. Make a strong statement by presenting nothing less and nothing more than the most relevant information.

- Most employers will spend no more than 2 minutes reading a job applicant's résumé. That is how long you have to sell yourself.

- Your résumé should showcase the qualifications that make you right for a particular job. This may mean preparing four or five résumés, all containing the same basic information, but each emphasizing a different aspect of your qualifications. If, for example, you are intent on a retail career, you may want to prepare two résumés. One might emphasize the impressive results you achieved during your summer job as a magazine sales representative, to get you that first sales-oriented job. The other might highlight your merchandising experience as assistant produce manager in a local supermarket, as a way of demonstrating your ability to handle a job in a buying office.

TABLE 14.2   A SAMPLE RESUMÉ

MICHAEL J. LANE
Campus Address (until June 5, 1992):
2745 Artis Road
St. Louis, Missouri 63167
(314) 821-4030

Home Address:
124 Kimberly Drive
Chicago, Illinois 60600
(312) 476-8765

Job Objective:
Industrial Relations/Human Resource Management Trainee
Available to enter position June 15, 1992

Education:
ST. LOUIS UNIVERSITY, St. Louis, MO
Degree: Bachelor of Business Administration, 1992
Major: Human Resource Management
Areas of Concentration: Labor relations, salary administration, union negotiations, benefits
administration, contract administration, professional training programs

Campus Activities and Honors:
Member, Society for Advancement of Management; President, 1991–1992
Beta Gamma Sigma Business Honorary
Dean's Honor List, 1990–1991, 1991–1992
Alpha Kappa Psi Business Fraternity
Member, University Debate Team, 1990–1992

Achievements:
Organized student negotiation teams for intercampus management conferences, 1990–1991.
Taught evening dorm course in computer programming for management
Served on hospitality committee for Parents Weekend, assisting 650 parent guests
Opened highest number of new charge accounts in 1 month
Maintained a 3.5 GPA in major while working 10–15 hours per week and being involved in
campus activities

Work Experience:
Part-Time Jobs:
Sales clerk, J.C. PENNEY AND COMPANY, 1988–1990
Computer operator, ST. LOUIS UNIVERSITY COMPUTER CENTER, 1990–1992
Summer Jobs:
Sales clerk, J.C. PENNEY AND COMPANY, 1988, 1989
Assistant to store manager, 1990

References: Available upon request.

In short, successful applicants market themselves. A fundamental truth about job hunting is that the most qualified person is not necessarily the person hired. Indeed, whether you are the *best* person for a job isn't the issue. The issue is whether you can convince the people doing the hiring that you are the *right* person for the job.

STEP 6: RESEARCH THE JOB MARKET

Begin by determining what jobs require your qualifications and where those jobs are located. Remember that at this point you are looking for a match between the qualifications you have to offer and a possible first rung on the ladder to the career objective you have set. Interview people who already hold these jobs to learn more about them. Once you have decided which jobs are best suited to your career objectives, investigate specific organizations that employ people in the field in which you are most interested. Request information from their public relations offices. Find out the career opportunities each has available.

At the same time, you should make use of all possible personal connections. This is known as **networking.** It involves using everyone you know (or can get to know) as a source of job information. Family members, friends, professors, and college advisors, parents of classmates, and acquaintances from church/temple and volunteer activities are all potential contacts. So are alumni. Think about beginning your own network immediately through involvement in student and professional groups, as well as attending professional conferences, campus lectures, and job fairs. The opportunities for networking are endless.

If you would like to work for a particular company, your placement office may be able to tell you who from your college or university already works there. Use that contact as a resource person to find out more about the company and if any opportunities are available. Remember, many positions, particularly at the entry level, are never advertised. Indeed, it is estimated that some 95 percent of all jobs are found by word of mouth. This hidden job market consists of jobs never advertised and never listed with agencies. These jobs could be existing openings or those resulting from expansion, upcoming promotions, or transfers.

Networking.
Using personal connections as a source of job information.

STEP 7: CONDUCT A JOB HUNT

To get the job you want, you must take the initiative. You should schedule as many interviews as possible at your college or university placement office. You should attend professional conferences and job fairs that feature placement services. Apply in person and by mail for advertised positions that interest you most. Your initial contact—whether by letter, over the telephone, or in person—should be carefully planned. You should be prepared to explain why you are applying and how your qualifications meet those required for the position.

It has been observed that job hunting bears more than a passing resemblance to courtship. From an organization's perspective, job candidates must be identified, evaluated, and wooed. From a job seeker's perspective, job openings must be identified, evaluated, and won. And like courtship, job hunting is laden with opportunities for missteps by both parties.

Research shows that first impressions are extremely important for both recruiters and job applicants. Recruiters begin making up their minds about applicants within 7 seconds of first meeting them. In turn, applicants' initial impressions are largely based on perceptions of an organization, its products or industry, its geographic location, and its training or advancement opportunities. Recruiters color these impressions in their recruiting efforts.[5]

As noted in Chapter 12, most organizations follow a deliberate procedure in selecting job candidates from available applicants. A mistake, as explained in Chap-

As America's 77 million baby-boomers move closer to retirement, employers search for the best workers the next generation has to offer. Motorola recruiters talk to a prospective applicant at the National Society of Black Engineers job fair in Los Angeles. Job fairs sponsored by professional organizations can be a good starting place for a job hunt.

ter 13, could cost them a considerable sum of money in training expenses and lost salaries. By contrast, a correct decision could help infuse an organization with new vitality and ensure its continued survival. It is up to you to determine whether you are the right person for a specific job. If you think you are, you must make a favorable first impression. The best advice for making a positive initial impression is simple: *Be prepared, be yourself, and be courteous.*[6]

Be prepared means learn all you can about the employers you are interviewing and have a clear idea of what you want to say about yourself. In most cases, you will have about 30 minutes to sell yourself. Practice how you wish to respond to questions such as those listed in Table 14.3 (Panel A). If you are asked a complicated or confusing question in an interview, you should ask for clarification rather than attempt to answer the question you *think* a recruiter is asking. Requesting clarification will not only buy you a few extra seconds to think, but show that you are treating the interview seriously.

If you are asked a potentially unfair preemployment question, concerning, for example, your spouse or children, maintain a dignified and professional demeanor. Remember that how you reply is as important as what you say. Experience suggests that it is best to recognize a recruiter's underlying concern rather than be evasive or confrontational. It is likely that a legitimate job-related requirement is being addressed, such as long hours, deadlines, or travel. If you remain cool, the recruiter will likely be more receptive to your response, and the interview can continue unimpeded.[7]

At the same time, you should have questions such as those listed in Table 14.3 (Panel B) ready for the recruiter. This will show a professional attitude and provide an insight into the interviewing process. Sources such as *Thomas Register of American Manufacturers, Moody's* manuals, *Poor's Register of Corporations, Directors and Executives, Million Dollar Directory, Dun & Bradstreet America's Corporate Families, Billion Dollar Directory,* and company annual reports are excellent starting points for gathering the information you will need to be prepared to ask intelligent

TABLE 14.3   AT THE JOB INTERVIEW

A. Questions Recruiters Ask	B. Questions You Should Ask

A. Questions Recruiters Ask

1. What are your future career plans?
2. In what school activities have you participated? Why? Which did you enjoy the most?
3. Why do you think you might like to work for our company?
4. What jobs have you held? How were they obtained, and why did you leave?
5. Why did you choose your particular field of work?
6. What percentage of your college expenses did you earn? How?
7. How did you spend your vacations while in school?
8. What qualifications do you have that make you feel that you will be successful in your field?
9. What are your ideas on salary?
10. If you were starting college all over again, what courses would you take?
11. Can you forget your education and start from scratch?
12. Do you prefer any specific geographic location? Why?
13. How much money do you hope to earn at age 30? 35?
14. Do you think that your extracurricular activities were worth the time you devoted to them? Why?
15. What is your greatest weakness?

B. Questions You Should Ask

1. What percentage of sales does your company spend on research? (New products spring from research, and your future can be in the test tube.)
2. How many new products has your company introduced in the last 5 years? Tell me about some of them. (Developing new products means the company is alert.)
3. About how many people go through your company's training program each year? (This will give you an idea of the size of your competition for reaching top management.)
4. How does your company make use of employee testing procedures? (Although sometimes resented, testing, when properly administered, can be a valid selection tool that can help you avoid a career mistake.)
5. How often will I be evaluated in my job? (Organizations are finally realizing that the need for employees to know how they are doing is a strong psychological factor.)
6. What is your company's general turnover rate in positions comparable to the one for which I am being considered? (Be sure you're not about to become one more person subject to a revolving-door policy.)
7. What position can someone like myself reasonably expect to hold in your company 2 years from now? (If the answers appear too optimistic, watch out.)
8. Do you enjoy your own job? Would you take any other in your company? (Ask the recruiter about his or her past experience and future directions—the answers can be revealing about a company's development program.)
9. What is your company's record for providing continuous employment? (A record of continuous employment means a company recognizes the irreplaceable value of its human resources.)
10. How frequently do you relocate professional employees? (Transfers often mean promotions, but also require uprooting one's family.)

Source: "Questions Interviewers Ask," adapted with permission from *The Northwestern Lindquist-Endicott Report* published by The Placement Center, Northwestern University, Evanston, IL.

questions about the employer you are interviewing. In addition, your college or university placement office may have booklets and other materials prepared by organizations detailing the career opportunities they offer. Researching an organization and its direction lets a recruiter know you care enough about a prospective job to spend time preparing for an interview. Such preparation can easily make the difference between a mediocre and a successful interview. Table 14.4 identifies the *minimum* information every job applicant should know about an organization.

Be yourself means do not put on false pretenses or overstate your qualifications. Show a sincere interest in the job opening for which you are interviewing. Don't hesitate to show enthusiasm. Try to display a positive self-image of assurance and competence. Above all, try to convey your maturity and stability.

Be courteous means use good manners. An extension of good manners are proper dress and meticulous grooming. Keep your interview outfit and all its accessories in ready condition. If an interview is scheduled unexpectedly, the last thing you will want to worry about is running to the cleaners for a touchup. Conservative styles of dress are generally recommended for both men and women; you will want to look your best and to feel at ease in a professional environment.

It's a good idea to arrive at least 15 minutes early for your interview. This will give you a chance to mentally practice your introduction and possibly size up your competition. You also can use this time to relax. If you're not sure of an interview's location, do a practice run ahead of time. Promptness is essential, and you don't want to arrive out of breath because you couldn't find the right office. Be sure to be friendly to everyone you meet, including secretaries and receptionists. You want to project the image that you would be a welcome co-worker, a pleasant person to

TABLE 14.4 THE MINIMUM INFORMATION EVERY JOB APPLICANT SHOULD KNOW ABOUT AN ORGANIZATION

1. *Organization identification.* Name, address, phone number of home office. Local address and phone number if target job is with a branch or regional office. Name and title of person with whom you will interview.
2. *Organization classification.* Is it a public, private, profit, or not-for-profit organization?
3. *Number of employees.* This provides an idea of an organization's scope of operations and adds to a job applicant's professionalism.
4. *What does the organization do?* Is its main activity production, sales, or service? It may be involved in all three. What brand names, if any, are associated with the organization?
5. *Where is the organization going?* Is it currently showing a profit or loss? Is there expansion on the horizon? What are its stated goals for the future? How do these fit predictions for the future?
6. *Where has the organization been?* Organizations, like people, are best understood by researching their past. Understanding how, why, and by whom an organization was formed is invaluable in identifying its current stage of development. Such understanding is also important in comprehending an organization's culture.
7. *What is the organization's stated philosophy?* Understanding an organization's stated philosophy will enable job applicants to tie their strengths, values, and career goals to those of the organization.
8. *Who owns and runs the organization?* This includes the parent organization, top managers, members of the board of directors, and other people significant to a job applicant's search.

Source: Based on Virginia M. Hall and Joyce A. Wessel, "Researching Possible Employers Doesn't Have to Be a Tedious Task," *Atlanta Journal and Constitution,* January 20, 1985, 45-L.

know. Finally, being courteous means sending a thank-you note to recruiters. At interviews, be sure to request recruiters' business cards so you will have the recruiters' correct name, title, and address. A short typewritten note expressing appreciation for the recruiters' time, restating your interest, and reemphasizing your qualifications will leave a final favorable impression about your professionalism. This simple act puts your name back in front of recruiters in a positive way and gives you the opportunity to add anything overlooked during the interview.

A final bit of advice is to maintain a log noting each interview, when it was held, and your general impressions. Job hunting can be an exciting, challenging experience if approached with confidence and determination. Take advantage of every opportunity to interview because each can be a learning experience, making you a better job candidate. Above all, don't sell yourself short. You've worked hard to earn your degree, and you have more to offer a future employer because of it. Go after the job you want. Others have done it before you and succeeded. So can you.

SMART MANAGEMENT 20 REASONS WHY JOB APPLICANTS AREN'T HIRED

To learn why job applicants aren't hired, Northwestern University's former placement director, Frank S. Endicott, surveyed 153 human resource managers. The following, listed in order of importance, are the most common reasons managers cited for not hiring a job applicant.

1. Poor personal appearance
2. Overaggressiveness
3. Inability to express information clearly
4. Lack of interest and enthusiasm
5. Lack of career planning; no purpose and no goals
6. Nervous, lack of confidence and poise
7. Overemphasis on money
8. Unwillingness to start at the bottom
9. Makes excuses
10. Lack of tact and courtesy
11. Immaturity
12. Condemns past employers
13. No genuine interest in company or job
14. Fails to look interviewer in the eye
15. Sloppy application form
16. Little sense of humor
17. Arrives late for interview
18. Fails to express appreciation for recruiter's time
19. Fails to ask questions about the employer and job
20. Vague responses to questions

Source: *The Northwestern Lindquist-Endicott Report,* published by The Placement Center, Northwestern University, Evanston, IL. Reprinted with permission.

STEP 8: IMPLEMENT AND MONITOR YOUR CAREER

After you have found the job that is right as a first step in meeting your career objectives, you must continue to implement your career plan and begin to monitor your career success. Some organizations offer programs to help their employees to develop their careers. Warner-Lambert, for example, offers a 2-day program titled "Managing Your Career." Sessions examine a variety of topics, including employee values, allowing employees to better match their personal and professional goals with career opportunities within the company. Additionally, top managers serve on panels where they discuss their jobs and career experiences. 3M has an entire department devoted to meeting individual career needs. Its Career Resources Department provides services in three functional areas: career development, career transition, and career information systems.

To complement formal career planning programs, some organizations assign employees, formally or informally, to a higher level manager for personal advice, counseling, and role modeling. This is known as **mentoring** and may involve an occasional after-hours conference, special assignments, development projects, and simple, daily one-on-one discussions of career plans. A mentor-protégé relationship with a successful, experienced employee can be an invaluable benefit to the lower level manager. Indeed, research suggests that employees are more satisfied in their work and progress faster in their careers when they are assigned a mentor than when they are not. Research also suggests that mentoring is particularly helpful in furthering the careers of women and minorities. Indeed, the lack of mentoring relationships is believed to be a major cause of disparity in advancement between men and both women and minorities.[8]

It is also important to monitor your progress in achieving the actions necessary to reach your career objectives. A word of caution: Don't become inflexible. It is estimated that each rung up the career ladder offers 30 percent fewer jobs than the step below. At some point it may become necessary to reassess your career aspirations in light of changes in career opportunities and your personal qualifications. Indeed, you are likely to reach a point in your career when further advancement is unlikely or impossible. This is a **career plateau.** For some, this is a career shock of major magnitude, resulting in agonizing soul-searching. For others, it is a relaxing time when family and friends emerge as the most important thing in their lives.

Career success is typically the result of hard work with perhaps a touch of luck. It demands more than just a desire to "play the game." It requires a complete plan to win. Effective career planning is much like success in chess. The ultimate champion is the one who visualizes potential opportunities and pitfalls and plans each move in advance. The following are selected guidelines for playing "success chess":[9]

Mentoring.
An arrangement whereby a higher level manager acts as an adviser, counselor, and role-model for a lower level employee.

Career plateau.
A point in someone's career when further advancement is unlikely or impossible.

1. Maintain the largest number of job options possible.
2. Do not waste time working for a superior who is unlikely to be promoted.
3. Become a crucial subordinate to an upwardly mobile superior.
4. Always favor increased exposure and visibility.
5. Be prepared to nominate yourself for open jobs. An organization is a market of jobs.
6. Leave an organization when your career slows.
7. Do not hesitate to rehearse quitting. It is a crucial act.
8. Do not let success in your present job preempt your career plan. You will stop moving up.

SPECIAL CAREER CHALLENGES

INITIAL PRESSURES

The first months on a new job can often determine the prospects for an employee's future job success. Because this initial period of adjustment is so critical, it is important to be aware of the feelings and pressures you are likely to experience when beginning a new job. These feelings are common both to new graduates and experienced managers. Understanding the reasons for these pressures may help put them in perspective and make this transitional period less trying.

Anxiety

It is not unusual, as noted in Chapter 13, for new employees to be anxious about their ability to perform as expected.[10] Indeed, it is quite normal for new employees to experience a "free-floating anxiety"—that is, anxiety without a known, specific cause. Experience suggests that it takes anywhere from 3 to 6 months for new employees to feel "at home." To minimize this transition period, it pays to ask questions. Don't be afraid to request detailed directions from your boss for fear of being considered unresourceful. It is much better to ask questions and learn to do a job correctly than to perform poorly because you are unsure of what is expected. Remember, too, you don't always have to ask your boss for assistance. Often a peer or subordinate can help.

Be sure to accept early assignments without complaint. It is important to establish from the beginning that you are flexible and cooperative. Note, however, that being flexible and cooperative does not mean being passive. Take cues from your peers. Is participation at department meetings encouraged? Are informal suggestions welcomed by your boss?

By participating as fully as possible, you will show that you fit into your new work group. At the same time, it is also important to participate socially. Don't isolate yourself by drinking coffee at your desk and brown bagging it at lunchtime. Meet everyone you can in your department and even the entire organization. If appropriate, ask co-workers to lunch. Seek their advice about community services. Attend company-sponsored seminars, join the softball or bowling team, or volunteer to collect for the United Way. All are good ways to know and become known, thereby reducing the anxiety common to a new job.

Unrealistic Job Expectations

A second career pressure that may affect new graduates, as well as more experienced job changers, is a condition often termed *reality shock*. New managers, especially recent graduates, often have unrealistic job expectations. Business school graduates, for instance, are trained to think like managers and to solve complex problems. On taking their first job, they expect to find the same level of challenge and to wield authority equal to the artificial authority they had in class. They also have high expectations about how quickly they will be able to scale the ladder to success. The reality, however, is that this usually takes years, not months, to achieve. This problem is compounded by a difference in time horizons. As recent students, many new managers are accustomed to almost immediate gratification and limited time spans—10- to 15-week school terms, an academic year, 4 years to graduate.

Of course, a permanent job is quite different. There are no predetermined time horizons, fewer events mark the passing seasons, and a full year's employment is required for a 2-week vacation. Thus, if your first job finds you assigned to a routine set of duties with little or no exposure to major decisions and an indifferent boss who may "review your progress" only annually (if that often) and on unknown criteria, do not be surprised if you develop an acute case of restlessness.

If your initial expectations have not been met, don't sulk. Speak up before your disenchantment affects your work. Your boss may not know a problem exists. Realize, too, that some organizations, burned in the past by the quick departure of self-proclaimed hotshots, like to season new employees for a year or two before considering them for the fast track. Various organizations have different philosophies when it comes to developing new employees.

JOB-RELATED STRESS

With their heavy emphasis on career winners and losers, organizations of all types exact a high personal price. This price is increased by the unrelenting pressure for high performance that exists in many organizations and the seemingly ceaseless urgency to accomplish more and more. As we have explored career success in this chapter, we have learned that managers live in a competitive world with intense rivalry for position and power. Those who lose the competitive struggle for position and power may feel defeated and defenseless.

At Southern California Edison Company's health-care center, staff physician Dr. Carol Peebles oversees a treadmill test. Southern California Edison encourages employees to maintain healthy lifestyles, promoting exercise, relaxation, and stress management through use of the center.

At least 45 percent of all U.S. managers suffer from excessive stress. Such stress is so common at Citibank that it has installed blood pressure monitors for its employees. Those showing signs of hypertension are provided medical assistance. The annual cost to business of stress-related problems is estimated at $150 billion in medical insurance, disability claims, lost productivity, and other expenses.[11]

Stress is the body's total response to any stimulus. Most normal activities—a game of chess or a passionate kiss—produce stress without causing harmful effects. Damaging stress—or distress—occurs when we undergo what is termed the "fight or flight response." In prehistoric times, stress was the caveman's response to danger. When faced with danger, he instinctively prepared either to stand his ground or to run. In today's world, no one can avoid unpleasant stress any more than the caveman. However, there are differences. Our adrenaline flows, our heart pounds, our breathing quickens, and our muscles go tense, just as his did. But we generally do not attack or run. As a consequence, an imbalance is likely to exist between demand and capacity as pressure builds. To the extent such a condition prompts a person to devise creative solutions, stress can be quite positive. It even may be regarded as a valued impetus to goal accomplishment.

Often, however, stress is not used positively. Research has linked excessive stress to a host of maladies. Consider the following partial list of problems that are either caused or aggravated by negative stress:

Stress.
The body's total response to any stimulus.

- Alcoholism
- Anxiety
- Arthritis
- Bronchial asthma
- Cancer
- Chest and neck pains
- Colitis or ulcerative colitis
- Depression
- Dermatitis
- Diarrhea
- Drug abuse
- Family abuse
- Fatigue
- Headaches
- Hypertension
- Insomnia
- Irregular heartbeat
- Peptic ulcers
- Sexual impotence
- Suicide
- Swollen glands
- Uncontrollable rage

In the workplace, excessive stress has been tied to absenteeism, inactivity, job dissatisfaction, increased accidents, tardiness, antagonism, turnover, and poor decisions. Common causes of on-the-job stress include tight deadlines, job insecurity, lack of a clear job description, imbalance between authority and responsibility, poor relations with colleagues, unpleasant environmental conditions (cigarette smoke and other air pollution, crowding, noise, exposure to chemicals), commuting difficulties, and the "FUD Factor" (fear, uncertainty, and doubt). Experts estimate that some 15 percent of all managers suffer from levels of stress that will ultimately affect their job performance.[12] Table 14.5 presents a questionnaire for assessing your own level of stress. Take the time to consider your likely behavior in the described situations.

Although stress is unavoidable, there are ways to manage it:[13]

CLOSE UP: INTERNATIONAL MANAGEMENT OVERWORK CAN BE FATAL: THE JAPANESE WAY

Overwork is a widespread condition in Japan. More and more commentators speak of it as one of the little-discussed keys to Japan's post-World War II "economic miracle." It is generally believed that at least tens of thousands of Japanese become seriously ill from overwork every year. Possibly thousands die. Death from overwork even has its own name, *karaski.* This is the other reality behind the economic success of Japan.

Underlying this problem is a set of on-the-job norms that demand an ethic of self-sacrifice far beyond the workaholism seen in Europe and North America. Japanese white-collar workers seldom have two-day weekends and commonly have to spend two or more hours a day standing on stifling crowded commuter trains. Employers often demand that they arrive for work early to sing songs and do calisthenics with fellow-workers, to instill the sense of teamwork and discipline that many managers think keeps production flowing.

The work culture of self-sacrifice has produced an environment in which millions of Japanese refuse to take as many as half of their paid vacation days in fear that work would pile up in their absence or that colleagues who didn't take their vacations would get ahead of them or look down on them.

Employees routinely falsify their time sheets to keep them in line with legal limits. Even in recorded time, the average Japanese worker puts in 2,150 hours annually, the average American worker 1,924, and the average French worker 1,643. At the French pace, the average Japanese worker annually puts in what amounts to an additional three months of work.

Source: Adapted from John E. Woodruff, "Overwork Becoming Widespread Condition Among Japanese," *Sunday Advocate* (Baton Rouge), January 13, 1991: 4E.

- *Control the situation.* Do your own stress audit by listing the things that bother you. Which of them can you do something about? Concentrate your time and talent on those and try to avoid the others.

- *Open up to others.* Freely discuss your problems, fears, frustrations, and sources of anxiety with those who care about you. When in doubt, smile! A sincere smile often can defuse tension and build a bridge of goodwill.

- *Pace yourself.* Allow for a certain amount of flexibility in your day's schedule. Don't try to do two or more things at the same time. Counter unproductive haste by forcing yourself to slow down. Stop and think before reacting rashly to negative situations or people. Try to live on a day-to-day basis, rather than on a minute-to-minute basis.

- *Exercise and relax.* Regularly engage in some form of healthy relaxation—transcendental meditation, yoga, a hobby—or a noncompetitive sport—walking, jogging, swimming, cycling, or aerobic dancing. If you prefer competitive sports, such as tennis, handball, or racquetball, remember that the point of such exercise is to have fun—not necessarily to win. If you have any doubts about your physical condition for such activities, you should, of course, see your doctor first.

DUAL-CAREER COUPLES

Just as the stresses of an individual's work life can cause personal discontentment, so too can factors in an individual's personal life affect how he or she performs at

TABLE 14.5   DO-IT-YOURSELF STRESS TEST

Circle the response alternative that best describes your likely behavior in each of the following situations.

1. When playing a competitive sport, do you
   a. Find yourself wasting energy through tension?
   b. Assume you will do well and throw yourself into the game without much worry?
   c. Worry about how your performance may be viewed?
   d. Need to win at all costs and suffer profound disappointment if you don't?
2. When driving in heavy traffic, do you
   a. Remain calm, alert, and relaxed?
   b. Find your heart beating faster and feel irritated?
   c. Find yourself getting actively angry with other motorists and want them to get out of your way?
   d. Become tired and worried about wasted time?
3. When meeting new people at work or a social event, do you
   a. Feel relaxed and face the meeting with a sense of excitement?
   b. Become tense, find your heart pounding?
   c. Worry about what they will think about you?
   d. Find yourself becoming bored and listless?
4. When you wake up in the morning, do you feel
   a. Alert and happy, looking forward to the day ahead?
   b. Anxious, with lots of different thoughts about what you have to do?
   c. Hoping desperately that the day ahead will hold something of interest to you?
   d. Not too bad, but resigned to the fact that each day is much like any other?
5. When demanding what you want from a colleague, friend, or marriage partner, do you
   a. Feel it is too much of an effort to pursue your demands?
   b. Try to convince yourself that you shouldn't feel too strongly about anything?
   c. Insist that this is what you are going to have or do, without regard for others?
   d. Enter into the confrontation eager to state your side of things but also listen to the other's side, relatively confident the two of you can come to a mutual agreement?
6. When planning a piece of work or organizing a fairly complex event at work or home, do you usually
   a. Easily and quietly gather together all the necessary materials and facts and proceed to sort them out?
   b. Find it difficult to get started?
   c. Become tense and uncomfortable, unsure that you will be able to handle it all?
   d. Treat it all as a matter of course, preparing yourself well and then carrying it out?
7. When having to deal with children's questions and difficulties, do you
   a. Become irritable?
   b. Find yourself bored and uninterested?
   c. Dismiss them as fast and curtly as possible?
   d. Listen wholeheartedly and then do everything possible to help them handle the problem effectively?
8. When a child does something you don't like, do you
   a. Calmly tell him how you prefer him to behave?
   b. Find it hard to summon up the energy to do anything?
   c. Feel confused and at a loss about what you should do?
   d. Find your temper rising and fly off the handle easily?
9. When after a long day you get in bed ready to go to sleep, do you find
   a. Thoughts keep racing through your head?
   b. You can relax and drift off easily?
   c. You turn and have trouble relaxing?
   d. You don't feel tired?
10. Do you feel you respond effectively to challenges
    a. Almost always?
    b. Rarely?
    c. Usually?
    d. Almost never?

Continued on next page.

TABLE 14.5 *continued*

11. Do you smoke
    a. Not ever?
    b. Fewer than ten cigarettes each day?
    c. Fewer than 20 cigarettes each day?
    d. More than 20 cigarettes each day?

12. Is your alcohol intake
    a. Frequent (every day) and heavy (more than three mixed drinks)?
    b. Frequent but not heavy?
    c. Occasional, not more than 3 days a week?
    d. Light, only the rarest glass of something?

To compute your stress score, total the values assigned to your individual item responses.

Item	Response			
	A	B	C	D
1	−2	+5	−1	+4
2	+5	−1	−4	−3
3	+5	−4	−2	−1
4	+5	−3	−2	−1
5	−2	−1	−4	+5
6	+4	−1	−3	+5
7	−4	−1	−3	+5
8	+5	−1	−2	−4
9	−4	+5	−2	−1
10	+5	−2	+3	−4
11	+5	+2	+1	−4
12	−4	−2	+1	+5

What Your Score Means

- If you scored more than 58, you are wonderfully free of excess stress and cope very well with day-to-day challenges. Congratulations!
- If you scored between 26 and 57, you are above average in being free of excessive stress.
- If you scored between 7 and 25, your stress load is too much although you are still within the "safe" zone, provided you don't have to face too many serious changes in your life all at once.
- If you scored below 7, you are definitely overstressed. You should take steps to improve your resistance to what could become prolonged strain.

Source: Adapted from Thomas S. Bateman and Robert C. Dailey, "Attacking Job Stress," *Louisiana Business Survey* 11 (October 1980), 6–7. Used with permission.

work. An increasingly arising problem is the need to balance life-style and career to accommodate a spouse's career.

The U.S. Department of Labor predicts that by 1995, 81 percent of all marriages will be dual-career partnerships. Although many dual-career couples have lives that are stimulating, exciting, and financially rewarding, they also face some formidable challenges. If, for example, their career opportunities clash, which career is to be given priority? One study of 815 dual-career couples found that 40 percent of the men surveyed had moved for their jobs, versus only 21 percent of the women. Such statistics may lead organizations to argue that it is wasteful to train a woman and then be unable to promote her because she won't move to take the new job.[14]

Time management also becomes a critical issue to two people leading lives in the fast track. For couples whose jobs require long hours and frequent travel, scheduling time together may resemble trying to book a flight to Florida during spring break. What at first may seem an amusing dilemma quickly loses its charm.

But all these issues pale next to the central dilemma faced by most dual-career couples: to have or not to have a child. For people accustomed to having a great deal of control over their lives, the upheaval posed by the prospect of children can be unsettling. This is especially true as a woman's biological clock forces a couple to face the issue at just about the time the woman is making great strides in her career. It has been suggested that employers should establish different career tracks to nurture two separate groups of women.[15] High-potential "career-primary" women, the first group, would put their careers ahead of all else. They would make a conscious decision to largely sacrifice their personal lives for maximum professional development. Most would remain single or childless, or, if they do have children, be content with others rearing them. "Career-and-family" women, the second group, would follow a so-called "mommy track." They would be high-performing women who wish to have children and are willing to trade off some career growth and compensation to do so. At certain times, they would be dedicated to their family and other times to their career.

Faith Wohl, Du Pont's Director of Work Force Partnering, has pushed her company to set up day-care centers near its major work sites around the country. Wohl's job is to listen to needs, especially personal and social concerns, and create company programs to meet those needs.

The notion of separating women into two separate groups, only one of which is likely to make it to the top, upsets some critics. They feel that fathers should assume more responsibility for home and children and recommend instead either a "daddy track" or "parent track." In any instance, the current reality is that, when faced with a choice between pursuing the fast track at work and raising a family, many women will choose the latter. Employers, in turn, will have to either devise flexible working arrangements for them or lose them. Beyond the human reasons for providing such arrangements, there is an equally compelling economic reason. Women are a very important part of our nation's human capital.

A growing number of employers are rising to this challenge by changing their human resource practices in consideration of the increasing number of dual-career couples. Du Pont, for example, has a "director of work force partnering," one of a new group of specialists known as "work-family coordinators." Some of the changes that will be necessary for employers to become more "family-friendly" include:

1. The modification of nepotism rules prohibiting the employment of two members from the same immediate family.

2. A willingness to expand special services, including dual-career counseling, child-care options, parental leave, and family-care leave-of-absence programs.

3. The development of clear conflict-of-interest rules that apply to dual-career couples who work for competitors.

4. The adjustment of employee benefit programs to avoid unnecessary duplication between partners.

5. Sensitive recruiting and a willingness to help find a position for both partners.

6. A willingness to schedule career changes, transfers, and promotions flexibly in consideration of both partners' needs.

7. Restrictions on the amount of required travel.

8. Workplace flexibility, including flex-time schedules, telecommuting, compressed workweeks, part-time work, and job sharing.

Companies have found that assisting employees with their family commitments reduces turnover and fosters company loyalty. Genentech's 2nd Generation is a child development and daycare center for employees' infants, toddlers, and preschoolers. It is located a few blocks from the company's offices and labs.

Source: Courtesy of Genentech, Inc.

It appears reasonable to believe that just as dual-career couples are learning to adapt, so will many more employers. There seems to be little question that, unless employers acknowledge the special nature of dual-career couples as a unique employee group, they will lose the services of some extremely talented people.

The Midlife Crisis

For many persons, the period between the mid-30s and late-40s is an unstable, troubled time. Since we spend most of our waking hours at work, this condition sometimes manifests itself there more than at home. It is important for managers to understand **midlife crisis** because it will help them appreciate a time in their peers' lives, their spouse's life, and a period they will likely experience themselves.

The great Italian poet Dante wrote, "Midway on the path of life I found myself in a dark woods." He expressed the midlife crisis well. Studies indicate that almost everyone experiences midlife crisis. Although part of the difficulties encountered during this time result from aging, research suggests there also are complex underlying psychological forces involved. These seem to manifest themselves as individuals begin to realize that they are inevitably on a descending path and the reality of life does not always measure up to one's dreams.[16]

Midlife crisis.
An unstable and troubled period in many persons' lives occurring between their mid-30s and late-40s.

What is midlife crisis like? In a word, *depression*. This does not mean merely "feeling down"; this depression may lead to insomnia and vulnerability to illness. In the more serious cases, it can lead to abandonment of one's career, alcoholism, mental illness, marital difficulties, divorce, and suicide. Midlife crisis is likely to be most serious when a person is under job stress or experiencing problems at home. Even those individuals who undergo a mild midlife crisis lasting for a few months may have trouble concentrating on their work and be unable to find meaning in their jobs or life itself.

How does midlife crisis beset its victims? Four factors seem to come together at this time. Each can set off the crisis, and each reinforces the others to make it worse.

1. *Personal problems*. At age 40 a person is likely halfway through life. The future is no longer of unlimited duration. For the first time, life may be viewed in terms of time left to live rather than time since birth. This sense of the loss of youth often is reinforced by the death of one's parents. Additionally, one's children may begin to leave home and marital problems may develop. Aging has set in: Vision becomes less sharp, hair grays and thins, weight is hard to lose, and sexual activity declines. A person recognizes that he or she has stopped growing up and begun to grow old. From here on, it seems everything is downhill. In short, the fact of human mortality becomes abundantly clear.

2. *Broken dreams*. Most of us, but especially managers with a high need for achievement, have dreams of reaching certain job, status, and money goals. Rarely, however, are these dreams completely met. The more ambitious a person is, the higher his or her goals and the harder it is to reach them. Around 40, many managers suddenly realize that they "didn't make it." Feelings of failure arise and they ask, "What's the use?" These feelings are compounded when they compare themselves to the few people who have achieved much more, a very unfavorable comparison indeed.

3. *Broken relationships*. Many managers receive help during their early years from a mentor. This relationship tends to be broken at the midlife stage because the mentor is older and less influential, or perhaps retired. It also may be broken when a manager decides that "it's time I grow up and achieve on my own." This break has even been compared by psychiatrists with the break from one's parents. Thus, midlife crisis may be considered a second painful adolescence.

4. *Increased competition*. Job competition seems especially tough at the midlife stage. Everyone may seem to be after a manager's job. There is often a terrible feeling of rivalry, a feeling that one has no friends and must constantly defend oneself and one's job. In many situations this may be compounded by a deepening concern about the obsolescence of one's technical skills, especially when compared with younger managers. This concern can be especially heightened by the naming of a young president. If the president is 38 and you are 42, what future do you have?

The first step toward overcoming midlife crisis is awareness. This should be coupled with a realization that, for the majority who survive (and a majority do), although life (and work) is different, it is not over. After Dante went through the "dark woods," he wrote his masterpiece, *The Divine Comedy*. In a few fields (notably the sciences) major contributions are typically made before age 40. But in most jobs, including management, a person's highest output often comes later in life.

Individual organizations can help employees overcome midlife crisis by offering career counseling programs. One's spouse and friends also can help. This is a time when an individual's personal life should be enriched by "renegotiating" and renewing one's marriage and developing new and closer friendships. Almost all research indicates that we survive life's traumas better with friends. People without friends may literally die of loneliness—sometimes immediately, but in most cases a little at a time.

Midlife crisis can be serious. However, by following the right steps it can be conquered, and an individual can go on to a rewarding life.

SUMMARY

In this chapter we considered how to build a successful career and discussed various challenges and crises that affect a great many managers. We emphasized that finding the right job—especially the right first job—is a skill.

Learning Objective 1:   List the steps in developing a career plan.
At least eight steps are necessary for developing a career plan: (1) take charge, (2) examine your career aspirations, (3) inventory your career assets and liabilities, (4) set career objectives, (5) "package" your qualifications, (6) research the job market, (7) conduct a job hunt, and (8) implement and monitor your career.

Learning Objective 2:   Explain what is meant by *networking*.
Networking involves using everyone a person knows (or can get to know) as a source of job information.

Learning Objective 3:   Know what is meant by *mentoring*.
Mentoring is an arrangement whereby a higher level manager acts as an adviser, counselor, and role-model for a lower level employee.

Learning Objective 4:   Outline guidelines for playing "success chess."
Selected guidelines for playing "success chess" are (1) maintain the largest number of job options possible, (2) do not waste time working for a superior who is unlikely to be promoted, (3) become a crucial subordinate to an upwardly mobile superior, (4) always favor increased exposure and visibility, (5) be prepared to nominate yourself for open jobs, (6) leave an organization when your career slows, (7) do not hesitate to rehearse quitting, and (8) do not let success in your present job preempt your career plan.

Learning Objective 5:   Recognize the pressures faced by new managers.
New managers are likely to encounter a number of pressures. An understanding of these pressures will help put them in perspective and make this transitional period less trying. Among the most common sources of pressure are anxieties about one's ability to perform as expected and unrealistic job expectations.

Learning Objective 6:   Describe the impact of job-related stress.
Excessive job-related stress can have a strong negative impact on individual performance and thus on achieving organization objectives. Aside from diminished performance, research has linked stress to a host of maladies, such as alcoholism,

cancer, dermatitis, and insomnia. The consequences of job-related stress are easy to predict. They include absenteeism, inactivity, job dissatisfaction, increased accidents, tardiness, antagonism, turnover, and poor decisions.

Learning Objective 7: Appreciate the challenges faced by dual-career couples.
Dual-career couples face many challenges, including resolving career opportunity clashes, managing time effectively, fulfilling family responsibilities, and overcoming disadvantageous staffing and human resource management policies.

Learning Objective 8: Answer the question, "What is midlife crisis like?"
What is midlife crisis like? In a word, *depression*. This does not mean merely "feeling down"; this depression may lead to insomnia and vulnerability to illnesses. In the more serious cases it can lead to abandonment of one's career, alcoholism, mental illness, marital difficulties, divorce, and suicide. Midlife crisis is likely to be most serious when a person is under job stress or experiencing problems at home. Even those individuals who undergo mild midlife crisis may have trouble concentrating on their work and be unable to find meaning in their jobs or life itself.

KEY TERMS

career 406

career plateau 417

mentoring 417

midlife crisis 425

networking 412

stress 420

THE MANAGEMENT EXPERIENCE WHERE ARE YOU IN YOUR JOB SEARCH? A SELF-ADMINISTERED CHECKLIST

This checklist is designed to help you find where you may be off target in your job search. The way you answer the following questions may yield some important clues. Answer each question "Yes" or "No." Then tally your "Yes" answers at the end of the form and discuss the results with your placement office adviser.

I. What You Know about Yourself and Your Preferences
1. Can you clearly state your career goals? _____
2. Can you explain why you chose your major? _____
3. Can you describe your greatest strength? _____
   Your greatest weakness? _____
4. Can you name the work activities you do most well and most enjoy? How about nonwork activities? _____
5. Can you list at least five job skills and abilities you have?_____
6. For each of your most important job-related experiences, can you list:
   a. Five things you did? _____
   b. Five things you learned? _____
   c. Several contributions you made or things you accomplished? _____
7. Have you clearly defined your geographical preferences and limitations?_____
8. Have you determined the salary range you will consider?_____

II. What You Know about Employers
9. Can you name at least three fields of employment into which you might fit?
   _____

Continued on next page.

10. Can you name at least 10 kinds of employers that might hire a person with your background? _____
11. Can you name at least 10 position titles that might fit you? _____
12. Do you know four or five resources to help you find answers to Questions 9, 10, and 11 above? _____
13. Can you name at least four sources or information that could help you discover potential employers in a particular geographical area? _____
14. In the last month, have you talked to at least three people who are employed in your field of interest with the purpose of learning more about what they do? _____
15. Can you name at least five employers to whom you have applied for work in the last 2 weeks? _____
16. Are any of these employers curious as to how your abilities, skills, and knowledge could help their organization? _____

III. Your Job Seeking Contacts to Employers

17. Do you rely on advertised job vacancy listings as your major source of job leads? _____
18. Have you prepared a résumé with which you are satisfied? _____
19. Have you asked anyone for feedback on your résumé? _____
20. Have you asked employers for feedback on your résumé? _____
21. When you apply to an employer, do you send your résumé to the human resource management office? _____
22. Are you familiar with the management structure, management, goods/services of the employers to whom you are applying? _____
23. Do you know the questions employers are likely to ask you in an interview? _____
24. Can you clearly state why you are interested in working for each employer to whom you apply? _____
25. Have you used any of the following methods to prepare for an interview:
    a. Role-playing with a friend or relative? _____
    b. Writing out answers to common interview questions? _____
    c. Role-playing by yourself in front of a mirror? _____
    d. Reading manuals and using services offered by your placement office? _____

Add up your "Yes" answers for each section and enter them below:

Section I—Yourself _____

Section II—Employers _____

Section III—Contacts _____

What Your Score Means

Score:

26–31 On the right track. Keep up the good work!

11–25 Close. Why not discuss these results with your placement office adviser?

0–10 Definitely discuss these results with your placement office adviser.

Source: From the *Placement Manual*, a career planning and placement resource for college seniors used at 115 universities, University Communications, Inc. Rahway, NJ 07065. Reprinted with permission.

REVIEW AND DISCUSSION QUESTIONS

1. As a prospective job hunter, describe how you would prepare for a job interview at your college or university placement office.

2. Select a *Fortune* 500 company. Visit your college or university library and prepare a one-page summary of information about the company from sources such as *Moody's Industrial Manual* or *Moody's Handbook of Common Stocks*.

3. Given your career objectives, prepare a list of questions to ask a campus recruiter.

4. One prominent university placement director advises that college students regard campus recruiters the same way they would regard army recruiting sergeants—that is, with some cynicism about the rosy picture a recruiter might paint. He observes, however, that few do. Acknowledging that some campus recruiters do exaggerate the attractiveness of open positions, how do you plan to avoid so-called reality shock resulting from unrealistic job expectations?

5. In drawing a profile of a typical prime prospect for a CEO's job, Russell Reynolds Associates, an executive search firm, lists nine attributes: "an advanced degree, profit and loss experience, steady progress through the operating ranks with an occasional detour to the staff, some background in international business, excellent communication skills, a vision that can be imparted to others, self-confidence, the ability to take risks without undue worry, and high integrity."[17] How can you take charge of your career to acquire these attributes?

6. Explain how you would go about developing a career plan. In doing so, prepare an inventory of your assets and liabilities.

7. In responding to a *Financial Times* reporter's question about why she quit her $180,000-a-year job as a bond trader with the Bank of America in London to become a $7,200-a-year nursery school teacher, Soo Pickett answered: "My adrenaline gland has disappeared. I no longer blow my car horn in frustration whenever I'm wasting time. I'm actually meeting people with normal jobs in the outside world."[18] What are some of the job-related stresses a bond trader might encounter?

8. Outline a personal plan for coping with job-related stress.

9. Interview a dual-career couple and prepare a one-page summary of the special challenges they face.

10. John Z. DeLorean was one of the more interesting mystery stories of the automobile industry. At age 40 he became the youngest general manager in Pontiac's history. Some 8 years later, he resigned from General Motors (GM) to found the ultimately ill-fated DeLorean Motor Co. For a person of DeLorean's drive, midlife crisis was a particularly trying experience. Gail Sheehy describes this crisis in her best-selling book *Passages: Predictable Crises of Adult Life.*[19] After reading the following excerpt, comment on DeLorean's behavior.

    > As the midlife crisis closed in, DeLorean grew more frenzied about making external changes. He tightened the pressure on dealers and drove up sales, hoisted heavier weights, raced more motorcycles, divested himself of a wife his own age, lifted his face, dyed his hair, turned up in discotheques with bosomy film stars, turned around the failing Chevrolet division in a virtuoso performance, and took a wife younger than

most GM officers' daughters. Having retooled the whole package, he adopted a son, his first child. Still he ran, pausing only for a few moments at dawn to see the boy before he left for marathon days of work. Soon enough, lonely and shunned by the older wives of Detroit, his beautiful child bride fled back home to California. . . .

Plunging deep into his second adolescence, he entered a sexual olympics of dating and discarding name beauties. He called up the Max Factor cover girl, a model half his age, and by May had taken her for his third wife. Three weeks later, he walked out on GM. In what would seem another projection of fears he was fighting in himself, he announced, "The automobile business has lost its masculinity."

CASE 14.1 A TALK WITH KIRKEBY'S SON

"Did you want to see me?" Brad Kirkeby poked his head into the open doorway of his boss's office.

"Sure did, Brad. Come on in. I'll be finished with these overtime authorizations in a minute." Anthony Carboni continued initialing time cards while Kirkeby came in and sat down. Putting the cards in a neat stack to one side of his desk, Carboni looked up and smiled.

"Well, Brad, how's it going?"

"Boring as heck!"

Carboni retained his composure. He cared little for the disrespectfulness of so many young people and their total lack of tact. But Carboni had two reasons for restraint in this case. First, Brad Kirkeby was recently out of college and on an 18-month company rotational training program. He would be in Carboni's section for only another 45 days. Second, Brad was the son of Lawrence Kirkeby, one of Lockport Aircraft's most capable designers.

"I'm sorry to hear that," replied Carboni. "What seems to be the problem?"

"I'm going out of my mind with blueprint check." Kirkeby's response was emphatic but not hostile.

"Well," said Carboni, "someone has to check blueprints."

"But why me?" replied Kirkeby. "Can't a draftsman or a clerk do it?"

"Oh, I suppose he could," said Carboni, "but this is the way we've always developed potential structure designers . . . by having them learn all phases of the business from the bottom up."

"No disrespect intended, Mr. Carboni, but that argument escapes me. It's like saying that if you want to be an actor, you have to have experience as

a stagehand. I joined Lockport Aircraft to design airplanes, not to check blueprints."

"And so you will, Brad . . . eventually."

Kirkeby laughed. " 'Eventually . . . in time, Brad . . . wait your turn, Brad.' In the long run it will all work out. Mr. Carboni, do you know what Lord Keynes, the famous British economist, said about the long run?"

"No," replied Carboni, growing less patient each moment.

"Lord Keynes said, 'In the long run we'll all be dead!'"

"Meaning?"

"Meaning that I don't want to die or retire before I'm given a meaningful job to do."

Carboni lit a small cigar and puffed several times while looking directly at Kirkeby.

"I'm trying to understand you, Brad," he replied at last. "But you are simply going to have to adjust to the fact that you are out of college and in the real world now. It takes years of experience before you assume major structural design responsibility."

"That's because what they call experience in the Lockport Aircraft training program is merely a succession of routine tasks that could be done as well by a moron. Experience is learning and I'm not learning anything!"

"Look, Brad. I know you get all those aeronautical design theory courses in college, and you expect to design planes your first week out of college. Face it, there's a certain amount of routine work in any job. Every day can't be a learning experience like it was in college."

"I don't see why not," replied Kirkeby. "If I was hired to eventually design planes, shouldn't I be working next to designers instead of piddling around with trivia?"

"The work in this section is hardly trivia!" Carboni was angry now but forced himself to keep from shouting. "But the work in this section is not the issue. You want to design airplanes like your father . . . right?"

"Right."

"Well," said Carboni, "your father has been with Lockport Aircraft for 25 years . . . 8 years longer than I have. He started at the bottom and worked himself up step by step. Now he's one of the most respected designers in the industry."

"My father is living proof of how ridiculous the system is. He had models at home when I was a boy . . . models he built in his spare time of wing and fuselage structures for as yet undreamed-of Mach I and Mach I.5 power plants."

"Lawrence Kirkeby was always considered to be a very talented person," replied Carboni calmly.

Brad Kirkeby continued, "He was way ahead of his time. And what did this company have him doing for most of those years? Did they use his creative talents to design planes, or on research to advance the state of the art? No. That would have been too obvious. They made him waste nearly 20 potentially creative years on trivial assignments before he became a designer with the authority to control technical considerations."

"How naive can you be, Brad Kirkeby? Do you really believe that your father alone came upon this advanced design information and was frustrated for years by a repressive and unresponsive management?" Carboni was angry now and let it show as he continued.

"Sure, your father was talented. That's how he got to be chief designer at Lockport Aircraft. But he was and still is a mortal like the rest of us. Lawrence Kirkeby made his share of mistakes along the line. It was only after years of detailing and understudy with our top designers that his own ideas began to evolve and his real talents began to show. That's

when he was moved to a responsible design position."

Brad Kirkeby started to reply, but Carboni cut him off.

"That's the trouble with you kids nowadays. You want everything in life without having to pay the price for it. You tell me you're bored with your job and ought to be designing planes instead. For your information, there are at least 30 bright young people currently in the company who have already passed this apprenticeship that you consider so useless and are now on detailing and limited design activity. Do you suggest I pass them up and promote you to the head of the class, simply because you're bored with your present assignment?"

"Of course not, but . . ." Brad Kirkeby made an attempt to intervene.

"You're darn right, I won't," shouted Carboni, answering his own question. "You've been in my section two months now and have turned in only mediocre work at best. You probably can justify that to yourself on the grounds that the work doesn't turn you on. Well, let me tell you something, Brad Kirkeby, talent is one heck of a lot more than just saying you have it. Talent is proving it in the work you do *now* . . . not the work you say you'll do next year or the year after! For all of your big talk about how great you are and how dull the work is, you have yet to prove to me you're anything but a phony!"

Problems

1. What issues are involved in this case?
2. To what extent do you agree with the basic position(s) taken by Brad Kirkeby?
3. To what extent do you agree with the basic position(s) taken by Anthony Carboni?
4. Can these two viewpoints be reconciled?
5. What is relevant job experience as you see it?

Source: Robert D. Joyce, *Encounters in Organizational Behavior* (Elmsford, NY: Pergamon Press, 1972), 151–154. Reprinted with permission of the publisher.

NOTES

[1] David Charlson, quoted in Terri Minsky, "More People Face Career Plateaus, a Relief for Some, Shock for Others," *Wall Street Journal,* August 2, 1982, 17.

[2] Ronald Bailey, "In Praise of the Conventional Life," *Forbes,* October 17, 1988, 158.

[3] Virginia Hall and Joyce Wessel, "For the Recent Graduate, Finding a Job Means Work," *Atlanta Journal and Constitution,* July 22, 1984, 49-J.

[4] Adapted from "The Chrysler-Plymouth Guide to Building a Résumé," *Business Week's Guide to Careers* 4 (March 1986): 3.

5 Roger Ailes, "Making a Good Impression," *Hyatt Magazine* 3 (March–April 1989): 16; and Sara Rynes, Robert Bretz, and Barry Gerhart, "The Importance of Recruitment in Job Choice: A Different Way of Looking," *Personnel Psychology* 44 (Autumn 1991): 487–521.

6 Hall and Wessel, "For the Recent Graduate."

7 Joann Keyton and Jeffrey K. Springston, "What Did You Ask Me?" *National Business Employment Weekly* (College Edition; Spring 1991): 32–34.

8 Gerard R. Roche, "Much Ado about Mentors," *Harvard Business Review* 57 (January–February 1979): 14–28.

9 Eugene E. Jennings, "Success Chess," *Management of Personnel Quarterly* 9 (Fall 1970): 4–8.

10 Peggy J. Schmidt, *Making It on Your First Job* (New York: Avon Books, 1981); this section also draws on Peggy J. Schmidt, "Don't Be Blue If You're Green at Work," *Family Weekly,* July 1, 1984, 9.

11 Sana Siwolop, "Stress: The Test Americans Are Failing," *Business Week,* April 18, 1988, 74.

12 Ibid.

13 Adapted from Robert Kreitner, "Personal Wellness: It's Just Good Business," *Business Horizons* 25 (May–June 1982): 33; and Donald Robinson, "Stressbusters," *Parade Magazine,* July 22, 1990, 13.

14 Susan Fraker, "Why Women Aren't Getting to the Top," *Fortune,* April 16, 1984, 40–45.

15 Felice N. Schwartz, "Management Women and the New Facts of Life," *Harvard Business Review* 67 (January–February 1989): 65–76.

16 Harry Levinson, "On Being a Middle-Aged Manager," *Harvard Business Review* 47 (July–August 1969): 51–60; and Manfred F. R. Kets de Vries, *Organizational Paradoxes* (London: Tavistock Publications, 1980), 133–164.

17 Roy Rowan, "America's Most Wanted Managers," *Fortune,* February 3, 1986, 18.

18 Quoted in "Now Hear This," *Fortune,* February 3, 1986, 11.

19 Gail Sheehy, *Passages: Predictable Crises of Adult Life* (New York: Dutton, 1976), 275–278.

PART
FIVE

LEADING AND INTERPERSONAL INFLUENCE

LEARNING OBJECTIVES

Upon completing this chapter, you should be able to:

- Explain various ways motivation plays a role in most organizations.
- Identify the five categories in Maslow's need-hierarchy theory.
- Differentiate between motivators and hygienes in Herzberg's two-factor theory.
- Describe the concepts of expectancy and valence as used in Vroom's expectancy theory.
- Distinguish between equality and equity as defined in Adams's equity theory.
- Explain the guiding principle behind Skinner's reinforcement theory.

ou have been a chemicals handler for a high-tech manufacturing company for less than a year. One day, in a flash of inspiration, you see how the company could reuse a solvent, cutting the need for expensive, dangerous hazardous-waste disposal. At home, you conduct a thorough cost-benefit analysis of the scheme to present to your supervisor. But you are an employee, not an owner or top manager of the company. What could possibly motivate you to take the initiative to work up a proposal on your own time?

At Reflexite Corp. in New Britain, Connecticut, your motivation would be evident because you would be a part-owner. To a degree that varies with seniority, Reflexite's 275 employees own 59 percent of its stock; the longer they stay, the more they own. And the longer they stay, the more likely they are to stay even longer because they have an ever-growing stake in Reflexite's success. For Reflexite, this means low turnover and a dependable supply of high-tech knowledge.

MOTIVATING HUMAN BEHAVIOR

Reflexite's unusual ownership arrangement was developed by its president, Cecil Ursprung. Early in his career, Ursprung found himself wondering whether traditional top-down direction was the best way to manage in the twentieth century. This method had been developed in the early years of the Industrial Revolution, when many available employees had nothing to offer except a strong back or nimble fingers. Today's employees are better educated and want more power over the decisions affecting their work lives. To tap into the desire of Reflexite employees for "a piece of the action," Ursprung convinced the company's owners to let the employees buy shares of the company's stock.

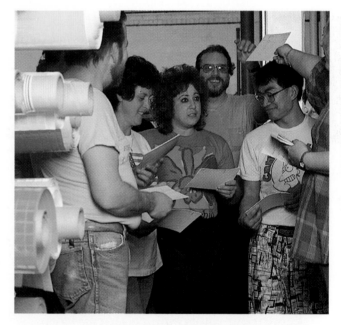

Because employees see how Reflexite is doing every month—their share of Reflexite's profit is distributed monthly—they are much more sensitive to costs and incomes than other employees would be. When they save money or make an improvement, they see the results. When somebody else does so, they also see the results. They do not feel that they are working for someone else; they know they are all in it together.

Does it work? Between 1986 and 1991, Reflexite's sales quadrupled. Subsidiaries in Canada, Europe, and Mexico are continually adding new customers. Even in lean times, a steady stream of outsiders have offered to buy Reflexite, only to be stymied when they are told that it is employee owned.

Employee ownership won't necessarily work for every company, but there are many other ways of inspiring employees to do their best. In this chapter, we will investigate past and current theories about what motivates people in the work environment.

Source: John Case, "Collective Effort," *Inc.*, January 1992, 32–35, 38, 42–43.

Motivation, meaning the will to achieve, is one of the most important challenges you will confront as a manager. We often tend to think of motivation in rather limited terms: motivating a sales force to promote a new product, for example, or motivating assembly-line workers to meet a quota. But in actuality, there are many way motivation plays a role in most organizations:

1. People must be attracted—or motivated—to join an organization and remain in it.

2. Once on the job, employees must be induced—or motivated—to exert energy and effort at an acceptable rate.

3. An organization's human resources must be maintained and developed. Company-sponsored training programs and conferences are often used for this purpose. Highly motivated employees are an essential element in the success of all such activities.

As the preceding reasons suggest, motivation is a central issue that pervades all aspects of employee behavior. As one observer noted, "The question, 'How can I motivate my people?' has been philosophically and practically posed in many eras and many tongues."[1] The many theories that have been advanced to answer this question can be grouped into two categories: the **content approach to motivation** and the **process approach to motivation.** These approaches and the major theories of motivation with which they are associated are summarized in Table 15.1 and form the basis for the following discussion. It is important to realize that a full understanding of motivation requires an appreciation of both content and process—that is, an appreciation of *what* motivates people, as well as *how* people are motivated.

Motivation.
The will to achieve.

Content approach to motivation.
An approach to motivation concerned with what motivates people.

Process approach to motivation.
An approach to motivation concerned with how people are motivated.

CONTENT APPROACH TO MOTIVATION

The content approach to motivation attempts to answer the question "What prompts people to behave as they do?" To answer this question, one must identify

TABLE 15.1 MAJOR APPROACHES TO MOTIVATION		
Approach	**Theories**	**Primary Concern**
1. Content	1. Need-hierarchy theory 2. Two-factor theory	Concerned with *what* motivates people
2. Process	1. Expectancy theory 2. Equity theory 3. Reinforcement theory	Concerned with *how* people are motivated

CLOSE-UP: QUALITY GRANITE ROCK IS HERE TO STAY!

In 1987 Granite Rock's Bruce Woolpert needed to adapt to some big changes. His family-controlled asphalt, concrete, and retail building supply business was facing stiff new competition from well-financed conglomerates. The State of California was tightening industrial air and water regulations, and customers were demanding ever higher quality materials and more responsive service. In addition, computer technology that would automate quarry work and concrete production was becoming available, but at a substantial investment.

Unfortunately, Woolpert, who served as joint CEO with his brother Steve, had limited time and few options. He would have to find a way to stay ahead of the competition, or Granite Rock might disappear.

Believing that a key management duty was to make certain that plenty of information flowed into the company, Woolpert transformed Granite Rock into a formidable apparatus for collecting and acting on gathered data. He asked customers to rate the company against competitors and even issued report cards. Where other high-tech manufacturers charted a dozen internal process controls, Granite Rock kept track of a hundred. And on the human side, he emphasized ongoing individual training, bringing in instructional speakers and urging employees to attend seminars on company time. They could even sign up for courses at the local college on the company tab. And it seemed that the more interested Woolpert got in his employees, the more interested they became in improving Granite Rock's operations. Very few left, except to retire.

Woolpert also picked up some information on his own. Visiting the company's cement plants and quarry, he asked his employees what they liked and didn't like about their jobs, their company, and even other companies. He established communication from the top down while encouraging feedback in the other direction as well. He set up teams of managers and hourly employees and tasked them with analyzing and acting on decisions within their departments. The joint makeup of the groups enhanced perspective and went a long way toward eliminating the "us vs. them" mentality between white- and blue-collar employees.

The results: Granite Rock's technologies made it the region's low-cost producer of crushed rock. Quality and service levels allow it to charge a 6 percent premium for concrete and asphalt while gaining market share every year since 1987. The workforce is highly motivated, with many employees acting on personal initiative alone to learn more than one job.

Source: Adapted from John Case, "The Change Masters," *Inc.*, March 1992, 59–61, 64, 66, 70.

people's needs. The needs for security and recognition are just two examples of forces that may motivate people and determine their actions. The two content theories that have generated the most interest are Maslow's need-hierarchy theory and Herzberg's two-factor theory.

MASLOW'S NEED-HIERARCHY THEORY

Abraham Maslow's *need-hierarchy theory* is one of the most widely known theories of motivation.[2] According to Maslow, people are motivated to satisfy five categories of inborn needs:

1. **Physiological needs,** including the needs for sleep, rest, food, water, and air. These are survival needs—without them, we die. They underscore the ancient generalization that self-preservation is the first law of life.

Physiological needs.
The needs for food, water, rest, air, and so forth.

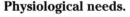

Long's Drug Stores meets the higher level needs of employees with opportunities for recognition and personal growth. This photo appeared in an ad titled "Our Priceless Ingredient" that was mailed to thousands of customers. It recognizes individual employees and indicates how the company feels about its workforce. Purchasing, pricing, promotions, and training are determined at the store or district level, providing opportunities for employee responsibility, achievement, personal growth, and recognition.

2. **Safety needs,** including the needs for security and stability, as well as freedom from fear or threat. In our culture, these needs are probably most active for children.

3. **Social needs,** including the needs for friendship, affection, acceptance, and interaction with others.

4. **Esteem needs,** including both a need for personal feelings of achievement or self-esteem and a need for recognition or respect from others.

5. **Self-actualization needs,** including feelings of self-fulfillment and the realization of one's potential.

Maslow held that these needs form a hierarchy of ascending importance, from low to high, as shown in Figure 15.1. He contended that a "lower" need must be relatively satisfied before the next "higher" need can motivate behavior. For example, a person's safety needs would have to be generally satisfied before the next level of need (social) can motivate behavior. Thus, the strength of any need is determined not only by its position in the hierarchy but also by the degree to which it and all lower needs have been satisfied. Relative satisfaction of a need, however, triggers dissatisfaction at the next higher level. This sequence of "increased satisfaction, decreased importance, increased importance of the next higher need" repeats itself until the highest level of the hierarchy (self-actualization) is reached.

Maslow suggested that a person can progress down as well as up the various need levels. If a lower level need (safety, for instance) were threatened at some later point in time, it again would become dominant and assume an important position in a person's total motivational system. Thus, sudden unemployment or loss of a loved one could shift one's concern from a pursuit of personal recognition to a preoccupation with providing for home and family.

Maximum personal motivation involves what Maslow termed *self-actualization.* He used this term to describe the need people have to grow and develop, or, as he put it, the "desire for self-fulfillment, namely . . . the tendency [for a person]

Safety needs.
The needs for security and stability, as well as freedom from fear or threat.

Social needs.
The needs for friendship, affection, acceptance, interaction with others, and so forth.

Esteem needs.
The needs for a personal feeling of achievement or self-esteem, as well as for recognition or respect from others.

Self-actualization needs.
The needs for a feeling of self-fulfillment, or the realization of one's potential.

FIGURE 15.1 MASLOW'S NEED-HIERARCHY THEORY

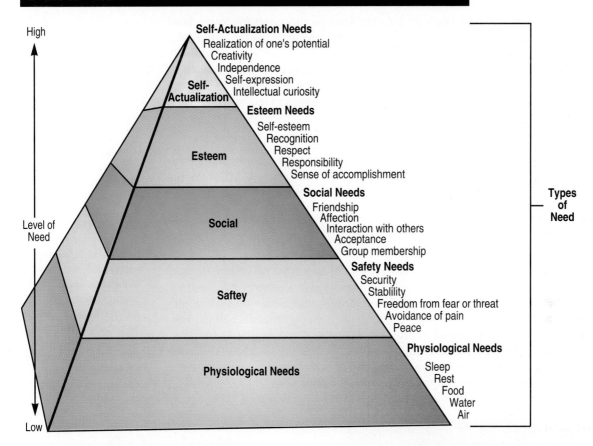

to become actualized in what he is potentially . . . the desire to become more and more what one is, to become everything that one is capable of becoming."[3] Maslow believed the drive to become self-actualized was universal, but that it is only rarely reached and never fully fulfilled. He cited Albert Einstein, Abraham Lincoln, Thomas Jefferson, Johann Sebastian Bach, and Ludwig van Beethoven as examples of people who had at least partially become self-actualized.

Assessment

Although the concept of people being motivated by a set of increasingly important needs is appealing, little evidence exists to support Maslow's need-hierarchy theory. Three points are particularly pertinent in this regard:

1. Researchers have been unable to prove that the five need levels Maslow proposed exist, suggesting instead that there are no more than two or three levels.

2. Although people do generally place a great deal of emphasis on satisfying their lower level needs (for example, hunger and thirst), research suggests that once these needs are satisfied, most people do not climb Maslow's need hierarchy in the proposed manner. Indeed, there appears to be no particular pattern governing which needs will become dominant once a person's lower level needs are satisfied. By assuming that all people have the *same* hierarchical order of

needs and respond to need deprivation in the *same* manner, Maslow's theory fails to allow for individual differences.

3. Research indicates that contrary to what Maslow proposed for lower level needs, at the highest level of the need hierarchy a reversal occurs in the satisfaction-importance relationship. Simply stated, as people experience self-actualization, they want more. Unlike motivation based on lower level needs, motivation based on self-actualization does not decrease as people become satisfied. Thus, for self-actualization, increased satisfaction leads to increased rather than decreased motivation.

Managerial Implications

Despite its questionable validity, Maslow's need-hierarchy theory continues to exert a significant influence on current thinking about motivation. Certainly its basic ideas have some valid managerial implications:

1. Managers should bear in mind that motivation is generally determined by multiple needs. The belief that one, and only one, factor accounts for motivation is usually an oversimplification.

2. Managers should identify their employees' most important needs and link satisfaction of those needs to desired performance. For instance, if a need for recognition (esteem) has been identified, opportunities offering such gratification should be made available and contingent on performance. Titles, pins, badges, and medals are all examples of awards that companies such as McDonald's, Tupperware, and IBM use to satisfy employee needs. IBM is especially noted for satisfying employee needs in effective, sometimes spectacular ways. There was the time, for example, when the manager of a 100-person IBM sales unit rented a stadium in New Jersey's Meadowlands Sports Complex for

A team of Humana Inc. managers meet to discuss progress on a project. This service enhancement team was charged with developing strategies to ensure Humana becomes the health care field's preeminent provider of superior, cost-effective customer service. Opportunities to work on special projects, take on additional responsibilities, achieve personal and organization goals, and receive recognition can increase employee motivation.
▼

an evening. Before spouses, children, and various top managers, all the sales representatives ran through the players' tunnel onto the field while their names were flashed on an electronic scoreboard to the cheers of the crowd.

3. Managers should be aware that what motivates one person may not motivate another. Different people have different desires. Managers must be sensitive to differences in individual preferences if they want to motivate their subordinates. Thus, the rewards in the previous examples might not motivate some employees.

4. Managers should realize that a person's needs are likely to change from time to time and from situation to situation. Thus, in Maslow's terms, people will be at different levels of the need hierarchy at different times.

5. It is a manager's responsibility to create a climate in which employees can maximize their potential. This may require creating opportunities for satisfying several different needs. Table 15.2 identifies different means a manager can use to motivate employees at each of the five levels in Maslow's hierarchy.

6. Certain needs are present at birth. People are born needing relationships with others, and with the need to be accepted and esteemed by other people. Accordingly, failure to provide work-related opportunities for such need satisfaction is likely to lead to employee frustration, diminished output, and increased turnover.

TABLE 15.2   EXAMPLES OF MEANS MANAGERS CAN USE TO MOTIVATE EMPLOYEES (BASED ON MASLOW'S HIERARCHY OF NEEDS)

Need	Means
1. Self-actualization	1. Opportunities for achievement 2. Encouragement of creativity 3. Chance for advancement 4. Autonomy 5. Challenging job
2. Esteem	1. Promotions 2. Praise 3. Name in company newsletter 4. Private office 5. Job title
3. Social	1. Sponsor athletic teams 2. Permit informal group activities 3. Encourage employee interaction 4. Develop professional friendships 5. Hold office parties
4. Safety	1. Medical insurance 2. Guaranteed compensation 3. Retirement plan 4. Safe working conditions 5. Job security
5. Physiological	1. Adequate salary 2. Comfortable working conditions 3. Free meals 4. Clothing allowance 5. Company housing

HERZBERG'S TWO-FACTOR THEORY

A second historically significant content theory of motivation was developed by Frederick Herzberg.[4] Generally referred to as the *two-factor theory,* it was first introduced in the late 1950s and enjoyed continuing popularity through the early 1970s. More recently, it has fallen out of vogue for reasons we will discuss.

The initial framework for the two-factor theory was derived from interviews with 200 accountants and engineers in the Pittsburgh area. Using what is known as the *critical-incident method,* the accountants and engineers were asked to provide interviewers with examples of times they felt exceptionally good or exceptionally bad about their jobs. The examples were analyzed and showed that the factors producing job satisfaction were entirely separate from those producing job dissatisfaction. That is, although an unpleasant work environment might be a reason given for job dissatisfaction, a pleasant work environment is rarely cited as a reason for job satisfaction. This suggested that job satisfaction and job dissatisfaction are not simple opposites. Because Herzberg, like Maslow, assumed a relationship between satisfaction and motivation, he concluded that a two-factor theory was needed to explain employee motivation.

Traditionally, managers had viewed job satisfaction and job dissatisfaction as opposite ends of the same continuum. This traditional view is illustrated in Figure 15.2 (Panel A). In contrast, Herzberg's findings suggested the opposite of satisfaction is not dissatisfaction, but rather simply "no satisfaction." This view is illustrated in Figure 15.2 (Panel B).

Herzberg labeled the factors that produced job satisfaction **motivators.** His analysis indicated these factors are directly related to *job content,* reflecting a need for personal fulfillment. Motivators included achievement, recognition, the work itself, responsibility, advancement, and personal growth. He labeled the factors that led to job dissatisfaction **hygienes** and found they are related more to the work setting, or *job context,* than to job content. Hygienic factors include company policies and administration, supervision, relations with one's peers, working conditions, pay, and job security (see Table 15.3).

Motivators. Factors that produce job satisfaction.

Hygienes. Factors that produce job dissatisfaction.

FIGURE 15.2 TWO VIEWS OF JOB SATISFACTION AND JOB DISSATISFACTION

A. Traditional View

Satisfaction — Dissatisfaction

B. Herzberg's View

Satisfaction — No Satisfaction

Dissatisfaction — No Dissatisfaction

TABLE 15.3 HERZBERG'S MOTIVATORS AND HYGIENES	
Motivators Leading to Job Satisfaction	**Hygienes Leading to Job Dissatisfaction**
1. Achievement	1. Policies and administration
2. Recognition	2. Supervision
3. Work itself	3. Relations with peers
4. Responsibility	4. Working conditions
5. Advancement	5. Pay
6. Personal growth	6. Job security

Based on this dichotomy, Herzberg concluded that only motivators produce job satisfaction, whereas hygienes merely prevent job dissatisfaction. In other words:

1. To the degree that motivators are present in a job, satisfaction will occur. When absent, motivators do not lead to dissatisfaction.

2. To the degree that hygienes are absent from a job, dissatisfaction will occur. When present, hygienes prevent dissatisfaction but do not lead to satisfaction.

As shown in Figure 15.3, Herzberg's two-factor theory basically reduces Maslow's five need levels to two. Herzberg's hygienes are roughly equivalent to Maslow's three lowest needs. Similarly, his motivators are roughly equivalent to Maslow's two highest needs. Herzberg's two-factor theory suggests that in modern society most employees have achieved such social and economic progress that their lower level needs are adequately satisfied. Consequently, lower level needs are no longer strong motivators for the typical employee. Rather, today's employees are likely to be primarily motivated by higher level needs, such as esteem and self-actualization.

Assessment
Research, however, has not supported Herzberg's conclusion about motivators and hygienes. Three points are particularly pertinent in this regard.

1. Evidence fails to support Herzberg's contention that hygienes can prevent dissatisfaction but cannot satisfy employees. Consequently, the question has emerged as to whether the factors leading to satisfaction and dissatisfaction are really different from each other. Certain factors, such as supervision, achievement, and pay, have been proven important for both satisfaction and dissatisfaction.

2. Although Herzberg has reported replications of his original study in countries located in Europe, Africa, the Middle East, and Asia, as well as in numerous professional and nonprofessional employee groups representing various economic and educational categories, research conducted by other investigators shows wide diversity in the work preferences of different people in different situations, thus casting doubt on the general applicability of his findings.

3. Doubts have been raised about Herzberg's methodology (that is, his use of the critical-incident method). Other investigators using techniques less

FIGURE 15.3 A COMPARISON OF MASLOW'S NEED-HIERARCHY THEORY AND HERZBERG'S TWO-FACTOR THEORY

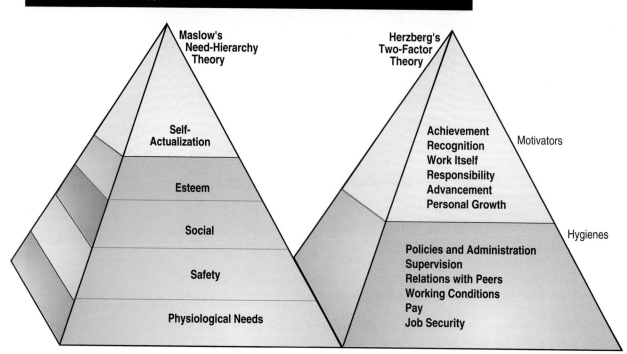

susceptible to respondent bias have failed to replicate his findings. In this regard, critics note that people are more likely to credit their own achievements as reasons for job satisfaction. Similarly, they are likely to blame poor policies or supervision for their dissatisfaction, rather than admit to their personal inadequacies. This suggests that Herzberg's findings may result from the manner in which he gathers his data. Indeed, other investigators, using different methods, have obtained findings contrary to what Herzberg's theory would predict.

Managerial Implications

Although there is obviously some question regarding the present status of Herzberg's two-factor theory, certain implications of the theory do merit managerial consideration. These include:

1. The two-factory theory suggests that an individual can be both very satisfied and very dissatisfied at the same time. A nurse, for example, may enjoy her work but be unhappy every time she opens her pay envelope. Thus, employees may be *either* satisfied *or* dissatisfied *or* both.

2. Managers often ask why their subordinates are not motivated. The traditional managerial response to motivation problems has been to alter company policies and improve working conditions, with little result. Herzberg's theory offers an apparent explanation to this puzzle. Improved hygienic factors may not strike at the root of the motivation problem at all.

3. The two-factor theory suggests that motivation can be increased by designing jobs to provide opportunities for achievement, recognition, responsibility, ad-

vancement, and personal growth. Indeed, Herzberg's ideas have inspired many successful projects involving the redesign of jobs and even entire organizations. In this connection, the message of the two-factor theory is direct, simple, and persuasive. As discussed in Chapter 10, for certain jobs and employees, job enrichment offers the promise of increased motivation.

PROCESS APPROACH TO MOTIVATION

Whereas the content approach is concerned with *what* motivates people, the process approach is concerned with *how* people are motivated. It focuses on how behavior is energized, how it is directed, how it is sustained, and how it is stopped. The three process theories that have generated the most interest are Vroom's expectancy theory, Adams's equity theory, and Skinner's reinforcement theory.

VROOM'S EXPECTANCY THEORY

Of the motivation theories identified in Table 15.1, *expectancy theory* is perhaps the most respected. Popularized by Victor H. Vroom, expectancy theory is based on the belief that people will act to maximize their rewards.[5] Accordingly, as shown in Figure 15.4 (Panel 1), expectancy theory holds that motivation is determined by:

1. *Expectancy.* The belief that effort will be rewarded.
2. *Valence.* The value attached to specific rewards.

Expectancies can be separated into two types: **Expectancy 1** is the belief that effort will lead to performance. **Expectancy 2** is the belief that performance will lead to rewards. Expectancy 1 is actually a belief in personal effectiveness; that is,

Expectancy 1.
The belief that effort will lead to performance.

Expectancy 2.
The belief that performance will lead to rewards (outcomes).

FIGURE 15.4   VROOM'S EXPECTANCY THEORY

1. **Basic Model**
   Motivation = Expectancy x Valence

   or

$$\text{Motivation} = \begin{pmatrix} \text{Belief that effort will} \\ \text{be rewarded} \end{pmatrix} \times \begin{pmatrix} \text{Value attached to} \\ \text{specific rewards} \end{pmatrix}$$

2. **Expanded Model**
   Motivation = [(Expectancy 1) (Expectancy 2)] (Valance)

   or

$$\text{Motivation} = \begin{pmatrix} \text{Belief that effort will} \\ \text{lead to performance} \end{pmatrix} \times \left[\begin{pmatrix} \text{Belief that performance} \\ \text{will lead to rewards} \end{pmatrix} \right] \begin{pmatrix} \text{Value attached to} \\ \text{specific rewards} \end{pmatrix}$$

an individual can perform well if he or she makes the effort. Expectancy 2 is the belief that good performance will be rewarded.

The opposite, of course, may be true. A person may feel that working harder does not produce better results and, in any case, higher performance is not directly related to rewards. In such a situation, a person would be low in both Expectancy 1 and Expectancy 2. An expanded version of the basic expectancy model, showing Expectancy 1 and Expectancy 2, is presented in Figure 15.4 (Panel 2).

Valence, the second determinant of motivation, is the value placed on an outcome (reward). It can be either positive or negative. Thus, a person may attach a negative value to an outcome (for example, being fired) or a positive value (for example, a promotion). Other things being equal, the more positive the value, the more likely a person will be highly motivated. On the other hand, the more negative the value, the less likely a person will be highly motivated.

Together, these concepts provide a basis for understanding motivation. In general, an individual's motivation to behave in a certain way will be greatest when:

1. The individual believes that the desired behavior is possible (Expectancy 1).
2. The individual believes that the behavior will lead to certain outcomes (Expectancy 2).
3. The individual places a positive value on these outcomes (valence).

An Example

The following example illustrates how Vroom's expectancy theory works on the job. Assume that you are a door-to-door sales representative for a brush company. You realize that the more calls you make each day, the more brushes you are likely to sell. That is, the more effort you expend, the greater the likelihood of desired performance—namely, increased sales. Thus, you see a direct relationship between effort and performance (Expectancy 1). Since you are on a straight commission, you also see a direct relationship between performance and rewards (Expectancy 2). Further, suppose a friend has offered to sell you his late model sports car that you have always admired. The only problem is that you are a little short of cash. Hence, you are really eager to make some extra money. In expectancy theory terms, you really value the increased income you will receive (valence). With these three factors combined (Expectancy 1, Expectancy 2, and valence), expectancy theory suggests you would be highly motivated to perform.

Assessment

Overall, expectancy theory is generally considered to be one of the better frameworks for understanding motivation. This is not to say that expectancy theory cannot be criticized. Three points are particularly pertinent in this regard:

1. The very complexity of expectancy theory has made its practical application particularly difficult.
2. Researchers have found that the complexity of expectancy theory makes it very difficult to test.
3. It is doubtful if managers actually attempt to calculate Expectancy 1, Expectancy 2, and valence estimates in making decisions. Moreover, since expectancy theory involves individual decision making, it is subject to all the limitations of bounded rationality discussed in Chapter 7. Critics note that human decision makers are incapable of processing the information required to

Valence.
The value placed on an outcome (reward).

know all alternative outcomes, their likelihood of occurrence, or their desirability, even if it were available.

Managerial Implications

Despite its complexity, expectancy theory has a number of valuable managerial implications:

1. Focusing on Expectancy 1, it is important that employees judge expected performance to be attainable. If employees view performance goals as unreasonable, motivation will suffer. This point carries implications for both the selection and training of qualified employees, as well as managers who set performance objectives.

2. Focusing on Expectancy 2, it is important that desired performance be clearly linked to positive outcomes, thus rewarding good work and giving mediocre performers an incentive or goal to do better. Moreover, if those who fail to perform quit, an organization benefits. In any case, failure to appropriately and fairly reward good work will severely diminish the motivation of high performers. Companies such as Lotus Development Corp. clearly appreciate this point. Accordingly, it has developed numerous programs tying performance to rewards. For instance, a system of financial rewards tied to unit sales of new products can earn the lead developer of a hit product a bonus of up to 2 years' salary.

   Establishing a link between performance and rewards also has clear implications for the role of performance appraisal as well as open (versus secret) compensation practices. If based on a sound performance-appraisal system, open compensation practices serve to reinforce the link between performance and rewards by making public the fact that those who perform are those who are rewarded. To make this point, Abt Associates annually passes around a list of everyone's salary and bonus. At NeXt Inc., lists of all employees' salaries hang in offices and anyone can consult them. Both Abt and NeXt are atypical. However, they put verifiable meaning into the slogan "We pay for performance" and acknowledge that employees tend to behave like fellow employees whom they see being rewarded.

3. Focusing on valence, rewards must be meaningful to employees. It is here that content theories of motivation can be put to work. By understanding individual employee needs, managers can match them to rewards for maximum motivation. This point also contains direct implications for the design of compensation programs.

4. As a whole, expectancy theory underscores the realization that different people have different desires and that they are likely to perceive different connections between actions and their fulfillment of these desires. In doing so, it points out important factors (that is, expectancies and valences) and suggests ways in which these factors alone and in combination influence behavior. In this respect alone, it has made a valuable contribution to understanding motivation.

ADAMS'S EQUITY THEORY

A second process theory of motivation was popularized by J. Stacy Adams. Generally referred to as *equity theory*, it attempts to explain satisfaction with outcomes

and to predict resulting changes in behavior.[6] It defines motivation in terms of the perceived equity between the effort a person puts into a job and what he or she receives in return, especially as compared to other persons in similar positions. Equity theory holds that perceived inequity creates tension within a person, this tension motivates a person to restore equity, and the strength of the resulting behavior will vary directly with the magnitude of the perceived inequity. Thus, the greater the tension a person feels, the harder he or she will work to restore equity and, thereby, reduce the tension. This process is shown in Figure 15.5.

According to equity theory, the "other person" an individual uses as a comparison could be one person (for example, a co-worker), a group (for example, workers on another shift), or someone from a previous, or even hypothetical, work situation. Two points are important to mention here:

1. Note the emphasis on "perceived" as compared to "actual" equity. With equity theory, it matters little whether an individual's comparisons are based on subjective perception or objective reality.

2. Equity and equality are not the same. **Equality** is said to exist when an individual perceives outcomes she receives as being equal to outcomes received by another person. That is,

$$\text{Outcomes}_{self} = \text{Outcomes}_{other}$$

Equity is attained when the ratio of an individual's perceived outcomes to inputs equals the ratio of the other person's outcomes to inputs. That is,

$$\frac{\text{Outcomes}_{self}}{\text{Inputs}_{self}} = \frac{\text{Outcomes}_{other}}{\text{Inputs}_{other}}$$

▲
Nucor Corporation believes that employees should be treated fairly. Production employees receive bonuses that are directly tied to productivity. Employees who do not make a full contribution to a day's production due to tardiness lose their daily bonus. Nucor's approach to equity is successful. The average employee earns over $32,000 per year, and there is rarely a shortage of applicants for job openings.

Equality.
When an individual's perceived outcomes are equal to outcomes received by another person.

Equity.
When the ratio of an individual's perceived outcomes to inputs equals the ratio of another person's outcomes to inputs.

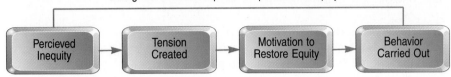

FIGURE 15.5   MOTIVATIONAL IMPLICATIONS OF PERCEIVED INEQUITY

Strength of behavior depends on perceived inequity

Percieved Inequity → Tension Created → Motivation to Restore Equity → Behavior Carried Out

Perceived inequity may exist in either of two cases:

1. When a person judges the ratio of her perceived outcomes to inputs as being too low relative to another.
2. When a person feels the ratio of her perceived outcomes to inputs is excessive relative to another.

This suggests that people will experience inequity when they are either relatively underpaid or overpaid. Examples of possible inputs and outcomes are given in Table 15.4. Note that two outcomes, monotony and fatigue, are negative.

An Example

Examples of perceived inequity are quite common. For instance, consider an episode that occurred in professional football several years ago. All-star Dallas Cowboys running back Tony Dorsett reacted bitterly to the team's signing of rookie Herschel Walker to a 5-year multimillion-dollar contract, the largest in the Cowboys' history. By comparison, Dorsett's contract was 9 years for half as much pay.

"What's he ever done?" asked Dorsett of Walker. "Heisman Trophy? Well, I've got one of those . . . I'm on the verge of becoming the NFL's second all-time rusher. Herschel hasn't contributed one yard to this team's success." Acknowledging that Dorsett may have had a legitimate gripe, Dallas quarterback Danny White added, "Tony's been one of the premier backs in the league for 10 years and Herschel hasn't played a down here yet." As this episode suggests, people are quick to become distressed, and thus motivated to some sort of action (whether it's making a verbal protest or even leaving a job), when they feel they are being treated inequitably.[7]

TABLE 15.4   EXAMPLE INPUTS AND OUTCOMES UNDER EQUITY THEORY

Inputs	Outcomes
1. Effort	1. Pay
2. Experience	2. Promotion opportunities
3. Education	3. Increased status
4. Seniority	4. Co-worker esteem
5. Status	5. Monotony
6. Intelligence	6. Fatigue
7. Time	7. Benefits
8. Loyalty	8. Satisfaction
9. Skills	9. Prestige
10. Productivity	10. Recognition

Restoring Equity

As just hinted, inequity produces a tension that motivates a person to take action to eliminate or at least reduce the tension. This action can be viewed as an attempt to *restore equity.* It may take one or more of the following forms:[8]

- *Altering inputs.* People may increase or decrease their inputs depending upon whether the perceived inequity is advantageous or disadvantageous. For instance, underpaid employees may work less, while overpaid employees may work harder.

- *Altering outcomes.* Employees may attempt to increase or decrease outcomes received on the job. The lawsuits brought by women and minorities against organizations that paid different wages for comparable work are an example of an attempt to alter outcomes. Subsequent state legislation requiring equal pay for equal work was designed to address this type of inequity.

- *Distorting inputs or outputs.* Employees who feel inequitably treated may rationalize, or mentally readjust their perceptions of, their input-outcome ratios. For example, people who perceive themselves as underpaid may inflate the status attached to their job ("This is really an important job") or deny the real effort they expend ("I really don't work that hard on this job").

- *Leave the field.* Employees who feel inequitably rewarded may decide to leave the field by requesting a transfer or simply quitting outright so as to find a more favorable balance of inputs to outcomes elsewhere. A computer science professor, for example, may decide to leave academe for industry when she realizes what her counterparts in high-tech firms are earning. This is essentially the action that Tony Dorsett took to restore equity in the episode described above. Dorsett wanted to leave Dallas after losing his starting role to Walker and was ultimately traded to the Denver Broncos.

- *Distort inputs or outcomes of others.* In the face of inequity, people may rationalize, or mentally readjust their perceptions of, other people's input-outcome ratios. The previously mentioned computer science professor may rationalize her comparatively lower earnings by noting that her counterparts in industry probably work longer hours and have fewer vacations than she does and thus deserve higher salaries. Or she may downplay the importance of a higher salary as compared to the greater satisfaction she perceives herself receiving from her work.

- *Change object of comparison.* An individual may decide the person he or she has chosen as a basis of comparison is not really an accurate counterpart and may select another who will yield a more favorable comparison of inputs to outcomes. For example, if a human resource manager finds his salary compares unfavorably with that of a sales manager, he may note that since the sales manager must travel a great deal, she deserves additional compensation. Instead, the human resource manager may choose to compare himself with a product manager whose salary is comparable to his own.

Assessment

Equity theory has received a great deal of attention. Its popularity can be partially explained by its ease of understanding and appeal to common sense. However, it also has been criticized. Four points are particularly pertinent in this regard:

1. Little is known about how people decide with whom to compare themselves. Available evidence suggests that the selection of an individual to use as a comparison is a function of both the availability of information concerning others and their attractiveness or relevance for comparison. However, evidence further intimates that the person with whom an individual compares himself or herself may change with the prevailing circumstances. Moreover, the comparison may be the consequence, as well as cause, of an individual's dissatisfaction. To add to the complexity, a feeling of inequality may stem not only from comparison with another person, but also from comparison of current outcomes with past outcomes.

2. It is difficult to define inputs and outcomes.

3. Other than saying that people may be expected to follow a cost-benefit strategy, very little is known about how inputs and outcomes are combined to resolve a perceived inequity.

4. Little is known about when and how combinations of inputs and outputs change over time.

Managerial Implications

Although equity theory has been criticized, it underscores several important implications for managers:

1. Employees make conscious equity comparisons that influence their motivation. Such comparisons are based on subjective perceptions, not objective reality. Thus, if two employees receive the same outcomes (rewards), but each thinks the other receives more, they will each base their feelings of inequity on their subjective perceptions rather than on objective reality.

2. Employees take a multifaceted view of their inputs and outcomes. Hence, compensation systems need to take into account a variety of inputs and outcomes.

3. When employees feel they are being treated inequitably, attitude and performance problems are seemingly inevitable. As Staton Corp. vice-president James Walls states, "When someone gets embedded in their mind that they are not being treated fairly, then they look for ways to strike back."[9] Such disaffection may manifest itself in an employee's refusal to relocate, for example, or even in an employee's departure. A few resort to fraud, theft, or other dishonest activities.

4. Rewards are judged in a relative rather than absolute fashion. Hence, it is not how one is paid in absolute terms that is important, but how much one is paid relative to others in identical or similar positions. An employee may be paid $75,000 a year for answering the telephone, but if a person in the next office is getting $76,000 for the same job, the employee probably will be dissatisfied.

5. Since rewards are judged in a relative rather than absolute fashion, it is important to influence employee perceptions of equity by making the inputs required for outcomes (rewards) as explicit as possible. This is another argument for open compensation practices. Further, it suggests the possibility that by paying above-market wages, an organization may be able to prompt extra workplace effort as employees strive to reduce feelings of inequity resulting from being relatively overpaid.

6. If rewards such as pay incentives or bonuses are to be effective, they must be perceived as substantial enough to justify the additional effort required to obtain them. Moreover, they must be perceived as equitable by other employees who do not receive them.

7. Actions intended to reduce perceived inequity can take one or more forms. Understanding and possibly influencing the alternatives available is an important part of a manager's job. Ideally, if such choices have to be made, they can be developed to benefit an organization and its employees.

SKINNER'S REINFORCEMENT THEORY

A third process theory is based largely on the work of B. F. Skinner. Known as *reinforcement theory*, its guiding principle is that human behavior is a function of its consequences.[10] Or, stated more formally, "behaviors that result in desirable consequences will likely recur; those that result in undesirable consequences will be less likely to recur." This last statement is popularly known as the **law of effect**.[11] In essence, it argues that people's behavior is determined by their reinforcement histories; they behave as their reinforcement histories have programmed them to behave. For reinforcement theory advocates, this explains why the best predictor of future behavior is past behavior. They view even seemingly spontaneous action as a response to past rewards and punishments.

Although various revisions have appeared in recent years, the basic concept behind reinforcement theory remains quite simple: Behaviors that lead to desirable consequences are likely to be repeated, and behaviors that lead to undesirable consequences are less likely to be repeated. This reasoning involves three components:

1. **Stimulus**—an event that leads to a response.
2. **Response**—a unit of behavior that follows a stimulus.
3. **Reinforcement**—a consequence of a response.

The relationship between these components is diagrammed in Figure 15.6. As indicated, a stimulus (event) leads to a response (behavior) that is reinforced (by a consequence). Note that none of these three components involves thinking. As noted, reinforcement theory holds that current behavior is solely determined by a person's reinforcement history. Thus, according to reinforcement theory, if a particular stimulus-response pair is followed by a desirable consequence, it will be more likely that the stimulus involved will prompt the same response in the future. Conversely, if the consequence is undesirable, the response will be less likely to recur. In sum, the consequences of a person's behavior are made dependent upon his or her response to a stimulus and determine the likelihood of the behavior recurring.

Types of Reinforcement

From a managerial perspective, there are at least four types of reinforcement

Law of effect.
Behaviors resulting in desirable consequences will likely recur and those resulting in undesirable consequences will be less likely to recur.

Stimulus.
An event that leads to a response.

Response.
A unit of behavior that follows a stimulus.

Reinforcement.
A consequence of a response.

FIGURE 15.6 THREE COMPONENTS OF REINFORCEMENT THEORY

Companies frequently motivate employees by rewarding them with trips and other prizes, positively reinforcing desired behaviors. This ad for United Airlines promotes such rewards.

available for modifying employee behavior. As summarized in Table 15.5, two of these strengthen or increase behavior, whereas the other two weaken or decrease it.

1. **Positive reinforcement.** A means of strengthening behavior, positive reinforcement provides a desirable consequence when a desirable behavior occurs. It thus increases the likelihood that a desired behavior will be repeated. If, for example, employees surpass sales goals, they may be rewarded with a prize. If the prize is attractive, they are likely to expend a similar effort in the next sales period. To illustrate, at Chick-fil-A, any franchise manager who increases a restaurant's annual sales by 40 percent is given a new Lincoln Continental for a year. If the manager repeats this increase the following year, she gets title to the car. Assuming a prize of a Lincoln is attractive, the manager is quite likely to repeat her first year's effort. Or, as shown in Figure 15.7, a

Positive reinforcement.

A type of reinforcement that strengthens behavior by providing a desirable consequence when a desirable behavior occurs.

TABLE 15.5 TYPES OF REINFORCEMENT

1. *Positive reinforcement.* Strengthens behavior by providing a desirable consequence when a desirable behavior occurs.
2. *Avoidance learning.* Strengthens behavior by teaching individuals to respond in ways to avoid undesirable consequences.
3. *Extinction.* Weakens behavior by withholding a desirable consequence when an undesirable behavior occurs.
4. *Punishment.* Weakens behavior by providing an undesirable consequence when an undesirable behavior occurs.

manager may praise an employee for consistently filing sales reports on time. According to Skinner, this response-consequence pattern will reinforce the employee's desire to keep on being punctual in the hope of receiving future praise. In a similar application, every employee at Mars, Inc., including the president, receives a 10 percent daily bonus for reporting to work on time. Similar reinforcement is provided by both Worthington Industries and the City of Memphis. At Worthington, anyone with perfect attendance for the year is awarded six shares of stock. Employees with no more than one absence pocket four shares each. The City of Memphis awards bonus days for perfect attendance. Employees who don't miss a day for illness or an unexcused attendance can earn up to four extra days off each year. Other examples of positive reinforcers would include pay increases, promotions, awards, extra time off, and extra vacation time.

2. **Avoidance learning.** A second means of strengthening behavior, avoidance learning, occurs when individuals respond in ways to *avoid* undesirable consequences. Referring to Figure 15.7, we see that if the employee in question consistently files the requested sales reports on time, the manager will avoid harassing or reprimanding the employee. The employee presumably will soon learn that being on time diminishes the likelihood of being "chewed out."

3. **Extinction.** A means of weakening behavior is extinction, which attempts to eliminate an undesirable behavior by withholding a desirable consequence when the behavior occurs. Under such conditions, the undesirable behavior will diminish and eventually become "extinct" as a result of not being positively reinforced. For example, managers who wish to discourage employees from making suggestions for workplace improvement can eliminate this behavior by ignoring those who make the suggestions. The suggestions will become extinct when they are invariably met with an absence of reinforcement. Presumably, the employee in Figure 15.7 will eventually realize that chronic

Avoidance learning.
A type of reinforcement that strengthens behavior by teaching individuals to respond in ways to avoid undesirable consequences.

Extinction.
A type of reinforcement that weakens behavior by withholding a desirable consequence when an undesirable behavior occurs.

FIGURE 15.7 EXAMPLES OF REINFORCEMENT

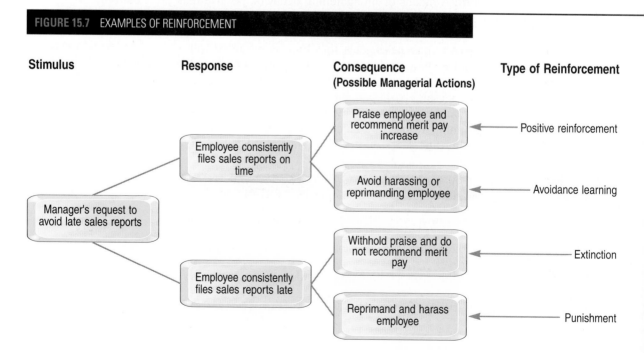

lateness is not producing a desired consequence and will discontinue the undesirable behavior.

4. **Punishment.** A second means for weakening behavior, punishment provides an undesirable consequence when an undesirable behavior occurs. For instance, W. T. Grant, the giant retailer that went bankrupt, made it a practice to cut the necktie of any sales manager who did not meet his quota. The reprimand or harassment of the employee in Figure 15.7 for consistently filing the requested sales report late is also an example of punishment. Fines, suspensions, pay cuts, probation periods, and demotions are other examples. According to Skinner, punishment has the effect of reducing the tendency to act in a given way, at least in the short run. An ardent opponent of punishment, except in the most extreme situations, Skinner noted that although punishment typically works immediately, it gives no beneficial long-term result. The responses to punishment—the urge to escape, the urge to counterattack, or a stubborn apathy—are all undesirable. Research into if, how, and when punishment should be used in work situations has yielded few definitive answers. As noted in Chapter 13, punishment in the form of discipline (oral and written warnings, suspensions without pay, and discharges) is occasionally necessary to maintain organization performance. Research indicates that mild to moderate forms of discipline, such as informal discussions oriented toward problem resolution and brief suspensions, can defuse tense situations and increase subsequent employee performance. In contrast, more severe forms of discipline, such as written warnings and longer suspensions, generally have negative effects, possibly because of the reasons mentioned above.[12]

Punishment.

A type of reinforcement that weakens behavior by providing an undesirable consequence when an undesirable behavior occurs.

SMART MANAGEMENT   CONGRATULATIONS! THE POWER OF POSITIVE REINFORCEMENT

The following story was overheard at a business meeting.

Last April, a company president decided to have a little fun with April Fool's Day. As a joke, he mailed his business card to several friends, and on the back of each card he wrote, "Well done . . . Congratulations!"

But the joke backfired because each of his friends telephoned to express appreciation for the pat on the back. Yes, each believed that he or she had done something important enough to deserve commendation.

That gave the company president another idea—but not as a joke. He wrote the very same congratulatory message on about a dozen pieces of personal stationery and sent them to various employees in separate interoffice envelopes.

Believe it or not, the same thing happened! Each person who received the message thanked the president for his kind words and said something like this: "I didn't realize you knew I graduated from the advanced computer course" or ". . . won the baking contest" or ". . . finished second in the marathon" or ". . . was named best bowler on the company team" or ". . . sold more than any sales rep in the field."

All felt they had accomplished something of sufficient importance to be praised. All deserved recognition.

What would you say is the moral of this story?

Source: Adapted with permission from Fred G. Lippert, "Management Comments," *Supervision* 46 (April 1984): 18.

Schedules of Reinforcement

A final, but important, aspect of reinforcement theory concerns the timing and frequency of reinforcement. **Continuous reinforcement** occurs when a desired behavior is always followed by a specific result. An example of continuous reinforcement would be praising a subordinate for every unit of output. Because it is not feasible in a typical work situation to reinforce every desired behavior, workplace reinforcement is seldom continuous. Rather, it is reinforced intermittently. **Intermittent reinforcement** occurs when a desired behavior is rewarded on an intermittent or periodic basis, as opposed to every time it is performed. There are four basic kinds of intermittent-reinforcement schedules (each is summarized in Table 15.6):

- **Fixed-interval schedules** apply reinforcement on the first response made after some fixed time interval. The critical variable is time, and it is held constant. Performance under a fixed-interval schedule of reinforcement tends to be poor since the absence of a direct link between performance and reward typically results in individuals exerting effort shortly before the set amount of time has gone by, in anticipation of the reinforcement that is to come. Likewise, performance tends to fall off immediately after reinforcement and tends to pick up again as the time for the next reinforcement draws near. In somewhat the same way, students often stop studying right after an exam and then gradually start up again as the date of the next test approaches. Fixed-interval schedules of reinforcement have been compared to weekly, semiweekly, or monthly paychecks because employee effort tends to drop off immediately following payday, only to pick up again immediately preceding payday.

- **Variable-interval schedules** apply reinforcement on the first response made after some variable, or changing, time interval. The actual times between pairs of reinforcers differ widely and unpredictably. One reinforcement might be given after 2 days, the next after 1 day, the next after a week, the next after a month and so on. Consequently, the time interval between reinforcement cannot be predicted in advance. At best, only the average time may be calculated. One example of a variable-interval schedule of reinforcement would be weekly pop quizzes given on random days of the week. A second would be a health inspector's unannounced quarterly visits to a restaurant. The instructor's students cannot predict precisely when they'll have another pop quiz, and neither can the restaurant's managers predict the health inspector's next visit. Nonetheless, the students can expect that *on the average* they will have one pop quiz a week, and the restaurant's managers can likely expect that *on the average* the health inspector will visit once every 3 months. Given these expectations, performance typically drops somewhat after reinforcement is ap-

---

Continuous reinforcement.
When a desired behavior is always followed by a specific result.

Intermittent reinforcement.
When a desired behavior is rewarded on an intermittent or periodic basis, as opposed to every time it is performed.

Fixed-interval schedules.
Reinforcement applied on the basis of time elapsed, with the amount of time specified in advance.

Variable-interval schedule.
Reinforcement applied on the basis of time elapsed, with the amount of time varying.

TABLE 15.6 INTERMITTENT-REINFORCEMENT SCHEDULES

1. *Fixed interval.* Reinforcement applied on the first response after some fixed time interval.
2. *Variable interval.* Reinforcement applied on the first response after some variable, or changing, time interval.
3. *Fixed ratio.* Reinforcement applied on the basis of number of behaviors performed, with the number specified in advance.
4. *Variable ratio.* Reinforcement applied on the basis of number of behaviors performed, with the number varying.

plied. Neither the students nor restaurant managers, for instance, expect a quiz or health inspection 2 days in a row, but they aren't likely to stop preparing for any great length of time.

- **Fixed-ratio schedules** apply reinforcement on the basis of the number of behaviors performed, with the number specified in advance. The most common example of a fixed-ratio reinforcement schedule is a piece-rate incentive pay scheme. Under such a scheme, an employee receives a reward for each unit of output. If the piece rate for a needleworker installing collars in a shirt factory is $1 for ten collars, the reinforcement (money, in this case) is fixed to the number of finished collars. For every 100 collars installed, the needleworker earns $10. Performance under a fixed-ratio reinforcement schedule tends to be higher than it is under either a fixed-interval or variable-interval reinforcement schedule. However, performance typically drops temporarily after fixed-ratio reinforcement since individuals are likely to exert effort in spurts to attain a specified level of output. Sales commissions are a second example of a fixed-ratio performance schedule.

Fixed-ratio schedules. Reinforcement applied on the basis of number of behaviors performed, with the number specified in advance.

- **Variable-ratio schedules** apply reinforcement on the basis of the number of behaviors performed, with the number varying. To receive reinforcement, an individual might have to repeat a desired behavior 10 times in one instance, 12 times the next, 6 times the next, and so on. The exact number of repetitions is unknown. Slot machines are a classic example of variable-ratio reinforcement. They are programmed to provide payoffs (jackpots) just frequently enough to reinforce the behavior of dropping a coin into a slot and pulling a handle. The exact number of plays (desired behaviors) required to win in a particular instance, however, is unknown.

Variable-ratio schedule. Reinforcement applied on the basis of number of behaviors performed with the number varying.

Few, if any, organizations use a variable-ratio schedule of reinforcement as their principal compensation strategy. Variable-ratio reinforcement, however, is used in other ways. For example, a manager might use a variable-ratio schedule for praising employees. In consequence, the employees are uncertain beforehand which of their actions (getting the fifth, twelfth, or twentieth order) might be praised. Of the various schedules of reinforcement, variable-ratio is generally considered the most effective in producing a consistently high level of performance. Indeed, individuals operating under a variable-ratio schedule often display an addiction to behavior that may be reinforced. This, of course, explains the addictive quality of gambling for many people.

Assessment

Reinforcement theory is unquestionably the most controversial of the motivation theories we have examined. Not unexpectedly, it has received a fair measure of criticism. There are six particularly pertinent criticisms:

1. By maintaining that human behavior is controlled by various factors outside the person and that conscious choice is thus irrelevant, it renders concepts such as free will and moral responsibility meaningless.

2. It is too rigid and programmed in its methods, failing to consider the importance of individual needs, expectancies, and valences.

3. It overemphasizes the importance of external outcomes (for example, pay and promotions) and ignores the role of internal outcomes (for example, feelings of accomplishment and recognition) that result from doing a task.

4. It fails to recognize that while various reinforcers may be initially effective, with time they lose their significance and people no longer respond to them.

5. It raises ethical concerns. Many critics feel the terms *extinction* and *punishment* themselves smack of employee manipulation. They fear reinforcement theory may be used to exploit employees.

6. It does not acknowledge that, once manipulated, people soon learn to manipulate back. Thus, as long as an organization has rewards to give, employees will play along. But when the rewards run out, motivation can, too.

Managerial Implications

The preceding criticisms notwithstanding, reinforcement theory is a legitimate motivation theory. As such, it carries several important implications for managers:

1. Behaviors that are rewarded will be repeated. Behaviors that are not rewarded will not be repeated. This has obvious implications for the design of compensation schemes since employees can be expected to behave as they are rewarded for behaving.

2. It is important for employees to be told which behaviors are desirable and will be rewarded, and which behaviors are undesirable and will not be rewarded. If employees are to be rewarded for high-quality work as opposed to quantity per se, this needs to be clearly communicated.

3. Rewards should be based on performance. If identical rewards, such as across-the-board raises, are given for all grades of performance, average and below-average performance will be strengthened and above-average performance weakened. Standardized compensation schemes, such as the federal government's Grade and Pay Scale, in essence endorse equal pay regardless of performance for all employees at the same organization level. They thereby encourage employees to do nothing more than the minimum necessary to keep their job.

4. The failure to reward also can modify behavior. If behavior (either desired or undesired) goes unrewarded, it will diminish and eventually become extinct. This has clear implications for the introduction of change, as well as for training efforts and other programs aimed at altering behavior.

SUMMARY

Motivation, meaning the will to achieve, is one of the most important concerns confronting a manager. This chapter has examined two content and three process theories of motivation.

Learning Objective 1: **Explain various ways motivation plays a role in most organizations.**

Motivation plays a role in most organizations in at least three ways: (1) people must be attracted—motivated—to join an organization and remain in it; (2) once on the job, employees must be induced—or motivated—to exert energy and effort at an acceptable rate; and (3) an organization's human resources must be maintained and developed. Company-sponsored training programs and conferences are often used for this purpose. Motivation is an essential element in the success of all such activities.

Learning Objective 2: Identify the five categories in Maslow's need-hierarchy theory.

The five categories in Maslow's need-hierarchy theory are physiological needs, safety needs, social needs, esteem needs, and self-actualization needs.

Learning Objective 3: Differentiate between motivators and hygienes in Herzberg's two-factor theory.

Herzberg labeled the factors (achievement, recognition, the work itself, responsibility, advancement, and personal growth) that produced job satisfaction *motivators*. His analysis indicated that these factors are directly related to job content. He labeled the factors (company policies and administration, supervision, relations with one's peers, working conditions, pay, and job security) that led to job dissatisfaction *hygienes*. His analysis indicated that these factors are more related to the work setting, or job context, than to job content.

Learning Objective 4: Describe the concepts of expectancy and valence as used in Vroom's expectancy theory.

Expectancies are beliefs that performance will be rewarded. They can be separated into two types: Expectancy 1—the belief that effort will lead to performance—and Expectancy 2—the belief that performance will lead to rewards. Valence is the value placed on an outcome (reward). It can be either positive or negative. Thus, a person may attach a negative value to an outcome (for example, being fired) or a positive value to an outcome (for example, a promotion).

Learning Objective 5: Distinguish between equality and equity as defined in Adams's equity theory.

Equality is said to exist when an individual perceives outcomes he or she receives to be equal to outcomes being received by another person. Equity is attained when the ratio of an individual's perceived outcomes to inputs equals the ratio of the other person's outcomes to inputs.

Learning Objective 6: Explain the guiding principle behind Skinner's reinforcement theory.

The guiding principle behind Skinner's reinforcement theory is that human behavior is a function of its consequences. That is, behaviors that lead to desirable consequences are likely to be repeated. Behaviors that lead to undesirable consequences are less likely to be repeated.

KEY TERMS

avoidance learning 456	fixed-ratio schedules 459	reinforcement 454
content approach to motivation 438	hygienes 444	response 454
	intermittent reinforcement 458	safety needs 440
continuous reinforcement 458	law of effect 454	self-actualization 440
equality 450	motivation 438	social needs 440
equity 450	motivators 444	stimulus 454
esteem needs 440	physiological needs 439	valence 448
expectancy 1 447	positive reinforcement 455	variable-interval schedule 458
expectancy 2 447	process approach to motivation 438	variable-ratio schedule 459
extinction 456	punishment 457	
fixed-interval schedules 458		

THE MANAGEMENT EXPERIENCE   WHAT EMPLOYEES WANT MOST

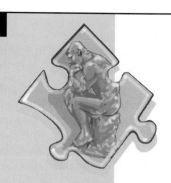

Over the years, several studies have attempted to determine what people want from their work. In one such study a list of ten work-related items was given to 1,000 employees and their 100 immediate superiors. The employees were asked to rank the items in order of importance to them. The superiors were asked to rank the items as they thought their employees would.

Here is a chance to rank the items yourself and compare your list with those of the employees and their superiors. In the space provided, enter the items in what you would expect to be their *descending* order of importance to the *employees*.

Feeling of being in on things	1. _____
Full appreciation of work done	2. _____
Good wages	3. _____
Good working conditions	4. _____
Interesting work	5. _____
Job security	6. _____
Personal loyalty to employees	7. _____
Promotions and growth in the company	8. _____
Sympathetic help with personal problems	9. _____
Tactful discipline	10. _____

Now, compare your list with the following two: This is how the superiors thought their employees would answer:

1. Good wages
2. Job security
3. Promotions and growth in the company
4. Good working conditions
5. Interesting work
6. Sympathetic help with personal problems
7. Personal loyalty to employees
8. Full appreciation of work done
9. Tactful discipline
10. Feeling of being in on things

This is how the employees actually answered:

1. Interesting work
2. Full appreciation of work done
3. Feeling of being in on things
4. Job security
5. Good wages
6. Promotions and growth in the company
7. Good working conditions
8. Personal loyalty to employees
9. Tactful discipline
10. Sympathetic help with personal problems

How did you do? Surprised? Does your list resemble that of the employees or their superiors? Did you list "good wages" either first or second, or did you realize intuitively that to many employees money is not the primary concern, important though it may be? Did you fall into the trap of assuming that employees respond most favorably to material rewards, or did you correctly predict their distinct preference for intangibles?

If you were wrong in most of your listing, you can see how easy it is to think you know someone when, in reality, you do not.

Source: Based on Kenneth A. Kovach, "What Motivates Employees? Workers and Supervisors Give Different Answers," *Business Horizons* 30 (September–October 1987): 58–65.

REVIEW AND DISCUSSION QUESTIONS

1. You are a leading sales representative for a major manufacturer of photocopiers. While attending a company-sponsored training program on motivation, you are told by your boss, "All I want from you is strong motivation. That's what makes a successful sales representative." Comment.

2. As a future manager, why should you want to know more about motivation?

3. In his book, *High Output Management*, Andrew S. Grove, president of Intel Corporation, notes that "the title of a movie about athletes, *Personal Best*, captures what self-actualization means." He goes on to observe that "once someone's source of motivation is self-actualization, his drive to perform has no limit."[13] Comment on this observation.

4. Mary Kay Cosmetics is especially known for the many awards and titles it gives to its high-performing saleswomen. Mary Kay's saleswomen flock to Dallas every August at their own expense to take part in a meeting that is much more than a sales meeting. During elaborate sessions called "Mary Kay seminars," gold-and-diamond pins, fur stoles, and even Cadillacs painted in a distinctive shade, called "Mary Kay pink," are awarded to top saleswomen. The awards are presented in a setting reminiscent of a Miss America pageant—in a large auditorium, on a stage in front of a cheering audience, and with everyone dressed in glamorous evening clothes. Drawing on your knowledge of Maslow's need-hierarchy theory and Herzberg's two-factor theory, explain how the behavior of Mary Kay's saleswomen is influenced more by factors related to job content than job context.

5. Suppose you are a wage and salary specialist in the compensation section of a large corporation. Your boss has just read an article titled "Modern Motivation Theories." Based upon what she has read, she has begun to wonder about the corporation's compensation practices. As a result, she has asked you to prepare a report discussing the motivational pros and cons of making all employee pay records public. Taking an expectancy-theory perspective, what will your report conclude?

6. Comment on the following quote by Ricardo Semler, president of Semco S/A, Brazil's largest marine and food-processing machinery manufacturer:

   If executives are embarrassed by their salaries, that probably means they aren't earning them. Confidential payrolls are for those who cannot look themselves in the mirror and say with conviction, "I live in a capitalist system that remunerates on a geometric scale. I spent years in school, I have years of experience, I am capable and dedicated and intelligent. I deserve what I get."[14]

7. Imagine that you are on your first job following graduation. You are excited about your work, your prospects for the future, and your salary—the highest starting salary in your graduating class. However, after 2 weeks on the job you accidentally learn that your officemate, another new college graduate hired for a position identical to yours, is earning some $125 a month more than you. Calling upon Adams's equity theory, predict your reaction to this information. What would your reaction be if the tables were turned?

8. The text notes that people will experience inequity when they are either relatively underpaid or overpaid. With this in mind, reflect on the following sentiment as expressed by Jim Harbaugh when serving as the Chicago Bears' first-string quarterback:

> I want a chance to contribute to this team. I wake up Monday morning and I have no bruises. That ain't right. I should be bruised. I feel I'm getting paid darn well, and I'm not able to do anything for my money. I feel underworked and overpaid. I want to feel like I'm pulling my share of the load.[15]

9. For the past several months, you have been unsuccessful in your attempts to persuade a subordinate in your retail sales department to increase his productivity. How could you use behavior modification for this purpose?

10. In his book, *Managing,* former ITT chief executive Harold Geneen contends, "The person who heads a company should realize that his people are really not working for him; they are working *with* him for themselves. They have their own dreams, their own need for self-fulfillment. He has to help fill their needs as much as they do his."[16] Do you agree with this contention? Why or why not?

CASE 15.1 — A TALE OF FRED AND WIL

The following two situations illustrate two types of employees with different motivations. They both cause problems for management in their own ways.

Fred Mengel, Tennessee Revenue Officer

An office of the Tennessee State Department of Revenue is located in Memphis. This unit is responsible for collecting Tennessee taxes for the region and enforcement of tax laws.

One of the employees of this office is Fred Mengel. Mengel, a civil service employee, is 51 years old. He has worked for the state for 20 years. He could not afford to go to college, but he has taken all the training the department offers and has occasionally attended night courses at Memphis State University, especially when the state paid for the course, and if it raised his pay grade.

Mengel was divorced some years ago. Between his job and an inheritance, he has more than enough money to live on. He has no children and his parents are dead. His wife moved to California after the divorce. He likes television. Every Thursday night he plays cards with friends. On Saturdays he usually has a date to go dancing or to a movie. Mengel feels that life is quite pleasant, especially when nobody pushes him.

The preceding is a preliminary description of a problem employee written to the casewriter by Mengel's superior, Bernie Lovell. Lovell is 38 years old, a graduate of Memphis State with a master's degree. He has been Mengel's boss for a year. He has discussed "the Fred problem" with his two previous supervisors. Their analysis is the same as his.

As he sees it, Mengel is a classic case of the ineffectual employee that you cannot do anything about. But he pulls morale and performance down. Lovell says,

> Fred is a 20-year civil service veteran. You really can't do anything about him. He slides through his job, never straining himself for anyone or anything. He drifts in about on time. He fiddles around his desk for half an hour or so. He starts the 9:30 coffee break early and stretches it late. He does the same at lunch and at the afternoon coffee break. He starts getting ready to leave 45 minutes early with the going-to-the-rest-room-and-straightening-up-his-desk routine. He has never, never left late. He has a good time with a circle of friends at breaks and lunches. He calls them during the day, too, though I've never caught him at it.
>
> Fred knows how to work the system. He does just enough so you can't do anything about him. Have you ever tried to discipline a civil servant, much less a 20-year veteran?

I've tried to talk to him. His attitude, never spoken, is: "I've seen bosses come and go and I'm still here. I'll listen, appear hurt, may even agree to try harder, but there's nothing you can do and we both know it. We're playing a game."

Mengel's job involves routine checking of tax payments. He has never received a bad performance evaluation or a good one. It is always average, slightly above, or slightly below.

But Lovell is perturbed because the other employees tend to emulate Mengel after awhile. Even if they are enthusiastic and hardworking at first, pretty soon they begin to follow his behavior patterns.

Wil Michaels of Foreign Autos, Inc.

Ralph Johnson, owner of Foreign Autos, Inc., was sitting alone in his office late one Friday night pondering what he should do about Wil Michaels, who had been with Foreign for some 20 years.

History

Foreign Autos, Inc., a medium-sized sales and service dealership for several makes of prestigious foreign automobiles, was founded in Virginia soon after World War II. From the sale of his very first automobile, Ralph Johnson realized a potential market existed among consumers who found themselves ready to purchase durables, especially automobiles, after the hardships of the war ended. Johnson knew that to develop a successful auto business, he not only must sell autos but also must be prepared to offer service commensurate with the prestigiousness of these autos. To do this, he very carefully hired auto mechanics who were familiar with his products. This was not an easy task for him, a salesman with a degree in business administration from a midwestern university. But with the help of a former army buddy, he was able to locate two mechanics who were familiar with foreign autos. Franz Hendrick, a former mechanic from Munich, Germany, was a middle-age widower who lost his wife just before the war and was able to immigrate to the United States. Hendrick was happy to have the chance to work on engines with which he was so familiar. Although his ability to communicate was restricted by his heavy German accent, he welcomed the opportunity to teach his trade to a young mechanic from Wisconsin, Wilson Michaels.

Hendrick and Michaels carried the service end of Foreign Autos for almost 5 years. One day,

however, in a conference with Johnson, both men requested an oil change and grease mechanic to relieve them of these more mundane duties. Foreign Autos had grown to the point where Hendrick and Michaels were working 10–12 hours a day and barely meeting customer time demands. They felt a grease mechanic would allow them to handle the mechanical work in a more efficient manner. Johnson, who was somewhat surprised at the request, said he certainly would look into the matter and apologized to Hendrick and Michaels for not spending more time with his service responsibilities.

Johnson realized then that he could not be a salesman and a service manager at the same time. Therefore, he was willing to relinquish his sales duties to his son and his service duties to a newly hired service manager. By 1976 the family business had burgeoned into a corporation with six salesmen headed by a sales manager and five mechanics headed by a service manager. Although Hendrick retired just before the service manager's coming, Michaels, now a 20-year veteran, remained as a valuable product of Hendrick's careful teaching.

Although attrition had been minimal before 1976, Foreign Autos, Inc., experienced considerable turnover in its service department during the following 10 years. It lost three service managers during that time, and none of the mechanics other than Michaels had more than 3 years with Foreign Autos.

Ned Thomas, Foreign's current service manager, was a young mechanic with a 2-year associate degree in auto repair. In addition, Thomas minored in management at college. Although Johnson felt that Thomas was well qualified to handle the service manager's job, problems continued in the service department.

The Issue

Thomas stormed into Johnson's office late last week and told Johnson that he had to get rid of Michaels. While Michaels was an outstanding mechanic, the other mechanics would not work with him. "Wil is trying to show us up," said Thomas. He comes in at 7:00 a.m. and works 'til 6:00 at night or later. That stuff can be done the next day."

"He won't even eat lunch with the rest of us guys," Thomas continued. "He eats while he works. Granted, a lot of people ask for Wil because he's been here so long, but if he would not tinker on a job, he would get through. The other day he was fixing a door lock and he said it just didn't sound right when he got it back together, so he took the whole thing apart again. It worked, and that's what matters."

"This is creating a problem, Ralph," said Thomas. "Let me cite a few other instances."

"One day about 2 weeks ago, a lady came in to get new wiper blades. She walked into the service area and was greeted by a big hello from Wil. You've got to admit, Wil's mighty friendly. To make a long story short, Wil left his job and put the wiper blades on for her. We've got people to do those small tasks. It was okay for him to retorque her engine after the head replacement, but why this nonsense? We've got a minimum charge for labor, and he puts those blades on for just the cost of the parts. We'll go bankrupt this way.

"You'll probably remember last Friday night when we were going to leave exactly on time to go to the ball game. Well, Wil was still working on this car he promised to have done. He had all the major work done by 4:45. Instead of quitting, he started tinkering with the seat belt adjustment. The customer told Wil that he would be very happy to bring the car in some other more convenient time—but, no, Wil had to fool around with that, too. You know, I don't leave until all the mechanics are gone, but I just couldn't stay and I decided to leave about ten after five. I don't know how long he kept the cashier there, on top of which he had me blocked in the parking lot with his car. Boy, I burned rubber when I got out of there!

"What concerns me most right now, Ralph, is that I overheard some of the guys planning to place one of Wil's wrenches in the cowl behind the fan. You know what that will do.

"I guess this problem is just getting too big for me to handle. I'd fire him immediately, but I learned in business school not to overstep my authority, so I'm coming to you to ask you to do it."

Johnson's train of thought suddenly was interrupted by the pile of mail on his desk. He had been so involved in his thoughts about his service department that he failed to look through the day's mail. Only bills, he thought, until he came to a postcard—a glossy color print of Vancouver—addressed to Michaels! Curiosity forced him to read the card. "We're having a lovely trip—no car trouble thanks to your wonderful service, time, and effort on our car. We'll always be your loyal customers."

Johnson turned back to his thoughts. He really didn't know what to do. Should he say something to Michaels tomorrow during their fishing trip?

Problems

1. What motivates Mengel?
2. What motivates Michaels?
3. As a manager, how would you attempt to modify the behavior of Michaels (or would you)? What theoretical framework would guide you in the effort?

Source: Mary Ann Lederhaus, University of North Florida, Jacksonville.

NOTES

[1] David E. Terpstra, "Theories of Motivation—Borrowing the Best," *Personnel Journal* 58 (June 1979): 376.

[2] Abraham H. Maslow, "A Theory of Human Motivation," *Psychological Review* 50 (July 1943): 370–396; Abraham H. Maslow, *Motivation and Personality*, 2d ed. (New York: Harper & Row, 1970); Abraham H. Maslow, *Eupsychian Management* (Homewood, Ill.: Irwin, 1965); and Abraham H. Maslow, *Toward a Psychology of Being*, 2d ed. (Princeton, N.J.: Van Nostrand Reinhold, 1968).

[3] Maslow, "A Theory of Human Motivation," 382.

[4] Frederick Herzberg, Bernard Mausner, Barbara B. Snyderman, *The Motivation to Work* (New York: Wiley, 1959); Frederick Herzberg, *Work and the Nature of Man* (Cleveland: World, 1966); Frederick Herzberg, *The Managerial Choice*, 2d ed. (rev.) (Salt Lake City, Utah: Olympus, 1982); and Frederick Herzberg, "Workers' Needs: The Same around the World," *Industry Week*, September 21, 1987, 29–32.

[5] Victor H. Vroom, *Work and Motivation* (New York: Wiley, 1964). Also see David Nadler and Edward E. Lawler III, "Motivation: A Diagnostic Approach," in J. Richard Hackman, Edward E. Lawler III, and Lyman W. Porter, eds., *Perspectives on Behavior in Organization*, 2d ed. (New York: McGraw-Hill, 1983), 67–78.

[6] J. Stacy Adams, "Toward an Understanding of Inequity," *Journal of Abnormal and Social Psychology* 67, no. 5 (1963), 422–436; and Richard T. Mowday, "Equity Theory Predictions of Behavior in Organizations," in Richard M. Steers and Lyman W. Porter (eds.), *Motivation and Work Behavior*, 3d ed. (New York: McGraw-Hill, 1983), 91–112.

[7] Quoted in Randy Galloway, "Dorsett: Mutiny over the Bounty," *Dallas Morning News*, August 14, 1986, 1B.

[8] Adapted from J. Stacy Adams, "Injustice in Social Exchange," in Leonard Berkowitz (ed.), *Advances in Experimental Social Psychology*, vol. 2 (New York: Academic Press, 1965), 283–296.

[9] Quoted in Thomas F. O'Boyle, "Loyalty Ebbs at Many Companies as Employees Grow Disillusioned," *Wall Street Journal,* July 11, 1985, 27.

[10] B. F. Skinner, *Science and Human Behavior* (New York: Free Press, 1953).

[11] Edward L. Thorndike, *Animal Intelligence* (New York: Macmillan, 1911), 244.

[12] Janice M. Beyer and Harrison M. Trice, "A Field of Study of the Use and Perceived Effects of Discipline in Controlling Work Performance," *Academy of Management Journal* 27 (December 1984): 743–764.

[13] Andrew S. Grove, *High Output Management* (New York: Random House, 1983), 164.

[14] Ricardo Semler, "Managing without Managers," *Harvard Business Review* 67 (September–October 1988): 83.

[15] "End Quote," (New Orleans) *Times-Picayune,* September 13, 1988, E-2.

[16] Harold S. Geneen, *Managing* (New York: Doubleday, 1984), 145.

osing weight is not easy for most people, but Jenny Craig has put a friendly face on this odious task. Jenny Craig International, Inc., offers an effective weight-loss program combined with counseling and support.

Craig became interested in weight loss after she had gained 45 pounds during her second pregnancy. At the time, she was a dental assistant at Louisiana Health Care Authority–Medical Center of Louisiana at New Orleans. She joined a fitness club and met other women who were also trying to lose weight. There she listened to their stories and offered them support while they all became slimmer and happier. She found the experience so inspiring that she applied for a job at the club. She soon became a manager, and within a few years, she was supervising several clubs.

In 1970 Craig took a job supervising health clubs for entrepreneur Sid Craig, whom she eventually married. By 1983 they had decided to sell the health-club business and move to Australia. There they started a weight-loss program consisting of nutritional guidance, counseling and support, and recommendations for exercise (no exercise facilities were provided). The program was a complete success. When the Craigs returned to the United States in 1985, they

EFFECTIVE LEADERSHIP

owned 50 centers in Australia and a $25 million per year business. Since then their empire has grown to 645 centers around the world, with an income of $431 million.

Obviously, Craig has more than just good ideas. She has 30 years of experience in the weight-loss business, at every level and in many locations. She has provided counsel and managed counselors; she has run established businesses and started new ones; she has worked in the United States and abroad. And she has probably talked to more dieters than anyone else in the world.

Craig radiates warmth and caring. Most people who meet her like her. And she has managed to suffuse this quality throughout the corporation—both in staff and in program design. Even Jenny Craig International's advertising reflects this quality. But just because Craig is sensitive to client needs does not mean that Jenny Craig International, with its thousands of employees, will be. Craig has therefore developed hiring policies that recruit caring individuals as counselors. Craig has developed a leadership style that successfully matches the demands of both her industry and its clients. She speaks smoothly but looks people right in the eye. She not only commands respect, but people like her. Craig is a recognized world leader in the weight-loss industry.

In this chapter, we will investigate what makes a person effective as a leader and how leaders transmit to employees not only the knowledge of what is to be done but the drive to actually do it.

Source: Gayle Sato Stodder, "Dieting's Diva," *Entrepreneurial Woman* 3, (March 1991): 42–44.

Effective leadership is essential to business, government, military, the arts, and all the other institutions that influence the way we live, work, and play. From a managerial perspective, **leadership** is the process of influencing others toward the accomplishment of goals. Although authority and power can also be used to shape the behavior of others, there are many circumstances when they are inappropriate for achieving desired results. Under such circumstances, leadership provides an alternative that is typically less threatening and generally more acceptable. In this respect, leadership is something more than either authority or power in that it implies some degree of voluntary compliance by followers.

Thus, the essence of leadership is the "influential increment" over and above routine compliance with management directives.[1] All managers at a given hierarchical level are equal with respect to formal authority and managerial power. They do not remain equal, however. Some have a much better understanding of people than others, as well as traits that are more acceptable to superiors and subordinates. The most effective managers have the ability to use more than their formal role in relating to people. Stated simply, they are able to act as leaders.

The importance of effective leadership has been demonstrated repeatedly. In the business world, Andrew Carnegie, John D. Rockefeller, Olive A. Beech, J. C. Pen-

Leadership.
The process of influencing others toward accomplishing goals.

In 1932 Olive A. Beech founded Beech Aircraft Corporation with her husband, Walter. She served as secretary-treasurer and director, arranging millions of dollars in financing as the corporation grew into a multi-million dollar enterprise. In 1950, upon the death of her husband, Beech became president and chairman of the Beech Aircraft board of directors. She continues to serve as chairman emeritus.

ney, J. Pierpont Morgan, and Lee A. Iacocca have made reputations for themselves as strong leaders. In the military, H. Norman Schwarzkopf, George S. Patton, Robert E. Lee, Ulysses S. Grant, Joan of Arc, Napoleon Bonaparte, and Julius Caesar are names associated with effective leadership. Thomas Jefferson, Abraham Lincoln, Mohandas K. Gandhi, and Winston Churchill are all well-known political leaders. Of course, the names of other leaders whose contributions have been less positive (Josef Stalin, Adolf Hitler, and Mao Zedung) also come to mind.

The purpose of this chapter is to explore the nature of effective leadership. We begin by reviewing the major theories of leadership, noting their strengths and limitations. In addition to assessing each theory, we will explore its managerial implications. We will then briefly examine several emerging perspectives on leadership. Finally, we will identify various "substitutes for leadership."

LEADERSHIP THEORIES

Leadership has been studied for thousands of years. As indicated in Figure 16.1, our knowledge of leadership has progressed through three principal research phases: the trait phase, the behavioral phase, and the situational phase. Because this knowledge has been largely cumulative across time, we will discuss the phases in chronological order. A thorough knowledge of the major theories of leadership associated with each phase will provide the background necessary to evaluate alternative leadership styles and to make an informed decision regarding their appropriate application. Additionally, it should be valuable in understanding why certain leaders are effective and others are not.

TRAIT PHASE

As viewed by many, history is shaped by the leadership of great people. Without Moses, the Jews would have remained captive in Egypt. Without Churchill, the British would have succumbed to the German Blitz in 1940.

We have all marveled at the achievements of great people, so it is not surprising that the earliest attempts to understand leadership centered on determining what specific traits make a person an effective leader. Consequently, early investigations sought to discover how people in leadership positions had attained them and whether the people had certain traits in common. In general, these investigations defined a **trait** as a distinctive physical or psychological characteristic that accounts for a person's behavior.

In its pure form, the trait phase grew out of the **"great man" theory of leadership,** which held that a person was born either with or without the necessary traits to be a successful leader. Thus, leadership was thought to be derived from

Trait.
A distinctive physical or psychological characteristic that accounts for a person's behavior.

"Great man" theory of leadership.
The view that a person is born with or without the necessary traits to be a successful leader.

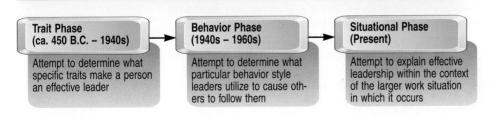

FIGURE 16.1 MAJOR PHASES IN LEADERSHIP RESEARCH (450 B.C.–Present)

Trait Phase (ca. 450 B.C. – 1940s)	Behavior Phase (1940s – 1960s)	Situational Phase (Present)
Attempt to determine what specific traits make a person an effective leader	Attempt to determine what particular behavior style leaders utilize to cause others to follow them	Attempt to explain effective leadership within the context of the larger work situation in which it occurs

nature. Learned behavior was considered irrelevant. People such as Alexander the Great, Hannibal, and Napoleon were said to be "natural leaders" who were born to lead. It was believed they were endowed with inborn qualities that would have enabled them to be effective leaders in any situation. (Despite the examples of Joan of Arc, Elizabeth I, and Catherine the Great, women leaders were ignored.)

The great-man theory held sway well into the late 1890s. At that time, belief in inborn leader traits began to diminish, although interest in traits themselves greatly increased. Under the influence of the promising new behavioral school of psychology, researchers began to reevaluate the great-man theory. There were two principal reasons for this:

1. It was contended that if there were indeed "great men," or "natural leaders," it should be possible to investigate the traits that set them apart from the masses.

2. It was believed that if these unique traits could be identified, other individuals should be able to acquire them through learning and experience.

Contrary to the great-man theory, many researchers contended that leadership could be *learned*. A host of studies ensued to discover the traits that, if acquired, would transform followers into leaders. Most of these studies attempted to identify the traits that distinguish leaders (usually persons holding a high office) from their followers. On the whole, however, such attempts have been disappointing. The only conclusions that receive support are that leaders tend to have a high effort level, a strong desire to lead but not to seek power as an end in itself, an undisputed honesty and integrity, a secure self-confidence, a reasonable cognitive ability, and a high degree of task-related knowledge.[2]

BEHAVIORAL PHASE

Since the study of traits offered little evidence for distinguishing leaders from followers or for making the latter into the former, researchers in the 1940s began to question the existence of unique leader traits and shifted attention instead to leader behavior. This shift marked the beginning of the *behavioral phase* of leadership research, which held that leaders may be best characterized by how they behave, rather than by their personal traits. Underlying this phase was the assumption that effective leaders utilize a particular behavioral style that causes others to follow them. The behavioral phase is perhaps best represented by the Ohio State Leadership Studies.

The Ohio State Leadership Studies

Begun in 1947, the Ohio State Leadership Studies were conducted under the primary direction of Ralph M. Stogdill. Their purpose was to determine the relationship between effective leader behavior and subordinates' satisfaction and performance.[3] From observations of managers typifying a wide variety of types and situations, some 1,800 examples of leadership behavior were compiled. Based on these examples, a questionnaire was constructed containing statements illustrating basic categories of leader behavior. A diverse sample of respondents was then asked to use the questionnaire to describe the behavior of their leaders. Their answers were statistically analyzed and revealed that the respondents perceived their leaders' behaviors to be composed of two principal dimensions:

1. **Consideration**—Leader behavior oriented toward developing mutual trust, two-way communication, respect for subordinates' ideas, and concern for their feelings. Examples of leader behaviors indicating consideration are given in Table 16.1 (Panel A).

2. **Initiating structure**—Leader behavior oriented toward structuring subordinates' activities for the purpose of goal attainment. Examples of leader behaviors indicating initiating structure are given in Table 16.1 (Panel B).

Figure 16.2 illustrates the relationship found between consideration and initiating structure. Since consideration and initiating structure are independent dimensions, it is possible for a leader to be high in initiating structure and low in consideration (Cell 1), low in initiating structure and high in consideration (Cell 4), or high or low in both (Cells 2 and 3). For example, a leader might do a good job of scheduling work to be done but mistreat subordinates (Cell 1). Alternatively, a leader might treat subordinates as equals while failing to maintain performance standards (Cell 4). Finally, a leader might do both (Cell 2) or neither (Cell 3).

At first, one might assume, as did the Ohio State researchers, that the most effective leaders would be those who ranked high on both consideration and initiating structure. Surprisingly, this was not always true. Further research indicated that while both are necessary for effective leadership, it is more important for a leader to know how to strike a balance between the two that is appropriate for a particular situation, than it is to exhibit a high degree of both at all times. A summary of conclusions concerning how effective leader behavior relates to employee satisfaction and performance in different situations is given in Table 16.2.

In retrospect, the Ohio State Leadership Studies added immensely to our knowledge about effective leadership. Moreover, the systematic methodology that they introduced and the increased awareness they generated concerning the importance of leader behavior served as a springboard for the leadership research that followed. The major drawback to the Ohio State studies was the limited attention given to situational differences that might influence leader effectiveness. By the late 1960s, this realization was widely acknowledged and leadership research began to shift toward a decidedly situational perspective.

Consideration.
A dimension of leader behavior oriented toward developing mutual trust, two-way communication, respect for subordinates' ideas, and concern for their feelings.

Initiating structure.
A dimension of leader behavior oriented toward structuring subordinates' activities for the purpose of goal attainment.

TABLE 16.1	TWO DIMENSIONS OF LEADER BEHAVIOR	
Dimension	**Meaning**	**Sample Leader Behaviors**
A. Consideration	A psychological closeness between leader and followers	Listens to subordinates Treats subordinates as equals Gives advance notice of changes Looks out for subordinates' personal welfare
B. Initiating structure	A concern for actively directing subordinates toward getting work done	Schedules work to be done Maintains performance standards Encourages use of uniform procedures Decides what will be done and how to do it

FIGURE 16.2 THE RELATIONSHIP BETWEEN CONSIDERATION AND INITIATING STRUCTURE

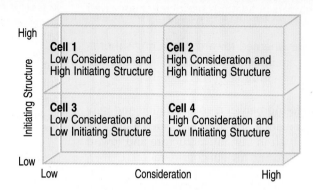

SITUATIONAL PHASE

By the late 1960s, it was widely acknowledged that situational differences that might influence leader effectiveness deserved greater attention. As a consequence, leadership research began to shift toward a decidedly situational perspective. In doing so, it became increasingly clear that there is no one best style of leadership. The most effective style depends on the total situation.

Contemporary leadership theories are almost entirely situational in nature. The three most prominent of these situational theories are Fiedler's contingency theory, House's path-goal theory, and Vroom and Jago's normative theory.

Fiedler's Contingency Theory

The first situational theory to be advanced was the **contingency theory of leadership,** developed by Fred E. Fiedler.[4] Directly consistent with the contin-

Contingency theory of leadership.

A leadership theory which holds that work group performance is contingent upon the match between a person's leadership style and the "favorableness" of the leadership situation.

TABLE 16.2 CONCLUSIONS CONCERNING EFFECTIVE LEADER BEHAVIOR

Consideration

1. Employee satisfaction with a leader is dependent on the degree of consideration displayed by the leader.
2. Leader consideration affects employee satisfaction more when jobs are unpleasant and stressful than when they are pleasant and unstressful.
3. A leader who is high in consideration can exercise more initiating structure without a decline in employee satisfaction.
4. Consideration given in response to good performance will increase the likelihood of future good performance.

Initiating Structure

1. Initiating structure by a leader that adds to role clarity will increase employee satisfaction.
2. Initiating structure by a leader will decrease employee satisfaction when structure is already adequate.
3. Initiating structure by a leader will increase performance when a task is unclear.
4. Initiating structure by a leader will not affect performance when a task is clear.

Source: Alan C. Filley, *The Complete Manager* (Champaign, Ill.: Research Press, 1978), 57–60.

gency approach to management introduced in Chapter 2, it defines leader effectiveness in terms of work group performance. It holds that work group performance depends (or is contingent) on the match between a person's leadership style and the "favorableness" of the leadership situation (see Figure 16.3). We will examine these two factors individually and then consider them together to explain how Fiedler's contingency theory works.

Leadership Style   The term **leadership style** refers to a leader's manner of acting in a work situation. According to Fiedler, one's leadership style depends upon one's personality and is, therefore, relatively fixed. To determine a person's leadership style, Fiedler has developed a simple measure called the **least preferred co-worker (LPC) scale.** This scale asks respondents to think of all the individuals with whom they have ever worked and, using the scale, rate the one person with whom they worked *least well*. LPC scale items are personality attributes like "friendly–unfriendly," "rejecting–accepting," and "distant–close." People who rate their least-preferred co-worker in a relatively unfavorable manner are described as **task oriented.** They derive satisfaction from successfully completing a task and give interpersonal relations a much lower priority. When under pressure, task-oriented leaders tend toward a more directive, structuring leadership style in an attempt to ensure task success. Conversely, people who rate their least-preferred co-worker in a relatively favorable manner are described as **relationship oriented.** They see good interpersonal relations as a requirement for task accomplishment and derive satisfaction from establishing close personal relations with fellow workers. When under pressure, relationship-oriented leaders are likely to adopt a participative, considerate leadership style, being more concerned with social acceptance and the positive regard of others than task success.

Situational Favorableness   The term **situational favorableness** refers to the degree a situation enables a person to exert control over a work group. Three factors are used to measure situational favorableness:

1. **Leader-member relations.** The quality of relations between a leader and group members is believed to be the most important determinant of situational favorableness. Fiedler maintains that leaders will have more control if they have the support of group members, the members of a group work well together, and group members can be relied upon to carry out orders.

2. **Task structure.** The second most important factor in determining situational favorableness is believed to be task structure. This is the degree to which a

Leadership style.
A leader's manner of acting in a work situation.

Least preferred co-worker (LPC) scale.
A scale that asks respondents to think of all the individuals with whom they have ever worked and, using the scale, describe the one person with who they worked *least well*.

Task-oriented leadership.
A leadership style in which satisfaction is derived from successfully completing a task and interpersonal relations are given a much lower priority.

Relationship-oriented leadership.
A leadership style in which good interpersonal relations are seen as a requirement for task accomplishment and satisfaction is derived from establishing close personal relations with fellow workers.

Situational favorableness.
The degree to which a situation enables a person to exert influence over a work group.

FIGURE 16.3   FIEDLER'S CONTINGENCY THEORY OF LEADERSHIP

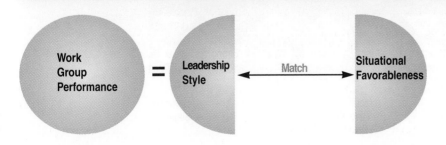

group's assignment is clear. Fiedler contends that highly structured tasks, which specify how a job is to be done in detail (for example, those of an assembly-line worker), provide a leader with more control over group actions than do unstructured tasks (for example, those of a research scientist) in which a leader may have no more knowledge than individual group members.

3. **Leader position power.** Leaders who have the right (legitimate power) to reward and punish subordinates, hire or promote them, and receive organization backing in their decisions have more power than those who do not. Position power can be readily measured in most instances. A ship's captain, for example, has more power than a deck hand, just as a department head has more power than a file clerk. Fiedler maintains that strong position power makes a leader's job easier to perform.

Group Situations When the favorableness of a situation is rated on the basis of leader-member relations, task structure, and leader position power, eight distinct *group situations* can be identified (see Figure 16.4). In other words, leader-member relations can be classified as either good or poor, task structure as either structured or unstructured, and leader position power as either strong or weak. This classification contains all possible combinations of the three situational variables incorporated in Fiedler's theory.

When comparing the eight group situations, note that the conditions at one end of the spectrum (Cell 1) are highly favorable to a leader: The leader is liked, has a structured task, and has position power. Examples would be a well-liked manager of an accounting department or a highly accepted supervisor of a production crew. At the opposite end of the spectrum (Cell 8), the conditions are highly unfavorable: The leader is disliked, has an unstructured task, and has little position power. The unpopular chairperson of an all-volunteer committee developing a new school curriculum might be an example of someone in this situation. In between (Cells 4 and 5), the conditions are only moderately favorable to a leader: The leader has a mixture of good and poor leader-member relations, an ambiguous task, and strong and weak position power. An example might be a respected research team leader or a respected army tank crew commander.

The Full Model To determine which leadership style is most effective in each of the eight group situations, Fiedler analyzed data from some 80 studies he

Leader-member relations.
Relations between a leader and work group members.

Task structure.
The degree to which a group assignment can be programmed and spelled out in a step-by-step fashion.

Leader position power.
The right to reward and punish, hire, or fire with organization backing.

FIGURE 16.4 FIEDLER'S EIGHT GROUP SITUATIONS

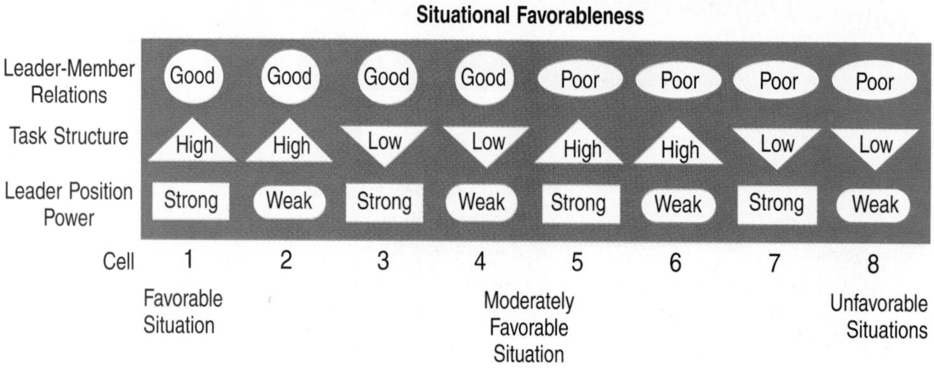

had conducted over more than a decade. These studies investigated a wide variety of groups and situations, including bomber crews, boards of directors, ROTC students, basketball teams, creative groups, and scientists engaged in pure research. The results suggest that neither task-oriented nor relationship-oriented leadership is consistently more effective. Each style works better under certain conditions.

Thus, judged on work group performance, task-oriented leaders do best in either favorable or unfavorable situations in which they have either relatively high control or low control. They are more effective in favorable situations (Cells 1, 2, and 3) because considerate behaviors are superfluous. They are also the most effective in unfavorable situations (Cells 7 and 8) because at least they ensure that "the job gets done." It is only in moderately favorable situations (Cells 4, 5, and 6) that relationship-oriented leaders are more effective because interpersonal relations are especially important.

Assessment Fiedler's contingency theory of leadership is especially appealing for at least two reasons. First, its results reflect everyday life. We all know people who have emerged as leaders in some situations, but not others. The contingency theory of leadership offers a possible explanation for this phenomenon. Second, by basing leadership style on personality attributes, it attempts to reconcile the trait approach to leadership with the idea of different situational requirements. However, caution must be exercised in blindly accepting its conclusions. As with the other theories that we've discussed, Fiedler's work is not without its problems or critics. Four points are particularly pertinent in this regard:

1. Evidence suggests that other situational variables, such as leader intelligence and experience, play a role in determining situational favorableness. Fiedler has recently turned his attention to addressing this weakness.[5]

2. There is some doubt whether the LPC scale is a true measure of leadership style. Critics contend its interpretation is speculative and inadequately supported. Moreover, they note that LPC scores are unstable, changing over time.

3. The exact meanings of the three factors used to measure situational favorableness are unclear. For example, at what point does a "good" leader-member relationship become a "poor" leader-member relationship, or a "structured" task become an "unstructured" task, or "strong" leader position power become "weak" leader position power?

4. The contingency theory of leadership is a "black box." That is, it fails to explain how and why the interaction of LPC and situational favorableness influence work group performance. As a consequence, it provides little guidance to leaders in performing their roles.

Managerial Implications Although Fiedler's contingency theory has been criticized, it carries several important implications for managers.

1. There is no such thing as a perfect leader for every situation. The leader who is highly effective in one situation may be totally ineffective in another. Thus, although General George Patton was a highly effective tank commander in World War II, one can hardly imagine his leadership style being successful in Mahatma Gandhi's protests against the British in India. Similarly, while Charles de Gaulle was highly effective as a general and president of France, one doubts

that his leadership style would have been suited to managing a small auto parts store on the outskirts of Paris.

2. Anyone can be a leader by carefully selecting those situations that match his or her leadership style.

3. A leader's effectiveness can be enhanced by "engineering the job to fit the manager." This is one way of saying that one's performance can be purposely affected by modifying the favorableness of a group situation in which one is placed. For example, by increasing or decreasing a leader's position power, changing the structure of a task, or influencing leader-member relations, a situation can be altered to better fit a leader's style. It should be realized, however, that in practice available actions may be limited. For example, an increase in a manager's position power may be unacceptable to her colleagues. Conversely, where a decrease is called for, a manager may find it unacceptable. Similarly, any change in task structure might require major alterations in job design that could result in mismatches elsewhere.

4. Fiedler contends that one's leadership style depends on one's personality and is, therefore, relatively fixed. Experience indicates that it may take from one to several years to permanently change someone's personality. This implies that a few lectures or even a few weeks of intensive training are unlikely to change a person's leadership style. The value of most leadership training would thus seem doubtful.

House's Path-Goal Theory

A second situational theory of leadership, the **path-goal theory of leadership,** has been developed by Robert J. House.[6] It reflects an attempt to combine basic elements of Vroom's expectancy theory of motivation with a situational perspective. As you will recall, according to expectancy theory, motivation depends on a person's belief that effort will lead to performance (Expectancy 1) and that performance will lead to rewards that are valued (Expectancy 2). Path-goal theory describes how leader behavior affects these expectancies, which in turn affect subordinate outcomes.

Thus, a leader's task contains two elements: a *path* element designed to influence Expectancy 1 and a *goal* element intended to influence Expectancy 2:

1. *Path element.* A leader must clarify and facilitate paths that will enable subordinates to achieve their own goals while simultaneously achieving organization goals.

2. *Goal element.* A leader must emphasize the relationship between subordinates' own goals and organization goals by increasing the number and kinds of rewards subordinates receive for work-goal attainment.

Leader Behavior and Situational Factors Like Fiedler's contingency theory of leadership, the path-goal theory does not specify one best way to lead. Rather, it stresses that to be effective, a leader should select the style most appropriate to a particular situation. The details of path-goal theory are summarized in Figure 16.5. This figure shows four styles of leadership and two situational factors: subordinate characteristics and environmental characteristics. *Subordinate characteristics* include knowledge, skills, abilities, and needs. *Environmental characteristics* include task structure, work group relations, formal authority system, and

Path-goal theory of leadership.
A leadership theory that describes how leader behavior affects a person's beliefs that effort will lead to performance and that performance will lead to rewards that are valued, which in turn affect subordinate outcomes.

The leadership effectiveness of the late Sam Walton exemplifies a successful match of leadership style, subordinate characteristics, and situational factors. Walton set high goals for Wal-Mart employees, known at all levels as "associates," and regularly met with store personnel to express his confidence in their capabilities. Wal-Mart associates are rewarded for performance by a system of stock purchase opportunities, profit sharing, and bonus incentives.

reward system. Together, leadership style and the situational factors influence subordinate outcomes, such as performance, job satisfaction, turnover, and grievances. The four styles of leadership are defined as follows:

- **Directive leadership.** Characterized by a leader who informs subordinates what is expected of them and provides specific guidance. This is similar to the Ohio State University researchers' *initiating structure*.

- **Supportive leadership.** Characterized by a leader who is friendly and approachable and shows concern for the status, well-being, and personal needs of subordinates. This is similar to the Ohio State University researchers' *consideration*.

- **Achievement-oriented leadership.** Characterized by a leader who sets challenging goals, expects subordinates to perform at their best, and shows confidence that subordinates will perform well.

- **Participative leadership.** Characterized by a leader who consults with subordinates and asks for their suggestions before making a decision.

Path-Goal Theory Predictions   Path-goal theory holds that, depending on subordinate characteristics, each of the four types of leader behavior will be used by an effective leader in different situations. *Directive leadership* is predicted to have a positive impact on subordinates in situations of high task ambiguity. When a task is ambiguous, directive leadership is needed to clarify role expectations and provide guidance. In doing so, a directive leader increases motivation by increasing the expectancy of subordinates that their effort will lead to performance (Expectancy 1).

Supportive leadership is predicted to have a positive impact on subordinates in situations that are stressful, dull, or dangerous. By acting supportive, a leader compensates for the negative aspects of a task, thereby making it more tolerable for subordinates.

Directive leadership.
A type of behavior in which a leader informs subordinates what is expected of them and provides specific guidance.

Supportive leadership.
A type of behavior in which a leader is friendly and approachable and shows concern for the status, well-being, and personal needs of subordinates.

Achievement-oriented leadership.
A type of behavior in which a leader sets challenging goals, expects subordinates to perform their best, and shows confidence that subordinates will perform well.

Participative leadership.
A type of behavior in which a leader consults with subordinates and asks for their suggestions before making a decision.

FIGURE 16.5 HOUSE'S PATH-GOAL THEORY OF LEADERSHIP

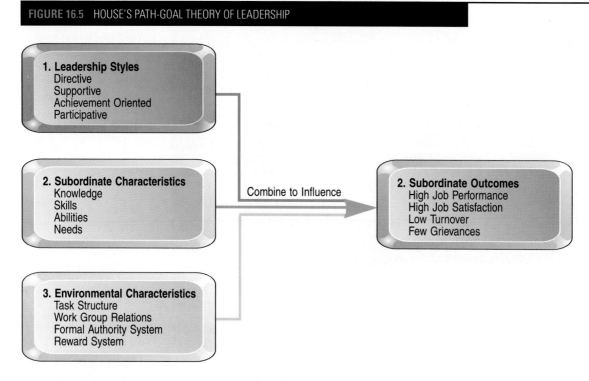

Achievement-oriented leadership is predicted to have a positive impact on subordinates in situations where subordinates have confidence in their ability to meet challenging goals and, thus, high performance standards. For subordinates performing difficult tasks, an achievement-oriented leader increases subordinate motivation by setting high standards of performance and expressing confidence that subordinates will perform well.

Participative leadership is predicted to have a positive impact on subordinates in situations of high complexity. By consulting with subordinates and asking for their suggestions on task-related matters, a participative leader builds subordinate commitment to task performance.

Assessment At present, path-goal theory is still in a developmental stage. Research conducted to test it has yielded mixed results. Some studies support the theory, but others do not. Three criticisms suggested by these studies are particularly pertinent:

1. Like expectancy theory, path-goal theory is complex. This has made its practical application extremely difficult.

2. Researchers have found the complexity of path-goal theory has made measuring the relevant variables contained in the theory especially trying.

3. Although many possible predictions are suggested by path-goal theory, not all have been thoroughly researched. Empirical research has largely concentrated on predictions associated with directive and supportive leader behavior. However, as noted, this research has produced mixed results.

Managerial Implications Despite its limitations, path-goal theory has contributed to the study of leadership by emphasizing the motivational function of leaders and by identifying situational variables that influence leader effectiveness. In the process, several valuable managerial implications have emerged:

1. An effective manager will find it necessary to use different types of leader behavior at varying times in different situations. In this respect, path-goal theory is more flexible than Fiedler's contingency theory, which holds that a person's leadership style is one-dimensional (task oriented or relationship oriented) and relatively fixed.

2. A leader can improve subordinate performance and satisfaction by enhancing subordinate competence through coaching and support, clarifying and facilitating paths that will enable subordinates to achieve their own goals while simultaneously achieving organization goals, and emphasizing the relationship between subordinates' own goals and organization goals by increasing the different kinds of rewards subordinates receive for work-goal attainment.

3. To be effective leaders, managers should be taught how to adapt their behavior to the task and subordinate characteristics of the situation at hand.

Vroom and Jago's Normative Theory

The final situational theory of leadership to be discussed was developed by Victor H. Vroom and Arthur G. Jago.[7] It is called a **normative theory of leadership** because it offers guidelines for how decisions *ought* to be made in specific situations. In doing so, it focuses on the extent to which a manager should allow subordinates to participate in decision making. In this sense, it is a limited theory of leadership because a manager's approach to decision making is only one facet of leadership.

Normative theory of leadership.
A leadership theory that offers normative guidelines for how decisions ought to be made in a specific situation.

UAL Corporation Chairman and CEO Stephen M. Wolf works closely with (left to right) Senior Vice-Presidents Paul G. George, Lawrence M. Nagin, Executive Vice-President James M. Guyette, and (seated) Vice-Chairman John C. Pope to manage United Airlines. Management teams such as this use the group participation method whereby team members work together to solve problems and make decisions.

Vroom and Jago identify five distinct decision-making methods that vary in the extent to which subordinates are allowed to participate in decision making. The five methods are presented in Table 16.3. The Roman numerals indicate variants of the same method. Thus, in both the **Autocratic I method** and **Autocratic II method,** a manager solves problems alone, but in the second method, she seeks information from subordinates first. Similarly, in both the **Consultative I method** and the **Consultative II method,** a manager shares problems with subordinates, but in the first method, she shares problems with subordinates *individually* and in the second as a *group*. In the **Group Participation method,** a manager not only shares problems with subordinates, but solves them together with the group.

According to Vroom and Jago, the appropriate decision-making method to use in a particular situation depends on answers to specific diagnostic questions associated with different "problem attributes." The questions are arranged as a decision tree. The decision tree suggested for a group problem without time constraints is shown in Figure 16.6. For simplicity, the decision tree treats each question as having only two answers: Yes or No and High or Low. The questions are intended to identify when it is useful to allow subordinates to participate in decision making and when it is not. As the questions suggest, if (1) subordinates possess pertinent information, (2) their commitment to a course of action is required, (3) they share an organization's goals, and (4) conflict over a preferred solution is unlikely, then participation is useful.

To solve a problem, one starts at the left-hand side of the decision tree, responds to the question associated with the problem attribute encountered, and follows the developing path. Each path ultimately leads to one of the given decision-making methods mentioned above.

Assessment Normative theory is especially attractive because it provides precise answers for dealing with the question of subordinate participation in

Autocratic I method.
A decision-making method in which a manager solves a problem alone, using whatever information is available at the time.

Autocratic II method.
A decision-making method in which a manager obtains necessary information from subordinates before making a decision alone.

Consultative I method.
A decision-making method in which a manager shares problems with subordinates *individually*, getting their ideas and suggestions before making a decision.

Consultative II method.
A method in which a manager shares problems with subordinates as a *group*, getting their ideas and suggestions before making a decision.

TABLE 16.3 DECISION-MAKING METHODS		
Method	**Definition**	**Degree of Subordinate Participation**
Autocratic I (AI)	Manager solves problem alone, using whatever information is available at the time.	Low
Autocratic II (AII)	Manager obtains necessary information from subordinates before making decision alone.	↑
Consultative I (CI)	Manager shares problem with subordinates *individually*, getting their ideas and suggestions before making decision.	
Consultative II (CII)	Manager shares problem with subordinates as a *group*, getting their ideas and suggestions before making decision.	
Group Participation (G)	Manager shares problem with subordinates as a group and *together* they make decision.	↓ High

FIGURE 16.6   VROOM-JAGO DECISION TREE FOR DETERMINING AN APPROPRIATE DECISION-MAKING METHOD—GROUP PROBLEMS

Decision-making methods

AI = Autocratic decision without subordinates' inputs
AII = Autocratic decision using information gathered from subordinates
CI = Consultative decision with problem discussed individually with each subordinate
CII = Consultative decision with problem discussed with subordinates as a group
G = Group decision

QR	Quality Requirement:	How important is the quality of this decision?
CR	Commitment Requirement:	How important is subordinate commitment to the decision?
LI	Leader's Information:	Do you have sufficient informantion to make a high-quality decision?
ST	Problem Structure:	Is the problem well structured?
CP	Commitment Probability:	If you were to make the decision by yourself, is it reasonably certain that your subordinates would be committed to the decision?
GC	Goal Congruence:	Do subordinates share the organization goals to be attained in solving this problem?
CO	Subordinate Conflict:	Is conflict among subordinates over preferred solutions likely?
SI	Subordinate Information:	Do subordinates have sufficient information to make a high-quality decision?

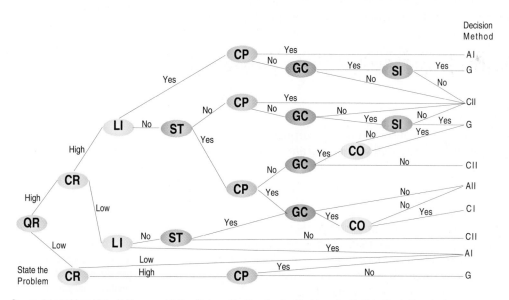

Source: Adapted from Victor H. Vroom and Arthur G. Jago, *The New Leadership: Managing Participation in Organizations* (Englewood Cliffs, N.J.: Prentice-Hall, 1988): 184.

decision making. In this respect, it represents a significant attempt to bridge the gap between leadership theory and practice. This is not to say that normative theory is without criticism. Three points are particularly pertinent in this regard:

1. There exist other decision-making methods besides the five identified by Vroom and Jago. For example, a manager could allow subordinates to make a decision alone.

2. Normative theory considers specific diagnostic questions associated with different problem attributes. Should other questions and attributes be considered? What about the assumption that managers have the skills to use each decision-making method? What about work group size? What about the need for secrecy?

3. Recognizing the limitations of bounded rationality, it is possible that managers are not sufficiently rational to apply normative theory under the best conditions, let alone given limited time and workplace pressures.

Managerial Implications In regard to the preceding considerations, one might wonder whether normative theory is of any practical value. Its value lies in its managerial implications:

1. Unlike Fiedler's contingency theory, which contends that a person's leadership style is relatively fixed, normative theory suggests that to be effective, a manager may find it necessary to be autocratic in one instance and consultative in the next. This implies that the key to effective leadership is the ability to correctly diagnose the prevailing situation before choosing a leadership style or, in normative theory terms, a decision-making method.

2. If the normative theory is valid, more effective leadership will result if managers are taught to use the theory for selecting an appropriate decision-making method. Moreover, having diagnostic questions laid out speeds up the learning process, allowing the development of leaders faster than is otherwise possible.

EMERGING THEORIES

Given the importance of leadership, it should not be surprising that new theories continue to emerge. Three theories currently emerging are *charismatic leadership, leader-member exchange,* and *transformational leadership.*

Charismatic Leadership Theory

Recent years have seen a resurgent interest in the traits or characteristics of leaders, especially those possessing *charisma.*[8] An aspect of referent power (see Chapter 9), **charisma** is a special quality that reaches people on an emotional, nonrational level, motivating them to extraordinary efforts. John F. Kennedy and Ronald Reagan are frequently cited examples of charismatic leaders. Both possessed intense magnetic charm that set them apart from others. By contrast, the four presidents between them—Lyndon Johnson, Richard Nixon, Gerald Ford, and Jimmy Carter—are generally considered to have had less charisma.

In general, it has been suggested that when a leader has charisma, followers perform better. In particular, charismatic leaders are seen as engendering favorable outcomes by modeling a value system for followers, exuding competence and suc-

Group Participation method.
A decision-making method in which a manager shares problems with subordinates as a group and together they make a decision.

Charisma.
A special quality of leaders that reaches people on an emotional, nonrational level, motivating them to extraordinary efforts.

cess, articulating an inspirational goal that is ideological rather than pragmatic, exhibiting high expectations, showing confidence in followers, and arousing their motivation. Whatever the consequences, charisma is likely a complex interaction of leader and follower characteristics, together with situational factors.

Critics note that effective leadership does not depend on charisma. Dwight D. Eisenhower and Harry S. Truman were singularly effective leaders, but neither was especially charismatic. At the same time, John Kennedy was one of the most charismatic people ever to occupy the White House, but few presidents were as ineffective. Effective leaders can evidently either be people who command attention and motivate others or those who quietly inspire through technical ability, insight, honesty, and other means.

Leader-Member Exchange Theory

Most leadership theories assume that a leader behaves in much the same way toward all followers. In contrast, **leader-member exchange theory** holds that leadership is a one-on-one exchange in which leaders behave differently with

Leader-member exchange theory.
A theory which holds that leadership is a one-on-one exchange in which leaders behave differently with different followers rather than behaving the same across the board.

CLOSE-UP: DIVERSITY DIFFERENT BUT TOGETHER

When Kinney Shoe Corp. decided it was time to teach its employees techniques for managing people from diverse cultural backgrounds, its first students were its top 60 executives.

By starting off with the highest echelon and working down, Kinney's human resource executives helped set the right tone for the whole company. Eventually, the 8-hour seminars, titled "Valuing Diversity," were offered to all the company's shoe executives and store managers.

The courses were the product of Kinney's Office of Fair Employment Practice. Established in 1990, the program intends not only to meet minority hiring goals, but to teach employees that talent is color and gender blind and culture neutral. Achieving this end can be as simple as disproving preconceived notions that a person's accent reflects a lack of intelligence, or as complicated as recruiting minorities from high unemployment areas.

Kinney executives say the program was necessary because the cultural and social backgrounds of most employees is different from those of the white males who still predominate management ranks. The program was also aimed at building on training theories that focus largely on homogeneity. Managers often are taught to treat workers exactly alike and to conduct identical evaluations, but such a management style can become problematic when a workforce is not homogeneous.

In the new program, Kinney managers learn that people react differently to situations in the workplace depending on their backgrounds. Through presentations and group discussions, managers learn that the reaction of Asians is often different from that of African Americans, and that women may react differently than men.

But Kinney's focus on cultural diversity goes beyond employee relations. Executives say that its work force in the year 2000 will be composed of greater numbers of women and minorities to reflect the composition of its customer base. "If you're going to be in a business that serves this mix of people, you had better have a mix of people who understand them," says John Kozlowski, Kinney's senior vice-president of human resources. "Today's retail environment needs a diverse work force to service a diverse customer base."

Source: Joyce E. Santora, "Kinney Shoe Steps into Diversity," *Personnel Journal* 69 (September 1991): 72, 74.

Wendy's founder and spokesman Dave Thomas spends over eight months each year visiting franchises, inspiring workers, and checking quality. Thomas is seen here flipping hamburgers. Leaders like Thomas are able to motivate employees with charisma, knowledge, and skills.

different group members rather than the same with each member.[9] It further holds that followers, based on the quality of their interpersonal relationships (exchanges) with a leader, form different groups, an *in-group* (higher quality) and an *out-group* (lower quality).

Insiders and outsiders experience very different work outcomes. Leader interactions with insiders resemble social transactions, with leaders and followers exchanging resources and enjoying higher levels of trust and support. For example, in return for leader-provided rewards, such as job autonomy, confidence, and participation in decision making, followers may expend greater than required time and energy, accept more responsibility, and so on. In this way, leader and follower become reciprocally interdependent.

On the other hand, in exchanges with outsiders, leaders act as supervisors, relying on formal authority to extract follower performance. At the extreme, leader exchanges with outsiders can be very mechanistic, arising from workplace rules, policies, and procedures, rather than spontaneous interaction. Such exchanges are typically characterized by low levels of trust, interaction, support, and leader-provided rewards.

Research suggests that, as a consequence of such contrasting treatment, in-group members perform better and are more satisfied than out-group members. More significantly, it underscores the fact that leader behavior originates, in part, in followers. That is, leadership is a mutual-influence process. Leaders respond differently to different followers and both leaders and followers alter their behavior depending on the performance of the other.

Transformational Leadership Theory

A third perspective has its roots in the belief that the challenges facing the world in the nineties require a new kind of leadership. Advocates of this belief describe what has been dubbed **transformational leadership** as consisting of two complementary roles: the mover-and-shaker and the gentle persuader.[10] In the first, the mover-and-shaker achieves a transformation in an organization's fortunes and is, therefore, described as a transforming leader. In the second, as a gentle persuader, the transforming leader converts followers into leaders by persuading them to look beyond their own self-interest for the good of the whole, to consider long-term rather than immediate needs, and to become more aware and accepting of an organization's goals.

Transformational leaders are in a sense a cross between a cheerleader and an evangelist. They achieve performance beyond expectations through four leadership factors: *charisma, inspiration, individualized consideration,* and *intellectual stimulation.*[11] Accordingly, transformational leaders use charisma to provide followers with a clear vision of a desired future state, instill pride, and gain respect and trust. They use inspiration to excite their followers with the idea that they can achieve great things with extra effort. Further, transformational leaders demonstrate individualized consideration. That is, they pay close attention to differences among followers, serve as mentors to those who need coaching and advising, and treat each follower as an individual worthy of respect. Finally, transformational leaders provide followers with intellectual stimulation by promoting new ways of looking at old problems, viewing difficulties as challenges to be met, and emphasizing creative thinking.

Advocates of transformational leadership believe it can make the difference between an organization's success or failure. They have found that followers are not only more satisfied when they believe their managers are transformational leaders, but they also do a better job. Lee Iacocca, who saved Chrysler with salesmanship, enthusiasm, and nerve, and Jack Welch, who seems to have revitalized General Electric, are obvious examples of the importance of transformational leaders to their organizations.

Transformational leadership.
A theory which holds that leaders can motivate followers to perform beyond expectations through charisma, inspiration, individualized consideration, and intellectual stimulation.

Lee Iacocca, credited with saving the Chrysler Corporation and rebuilding its fortunes in the 1980s, exemplifies transformational leadership. Iacocca is widely recognized as a charismatic and inspirational leader, as well as a persuasive spokesperson. Although retired from Chrysler, Iacocca is bound to exert an influence on American industry for some time to come.

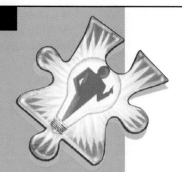

SMART MANAGEMENT SUBSTITUTES FOR LEADERSHIP: EXPERIENCE AND KNOWLEDGE

For 18 years Ginny had been doing about the same thing—packing expandrium fittings for shipment. She was so well practiced that she could do the job perfectly without paying the slightest attention. This, of course, left her free to "socialize" and observe the life of the company as it took place about her.

Today, however, she was breaking in a new packer. "No, not that way. Look, honey, if you hold it that way, well, then you have to twist your arm when you pack this corner, see. This way it's easier."

"But that's the way Claude Gilliam [the methods engineer] said we had to do it."

"Sure he did, honey. But he's never had to do it 8 hours a day like me. You just pay attention to what I say."

"But what if he comes around and says I should pack the other way?"

"Oh, that's easy. When he's here, you do it his way. Anyway, after a couple weeks, you won't see him again. Slow down, you'll wear yourself out. No one's going to expect you to do 80 pieces a week anyway."

"But Mr. Gilliam said 90."

"Sure he did. Let *him* do it. Look, here's how to pace yourself. It's the way I was taught, and it works. You know *The Battle Hymn of the Republic?*" (Ginny hummed a few bars). "Well, you just work to that, hum it to yourself, use the way I showed you, and you'll be doing 80 next week."

"But what if they make me do 90?"

"They can't. Y'know, you start making mistakes when you go that fast. No, 80 is right. I always say, a fair day's work for a fair day's pay."

Source: Adapted with permission from R. Richard Ritti and G. Ray Funkhouser, *The Ropes to Skip and the Ropes to Know,* 3d ed. (New York: Wiley, 1987), 71.

SUBSTITUTES FOR LEADERSHIP

Recent research has begun to question the belief that leadership is always important.[12] It has been suggested that there are instances when leaders are unnecessary. That is to say, in some situations there may be sources of support that make leadership behavior irrelevant to employee performance. Such "substitutes for leadership" would include:

- *Experience and knowledge.* Some employees have worked at a particular job for so long that they possess more knowledge about its requirements than anyone else—even their superiors. They have both the necessary knowledge and experience to deal with all anticipated and unanticipated problems. In such situations, leader influence may be sharply reduced. The accompanying "Smart Management" box demonstrates this point.

- *Technology.* Leader influence is also reduced in situations where work is either machine paced or highly standardized. Performance requirements in these instances (automobile assembly lines, automated bakeries, petroleum refineries) are delineated in such detail and change so infrequently that a leader's options in selecting a leadership style are clearly limited.

- *Work group norms and cohesiveness.* Certain factors are inherent in mature group structures. One of these is group norms. If a group is very cohesive, norms will be even more powerful. The effects of group norms and cohesiveness were discussed earlier. (Remember the "binging" that unwary "rate-busters" would experience in the Hawthorne Studies discussed in Chapter 2?). We will discuss the effects of group norms and cohesiveness further in Chapter 17. In any case, group factors can easily negate leader influence over employee behavior.

- *Job satisfaction.* The nature of a given job also can serve as a substitute for leadership. For example, where employees derive a great deal of satisfaction from their work, any attempt by a leader to influence performance probably will be unnecessary. Thus, to the extent a job is "intrinsically satisfying," the need for a leader may be decreased.

These substitutes should not be taken to imply that leadership is redundant or superfluous. They do suggest, however, that employee performance may be influenced by factors other than a leader's behavior. Exercise of leadership is but one (albeit important) element contributing to goal accomplishment. As we have seen in earlier chapters, an organization's success or failure also is influenced by a host of other forces.

SUMMARY

The purpose of this chapter has been to explore the nature of effective leadership. We have reviewed the major theories of leadership, briefly examined several emerging perspectives on leadership, and identified various "substitutes for leadership."

Learning Objective 1:   Define *leadership*.
Leadership is the process of influencing others toward the accomplishment of goals.

Learning Objective 2:   Describe the trait phase of leadership research, commenting on the "great man" theory.
The earliest attempts to understand leadership centered on determining what specific traits make a person an effective leader. In its pure form, the trait phase grew out of the great-man theory of leadership. This theory held that leaders were born, not made. The great-man theory held sway well into the late 1890s. At that time, belief in inborn leader traits began to diminish, although interest in traits themselves greatly increased. Researchers began to contend that leadership could be learned. On the whole, however, attempts to discover the traits that distinguish leaders from followers were disappointing, resulting in contradictory findings. As a consequence, in the 1940s researchers began to question the existence of leader traits.

Learning Objective 3:   Discuss the behavioral phase of leadership research.
The behavioral phase of leadership research held that leaders may be best characterized by how they behave, rather than by their personal traits. Underlying this

phase was the assumption that effective leaders utilize a particular behavioral style that causes others to follow them. The behavioral phase is perhaps best represented by the Ohio State Leadership Studies.

Learning Objective 4: Distinguish between *consideration* and *initiating structure* as identified by the Ohio State Leadership Studies.
The Ohio State Leadership Studies identified two dimensions of effective leader behavior: "consideration" and "initiating structure." Consideration is leader behavior oriented toward developing mutual trust, two-way communication, respect for subordinates' ideas, and concern for their feelings. Initiating structure is leader behavior oriented toward structuring subordinates' activities for the purpose of goal attainment.

Learning Objective 5: Describe the situational phase of leadership research.
In contrast to the earlier behavioral phase, which focused on leader behavior, the newer situational phase attempts to explain effective leadership within the context of the larger situation in which it occurs. The three most prominent theories of this phase are Fiedler's contingency theory, House's path-goal theory, and Vroom and Jago's normative theory.

Learning Objective 6: Describe Fiedler's contingency theory of leadership.
Fiedler's contingency theory of leadership holds that work group performance is contingent upon the match between a person's leadership style and the "favorableness" of the leadership situation.

Learning Objective 7: Discuss House's path-goal theory of leadership.
House's path-goal theory of leadership describes how leader behavior affects a person's beliefs that effort will lead to performance and that performance will lead to rewards that are valued, which in turn affect subordinate outcomes.

Learning Objective 8: Describe Vroom and Jago's normative theory of leadership.
Vroom and Jago's normative theory of leadership offers normative guidelines for how decisions *ought* to be made in a specific situation.

Learning Objective 9: Describe such emerging theories on leadership as charismatic leadership, leader-member exchange, and transformational leadership.
Charismatic leadership theory deals with a special quality of leaders that reaches people on an emotional, nonrational level, motivating them to extraordinary efforts. Leader-member exchange theory holds that leadership is a one-on-one exchange in which leaders behave differently with different group members rather than the same with each member. Transformational leadership theory holds that leaders can motivate followers to perform beyond expectations through charisma, inspiration, individualized consideration, and intellectual stimulation.

Learning Objective 10: Identify various so-called substitutes for leadership.
It has been suggested that there are instances when leaders are unnecessary. That is to say, in some situations, there may be sources of support such that leadership behavior is irrelevant to employee performance. Such "substitutes for leadership" include experience and knowledge, technology, work group norms and cohesiveness, and job satisfaction.

KEY TERMS

achievement-oriented leadership 479

Autocratic I method 482

Autocratic II method 482

charisma 484

consideration 473

Consultative I method 482

Consultative II method 482

contingency theory of leadership 474

directive leadership 479

great-man theory of leadership 471

group participation method 484

initiating structure 473

leader position power 476

leader-member exchange theory 485

leader-member relations 476

leadership 470

leadership style 475

least preferred co-worker (LPC) scale 475

normative theory of leadership 481

participative leadership 479

path-goal theory of leadership 478

relationship-oriented leadership 475

situational favorableness 475

supportive leadership 479

task structure 476

task-oriented leadership 475

trait 471

transformational leadership 487

REVIEW AND DISCUSSION QUESTIONS

1. Much has been written on the "what, when, how, where, and who" of leadership, but not nearly as much on the "why." Calling upon your personal experience, why do you think ideas about leadership should be of interest and practical value to those concerned with management?

2. Horatio Alger (1832–1899) was quite possibly the most popular author in the United States in the last 30 years of the nineteenth century and, without a doubt, one of the most influential of his generation. His stories were always about poor boys from humble beginnings who rose to success and riches by means of traits such as honesty, cheerful perseverance, and hard work. It was during the period of Alger's influence that groups such as the Girl Guides (1909), Boy Scouts (1910), and Girl Scouts (1912) were founded. The creed of each of these groups stresses the importance of traits such as kindness, reverence, obedience, and loyalty to success in life. Comment on the simultaneous popularity of Alger's books, the founding of groups such as the Boy Scouts, and attempts by contemporary leadership researchers to determine what specific traits make a person an effective leader.

3. One finding of early trait theorists was that leaders tend to be somewhat taller than followers. Interestingly, with the exception of the 1924, 1972, and 1976 presidential elections, the taller of the two major candidates was always sent to the White House. In 1976 Jimmy Carter (5 feet, 10 inches) defeated Gerald Ford (6 feet). However, in 1980 Ronald Reagan (6 feet, 1 inch) won over Carter. Could the early trait theorists have been right? Explain your answer.

4. The behavioral phase of leadership research attempted to determine what particular behavior style leaders utilize to cause others to follow them. Read the following descriptions of John F. McGillicuddy, chairman and CEO, Manufacturers Hanover Corporation, and comment on McGillicuddy's behavior as a leader.

    (1) "John is a rare person who combines unique talent as a businessman with a deep concern for the well-being of others. He is not only the leading

THE MANAGEMENT EXPERIENCE LEADERSHIP POTENTIAL

An effective leader is a valued asset in any organization. The deeds of leaders such as Dwight D. Eisenhower, Mao Zedung, John F. Kennedy, and Charles de Gaulle easily attest to their importance in shaping the world. The ability to influence makes leaders highly sought after and valued by society. Are you a potential leader?

To gauge your leadership potential, carefully read the following items. After each item, circle whether you would most likely agree or disagree with the item.

Leadership Potential

1. Good leaders are born, not made. Agree Disagree
2. I tend to treat my subordinates well so long as they do what I say. Agree Disagree
3. Good leaders depend on their followers as much as they depend on themselves. Agree Disagree
4. As a leader, I would always include the reasons why when asking a subordinate to perform a task. Agree Disagree
5. A good leader will achieve his or her objectives at any costs. Agree Disagree
6. As a group manager, I would never entrust a vital project to anyone but myself, even if that meant working overtime. Agree Disagree

7. A key to good leadership is being consistent in how one leads. Agree Disagree
8. If justified, I would recommend a subordinate for a promotion to a position equal to or even higher than my own position. Agree Disagree
9. Some subordinates can participate in the decision-making process without threatening a leader's position. Agree Disagree
10. If my group failed to achieve an objective because of a group member's failure, I would explain it as such to my superiors. Agree Disagree
11. I consider myself indispensable in my present position. Agree Disagree

Scoring:
To compute your score, add up the points assigned to each item.
1. Agree (0), disagree (1)
2. Agree (0), disagree (1)
3. Agree (1), disagree (0)
4. Agree (1), disagree (0)
5. Agree (0), disagree (1)
6. Agree (0), disagree (1)
7. Agree (0), disagree (1)
8. Agree (1), disagree (0)
9. Agree (1), disagree (0)
10. Agree (0), disagree (1)
11. Agree (0), disagree (1)

What Your Score Means
Bear in mind that this is not a test, but simply an indication of your leadership potential.
11–9 Excellent potential
8–6 Good potential
5–0 Drastic changes needed

Source: Reprinted by permission of the publisher, from "How to Measure Your Leadership Potential," by Oliver L. Niehouse. *Supervisory Management* 28 (January 1983), 4. © 1983 AMACOM Periodicals Division, American Management Association, New York. All Rights Reserved.

banker in New York, but also a man with an extraordinary measure of humanity who gives unstintingly of himself to the community."—Cyrus Vance, former U.S. Secretary of State.

(2) "John McGillicuddy is a terrific coach ... [He] sat on the bench in his day, and from that he learned humility. He's also been a star, and from that he learned the importance of recognition. I've never worked for anyone like Mr. McGillicuddy, who wants everybody to succeed and profit from the company's

successes. He's a great leader."—Charles H. McCabe, Jr., senior vice-president, Manufacturers Hanover Corporation.[13]

5. As noted in Question 4, the behavioral phase of leadership research attempted to determine what particular behavior style leaders utilize to cause others to follow them. Read the following descriptions of John Welch, Jr., chairman, General Electric Company. Having done so, comment on Welch's behavior as a leader.

(1) "High IQ, very abrasive, doesn't want 'I think' answers . . . I've never met a man with so many creative business ideas. I've never felt that anybody was tapping my brain so well. . . . He's a high-strung instrument. Misses the opportunity to get input from people who don't have the skill or courage to play him like a violin. . . . Too determined to get a notch on his six-gun. . . . Working for him is like a war. A lot of people get shot up; the survivors go on to the next battle."

(2) "Extraordinarily bright, penetrating in his questions, and determined to get results, Welch has carved out a reputation for abrasiveness. . . . Welch conducts meetings so aggressively that people tremble. He attacks almost physically with his intellect—criticizing, demeaning, ridiculing, humiliating."[14]

6. You are a popular first-line supervisor at a Ford Motor Company production plant. Given your knowledge of Fiedler's contingency theory of leadership, what leadership style would you expect to be most effective in your situation? Why?

7. You are a popular university department chairperson. Given your knowledge of Fiedler's contingency theory of leadership, what leadership style would you expect to be most effective in your situation? Why?

8. Who do you think are today's charismatic leaders? Why?

9. Reflecting on your own experience as a follower, comment on a situation in which an in-group and an out-group existed as predicted by leader-member exchange theory. How were leader-member relations different with respect to both groups?

10. As self-managing teams become more common, are leaders becoming increasingly unnecessary? Why? Why not?

CASE 16.1   WHICH STYLE IS BEST?

The ABC Company is a medium-size corporation that manufactures automotive parts. Recently, the company president attended a leadership seminar and came away deeply impressed with the effect various leadership styles could have on the output and morale of the organization.

In mulling over how he might proceed, the president decided to utilize the services of Paul Patterson, a management consultant who was currently reviewing the goals of the company. The president told Patterson about the leadership seminar and how impressed he had been and that a leadership survey of the company was desired.

It was determined that the division headed by Donald Drake should be the test case and that Patterson would report to the president after completing that survey. Some of the notes made by Patterson in his interviews with the key managers in Drake's division follow.

Ancil Able

Able is very proud of the output of his section. He has always stressed the necessity for good control procedures and efficiency and is very insistent that project instructions be fully understood by his subordinates and that follow-up communications be rapid, complete, and accurate. He serves as the clearinghouse for all incoming and outgoing work. He gives small problems to one individual to complete, but if the problem is large he calls in several key people. Usually, his employees are briefed on what the policy is to be, what part of the report each subordinate is to complete, and the completion date. Able considers this as the only way to get full coordination without lost motion or an overlap of work.

He considers it best for a boss to remain aloof from his subordinates and believes that being "buddy-buddy" tends to hamper discipline. He does his "chewing out" in private and his praising, too. He believes that people in his section really know where they stand.

According to Able, the biggest problem in business today is that subordinates just will not accept responsibility. He states that his people have lots of opportunities to show what they can do but that few really try.

One comment Able made was that he does not understand how his subordinates got along with the previous section head, who ran a very "loose shop." Able stated that his boss is quite happy with the way things go in his section.

Bob Black

Black believes that every employee has a right to be treated as an individual and espouses the theory that it is a boss's responsibility and duty to cater to the employee's needs. He noted that he is constantly doing little things for his subordinates and gave as an example his presentation of two tickets to an art show to be held at the City Gallery next month. He stated that the tickets cost $5 each but that it will be both educational and enjoyable for the employee and his wife. This was done to express his appreciation for a good job the man had done a few months back.

Black says that he always makes a point of walking through his section area at least once each day, stopping to speak to at least 25 percent of the employees on each trip.

He does not like to "knock" anyone, but he noted that Able ran one of those "tight ships" you hear about. He stated that Able's employees are probably not too happy, but there isn't much they can do but wait for Able to move.

Black said he had noticed a little bit of bypassing going on in the company but that most of it is attributable to the press of business. His idea is to run a friendly, low-keyed operation with a happy group of subordinates. Although he confesses that they might not be as efficient in terms of speedy outputs as other units, he believes that he has far greater subordinate loyalty and higher morale and that his subordinates work well as an expression of their appreciation of his (Black's) enlightened leadership.

Charles Carr

Carr says his principal problem is the shifting of responsibilities between his section and others in the division. He considers his section the "fire drill" area that gets all the rush, hot items, whether or not they belong in his section. He seems to think this is caused by his immediate superior not being too sure who should handle what jobs in the division.

Carr admits that he hasn't tried to stop this practice. He stated (with a grin) that it makes the other section heads jealous but that they are afraid to complain. They seem to think that Carr is a personal friend of the division manager, but Carr says that this is not true.

He said he used to be embarrassed in meetings when it was obvious he was doing jobs out of his area but that he has gotten used to it by now, and apparently the other section heads have also.

His approach to discipline is to keep everybody busy—then "you won't have those kinds of problems." He stated that a good boss doesn't have time to hold anybody's hand, like Black does, and tell the guy what a great job he's doing. Carr believes that if you promise people that you will keep an eye on their work for raises and promotion purposes, most of the problems take care of themselves.

He stated that he believes in giving a guy a job to do and then letting him do it without too much checking on his work. He believes that most of his subordinates know the score and do their jobs reasonably well without too much griping.

If he has a problem, it is probably the fact that the role and scope of his section has become a little blurred by current practices. He did state that he thinks he should resist a recent tendency for "company people above my division manager's level" to call him up to their offices to hear his ideas on certain programs. However, Carr is not too sure that this can be stopped without creating a ruckus of some kind. He says he is studying the problem.

Donald Drake

As division manager, Drake thinks things are going pretty well because he has not had any real complaints from his superiors in the company, beyond the "small problem" type of thing. He thinks his division is at about the same level of efficiency as the other divisions in the organization.

His management philosophy is to let the section managers find their own level, organizational niche, and form of operation and then check to see if the total output of the division is satisfactory. He stated that he has done this with his present section heads. This was the policy being used when he (Drake) was a section head, and it has worked fine for him.

Drake considers his function as that of a clearinghouse for division inputs and outputs, and sees his job basically as a coordinating one, coupled with the requirement for him to "front" for the division. He believes that you should let a man expand his job activities as much as he is able to do so. He noted that Carr had expanded greatly as a manager since he (Drake) had arrived. He says he frequently takes Carr with him to high-level meetings in the company, since Carr knows more about the division's operations than anyone else in it.

Drake noted that both Able and Black seem to do a creditable job in their sections. He has very little contact with Able's employees but occasionally has to see one of Black's employees about something the employee has fouled up. This results from the fact that Black considers such a face-to-face confrontation between the division manager and a lower level section employee a good lesson to impress upon the subordinate that he has let down his boss. Drake said he is not too keen on this procedure but that Black considers it a most valuable training device to teach the employee to do a good job every time, so Drake goes along with it.

Problems

1. How would you describe the leadership styles of Ancil Able, Bob Black, and Charles Carr?

2. What predictions would you make about the satisfaction and performance of Able's, Black's, and Carr's subordinates?

3. How can Able and Black seem to be doing a creditable job in their sections with such contrasting leadership styles?

4. Is it possible that Able's, Black's, and Carr's leadership styles are appropriate to the particular situation in which they work? Why or why not?

Source: Reprinted with permission from William D. Heier, Arizona State University.

NOTES

[1] Daniel Katz and Robert L. Kahn, *The Social Psychology of Organizations,* 2d ed. (New York: Wiley, 1978): 526–528.

[2] Shelly A. Kirkpatrick and Edwin A. Locke, "Leadership: Do Traits Matter?" *Academy of Management Executive* 5 (May 1991): 48–60.

[3] Carroll L. Shartle, "The Early Years of the Ohio State University Leadership Studies," *Journal of Management* 5 (Fall 1979): 127–134; and Chester A. Schriesheim and Barbara J. Bird, "Contributions of the Ohio State Studies to the Field of Leadership," *Journal of Management* 5 (Fall 1979): 135–145.

[4] Fred E. Fiedler, *A Theory of Leadership Effectiveness* (New York: McGraw-Hill, 1967); and Fred E. Fiedler and Martin M. Chembers, *Improving Leadership Effectiveness: The Leader Match Concept,* 2d ed. (New York: Wiley, 1984).

[5] Fred E. Fiedler and Joseph E. Garcia, *New Approaches to Effective Leadership* (New York: Wiley, 1987).

[6] Robert J. House, "A Path-Goal Theory of Leader Effectiveness," *Administrative Science Quarterly* 16 (September 1971): 321–338; and Robert J. House and Terence R. Mitchell, "Path-Goal Theory of Leadership," *Journal of Contemporary Business 3* (Autumn 1974): 81–97.

[7] Victor H. Vroom and Arthur G. Jago, *The New Leadership: Managing Participation in Organizations* (Englewood Cliffs, N.J.: Prentice-Hall, 1988).

[8] See, for example, Jay A. Conger, Rabindra N. Kanungo and Associates, *Charismatic Leadership: The Elusive Factor in Organizational Effectiveness* (San Francisco: Jossey-Bass, 1988); and Peter F. Drucker, "Leadership: More Doing than Dash," *Wall Street Journal,* January 6, 1988, 14.

[9] George B. Graen and Terri A. Scandura, "Toward a Psychology of Dyadic Organizing," *Research in Organizational Behavior* 9 (1987): 175–208.

[10] John Nicholls, "Eight Leadership Types and the Transforming Autocrat: As Derived from Burns' Basic Criteria," *Journal of General Management* 13 (Summer 1988): 45–56.

[11] Bernard M. Bass, "From Transactional to Transformational Leadership: Learning to Share the Vision," *Organizational Dynamics* 19 (Spring 1990): 19–31.

[12] Jon P. Howell, David E. Bowen, Peter W. Dorfman, Steven Kerr, and Philip M. Podsakoff, "Substitutes for Leadership: Effective Alternatives to Ineffective Leadership," *Organizational Dynamics* 19 (Summer 1990): 21–38.

[13] Robbie Vorhaus, "John F. McGillicuddy: Chairman & CEO, Manufacturers Hanover Corporation," *Sky* 13 (April 1984): 39.

[14] Steven Flax, "The Toughest Bosses in America," *Fortune,* August 6, 1984, 18–19.

CHAPTER 17

LEARNING OBJECTIVES

Upon completing this chapter, you should be able to:

- Answer the question *What is a group?*
- Distinguish between formal and informal groups.
- Explain why people join groups.
- Specify the stages of development a typical new group moves through from the time it is created to the time it disbands.
- Explain how work groups can contribute to an organization's success.
- State various factors that have been shown to influence work group effectiveness.
- Describe the so-called free-rider problem.
- Recount two situations in which work group behavior could be considered dysfunctional.
- Detail the major causes of conflict between work groups.
- List various conflict-resolution options.
- Outline the pros and cons of committees.
- Identify various ways to increase committee effectiveness.

All companies face the potential of their employees lapsing into bureaucratic inertia. This is especially the case if employees assume that the way they have always done their job is the only way. Organizing employees into teams helps prevent this problem to a certain extent, particularly when there is some turnover in the team's membership. But even teams can eventually stagnate if they are not challenged.

A number of Japanese companies have developed an alternative way of dealing with employee stagnation. They have developed a system of "checks and balances" in which different functions overlap. While these checks and balances may seem inefficient to Western eyes, the Japanese value this system because it stimulates communication and dialogue. In developing a new product, for instance, different divisions will work together, meeting and criticizing each other until they arrive at a consensus. At one company—Canon—teams are divided into groups, each of which prepares a different approach to devel-

GROUP DYNAMICS AND CONFLICT

oping the same product; then the groups review each other's pro-posals. Many, if not most Western companies would feel that such duplication wastes time, but in fact such a system can create and implement new ideas quite quickly.

Such systems, however, can create problems. Conflict and rivalry are likely to arise. However, sensitive management ensures that team members know they are respected even if their ideas are dis-carded. Conflict guarantees that the ideas finally accepted will have been considered thoroughly. At Canon, for example, a team working on the design of a mini-copier for personal use solved a dif-ficult problem through group interaction. Because the team mem-bers wanted to make the copier drum disposable, it had to be cheap. One day, finding themselves deadlocked, team members sent out for beer. Examining a beer can, one of the members noted that it, like the drum, had to be manufactured cheaply. The team be-gan to explore how the copier drum and the beer can were similar and how they differed. In the end, what had begun as a ludicrous comparison ended up as the basis for a manufacturable component.

Many other examples illustrating the value of conflict as well as co-operation in groups could be cited. In this chapter we will explore the dynamics of group interaction—both conflict and coopera-tion—in detail.

Source: Ikurjiro Nonaka, "The Knowledge Creating Company," *Harvard Business Review 69* (November–December 1991): 96–98, 101–102.

Chapters 15 and 16 discussed motivation and leadership, two forces that influence individual behavior. In most organizations, however, goals are achieved by groups of people working together, not by individuals acting alone. Indeed, most organizations largely consist of groups. Advisory boards, boards of directors, policy committees, special councils, and self-managing teams are only a few of the many groups that permeate a typical organization.

To be successful, managers must understand the dynamics that govern such groups. Thus, the purpose of this chapter is to examine work group behavior. We begin by briefly commenting on the two basic types of groups found in most organizations and by considering various reasons people join groups. We then explain how groups develop, and discuss how groups contribute to an organization's success. Next, we review ways that managers can help groups work effectively. The chapter then considers norms that oppose rather than support goals as well as various reasons for intergroup conflict. We conclude by discussing one of the most common forms of group interaction, committees.

BASIC FACTS ABOUT GROUPS

A **group** is defined as two or more people who interact regularly to achieve a common goal. Throughout your life, you have undoubtedly been part of many groups, some at school, some at church, some social and some political in nature.

The study of groups is important because the results of group activities cannot always be predicted from the performance of individuals outside a group situation.

Group.
Two or more people who interact regularly to achieve a common goal.

Kraft USA employees discuss a storyboard for a Kraft Macaroni & Cheese dinner commercial. This is a formal group, created by Kraft to achieve a specific goal—develop a commercial for a product.

Group influences can either enhance or diminish individual performance. We have all experienced the excitement, enthusiasm, and power of groups in getting things done. At other times, however, we have also experienced their inefficiency and ineffectiveness.

As a manager, you will be involved in group activities as a continuing part of your job. Indeed, you will rarely operate alone. In most organizations, getting a job done takes a group effort. In this regard, group influences on individual performance will be a prime consideration in ensuring work group effectiveness.

TYPES OF GROUPS

There are two primary types of groups in a typical organization: formal and informal. **Formal groups** are those deliberately created by an organization to achieve a specific goal. They are an official part of an organization's structure, with designated work assignments. Additionally, they emphasize authority and position and are characterized by specialized roles. Xerox's recently formed six-member "corporate office" is one example of a formal group. It is an official part of Xerox's structure and operates in place of a president. Each member of the corporate office has been assigned a specialized role with specific responsibilities. Other examples of formal groups include departments, sections, task forces, committees, special councils, and project teams.

Informal groups, on the other hand, are independent of an organization's structure and are created for their members' purposes. They generally emerge spontaneously and may not support an organization's goals. Members are attracted to informal groups because of common interests, social reasons, and friendship. Such groups emphasize personal and social relations as opposed to authority and position. They are held together by the mutual attraction of their members.

Informal Groups: An Example

Informal groups play a significant role in the work lives of most employees. The following example, based on a true story, reveals the dynamics that govern such groups and provides a basis for discussing why people join groups.

Consider a typical work group of 15 sales representatives who call on supermarket buyers. On an average day, the reps have very little time to spend with one another. They spend most of their day fighting to meet their sales quotas. The buyers they call on are clearly in a position of power, while the sales reps are suppliants, always asking for something—an order for a new product, a better shelf position, permission to erect a display. Occasionally, they can offer the buyers small gifts—a free lunch or tickets to sporting events.

Although the sales reps generally break the day's routine for the buyers, telling stories and jokes or repeating community gossip, the buyers are often busy and have little time to talk. In such instances, it is not unusual for them to respond either by being gruff or ignoring the sales reps altogether. Needless to say, on some days, the reps feel quite discouraged.

How does the work group function in this situation? The sales reps work alone, calling on stores by themselves. Nevertheless, the group influences each member's work life. The group informally gathers for coffee and lunch whenever possible, or members meet to talk after work. They also attend weekly sales briefings and national sales meetings together.

At national sales meetings, where the official purpose is to introduce new products, new advertising campaigns, or price changes, sales reps are encouraged to share their success

Formal group.
A group deliberately created by an organization to achieve a specific goal.

Informal group.
A group that is independent of an organization's structure and created for its members' purposes.

At Tyson Foods' annual employee softball tournament, two teams share an end-of-the-game "high-five." Informal groups like these softball teams provide opportunities for friendship as well as for developing interests and fostering communication and cooperation across a company.

stories. This is essentially viewed as an opportunity for experienced reps to "train" newer hires. Time and again, the experienced reps proudly recount their "classic" sales strategies. The common thread in these stories is how the rep fooled a buyer. Usually the main protagonist is an unpleasant buyer whom a rep oversells by playing on the buyer's weaknesses.

For example, one of Charlie's buyers, who represented an independent group of stores, continually berated him. One day, Charlie was asked to try to sell this buyer 500 cases of a new product. In a "classic" sales strategy, Charlie exploited one of the buyer's main weaknesses—a hatred of chain stores.

"Well, Frank," Charlie said, "this new line is guaranteed to sell. In fact, it's already on allocation [limited sale]. You're entitled to 500 cases, but I doubt your small stores can handle that many. I'd hate to see you overloaded, so I'll put you down for an order of 250 and give the other 250 to A&P or Kroger."

"The heck you will!" Frank retorted. "What do you mean my stores aren't big enough? I'm entitled to 500 cases, and, by darn, I get 500. Don't you dare give any of my cases to those . . . to A&P and Kroger."

Each time this story is told there is uproarious laughter. Charlie clearly had the buyer exactly where he wanted him. He met his quota, and the buyer couldn't complain since he had insisted on ordering all 500 cases. By telling his story, Charlie receives a great deal of personal recognition and teaches the new sales reps a "trick of the trade."

WHY PEOPLE JOIN GROUPS

As the preceding example suggests, groups can provide many benefits to their members. The exact benefits someone might derive from being a member of a particular group, of course, can vary widely. In general, however, people join groups to satisfy specific needs. Principal among these are social needs, esteem needs, security needs, and reality needs.

Social Needs

In Chapter 15, we discussed the importance of satisfying one's social needs. Through the friendship and support they offer, groups are a primary means for satisfying such needs. Groups offer an opportunity for understanding and camaraderie. Job problems, and even personal problems, may be discussed with fellow group members. The sales reps in our example are satisfying their social needs through the banter and kidding, common to most work groups.

Esteem Needs

Group membership also helps to satisfy esteem needs. In this regard, work groups make a significant contribution to defining a person's identity. Others may not understand what a biochemist does, for example, but a biochemist's co-workers know and provide personal feedback. Whether individuals identify themselves as teachers, hospital administrators, or engineers, through work groups they can attain recognition and maintain their self-esteem.

So other needs are being fulfilled when the sales reps in our example are encouraged to tell their success stories. Remember, they work alone, and no one else knows their achievements. Such bragging sessions help establish their identity and enhance their self-esteem.

Security Needs

Work groups also help individuals satisfy their security needs. As you will recall from Chapter 15, the need for security is one of the primary forces that motivates people. When a work group protects its members from the "arbitrary" demands of outsiders (other work groups, managers, clients), it provides them with a feeling of security, and, therefore, dignity. Evidence is fairly strong that most employees who join unions do so to protect themselves against forces they could not resist on their own. Joining a union makes these employees feel less anxious in the face of perceived threats. Similarly, the work group in our example provides its members with the reassurance necessary to continue dealing with hostile buyers.

Reality Needs

Groups also serve as an agent for establishing and interpreting reality. The world we live in contains a great deal of ambiguity. It is through group interactions that ambiguous events like pay raises, management directives, and workplace changes are clarified and made "real." Work groups, in particular, can define our reality and thus anchor our world. For example, group members may feel their boss overworks them or that their working conditions are inadequate. By interacting with each other, they can verify their feelings and, thus, reduce the ambiguity associated with their jobs, as well as establish which responses are appropriate. By creating such shared understandings through their storytelling and informal get-togethers at lunch and over coffee, the sales reps in our example learn a great deal about the "real" world.

STAGES OF GROUP DEVELOPMENT

In reflecting back on our example, the value of learning to work with and through groups for satisfying important individual needs should be clear. To do so effectively, however, it is helpful to understand the dynamics of group development.

Research suggests that new groups typically progress through five developmental stages from the time they are created to the time they are disbanded.[1]

This is not to imply that all five stages are so clearly marked that there is no overlap between them or that groups do not vary in the speed with which they progress through each stage. A group still may have some characteristics of the first stage and already be showing signs of the third while still largely in the second. Moreover, issues not resolved at one stage may reappear at another. The five stages of group development and the major processes and characteristics associated with each are summarized in Table 17.1.

Stage 1: Forming. The first stage of development for a new group is a period of orientation and testing. Group members attempt to determine what behaviors are acceptable to the group and what is to be gained from group membership. Acquaintanceships are established ("Hi! My name is Pat. What's yours?"), and the skills of each member are identified ("I'm a new auditor in the accounting department. What's your department?"). This is also a time for establishing "ground rules" for task performance ("How much am I expected to do?") and resolving questions regarding group structure ("Who has the real power?"). Though some initial work may be accomplished, members do not feel responsible for the group as a whole, still seeing themselves as individuals.

Stage 2: Storming. This stage of development is marked by a period of intragroup conflict and interpersonal differences as members vie for particular roles. There is disagreement with respect to relative goal priorities, who is to be responsible for what, and how such differences are going to be resolved. Competition for leadership positions is likely as a "pecking order" begins to emerge. Ideas are criticized, and hostility is overt. A group in this stage is likely to have difficulty making decisions and communicating effectively.

Stage 3: Norming. The conflict of Stage 2 ("storming") is typically followed by a sense of heightened solidarity. It is during this third stage of group development that a feeling of cohesiveness emerges. Members develop increasing trust in each other and begin to develop a team spirit. Norms emerge regarding when to

Forming.
A stage of group development characterized by orientation and testing.

Storming.
A stage of group development marked by intragroup conflict and interpersonal differences as members vie for group and task roles.

Norming.
A stage of group development characterized by a sense of heightened solidarity.

Stage	Major Processes	Characteristics
TABLE 17.1 FIVE STAGES OF GROUP DEVELOPMENT		
Forming	Development of attraction bonds, exchange of information, and orientation toward others and the situation	Tentative interactions, polite discourse, concern over ambiguity, and silences
Storming	Dissatisfaction with others, competition among members, disagreement over procedures, conflict	Criticism of ideas, interruption of speakers, poor attendance, and hostility
Norming	Development of group structure, increased cohesiveness and harmony, and establishment of roles and relationships	Agreement on rules, consensus seeking, increased supportiveness, and a feeling of unity with other group members.
Performing	Focus on achievement, high task orientation, and emphasis on performance and productivity	Decision making, problem solving, increased cooperation, and decreased emotionality
Adjourning	Termination of duties, reduction of dependency, and task completion	Regret, increased emotionality, and disintegration

meet, how to behave, what work procedures are to be used, and so forth. Cooperation prevails as previous hostility is overcome. A sense of shared responsibility for "our" group surfaces. Personal opinions are openly expressed. Group structure and harmony solidify. It is during this stage, however, that a group runs the greatest risk of falling victim to groupthink.

Stage 4: Performing. This stage is heralded by increased cooperation, problem solving, and task performance. Decisions are made with the full participation of everyone and after a comprehensive discussion of all alternatives. Roles are flexible, and group energy is focused on productivity. Emotionalism is minimized. This is the most difficult stage for most groups to achieve. In fact, groups unable to perform at an acceptable level will likely regress back to Stage 3 or even Stage 2 in an effort to achieve the maturity required for goal accomplishment.

Stage 5: Adjourning. For permanent groups, performing is the last stage in their development. However, for groups with a specific task to perform, there is an adjourning stage. This stage is exemplified by task completion. Duties are terminated, group members move on to other assignments, and the focus of any remaining members switches to "wrapping things up." The reactions of group members vary. Some are upbeat over the group's accomplishments. Others regret the loss of friendships and camaraderie fostered throughout the group's development.

It is quite likely that anyone who has been in a social club or on a sports team or participated in any other group activity is familiar with the five stages of group development. Indeed, you may have even experienced most of these stages in your present classroom situation. Although these stages do not necessarily occur in a clear-cut or linear manner, neither do they occur in a random fashion. By better understanding the major processes and characteristics of each stage, groups can anticipate problems and focus on task performance. Further, by understanding the forming-storming-norming-performing-adjourning sequence, groups can consciously design their activities so that issues at each stage can be openly addressed and resolved. Thus, they will be able to operate more smoothly and productively than might otherwise be the case.[2]

Performing.
A stage of group development heralded by increased cooperation, problem solving, and task performance.

Adjourning.
A stage of group development exemplified by task completion.

USING GROUPS EFFECTIVELY

Group dynamics can influence the performance of not only individual groups, but also entire organizations. From an organization standpoint, work groups perform at least three activities that contribute to an organization's success: They help "get the job done," they socialize new employees, and they aid in decision making.

HELP "GET THE JOB DONE"

Perhaps the most important function of work groups is that they provide a means for accomplishing complex jobs beyond the capacity of any single individual. In this respect, work groups not only can fill gaps in a manager's abilities, but they can be a source of strength for group members who are unsure of their assignments. Further, they can lighten a manager's work load by assisting in activities such as training. As discussed in Chapter 13, green recruits typically receive at least some

SMART MANAGEMENT THE "HIDDEN HIERARCHY"

Writing in their book *Corporate Cultures: The Rites and Rituals of Corporate Life,* Terrence E. Deal and Allan A. Kennedy estimate that 90 percent of what occurs in an organization has nothing to do with formal events.

Rather, the real process of operating an organization goes on in its informal network. Within this network, various characters form a hidden "hierarchy of power." Here are some of the characters in this informal network.

Storytellers. Storytellers interpret what goes on in an organization. And they can tell you a lot with their stories about what it takes to get ahead.

Thomas Watson, Jr., son of the founder of IBM, often told a story about a nature lover who liked watching ducks fly south. The nature lover started feeding the ducks in a nearby pond. After awhile, the ducks no longer bothered to fly south; they simply wintered in the pond.

As time passed, the ducks flew less and less. And after many years, they grew so lazy and fat they no longer could fly. Watson would end the story saying, "The duck who is tamed will never go anywhere anymore. We are convinced that business needs its wild ducks. And in IBM we try not to tame them."

Watson's story communicated informally that IBM should tolerate—and even encourage— some deviate behavior.

Priests. Like priests in church, they are guardians of an organization's cultural values. They are designated worriers, always trying to keep the flock together.

Priest figures are usually mature and serious, and they know organization history as they know their front yards. Priests seldom have powerful formal positions or titles, but people in power respect their sense of history and judgment.

In describing how he made tough personnel decisions, a manager said, "I ask Harriet." Who is Harriet?

"She is an assistant in personnel. She has been here 15 years, and she is an excellent judge of people. When in doubt, I simply ask Harriet. She knows what we are looking for."

Even though she is almost invisible in the structure, Harriet has a lot of influence.

Whisperers. Whisperers are powers behind the throne, people like Lyndon Johnson's Clark Clifford or Richard Nixon's John Ehrlichman. Whisperers are movers and shakers, but they do not hold formal authority. They wield power because people know they are doing the boss's bidding. No one wants to cross a whisperer because of the influence he or she has on the boss.

Gossips. The gossips are the troubadors of an organization's hidden hierarchy. They pass the latest "have you heard . . . ?" like lightning throughout a company. People do not always take them seriously, and they are not always right; but they entertain and are tolerated.

Source: Terrence E. Deal and Allan A. Kennedy, *Corporate Cultures: The Rites and Rituals of Corporate Life* (Reading, Mass.: Addison-Wesley, 1982), 85–98.

Members from two Santa Fe Pacific Pipeline departments, Systems and Programming and Business Development, join together as a work group to review plans for installing an electronic data interchange system. Work groups created to oversee such complex projects are frequently composed of group members from different departments. The idea is that each member has a combination of unique skills, knowledge, and experiences which can be tapped to complete the group's work efficiently and effectively.

training in their new job assignments. Rarely, however, is this training thorough enough to enable an individual to perform a job without further assistance. In a majority of cases, just as in our example, it is the work group that teaches new employees how to cope with a job and handle the innumerable "tricks of the trade" necessary to perform satisfactorily. Indeed, along this same line, a study by Xerox revealed that its repairmen learn more about fixing copiers from swapping stories with one another than from reading company manuals.[3]

SOCIALIZE NEW EMPLOYEES

Socialization is the process by which new employees are made part of an organization's culture. At the work group level, socialization provides new employees with an understanding of group norms and sanctions. Just as in the Hawthorne Studies, new recruits who ignore established norms typically encounter group pressure to conform. This pressure may take the form of a "heart-to-heart" talk, shunning, or even physical abuse. Work groups may use such pressures to slow down new employees who are "working too hard," or to persuade an employee who is not working hard enough to "get in line." Few work groups want their reputation tarnished by "goof-offs" and "troublemakers." Through such socialization, employees learn just what is expected of them. From an organization standpoint, this process serves to increase the predictability of individual behavior. It also helps to facilitate performance, since a work group can be counted on to monitor an individual employee's actions in a boss's absence.

Socialization.
The process by which new employees are made part of an organization's culture.

AID IN DECISION MAKING

As discussed in Chapter 7, groups such as councils, boards, and committees are often used to make decisions. When the situation is appropriate, group decision making can be extremely useful. Just as the Vroom and Jago normative theory of leadership suggests, this is especially the case when (1) group members possess pertinent information, (2) their commitment to a course of action is required, (3) they share an organization's goals, and (4) conflict over a preferred solution is unlikely.

INFLUENCING WORK GROUP EFFECTIVENESS

The primary standard by which a group is judged is its effectiveness. A work group is generally said to be effective when its members function as a team and accomplish assigned goals. In a group context, effectiveness must be regarded as complex and multidimensional. Obviously, not all groups operate with equal effectiveness. With these points in mind, we will briefly discuss four factors that have been shown to particularly influence group effectiveness. These factors are group size, spatial constraints, group cohesiveness, and group norms.

GROUP SIZE

Research into the influence of size on group effectiveness has largely focused on the impact that size has on interpersonal relations among group members.[4] Findings suggest that as group size increases:

1. Members often feel threatened and reluctant to participate. These feelings may arise because as a group's size increases, the relationships between individual members are apt to be less intimate.

2. The sheer volume of interactions necessary to keep everyone informed tends to make any concerted action much more difficult.

3. Members have less of an opportunity to participate in discussions.

4. Communication tends to be dominated by a few members.

5. Some individuals will seek the benefits of group membership without contributing their fair share of the costs involved. This is referred to as the **free-rider problem.**[5] Free riding is more likely in larger groups because the contributions of individual members cannot be as easily identified. Group productivity will decrease unless coercion or special incentives are used to counter free riding.

Free-rider problem. The tendency for some individuals to seek the benefits of group membership without contributing their fair share of the costs involved.

Evidence dealing with the influence of size on group effectiveness does provide some guidance on the best number of individuals to place in a group. For instance, it is generally concluded that:

1. Disagreement is more common in even-numbered groups than odd-numbered groups because of the likelihood for equal-size subgroups to become pitted against each other.

2. The best group size in most situations is either five or seven. Studies suggest that groups of this size provide maximum member satisfaction because they

are large enough for members to freely express positive and negative feelings and to aggressively solve problems, even at the risk of antagonizing each other, yet small enough that a legitimate concern will be shown for the needs of others. Also, such groups are large enough that the loss of a member can be tolerated, but small enough that the loss cannot be altogether ignored. Additionally, in such groups free riding can be more easily noticed and hence is less likely. An obvious managerial implication of this conclusion is that if work groups have to be larger than five to seven members, subgroups should be formed. In the case of a committee, this might mean empowering an executive group to act for the committee as a whole.

SPATIAL CONSTRAINTS

A job's physical characteristics may require that it be performed in a specific area. Employees feel space restrictions most noticeably when they must remain in a single location to manipulate controls or move between machines or work stations. Such requirements establish physical distances between workers and thus restrict the amount and quality of interaction that can take place among group members. As the physical distance separating workers increases, group effectiveness tends to decrease. That is, work groups whose members are located close together and can interact frequently and easily are likely to be more effective than those whose members are separated by a greater distance. If work group members can talk to each other face to face often, problems of coordination related to faulty communication are less likely to occur.[6]

GROUP COHESIVENESS

A third factor influencing group effectiveness is cohesiveness. **Group cohesiveness** refers to the degree to which group members form a strong collective unit reflecting a feeling of "oneness." Cohesiveness is often associated with group loyalty

Group cohesiveness.
The degree to which group members form a strong collective unit reflecting a feeling of "oneness."

At Compaq Computer Corporation's Houston, Texas, plant the assembly line is U-shaped so that workers at the beginning and end of the line can easily confer. This arrangement facilitates group interaction as in the quality circle meeting pictured here.

or group pride, being typical of Stage 3 group development. It is a result of the various forces acting on individual members to remain in a group. A group is low in cohesiveness when the forces acting on members to remain in a group are not strong enough to counteract those forces acting on them to depart.

Various forces that either enhance or diminish group cohesiveness are identified in Figure 17.1.[7] As suggested, an individual's decision to remain in a group is a result of forces pushing in opposing directions. The enhancing forces push one way, and the diminishing forces push the other. A person will remain a group member only as long as the enhancements to do so are as great as or greater than the forces not to do so.

The positive consequences of group cohesiveness include more and better group interaction, less intermember conflict, and greater interpersonal coordination. In a cohesive work group, employees value their membership and are strongly motivated toward advancing its goals and participating in its activities. Perhaps the greatest advantage of a cohesive group is that its members can find in group achievement satisfaction for their individual esteem, as well as social and security needs. From an organization's perspective, cohesiveness contributes to a work group's vitality—and thus its effectiveness.

The multiplier effect of cohesiveness was especially evident during the early financially pressed days of Federal Express Corp. Stories abound of Federal employees who delayed cashing their paychecks, and pilots who became station managers until there were planes to fly. No one at Federal wanted to disappoint their colleagues. The esprit de corps that develops from such cohesiveness can be a very powerful motivating force. Indeed, Federal Express continues to be known as perhaps the closest thing in corporate America to the Green Berets.

FIGURE 17.1 FORCES THAT ENHANCE OR DIMINISH GROUP COHESIVENESS

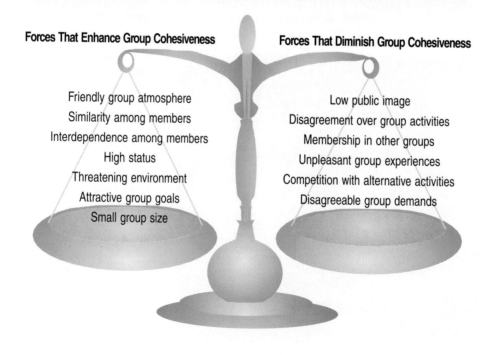

Forces That Enhance Group Cohesiveness

Friendly group atmosphere
Similarity among members
Interdependence among members
High status
Threatening environment
Attractive group goals
Small group size

Forces That Diminish Group Cohesiveness

Low public image
Disagreement over group activities
Membership in other groups
Unpleasant group experiences
Competition with alternative activities
Disagreeable group demands

GROUP NORMS

Norms are standards of behavior accepted by a group's members. By defining the kinds of behaviors that are acceptable or unacceptable, norms are a powerful and efficient means of influencing work group behavior. Norms develop over time and are reinforced or weakened by group pressures, which are in turn related to group cohesiveness. In a highly cohesive group, the influence of norms will likely be greater than in a less cohesive group.

As an important basis for control, norms naturally influence work group effectiveness—either positively or negatively. Table 17.2 identifies ten categories of norms that can influence group effectiveness. For each category, an example positive or negative norm is given. Research indicates that work groups, departments, and even entire organizations with positive norms in these categories tend to be more effective than those with negative norms.

Norms.
Standards of behavior accepted by a group's members.

TABLE 17.2 TEN CATEGORIES OF WORK GROUP NORMS WITH POSITIVE AND NEGATIVE EXAMPLES

Category	Example	
	Positive Norm	**Negative Norm**
1. Organization and personal pride	Group members stand up for the organization when it is unfairly criticized.	Group members don't care about organization problems.
2. Performance/excellence	Group members try to improve, even when doing well.	Group members are satisfied with the minimum acceptable performance.
3. Teamwork/communication	Group members listen and seek the opinions of others.	Group members talk about others behind their backs rather than confronting issues.
4. Leadership	Group members ask for help when they need it.	Group members hide their problems and avoid superiors.
5. Profitability and cost effectiveness	Group members are concerned with increasing profitability and cost effectiveness.	Group members don't care about profits; that's someone else's problem.
6. Colleague relations	Group members refuse to take advantage of one another.	Group members don't care about one another's well-being.
7. Consumer relations	Group members feel the customer is No. 1.	Group members are indifferent to customer satisfaction.
8. Honesty and security	Group members refuse to tolerate pilferage or lax security.	Group members are unconcerned with pilferage or security.
9. Training and development	Group members care about training and development.	Group members talk about training and development, but don't take it seriously.
10. Innovational change	Group members are always looking for better ways to do things.	Group members don't have new ideas.

Source: Adapted with permission from Robert F. Allen and Saul Pilnick, "Confronting the Shadow Organization," *Organizational Dynamics* 1 (Spring 1973): 6–10.

DYSFUNCTIONAL WORK GROUP BEHAVIOR

Until now, we have focused primarily on the positive aspects of work group behavior. However, as our discussion on norms suggests, work group behavior can also be dysfunctional. Two situations are of major concern:

1. Work groups that oppose rather than support organization goals.
2. Work groups in conflict with one another.

WORK GROUP OPPOSITION

Work groups can oppose as well as support organization goals. What is good for an organization may not be good for group members. Consequently, even though a group member may wish to support both organization and work group goals, to do so might be impossible. For example, group members who would like to work harder might run into opposition from their peers who could reason that increased individual output will result in a need for fewer workers. This would obviously be counter to the desire for work group job security.

The management literature contains numerous illustrations of work groups opposing organization goals. The following true story will suffice to show to what lengths a cohesive work group, in this case a tank platoon, will go to achieve its own goals.

> Following the completion of basic training, Jim was assigned for advanced training to the Armor Center at Fort Knox, Kentucky. He was part of a typical tank platoon. The platoon members got along well and were a cohesive group. All seemed fine until the platoon was assigned a new second lieutenant—an ROTC graduate with a swagger stick, an exaggerated opinion of himself, and a low opinion of the men in the company. He made them work long hours, punished them frequently, and never praised them. The men let their efficiency rate drop to send him a message. His response was to berate and work them even harder.

> The men then decided to take action. They met after-hours and planned a reprisal. The lieutenant (whom they called "Little Napoleon") took special pride in the platoon dayroom, a place designed for troop relaxation, consisting of pool tables, magazines, games, and so on. For the most part, the dayroom was little used and little noticed. Nevertheless, Little Napoleon demanded that it be waxed and polished daily.

> The group's plan was to send Napoleon a stronger message than had been sent before. Late one evening the men emptied the dayroom of its chairs, Ping-Pong table, pool tables, and other items and dumped them into the Ohio River. Napoleon was legally and financially responsible for every item taken. This still produced no change in his behavior. He redoubled his efforts to drive the men even harder.

> At about this time, the platoon was scheduled for rotation to Europe. After all the platoon's equipment had been prepared for shipment overseas, several group members slipped into the loading area and changed the serial number on one of the tanks under Napoleon's charge. As a result, it was sent to the wrong unit in West Germany. Napoleon was now out $1.3 million. This incident finally convinced him that he was doing something wrong.

As this story attests, work group behavior can become gravely misdirected when group members oppose rather than support organization goals. However, the question remains: Why does such opposition develop?

The first thing to learn around here,   kid, is don't try to break any records.

Sage advice to the new union card holder? The way to protect his job?

Not really.

Artificial restraints on productivity are losing jobs for Americans. Jobs formerly performed here have been exported to Brazil, Japan and to the foreign-flag shipping companies that haul freight all over the world.

The most apparent cause for our loss of jobs, tax sources and wealth generation has been the power and the inflexible attitude of labor unions. Demands for wages and benefit increases have far exceeded productivity gains.

And it's about time you, Mr. Industry Manager, speak up about it.

To do it effectively, you need the best communications help you can get. As soon as you can get it.

Penton

Industry Week, Foundry, Automation, Machine Design, New Equipment Digest, Education Division, Press Division.

One explanation can be found in Adams's equity theory. If work group members feel they are unappreciated, overworked, and receiving less than a fair outcome (praise, rewards, and so on) for their inputs (effort, dedication, and so on), opposition is likely to develop in all but the most uncohesive work groups. From a managerial perspective, there is only one way to confront such a situation: Determine the *cause* of the perceived inequity, and do something about it. This may involve actions such as redesigning specific jobs, reevaluating relevant pay scales and employee benefits, or even disbanding and reforming the group.

INTERGROUP CONFLICT

Conflict, which may be defined as a situation in which two or more parties are in opposition, is a normal and natural consequence of human interaction. From a managerial perspective, conflict is dysfunctional when it impairs relationships among parties that need to interact effectively. Although conflict may occur between individuals, between individuals and groups, or between groups, our present focus is on the latter.

Causes of Conflict

Managers report spending up to 30 percent of their time and energy dealing with conflict.[8] Although there are many causes of conflict between work groups, the following four are perhaps the most common (see Figure 17.2):

▲
Conflict, which may be defined as a situation in which two or more parties are in opposition, is a normal consequence of human interaction. Often, the pursuit of different goals, such as those typically pursued by management and by labor unions, is a major source of conflict.

Conflict.
A situation in which two or more parties are in opposition.

CLOSE UP: DIVERSITY

In today's multinational business environment, managers are as likely to have colleagues from across town as from halfway across the world. While certain nuances of group dynamics are the same, there are several key differences that could create obstacles.

Here are some things to keep in mind when dealing with people from different cultural or ethnic backgrounds.

- Before giving a colleague a piece of your mind, consider that not all cultures value candor above consensus. In some countries, "saving face" is far more important than the benefits derived from constructive criticism. That may mean you'll be dealing with people who prefer to gloss over conflicts rather than confront problems candidly.

- There's an old saying, "When God made time, he made a lot of it." To some people that means an 8 o'clock meeting can just as easily get under way at 8:30 or 9. What does that mean for an American manager who demands punctuality? If you want a meeting to begin on time, say so. Then hope for the best.

- Which is more important? Tradition, the past, and ancestors? Or progress, the future, and contemporaries? This depends on who you ask. Some cultures abide by the belief that unless something has withstood the test of time, it can't possibly be worthwhile. For others, old ideas are outdated. A compromise might be to mix the old with the new.

- Groups provide an ideal forum for exchanging ideas. But what happens when expressing an opinion is tantamount to an unthinkable breach of etiquette and decorum? That's the case in some countries where the opinions of those in high-status positions are always held in higher esteem than the opinions of those of lower status, regardless of expertise. One of the best ways to get around hierarchical obstacles is to stress the advantages of specialization.

- A signature on the dotted line is a deal clincher in the United States, but there are some countries where personal commitment and a handshake carry more clout. In that case, executives are better off spending their time building long-term friendships rather than poring over meticulously worded legal documents.

Source: Adapted from "A 'Primer' on Cultural Dimensions," by Leonard Sayles, *Issues & Observations*, Fall 1989, 8–9.

Differences in Goals   The work groups involved in a conflict may be pursuing different goals. Labor-management disagreements are perhaps the most frequently cited example of this situation. However, it should be noted that because of in-group loyalty, the competitive nature of intergroup relationships often contributes to distortions in perception and judgment. As a result of being convinced that its position is correct or superior to the claims of others, work groups unwittingly may enter win-lose situations where one side is destined to be a loser. Such conflicts can be the most trying that an organization experiences.

Differences in Perspective   Two groups may share the same goals but differ over how the goals should be achieved. As a result, they are likely to disagree on what method is best for an organization. For example, both an organization's sales and production departments may want to increase profits but disagree on how to do so. Sales may believe the answer is to increase product sales through customer service. Production, however, may believe the answer is to cut costs. So,

FIGURE 17.2 SELECTED CAUSES OF CONFLICT BETWEEN WORK GROUPS

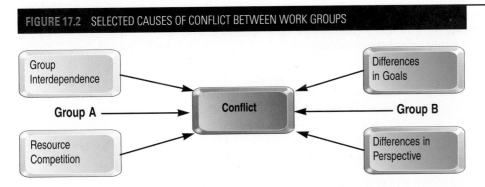

when a customer requests a small run of a specialized product, sales says, "No problem." Production, on the other hand, says, "No way!" Neither side is being quarrelsome; both are simply doing what, from their perspective, is best to increase profits. Incidentally, as discussed in Chapter 9, this type of conflict is typical of line-staff relations. In general, such conflict is attributable as much to different perspectives and training as it is to separate roles and career paths.

Resource Competition When one group sees the prospect of either incurring a loss or being denied a gain as the result of another's actions, conflict is likely. This is often precisely the case in situations involving limited resources. If a larger or increased resource allocation to one group represents a commensurate loss to another, conflict between the two groups can be anticipated. Such intergroup conflict may develop over the allocation of capital, labor, supplies, and so on.

Group Interdependence In Chapter 9, we identified three types of task interdependence: pooled, sequential, and reciprocal. Just as increased interdependence requires more coordination, it also increases the potential for conflict. In situations of pooled interdependence, conflict is typically infrequent because the degree of coordination required between groups is minimal. The advertising department at a Neiman-Marcus store is essentially independent from the shipping and receiving department, so the two departments seldom have a reason to interact and, thus, disagree. When they do interact, their interchanges typically are governed by standing policies and procedures.

Greater coordination is required in situations of sequential interdependence. In such situations, the outputs from one group are the inputs for another group. Thus, the first group must finish its work before the second can begin its assigned task. The opportunity for conflict is understandably high in such situations. The most obvious example of sequential interdependence is the automobile assembly line. Other examples include cafeterias, petroleum refineries, food and beverage processors, and meat packing plants. To avoid conflict between groups in such highly interdependent organizations, scheduling is particularly important.

In situations of reciprocal interdependence, the potential for conflict is typically the highest. In such situations, outputs from one group may serve as inputs for another and vice versa. In other words, there is a two-way interdependence. As a consequence, the degree of coordination required between groups is quite extensive. Examples of situations in which reciprocal interdependence is common include hospital emergency rooms, mental health centers, computer service firms, and certain research and development labs. Coordination to avoid conflict between groups in such situations requires the continuous monitoring of input/output transactions above and beyond the schedules, policies, and procedures generally associated with pooled and sequential interdependence.

Benefits of Conflict

It should be stressed that conflict is not always detrimental. Properly managed, conflict can have constructive consequences.[9] These include:

1. Serving as a "safety valve" to release pent-up emotions.
2. Increasing group cohesion when directed at an external force.
3. Making change more acceptable and even desirable.
4. Bringing hidden issues to the surface.
5. Mobilizing and energizing group members.
6. Triggering creativity and innovation.
7. Enhancing communication.
8. Resolving or ending an unproductive relationship.

Managing Conflict

Because conflict may impede an organization's effectiveness, it needs to be managed. There are essentially five conflict-resolution options: *avoidance, accommodation, competition, compromise,* and *collaboration.*[10] Each has particular strengths and weaknesses, and no one option is ideal for all situations.

- **Avoidance** involves withdrawing from or suppressing a conflict. This option is likely to be chosen when a conflict is judged unnecessary and irrelevant and its resolution is therefore considered unimportant.

- **Accommodation** involves one party maintaining harmony by giving in to another. This option is likely to be chosen when the issue in question is deemed relatively insignificant, especially given the risk of disrupting an important ongoing relationship.

- **Competition** involves attempting to win a conflict at the expense of another. This option is likely to be chosen when one or more parties has high concern for the issue in question but little concern for the relationships involved.

- **Compromise** involves reaching an agreement that gives all parties to a conflict at least some of what they want. This option is likely to be chosen in situations where the parties involved have some concern for the issue in question, as well as for the relationships involved. Compromise is a principal means for resolving conflicts in highly formalized bargaining situations, such as in negotiations for labor-management contracts. It is also applicable in less formal circumstances. Consider two parties working together on a sales plan. They are at odds on how to best forecast economic trends. A possible compromise might be to have each party forecast different economic trends and then combine the results in an integrated report.

- **Collaboration** involves reaching an agreement that permits all parties involved in a conflict to achieve their desired outcomes. The option is likely to be chosen in situations where the issue at hand is too important to be compromised and the cooperation of all parties is required. For example, two par-

Avoidance.
A conflict-resolution option that involves withdrawing from or suppressing a conflict.

Accommodation.
A conflict-resolution option that involves one party maintaining harmony by giving in to another.

Competition.
A conflict-resolution option that involves attempting to win a conflict at the expense of another.

Compromise.
A conflict-resolution option that involves reaching an agreement that gives all parties at least some of what they want.

Collaboration.
A conflict-handling option that involves reaching an agreement that permits all parties involved to achieve their desired outcomes.

ties may disagree on which of two suppliers to use when upgrading an existing computer system. A possible compromise solution is to use both suppliers for different parts of the system.

COMMITTEE MEETINGS

In general, a **committee** may be defined as a group assembled to consider, investigate, take action on, or report on some matter. Committees are involved in the bulk of the 11 million meetings that take place daily in the United States.[11] It is estimated that the average top-level manager spends between 840 and 1,200 hours a year in meetings. That's the equivalent of twenty-one to thirty 40-hour workweeks.[12]

Committee.
A group assembled to consider, investigate, take action on, or report on some matter.

THE PROS AND CONS OF COMMITTEES

A list of the most common reasons for using committees is presented in Table 17.3. In many ways the pros in the table resemble the list of advantages of group decision making presented in Chapter 7. Despite these reasons, many managers still have negative feelings about committees. "J. B." Fuqua, chairman of the board and CEO of Fuqua Industries, for example, does not believe in committees, seeing them as an excuse by management to avoid responsibilities. As he commented in an address at the University of Pennsylvania's Wharton School of Business: "I just don't believe in committees. You can spend all tomorrow hunting around Philadelphia, and you won't find the first monument to a committee. This school isn't named after a committee; it's named after a man who made his mark on the free-enterprise system."[13]

TABLE 17.3 COMMITTEE PROS AND CONS

Pros

1. Committee decisions are likely to be accepted by their members. This makes implementation much easier.
2. Committees composed of affected work group representatives can identify potential coordination problems.
3. Committees diffuse power. Some decisions are too significant (and complex) to be decided by a single person.
4. Committees that are purposefully constituted can bring divergent experiences and training to bear on a single issue.
5. Committees can rapidly disseminate information.
6. Committees can help to train new managers.
7. Committees can avoid placing all the blame on one person for an unpopular decision.

Cons

1. Committees are expensive.
2. Committees are time consuming; poorly structured committee meetings can be a waste of time.
3. Committees can result in mediocre decisions. (Like groups, committee decisions are subject to the *leveling effect*.)
4. Committees can amplify differences and generate conflicts that might not otherwise occur.
5. Committees can be used as a guise to avoid assuming responsibilities.

The various reasons managers cite for disliking committees are also listed in Table 17.3. In reviewing this list, remember that committees are like people. They can be effective or ineffective. It is a manager's job to make them effective both as a committee chairperson and a committee member.

INCREASING COMMITTEE EFFECTIVENESS

There are several commonsense ways to increase committee effectiveness. Both committee chairpersons and committee members can contribute to the effectiveness of committee meetings by following the guidelines given in Table 17.4. As the table suggests, there is more to an effective committee meeting than what takes place when it convenes. Both committee chairpersons and committee members should prepare for meetings in advance and review—and sometimes even re-think—a committee's actions after it meets.

Recognizing how much of a typical manager's day is spent in meetings, some organizations have developed techniques to increase meeting effectiveness by making sure that meetings run no longer than necessary. Here are some of the techniques they use:

- At Manco Inc., a cowbell is placed in the middle of all meeting rooms. Anytime committee members feel someone has droned on too long, they can ring the bell and the speaker must stop talking.

- Merck & Co. holds *stand-up* meetings with a 20-minute time limit.

- General Electric's medical-health group has declared Wednesday a "no meeting" day. In addition, when meetings are held, participants outnumber chairs by one. This means that the last person to arrive must stand—but meetings start on time.

Finally, to increase its effectiveness, a manager who creates a committee and selects its members must also be sensitive to factors that will influence the committee's interpersonal dynamics. A committee chairperson should be chosen carefully, with consideration given to ability and leadership style. Committee members should be selected with equal care for their problem-solving insight and expertise.

▲
Organizations often establish permanent committees with members drawn from top management. J. P. Morgan & Co.'s Credit Policy Committee meets weekly to review significant developments in commercial banking and is charged with major credit-related decisions. Committee members include vice-presidents and senior vice-presidents.

TABLE 17.4 GUIDELINES FOR INCREASING COMMITTEE EFFECTIVENESS		
Committee Chairperson		
Before Committee Meeting	**During Committee Meeting**	**After Committee Meeting**
Limit committee size. (Research indicates ideal size is 5 or 7.)	Set the right tone; encourage participation by all members.	See that meeting notes are promptly distributed.
Select informed members who can act in a conscientious and reasonable manner.	Avoid dominating meetings.	Make the same preparations for any followup meetings as for the first meeting.
Define committee responsibility and authority.	Avoid competing with members for "equal time."	Schedule meetings so that committee work conforms to a specified timetable.
Communicate this definition along with agenda and supporting documents so members can prepare in advance of meetings.	Summarize discussion from time to time.	After a committee's final meeting, thank members in person as well as in writing.
Contact members, remind them of meeting times and locations, and answer any questions.	Keep discussion on appropriate subject.	Communicate results of a committee's work to the right authorities orally and in writing, as required.
Appoint a secretary to take and distribute notes to members after each meeting.	Be interested and alert.	
Start meetings on time.	End on time.	
Committee Members		
Before Committee Meeting	**During Committee Meeting**	**After Committee Meeting**
Read preparatory materials and develop preliminary ideas.	Be alert and attentive.	Rethink your initial position; reread meeting notes.
Consult with those you represent to learn their ideas and responses to your preliminary ideas.	Participate, being sure to clearly state your position.	Consult with those you represent for their responses and suggestions.
Arrive at meetings on time.	Try to be rational, especially when responding to persons you do not like or to those who are severely critical of your position.	
	Avoid dominating discussions.	
	Encourage other members to participate.	

SUMMARY

In most organizations, goals are achieved by groups of people working together, not by individuals acting alone. To be successful, managers must understand the dynamics that govern groups. Thus, the purpose of this chapter was to examine work group behavior.

Learning Objective 1:   Answer the question *What is a group?*
A group is two or more people who interact regularly to achieve a common goal.

Learning Objective 2:   Distinguish between formal and informal groups.
Formal groups are those deliberately created by an organization to achieve a

specific goal. Informal groups are ones that are independent of an organization's structure and created for their members' purposes.

Learning Objective 3: Explain why people join groups.
People join groups to satisfy specific needs. Principal among these are social needs, esteem needs, security needs, and reality needs.

Learning Objective 4: Specify the stages of development a typical new group moves through from the time it is created to the time it disbands.
The five developmental stages a typical new group moves through are forming, storming, norming, performing, and adjourning.

Learning Objective 5: Explain how work groups can contribute to an organization's success.
Work groups can contribute to an organization's success in at least three ways: helping to "get the job done," socializing new employees, and aiding in decision making.

Learning Objective 6: State various factors that have been shown to influence work group effectiveness.
Various factors that have been shown to influence work group effectiveness are group size, spatial constraints, group cohesiveness, and group norms.

Learning Objective 7: Describe the so-called free-rider problem.
The free-rider problem occurs when individuals seek the benefits of group membership without contributing their fair share of the costs involved.

Learning Objective 8: Recount two situations in which work group behavior could be considered dysfunctional.
Two situations in which work group behavior could be considered dysfunctional are work groups that oppose rather than support organization goals and work groups in conflict with one another.

Learning Objective 9: Detail the major causes of conflict between work groups.
Four major causes of conflict between work groups are differences in goals, differences in perspective, resource competition, and group interdependence.

Learning Objective 10: List various conflict-resolution options.
There are essentially five conflict-resolution options: avoidance, accommodation, competition, compromise, and collaboration.

Learning Objective 11: Outline the pros and cons of committees.
The pros and cons of committees are outlined in Table 17.3.

Learning Objective 12: Identify various ways to increase committee effectiveness.
Guidelines for increasing committee effectiveness are given in Table 17.4.

KEY TERMS

accommodation 514
adjourning 503
avoidance 514
collaboration 514
committee 515
competition 514
compromise 514

conflict 511
formal group 499
forming 502
free-rider problem 506
group 498
group cohesiveness 507

informal group 499
norming 502
norms 509
performing 503
socialization 505
storming 502

REVIEW AND DISCUSSION QUESTIONS

1. It is generally conceded that the primary benefit accorded an individual by group membership is the opportunity to satisfy personal needs. Prepare separate lists of the formal and informal groups to which you belong and identify the needs that your membership in each group satisfies.

2. Work groups take many different forms. Although you may not have thought of it as such, for the last several weeks you have been a member of a work group—your class in management. Describe how this work group has developed through the various stages of group development discussed in this chapter.

3. Size is one factor that has been repeatedly shown to influence work group effectiveness. During your career as a student you've probably been enrolled in classes that have varied in size from perhaps as few as 15 to several hundred. Considering a class at either extreme, how did the difference in size affect (1) your willingness to participate, (2) the ease or difficulty of concerted actions, (3) your opportunity to participate in discussions, and (4) the tendency for communication to be dominated by a few people (perhaps even solely by your instructor)?

4. "This is small company," Chris, a supervisor at a TV production company, says. "So we work our fingers to the bone. You could spot in a minute anyone who was dragging his feet. The others would resent it and wouldn't stand for it. There's just too much to do for the rest of us to carry someone like that." Relate Chris's comment to the so-called free-rider problem. What has your own experience been in this regard?

5. Dr. Allen E. Puckett is chairman and CEO of the aerospace megacompany Hughes Aircraft. According to Puckett, the way Hughes Aircraft is run "revolves around its people." He goes on to say that "in dealing with projects as complex as those in which we are typically involved, it is absolutely essential that we maintain a strong team effort and a real spirit of teamwork in everything we do." To further make his point, Puckett uses a sports analogy: "On a sailboat of any size at all, where you have eight or ten crewmembers working, if they aren't a cohesive team, you might as well forget it."[14] Reflecting on Puckett's comments, how valuable do you think such cohesiveness—what Puckett terms a "sink or swim together attitude"—is to an organization's success?

6. As noted in this chapter, norms can be positive or negative, healthy or unhealthy, productive or unproductive. Prepare a list of norms that govern behavior in your residence hall, fraternity/sorority, campus clubs, place of employment, or classroom. Indicate those you feel are productive and should be enforced.

7. Most people have violated informal group norms at one time or another. As a consequence, they have probably incurred the informal group's wrath. This wrath may take the form of open sanctions or punishment, such as telling a person he is out of bounds or ignoring him. More subtle enforcement, such as joking or warning the person about the punishment due norm violators, also may be used. Recount an instance of norm enforcement with which you are familiar.

8. Conflict is pervasive both on and off the job. Drawing on either your own experience or the daily papers, describe a situation in which someone capitalized on its positive aspects.

9. A humorist once observed, "Committees keep minutes but waste hours." Reflect on your own experiences as a committee member. What pros and cons do you associate with committees?

10. Andrew S. Grove is president of Intel Corporation, a manufacturer of microprocessors and computer memory devices, renowned for good management. Writing in *Fortune*, Grove states: "Meetings have a bad name." Despite this bad name, he argues that meetings are the medium through which managerial work is performed. To ensure that committee meetings are productive and not a waste of time (and money), Grove advises that "most of what the chairman contributes should occur before the proceedings begin."[15] Explain what Grove means by this statement.

THE MANAGEMENT EXPERIENCE   NORMS: DO'S AND DON'TS

There are literally hundreds of norms in every organization, department, or work group. Norms can be positive or negative, healthy or unhealthy, productive or unproductive. With this in mind, examine the following norms of one large company as perceived by more than 100 top managers. As you review them, put a check mark beside those that you feel are productive and should be enforced. *Compare and discuss your answers with those of your classmates.*

Do	Don't
• Dress conservatively	• Turn down promotions
• Be punctual	• Associate with lower level employees
• Be frugal	• Discuss salaries
• Stress accepted values or be quiet	• Ask embarrassing questions
• Operate through the chain of command	• Admit weakness
• Eat with a work-defined group	• Use profanity
• Consider an invitation a command	• Be overly negative
• Be a self-starter	• Cross departmental lines to handle a problem
• Answer your own phone	• Work late in the office
• Be prompt in answering mail	• Disagree with immediate supervisor
• Be available	• Go over boss's head
• Be cooperative and diplomatic with other departments	• Grow a beard
• Be conservative with expenses	• Socialize with your boss
• Be accurate	• Eat lunch with clerical employees
• Stay at your desk and look busy	• Leave the lunch table until the boss does, even if he or she arrives late
• Be discreet about goofing off	• Leave early
• Decorate your office conservatively	• Spread rumors
• Defer to superiors	• Moonlight
• Respond instantly to vice-presidents	• Lose your self-control
	• Close your office door
	• Call in sick on a long weekend

Source: Adapted from Robert W. Goddard, "Everything Swings off #1," *Manage* 36 (January 1984): 8.

CASE 17.1   SHEPHERD MANUFACTURING COMPANY

Charles Johnson, the new supervisor of the drill press department at Shepherd Manufacturing Company, was wondering how to deal with what appeared to be a solidly formed clique comprised of ten of the 21 drill press operators in his department. These particular operators all worked on adjacent drill presses, bantered back and forth during working hours, ate lunch together, and frequently were involved together in after-hours social functions.

Ike Ramey, the union shop steward for the drill press department, seemed to organize most of the clique's after-hours functions, and his leadership within the group also was quite apparent on the job. It appeared obvious to Johnson, after only a week in this department, that every time he made a request of any of these ten men, the operator would look to Ramey for his approval before he would cooperate. Already, on two occasions, Ramey had come to Johnson as spokesman for "his men" regarding matters having nothing to do with the union or his position as steward.

The situation appeared particularly intolerable to Johnson after the youngest man in the department visited him at lunchtime today while the others were out. He complained that he was being forced to hold down his output. This young man, Johnny Rivers, said that Ramey had mentioned to him on several occasions that he should hold his completed plates down to 15 an hour. Rivers had told his supervisor that it was easy for him to turn out 25 an hour, even though he had been on the job for only 3 weeks. He found the work much more boring and even made more mistakes when working at such a slow pace. Yesterday he had resumed his former pace of 25 plates an hour and had already today been called a "fink" by one of his coworkers and a "rate buster" by another. Then shortly before lunchtime, he found that his lunch box had mysteriously disappeared. Although he knew exactly where it had been left, his questions of his fellow workers had brought only knowing smiles but not his lunch.

As Johnson leaned back in his chair thinking over the situation existing in his department, he could hear the men laughing and talking as they returned from lunch.

Problems

1. What can Charles Johnson do to increase productivity at Shepherd?
2. What can he do to better manage Ike Ramey?

Source: Roland B. Cousins, University of Southwestern Louisiana, Lafayette, La. Reprinted by permission.

NOTES

[1] Bruce W. Tuckman, "Developmental Sequence in Small Groups," *Psychological Bulletin* 63 (November 1965): 384–399; and Bruce W. Tuckman and Mary Ann C. Jensen, "Stages of Small-Group Development Revisited," *Group & Organization Studies* 2 (December 1977): 419–427.

[2] Marshall Saskin and William C. Morris, *Organizational Behavior: Concepts and Experiences* (Reston, Va.: Reston, 1984), 186–187.

[3] Thomas A. Stewart, "Brainpower," *Fortune*, June 3, 1991, 50.

[4] For a review of findings in this area, see A. Paul Hare, *Handbook of Group Research*, 2d ed. (New York: Free Press, 1976), 214–219; and Marvin E. Shaw, *Group Dynamics: The Psychology of Small Group Behavior*, 3d ed. (New York: McGraw-Hill, 1981), 168–177.

[5] Robert Albanese and David D. Van Fleet, "Rational Behavior in Groups: The Free-Riding Tendency," *Academy of Management Review* 10 (April 1985): 244–255.

[6] Robert Sommer, "Spatial Behavior," Herbert H. Blumberg, A. Paul Hare, Valerie Kent, and Martin F. Davies (eds.) in *Small Groups and Social Interaction*, vol. 1, (Chichester, U.K.: Wiley, 1983), 9–15.

[7] Dorwin Cartwright, "The Nature of Group Cohesiveness," Dorwin Cartwright and Alvin Zander (eds.), in *Group Dynamics: Research and Theory*, 3d ed., (New York: Harper & Row, 1968), 98–103.

[8] William Friend, "Managing Conflict," *Association Management* 37 (June 1985): 87.

[9] Dennis King, "Three Cheers for Conflict!" *Personnel* 58 (January–February 1981): 13–22.

[10] Kenneth W. Thomas, "Toward Multi-Dimensional Values in Teaching: The Example of Conflict Behavior," *Academy of Management Review* 2 (April 1977): 484–490; and Douglas E. Wolfe and Stephen C. Bushardt, "Interpersonal Conflict: Strategies and Guidelines for Resolution," *Journal of American Medical Records Association* 56 (February 1985): 18–22.

[11] Anthony Jay, "How to Run a Meeting," *Harvard Business Review* 54 (March–April 1956): 46.

[12] Peggy Scott, "Average Executive Wastes Six Weeks in Meetings," *Baton Rouge Business Report* 4 (January 1986): 101; and Carol Hymowitz, "A Survival Guide to the Office Meeting," *Wall Street Journal*, June 21, 1988, 31.

[13] Quoted in Jasper Dorsey, "J. B. Fuqua: Chairman & CEO, Fuqua Industries, Inc.," *Sky* (May 1985): 45.

[14] Quoted in Charles Gordon, "Allen E. Puckett: Chairman & CEO, Hughes Aircraft Company," *Sky* 12 (December 1983): 39–40.

[15] Andrew S. Grove, "How (and Why) to Run a Meeting," *Fortune*, July 11, 1983, 138.

CHAPTER 18

LEARNING OBJECTIVES

Upon completing this chapter, you should be able to:

- Describe the communication process.
- Identify various barriers to effective communication.
- List various do's and don'ts of effective listening.
- Detail several grapevine characteristics.
- Recount different strategies for dealing with misinformation.
- Name several techniques to improve an organization's communication effectiveness.

earning how to communicate effectively is a challenge even under normal circumstances. But when a company's workforce is made up of employees who don't speak English, the barriers may seem insurmountable.

Take the case of Pace Food, Inc., maker of the popular hot sauce that bears the company name. Nearly three-quarters of the employees at the San Antonio firm are Mexican Americans, but they are managed by a white male, President Kit Goldsbury.

Despite the obvious drawbacks, Goldsbury is undaunted by the challenge. He has responded by making Pace Food bilingual, with company publications printed in Spanish and English and even meetings conducted in both languages. That's no problem for Goldsbury: He learned Spanish on the family-owned ranch in Mexico where he spent much of his youth.

But allowing workers to speak their native languages is not always that easy. Management experts say that relationships can be harmed when one group of employees speaks a foreign language, especially when those who don't understand it believe they are being deliberately excluded. On the other hand, it is difficult to bar

EFFECTIVE
COMMUNICATION

employees from speaking their native tongues. One solution is for all employees either to speak English or to let others know what they are discussing. And those who understand only English should be more sensitive to the need of others to speak their own language. Banning the use of foreign languages altogether usually is not a good idea, unless it's necessary for employees to get their jobs done.

Sometimes barriers to effective communication can be more subtle. For example, a white male supervisor might be reluctant to promote an Asian who is disinclined to talk about his accomplishments. To the white manager, the taciturn worker lacks leadership qualities; to the Asian, such self-promotion is equivalent to bragging and is considered inappropriate.

The key to managing a diverse workforce successfully is to encourage understanding on all sides. For example, Pace Foods gives English lessons to its Hispanic employees but also offers Spanish classes to its English-speaking employees.

In the final analysis, companies must adopt policies that reflect the unique needs of their employees. But even though the policies may be different, their aim should be the same: to create an environment where race and ethnic origin are neither an advantage nor a disadvantage. In this chapter, we will discuss the importance of good communication for creating such an environment. We will identify some barriers to communication and discuss alternatives for increasing communication effectiveness.

Source: Sharon Nelton, "Meet Your New Workforce," *Nation's Business* 77 (July 1988): 14–21.

Although all jobs involve communication to some extent, by its very nature a manager's job requires more time spent communicating than most. In previous chapters, we focused on the interpersonal skills a manager must develop to be successful. Implicit in the discussion was the need for effective communication. The success of every manager and every organization depends on communication because in any undertaking involving two or more persons, it is essential for the coordination of individual activities. Accordingly, this chapter discusses how the communication process works, barriers to effective communication, the importance of effective listening, and the so-called grapevine, and it suggests several ways for an organization to improve its communication effectiveness.

THE COMMUNICATION PROCESS

Communication is defined as the process of transmitting understood information among two or more people. As such, it always involves at least two parties—a sender and a receiver. Technically speaking, communication is successful only when mutual understanding results, that is, when one not only transmits information, but also makes oneself understood by others.

In most organizations, communication is clearly a dynamic and vital process. The complex nature of this process must be understood if it is to be effective and meaningful. We can best appreciate the communication process if we break it into various steps and diagram them as in Figure 18.1. Bear in mind, however, that any attempt to diagram the sequence of communication between two individuals is necessarily an oversimplification. Moreover, the steps in a communication episode not only occur individually, but also interact with each other. Though we must discuss the steps separately, we must beware of thinking of them as being separate from one another, or we will distort the true picture of the communication process.

- *Step 1.* The first step in the communication process is **ideation.** A sender has information for, or needs information from, another person. This information may consist of ideas, facts, opinions, and so on. As a consequence, a decision is made to communicate.

- *Step 2.* The next step is **encoding.** At this point in the communication process, the sender translates the message to be conveyed into a set of symbols, which it is believed an intended receiver will understand. To be most effective, the symbols selected are adapted to the medium used to transmit the message. If the medium is a written report, for instance, the encoding symbols will be words, tables, diagrams, and, perhaps, pictures. If the medium is a lecture, encoding might involve words, overhead transparencies, and written handouts.

- *Step 3.* The third step is the actual **transmission** of the message as encoded. As suggested, messages can be transmitted in several different forms. They may be presented in writing (electronic mail, faxes, letters, memoranda,

Communication.
The process of transmitting understood information among two or more people.

Ideation.
A step in the communication process wherein a sender has information for, or needs information from, another person.

Encoding.
A step in the communication process wherein a sender translates the message to be conveyed into a set of symbols, which it is believed an intended received will understand.

Transmission.
A step in the communication process wherein a message is sent.

FIGURE 18.1 STEPS IN THE COMMUNICATION PROCESS

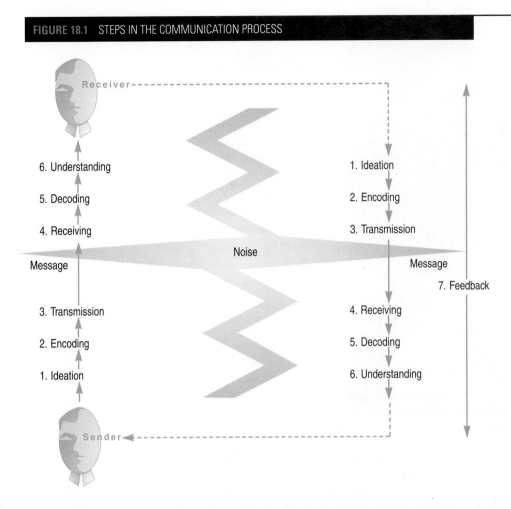

Receiver

6. Understanding

5. Decoding

4. Receiving

Message

3. Transmission

2. Encoding

1. Ideation

Sender

1. Ideation

2. Encoding

3. Transmission

Noise

Message

7. Feedback

4. Receiving

5. Decoding

6. Understanding

charts, diagrams, bulletins, company newspapers), or they may be delivered orally (face-to-face discussions, telephone conversations, lectures, videoconferences). Messages also may be communicated through body movements such as gestures, facial expressions, and posture. As any latecomer to class can surely attest, one frown from a disgruntled professor can speak volumes!

- *Step 4.* Next, the person with whom communication is intended **receives** the message. Obviously, if there is to be any communication at all, the intended receiver must perceive the message. If the message is oral, for example, the receiver must be listening. If the intended receiver is not listening, the message will be lost.

- *Step 5.* The fifth step is **decoding.** At this point in the communication process, the receiver of a message interprets it. Thus, the receiver perceives certain words or sees certain actions and interprets them to have a particular meaning. Depending on the skills of the sender in encoding and transmitting and those of the receiver in receiving and decoding, the interpretation may not be what was intended.

- *Step 6.* **Understanding** is the sixth step in the communication process. As noted, communication is successful only when mutual understanding results.

Receive.
A step in the communication process wherein an intended message is perceived by a receiver.

Decoding.
A step in the communication process wherein the receiver of a message interprets it.

Understanding.
A step in the communication process wherein mutual understanding results.

These Rockwell International employees discussing engineering drawings highlight several steps in the communication process. The words used by the employees and the pictures and words displayed on the drawings are symbols which encode messages. These messages are transmitted by way of conversation, writing, and drawing. The employees could be discussing the decoding of the symbols.

- *Step 7.* The final step is **feedback.** Although feedback technically is not necessary for successful communication, it does allow a sender to verify that an intended message has been accurately received. A message may be inaccurately received because of **noise,** meaning any factor that disturbs or distorts a message. This term includes actual auditory noise that makes a message difficult to hear, as in a noisy textile mill, or an obstacle to reception, such as a receiver who is not paying attention. Feedback tells a sender to what degree a message has been understood. It can be delivered orally, in writing, or nonverbally through body movements. The feedback loop in Figure 18.1 recognizes that communication involves a two-way flow of information. The preceding steps also must be followed in the communication of a return message.

Feedback.
A step in the communication process which allows a sender to determine if an intended message has been accurately received.

Noise.
Any factor that disturbs or distorts a message.

BARRIERS TO EFFECTIVE COMMUNICATION

As the preceding discussion suggests, effective communication requires overcoming various barriers. An examination of all the possible barriers to effective communication is beyond the scope of this chapter. For this reason, only those communication barriers common to a typical organization will be discussed. As shown in Figure 18.2, they may be placed in four categories: intrapersonal, interpersonal, structural, and technological.

FIGURE 18.2   BARRIERS TO EFFECTIVE COMMUNICATION

Effective Communication

Intrapersonal Factors	Interpersonal Factors	Structural Factors	Technological Factors
1. Selective perception 2. Individual differences in communication skills	1. Climate 2. Trust 3. Credibility 4. Sender-receiver similarity	1. Status 2. Serial transmission 3. Group size 4. Spatial constraints	1. Language and meaning 2. Nonverbal cues 3. Media effectiveness 4. Information overload

INTRAPERSONAL FACTORS

Selective Perception

The relationship between perception and communication is complex. The way in which we perceive an object or an event involves not only the way we see it but also the way in which our thoughts about it are converted into meaningful communication. For example, researchers have often demonstrated that people have a tendency to see and hear only what they are emotionally prepared (or want) to see or hear. Furthermore, research suggests that people seek out favorable messages and ignore unpleasant ones.[1] In other words, they reject or inaccurately perceive information that is inconsistent with their previously established expectations. This phenomenon is known as **selective perception.**

An interesting example of selective perception and its impact on communication was a study that asked 23 executives from a single firm to analyze a standard business case from the company-wide perspective of a new president. They were then asked to identify "the most important problem" presented by the case.[2] Despite this deliberate attempt to influence the scope of their analyses, the executives still tended to perceive the most important problem facing the company in terms of the goals of their own particular departments—and consequent self–interest. Sales executives identified a sales problem, manufacturing executives described a problem of internal organization, and public relations and industrial relations executives considered a human relations problem to be the central issue. With evidence such as this, it is easy to understand how selective perception can cause miscommunication. This study also illustrates two additional points:

1. People see what they are skilled at seeing.

2. Complex situations can be viewed from various perspectives, and the perspective one selects strongly influences problem identification.

Likewise, two managerial implications are clear:

1. While different specialist groups may be correct in their own area of expertise, the coordination of higher management will likely be required when final decisions are made.

Selective perception.

A phenomenon wherein people reject or inaccurately perceive information that is inconsistent with their previously held expectations.

2. Unless effective interdepartmental communication takes place, conflict is likely to develop as each specialist group views other specialist groups as not understanding the "true" meaning of a situation.

Individual Differences in Communication Skills

Besides differing in their perceptual ability, people also differ in their ability to develop and apply basic communication skills. Some people are incapable of expressing themselves orally but are able to write clear and concise messages. Others are effective speakers but poor listeners. In addition, many read slowly and find it difficult to understand what they have read. Such difficulties are potential barriers to effective communication. These difficulties and their effects on employee communication appear to have been inadequately taken into account. Moreover, many studies have shown that the reading level of collective bargaining agreements, company bulletins and magazines, and employee handbooks and training manuals is often at the second or third year of college.[3] This is despite the fact that some 65 percent of the U.S. workforce reads below the ninth-grade level. At General Motors, for instance, some 15 percent of hourly employees—and as much as 30 percent at some plants—can't read or write. As a consequence, some employees can't even read simple safety signs, such as "Do not enter." Obviously, unless employees comprehend the information directed at them, they cannot be expected to react effectively.

Recognizing that they have a problem, many organizations (as noted in our Chapter 13 discussion on training) are trying to address it. Motorola has invested $5 million to teach production workers basic reading and math skills. Over the past 10 years, Ford Motor has trained over 32,000 workers to read. Overall, it is estimated that corporations spend $500 million each year on remedial reading and other basic skills programs.

INTERPERSONAL FACTORS

Climate

The relationship between superior and subordinate is often based on the way each treats the other and how this reciprocal behavior is interpreted. As superior and subordinate interact, the feelings that arise either limit or encourage the content and frequency of their communications, as well as the methods in which they attempt to communicate with each other. This combination of elements comprises the climate of an interpersonal relationship. A negative climate can easily lead to a restricted flow of communication, subordinate attempts to manipulate information, and widespread distrust and antagonism. The result can be a decay in both group and organization effectiveness.

A favorable communication climate often starts with an insistence on informality. This is the case in well-known companies such as Walt Disney Productions, where everyone from the president on down wears a name tag with only his or her first name on it. Hewlett-Packard is equally emphatic about first names. In a parallel fashion, IBM devotes a tremendous amount of time and energy to its **open door policy,** which permits employees free access to higher level management so that they can speak out on organization affairs. IBM CEO John F. Akers personally answers all inquiries that come to him from the company's over 400,000 employees.

Trust

The communication process is a give-and-take relationship between a sender and receiver. Information transmitted is meant to have a reciprocal effect on both

Open door policy.
A policy that permits employees free access to higher level management so that they can speak out on organization affairs.

parties. A major requirement for all such relationships is trust. Distrust between a superior and subordinate can serve only to increase defensiveness, decrease the frequency of open expression, and subsequently decrease the likelihood of effective communication. Anxious subordinates who must communicate information that could be damaging to their careers, for example, may tend to distort such information. And research in the area of superior-subordinate communication suggests that many managers automatically assume that the messages they receive are in some way biased; therefore, they tend to apply counterbiases to adjust for the perceived distortion.[4] For instance, many superiors perceive messages that are favorable to their subordinates as probably less accurate than messages that are unfavorable. Subordinates, they have observed, are more likely to screen information that makes them look bad and highlight information that makes them look good.

From an overall organization perspective, it is apparent that the elimination of this type of distortion is essential for effective performance. From a more basic interpersonal perspective, establishment of trust is crucial to individual and work group development. In this regard, it is important to realize that trust cannot be mandated or bought; it must be earned. To be truly effective, managers must earn the trust not only of their subordinates, but also of all the constituencies with which they interact. In the public sector, the Watergate experience is a classic example of how quickly a manager (President Nixon) can fall when the trust of key constituencies is lost.

Credibility

Closely related to trust, **credibility** refers to the perceived characteristics of an information source. As shown in Figure 18.3, source credibility is composed of four distinct elements: honesty, competence, enthusiasm, and objectivity.[5] These characteristics are not necessarily possessed by a given source, but are attributed to the source by individual receivers. Thus, a source's credibility is actually receiver determined. For example, when presented with identical communications from different sources, employees will most often believe (trust) that one coming from the source that *they perceive* to be most honest, competent, enthusiastic, and objective.

Of particular importance to the study of communication are findings that relate credibility to individual and group behavior.[6] At the individual level, a subordinate's belief in a superior's credibility is often a key factor in that employee's satisfaction with her boss. At the group level, highly credible work units or departments have been shown to experience greater communication openness and information accuracy and higher within-group interaction rates than do other units. As a result, they are generally found to be more accurate in information

Credibility.
The perceived characteristics of an information source as related to four distinct elements: honesty, competence, enthusiasm, and objectivity.

FIGURE 18.3 ELEMENTS OF SOURCE CREDIBILITY

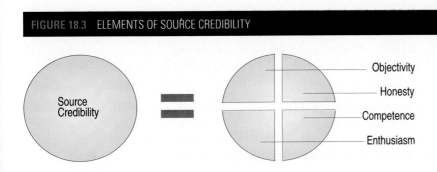

transmission and more efficient in problem solving. They also experience a greater degree of group accomplishment.

Sender-Receiver Similarity

The accuracy and frequency of communication between two communicators also are directly related to the extent that the communicators perceive themselves to be similar.[7] The degree of similarity between communicators in terms of characteristics such as age, gender, intelligence, race, and socioeconomic status, as well as common attitudes, interests, values, and abilities, influences the ease and openness of their communication. Communicators who perceive themselves as being similar are generally more willing to accept the viewpoints of one another and to express common agreement.

For example, in the mid-1980s, age differences posed a new wrinkle in the fabric of communication. The increased number of older women going to work for young female superiors resulted in discomfort on both sides and some thorny communication difficulties. One young manager claimed that the older women she supervised resisted her directives and were dismayed when she treated them as employees instead of sisters. "They say, 'I expected something different from a woman,'" she said, and they accuse her of being "pro-male" in making assignments and doling out criticism.[8] Similar difficulties may arise today when subordinates of one race or nationality are supervised by superiors of a different race or nationality, or when women supervise men or vice versa.

STRUCTURAL FACTORS

Status

A person's status in an organization depends largely upon the prestige associated with the position he occupies. The influence of status on the direction and frequency of communication has been the subject of many studies.[9] Evidence indicates that (1) people generally prefer to communicate with individuals of higher status; (2) people of high status generally communicate more with one another than they do with people of lower status; (3) the wider the status difference, the greater the likelihood that information will flow from higher to lower status people than vice versa; (4) high-status people generally dominate conversations with lower status people; and (5) low-status people often attempt to gain the favor of those with higher status by displaying respect, offering praise, and agreeing with their views.

These findings clearly suggest that status is a major barrier influencing communication. From a managerial viewpoint, there are at least two reasons that employees prefer to communicate with individuals of higher status:

1. Such interactions can be one way to gain peer group recognition and prestige.
2. Communicating with higher status superiors who possess the capacity to enhance or hinder one's career is often perceived as a way of increasing one's chances of success.

Since status differences are inherent in an organization's chain of command, managers should be keenly aware of the influence status has upon their communications with subordinates and superiors. All managers should take special care to avoid being isolated from the people below, many of whom may be in better touch with what is going on. In this regard, organizations can do a lot to deemphasize status differences and thereby improve internal communications. For instance, the status differential between top managers and others can be reduced by making top-management offices less imposing and locating them closer to other offices. Intel purposely avoids high-status perks such as limousines, plush offices, and private dining rooms for its top managers in an effort to reduce status differences.

CLOSE-UP: DIVERSITY   A GENDER-NEUTRAL UPDATE

Political correctness is one of the most popular and controversial topics of the 1990s. Not surprisingly, its influence is apparent in the modern use of language. Gender specific is out: gender neutral is in.

So what is gender-neutral language? It's language that gives equal importance to both male and female by ignoring gender and instead emphasizing position. Referring to females in the abstract generic *he* is unacceptable, even with an attached disclaimer. And suffixing titles with *person,* as in *councilperson* or *chairperson,* is also taboo because it suggests that a position holder is female.

Does this mean that effective communication will be hamstrung by some sanitized lexicon designed to offend no one? Probably not, but stay tuned, and be prepared to make some adjustments. For example, a modern manager should find new ways of addressing employees, now that women make up about half of the workforce. Salesmen, repairmen, and garbagemen are better known today as sales representatives, technicians, and sanitation workers. The same goes for foremen, businessmen, and chairmen. More acceptable terms for these positions are *supervisor, member of the business community,* and *chair.*

The new rules also apply to job descriptions that are gender specific for females. Forget titles like *meter maid, stewardess,* and *paper girl.* Better terms might be *parking meter attendant, flight attendant,* and *newspaper carrier.* On the other hand, if a title is already gender neutral, it should be left that way. Titles like *president, governor,* or *mayor* rarely offend anyone, whether male or female.

Perhaps the gender-specific term that's still used most often today is the masculine pronoun *he.* Even though it may be grammatically correct to refer to someone of either sex as *he,* some women resent it. Conversely, some men don't appreciate being referred to as *she.* Avoiding the use of these pronouns takes some thought, but like anything else, it can become routine. Then a sentence like *Every employee must sign his time card* becomes *Employees must sign their time cards.* There are plenty of other ways to eliminate the use of the masculine pronoun. Gender-specific pronouns should be used, however, when appropriate. That means *he* can be used when referring specifically to a man.

Gender-neutral language is designed to give equal recognition to both men and women and differs from feminist language, which emphasizes the role of women. So there is no need to drop words like *manufacture, manual,* and *manuscript.* The root of these words is the Latin *manu,* meaning hand, and that has nothing to do with the male gender.

If it all sounds like a lot to keep up with, that's because it does take some practice. But with a bit of thought before speaking or writing (always a good idea), gender-neutral language can become both a habit and an enhancement to effective communication.

1989–1990 Meeting Administration Committee, International Institute of Municipal Clerks, chairman: Christina N. Wilder, CMC/AAE, Hamilton Township, N.J., "The Language of Local Government," 9–14.

Mattel CEO John Amerman regularly eats in the company's cafeteria and chats with employees. Amerman has been able to keep in touch with employees by creating an informal communications climate in which he can be approached while de-emphasizing the effects of his status. His efforts have paid off. When he asked employees for ways to trim layers in the company they suggested reducing or eliminating departments, sometimes their own.

On balance, however, the most important factor in overcoming status as a barrier to effective communication may be a manager's demeanor. Some wisely make it a point to avoid becoming isolated and to solicit feedback on their decisions. For their part, subordinates must be assured that their opinions are honestly desired and that they will not receive "their head on a platter" if those opinions are viewed unfavorably.

Serial Transmission

As noted in Chapter 8, experience shows that the greater the number of management layers a message must pass through, the longer it will take to reach its destination and the less likely it is to be accurate. In effect, successive layers of management often act as communication filters that distort the transmission of information. The changes that messages undergo as they are successively communicated from layer to layer is known as the **serial transmission effect.** One study of the transmission of information in 100 business and industrial companies calculated the average loss of information sent from the top of these companies through five layers of management to operative employees to be an astonishing 80 percent.[10] On the average, only 67 percent of a message sent by their board of directors was understood at the vice-presidential level. At the general supervisory level, 56 percent was understood; at the plant manager level, 40 percent was understood; at the general first-line supervisory level, 30 percent; and at the operative level, only 20 percent (see Figure 18.4).

In addition to the *Challenger* disaster mentioned in Chapter 8, other dramatic examples of the serial transmission effect can be cited. At My Lai, for instance, the order sent down from the U.S. Army's 1st Air Cavalry Division headquarters to brigade was "On no occasion must hamlets be burned down." Brigade radioed battalion, "Do not burn down any hamlets unless you are absolutely convinced that the Viet Cong are in them." Battalion radioed the infantry company at the scene, "If you think there are any Viet Cong in the hamlet, burn it down." The company commander told his troops, "Burn down that hamlet."[11]

Serial transmission effect.

The change that a message undergoes as it is successively communicated from one management layer to another.

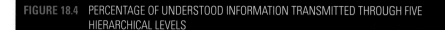

FIGURE 18.4   PERCENTAGE OF UNDERSTOOD INFORMATION TRANSMITTED THROUGH FIVE HIERARCHICAL LEVELS

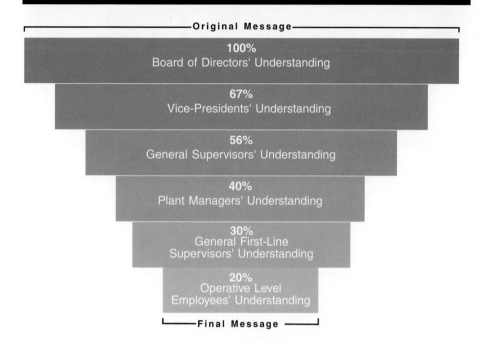

As this example suggests, as people transmit information through a chain of command, they drop details, add interpretations, and alter implications. These losses and alterations result from systematic processes that contribute to the retention and exaggeration of certain aspects while simultaneously contributing to the addition or omission of others.[12] These processes are discussed in the following paragraphs and summarized in Figure 18.5.

Condensation   Research indicates that the recipient of a message who, in turn, is responsible for passing it on to another person typically summarizes (condenses) its content (especially in word-of-mouth transmissions) in a predictable manner. That is, what he or she reports will be shorter, less detailed, and more easily grasped and repeated. In successive versions, fewer words will be used and fewer details mentioned. This process is known as **leveling.** As leveling progresses, those details retained become relatively more prominent or central to a message's main theme. This is referred to as **sharpening.**

Leveling and sharpening, of course, are two sides of the same coin. Predictably, the longer the period between the time a message is received and the time it is relayed to the next hierarchical level, and the larger the number of people involved in its transmission, the more likely it is to be condensed as a consequence of leveling and sharpening.

Closure   Relayers of ambiguous messages tend to fill in—that is, close gaps—in the information they are transmitting in order to make it more plausible and coherent. Most people have a low tolerance for ambiguity and will make whatever inferences are necessary to reduce prevailing uncertainty to an acceptable level. A tendency for closure often occurs in situations where inferences are drawn from a fragment of actual evidence.

Leveling.

The tendency for a message to become shorter, less detailed, and more easily grasped and repeated as it is passed from one person to another.

Sharpening.

The tendency for certain details to become relatively more prominent or central to a message's main theme as a consequence of leveling.

FIGURE 18.5 SYSTEMATIC PROCESSES CONTRIBUTING TO THE SERIAL TRANSMISSION EFFECT

As an illustration, say information leaks that an unknown official from headquarters will arrive sometime in the near future on an unannounced inspection tour. The news may be subsequently transmitted that a staff manager, *probably* John Henry, is coming *next week* to conduct a surprise inspection. After several transmissions, the message may be that John Henry is *definitely* coming on *Monday* to conduct a surprise inspection. The first communicators in this episode took the facts about an unannounced inspection tour and made certain inferences. The messages that were then transmitted to others were composed of conclusions based on the inferences rather than the available evidence.

Expectations Evidence further suggests that relayers of information often attach meaning to communications according to their expectations. As a message flows up or down the levels of an organization, it passes through various human "links," or "way stations," each with unique expectations. Like perceptions, expectations differ because of variations in attitudes, interests, and values, as well as job requirements.

A study involving 32 graduate business students provides an interesting example of this point as it relates to job requirements.[13] The students were asked to make either cost or sales estimates using identical figures, at one time taking the role of a chief market analyst, at another taking the role of a chief cost analyst. Study results clearly highlight the influence of job requirements on expectations. When acting as cost analysts, the students tended to overestimate costs. When acting as sales analysts, they tended to underestimate sales. In other words, the students interpreted the same information according to the biases inherent in two different roles and arrived at two very different conclusions. In an organization, this sort of prejudice inevitably exists in information transmission and reception.

Association Research further indicates that when events or outcomes have occurred together in the past, they are often associated with one another at a later date. If, for instance, a particular person has been responsible for certain errors, that person is likely to be linked to any recurrence of the errors, often without justification. In such instances, corresponding cues serve to suggest guilt by prior association. Thus, people who have acted honestly in one situation are apt to be viewed as honest in another. Conversely, people who have acted dishonestly in one situation are likely to be viewed as dishonest in another. Such strong associations act as communication barriers by stereotyping human behavior rather than viewing it as the result of situational forces operating at a specific time. As one manager has observed, "In organizations we label people. . . . It's a gradual, insidious kind of process . . . but, over time labels stick and become well-known, unspoken fact."[14] Labeling a subordinate based solely on past events rests on the faulty assumption that people are unable to change over time, and such labeling will impede future communication.

Managerial Implications The serial transmission effect clearly suggests that managers should be suspicious about secondhand information, circumvent the chain of command as necessary to get credible information, avoid basing judgments on inferences rather than complete evidence, double-check information based on memory, personally cross-check information with several sources, avoid drawing stereotypes based on past associations, and always expect differences between sent and received information. These recommendations have obvious costs. Constraints on a manager's time, energy, and mental ability will make it difficult to pursue multiple sources, assess what each has to say, and take their advice into account.

Group Size

As our earlier discussion of work group behavior indicated (Chapter 17), interpersonal communication becomes increasingly difficult as the size of a work group increases. This occurs in part because the sheer volume of interactions necessary to keep everyone informed tends to make concerted action more difficult. As work groups become larger, the number of possible communication channels between individual members increases more rapidly than does group size. For a group of five people, there are $n(n - 1)/2$, or ten, channels of communication possible. When group size increases to ten, 45 potential channels exist. When a group is composed of 20 members, 190 channels are opened. Furthermore, as the size of a group increases, communication patterns become increasingly complicated by the formation of subgroups. Their development not only creates additional communication channels (for instance, between subgroups or between an individual

This 3M research and development facility in Austin, Texas was designed to encourage communication among the research and marketing personnel employed there. The open areas encourage informal gatherings and interaction which should stimulate the flow of ideas and lead to innovative new 3M products.

and a subgroup), but also increases the likelihood of intragroup conflict. Allowing for formation of inner circles, the number of possible communication channels within a gathering of five people is $(3^n - 2^{n+1})/2$, or 90. This represents a rapid increase over the number of potential relationships calculated when consideration is given only to interactions between individuals. In most groups, however, not all possible communication channels are utilized; indeed, available evidence suggests the existence of a negative relationship between group size and the percentage of total possible communication channels employed.[15] In any case, the influence of work group size on effective communication is often underestimated.

Spatial Constraints

A job's physical characteristics may require that it be performed in a specific area. Spatial constraints are felt most noticeably in situations where it is necessary either to remain in a single location to manipulate controls or to move between machines or work stations. Such requirements establish physical distances between workers and thus not only restrict the amount and quality of interaction that can take place between individuals, but also the amount and quality of communication. In general, the shorter the physical distance between two individuals, the more frequently they will interact.[16] Therefore, an engineer in a design laboratory is more apt to discuss a technical problem with an officemate than with someone down the hall. Likewise, she is more apt to discuss it with someone down the hall than with someone on another floor.

This suggests that an organization may be able to influence interaction, and therefore communication, between individuals or groups by manipulating spatial constraints. Indeed, as one author has observed:

> Arranging for people to share common facilities (copying machines, elevators, eating areas, desks) is a common method of encouraging communication. Separate facilities, physical distance, closed doors, walls, indirect lines of communication, and different working hours are devices which will usually discourage communication. Many of these factors are controllable by managers and administrators, and they are more effective than telling people that they should not communicate.[17]

Corning Glass Works is an example of one company that recognizes that spatial constraints can serve as a barrier to effective communication. It installs escalators rather than elevators in its buildings to increase the chance of face-to-face contact. Mars, Inc., goes even further. *No one* at Mars has an office. Desks are spread across an open floor in concentric circles, with the president and his staff at the center and their subordinates in the next circle, their subordinates at the next, and so on. Operating in close proximity, everyone is totally visible and accessible. Communication is fast and almost exclusively verbal.

TECHNOLOGICAL FACTORS

Language and Meaning

The accuracy of most communication is largely dependent on the extent to which communicators assign similar meanings to the same words. Because language, like mathematics, is a symbol system, words in and of themselves have no meaning. They are simply labels we use to describe or symbolize our personal view of reality. The meaning a person attaches to a message is uniquely determined by prior experiences, individual needs, social background, and so on. For this reason, the words used in a message rarely have exactly the same meaning to a sender as they do to a receiver; neither do they have the same meaning for different receivers.

The imprecision of language is further complicated by the fact that, besides simply serving as labels, words are capable of evoking a vast array of emotions that may bias the interpretation of a message. One study examined reactions of 488 hourly paid employees to 61 commonly used managerial terms.[18] Managers, it found, typically use the word *capitalism* to mean "private ownership of business . . . equal opportunity for all." But 74 percent of the hourly employees felt the term meant things such as "the wealthiest people take over," "big business has so much money they freeze out the little fellow," and even "a dictatorship by the rich." The phrase *free enterprise* was much more acceptable to the hourly employees. The word *corporation* carried a strong connotation of money, power, and selfishness; the term *company* was preferred. The phrase *work stoppage* was considered to be unfair; however, *strike* was seen as a practical means to an end.

Recognizing that words convey emotions as well as meaning, companies like Du Pont, McDonald's, Disney Productions, Wal-Mart, and J.C. Penney steer away from the use of *employee* in favor of *associate* and *team member.* They feel that words like *employee* and *management* create a we-they mind-set that destroys the team spirit they wish to encourage.

There are other obstacles to comprehension. Although it is correct to say that no two people assign exactly the same meaning to the same word or symbol, unless there is some uniformity in meanings—some public dimension—we would be unable to communicate. Indeed, use of common language implies a certain degree of regularity or agreement in word meanings. The extent of this regularity, however, varies widely. Few words have only one common meaning. One study reports that for each of the 500 most frequently used words in the English language, the *Oxford English Dictionary* records an average of over 28 separate and different meanings.[19] The simple word *set* has the most definitions—58 as a noun, 126 as a verb, and 10 as an adjective.

But even a dictionary is often not an accurate guideline to a word's current meaning. Most lexicographers (dictionary editors) would readily admit that dictionaries are merely history books that show how *some* words have been used at different times and in certain contexts. Dictionaries are typically incomplete when it comes to slang, colloquialisms, high-tech terminology, and the jargon prevalent in certain professions.

Professional jargon can easily cause miscommunication by a new employee.[20] Consider the embarrassment of the supervisor who instructed a new employee to go to the next room and begin *stripping*—an entirely appropriate technical term in their work setting for the processing of raw materials, but whose meaning left considerable room for interpretation.

Nonverbal Cues

When people speak, their words are usually accompanied by a variety of meaningful nonverbal cues, such as physical posture, head orientation and gestures, facial expressions, body movements, touch, and visual behavior. These silent messages assist in the accurate transfer of meaning. For example, the degree of eye contact between communicators may indicate interest, liking, involvement, or aggression. Facial expressions may show surprise, fear, joy, sadness, anger, or disgust. Similarly, body movements (shifts in position, hand gestures, head nods) may convey eagerness, anger, or feelings of relaxation.

The importance of nonverbal communication is underscored by evidence that suggests that in face-to-face communication only 7 percent of the content of a typical message is transmitted by words.[21] The remaining 93 percent is transmitted by tone of voice (38 percent) and facial expression (55 percent). Verbal and nonverbal cues interrelate to create a total message.

Research indicates that in most cases verbal and nonverbal cues will be in harmony to carry the same meaning. That is, they will repeat, complement, or accent one another. For example, a verbal expression of anger may be accompanied by a look of disgust, a rigid body stance, and a clenched fist accenting particular phrases. Sometimes, however, nonverbal stimuli may contradict and even negate the intended meaning of a verbal message. For example, the statement "That's great, just great!" said in a sarcastic tone of voice in response to some organization catastrophe is unlikely to be taken literally. In general, evidence suggests that when nonverbal cues don't fit with an accompanying verbal message, most people will rely primarily upon the nonverbal portion of a total communication, probably because nonverbal cues are less subject to conscious control. Research suggests that when discrepancy between a sender's verbal and nonverbal behavior persists, the resulting ambiguity will almost invariably lead to feelings of tension and anxiety on the part of affected observers.

Table 18.1 offers several suggestions for making nonverbal cues work for you. The accompanying Globetrotting box, titled "International No-No's," stresses that the meaning and acceptability of nonverbal cues varies widely from culture to culture.

Media Effectiveness

Managers have long been concerned with the comparative effectiveness of different communication media. Amid often conflicting results, evidence suggests that written and oral media are each preferred for specific tasks (see Table 18.2).[22] Written media (electronic mail, faxes, letters, memoranda, charts, diagrams, bul-

TABLE 18.1 MAKING NONVERBAL CUES WORK FOR YOU

Here are some suggestions for making nonverbal cues work for you:

1. Recognize that nonverbal cues include movement, appearance, dress, facial expression, gestures, posture, use of silence, use of touch, timing, distance between speakers and listeners, and tone and rhythm of speech.

2. Make sure your nonverbal cues match your verbal cues. If you're insincere in what you're saying, your nonverbal cues will likely reveal your true feelings.

3. Become a student of nonverbal cues. Observe others' nonverbal cues. Try to describe your own nonverbal cues. What do you reveal about yourself without speaking?

4. Use eye contact. However, don't stare. Good eye contact signals that you think a person is important and that you want to cooperate.

5. Keep an acceptable distance between you and your audience. In the United States this means 3–8 feet. If your are closer, you risk invading another's "personal bubble." If you're farther away, conversation will be awkward and unclear.

Source: Adapted from Paula Ancona, "Language Isn't Always Spoken," (Baton Rouge) *Sunday Advocate*, March 24, 1991, 7E.

TABLE 18.2 COMMUNICATION MEDIA		
Type	**Effectiveness**	**Examples**
1. Written media	Most effective for transmitting lengthy and detailed material	Memoranda, charts, e-mail, diagrams, bulletins, company newspapers
2. Oral media	Most effective for communications requiring translation and elaboration to be understood by recipients with varying orientations and language skills	Face-to-face discussions, telephone conversations, lectures, conferences
3. Multimedia	Most effective in situations such as settling work disputes, communicating major policy changes, and reprimanding work deficiencies	Written/oral, written/visual, oral/visual, written/oral/visual

letins, company newspapers) have been found to be most effective for transmitting lengthy and detailed material. When used appropriately, written media offer several advantages:

1. They provide readers with the opportunity to achieve understanding at their own rate (even rereading as needed) and by their own methods.
2. They allow ideas to be conveyed over distance and time.
3. They are easy to store and retrieve for use in making future decisions.
4. They can be made more exact since they are open to the scrutiny of more than one person.

Oral media (face-to-face discussions, telephone conversations, lectures, video-conferences) are especially effective for communications that require translation or elaboration to be understood by recipients who possess varying orientations and language skills. When used appropriately, oral media offer several advantages:

1. They are particularly effective when rapid transmission of information and immediate feedback are desired.
2. They are especially appropriate for handling sensitive or confidential matters because their transitory nature makes discussion of ticklish issues more acceptable.
3. They make possible a measure of personalism that is difficult to achieve through written media.
4. They are better suited to communicating feelings and ideas than written media because oral media provide a maximum opportunity for interaction on the basis of both verbal and nonverbal cues.

Multimedia transmissions (written/oral, written/visual, oral/visual, written/oral/visual) have proven to be the most effective in situations such as settling work disputes, communicating major policy changes, and reprimanding employees for work deficiencies. Some multimedia transmissions employ different media consecutively to accomplish objectives. For example, a face-to-face discussion of work problems might be followed by a written memorandum specifying the means of overcoming problems that were discussed. This format serves first to verify understanding and second to ensure that compliance is agreed upon. An oral presentation of an annual operating report, accompanied by a written handout, and further complemented by charts and graphs depicting important trends, is a particularly effective means of getting a message across. Repetition of a transmission through various media increases the likelihood that it not only will be received and comprehended, but also accurately recalled.

Soon after taking over at ITT, its former CEO Harold Geneen learned the benefit of face-to-face discussions (permitting both oral and visual transmission) over written communications. More specifically, he discovered that the way he communicated with ITT's European subsidiaries made a big difference in his subsequent decisions.

> One of the first things I learned in those early days was that when I responded to a question or request from Europe while sitting in New York, my decision was often different from what it would have been had I been in Europe. In New York, I might read a request and say no. But in Europe, I could see the man's face, hear his voice, understand the intensity of his conviction, and the answer to the same question might be yes.[23]

Managerial Implications   Drawing on the available evidence, at least three managerial implications emerge for deciding which medium to use:

1. Both sending and receiving information through a communication medium are decisions that affects the information's meaning.

2. The effectiveness of a communication medium depends on the type and purpose of the information being transmitted, as well as the circumstances and individuals involved.

3. With respect to putting the word out, just because you think it, write it, or say it doesn't mean others will hear it, understand it, or believe it.

Information Overload

As suggested by our discussion of bounded rationality in Chapter 7, there is clearly a limit to the amount of information an individual can process and absorb at any given time. It has been observed that a typical executive can receive and absorb only $\frac{1}{100}$ to $\frac{1}{1000}$ of the available information relevant to his or her decisions.[24] Information overload is partly a product of the technological and scientific knowledge explosion of our times. The number of scientific journals has increased from one in 1665 to well over 100,000 today. More than 500,000 books and about 10,000 general-interest newspapers are published annually. Cable News Network broadcasts 24 hours a day.

The result is an "information squeeze," with the volume of information managers need to absorb continuing to grow. Although facsimile machines, cellular

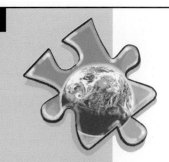

CLOSE UP: INTERNATIONAL MANAGEMENT: INTERNATIONAL NO-NO'S

Nonverbal cues tell a lot about what people really are feeling. Although we may not realize it, we usually gain more information from nonverbal cues than from the words someone is actually saying. This is probably why we give credence to such well-worn phrases as "a picture is worth a thousand words" and "actions speak louder than words." Even in our language we recognize the importance of nonverbal cues by using such body-oriented phrases as "keeping someone at arm's length" or "giving someone the cold shoulder." People are also counseled to "keep a stiff upper lip," "keep your chin up," "grit your teeth," "face up to it," and "get it off your chest."

Such phrases have a generally established meaning in the United States. Nonverbal cues, however, do not communicate the same meaning internationally. Take the case of body language. When a visitor from Bulgaria or Sri Lanka nods his head, that means "no." A head shake connotes "yes." A Turk signifies "no" by raising his chin, shutting his eyes, and tilting the head backward.

Ordinary gestures in our culture can convey extraordinary meanings to a foreign visitor. Placing your hands on your hips is an aggressive gesture in Mexico. Thumbs up is a rude gesture in Bangladesh, as is winking or beckoning with the middle finger in Hong Kong and Malaysia.

The Japanese dislike being slapped on the back—touching is unacceptable. Likewise, an open mouth is offensive, so yawns, belly laughs, and gum chewing are out.

An astute manager recognizes differences in cultures. Doing business in the global marketplace means learning what is and what is not proper behavior. Inadvertently committing a cultural gaffe can suddenly make a line jagged on an organization's sales chart and cause great embarrassment.

Sources: Adapted from Hugh A. Mulligan, "Ordinary Gestures Can Shock Foreign Visitors," (Baton Rouge) *Sunday Advocate*, August 5, 1990, 6E; and Madeline J. Trimby, "'What Do You Really Mean?'" *Management World* 17 (July–August 1988), 12–13.

phones, and electronic mail can be time savers, they can also contribute to information overload. One manager at Digital Equipment Corp. returned from a 3-week assignment to find 1,000 electronic mail messages awaiting his response.

Electronic mail, or, as it is commonly called, e-mail, is rapidly growing in worldwide popularity. Indeed, it has been called "the lifeblood" of companies such as Microsoft. All Microsoft employees have access to e-mail and are encouraged to share ideas and information. Employees are likely to receive personal messages from founder Bill Gates at any time. Wherever he is, Gates uses e-mail to keep up with his empire. In an innovative twist, Apple Computer chairman John Sculley uses e-mail to electronically communicate with customers. He answers a dozen or so customer questions a day using the AppleLink e-mail system.

E-mail is transmitted via computers that are linked together by telephone lines. Messages are transmitted instantly to recipients who receive them on their PC screens. The recipients may then read and respond to the messages at their leisure. E-mail is fast, convenient, inexpensive, and, typically, informal. However, because it is a form of writing, its restrictions are like those of letters or memos. For example, it does not incorporate any elements of body language or allow sender-recipient interaction, which often clarifies oral communication. It does, however, allow one to

Electronic mail.

Instantaneous transmission of written messages via computers that are linked by telephone lines. Also known as e-mail.

In the state-of-the-art video conference center at Hoffmann-La Roche's U.S. headquarters in Nutley, New Jersey, scientists discuss research goals and results with Roche colleagues in Basel, Switzerland. Video-conferencing often allows conferees who would normally not travel to other company facilities to communicate face-to-face with colleagues, quickly transmitting information and receiving feedback.

make a complete statement without interruption, as well as give recipients time to decide on a thoughtful response. Like other forms of written communication, e-mail can easily be printed, reproduced, forwarded, and saved for future reference.

It should be noted that, whatever its cause, information overload also has consequences for effective work group communication. Overloaded individuals may forget to forward necessary information to other group members, thereby increasing their errors. Errors prompt information-seeking questions. These questions, because they require answers, further increase the communication load. The result is often a self-perpetuating state of communication confusion.

EFFECTIVE LISTENING

Listening is never an easy task. Failures in listening include not hearing what was said, hearing only part of what was said, and hearing information incorrectly. Unfortunately, they are common.

Research suggests that the typical person listens at about 25 percent efficiency.[25] The principal reason for this is that most people talk at about 125 words a minute, whereas they listen and understand at four times that rate. Thus, they can think about many other things while a message is being transmitted.

It has been estimated that we spend as much as 80 percent of our waking hours communicating in one form or another. About 9 percent of our time is spent in writ-

TABLE 18.3 SOME DO'S AND DON'TS OF EFFECTIVE LISTENING	
Do	**Don't**
1. Show interest.	1. Argue.
2. Express empathy.	2. Interrupt.
3. Be silent when silence is needed.	3. Engage in other activities.
4. Eliminate distractions by holding telephone calls and choosing a quiet place to talk.	4. Pass judgment too quickly or in advance.
5. Allow adequate time for discussion.	5. Jump to conclusions.
6. Take note of accompanying nonverbal cues.	6. Let the other person's emotions act too directly on your own.
7. When you are unsure of what was said, restate what you think you heard in the form of a question.	
8. When you feel that something is missing, ask simple, direct questions to get the necessary information.	

ing, 16 percent in reading, 30 percent in speaking, and *45 percent* in listening.[26] Yet, of all these skills, most people have had the least training in listening.

Training for effective listening is invaluable preparation for a successful managerial career. Much valuable time and information, not to mention money, are wasted as a result of poor listening habits. Table 18.3 lists some do's and don'ts of effective listening. By practicing the advice given, you should be able to become a better listener. Always remember, one way to know more is to listen more. Listening is a key to knowing and understanding.

INFORMAL COMMUNICATION: THE GRAPEVINE

In addition to formal communication channels, every organization contains various informal channels. Formal channels largely duplicate an organization's chain of command. Informal ones, on the other hand, are more flexible and move in all directions.

Commonly called the **grapevine,** informal channels of communication are a natural outgrowth of the informal relationships that develop between employees who have no reporting responsibility to one another but nevertheless share information. The term *grapevine* originated during the Civil War. For concealment, telegraph lines were strung between trees to resemble wild grapevines. Today the term applies to all informal means of transmitting information from person to person.

Just as both formal and informal work groups are necessary for effective organization performance, formal and informal channels of communication complement one another. Even when formal channels are sufficient to deliver the bare bones of some information, the grapevine is often necessary to explain the whys and wherefores. It provides a varied assortment of facts, scuttlebutt, inferences, opinions, suspicions, and otherwise unavailable information that typically could not pass through formal channels of communication without causing hostile feelings and open conflict, or threatening managerial prestige. The official announcement might be that the vice-president of sales resigned to pursue other opportunities. Within hours after the announcement, however, the grapevine has circulated the

Grapevine.
An informal channel of communication that develops between employees who have no reporting responsibility to one another but nevertheless share information.

"truth": the vice-president missed his sales quota for the third straight year—a performance that entitled him to seek "other opportunities" at the unemployment office!

GRAPEVINE CHARACTERISTICS

The grapevine's prime function is to disseminate information of interest to employees (both managerial and nonmanagerial) and relevant to their needs. The grapevine derives its existence from employees' social and personal interests, rather than from formal organization requirements. In this respect, it has certain characteristics:

1. *The grapevine is fast.* It exists because it gets information to people much faster than formal communication channels. "With the rapidity of a burning powder train, information flows like magic out of the woodwork, past the water fountain, past the manager's door and the janitor's mop closet."[27] As an example of its speed, an accountant was in her boss's office resigning. While they were talking, the boss received a telephone call from across town specifically concerning the accountant's job, which was understood to be open.

2. *The grapevine is accurate.* Recognizing the difficulties inherent in verbal communication, studies indicate that the grapevine is nevertheless up to 95 percent accurate.[28] Any inaccuracy normally takes the form of incompleteness rather than wrong information. Grapevine reliability often is underestimated because its misses tend to be more dramatic than its hits. In this respect, it should be made clear that rumor and grapevine are not the same. **Rumors**—information without a factual base—may just as easily be communicated via formal as informal channels of communication. The grapevine by no means has a monopoly on unfounded hearsay and inaccurate scuttlebutt.

3. *The grapevine is efficient.* It selectively routes information to those who would find it of the greatest interest. By contrast, formal channels have a way of sending information to people who do not need it. As a result, unwanted information may sit on a desk for an extended period before it is passed on. Formal communication channels are almost never more efficient than the grapevine.

4. *The grapevine fulfills employee needs.* It is based not on managerial authority but on the need or desire to communicate. It is made up of people who like each other and want to communicate. Thus, it serves social needs, and through speed and accuracy it helps fulfill security needs as well. In a way it satisfies esteem needs, too. The "communication center" gets recognition when people call him or her to find out "what's going on."

Rumors.
Information without a factual base.

FEEDING THE GRAPEVINE

Whether viewed as an asset or a liability, the grapevine is important for managers to understand. Since it is always present, speedy, and largely accurate, managers should effectively use it as another means of transmitting information. They should tune it in and learn what is being said. They should learn who is likely to spread information and "feed" these individuals selected messages. Office memos are one method:

> Memos are commonly used by management to initiate plays in the game of corporate politics. "Confidential" information or rumors may float to the grapevine via planted memos which are calculatingly used by management. Usually several executives work in collusion.

All decide what information they want to disburse, and the one with the least "reliable" secretary (she who can be counted on to whisper this highly confidential news to a friend, thereby activating the grapevine) is chosen as writer of a "confidential" memo to his management collaborators. Popular subjects of planted memos have to do with projected losses in a quarter (i.e., looks like no raises will be possible) or "plans" for staff cutbacks (i.e., everybody better start humping it lest they be the first to go.)[29]

PRUNING THE GRAPEVINE

In certain instances, it may be necessary to prune an organization's grapevine to halt the circulation of misinformation. Experience suggests at least three strategies for this purpose:[30]

1. Ignore misinformation in the hope that it will either pass with time or collapse from obvious absurdity. However, this strategy cannot be counted on to work.
2. Take the offensive by identifying the misinformation and discrediting it as often as possible to the largest number of people. This may involve sending out a memo to dispel the misinformation, calling employee meetings to counter-

---

SMART MANAGEMENT   "I HEARD IT THROUGH THE GRAPEVINE"

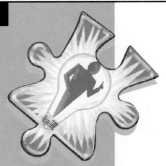

"Secretary" comes from the word "secret," but when William A. Delaney got his first secretary, he discovered that the two terms were not necessarily related. Indeed, as a result of her access to the grapevine, his secretary was giving him invaluable information unavailable anywhere else: advance notice on reorganizations, firings, and promotions.

It's a typical managerial response to sneer at the grapevine as a gossips' playground, but Delaney pragmatically asks, "Why ignore this source if it is there anyway and others know about it and use it?" As long as the grapevine is used sparingly and discreetly, it can be an aid to managers. Delaney suggests these techniques:

1. Leak potentially unwelcome changes in procedure through the grapevine. Then you can get feedback on them before they become official policy.
2. About once a week ask your secretary, "What's new?" It demonstrates a guarded interest in the grapevine without labeling you a busybody. It also gives managers a chance to develop counterstrategies to potential problems before they are officially publicized. Delaney recalls when his secretary warned him that he would be reporting to a new, unpopular boss. He discussed the matter in private with the manager and blocked the change.
3. Release good news into the grapevine whenever possible. It buoys employee morale.

It is important, of course, to know exactly how much one can trust his or her secretary before confiding classified information. It is also important not to overuse the grapevine, since chronic gossips rarely ascend into top management. Used in moderation, however, the grapevine can be an effective managerial tool. Remember, says Delaney, the grapevine "is morally neutral, not good or bad. It's just there for you to use to your advantage when and how you choose."

Source: Adapted by permission of the publisher from "I Heard It through the Grapevine," *Management Review* 72 (August 1983): 5. © 1983 American Management Association, New York. All rights reserved.

act the rumor mill with straight talk, holding press conferences to quash gossip, taking out a newspaper ad denying untruths, and prosecuting rumor-mongers. This strategy, however, has its own hazard. Denying misinformation has the perverse effect of also spreading it.

3. Outflank the misinformation by refuting it without really repeating it. In one company, it was rumored that an employee had lost a hand in a machine accident. To spike the rumor, management released a "weekly accident report" simply indicating that there had not been a single accident during the week. Experts advise that in rebutting misinformation it should never be repeated or referred to directly. This thus avoids spreading the misinformation.

MANAGERIAL IMPLICATIONS

The wise manager will try to live with and make good use of the grapevine. Failure to recognize the grapevine as a normal means of communication is a serious mistake. Attempts to eliminate it are foolhardy and misdirected. As one author has concluded, the grapevine "cannot be abolished, rubbed out, hidden under a basket, chopped down, tied up, or stopped. It is as hard to kill as the mythical glass snake that, when struck, broke into fragments and grew a new snake out of each piece."[31] Increasingly, managers are learning that they should "feed, water, and cultivate the grapevine," to reap the benefits that it offers.

IMPROVING COMMUNICATION EFFECTIVENESS

Communication can be improved in several ways. In this, the final section of the chapter, we will review techniques beyond traditional videotapes, bulletin boards, company newspapers, and such that organizations can use to improve their communication effectiveness.

SATELLITE TRANSMISSION

With the advent of increasingly sophisticated electronic technology, many organizations are using television technology to communicate via satellite with employees. Co-founders Bernard Marcus and Arthur Black annually deliver fiscal year results to all 24,000 Home Depot employees via satellite link to their 145 stores. Wal-Mart beams company news directly to employees over its own six-channel satellite-television network. Similarly, Ford Motor Company uses its own private television system, Ford Communications Network, to telecast programs to more than 200 Ford facilities. Federal Express founder Fred Smith gives pep talks in periodic "family briefings" beamed internationally on FXTV, Federal's own television network. The idea in each instance is to tell employees about significant happenings, thereby promoting a sense of community.

PRIVATE LINES

The technique of using *private lines* enables employees anonymously or otherwise to question or comment on any issue ranging from job assignments to promotions, either by calling a special telephone number or by mailing remarks on company-prepared forms. There may even be certain time periods when top managers are available to answer telephone calls personally. Responses are either sent to employees directly or published in a company newsletter or other publication. The popularity of private lines is apparent from their high use. In Bank of America's "Open Line" program and IBM's "Speak Up" program, employees submit questions or complaints on forms dropped into slotted boxes. General Electric has long used "I Want to Know" letters. General Mills maintains a telephone service called "Fact-Fone."

SPECIAL COUNCILS

Composed of both managers and operative employees, *special councils* provide an opportunity for managers and lower level employees to get together regularly to discuss issues of mutual concern. Generally scheduled to meet two to six times a year, these councils normally have a formal agenda jointly prepared by both groups. The agenda is published before council meetings, and the subsequent outcome for each item is publicly announced. In many organizations, the main council is undergirded by subcouncils of lower level employees. Issues that cannot be settled at lower levels flow up to the main council for resolution. Pitney-Bowes established its "Personnel Council" more than 40 years ago. In the Royal Corporation, special council sessions are called "Employee-Management Meetings"; at Lockheed Aircraft, "Roundtable Sessions"; at Lear Siegler, "ROI (Return on Involvement) Sessions"; and at Southern California Gas Company, "Interact."

EMPLOYEE ANNUAL MEETINGS

Employee annual meetings are conducted at about the same time of year and in the same manner as regular stockholders' meetings. In addition to being available for questions, an organization's president and other top managers brief employees on the state of the organization and outline future organization plans. Pitney-Bowes and Dana Corporation are among the companies that hold such annual meetings. Pitney-Bowes goes so far as to issue an annual employee report describing the company's progress, citing employee achievements, reporting on new or expanded employee benefits, and so forth. In geographically dispersed organizations, such as Union Pacific Railroad, several meetings may be held. Union Pacific calls these annual get-togethers "town hall" meetings. They are held throughout the 19 states in which it operates. Although these meetings involve considerable time and expense, they serve to underscore management's interest in improved communication.

Some companies hold employee meetings several times a year. For instance, every other month Lotus Development Corporation has an all-employee meeting at which company founder Mitchell Kapor and CEO Jim Manzi field questions. 3M regularly holds "town hall" meetings for its more than 5,000 managers in the Twin Cities area. Questions submitted in advance or spontaneously asked from the floor are answered by top managers, including 3M president Allen F. Jacobson. Fel-Pro Inc.'s "Employee Forum" has met monthly since 1952 to consider employee grievances and suggestions. Explains Fel-Pro co-CEO Lew Weinberg, "Employees must have answers. The minute we don't fulfill that role, we sign our death warrant."[32]

NONMANAGERIAL TASK TEAMS

Nonmanagerial task teams are generally formed in response to specific high-priority employee problems. Typically, formation of these task teams and the problems they are to study are widely publicized. Most often, they are composed of volunteers who are allowed to use a certain amount of their work time to conduct their investigation and report to management. In turn, management has a specified period of time to respond publicly. Teams deal with problems such as labor-management relations, scheduling of maintenance work, and interdepartmental conflicts. At General Electric, nonmanagerial task teams are known as "Sounding Boards"

Former Union Pacific Railroad CEO Michael Walsh (standing) instituted town hall meetings like this one. Such meetings allow managers to explain industry changes, company strategies, and how these affect employees.

and have dealt with topics such as developing a new vacation scheduling procedure and studying causes of industrial accidents.

INTERDEPARTMENTAL MANAGEMENT TEAMS

Designed to facilitate horizontal communication, *interdepartmental management teams* meet regularly to coordinate work flow operations. These groups, which are also called *coordinating action teams*, generally have proven to be particularly successful as a vehicle for stimulating meaningful and effective first-line management participation. Furthermore, because of their person-to-person nature, coordinating action teams have been especially effective in resolving sensitive human resource management issues.

SUMMARY

Communication is the process of transmitting understood information among two or more people. Although all jobs involve communication to some extent, by its very nature a manager's job requires more time spent communicating than most. This chapter discussed how the communication process works, barriers to effective communication, the importance of effective listening, the so-called grapevine, and several ways for an organization to improve its communication effectiveness.

Learning Objective 1: Describe the communication process.

The communication process is composed of seven steps: ideation, encoding, transmission, receiving, decoding, understanding, and feedback. These steps are diagrammed in Figure 18.1.

Learning Objective 2: **Identify various barriers to effective communication.**

Various barriers to effective communication may be placed in four categories: (1) *intrapersonal,* including (a) selective perception and (b) individual differences in communication skills; (2) *interpersonal,* including (a) climate, (b) trust, (c) credibility, and (d) sender-receiver similarity; (3) *structural,* including (a) status, (b) serial transmission, (c) group size, and (d) spatial constraints; and (4) *technological,* including (a) language and meaning, (b) nonverbal cues, (c) media effectiveness, and (d) information overload.

Learning Objective 3: **List various do's and don'ts of effective listening.**

Various do's and don'ts of effective listening are listed in Table 18.3.

Learning Objective 4: **Detail several grapevine characteristics.**

The grapevine is fast, accurate, and efficient, and it fulfills employee needs.

Learning Objective 5: **Recount different strategies for dealing with misinformation.**

Three strategies—not all of them consistently reliable—for dealing with misinformation are to ignore misinformation in the hope that it will either pass with time or collapse from obvious absurdity; take the offensive by identifying the misinformation and discrediting it as often as possible to the largest number of people; and outflank the misinformation by refuting it without really repeating it.

Learning Objective 6: **Name several techniques to improve an organization's communication effectiveness.**

Several techniques an organization can use to improve its communication effectiveness are satellite transmissions, private lines, special councils, employee annual meetings, nonmanagerial task teams, and interdepartmental management teams.

KEY TERMS

communication 524	grapevine 543	rumors 544
credibility 529	ideation 524	selective perception 527
decoding 525	leveling 533	serial transmission effect 532
electronic mail 541	noise 526	sharpening 533
encoding 524	open door policy 528	transmission 524
feedback 526	receive 525	understanding 525

REVIEW AND DISCUSSION QUESTIONS

1. Selective perception is a common barrier to effective communication. Moreover, evidence suggests that people see what they are skilled at seeing and that different perspectives strongly influence problem identification. How does professional training influence a person's perception of a problem? For example, how might an accountant, a sales manager, and an engineer approach the problem of reduced profits? What difficulties might their different approaches prompt if the three had to work together to solve this problem?

2. People admittedly differ in their ability to apply basic communication skills. Such differences may be the result of any number of factors. Read the following story and comment on the barrier blocking effective communication.

   > Foreigners in Tokyo have been chuckling over the announcement at the entrance of a new restaurant. The establishment is the last word in continental elegance, with an

army of waiters impeccably dressed in evening clothes, and a wine steward in festooned jacket and knee breeches.

The neatly printed English-language announcement reads: "To Our Distinguished Guests—Please be assured that the vegetables used in the preparation of the fine French dishes in our new restaurant have been washed in water personally passed by our chef."[33]

3. The present chapter notes that status can be a barrier to effective communication. This is especially so when low-status persons attempt to gain the favor of those with higher status by agreeing with their views. With this in mind, comment on the following incident, being sure to suggest how one might avoid the predicted outcome.

A man was elected president of a large corporation. One of the older directors said, "So now you are president!"

"So it seems," the man smiled.

"Then," said the director, "you have heard the truth for the last time."

4. The serial transmission effect is an especially difficult communication barrier to overcome in organizations that are composed of various managerial levels. Military organizations are a case in point. The chain of command is considered sacred in such organizations and thereby directly influences superior-subordinate communication.

Read the following story and comment on the systematic processes contributing to the obvious serial transmission effect.

Eclipse of the Sun

The Operation of the Chain of Command

The colonel to the executive: At nine o'clock tomorrow there will be an eclipse of the sun, something which does not occur every day. Get the men to fall out in the company street in their fatigues so that they will see this rare phenomenon, and I will explain it to them. In case of rain, we will not be able to see anything, so take the men to the gym.

The executive to the captain: By order of the colonel, tomorrow at nine o'clock there will be an eclipse of the sun; if it rains you will not be able to see it from the company street, so then, in fatigues, the eclipse of the sun will take place in the gym, something that does not occur every day.

The captain to the lieutenant: By order of the colonel in fatigues tomorrow at nine o'clock in the morning the inauguration of the eclipse of the sun will take place in the gym. The colonel will give the order if it should rain, something which occurs every day.

The lieutenant to the sergeant: Tomorrow at nine the colonel in fatigues will eclipse the sun in the gym, as it occurs every day if it is a nice day; if it rains, then in the company street.

The sergeant to the corporal: Tomorrow at nine the eclipse of the colonel in fatigues will take place by cause of the sun. If it rains in the gym, something which does not take place every day, you will fall out in the company street.

Comments among the privates: Tomorrow, if it rains, it looks as if the sun will eclipse the colonel in the gym. It is a shame that this does not occur every day.[34]

---

5. Spatial constraints can be a particularly strong barrier to effective communication. Recognizing this, 3M sponsors clubs for any group of 12 or more employees. 3M's sole purpose is to increase the likelihood of stray problem-solving sessions at club meetings. Suggest several other ways spatial constraints can be minimized.

6. (a) Specialized language, or jargon, is built into nearly every field of work. Physicians, computer specialists, waitresses, government employees, and sales representatives each have their own jargon. As a manager, it is important to remember that other people may not understand your language. The special terms that follow are all used in business. Provide a brief explanation for each in a business context.

1.	Bite the bullet	5.	Out in left field
2.	Team player	6.	Touch all bases
3.	Run it up the flagpole	7.	The ball is in your court
4.	Under the gun	8.	Put it on the back burner

(b) The sources of jargon are virtually limitless. They include the space program (all systems go, A-OK), computers (interface, GIGO, or garbage in, garbage out), and automobiles (grease the wheels, running on all cylinders). Prepare a list of jargon common to your college campus. Compare your list to those of your classmates.

7. What you wear sends a powerful nonverbal message. According to popular advice, men and women who are interested in getting ahead should consider their wardrobe a blue-chip investment that will pay high dividends. They should dress as fashionably as possible, attempting to appear as if they had already arrived at the top of their success pyramid. John T. Molloy, a noted expert in fashion images, states that there are "authority" outfits, "believability" outfits, and "popularity" outfits.[35] Looking around your classroom, classify the outfits of your instructor and fellow classmates.

8. Is more communication equal to better communication? Why or why not? Give an example to illustrate your answer.

9. As a successful manufacturing plant manager, you've recently been plagued by a rash of workforce rumors. First, it was "They're going to automate the entire plant." The next week it was "That foreign outfit is buying us out and closing this location." Now it is "They're cutting out all bonuses." What strategy will you use to deal with this latest rumor?

10. As a technique for improving communication effectiveness, 3M holds "town hall" meetings for its more than 5,000 managers in the Twin Cities area. At the 2-hour meetings, questions submitted in advance and spontaneous questions from the floor of a rented civic auditorium are answered by sector heads, other top executives, or the company president. The goal is to have everyone in the 3M network feel like an important part of a caring family. This involves getting to know one another and being totally aware of the company. Do you think that this is a realistic goal? If so, why? If not, why not?

THE MANAGEMENT EXPERIENCE   HOW DO YOU RATE AS A LISTENER?

Few virtues are more prized and less practiced than good listening. This checklist, though certainly not complete, will help you gauge your own listening habits. Try to answer each question objectively.

When taking part in an interview or group conference, do you:	Usually	Sometimes	Seldom
1. Prepare yourself physically by sitting facing the speaker and making sure you can hear?	☐	☐	☐
2. Watch the speaker as well as listen to him?	☐	☐	☐
3. Decide from the speaker's appearance and delivery whether or not what he has to say is worthwhile?	☐	☐	☐
4. Listen primarily for ideas and underlying feelings?	☐	☐	☐
5. Determine your own bias, if any, and try to allow for it?	☐	☐	☐
6. Keep your mind on what the speaker is saying?	☐	☐	☐
7. Interrupt immediately if you hear a statement you feel is wrong?	☐	☐	☐
8. Make sure before answering that you've understood the other person's point of view?	☐	☐	☐
9. Try to have the last word?	☐	☐	☐
10. Make a conscious effort to evaluate the logic and credibility of what you hear?	☐	☐	☐

Scoring Your Results

Questions 1, 2, 4, 5, 6, 8, 10—10 points for "usually," 5 for "sometimes," 0 for "seldom."

Questions 3, 7, 9—0 points for "usually," 5 for "some-times," 10 for "seldom."

What Your Score Means

A score below 70 indicates you have developed some bad listening habits.

A score of 70–85 suggests that you listen well but could improve.

A score of 90 or above means you're an excellent listener.

Source: Adapted from Ted Pollock, "Listener's Quiz," *Supervision* 33 (August 1971): 22. Reprinted by permission of *Supervision*. Copyright 1971 by the National Research Bureau, Inc., P.O. Box 1, Burlington, Iowa 52601-9989.

CASE 18.1   MY DOOR IS ALWAYS OPEN

Setting: The Production Manager's Office

Participants: Gilbert Steiner—
Production Manager
Harold Terry—
Production Scheduler

Time: Monday morning

Steiner: Good morning, Hal. Have a nice weekend?

Terry: Great, Mr. Steiner . . . took the family to the beach.

Steiner: Fine weekend for it . . . bet your kids enjoyed it.

Terry: They certainly did. My oldest boy loves the ocean.

Steiner: Billy?

Terry: *(surprised)* Yes, Billy. I didn't know you knew his name.

Steiner: You probably told me once.

Terry: You have a good memory.

Steiner: Thank you. Frankly, it's something I developed a long time ago. It's good management practice to get to know a little about your employees . . . their families . . . it brings you closer to them.

Terry: I can't argue with that. . . .

Steiner: Sounds a little phony at first . . . I mean a man could sound like a fool overplaying the concerned boss and carrying on about an employee's arthritic dog, Jasper . . . but I mean real interest and concern in the man and his family.

Terry: I'm sure it pays dividends in employee loyalty and productivity.

Steiner: It certainly does. When you become a supervisor, I'm sure you'll realize it even more . . . *(pause)* Well, we'd better get started before the week is over.

Terry: Right. I've already checked the Final Assembly Department, and we should be able to ship the Fedderson order by Wednesday and the A-B-N Industries order by Thursday or Friday.

Steiner: Good. I'll hold you to that. . .

Terry: We do have a couple of problems, though, which I want to talk to you about.

Steiner: Yes?

Terry: We can't ship to Ellis Industries as planned this week because . . .

Steiner: *(angrily)* What?

Terry: The parts we need still haven't arrived. . .

Steiner: Darn it, man! You told me that last week, didn't you?

Terry: Yes, I did but . . .

Steiner: And do you recall what I told you?

Terry: You said it was my responsibility to make sure the parts came in.

Steiner: And you blew it!

Terry: Well, I did review the problem with Purchasing and they suggested . . .

Steiner: To heck with Purchasing! Those paper work clerks only help foul up things worse. You should have contacted the vendor directly and . . . *(pausing and composing himself)* Look, Hal, you're a big boy. I don't have to do your job, do I?

Terry: Of course not, Mr. Steiner.

Steiner: Then you will get those parts this week, won't you?

Terry: Yes, I'll get the parts.

Steiner: And you'll ship by Friday?

Terry: We'll ship by Friday.

Steiner: *(smiling)* Good. Management by results is the only thing that counts . . . don't you agree?

Terry: Yes, sir.

Steiner: *(serious)* Look, Hal, I guess I come down hard on you sometimes but it's because I expect a lot from you. How can you grow without challenge . . . without difficult objectives to reach?

Terry: I suppose you're right.

Steiner: I know I'm right. It's a philosophy I learned from my father years ago . . . results count, not words.

Terry: True.

Steiner: Anything else I should know? I don't care for lots of detail but, at the same time, a man can easily get cut out of the communications loop if he gets too far from the action. And I don't like to get cut out of the loop.

Terry: Not really. Everything else is moving according to schedule. *(pauses)* The people in Shipping are a little upset, though, over the late Friday afternoon shipping schedules and were asking me if we in Manufacturing might not work out a more sequential shipping schedule. I thought that was information we could use, particularly with the planned production increase of next quarter . . .

Steiner: Ignore them. Those guys are always complaining, and they'll bend your ear all day if you let them. That's not information, Hal, that's *noise* you're getting. When a shipping clerk stops complaining, it means he's dead.

Terry: Yes, sir.

Steiner: Anything else?

Terry: No. As far as I know, we've covered everything.

Steiner: Hal, you know I like you. You've got tremendous potential in this department. I want to help you learn this business inside and out . . . I want to see you grow and develop . . .

Terry: Yes?

Steiner: Well, what I mean is . . . don't be reluctant to come to me if you have any problems which I can help you with . . . anything that you want to sit down and talk about . . . my door is always open.

Terry: Thank you, Mr. Steiner. *(turns to leave)*

Steiner: About the Ellis order . . . you did hear me, didn't you?

Terry: Yes, sir, I heard you. We'll ship by Friday.

Setting: The water fountain
Participants: Harold Terry—
 Production Scheduler
 Phil Siegel—
 Production Foreman
Time: A few minutes later

Siegel: *(at fountain)* Hi, Hal. Didn't see you behind me.

Terry: Move over, man. I've got some pills to take.

Siegel: Headache?

Terry: *(taking aspirins)* You wouldn't believe . . .

Siegel: I can guess. You've just had your Monday morning headbeating from Steiner.

Terry: Right.

Siegel: Why do you take it? Why don't you tell the tyrant off?

Terry: I need my job. Why don't you?

Siegel: I need my job, too. But I don't have to go in to see him and ask for it like you. When Steiner wants me for something, he has to find me out in production and ask. I'm not trapped in his office with regular scheduling reports.

Terry: But you always handle him so well. I get all torn up inside because I can't communicate with him.

Siegel: You're doing it all wrong. First, never tell him *anything* he can use against you. Never volunteer information, pal.

Terry: You mean *lie* about problems?

Siegel: Who said lie? I just said don't volunteer any information. What Steiner doesn't know won't hurt you.

Terry: And the second thing?

Siegel: If he asks a question, answer it exactly as he asked it. You'll stay out of trouble that way.

Terry: I don't follow you.

Siegel: When he says, "Siegel do you have any problems?" I say, "No, sir, Mr. Steiner, no problems at all." You see, he's saying that he doesn't want you to have any problems so I agree with him and he's happy.

Terry: And if you do have a problem?

Siegel: I get a friend to help me fix it. I have friends in every department.

Terry: What if it needs Steiner's attention?

Siegel: Boy, you are naive! Most everything is done without Steiner now. He's a title, not the real thing! He cut himself off from the company long ago.

Terry: It's sad. It really is. I respect the man. He's very intelligent and he's worked so hard to get where he is . . . and I know he's trying . . . he really does want to communicate . . . I'm sure he doesn't consciously intend to put everyone down the way he does . . . but that's how it usually comes out.

Problems

1. What is an open door policy?

2. Why does an open door policy usually fail to achieve its stated purpose?

3. Why does Steiner fail to see the results of his discussions with subordinates?

4. What is wrong with the way in which Siegel responds to Steiner?

5. What are the long-term implications for:
 a. Steiner?
 b. The company?

6. Is there any way to reach Steiner, that is, to let him know how he is cutting himself out of the communication loop?

7. Can an employee "level" with his or her boss?

8. Why is it difficult to "level" with one's boss?

9. Why is it difficult to "level" with anyone on subjects of mutual concern (for example, on problems in which each has an emotional stake, as opposed to "chit-chat")?

10. Define and discuss:
 a. Open communication
 b. Responsible feedback versus criticism
 c. Nonverbal communication
 d. Power, status, and ease of communication
 e. Hidden agendas

Source: Adapted from Robert D. Joyce, *Encounters in Organizational Behavior: Problem Situations* (New York: Pergamon Press, Ltd., 1972), 2–5. Reprinted by permission of the publisher.

NOTES

[1] Harold J. Leavitt, *Managerial Psychology*, 4th ed. (Chicago: University of Chicago Press, 1978), 25–54.

[2] DeWitt C. Dearborn and Herbert A. Simon, "Selective Perception: A Note on the Departmental Identifications of Executives,"

Sociometry 21 (June 1958): 140–144. For a more optimistic view, see James D. Walsh, "Selectivity and Selective Perception: An Investigation of Managers' Belief Structures and Information Processing," *Academy of Management Journal* 31 (December 1988): 873–896.

3 For example, see Debra L. Heflich, "Developing a Readable Employee Handbook," *Personnel Administrator* 28 (March 1983): 80–83; and James Suchan and Clyde Scott, "Readability Levels of Collective Bargaining Agreements," *Personnel Administrator* 29 (November 1984): 73–80.

4 Lyle Sussman, "Perceived Message Distortion or You Can Fool Some of the Supervisors Some of the Time. . . .," *Personnel Journal* 53 (September 1974): 679–682, 688.

5 Jack L. Whitehead, Jr., "Factors of Source Credibility," *Quarterly Journal of Speech* 54 (February 1968): 59–63.

6 Raymond L. Falcione, "The Relationship of Supervisor Credibility to Subordinate Satisfaction," *Personnel Journal* 52 (September 1973): 800–803; and Charles A. O'Reilly III, "The Intentional Distortion of Information in Organizational Communication: A Laboratory and Field Investigation," *Human Relations* 31 (February 1978): 173–193.

7 For a review of findings in this area, see Albert Mehrabian and Henry J. Reed, Jr., "Some Determinants of Communication Accuracy," *Psychological Bulletin* 70 (September 1968): 365–381; and Daniel B. Turban and Allan P. Jones, "Supervisor–Subordinate Similarity: Types, Effects, and Mechanisms," *Journal of Applied Psychology* 73 (May 1988): 228–234.

8 Lori King quoted in Amy Glickman, "Women Clash: Older Workers vs. Young Boss," *Wall Street Journal*, February 19, 1985, 37.

9 For a review of findings in this area, see Frederic M. Jablin, "Superior-Subordinate Communication: The State of the Art," *Psychological Bulletin* 86 (November 1979): 1201–1222.

10 Ralph G. Nichols, "Listening Is Good Business," *Management of Personnel Quarterly* 1, no. 2 (1962): 2–10.

11 James G. Miller, *Living Systems* (New York: McGraw-Hill, 1978), 649.

12 Donald T. Campbell, "Systematic Error on the Part of Human Links in Communication Systems," *Information and Control* 1 (December 1958): 334–369.

13 Richard M. Cyert, James G. March, and William H. Starbuck, "Two Experiments on Bids and Conflict in Organization Estimation," *Management Science* 7 (April 1961): 254–264.

14 Quoted in John F. Veiga, "Face Your Problem Subordinate Now!" *Academy of Management Executive* 2 (May 1988): 150.

15 For a review of findings in this area, see A. Paul Hare, *Handbook of Small Group Research,* 2d ed. (New York: Free Press, 1976), 214–219; and Marvin E. Shaw, *Group Dynamics: The Psychology of Small Group Behavior,* 3d ed. (New York: McGraw-Hill, 1981), 168–177.

16 George F. Faris, "Groups and the Informal Organization," in *Groups at Work,* ed. Roy Payne and Cary L. Cooper (Chichester, England: Wiley, 1981), 106.

17 H. Joseph Reitz, *Behavior in Organizations,* rev. ed. (Homewood, Ill.: Irwin, 1981), 311–312.

18 Martin Wright, "Do You Need Lessons in Shop Talk?" *Personnel* 42 (July–August 1965): 58–62. Also see Abraham K. Korman, "A Cause of Communication Failure," *Personnel Administration* 23 (May–June 1960): 17–21; and Carl H. Weaver, "The Quantification of the Frame of Research in Labor Management Communication," *Journal of Applied Psychology* 42 (February 1958): 1–19.

19 Charles C. Fries, *Linguistics and Reading* (New York: Holt, Rinehart and Winston, 1963), 57.

20 Stephen R. Axley, "Organizational Communicators: Blow Up the Communication Pipeline," *Industrial Management* 28 (January–February 1986): 16.

21 Albert Mehrabian, *Silent Messages* (Belmont, Calif.: Wadsworth, 1971), 44.

22 Dale A. Level, "Communication Effectiveness: Method and Situation," *Journal of Business Communication* 10 (Fall 1972): 19–25.

23 Harold Geneen, *Managing* (New York: Doubleday, 1984): 46–47.

24 Richard C. Raymond, "Betting on New Technologies," in *Technological Planning on the Corporate Level,* ed. James R. Bright (Boston: Graduate School of Business Administration, Harvard University, 1962), 21.

25 William K. Fallon, ed., *Effective Communication on the Job,* 3d ed. (New York: AMACOM, 1981), 4.

26 Stan Kossen, *The Human Side of Organizations,* 4th ed. (New York: Harper & Row, 1987), 77.

27 Joseph K. Shepart, "I Heard It on . . . the Grapevine," *The Indianapolis Star Magazine,* October 2, 1955, 4.

28 Keith Davis, "The Care and Cultivation of the Corporate Grapevine," *Dun's Review* 102 (July 1973): 44–47. Also see Fredrick Koenig, "Rumors That Follow the Sun," *Across the Board* (22 February 1985): 24–30; and Carol Hymowitz, "Managing," *Wall Street Journal,* October 14, 1988, B1.

29 Betty L. Harragan, *Games Mother Never Taught You* (New York: Rawson, 1977), 296–297.

30 Keith Davis, "Cut Those Rumors Down to Size," *Supervisory Management* 20 (June 1975): 2–6; Jim Montgomery, "'Did You Know . . . ?' Rumor-Plagued Firms Use Various Strategies to Keep Damage Low," *Wall Street Journal,* February 6, 1979, 1–22; and Larry Light, "Killing a Rumor Before It Kills a Company," *Business Week,* December 24, 1990, 23.

31 Keith Davis, *Human Behavior at Work: Organizational Behavior,* 5th ed. (New York: McGraw-Hill, 1972), 278, 280.

32 Quoted in Anthony J. Rutgliano, "Some Would Call It Paternalism," *Management Review* 75 (July 1986): 35.

33 "Laughter, the Best Medicine," *Reader's Digest* (May 1970): 104. Reprinted with permission.

34 Robert H. Howe, "Eclipse of the Sun," *Army* 13 (February 1963): 31. Reprinted with permission.

35 John T. Molloy, *Dress for Success* (New York: Warner, 1975).

PART

SIX

CONTROLLING

CHAPTER 19

Things did not go well for American Express in 1991. The standards of performance that managers, shareholders, and the public have come to expect were not met. Could American Express, once thought to be among the nation's best-managed service companies, have lost control?

Some might call American Express, with its AMEX and Optima credit cards and traveler's checks, the Mercedes-Benz of travel and credit services. All genuine and aspiring upscale business travelers would most certainly not leave home without the security and status of an American Express card.

But the successes of the 1980s for American Express were not to be realized in the early 1990s. One study shows the popularity of American Express dropping among business travelers from 52 percent in 1986 to 46 percent in 1991. Visa and MasterCard accounts, on the other hand, increased from 24 percent to 30 percent and from 11 percent to 17 percent, respectively. Another measure of performance, dollar volume of billings, shows American Express leveling off while MasterCard, Visa, and Discover are gaining. Market share, another performance measure, shows American Express losing 5 percent in the last 5 years, with Visa adding 3 percent and Discover adding 4.5 percent. In the third quarter of 1991, American Express had a 91 percent decline in earnings, triggered by poor handling of cardholder debt problems. The company's stock dropped from $27 to $19 a share after the announcement of its earnings problem.

The above performance measures served to raise a red flag at American Express, resulting in more detailed analyses of the situation. After identifying reasons for the variation from performance standards, American Express responded differently in two different areas:

EFFECTIVE CONTROL

■ Credit card companies make money from the fees charged merchants who accept credit cards from customers. When Visa lowered its fee to an average of 1.82 percent, American Express did nothing, believing that banks issuing Visa cards would find the low rate unprofitable and would eventually move back toward the 3–4 percent rate charged by American Express. But the decreasing cost of borrowing money to around 5 percent, combined with the 19 percent paid by card users on unpaid balances, allowed banks to stay at the lower merchant fee. The result was that merchants began to ask their customers for a card other than American Express; some even refused to accept American Express. The privileged status of being an American Express cardholder began to slip. When restaurants demanded lower merchant fees, American Express lowered the fee for restaurants who cleared their transactions electronically. This change helped reduce the number of merchants requesting other cards from diners, but led other merchants to ask for the same treatment.

■ American Express now provides less emphasis on increasing the number of its cardholders and more emphasis on taking care of its best users, the 20 percent of its cardholders who account for 80 percent of the company's charge volume.

Even the best-managed organizations have control problems. As we will discuss in this chapter, control is an ongoing process essential for the effective management of *all* organizations. We begin by defining and establishing the need for control. Next, the basic nature of the control process is described. After identifying various types of control, the chapter reviews the characteristics of effective controls. A variety of control methods are then examined. Finally, the value of financial ratios for interpreting an organization's performance is illustrated.

Source: Bill Saporito, "The Bill Is Due at American Express," *Fortune,* November 18, 1991, 99–112.

With the continued expansion of worldwide economic connections, organizations everywhere have come to recognize that they are competing not only domestically, but globally. Global linkages of financial markets, technology, and production have resulted in the emergence of previously unknown and unanticipated marketplace opportunities and threats. Only a few years ago, it would have been thought impossible to manufacture parts for an automobile in one country, assemble them in another, and sell the finished product in a third. Yet today such global strategies are commonplace.

The key to the success of such strategies goes beyond simply identifying marketplace opportunities. Rather, control is necessary to ensure that an organization's efforts succeed. To this end, control is essential for determining how well an organization is performing, whether improvement is needed, where it should occur, how much is needed, and how quickly.

CONTROL DEFINED

In the present context, **control** is the process of ensuring the efficient accomplishment of organization goals. If we lived in a perfect world, where all plans were fulfilled, control would be unnecessary. Such perfection is, of course, an ideal that cannot be achieved. Rather, as we have noted previously, factors both within organizations and within their surrounding environment are apt to divert an organization from its planned course unless it modifies its behavior. Experienced managers recognize, however, that change without order can also be equally disruptive. Control provides that order.

Control.
The process of ensuring the efficient accomplishment of organization goals.

THE CONTROL PROCESS

Control is a continuous process. It is through control that an organization channels the behavior of individual employees and units, making certain outcomes likely and minimizing the likelihood of others. The control process involves three general steps. They are illustrated in Figure 19.1.

FIGURE 19.1 THE CONTROL PROCESS

Setting Standards

Measuring and Evaluating Performance

Taking Action

STEP 1: SETTING STANDARDS

The first step in the control process is to set performance standards. A **standard** is a criterion against which actual performance can be compared. In this respect, standards are nothing more than yardsticks for measuring performance. Thus, just as par is used as a standard for gauging performance in a round of golf, an organization must use standards to judge its success in achieving stipulated goals.

Unless standards are set—and enforced—performance across units is likely to vary widely. A lack of standards regarding facilities, employees, franchisee selection, food preparation, maintenance, and service is commonly offered as a major reason for Burger Chef's loss of market share. Its failure to impose performance standards was especially evident in contrast to McDonald's, whose insistence on tight and vigorously enforced standards is legendary. Its 350-page operating manual specifies everything from how frequently door windows and restrooms are to be cleaned each day, to the width of hamburger buns (3-½ inches), to how many ounces of onions are permitted per hamburger (¼ ounce) and the holding time for cooked products. French fries are thrown out after 7 minutes, burgers after 10 minutes, and coffee after 30 minutes. To prevent damage to the McDonald's reputation, field consultants closely supervise store operations and make two 3-day inspections to each outlet every year, grading quality, cleanliness, quick service, and friendliness. Franchises can be terminated if prescribed standards are not met. Consistency in adhering to standards is inherent in the company's corporate strategy.

There are many different types of standards. As much as possible, standards should be derived from an organization's goals. Examples of standards for various areas in which an organization is likely to have goals include the following:

- *Quality:* Product deviations should not exceed 3.4 defects per million parts.
- *Productivity:* Annual sales volume produced per square foot of floor space should exceed $25,000.
- *Market share:* Sales volume should increase at a rate equal to or greater than total market demand.
- *Innovation:* At least 25 percent of annual sales should be from products less than 5 years old.
- *Employee performance and attitude:* Turnover of sales representatives should not exceed 4 percent per month and no more than 20 percent annually.

Determining appropriate performance standards is a difficult task. Given the many different areas in which standards must be set, no single method for establishing standards is universally applicable. Whatever the method, however, standards can be classified as one of three kinds: *historical, comparative,* or *engineering.*

Historical standards are based on an organization's past experience. Previous sales, costs, profits, production times, and so forth can be used as a basis for evaluating future performance. For example, based on past performance, an organization might set a profit standard of 8.2 percent per dollar in sales. The use of historical data to set standards rests on the assumption that the future will be a continuation of the past. Of course, abrupt changes within either an organization's internal or surrounding environment can easily make such an assumption false.

Comparative standards are based on the experiences of others. Such standards can be applied at the corporate, business-unit, or functional level. At the

Standard.
A criterion against which actual performance can be compared.

Historical standard.
A kind of standard based on past experience.

Comparative standard.
A kind of standard based on the experience of others.

Emerson Electric Co. produces the electronic control units being installed in these Whirlpool dishwashers as well as the motors that power the dishwashers. Emerson uses criteria for the Malcolm Baldrige National Quality Award as a comparative standard against which to measure its performance.

corporate level, the financial performance of organizations in the same industry is regularly compared to judge market value. At the business-unit and functional levels, trade associations typically publish information on the average yearly sales, costs of goods sold, wages, advertising expenditures, and so on of member organizations. Such information is invaluable in "benchmarking" a business unit's overall success, as well as its performance in specific functional areas, such as marketing and finance. Motorola is currently trying to use benchmarking to establish standards even in such areas as basic research and meetings, where standards are not easily set.

Engineering standards are based on technical analyses. They generally apply to production methods, materials, machinery, safety equipment, parts, and supplies. Quality limits, machine-output specifications, material requirements, and output volume are all examples of engineering standards. For a computer company, an engineering standard might be on-time delivery rates of 98 percent. Such standards are typically expressed in numerical terms and based on objective data. As with other standards, their intent is to improve performance, resulting in lower costs or higher sales volume.

Engineering standard.
A kind of standard based on technical analyses.

STEP 2: MEASURING AND EVALUATING PERFORMANCE

The second step in the control process is to measure and evaluate performance. Actual performance must be compared against the standards set in Step 1. This is essentially a comparison between "what is" and "what should be." Performance may surpass, meet, or fall below expectations. If performance fulfills expectations, no control problem exists. If performance exceeds or fails to meet expectations, fur-

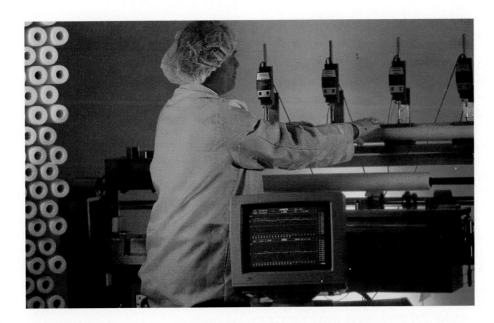

Pall Corporation uses computer-aided control in select manufacturing processes. This technology assists in monitoring and controlling key aspects of the production of Pall filters.

ther investigation is called for to determine the cause. Performance that exceeds expectations may mean either superior talent or inappropriately set standards. Performance that fails to meet expectations may likewise mean inappropriately set standards, but of greater concern is the possibility of either poor talent or the improper use of resources. The key question in both cases, however, becomes, "How much variation from standards is acceptable before action is taken?"

The answer to this question is not as direct as it might initially seem. In reality, actual performance seldom conforms perfectly to expectations. As a consequence, deviations both above and below expected performance are the normal state of affairs. Because management cannot react to every discrepancy from standards, performance ranges are typically employed. These ranges are defined by upper and lower control limits. Performance outside an acceptable range serves as a red flag. The setting of exact upper and lower control limits should be based on various relevant factors, including the absolute dollar amounts involved and the potential for loss. More will be said shortly about the importance of controls focusing on a manageable number of strategic activities in our discussion of *management by exception* in the section titled "Characteristics of Effective Controls."

STEP 3: TAKING ACTION

The final step in the control process is to take action based on the comparisons made in Step 2. In those instances where performance falls outside acceptable limits, one of three actions is typically appropriate: do nothing, correct the deviation, or revise the standard being used.

Do Nothing

Doing nothing generally is appropriate in those instances where an organization's plans are revealed to have been inappropriate for the actual conditions that subsequently prevailed or when mitigating circumstances occurred, such as labor problems or a disruption in the supply of necessary parts, that were beyond management control. Maintaining the status quo can also be an appropriate response in situations where deviations, although beyond established limits, prove too costly or time consuming to justify correcting.

Correct the Deviation

If a deviation does fall outside acceptable limits, it is more likely, however, that corrective action will be necessary. In this regard, a prudent manager acts on both positive and negative deviations. Positive deviations should be examined for new insights into such success. Negative deviations should also be a basis for learning. Perhaps an organization's expectations were realistic, but plans were poorly implemented. Employee resistance and poor communication might be contributing factors. Again, the prudent manager applies such knowledge to improve future performance.

Revise Standards

A final response when performance falls outside acceptable limits is to revise standards. Expectations may have been based on historical standards inappropriate to current conditions. In such instances, as noted earlier, the past is a poor basis on which to predict the future. Similarly, the use of comparative standards may prove to be problematic. Such standards are based on the experiences of others. No two organizations are ever alike. For this reason, trade association information and other secondary source data relating "average" performance figures can be quite misleading. Such figures are nothing more than the mathematical mean of different performance levels. Finally, engineering standards, despite their claim of objectivity, may also require revision. Too often, it seems, the qualitative aspects of performance are inappropriately weighted in establishing such standards. Indeed, it has often been noted that "not everything that counts can be counted, and not everything that can be counted counts."

CONTROL POINTS

The various steps in the control process indicate that control is necessary to anticipate problems, adjust plans, and take action as needed. This suggests that one way to further understand the control process is to place it within a systems theory framework. Naturally occurring systems, such as the human body, are self-regulating and, thus, exemplify the control process in its purest form. When a jogger's temperature exceeds 98.6° Fahrenheit, the body senses the difference and automatically takes corrective action by activating the sweat glands—the jogger begins to perspire. When normal temperature is regained, perspiration ceases.

Being self-regulating, the human body is, technically speaking, a **cybernetic system.**[1] By contrast, artificially created systems, such as business firms, health-care facilities, and educational institutions, do not have automatic controls. Their performance must be continually monitored to detect and adjust for deviations from set standards.

From a systems perspective, an organization's performance can be monitored and, thus, controlled at three points: before, during, or after an activity is completed. As Figure 19.2 shows, each of these points matches a different aspect of the input → transformation → output cycle that must be maintained if an organization is to exist over time.

Precontrols (also called *feedforward* or *preventive controls*) monitor inputs to ensure that they meet the standards necessary for successful transformation. In doing so, they regulate the quality and quantity of financial, physical, human, and

Cybernetic system.
A self-regulating system.

Precontrols.
Controls that monitor inputs to ensure that they meet the standards necessary for successful transformation. Also known as feedforward or preventive controls.

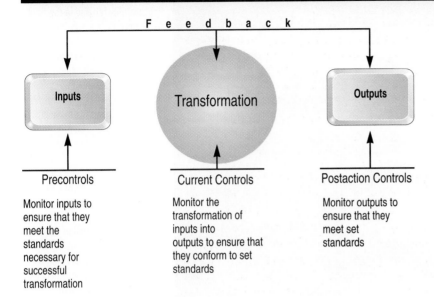

FIGURE 19.2 THREE CONTROL POINTS: PRECONTROLS, CONCURRENT CONTROLS, AND POSTACTION CONTROLS

information resources before they are transformed into outputs. Precontrols are designed to anticipate problems and take preventive action. Thus, to ensure the quality of its baked goods, Pepperidge Farms buys only the finest ingredients (inputs). To ensure the quality of its employees, Microsoft hires only the most outstanding job candidates—just one out of every 6,000 applicants. Similarly, Morgan Guaranty maintains rigid lending standards to protect its financial integrity.

Mrs. Fields Cookies and Wal-Mart also offer excellent examples of precontrol systems that detect deviations *before* they occur. At Mrs. Fields, store managers use a computer network to interact with headquarters hourly. They input hourly sales figures, customer counts, and average sales figures. If customer counts are up but sales are lagging, headquarters may suggest more aggressive sampling to ensure that all sales quotas are met by day's end. Wal-Mart has an around-the-clock precontrol system to ensure that the products customers want are always in stock. It maintains a computer center in Bentonville, Arkansas, the size of a football field that simultaneously tracks sales and inventories via satellite.

Concurrent controls (also called *screening* or *yes/no controls*) monitor the transformation of inputs into outputs to ensure that they conform to set standards. Because concurrent controls involve the monitoring of ongoing activities, they are the only controls that can cope with contingencies that cannot be anticipated. For this reason, they have a special significance.

When contingencies do arise involving activities in a transformation process, a "go, no-go" decision typically is required. That is, a decision must be made whether to continue as before, follow an alternative course, or stop work altogether. In this way, concurrent controls allow for adjustments to be made while work is being done. Moreover, they help avoid the waste of unacceptable outputs and, perhaps more importantly, help keep such outputs from reaching the marketplace.

To protect against shipping products (outputs) that do not meet quality standards, companies like Coca-Cola, Procter & Gamble, and Mars make extensive use of concurrent controls. When was the last time you opened a bottle of Coke that

Concurrent controls.

Controls that monitor the transformation of inputs into outputs to ensure that they conform to set standards. Also known as screening or yes/no controls.

Microsoft Corporation software goes through rigorous user testing in the company's usability lab and in the field as products are being developed. This type of concurrent control has been unusual in the software business because of the time it can take. Usability testing not only uncovers program errors but points out if a commonly used function requires more actions than necessary. Including usability testing in the development of software which demands that programmers be ready to rewrite codes as production deadlines approach, but it gives Microsoft products their user-friendliness that has become the industry standard.

didn't fizz? Or squeezed a tube of Crest that didn't squirt out onto your toothbrush? Or bite into a Snickers bar that didn't have a pleasant taste?

Postaction controls (also called *feedback controls*) monitor outputs to ensure that they meet set standards. They come into play after transformation has taken place. Thus, they focus on end results, as opposed to inputs and activities.

Such control is especially beneficial because it provides managers with a basis for evaluating the reasonableness of both organization goals and standards, as well as insights into past performance that can be used to avoid future mistakes. This type of knowledge is essential for refining an organization's planning capabilities. Information on number of units made and sold, production costs, quality levels, rate of return on assets, net profit, and so on is a basic necessity for revising goals and standards and formulating new plans. By documenting accomplishments, postaction controls also provide feedback for allocating employee rewards.

Postaction controls can be as simple as a maître d' asking diners leaving a restaurant if they enjoyed their meal or a store manager chatting with departing shoppers. Similar feedback is gathered somewhat more elaborately by Nissan Motor Co. and MBNA America. Nissan pays bonuses of up to $100,000 per year to its dealers based on customer satisfaction scores gathered from buyer surveys and from evaluators posing as shoppers. MBNA has a special unit that calls every customer who wants to drop an MBNA Visa card or MasterCard. Its customer-retention rate is twice the industry average.

A&P likewise uses postaction controls to gather feedback. Every Monday, chairman James Wood sits down with his top assistants and reviews the previous week's operating statistics for 1,300 stores. "It allows us to jump in very, very quickly to solve problems," explains Wood.[2] For instance, in a week's time, Wood can identify a problem of theft at a particular store. For competitors operating on a quarterly cycle, such a problem would go unnoticed for 13 weeks.

Postaction controls.
Controls that monitor outputs to ensure that they meet set standards. Also known as feedback controls.

CLOSE-UP: QUALITY   TO SPY OR NOT TO SPY—MANAGEMENT'S QUESTION REGARDING EMPLOYEES

Modern technology offers managers new techniques for monitoring employee performance. "Silent monitoring" can now be used to eavesdrop on employee transactions conducted via telephone or networked PC computers. Computerized devices and software programs are available, for example, to count the keystrokes of data entry clerks or secretly watch the screens of computer operators. Silent telephone monitoring is not new but is improved and spreading. An estimated 6 million workers are being subjected to electronic surveillance.

Is this a proper management practice? Critics say it is an unwarranted invasion of privacy that results in greater stress and stress-related health problems for employees and therefore in lower productivity. It is Big Brother at work, verifies management distrust of employees, and increases the adversarial "us vs. them" attitude between management and labor. There have been a growing number of class-action lawsuits against employers, and legislation to limit silent monitoring is being suggested.

Advocates say that proper monitoring can result in better employee relations. The bonus can be greater employee productivity, improved service quality, and increased sales and profits. For example, at General Electric's Answer Center in Louisville, Kentucky, 200 agents handle over 14,000 telephone calls each day from potential appliance buyers and fix-it-yourselfers. Ten "coaches" record conversations and play some of them back for training purposes. The center has a 96 percent customer satisfaction rating and generates $16 per call in appliance sales revenue and service savings compared to the $4 cost per call.

Experience suggests that managers who choose to use silent monitoring should observe the following guidelines:

- Select and train employees (including managers) carefully.
- Make clear to employees how and why they will be monitored.
- Use monitoring as an aid to coaching, not as a disciplinary tool.
- Use it more with newer employees, less with experienced employees.
- Involve employees in establishing a fair, workable system.
- Emphasize quality of work rather than quantity of work (quotas).

Control is important, but it must not break down trust or demean the employees being controlled. If it is to be effective and if productivity and quality are to be enhanced, it must be acceptable to all concerned. Once employee trust is lost, it is difficult to regain.

Source: Gene Bylinsky, "How Companies Spy on Employees," *Fortune,* November 4, 1991, 131–140.

MULTIPLE CONTROLS

In most complex organizations, it is desirable to exercise all three types of control— precontrol, concurrent control, and postaction control. Precontrol helps managers anticipate problems in the first place. Concurrent control allows them to cope with contingencies that cannot be anticipated. Finally, postaction control keeps them from repeating past mistakes.

Coca-Cola, which has already been cited for its excellent use of concurrent controls, also employs precontrol and postaction control systems. As a precontrol, Coke receives estimated monthly sales figures from around the world, for country after country, on the 15th of each month. As a postaction control, on the fifth working day of each month, it receives the previous month's market share figures and a sales estimate for the rest of the year.

CHARACTERISTICS OF EFFECTIVE CONTROLS

Regardless of type, effective controls share several basic characteristics. It is important to note, however, that controls must be tailored to the specific task and persons they are intended to serve. To be effective, controls should be cost effective, acceptable, appropriate, strategic, and reliable and valid.

Cost Effective

The benefits received from control should more than offset their expense. Most large department stores began tagging merchandise with electronic strips or ink disks to control shoplifting only after it became evident that the cost of doing so would be more than offset by the savings associated with reduced theft. An elaborate security system with one-way mirrors, closed-circuit television, guards, and alarms might be reasonable for a Las Vegas casino but would be overkill for a supermarket. In any case, the cost of controls must be weighed against their expected benefits.

Acceptable

Controls, much like laws, are doomed to ineffectiveness if the individuals whom they affect resent them or feel they are harmful to their personal and psychological well-being. Likewise, controls that appear arbitrary or unnecessary can lead to frustration and diminished motivation. The current drive to eliminate smoking in public places is a good illustration of the difficulty involved in enforcing controls that many find unacceptable. In this case, as in all others, true control is possible only if the people affected believe it is necessary and are willing to help make it work.

Appropriate

Controls should correspond to an organization's plans. Moreover, they need only be as detailed as the activities they monitor. Further, what will do for a vice-president of sales is likely to be inappropriate for a first-line supervisor. Controls designed for a finance department will differ from those appropriate for a purchasing department or an engineering department. It would seem that many organizations, fascinated with the power of sophisticated control systems, suffer from overly detailed feedback. One top manager relates that his company actually knew *less* about its operation after the installation of a new "state-of-the-art" control system.[3] One could look on page 67, Chart 112.6, for example, and see how much coffee its third shift consumed, but there were so many numbers no one bothered to read them. Today, the company has a simple accounting system providing limited but relevant information that can be grasped and acted on quickly. Gone are the 400 cost centers and hundreds of classifications.

Strategic

Controls should focus on a manageable number of strategic activities. As an organization becomes larger, the need for strategic controls increases because top managers can no longer personally monitor all aspects of its operations. As our discussion of the control process indicated, managers must direct their attention to significant deviations from what is expected at strategic control points. Such deviations may be positive or negative. This practice has long been known as **management by exception** and specifies that managers should concentrate on significant deviations from planned performance. In this way, those activities requiring immediate attention (the "exceptions") can be identified. Ordinary operations and less significant deviations can be handled by lower level managers. Management by exception thus improves upper management efficiency by allowing time to address the most important concerns, while permitting lower level managers to exercise greater authority.

At ITT, significant deviations from planned performance are "red-flagged" for immediate attention. Red-flag items remain on the first page of each division's monthly report, updated for changes, every month until their cause is determined. Management by exception operates somewhat differently at Alde & Company Ltd., a British company with worldwide offices. Information on sales of selected products from a number of "critical" markets is telexed daily to company headquarters and compared to planned performance. When significant deviations occur, further details are requested. Management by exception thus allows both ITT and Alde to quickly pinpoint specific problems (or opportunities) that need immediate investigating.

Reliable and Valid

Controls not only must be dependable (reliable), but they also must measure what they purport to measure (that is, they must be valid). Where controls cannot be relied on and are invalid, they are unlikely to be trusted and can lead to calamitous consequences. For example, a control system that reports unreliable sales figures for various regions can lead to serious inventory problems. Some regions will likely have too much inventory, while others will lose sales because of inventory shortages. Similarly, controls should be valid, that is, based on objective criteria. A regional manager who bases raw material orders on "how he thinks" things are going will be no match for a manager who computes needed raw materials based on a breakdown of units produced and sold.

METHODS OF CONTROL

There are a variety of control methods. Their appropriateness for various points in the input → transformation → output cycle will vary with the conditions and requirements of a particular undertaking. Some have been described in our previous discussions and will be mentioned only briefly here. Figure 19.3 identifies nine of these methods according to their frequency of use.

Control methods that are used *constantly* are self-control, group control, and policies/procedures/rules. Management information systems, external audits, and budgets provide information used to control on a *periodic* basis. Finally, three control methods used *occasionally* are special reports, personal observation, and project control.

Constant Controls

Self-Control No organization could exist for long unless its employees exerted the self-control required to perform their assigned tasks. The absence of such self-control would require an enormous investment in other control methods. To be effective, therefore, an organization must be able to achieve its goals by shifting

Management by exception.

The notion that controls should concentrate on significant exceptions from planned performance.

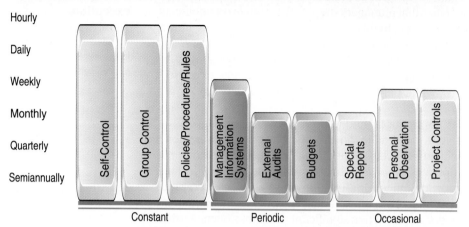

FIGURE 19.3   NINE METHODS OF CONTROL AND THEIR FREQUENCY OF USE

control away from management to the self-control within individual employees. For employees, self-control means giving a fair day's work for a fair day's pay, reporting to work on time, respecting property, and observing the rights of others. Personal pride and initiative are the main sources of self-control, though orientation and training contribute to it. Managers may be able to influence employees' self-control somewhat through the types of reinforcement mentioned in Chapter 15, but overall, the significance of self-control as the single most important method of control cannot be underestimated.

Group Control   As noted in Chapter 17, work groups also are a source of control. By defining the kinds of behavior that are acceptable or unacceptable, group-defined norms exert a strong influence on individual actions. Some organizations place great emphasis on work group control. They strive to develop a way of thinking that stresses adherence to group-established behavior patterns. We tend to associate this kind of influence with certain religious faiths, monastic orders, and volunteer agencies. However, many business organizations also stress group control. For example, IBM founder Thomas Watson, Sr., decreed what employees were to wear (dark business suits, white shirts, and striped ties) and to drink (no alcohol, even when off the job); plus, employees were urged in signs posted everywhere to THINK. Watson-instilled norms are still in effect today, although in a softened form. IBM sales representatives can now drink at lunch, but if they do, they are warned not to make further customer calls that day. Male employees still must wear suits and ties when meeting prospective customers, although their shirts need not be white. Still, a conservative appearance remains the IBM style. "I don't think I've ever seen an IBMer in a pink shirt or an outlandish tie," says a vice-president from another firm.[4] Watson's intention was to instill a way of thinking about one's job and even appearance that ensured a behavior pattern common to all IBM employees. That his intent still persists is a testimony to the effectiveness of group-based control.

Policies/Procedures/Rules   The role of policies, procedures, and rules was discussed in connection with planning in Chapter 5. Policies, procedures, and rules are also methods of control. Typically reflecting past managerial experiences, they may concern any number of things—how to make certain decisions, deal

Store owner Stew Leonard's business policy is literally written in stone. This clearly stated policy helps Leonard control employees' behavior by ensuring that they always keep customers satisfied.

with resources, handle difficult employees, and so on. Properly implemented, policies, procedures, and rules that are kept up to date, that are clearly communicated, and that incorporate employee input can effectively control individual and work group behavior.

A classic example of a policy that controls employee behavior is chiseled into a 6,000-pound rock standing next to the front door of Stew Leonard's dairy store in Norwalk, Connecticut. It reads:

OUR POLICY

Rule 1—The customer is always right.

Rule 2—If the customer is ever wrong, reread Rule 1.

This policy not only guides employee efforts to put customers first, but is the basis for Stew Leonard's corporate strategy.

Periodic Controls

Information Systems Each function within the management process is served by various information systems. Besides aiding in the effective control of organization resources, management information systems are important in planning, organizing, staffing and human resource management, and leadership and interpersonal influence. Simply put, an **information system** is a mechanism for

Information system.
A mechanism for collecting, analyzing, and disseminating data in the form of usable information.

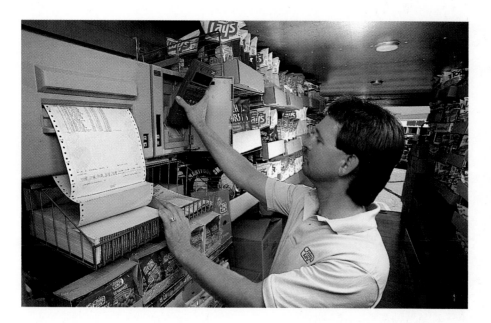

A Frito-Lay route salesman uses a hand-held computer to prepare invoices and relay sales data to Frito-Lay's mainframe computers. This sophisticated system allows up-to-the-minute transmittal of the detailed information managers need in order to assess the results of promotions, to spot trends, and to make informed decisions.

collecting, analyzing, and disseminating data in the form of usable information. As such, it links the various decision-making centers within an organization. Because of their significance, information systems are examined at length in Chapter 20.

PepsiCo's Frito-Lay has one of the most sophisticated information systems in the packaged-goods industry. Its 10,000 salespeople carry hand-held computers that plug into modems at their homes. Each night they zap information on their day's efforts to headquarters in Plano, Texas. Not only will the system tell top management how many bags of Doritos were sold throughout the United States on the day before, but it will provide more specific information on sales in Tennessee, in Shelby County, in the city of Memphis, in the local Kroger's, and in the special promotion at the end of aisle four.

External Audits Sound management requires the examination of an organization's finances on a regular basis by an outside accounting firm. The professionals in these firms, called *certified public accountants (CPAs),* are trained to ensure that an organization's financial statements are prepared in conformity with generally accepted accounting principles. Thus, they help protect the rights of present and future stockholders.

Rather than examining every detail in a financial statement, CPAs randomly audit sample items. They check to ensure that the assets claimed on financial statements actually exist. They verify the existence of inventory, equipment, furniture, and current assets, such as cash. External audits therefore help control the use of organization assets and resources.

Budgets As defined in Chapter 5, *budgets* are plans that deal with the future allocation and utilization of various resources to different organization activities over a given time period. Most people think of budgets in financial or monetary terms. However, they are also used to control the allocation and utilization of labor, raw materials, floor space, machine hours, and so on. Thus, in addition to being a type of plan, budgets are also a method of control. They exercise control by allocating resources across departments; specifying, in advance, how allocated

SMART MANAGEMENT CAN YOU TRUST THAT AUDIT?

Ever since news of the S&L crisis first broke, accounting firms have been the subject of considerable scrutiny. Many people who rely on the accuracy of financial statements are now confronted with the question: Can you trust that audit? Some are criticizing (and even suing) accounting firms that gave relatively clean bills of health on their outside audits of companies that later got into deep water. Others, however, believe that outside auditors are alive, well, and trustworthy.

Evidence of the problem is easy to find:

- In its analysis of 11 failed S&Ls, the General Accounting Office found instances where auditors inadequately checked oral assertions that problem loans were collectible. Auditors also failed to confirm doubts about appraisal values of collateral.

- The Federal Deposit Insurance Corporation (FDIC) has sued or settled with five of the Big Six accounting firms, in most cases alleging negligence. The sixth firm is embroiled in controversy because of an audit performed by its London affiliate.

- Competition among accounting firms for auditing clients in a sluggish economy has led to fee cutting. One accounting firm reportedly gained a client by offering a "first year free" package for a 3-year contract. It seems reasonable to suspect that an accounting firm that makes less money will commit fewer resources (that is, fewer auditor hours) to the audit, resulting in diminished audit quality.

- Auditors are reluctant to "blow the whistle" on managers when they find evidence of fraud. They prefer to resign quietly.

A closer look at the controversy reveals that accounting firms are being unfairly criticized. Allegations that auditors have been negligent run at less than 0.5 percent of all audits performed on more than 12,000 companies submitting financial statements to the Securities and Exchange Commission (SEC). In addition, courts have had difficulty finding a correlation between a failed S&L and a faulty audit. One judge threw out a $560 million suit by the FDIC against the auditors.

Many people, it seems, simply don't understand what an audit is. It is *not* a stamp of approval. It *is* reasonable assurance that the financial information is free of material misstatements. It is usually done through sampling techniques after an auditor learns a company's accounting system. And contrary to the belief that they must serve as accounting watchdogs, auditors are not required to look for fraud, and their sampling techniques are unlikely to uncover it.

Yes, auditors can be trusted. But rethinking to make the process more valuable is needed and underway. New methods of communicating conclusions regarding the risks and uncertainties that a company faces are being sought. Legislation has been submitted requiring auditors to report fraud to the SEC.

Audits, from internal and external sources, are valuable control tools. But smart managers will look beyond these audits if the controlling function is to be accomplished effectively.

Source: Rahul Jacob, "Can You Trust That Audit?" *Fortune*, November 18, 1991, 191–198.

resources are to be utilized; and providing a standard against which planned performance can be compared to actual performance. In so doing, budgets help preserve organization resources, promote efficient resource use, and assist in attaining organization goals.

Flexibility is much more important in enacting budgets than blind adherence to initial allocations. Moreover, what matters in budgets is how managers treat them. Budgets should be compared to monthly reports. By comparing expectations to results, managers can determine how well they know their units and, in the case of financial budgets, if there will be a profit. Some obviously disagree with this philosophy. At Campbell Soup, budgets are anything but guidelines. Make your "number," so it is said, and CEO David Johnson will "serve you cake on a plate." Miss it and he'll "serve your can on a platter."[5]

Occasional Controls

Special Reports When controls indicate a discrepancy between standards and performance, a special report may be prepared. Individual managers, nonmanagerial task teams, or interdepartmental teams may be asked to gather information as the basis for a special report. Data for special reports may be generated internally, obtained from government sources, gleaned from trade association publications, or purchased from private research firms.

Depending on their purpose, special reports vary in content and style. Some may be statistical, others descriptive. Topics of special reports might include:

- *Downtime*. An analysis of idle machine time, its causes, and its costs.

- *Sales*. A monthly summary of total sales in dollars and units, itemized sales by customer, forecast sales, "lost sales," and new accounts.

- *Quality*. A breakdown of defects per thousand parts, deviations in manufactured products, maintenance costs, and scrap performance.

- *Accounts receivable*. A summary of the number of sales pending final credit approval, number of overdue accounts, and average collection period for credit sales.

Personal Observation There are essentially two ways managers can determine what is happening in an organization: rely on information provided by others or find out for themselves. Effective managers recognize the importance of reliable, firsthand information and circumvent the chain of command as necessary to get it. This might require speaking directly to those performing various functions, or holding meetings with lower level employees. John W. Teets, Dial Corp. CEO, spends a day or more each week in the field talking with plant managers, supervisors, and production people. McDonald's late chairman Ray Kroc was legendary for regularly visiting stores and assessing them on the factors the company holds dear, Q.S.C.&V. (quality, service, cleanliness, and value). Motorola CEO William J. Weisz regularly walks the halls and laboratories of his company's different plants engaging in what United Airlines calls "Management by Walking About" or what is known at Hewlett-Packard as "Management by Wandering Around." Following the same pattern, James Renier, head of Honeywell's Control Systems Division, personally talks to more than 3,000 employees a year. "Eighty-five percent of the information I need comes through normal channels," he explains, "but the other 15 percent can be of vital importance."[6]

Other top managers who agree are former Singer Co. CEO William F. Schmied and Lanier Business Products CEO Gene Milner. A strong believer in hands-on management, Schmied likes to give lower level managers a great deal of latitude but states that "listening to a presentation on how things are going is a far cry from going out there and thumping the watermelon."[7] Milner shares Schmied's sentiments. He strongly feels that "hand-off" managers cannot effectively do their jobs. Milner says,

> I think management is sadly remiss when they delegate things and just look at profit-and-loss statements and so forth, and don't get down to finding out the cure part. No matter what anybody says, I don't believe an executive should keep hands off at any level. You can't really know what's going on unless you get down and work, walk through the building and see where people are just chatting on the phone with their friends and what-have-you. The top guy must know what's going on in order to take corrective action.[8]

The importance of personal observation as a form of control is evident in the actions of Debbi Fields, founder of Mrs. Fields Cookies. Fields makes unannounced visits to her stores, where she masquerades as a casual shopper to test the enthusiasm and sales techniques of her staff, as well as product quality. More than once, she has found a store's cookies unsatisfactory, dumped its entire inventory into the garbage, and closed the store until her exacting standards were met.

Project Controls Various methods have been developed for controlling specific projects. The three most popular are **Gantt charts,** developed early in this century by scientific management pioneer Henry L. Gantt; **PERT (Program Evaluation and Review Technique),** developed by the U.S. Navy, Lockheed Aircraft Corporation, and management consultants Booz, Allen & Hamilton for construction of the Polaris missile; and **break-even analysis,** popularized by Charles E. Knoeppel and Walter Rautenstrauch.

Gantt Charts Also known as *bar charts,* Gantt charts depict across time the occurrence of those activities comprising a project, as in Figure 19.4. Activities represented by overlapping bars can be performed concurrently to the degree they overlap. Activities represented by nonoverlapping bars must be performed in the sequence indicated. For instance, Activity D in Figure 19.4 cannot begin until Activity A is completed. However, it can be performed concurrently with Activities C and E, at least to the extent of their overlap.

Figure 19.5 shows a Gantt chart for building a house within 12 weeks. As indicated, the project is entering its ninth week. The black bars reflect the plan, and the

Gantt chart (bar chart).
A control method that depicts across time the occurrence of those activities comprising a project.

Program evaluation and review technique (PERT).
A control method that depicts the interrelationships across time among those events and activities comprising a project.

Break-even analysis.
A method of visualizing the relationship between costs and revenues.

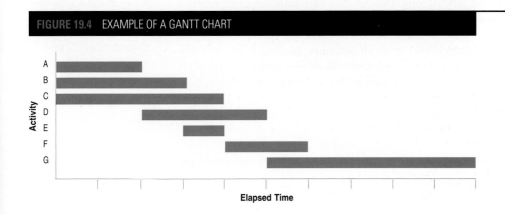

FIGURE 19.4   EXAMPLE OF A GANTT CHART

Elapsed Time

FIGURE 19.5 A GANTT CHART FOR CONSTRUCTING A HOUSE

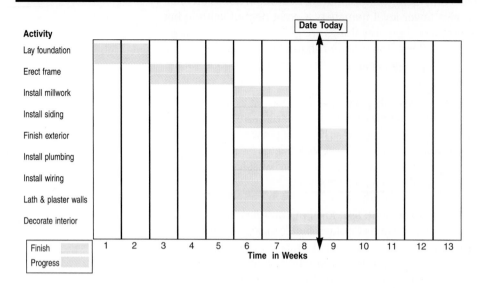

Source: Adapted from Kenneth L. Dean, *Fundamentals of Network Planning and Analysis* (St. Paul: Military Department, UNIVAC, Sperry Rand Corporation, 1962), 67.

blue bars denote progress against that schedule. All activities except installation of millwork are on schedule. The delay in millwork is no cause for alarm because 4 weeks remain in the project, and the chart shows only 2 weeks of millwork remaining.

By updating progress on the chart, one can see at a glance the activities that are behind schedule, on time, and ahead of schedule. Gantt charts facilitate the coordination of activities and scheduling of labor. However, they are best used in scheduling a series of unrelated activities. In our house-building project, for example, electricians can be doing their work whether or not the painters show up to paint the exterior of the house. A Gantt chart's value is much more limited when many activities must be interrelated. Thus, in situations where one activity (for example, erect frame) must be completed before another can begin (for example, install millwork), a Gantt chart is of limited use in controlling the two. PERT helps overcome this limitation.

PERT PERT offers as its basic tool a **network,** which is a diagram depicting the interrelationships across time among those events and activities comprising a project.[9] Figure 19.6 presents an example. *Events* (depicted by circles) mark the beginning and ending of activities; therefore, an event does not consume time. An event is not considered accomplished until all activities leading to it are completed. *Activities* (depicted by arrows) represent the work required to accomplish an event. An activity cannot begin until all preceding activities to which it is connected have been completed.

Designing a PERT network, such as that in Figure 19.7 showing the construction of another house, involves five steps:

1. Prepare a chronological list of each event that must be accomplished to complete a project.

Network.

A diagram showing the interrelationships between the events and activities that compromise a PERT project.

FIGURE 19.6   EXAMPLE OF A PERT NETWORK

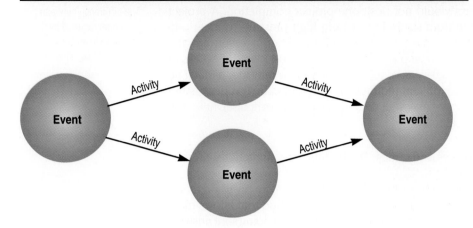

2. Based on this listing, draw a network, placing each event in chronological order. Two or more events may begin or end at the same time, and various activities can be going on at once. Connect the events with arrows to show the
   proper sequence of activities.

3. Estimate the time required to accomplish each activity after the preceding activity has been finished. Time estimates are usually expressed in weeks.

4. Total the required time for each activity along every sequence—or path—of
   activities in the network. The path having the longest time is the **critical path.**
   The critical path, therefore, indicates the earliest date that a project can be
   completed. In Figure 19.7, the critical path runs through Events 1, 2, 3, 7, 9, and
   11 and requires 14 weeks to complete. Having identified the critical path, a
   project manager can focus his or her attention on either reducing the time of
   activities in this path, or at least watching closely for any delays.

Critical path.
The largest path or sequence
of activities in a PERT network.

FIGURE 19.7   A PERT NETWORK FOR CONSTRUCTING A HOUSE

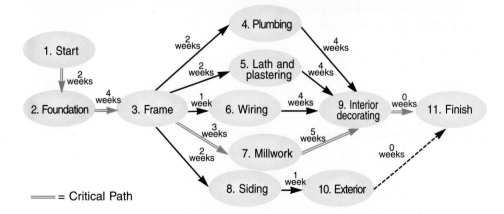

Source: Adapted from Kenneth L. Dean, *Fundamentals of Network Planning and Analysis* (St. Paul: Military
Department, UNIVAC Division, Sperry Rand Corporation, 1962),68.

5. If desired, the difference between the total time required by the critical path and other paths can also be calculated. Such differences are **slack times,** or margins in which delays would not postpone project completion. A project manager can determine from slack times where high pressure to meet estimated times may be unwarranted. In Figure 19.7, the difference between the total time required by the critical path and Path 1-2-3-8-10-11 yields 5 weeks of slack time (14 weeks minus 9 weeks). To a contractor, this may mean that if he can get a lucrative interim job that requires the carpenters he has designated for the exterior of a house, he may well decide to let them work elsewhere during the original job's slack time.

Slack time.
The difference between the total time required by the critical path and any other path in a PERT network.

PERT has both its advocates and critics. The benefits and limitations cited by each are summarized in Table 19.1.

Break-Even Analysis   One goal of both for-profit and not-for-profit organizations is to avoid suffering a loss. Break-even analysis is a method that allows managers to visualize the relationship between costs and revenues. In doing so, it answers the question "How many units or products must we sell before total costs exactly equal total revenues?" That is, how much must we sell before we break even, meaning that our organization neither loses nor makes money?

Total costs include fixed costs and variable costs. **Fixed costs** are costs that do not vary with levels of output (for example, depreciation, insurance, top management salaries, taxes, and maintenance). **Variable costs**—labor, materials, supplies, training, supervision, and fringes—are directly related to levels of output. As output increases, these costs increase, and as output decreases, they decrease. **Total revenues** are the income resulting from an activity and are computed by multiplying selling price per unit times the number of units sold.

Figure 19.8 shows a break-even analysis for a proposed project—a new product. The analysis graphically plots total revenues (based on a selling price of $6 per unit) and total costs ($100,000 fixed costs and $4-per-unit variable costs). The

Total costs.
The total of fixed and variable costs.

Fixed costs.
Costs that do not vary with levels of output.

Variable costs.
Costs that vary with levels of output.

Total revenues.
Income computed by multiplying selling price per unit times number of units sold.

TABLE 19.1   PERT: BENEFITS AND LIMITATIONS

Benefits

1. It is a detailed, easy-to-communicate means for controlling organization activities.
2. It focuses on activities that are most likely to delay a project's completion.
3. It highlights project resources that are not being fully utilized.
4. It provides a prompt means for determining a project's current status.
5. It often stimulates alternative plans and schedules.

Limitations

1. It is useful only when event times can be accurately estimated.
2. Time estimates generally prove to be less reliable when outside vendors and subcontractors are involved.
3. It may be impossible to make time estimates for unique projects.
4. It is impractical for projects involving a repetitive sequence of events (for example, assembly-line routines) since virtually all events fall along a single critical path.
5. It can be costly. A network for the building and equipping of a new manufacturing plant may involve 1,500 activities and 1,000 events.

FIGURE 19.8   EXAMPLE OF BREAK-EVEN ANALYSIS

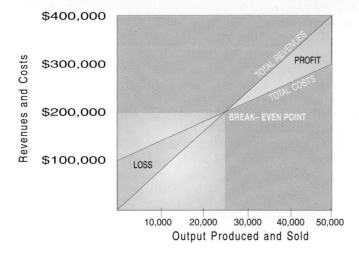

break-even point—the number of units that must be produced and sold for total costs to equal total revenues—is 25,000 units per year. If fewer than 25,000 units are sold per year, a loss is incurred (total costs are greater than total revenues). At output levels greater than the break-even point, a profit is generated (total revenues are greater than total costs).

Perhaps the greatest strength of break-even analysis is its simplicity. It is easily performed, easily explained, and quickly understood. In spite of its simplicity, break-even analysis allows managers to answer such subtle questions as: What selling price will allow us to break even if we estimate that 25,000 units will be sold? How much must we reduce our total costs to break even at our current level of annual sales? Break-even analysis thus provides a basis for monitoring an organization's performance.

Break-even analysis does have limitations. It is an effective method of control only if selling price and variable costs per unit are constant (total revenue and total cost functions are linear) over a broad range of output levels. Additionally, it must be possible to estimate the revenues and costs with some certainty. Despite limitations, however, break-even analysis is one of the most frequently used methods of control.

FINANCIAL RATIOS

Over the years, several types of control guidelines have been developed for interpreting an organization's performance. Finance and accounting courses typically focus on such control guidelines in depth. These guidelines facilitate control by serving as benchmarks for evaluating performance. Although they are most often used by financial analysts, managers should also be familiar with them to benefit from the insights they provide.

External audits and budgets, of course, provide a certain measure of control over an organization's finances. Additionally, **financial ratios** are commonly used to express relationships between single or group items on an organization's balance

Break-even point.
Number of units that must be produced and sold for total costs to equal total revenues.

Financial ratios.
Control guidelines commonly used to express relationships between single or group items on an organization's balance sheet and income statement.

sheet and income statement. These ratios provide financial guidelines for interpreting an organization's performance. There are four basic types of financial ratios: liquidity, activity, profitability, and leverage. Each of these ratios is summarized
in Table 19.2 and briefly explained in the following paragraphs, which use the ficti-
tious ABC Company as an example. ABC's balance sheet and profit and loss statement are presented in Tables 19.3 and 19.4, respectively.

LIQUIDITY RATIOS

An organization's **liquidity** is a measure of its ability to pay its short-term debts. A
popular indication of an organization's liquidity is its **current ratio.** This is simply
a comparison of its current assets with its current liabilities. To obtain an organization's current ratio, divide current assets by current liabilities. In the ABC balance
sheet, the figures are

$$\frac{\$464,259_{\text{Current assets}}}{\$121,570_{\text{Current liabilities}}} = \frac{3.82}{1}, \text{ or } 3.82 \text{ to } 1.$$

Therefore, for each $1 in current liabilities, there is an amount of $3.82 in current assets to back it up. Most financial analysts believe a current ratio of 2 to 1 is
desirable. A large current ratio is not necessarily a good sign; it may mean an orga-

Liquidity.
A measure of an organiza-
tion's ability to pay its short-
term debts.

Current ratio.
The ratio between an organization's current assets and
current liabilities. Used to
judge an organization's liquidity.

TABLE 19.2 FOUR BASIC TYPES OF FINANCIAL RATIOS		
Type	**Obtained by**	**Purpose**
1. *Liquidity Ratios*		
Current ratio	$\dfrac{\text{Current assets}}{\text{Current liabilities}}$	To determine an organization's ability to pay its short-term debts
Quick assets ratio	$\dfrac{\text{Quick assets}}{\text{Current liabilities}}$	To determine an organization's ability to cover a sudden emergency without selling its inventory
2. *Activity Ratios*		
Asset turnover ratio	$\dfrac{\text{Sales}}{\text{Total assets}}$	To determine how efficiently an organization is using its assets
Inventory turnover ratio	$\dfrac{\text{Cost of goods sold}}{\text{Inventory}}$	To determine the number of times an organization's inventory has been sold during a period
Accounts receivable turnover	$\dfrac{\text{Sales}}{\text{Accounts receivable}}$	To determine the average collection period on credit sales
3. *Profitability Ratios*		
Net profit ratio	$\dfrac{\text{Net profit}}{\text{Sales}}$	To determine the percent of profit per dollar of sales
Rate of return on assets	$\dfrac{\text{Net profit}}{\text{Total assets}}$	To determine the rate of return on assets
4. *Leverage Ratios*		
Debt-equity ratio	$\dfrac{\text{Total liabilities}}{\text{Total equities}}$	To determine the extent of an organization's debt financing

TABLE 19.3 BALANCE SHEET: ABC COMPANY, INC., DECEMBER 31, 19— (IN THOUSANDS OF DOLLARS)		

Assets

Current assets:		
Cash and short-term securities	$ 7,554	
Accounts receivable	97,182	
Inventory	359,523	
Total current assets		$464,259
Property, plant, and equipment, at cost	$224,654	
Less accumulated depreciation	67,118	
Net property, plant, and equipment		157,536
Goodwill, patents, trademarks		97,000
Total assets		$718,795

Liabilities and Stockholders' Equity

Current liabilities:		
Notes payable	$ 20,584	
Accounts payable	70,625	
Accrued expenses	8,996	
Federal income tax payable	21,365	
Total current liabilities		$121,570
Long-term liabilities		175,863
Total liabilities		$297,433
Stockholders' equity:		
Capital stock	$223,536	
Preferred stock	5,605	
Paid-in capital	124,314	
Retained earnings	67,907	
Total stockholders' equity		421,362
Total Liabilities and Stockholders' Equity		$718,795

nization is not efficiently using its assets. Current ratios will vary from industry to industry, being lower in those that are more volatile. For example, the average current ratio in the petroleum refining industry is 1.6 to 1 as compared to 3.4 to 1 for museums and art galleries.

Since slow-moving inventories could cause an organization's current ratio to overstate its liquidity, financial analysts sometimes prefer to use the **quick assets ratio** as a measure of an organization's ability to meet its financial obligations. **Quick assets** are those available to cover a sudden emergency, assets such as cash, short-term securities, and accounts receivable, which are highly liquid. This excludes inventories because they have yet to be sold. An organization's quick ratio is obtained by subtracting the value of its inventory from its current assets and dividing that figure by its current liabilities. Anytime an organization's quick assets ratio is as much as 1.0 to 1.0, it is said to be in a liquid condition. The larger the ratio is, the greater the liquidity. In the ABC balance sheet, the figures are as follows:

Quick asset ratio.
The ratio between an organization's net profit and total assets. Used to measure an organization's ability to meet its financial obligations.

Quick assets.
Highly liquid assets such as cash, short-term securities, and accounts receivable available to cover a sudden organization emergency.

$$
\begin{array}{ll}
\text{Current assets} & \$464{,}259 \\
\textit{Less:} \text{ Inventory} & \$359{,}523 \\
\text{Quick assets} & \$104{,}736
\end{array}
$$

$$
\frac{\$104{,}736_{\text{Quick assets}}}{\$121{,}570_{\text{Current liabilities}}} = \frac{0.86}{1}, \text{ or } 0.86 \text{ to } 1.
$$

As you can see, for each $1 of current liabilities, there are only 86 cents in quick assets available. The quick assets ratio reveals the protection afforded short-term creditors in cash or near-cash assets. It shows the number of dollars of liquid assets available to cover each dollar of current debt. In the present example, ABC appears to be overextended.

ACTIVITY RATIOS

The intent of **activity ratios** is to gauge how efficiently an organization is using its resources. Three measures of an organization's resource efficiency are its asset turnover ratio, inventory turnover ratio, and accounts receivable turnover ratio.

The **asset turnover ratio** indicates how efficiently an organization is using its assets. It is obtained by dividing total assets into sales. For ABC, the figures are

$$
\frac{\$908{,}785_{\text{Sales}}}{\$718{,}795_{\text{Total assets}}} = \frac{1.26}{1}, \text{ or } 1.26 \text{ to } 1.
$$

This means that each $1 invested in assets generated $1.26 in sales. Industry figures for asset turnover vary, with capital-intensive industries having small ratios.

Activity ratios.
One of several ratios used to gauge how efficiently an organization uses its resources.

Asset turnover ratio.
The ratio between an organization's sales and total assets. Used to indicate how efficiently an organization is using its assets.

TABLE 19.4 PROFIT AND LOSS STATEMENT: ABC COMPANY, INC., DECEMBER 31, 19—
(IN THOUSANDS OF DOLLARS)

Revenues

Sales	$908,785	
Other income	565	
Total revenues		$909,350

Costs and Expenses

Cost of goods sold		$602,378
Expenses:		
Selling and administrative	$201,425	
Research and development	2,203	
Depreciation	9,189	
Interest expense	18,863	
Income taxes	33,567	
Total expenses		265,247
Total costs and expenses		867,625
Net Profit		$ 41,725

If ABC were a chemical company or produced women's dresses, this ratio would be low.

The **inventory turnover ratio** measures the number of times an organization's inventory has been sold during a period. To obtain an organization's inventory turnover ratio, divide cost of goods sold by the inventory. For ABC, the figures are

$$\frac{\$602{,}378_{\text{Cost of goods sold}}}{\$359{,}523_{\text{Inventory}}} = \frac{1.68}{1}, \text{ or } 1.68 \text{ to } 1.$$

Inventory turnover ratio.

The ratio between an organization's cost of goods sold and inventory. Used to measure the number of times an organization's inventory has been sold during a period.

Thus the turnover is 1.68 times, meaning that ABC's inventory has been sold more than one and a half times in the past year. If ABC were a furniture manufacturer, this would be below the industry average of 7.3 times a year.

The **accounts receivable turnover ratio** measures an organization's collection period on credit sales. A ratio that is too high could indicate that an organization is losing sales because of a restrictive credit policy. Conversely, a ratio that is too low could indicate that it may be tying up excess capital in accounts receivable and increasing the chances of bad debts. Because of varying industry credit policies, comparing a single organization over time or several similar organizations within an industry are the only valid ways of estimating an appropriate accounts receivable turnover ratio. To obtain an organization's accounts receivable turnover ratio, divide sales by accounts receivable. For ABC, the figures are

$$\frac{\$908{,}785_{\text{Sales}}}{\$97{,}182_{\text{Accounts receivable}}} = \frac{9.35}{1}, \text{ or } 9.35 \text{ to } 1.$$

Accounts receivable turnover ratio.

The ratio between an organization's sales and accounts receivable. Used to measure an organization's collection period on credit sales.

Thus, the turnover is 9.35 times. This means that on the basis of a 360-day year, the average collection period for accounts receivable is 38.5 days (360 divided by 9.35). Any collection period more than one-third over normal selling terms (40.0 for 30-day terms) indicates slow-turning receivables.

PROFITABILITY RATIOS

Profitability is the result of numerous factors. In determining an organization's profit, the first measure typically computed is the **net profit ratio.** This ratio is a gauge of short-term profitability. It is obtained by dividing sales into net profit. In the ABC income statement, the figures are

$$\frac{\$41{,}725_{\text{Net profit}}}{\$908{,}785_{\text{Sales}}} = 0.0459 = 4.6\%.$$

Net profit ratio.

The ratio between an organization's net profit and sales. Used to measure an organization's short-term profitability.

This means that for every $1 in sales, 4.6 cents in profit are ultimately earned. During 1990, pharmaceuticals reported the highest net profit ratio (13.6 percent), followed by mining and crude-oil production (8.7 percent) and beverages (7.8 percent). The *Fortune* 500 all-industry net profit ratio median for 1990 was 4.1 percent.

A second useful profitability ratio is **rate of return on assets.** This ratio measures an organization's efficiency in generating profit. Return on assets is obtained by dividing total assets into net profit. For ABC, the figures are as follows:

Rate of return on assets.

The ratio between an organization's net profit and total assets. Used to measure an organization's efficiency in generating profit.

$$\frac{\$41,725_{\text{Net profit}}}{\$718,795_{\text{Total assets}}} = 0.0580 = 5.8\%.$$

This means that for every $1 invested in assets, 5.8 cents in profit are ultimately earned. An unacceptable rate of return on assets may be attributable to either a low asset turnover ratio or a low net profit ratio. If ABC were an aerospace manufacturer, a ratio of 5.8 percent would be lower than the 1990 *Fortune* 500 median of 6.9 percent.

LEVERAGE RATIOS

The intent of **leverage ratios** is to identify the source of an organization's capital—stockholders or outside creditors. **Leverage** refers to the increased rate of return on stockholders' equity when an investment earns a return larger than the interest rate for debt financing. The most popular measure of leverage is the **debt-equity ratio.** This ratio indicates the extent of an organization's debt financing. It is obtained by dividing total equities (liabilities plus shareholders' equity) into total liabilities. In the ABC balance sheet, the figures are

$$\frac{\$297,433_{\text{Total liabilities}}}{\$718,795_{\text{Total equities}}} = \frac{0.41}{1}, \text{ or } 0.41 \text{ to } 1.$$

This means that for every $1 in equity, 41 cents are borrowed capital. In general, total liabilities should not exceed total equities, since in such cases creditors have more at stake than owners. The average debt-equity ratio in the electronic components industry is 0.99 to 1. The average ratio in the candy and confectionery industry is 1.01 to 1.

Leverage ratio.
One of several ratios used to identify the source of an organization's capital—stockholders or outside creditors.

Leverage.
The increased rate of return on stockholders' equity when an investment earns a return larger than the interest paid for debt financing.

Debt-equity ratio.
The ratio between an organization's total liabilities and total equities. Used to indicate the extent of an organization's debt financing.

SUMMARY

Control is the process of ensuring the efficient accomplishment of organization goals. The present chapter began by defining and establishing the need for control. Next, the basic nature of the control process was described. After identifying various types of control, the chapter reviewed the characteristics of effective control. A variety of control methods were then examined. Finally, the value of financial ratios for interpreting an organization's performance was illustrated.

Learning Objective 1: Explain why control is essential.
Control is essential for determining how well an organization is performing, whether improvement is needed, where it should occur, how much is needed, and how quickly.

Learning Objective 2: Describe the control process.
The control process involves three general steps: setting standards, measuring and evaluating performance, and taking appropriate action.

Learning Objective 3: Identify three kinds of standards.
Standards can be classified as historical (those based on past experience), comparative (those based on the experience of others), or engineering (those based on technical analyses).

Learning Objective 4: Detail the three points at which an organization's performance can be monitored.
The three points at which an organization's performance can be monitored and,

thus, controlled, are before, during, and after an activity is completed. These three points correspond to the use of precontrols, concurrent controls, and postaction controls.

Learning Objective 5: Explain what is meant by a *cybernetic system*.
A cybernetic system is a system that is self-regulating.

Learning Objective 6: List the characteristics of effective controls.
Effective controls are characteristically cost effective, acceptable to those to whom they apply, appropriate, strategic, and reliable and objective.

Learning Objective 7: Recount various methods of control.
Control methods may be classified according to their frequency of use. Those that are used *constantly* are self-control, group control, and policies/procedures/rules. Control methods used *periodically* are information systems, external audits, and budgets. Finally, three control methods used *occasionally* are special reports, personal observation, and project controls.

Learning Objective 8: Explain management by exception.
Management by exception is the practice of concentrating on significant deviations from planned performance.

Learning Objective 9: Describe a Gantt chart.
A Gantt chart is a project control method that depicts the occurrence of various activities across time.

Learning Objective 10: Describe PERT.
PERT (Program Evaluation and Review Technique) is a control method that shows the interrelationships among the events and activities that comprise a project.

Learning Objective 11: Explain the basic types of financial ratios.
The four basic types of financial ratios, the formulas used to obtain them, and their purposes are presented in Table 19.2.

Learning Objective 12: Characterize break-even analysis.
Break-even analysis is a method for visualizing the relationship between costs and revenues.

KEY TERMS

accounts receivable turnover ratio 583

activity ratios 582

asset turnover ratio 582

break-even analysis 575

break-even point 579

comparative standard 561

concurrent controls 565

control 560

critical path 577

current ratio 580

cybernetic system 564

debt-equity ratio 584

engineering standard 562

financial ratios 579

fixed costs 578

Gantt chart (bar chart) 575

historical standard 561

information system 571

inventory turnover ratio 583

leverage 584

leverage ratios 584

liquidity 580

management by exception 569

net profit ratio 583

network 576

postaction controls 566

precontrols 564

program evaluation and review technique (PERT) 575

quick asset ratio 581

quick assets 581

rate of return on assets 583

slack time 578

standard 561

total costs 578

total revenues 578

variable costs 578

REVIEW AND DISCUSSION QUESTIONS

1. According to Robert Appleby, former chairman of Black & Decker (United Kingdom), "You only need control when you haven't got it."[10] Explain what he means by this statement.

2. Imagine that you are the CEO of the Coca-Cola Company. You are determined to maintain Coke's worldwide leadership position in the soft-drink industry and realize that strong controls, including personal observation, are a must if you are to do so. Given that Coca-Cola operates in some 155 countries and the South Pole, explain how you would, to borrow William F. Schmied's phrase, "go out there and thump the watermelon."

3. Assume you are a university professor. You teach a "Principles of Management" course with an enrollment of nearly 400 students. The course is taught in a large lecture hall with exactly 400 seats. Design a control system to ensure that there is no cheating on the final exam. Remember the characteristics of effective controls.

4. According to former ITT CEO Harold Geneen, "Any significant variation [from organization expectations] is a signal for action." Geneen advises, "If one of your products is selling above expectations, you may want to increase production immediately. If . . . one or more of your products is not selling as well as expected, then you may have to find some way to get those sales up or begin to reduce the costs and expenses involved, and the sooner the better."[11] This advice presents a good example of management by exception, emphasizing the need to be concerned with both positive and negative deviations from standards.

   You are a middle manager in a medium-size manufacturing firm. Your subordinates feel control only highlights negative outcomes. Explain why effective control spotlights both positive and negative results.

5. Former Black & Decker chairman Robert Appleby is considered one of the ablest managers in Great Britain. He believes in strong but subtle control, as well as the speediest possible response to any evidence of trouble. Simply stated, he believes in management by exception. Cite examples from your own experience demonstrating the merits of management by exception.

6. Explain how you could use the three-step control process to channel your academic performance.

7. Draw a Gantt chart depicting how you would either paint your home or prepare for a formal dinner. Your objective is to do whichever task you choose in the fastest possible time. Assume that you have two competent assistants.

8. As an aerospace engineer, you are responsible for developing a new airplane. The following tasks must be accomplished:

   1. Obtain program go-ahead.
   2. Initiate engine procurement.
   3. Complete fuselage drawings.
   4. Award tail assembly subcontract.
   5. Award wings subcontract.
   6. Complete fuselage manufacture.
   7. Complete assembly of fuselage-engine.
   8. Receive tail assembly from subcontractor.
   9. Receive wings from subcontractor.
   10. Unveil aircraft.

   Draw a PERT network showing how these tasks would be accomplished.

9. You've just finished your first year as an independent businessperson. Your net profit was $50,000 on $1,000,000 in sales. (a) What was your net profit ratio? (b) What does this ratio mean?

10. Suppose a business has two investments: (1) $10,000 investment in assets with $2,000 net profit, and (2) $10,000 investment in assets with $2,500 net profit. (a) What is the rate of return on assets for each investment? (b) What do these figures mean?

THE MANAGEMENT EXPERIENCE   SELF-CONTROL QUESTIONNAIRE

As suggested in the accompanying discussion, no organization could exist long unless its employees exerted the self-control required to perform their assigned tasks. Take a few moments to assess your own self-control tendencies. Respond to the following items by circling the number corresponding to the description (that is, "describes me very well," "describes me well," and so on) that you believe best reflects your position regarding each of the statements included. Some may seem a bit redundant to you. Try not to let this bother you. Respond to each one.

Describes Me:	Very Well	Well	Some-what	Not Very Well	Not at All
1. I try to keep track of how well I'm doing while I work.	5	4	3	2	1
2. I often use reminders to help me remember things I need to do.	5	4	3	2	1
3. I like to work toward specific goals I set for myself.	5	4	3	2	1
4. After I perform well on an activity, I feel good about myself.	5	4	3	2	1
5. I often practice important tasks before I actually do them.	5	4	3	2	1
6. I usually am aware of how I am performing on an activity.	5	4	3	2	1

Continued on next page.

Describes Me:	Very Well	Well	Some-what	Not Very Well	Not at All
7. I try to arrange my work area in a way that helps me positively focus my attention on my work.	5	4	3	2	1
8. I establish personal goals for myself.	5	4	3	2	1
9. When I have successfully completed a task, I often reward myself with something I like.	5	4	3	2	1
10. I like to go over an important activity before I actually perform it.	5	4	3	2	1
11. I keep track of my progress on projects I'm working on.	5	4	3	2	1
12. I try to surround myself with objects and people that bring out my desirable behaviors.	5	4	3	2	1
13. I like to set task goals for my performance.	5	4	3	2	1
14. When I do an assignment especially well, I like to treat myself to something or an activity I enjoy.	5	4	3	2	1

Continued on next page.

Describes Me:	Very Well	Well	Some-what	Not Very Well	Not at All
15. I often rehearse my plan for dealing with a challenge before I actually face the challenge.	5	4	3	2	1

Scoring:
To compute your "self-control" score, total the values assigned to your individual item responses. Your score could range from 15 to 75.

What your score means:
A score of 15 to 22 indicates a *very low* level of self-control.
A score of 23 to 37 indicates a *low* level of self-control.
A score of 38 to 52 indicates a *moderate* level of self-control.
A score of 53 to 67 indicates a *high* level of self-control.
A score of 68 to 75 indicates a *very high* level of self-control.

Source: Adapted with permission from Charles C. Manz, *The Art of Self-Leadership* (Englewood Cliffs, N.J.: Prentice-Hall, 1983), 16–19.

CASE 19.1   HONEST EMPLOYEES

Recently a fast-food chain that was concerned about robberies installed television cameras in some of its stores on an experimental basis. They were focused on the cash register. The chain explained the purpose of the experiment to its employees and said it did not know if it could justify the expense for the full chain.

A few months after the installation, one of the accountants pointed out an interesting phenomenon. The accountant had compared the cash register receipts before and after the installation of the cameras and found that the number of small sales rung up after the installation was substantially higher than before. "It seems to me that some of the employees were taking some sales as 'tips' before we installed the cameras. Now they think we're watching. This should help profitability."

At the same time, the human resource manager began to get complaints about "Big Brother" in the exit interviews of some of the employees who quit. He followed this up and found that a number of employees were really upset because they felt they were being watched by the bosses.

The security specialist pointed out that not one of the outlets with the cameras had been robbed. The stores had prominent signs warning thieves about the cameras.

The cameras are very expensive. The additional cash in the cash registers covered 10 percent of the cost of the cameras. At the stores without the cameras (used as "control" stores) there was one robbery. The total "savings" from additional cash and "lack of robberies" equaled 25 percent of the cost of the cameras.

Problem

You are the manager in charge of this company. Since the 3-month trial period is over, should you remove the cameras (they are leased)? Continue the experiment another 3 months? Expand the experiment? Explain your answer.

CASE 19.2   AJAX FOUNDRY

Ajax Foundry has a large plant in Arizona. Each employee's job has been analyzed using time and motion studies. Each employee, therefore, is responsible for a certain amount of output. The company also uses a common recording and control device: the time clock.

On one particular job, some of the employees, who had been selected on the basis of their skill, were getting the job done an hour and a half before quitting time. All but one of these employees would leave early. That employee would stay around and punch the whole section out on the time clock at the end of the shift. This "job" was rotated among the members of the section.

One day Paul Richards, the plant manager, caught one employee punching out all the employees in the section. The next day he met with them. He reminded them that according to company rules, this action justified firing them all. He explained that in this case he would just warn them that if it happened again he would have to fire them. At this point John Sikes, the informal group leader, spoke up: "Look, Mr. Richards, we do good work. We do all our work. Why not put this job on a 'get the work out, then go home' basis?"

Richards said, "I wish I could do that, but as you know, you guys are unionized. If I put the job on that basis, the senior men could apply for your jobs and bump you from them. The contract says they have that right, and you know this would happen because they would want to leave early. Frankly, many of the senior men are not as skilled as you guys, and product quality would drop."

The employees continued to work fast. But since they had to stay around, they tended to wander around the plant, distracting other workers, reducing their productivity, and lowering their morale ("those guys must have cushy jobs"). And as they started messing around, the accident rate increased by 5 percent.

Problem

You are the assistant plant manager. What recommendations would you give Richards on this control and morale problem?

NOTES

[1] Norbert Wiener, *Cybernetics, or Control and Communication in the Animal and the Machine* (Cambridge: MIT Press, 1949).

[2] Quoted in Jeffrey Zygmont, "A Detail for Retail," *Sky* 21 (February 1992): 54.

[3] Ricardo Semler, "Managing without Managers," *Harvard Business Review* 67 (September–October 1989): 83–84.

[4] Joseph Levy quoted in John Greenwald, "The Colossus That Works," *Time*, July 11, 1983, 46.

[5] Bill Saporito, "Campbell Soup Gets Piping Hot," *Fortune*, September 9, 1991, 144.

[6] Quoted in George H. Labovitz, "Want to Find Out What's Going On? Take a Walk," *Wall Street Journal*, December 20, 1982, 16. Also see Thomas F. O'Boyle and Carol Hymowitz, "Keeping in Touch: More Corporate Chiefs Seek Direct Contact with Staff and Customers," *Wall Street Journal*, February 27, 1985, 1, 20.

[7] Quoted in Lester Brooks, "William F. Schmied: President & Chief Operating Officer, The Singer Company," *Sky* 13 (February 1984): 56.

[8] Quoted in Donna Dupuy, "Gene Milner: Chairman of the Board & CEO, Lanier Business Products, Inc.," *Sky* 10 (November 1981): 61.

[9] This section draws on Harry F. Evarts, *Introduction to PERT* (Boston: Allyn and Bacon, 1964), 1–44.

[10] Quoted in Paul Johnson, "Robert Appleby—The King of D.I.Y.," *Director* 37 (February 1984): 56.

[11] Harold S. Geneen, "The Case for Managing by the Numbers," *Fortune*, October 1, 1984, 80.

ENHANCEMENT MODULE 2: CONTROLLING YOUR TIME

The most valuable resource that managers have is their own time. All too easily managers find themselves in a state of "timelock." This occurs when demands on a manager become so overwhelming that it feels impossible to wring one more second out of a crowded day. This enhancement module is intended to help you improve your on-the-job time control. The guidelines presented can also be applied to your off-the-job life.

To more effectively control your time you must determine how you use your time, analyze how you use your time, set priorities and develop a time-use strategy, and implement an effective time plan.

STEP 1: DETERMINING HOW YOU USE YOUR TIME

The first step toward better control of your time is to learn how you use your time now. Perhaps the easiest approach for this purpose is to keep a *time log*. Table EM 2.1 provides an example of a partial time log for a marketing supervisor. For your time log to be effective, keep the following hints in mind:

- Carry your log with you at all times.
- Note your comments immediately so you don't forget details.
- Make your entries short and specific.
- Record the *smallest* uses of time, *especially interruptions*.
- Subdivide long periods. For example, a meeting may cover three areas: finance, accounting, and marketing.

    Having logged your activities, you are ready for Step 2.

STEP 2: ANALYZING HOW YOU USE YOUR TIME

Time analysis can be done in several ways. The first way is to total the amount of time you spend in various activities, such as personal matters, telephone calls, conferences, and individual discussions. Then you can examine how you allocate your time to different activities. This includes a study of the time taken up by interruptions.

Next, your time can be divided into four categories: *creative, preparatory, productive,* and *overhead:*

- *Creative time* is devoted to planning future activities, new product ideas, and so forth.
- *Preparatory time* is spent in preparatory activities, such as gathering facts for a conference.
- *Productive time* is spent actually doing your job.
- *Overhead time* is spent on correspondence, reports, paperwork, public relations, and so forth.

| TABLE EM 2.1 | PARTIAL TIME LOG FOR A MARKETING SUPERVISOR |

Name	Jim Azarian				Title	Marketing Supervisor	
Date	May 2, 1992				Company	Buford Manufacturing	

Start	End	Time Elapsed	Activity	With Whom	Initiation	Action Taken/Notes
08:00	09:00	60	M	Region 1 Sales Reps	S	Discussed entry of Howard Brothers Region 1 market. Action; discuss with boss our reaction.
09:00	09:05	5	TP	Gatlin Wholesale	S	Set up appointment.
09:05	09:50	45	T,R	John Gunter (Sales Rep)	S	While on way, Gunter briefed me on Howard Brothers situation.
09:50	10:00	10	W,T	Gunter	—	Waiting for appointment.
10:00	10:30	30	C	Gunter; Tom Jackson (Buyer)	S	Discussed Howard Brothers market entry with buyer and how we should respond.

Initiation	Activity	Functional Code
O = Other	I = Individual discussion	P = Personal activities
S = Self	C = Conference	F = Financial/accounting problems
	TP = Telephone	M = Marketing/customer relations/logistics
	W = Writing correspondence, reports	E = External/public relations
	R = Reading	O = Operating problems
	T = Thinking	PP = Human resource problems

In examining how you allocate your time, you should ask yourself the following questions:

1. Should anyone be doing this activity at all? Does it serve any purpose? For example, suppose you always start the day by meeting with three assistants. Is this conference really needed? What purpose does it serve? Maybe it should be eliminated.

2. If the activity needs to be done, should I be doing it? If a subordinate can do it equally well (with a little experience), then you should not be doing it. If you decide to delegate the activity, do not oversupervise.

3. If I should do it myself, can it be done in less time? How?

4. Do I keep to my time schedule, or do I waste subordinates' time?

5. Do I keep a pile of overhead materials (for example, correspondence to be signed) at my elbow to be done while waiting for telephone calls or visitors to show up?

STEP 3: SETTING PRIORITIES AND DEVELOPING A TIME-USE STRATEGY

Step 2 should help you realize how you spend your time. Step 3, in which you decide what to do with your time, is much more difficult.

Your total available time can be divided into several categories: work, pleasure, sleep, personal hygiene, self-development, and travel. You must set personal priorities among these categories. Some people become workaholics and eliminate the pleasure and self-development categories and cut back on their sleep. Only you can set your own priorities, and your allocation of time is a reflection of your life-style, beliefs, and attitudes.

But how do you set priorities within the work category? The story is told of a top executive who asked a consultant to make his time use more efficient. He paid the consultant $25,000 for the following advice: At the end of each day, make a list of the important things you did not get done today. The next day use it as your job list. Do the jobs in order of their importance, starting with those that are the most important or difficult.

To take advantage of this advice, you must be able to set your priorities—to come up with a job list and then rank the jobs in order of importance. The list should be shorter as a result of Step 2. Still, if six items are on the list, which three should you do first? It is frequently pointed out that most people fulfill 80 percent of their accomplishments during the vital 20 percent of their activities. Thus, the importance of setting priorities should be evident.

STEP 4: IMPLEMENTING AN EFFECTIVE TIME PLAN

The most basic aspect of implementing an effective time plan is developing a time budget. This should be easier if you follow these suggestions:

- Assign long periods of uninterrupted time to major tasks (productive time). Control interruptions during crucial periods by not accepting either visitors or telephone calls.

- Block out time for creative planning, preparation, and overhead activities. Creative planning and preparation time should be used in a quiet place away from your desk, if possible.

- Group together related kinds of work, including telephone calls, to save starting and stopping time.

- Schedule top-priority projects early in the week.

- Schedule decision dates to reduce procrastination.

- Reserve a certain amount of time for unanticipated crises and events over which you have no control (for example, conferences initiated by others).

- Schedule your least interesting jobs at your peak energy periods so they will get done.

- Postpone beginning shorter projects until you have completed longer ones. This will motivate you to complete the longer ones.

- Make better use of meeting time. Prepare an agenda with time allocated to each topic. Schedule meetings so that they will be naturally cut off by lunch or the end of the workday.

The above suggestions constitute a strategy for controlling your time that can work on the job, in school, or during leisure pursuits. Managers who control their time generally get more done and are more effective.

CHAPTER 20

LEARNING OBJECTIVES

Upon completing this chapter, you should be able to:

- Discuss the information systems requirements of an organization's different hierarchical levels .

- Describe the different categories of software systems found in organizations.

- List the different hardware components in an information system.

- Compare the characteristics of the systems development life cycle with those of prototyping.

n 1988, after tripling its assets during several years of record growth through expansion and acquisition, Ryder Systems Inc. found its momentum stopped by the recession. While many executives would sell off recent acquisitions, chairman M. Anthony Burns refused to take short-term actions and abandon the company's long-term goal of dominance in truck leasing, aircraft maintenance, and school bus operation. Greatly reduced profits in 1990 and 1991 have resulted in pressure to cut costs, but management is trying to do so without compromising long-term operations.

One of the key areas requiring ongoing investment is information services. While many companies have gone overboard with state-of-the-art technologies, Ryder has kept its eye on the need to reduce costs, add value to other services, and promote quality. It has a solid technological base and can pursue what CIO Dennis Klinger calls the practical, blue-collar applications. Ryder is investing in its own software development in many areas, believing that this will give it an edge over competitors that have fewer resources available within their organizations.

In its truck leasing operations, Ryder not only leases vehicles but also maintains customer-owned vehicles and warehouses and distributes goods for customers. To demonstrate its efficiency, Ryder has developed software for high-end PCs that will analyze a cus-

INFORMATION SYSTEMS FOR MANAGING

tomer's operations and show how to manage them better, using high-resolution graphics to demonstrate the savings. Many customers have said that this technological advantage over its competitors has been a key factor in their decision to use Ryder.

In the car-carrier industry, the one absolutely unacceptable error is car damage—car dealers have a very difficult time selling damaged new cars. In 1991 Ryder's damage claim payments totalled $10 million. Ryder's Statistical Process Control (SPC) program now tracks all shipments, recording any damage (including the location of the car on the carrier), and analyzes the data to determine how to avoid future damage. Since it implemented SPC, Ryder's damage rate has dropped to 1 percent, compared to 3 percent for the industry as a whole.

Through sensible, innovative use of information services, Ryder is hoping to lessen the impact of the recession and maintain its dominance when the economy turns around. In this chapter we will discuss these and other aspects of information systems.

Source: Pete Engardio and Eric Schine, "Suddenly Ryder's Engine is Sputtering," *Business Week,* June 19, 1989, 56; and Jon Pepper, "On the Road to a Rebound," *Information Week,* September 2, 1991, 32.

The contributions of M. Khris McAlister and Julio C. Rivera, University of Alabama at Birmingham, in the preparation of this chapter are gratefully acknowledged.

Market forces, technology, etc., are inducing companies to move and innovate with light-ning-fast speed, and to make operational and strategic decisions with lightning-fast speed.[1]

The foregoing quotation from Tom Peters dramatizes the importance that is being placed on "information" in shaping organizations and the way in which they are managed. The importance of information in popular culture as well is revealed in television advertisements showing managers anxious about not receiving the information they need to make necessary decisions. In a slight twist on this theme, one advertiser exclaims how wonderful life must be in Phoenix since all departments of the city government have been "linked together." These illustrations support Peters's contention that information is or soon will become the central focus of all organizations.

Today's organizations operate in environments characterized by requirements of speed, innovation, cost competitiveness, and quality emphasis. Marketplace strategies are directed toward competing on the basis of cost, product differentiation, or customer focus. **Information systems (IS),** through their many and varied applications, are a major resource for competing in this environment. In fact, many organizations are using IS technology as the basis for defining the terms of their particular strategic initiatives. In other organizations, IS are used for maintaining operational efficiency and effectiveness.

In a more general sense, the topic of IS is about decision making, because information provides the basis for decisions, and the purpose of an IS is to provide information that will foster high-quality decisions. Indeed, when managers from all hierarchical levels and functional perspectives are questioned concerning the nature of their jobs, a typical thread in their responses is that they make decisions directed toward achieving organization goals based on available information.

Information system (IS).

A system of people, computer hardware, software, and procedures to provide an organization with required information.

THE LINK BETWEEN INFORMATION SYSTEMS AND DECISION MAKING

In the late 1940s, Herbert A. Simon popularized the notion that management was primarily a decision-making process (see Chapter 7). Simon later received the Nobel Prize in economics for his work on managerial decision making. Simon argued convincingly that all managerial activities involve a conscious or unconscious selection of particular actions. In many cases, the selection process consists simply of an established reflex action or habit. In other cases, the selection is itself the product of a complex chain of activities. Further, Simon suggested that for any decision there are a multitude of possible alternative actions, any of which may be selected. By some process, the numerous alternatives are narrowed down to the one that is, in fact, selected.[2]

Essential to this process of narrowing down alternatives is information—which is provided by an organization's IS. The quality of the information provided depends on the manner in which data are gathered, coded, stored, processed, and

Dun and Bradstreet's European customers wanted to receive information at a level appropriate for the risk associated with a given business decision. In response, Dun and Bradstreet has introduced "A La Carte" service throughout Europe, providing information services in an adaptable, flexible format that facilitates different kinds of decision making.

presented—the various elements of an IS. These elements are valuable only if they relate to effective decision making. Of course, the quality of decision making depends also on the way information is used after it is provided by an IS. Accordingly, one way to understand the management of organizations is to understand first the nature of decision making and second the manner in which an organization's IS work.

Figure 20.1 indicates the relationship between an organization's IS and decision making. Decision making is supported by IS, which receives their raw materials from an organization's internal and external environments. From within an organization, IS gather data about marketing, finance, production, and human resource matters; and from outside an organization, it gathers data about governmental, technological, social, and economic factors. These data are integrated in various forms and reporting formats to support managerial decisions.

DEFINING INFORMATION SYSTEMS

For the present discussion we propose the following alternate definition of an IS: an integrated user/machine system (usually computerized) for providing information to support decision making in an organization.

The key elements of this definition are:

- An integrated user/machine system
- For providing information

FIGURE 20.1 THE RELATIONSHIP BETWEEN AN ORGANIZATION'S IS AND DECISION MAKING

Information Sources

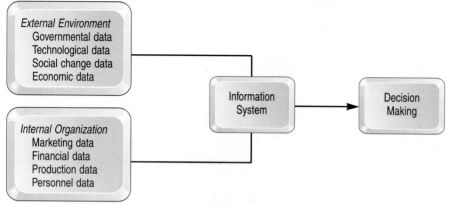

- To support decision making
- In an organization

An IS utilizes:

- Computer hardware and software
- Manual procedures
- Models for analysis
- A data base

INFORMATION NEEDS OF AN ORGANIZATION

If one tried to visualize the hierarchy of an organization in terms of the activities performed and the information related to those activities, the result might look similar to Figure 20.2.

At the *operational control level,* IS process transactions as they occur to update internal records and provides reports and documents. For example, today the details of each sale in a fast-food restaurant are captured at a cash register, customers are provided with a receipt of the transaction, food preparers are provided with the details of customer orders (usually on a CRT screen), and internal records are adjusted to reflect the order (inventory records, daily sales records, and so forth are changed). At the end of the day, summary records are produced and, in some cases, orders are electronically transmitted to suppliers to replenish inventories.

At the *management control level,* managers receive results from the operational control level (collected by transaction processing systems or from operations managers), summarize them, and pass them on to top managers who establish goals to be transformed into plans. In addition, managers also access data from internal and external sources to support top management and their own planning and control activities.

At the *strategic control level,* strategic-planning and decision-making information is required. This information comes from internal and external sources and is

FIGURE 20.2   INFORMATION NEEDS OF AN ORGANIZATION

— Strategic Controlling Information

— Management Control Information

— Operational Control Information

Source: Based on Robert V. Head, "Management Information Systems: A Critical Appraisal," *Datamation* 13 (May 1967): 22–27.

used to gauge an organization's strengths and weaknesses, as well as market opportunities and threats.

In actual practice, the information requirements of these three hierarchical levels are somewhat fuzzy. An alternative picture of the information activity at a specific level may be provided by looking at two types of supporting information systems: those that support specific hierarchical levels and those that support a whole organization (see Figure 20.3).

INFORMATION SYSTEMS THAT SUPPORT SPECIFIC HIERARCHICAL LEVELS

If we start at the bottom level (see Figure 20.3), we find data concerning the thousands (and in many cases, hundreds of thousands) of events critical to an organization. These **transaction-processing and reporting systems** are the foundation IS applications for an organization's operations. Events such as a sale, a shipment, an order, an employee transfer, an employee marriage, issue of a paycheck, or an employee dismissal all require that specific data be gathered, stored, processed, and retrieved. In the history of using computers to provide the solutions for organization problems, it is in the area of transaction processing that computers had their first significant impact. Even today, in most organizations the largest single use of computing resources is for transaction processing. The data gathered become the raw material to supply many of the IS that support first-line, middle, and top management.

The middle level in Figure 20.3 highlights **decision support systems (DSS)** and **group decision support systems (GDSS).** Although each of these applications may be used at other levels, the primary impact of these systems has been at the management control level. DSS are usually interactive systems designed to support the decision-making activities of a particular manager. These systems permit a manager to apply models to data to help identify unstructured and semistructured problems. Moreover, DSS typically are designed to support all phases of decision making (intelligence, design, choice, and implementation). Although there are large system equivalents, probably the most frequently used DSS is a microcomputer spreadsheet program such as Lotus or Excel. Users can develop, for example, multiple versions of budgets under different assumptions. A final budget is selected by the appropriate decision makers. The key characteristic of all DSS is that they are designed to aid but not make decisions for managers.

GDSS are a recent but significant part of DSS. As noted, DSS tend to focus on individual managers. In reality, many of the decision processes are group (or meeting) based. GDSS assist the typical group work in idea generation, critical

Transaction-processing and reporting system.
An information system that gathers, stores, and processes transaction data.

Decision support system (DSS).
A system for providing information to help managers with new, unstructured decision making.

Group decision support system (GDSS).
An information system that supports collective decision making by managers working as a group on unstructured problems.

Independent retailers benefit from the Fleming Companies' expertise in retail electronics and information systems. Fleming is a service-oriented wholesaler that offers a package of electronic services that includes point-of-sale scanning support and computer applications for better planning and control. Inventory control and retail pricing are among the transactions that occur at the operational level through information systems technology.

evaluation, and selection. Experience has indicated that GDSS make meetings more productive.[3]

At the apex of Figure 20.3 are **executive information systems (EIS).** These systems are designed for hands-on use by top managers and provide both strategic and management control information. Typically, these systems are designed to focus on key success factors and use graphics, communications, and data storage coupled with a simple, friendly (one-finger-controlled) interface for the top management user. Although many organizations use EIS, the most famous is one of the first systems noted in the literature: the management information and decision support system at Lockheed-Georgia. Lockheed top and middle managers can retrieve various of key facts via microcomputers in their offices connected to a large computer system.[4]

INFORMATION SYSTEMS THAT SUPPORT A WHOLE ORGANIZATION

The preceding view, however, meaningful, does not capture the full penetration of information systems into an organization's fabric. Some IS span more than one level. Figure 20.3 identifies four categories of systems: office automation systems, manufacturing automation systems, expert systems, and strategic systems.

One of the most common IS that support all levels of an organization are **office automation systems.** Under this umbrella term are a number of different applications. The most common, of course, are word processing and desktop publishing. Electronic filing, copying, document storing, electronic calendaring, and electronic mailing are additional applications commonly categorized as office automation systems. These systems have greatly increased the productivity and effectiveness of office and white-collar employees.

In a factory or manufacturing environment, **manufacturing automation systems** have been used primarily at the lower and middle management levels, but they have significantly affected whole organizations. Such systems support an or-

Executive information system (EIS).
A system designed to meet the information needs of top managers through direct hands-on contact with a computer.

Office automation system.
An information system that supports the varied activities and work requirements of office and white-collar employees.

Manufacturing automation system.
An information system that supports manufacturing scheduling and planning activities as well as the automation of machines and product transportation in an organization.

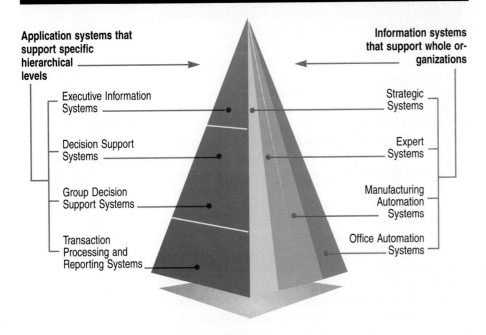

FIGURE 20.3   INFORMATION SYSTEMS SUPPORTING AN ORGANIZATION

Application systems that support specific hierarchical levels

Information systems that support whole organizations

Executive Information Systems

Decision Support Systems

Group Decision Support Systems

Transaction Processing and Reporting Systems

Strategic Systems

Expert Systems

Manufacturing Automation Systems

Office Automation Systems

ganization's manufacturing scheduling and planning activities (MRP systems), as well as the automation of machines and product transportation (flexible manufacturing systems). Some newer installations combine these two areas, allowing the use of computer software to schedule and plan the actual parts manufacturing. Caterpillar uses flexible manufacturing systems to reduce the parts it maintains in inventory (and the corresponding amount of money invested in parts) and still make sure that parts are available when a dealer places an order.

Manufacturing automation systems are a vital to the operations of Delco Electronics, division of GM Hughes a leading supplier of automotive instrumentation and air controls. In this picture, computerized packaging of air control modules ensures precise product tracking in the assembly process.

It is interesting to note that although these systems have a direct impact on the duties of middle and first-line managers, they typically provide a strategic advantage for an organization. For example, through computer support, orders are scheduled and products manufactured. The advantage lies in faster order filing for customers and more consistent quality. In addition, organizations do not have to make large production runs and thus can keep their in-process and final goods inventories at lower levels. IS technology permits the use of computer-controlled robots in the manufacturing cycle for potentially dangerous jobs.

Efforts to make computers perform the duties and the actions of people typically are called **artificial intelligence.** One of the first applications of these efforts to real-world problems is through **expert systems.** Expert systems focus on building systems that incorporate the same decision-making logic as people. For example, Digital Equipment Company uses an expert system called XCON to review sales orders and design the layout of each computer order it analyzes. The impact of XCON is that Digital can ship components directly to customer sites for final assembly, eliminating the need for final assembly facilities. As another example, American Express, uses an expert system to assist its credit authorization staff in sorting through data from up to 13 data bases. Because American Express must review cardholder credit history and authorize the purchase each time a cardholder makes a large purchase, response time is essential. With an expert system, the credit review and authorization take only seconds. These systems permit an expert's knowledge to be available in many locations at once—to assist an inexperienced or less knowledgeable employee, to train employees, or to provide more consistent decision making. Because of excessive development costs, expert systems technology typically is applied to repetitive, high-value decisions in a narrowly defined area. With the environmental pressures on many organizations to do more with less, expert systems will be a significant benefit and will gain more widespread application in the future.[5]

Although many of the information systems mentioned above can have strategic importance, it is appropriate to treat strategic systems differently because of their importance to organizations. A classic example of a strategic system is the SABRE reservation system. American Airlines developed the SABRE system at great expense to handle customer reservations. In addition to handling American's own reservation needs, SABRE also is used in travel agencies to facilitate their placing flights on American. American, for a fee, also allowed other airlines to use SABRE. Because American controlled the software, it also controlled the order of possible flights for travel agent consideration. Because of SABRE's sheer size and expense, American has an advantage over many of its competitors. In addition, for those competing airlines that list flights on SABRE, American collects a fee for each reservation—making additional revenue while driving its competitors' costs higher.[6]

> **Artificial intelligence.**
> Efforts to make computers perform the duties and the actions of people.
>
> **Expert system (ES).**
> An information system that uses special symbolic reasoning to solve problems.

SYSTEMS INFRASTRUCTURE

Information systems are supported by *computer hardware* and *telecommunications systems.* Without these systems, software applications could not function. The following sections describe various hardware and telecommunications basics.

Computer hardware is a broad term to denote the physical components of a computer system. The four primary categories of computer system components are a **central processing unit (CPU),** *input devices, output devices,* and *auxiliary storage.* These are graphically depicted in Figure 20.4.

> **Computer hardware.**
> A broad term to denote the physical components of a computer system.
>
> **Central processing unit (CPU).**
> The control, arithmetic, and logic unit of a computer.

Behind most successful entrepreneurs with vision stands a technical partner who turned vision into reality. The success of Cannondale Corp., a $40 million manufacturer of high-priced bicycles for cycling devotees, is built on such a partnership.

When Cannondale, based in Georgetown, Conn., first went into business in 1971, it had "terrible cash-flow problems," recalled founder Joseph S. Montgomery. "We were going broke because I couldn't see any more than five [bicycle] stores a day. The cost of the sale was just too high."

Montgomery envisioned a technological solution to his financial problem. A lean telemarketing sales force, backed by an IS that provided salespeople with customer information, would be able to pitch his bicycles to hundreds of stores at little cost.

His first attempt at creating the IS was a fiasco. The Burroughs IS he installed repeatedly crashed, wiping out weeks of work. Then Montgomery lucked out. He returned the computer to Burroughs and called IBM who brought in John Drahzal, an independent systems programmer, to set up a new system. When Drahzal got the job done in two weeks, Montgomery knew he had found someone with the right mix of technical skills and business moxie to help him build his company. It took a good deal of courting and persuasion—and ultimately, the purchase of half of Drahzal's business—before Montgomery managed to convince Drahzal to join his company. But it appears to have been worth it; the system set up by Drahzal helped lift Cannondale off the ground. In fact, it performed so well that the company got by with only two salespeople until it reached the $6 million sales mark.

Since then, when Cannondale's sales staff boot up their computers in the morning, the IS provides them with a list of dealers to call and indicates what should be discussed. The IS, said Drahzal, provides "everything you'd want to know about the dealer"—previous orders, credit history, notes from earlier discussions, and any items ordered in previous years but not yet ordered this year. The system also reminds sales staff of any specials Cannondale is offering.

Still, it takes more than a savvy sales force to win against giant competitors like the Schwinn Bicycle Co. So, since 1975, the IS has been expanded so that it can pinpoint lucrative markets and secure dealer loyalty. For example, Cannondale uses regional demographic data base and analysis tools from Rand McNally & Co. of Skokie, Ill., to scour Cannondale's sales data and pinpoint where to focus marketing efforts.

"Lots of Midwestern mid-size cities are neglected [by sales forces] because nobody knows who is there. We do, and we're getting them," said Drahzal.

The IS aids dealers by helping them calculate which models and colors to carry. It also helps them take advantage of Cannondale's discount programs. It's a win-win situation, according to Drahzal. The dealers get the best prices when they order in advance of the cycling season, and by doing so they ensure they will have the bicycles they need in stock.

And Cannondale's manufacturing operation in Bedford, Pa., knows which models to build. Plant managers can plan their runs, perform manufacturing cost analyses, and provide gross profit-margin guarantees to both Cannondale and its clients. Still, Montgomery doesn't believe information technology reduces costs. "We have not been successful in that regard. What IS does is allow you to grow. It removes the hurdles and bridges the pitfalls of growth, because it allows you to control the growth."

Source: Allen E. Alter, "Compact Competitors," *CIO*, July 1989, p.49. Reprinted through the courtesy of *CIO Magazine* © 1989 CIO Publishing.

Microcomputers have been a part of Southwestern Electric Power Company's continuing investment in new equipment to increase efficiency. In East Texas, Welsh Power Plant employees used their new computerized maintenance system to dramatically improve scheduling and performance of preventative maintenance at the company's largest generating facility.

A CPU consists of electronic components that interpret and execute computer program's instructions. In addition, a CPU works in conjunction with MAIN Memory, where programs and data must be stored before a CPU can execute a computer program. Input devices are those components used to enter data directly into a computer. Typical input devices include keyboards, page scanners, optical scanning devices, and magnetic ink character readers. Output device produce human-usable symbols (words, pictures, graphs, and so forth). These components include display screens (CRT or LCD), printers, audio devices, and plotters. **Auxiliary storage** devices (hard and floppy magnetic disk drives, magnetic tapes, and optical disks) hold data and programs in a form quickly usable by a computer but directly accessible when required.

Although these basic components are consistent for all computers, it is ap-

Auxiliary storage. Devices such as magnetic disk and tape and optical disks that store data and programs for later processing.

FIGURE 20.4 COMPUTER HARDWARE

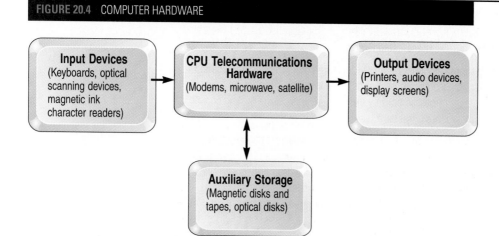

CLOSE-UP: SOCIAL RESPONSIBILITY   PIRATING SOFTWARE

Almost everyone who has ever used a personal computer has faced the legal and ethical dilemma of whether to copy copyrighted software. The specific code in a software program is classified as "intellectual property" and, when documented and registered, is subject to the copyright protection laws. In addition, computer users, because of their independence, must personally decide whether or not to pirate software.

From a software developer's perspective, the development of computer software represents a significant expenditure of resources that must be offset by software sales. In addition, the unauthorized copying and subsequent loss of revenue acts as a disincentive to develop advanced revisions of existing software or completely new programs. For an indication of the extent of software piracy and its impact on software developers, we need look only at the case of Micropro, developer of one of the early dominant IBM compatible word processing packages, Wordstar. Although there is no definitive measure, a widely used but unofficial estimate suggests that two out of every three copies of Wordstar in use were pirated. If this estimate is reasonably accurate, one can imagine the tremendous revenue loss for Micropro.

When viewed from a user's perspective, the use of copied software does offer significant short-term savings. For example, a user could try a package at little or no cost before making a major cash outlay. There are, however, three major disadvantages to pirating software: it is clearly illegal; it limits the future availability of software; and illegal copies do not have documentation and are not vendor registered, thus depriving copiers of subsequent upgrades and vendor support.

To fight software pirating through legal action, the development of more effective copy protection mechanisms, and public persuasion, software vendors formed the Association of Data Processing Service Organizations (ADAPSO). ADAPSO and its members have started litigation against organizations that violate their copyrights.

In one noteworthy study, the attitudes of college and university IS faculty members on the ethics of unauthorized software copying were compared to those of IS managers. The findings indicated that the IS managers were more sensitive to copyright issues and much less tolerant of pirating than their academic counterparts. This perspective may be attributable, in part, to the relative availability of legal software in the business community. In addition, many of the IS managers were sensitive to the ramifications of the adverse publicity from a lawsuit. In essence, the typical attitude in business is that pirating is just not worth the risk.

Sources: Susan L. Soloman and James A. O'Brien, "The Effect of Demographic Factors on Attitudes toward Software Piracy," *Journal of Computer Information Systems* 30, 40–46; and J. P. Shim and G. Stephen Taylor, "A Comparative Study of Unauthorized Software Copying: Information Systems Faculty Members' vs. Practicing Managers' Perceptions," in *Ethical Issues in Information Systems,* ed. Roy Dejoie, George Fowler, and David Paradice (Boston: Boyd & Fraser, 1991).

propriate to note that computers come in different size and performance categories. Although the boundaries between the different computer categories are somewhat clouded, there are some clear attributes. *Microcomputers* are the familiar IBM personal computers and clones and Macintoshes. These computers usually cost from $600 to $10,000. They are self-contained and often support a single user at a time.

Minicomputers can be purchased for about $10,000 to $100,000. They have greater capacity than microcomputers and often support a complete business unit or function. In the most common installations, minicomputers support many users at the same time. The vendors of minicomputers include IBM (AS 400), DEC, and Hewlett-Packard.

Mainframe computers are the large computers used by many organizations to support their transaction processing and other large applications. These are expensive systems (costing between $500,000 and $10,000,000) that can handle hundreds of terminals and users.

At the top of the computer hierarchy are *supercomputers.* These computers are high-speed "number crunchers" that usually run engineering, science, and research applications having very intensive numerical calculations. They are very expensive and very fast. The most famous supercomputer manufacturer is CRAY, which is the dominant vendor in the market. Typically, even the largest corporation would not use a supercomputer for its business and IS applications.

Telecommunications systems permit computing devices at dispersed locations to communicate with each other. For example, Wal-Mart uses telecommunications to transmit data from its individual stores to its regional offices to speed inventory management and control.

A simple telecommunications system is depicted in Figure 20.5. Two computers are connected via telephone lines. The two devices used to transform the digital electrical signals into an analog-transmittable system are called **modems** (an abbreviation of modular-demodulator). It should be noted that the U.S. telephone system is slowly being converted from an analog system to a digital system, which permits data to be transmitted directly over different channels.

Different transmission channels are available for data transmission. Probably the most common are twisted pairs of wires, or *coaxial cables.* The transmission speed and, therefore, the amount of data that can be transmitted in a given period, will vary greatly. For example, on standard voice-grade telephone lines, transmission takes place at from 300 *bps* (bits per second) to 9,600. In contrast, special high-speed lines can carry up to 500 million bps.

Telecommunications.
The electronic transmission of data from one computer device to another.

Modems.
Two devices used to transform the digital electrical signals into an analog-transmittable system that connects two computers via telephone lines.

FIGURE 20.5 BASIC ELEMENTS OF A TELECOMMUNICATIONS SYSTEM

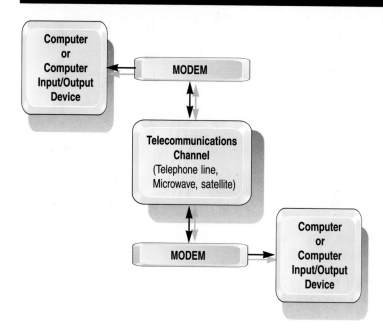

Employees of Eli Lilly and Company use a videoconferencing system supported by Indiana Bell to link Lilly's world headquarters in Indianapolis with its offices around the globe. The network uses Ameritech's OPTINET DS1 service, and enables participants to see, hear, and interact with one another from widely separated locations throughout the world, saving time and cutting travel costs.

Another alternative for data transmission is through *microwaves*. Essentially, microwaves are radio waves that are transmitted through the air. As with FM radio, a microwave transmission travels in a straight line—so microwave towers have to be erected every 25–50 miles to allow microwave signals to follow the earth's curvature. As you might guess, this is an expensive option. In the long run, however, it may be less costly than burying cable or stringing telephone lines on poles. Microwaves are widely used for long-distance telephone communications and for voice and data transmissions.

Satellite transmission is similar in nature to microwave transmission. Instead of being transmitted to a tower a few miles away, however, the transmission is sent to a satellite in space. The great distances cause a time delay (as low as one-third of a second) over conventional earth-based towers. The inconvenience of this delay may be offset by less expensive telecommunications costs or by convenience.

Fiber-optic cable is preferable to conventional wire cable for telecommunications. Data are transmitted as pulses of light through tiny glass fibers. Fiber-optic cable has advantages for telecommunications: They provide high-speed transmission and a high message capacity while being less subject to interference.

The different needs of organizations are reflected in more common telecommunications networks. In one case, there is a need to directly link computers and attendant devices (for example, printers) in an office or building to allow users to share devices or data. This particular kind of network is called a **local area network,** or **LAN.** In contrast to a LAN, a **wide area network (WAN)** is designed to permit both voice and data communications between computing equipment across great distances.

Local area network (LAN).

A group of computers and terminals that are interconnected in a small geographic area.

Wide area network (WAN).

A group of computers and terminals that are interconnected in a large geographic area.

The impact of telecommunications is becoming increasingly important. For many activities, it is important to have fast on-line operations. For example, banks need to update customer accounts as transactions occur at branches far removed from a home computing center. With the current emphasis on speed and fast response to customer needs, organizations of all types are recognizing the necessity for a telecommunications system to link computing operations at remote sites.

A second issue of importance is **connectivity,** that is, the compatibility of hardware components to be linked into a network. In fact, one of the basic features of the just-in-time inventory systems is the linking of suppliers to manufacturers. This is required to coordinate schedules and parts delivery.

A third major issue for management is the use of **electronic data interchange** (EDI). EDI is a set of standards as well as hardware and software designed to permit the transfer of data such as purchase orders, invoices, and so forth between computers in different organizations. By using EDI technology, organizations can increase the speed at which they process payments and reduce the associated costs.

Connectivity.
The compatibility of hardware components to be linked into a network.

Electronic data interchange.
Set of standards as well as hardware and software designed to permit the transfer of data between computers in different organizations.

DEVELOPING INFORMATION SYSTEMS

The vast majority of this text's readers will not be IS specialists. They will, however, be IS users in line and staff departments, such as accounting, manufacturing, marketing, and so forth. Their performance will, in part, depend on the quality of the IS support available. To be an educated user, they will need to participate in developing IS applications. For this reason, they should be familiar with the basic methodologies IS development. This section will discuss two of the more common development methodologies: the *systems development* life cycle and *prototyping*.

The traditional methodology for developing large information systems is to follow the **systems development life cycle (SDLC).** Although there are many different versions of the SDLC, they are all similar. Figure 20.6 describes the steps that are usually followed in developing a typical SDLC.

Systems development life cycle (SDLC).
A procedure for proposing, analyzing, designing, and implementing computer software.

FIGURE 20.6 STEPS IN THE SYSTEMS DEVELOPMENT LIFE CYCLE

Problem definition — Define problem and determine project feasibility.

Systems analysis — Document and analyze IS being used, define performance specifications of the new IS, and develop a conceptual design for the new IS.

Design — Detail design of IS, including inputs, outputs, data storage, and processing specifications. In addition, specify any hardware and facilities.

Implementation — Program, test, and convert the old IS to the new IS.

Operation and maintenance — Maintain and operate IS.

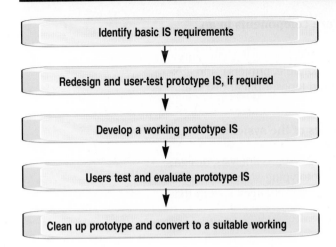

FIGURE 20.7 STEPS IN PROTOTYPING

Identify basic IS requirements

Redesign and user-test prototype IS, if required

Develop a working prototype IS

Users test and evaluate prototype IS

Clean up prototype and convert to a suitable working

A user's role in information systems developed following the SDLC is quite extensive for two important reasons. First, and foremost, users have the most firsthand knowledge of an organization's current IS, their deficiencies, and opportunities for improvement. Second, their participation in developing an IS will greatly increase their acceptance of the system. At almost every step of the SDLC, users have significant opportunities for participation. This participation may range from contributing to the design to helping to test and convert the SDLC.

An alternative to the SDLC is **prototyping,** or building a working IS with the most important features in a short time. The purpose of this "quick and dirty" system is to provide users with an IS so they can examine and, through fast changes, specify that it meets their needs. A simple representation of the prototyping development methodology is shown in Figure 20.7. Prototyping is especially helpful in developing decision support systems and other interactive information systems.

Prototyping.
A shortened software development procedure that relies on advanced software development tools to quickly provide a working system for users to examine.

SUMMARY

Today's business environment requires that organizations provide products that meet or exceed their customers' quality standards. This chapter has discussed the types of IS used to support these requirements and to facilitate managerial decision making.

Learning Objective 1: Discuss the information systems requirements of an organization's different hierarchical levels.
The operational control level of an organization processes transactions as they occur to update internal records and provide reports and documents. The management control level of an organization receives information from the operational level and combines and summarizes this information for the strategic control level.

Learning Objective 2: Describe the different categories of software systems found in organizations.
At the operational level, transaction processing is used to gather data and provide routine reporting services to management. The management control level uses

decision support systems and group decision support systems. At the top management level, a primary support system is executive information systems.

Learning Objective 3: List the different hardware components in an information system.
The major hardware components of an IS are the central processing unit, input devices (for example, keyboards), output devices (for example, printers), and auxiliary storage devices (for example, magnetic disks and tapes, optical disks, and so forth).

Learning Objective 4: Compare the characteristics of the systems development life cycle with those of prototyping.
The SDLC is a structured set of steps (problem definition, systems analysis, design, implementation, and operation and maintenance). Prototyping is quickly developing a working system for users to examine and, through fast changes, specify that a system meets users' needs.

KEY TERMS

artificial intelligence 602

auxiliary storage 604

central processing unit (CPU) 602

computer hardware 602

connectivity 608

decision support system (DSS) 599

electronic data interchange 608

executive information system (EIS) 600

expert system (ES) 602

group decision support system (GDSS) 599

information system (IS) 596

local area network (LAN) 607

manufacturing automation system 600

modems 606

office automation system 600

prototyping 609

systems development life cycle (SDLC) 608

telecommunications 606

transaction-processing and reporting system 599

wide area network (WAN) 607

REVIEW AND DISCUSSION QUESTIONS

1. Explain how management and decision making may be viewed as synonymous terms.

2. How does an organization's external environment influence its internal decision making? What are some important external environmental influences that managers should monitor?

3. Explain the difference between data and information.

4. What is the purpose of an information system? Show how DSS, GDSS, expert systems, office automation systems, and executive information systems fit into a definition of IS.

5. Explain the difference between local and wide area networks.

6. Compare the SDLC to prototyping.

THE MANAGEMENT EXPERIENCE   DATA BASE MAGIC

A data base is a collection of data structured for rapid search and retrieval. Within an IS framework, data bases are used to generate decision-relevant information. Over the past decade, data bases have been discovered by an increasing number of diverse users in government, law, business, education, and private life. Data bases are available in many subject fields and correspond to printed indexes or abstracts.

Chances are that you have access to a variety of data bases through your academic library. DIALOG, developed by the Lockheed Palo Alto Research Laboratory, is perhaps the most popular data base search service. With over 180 data bases containing 80 million searchable records, DIALOG is the largest vendor in the field. Other popular data base search services include System Development Corporation's ORBIT (On-Line Retrieval of Bibliographic Information Timeshared) and Indian Head Inc.'s BRS (Bibliographic Retrieval Services).

To learn more of the contents of these or other data base search services, do the following:

1. Visit an academic library.

2. Prepare a list of the available data base search services.

3. Select a topic related to your major area of academic study.

4. Formulate a question on this topic to which you would like to know the answer.

5. Based on the descriptions of the data bases to which your library has access, identify those data bases that would most likely contain information necessary for answering the question.

6. Prepare a one-page report on what you have done and learned. Be sure to identify the academic library visited, the available data base search services, the topic you chose in your major area of academic study, the question you wished answered, and the data bases you judged most likely to be of value for answering your question.

CASE 20.1   S-K-I LTD.

An informating firm—one that uses IT to constantly track its performance—can set a virtuous cycle in motion. It can use the information it gathers to take corrective actions, then monitor the results. The cycle may lead to a sizable IT investment as the company seeks more and more data, but the end result can be better customer service, a more productive work force and steady profitability.

Such has been the case at S-K-I Ltd., the company that runs Vermont's two largest ski resorts, Killington and Mt. Snow, as well as California's Bear Mountain ski area. The $76 million company has been profitable for 29 consecutive years.

In the early 1970s, said S-K-I's chief financial officer, Martel Wilson, the pressures of running a highly seasonal business led the firm to close its books on a weekly basis rather than monthly or quarterly. It didn't make sense, he said, to discover "you were off-track halfway into the season."

Today, S-K-I's financial-reporting system has evolved to the point where managers have detailed weekly profit plans comparing performance to the budget and historical benchmarks. "We know by Wednesday how far off this week might be in revenue," said Wilson. On Thursday, managers meet to discuss targets and how to attain them.

"A good analogy is celestial navigation in the open ocean," Wilson said. "Do your sights every day, and you won't be too far off."

But navigation is useless unless the captain steers the ship. The issue, said Wilson, is to apply information to set objectives, and then correct problems and change behavior. This has led S-K-I to create new systems that feed into its financial-controls system. Since 1984, when Ivars "Ike" Eichvalds became S-K-I's MIS manager, the company has developed 27 such systems.

A staffing system helps S-K-I to get the most out of the fewest number of employees possible—a critical function because of the "Baby Bust," said Wilson.

Staff levels at Killington can balloon from 600 to 1,500 at the height of the season. The staffing system, said Eichvalds, "tells us what our staff levels should be in each department. When the level of business drops off, it [indicates] that our part-time people should be laid off." It also directs staff to where they are needed—be it the lift area, maintenance or food service. If the lift-ticket tracking system reports 5,000 skiers by 10 a.m., said Eichvalds, "we can project 10,000 by 11. We know we will have a big day in our food retail areas, and [that we] have to be covered for that."

Other systems help maintain optimal skiing conditions. Sensors beneath Killington's 16 lifts record the number of skiers on each slope by the hour. By tracking skiers and using historical data, said Eichvalds, "you know where the most efficient routing and snow-making needs to be done." S-K-I also records the amount of snow generated at each hydrant on the slopes. Man-made snow is expensive, said Wilson, and a spot on the slope that requires more man-made snow might be a candidate for landscaping.

Finally, since business depends on attracting skiers, said Eichvalds, S-K-I has set up computerized reservation and marketing systems. The hotel-reservation system not only includes S-K-I's own ski areas and the condos it manages, but it also handles reservations for other hotels and inns in the area. The reservation system is designed to avoid long check-in lines. Rooms are assigned in advance, and payment is made up front.

As for the marketing system, Eichvalds was unwilling to say anything more than that S-K-I keeps track of where its customers are from, and targets advertising and direct mail accordingly.

Problems

1. How does S-K-I Ltd. use IS to support its corporate strategy?

2. How does it use IS to help its managers make better decisions?

Source: Allan E. Alter, "Compact Competitors," *CIO*, July 1989, p.40–49. Reprinted through the courtesy of *CIO Magazine*. © 1989 CIO Publishing.

NOTES

[1] Allan E. Alter, "Peter's Principles," *CIO* 2 (August 1989): 12–18.

[2] Herbert A. Simon, *Administrative Behavior,* 2nd ed. (New York: Free Press, 1957), 3–4.

[3] Gerardine DeSanctis and Brent Galupe, "Group Decision Support Systems: A New Frontier," *Data Base* 3 (Winter 1985): 3–10.

[4] George Houdeshel and Hugh J. Watson, "The Management Information and Decision Support (MIDS) Systems at Lockheed Georgia," *MIS Quarterly* 11 (March 1987): 127–140.

[5] Dorothy Leonard-Baron and John J. Sviokla, "Putting Expert Systems to Work," *Harvard Business Review* 66 (March–April 1988): 91–98; and Robert C. Ford and M. Khris McAlister, "Tapping into Expert Systems," *Personnel Administrator* 34 (January 1989): 26–32.

[6] Max D. Hopper, "Rattling SABRE—New Ways to Compete on Information," *Harvard Business Review* 68 (May–June 1990): 118–125.

CHAPTER 21

LEARNING OBJECTIVES

Upon completing this chapter, you should be able to:

- Describe the kinds of organizations that have production systems.
- Outline the general nature of the operations management process.
- Identify various questions that must be considered before designing a production system.
- Understand the basic elements of a manufacturing resource planning (MRP II) system.
- Illustrate how an organization's strategic plan should influence the design of its master production schedule.
- Explain the major difference between service and manufacturing organizations.
- Define the term *productivity.*

A Big Mac is a simple item, isn't it? After all, Big Macs are often assembled, packaged, and sold by unskilled high school students. And, apart from the secret "special sauce," even a novice cook shouldn't have much trouble making a fairly decent replica at home.

But is making a Big Mac really so simple? The folks at McDonald's don't think so. They have spent years working on a production system that will ensure that the Big Mac you eat in Bangor, Maine, will taste just the same as the one you eat in Bangkok, Thailand. Designing a production system that can consistently meet a rigorous set of specifications for ingredients, quality, and delivery speed, as well as packaging, advertising, and price, and to do it worldwide is a feat worthy of a four-star general.

Just think of the dozens of questions that needed to be resolved to successfully design, produce, and distribute the Big Mac. First, how should it have been designed? The "sesame seed bun," the "all-beef patty," the "special sauce," and even the wrapper it comes in had to be perfected. Then rigid standards as to size, weight, and material requirements had to be set.

Secondly, McDonald's planners had to ask, should Big Macs be customized, with many variations available, or be a standard burger where variations are available, or be a standard burger where variations are available but not encouraged? For the most part, Big Macs are standardized, which allows them to be assembled without a specific customer in mind. Chief competitor Burger King, on the other hand, has built its strategy around customized burgers. At Burger King, for example, you can request a Whopper and "hold the pickle." At McDonald's you are best advised to remove the pickle yourself.

OPERATIONS MANAGEMENT AND PRODUCTIVITY

Once the Big Mac was designed, equipment had to be devised and purchased to produce it efficiently. To determine what equipment was needed, McDonald's had to first decide whether it was going to make all the Big Mac's components itself or buy some or all from suppliers. For example, should buns be baked at each restaurant, baked at a McDonald's-owned central bakery, or subcontracted out to local bakeries who would produce buns to McDonald's specifications? Should the same grill used for cooking beef patties be used for pancakes and eggs, or should there be separate equipment for different menu items?

Once equipment was chosen, McDonald's planners had to decide how many burgers to produce at a time. To meet its rigorous quality standards, McDonald's corporate policy requires that a Big Mac's life, from the time it is prepared until it is in the hands of a customer, is not to exceed 10 minutes! Those 11 minutes or older are destroyed.

To ensure a ready supply of menu items—and a minimum amount of waste—a production planner (usually a store manager) needs to be able to forecast demand for each item based on historical sales data. These data may vary with the time of day, week, and year, or with the amount of promotion an item is being given.

To run a McDonald's successfully, other questions also must be answered. In what order should ingredients be assembled? How many cash registers should be open at any given time? What should each employee's job be, and how much output should be expected from each employee? Should the special sauce be applied with a spatula or squirted in precisely determined amounts from a specially designed dispenser?

The collaboration of Thomas E. Hendrick, Arizona State University, and Byron J. Finch, Miami University, in the preparation of this chapter is gratefully acknowledged.

We could go on asking such questions indefinitely, but, as you have no doubt begun to realize, producing a Big Mac is not so simple after all. The kinds of questions we have been asking could have been applied as well to organizations such as Federal Express, which provides a service, but no goods, or to Mattel, which produces goods, but no services. Even organizations such as banks, universities, and hospitals must ask themselves similar questions to determine the kind of production system required to keep their operations running efficiently. In each case, a wide range of complex decisions must be made to design and implement a production system that transforms inputs (people, materials, money, and information) into outputs (goods and services), and does so with a high rate of productivity. This set of activities is known as **operations management.**

In this chapter, we will look at the design and implementation of the operations management process. We also stress the importance of high productivity.

Figure 21.1 shows the general nature of the operations process and how it relates to both the management process and an organization's environment. To understand Figure 21.1, begin at the left side, "Demand for goods/services." Demand is an absolutely essential condition for an organization's long-run survival. The next box provides a sampling of inputs that are transformed into outputs (that is, goods and services). Feedback from an organization's environment allows it to adjust its performance to meet future demand and reinitiate the input, transformation, and output sequence.

Operations management.

The design and implementation of a production system that transforms inputs (people, money, and information) into outputs (goods and services) with a high rate of productivity.

STRATEGIC PLANNING AND THE OPERATIONS PROCESS

The nature of the goods and services an organization produces will have a major effect on its strategic plan, and, thus, on the components of its operations process. For example, before designing a production system, an organization would need answers to various questions. For example:

- Do we produce custom or standard goods/services or both (custom microprocessors for space vehicles or standard microprocessors for inexpensive calculators)?

- Are we capital intensive (an automated factory) or labor intensive (a hospital)?

- What mix of materials and component parts do we make ourselves and buy from others? (A restaurant may make its own pies but buy ketchup from suppliers.)

- How much stability (disposable diapers) or variability (ski lift tickets) is there in the demand for our goods/services?

- What mix of skilled (electronics engineers), semiskilled (truck drivers), and unskilled (college sophomores) employees do we need?

FIGURE 21.1 OPERATIONS MANAGEMENT PROCESS: INPUTS ARE TRANSFORMED INTO OUTPUTS

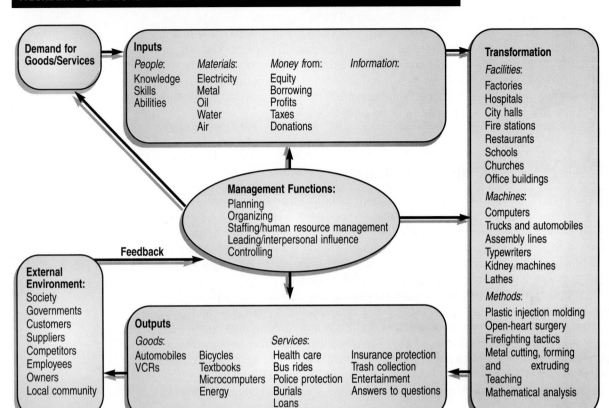

- Are we producing a good/service with a stable design (aspirin) or one that is changing rapidly (microcomputers, income tax services), and at what stage is our good/service in its life cycle (computer disks or Indiana Jones Halloween costumes)?

- Are our goods/services unique and copyright protected, or is entry into our market easy (gas and electric service or gas stations)?

- Are our suppliers reliable as to delivery and quality (local steel mill or herbs from a developing country)?

- What level of quality, reliability, durability, and product life are we targeting (a microchip for a $12 watch or a microchip for a navigation system on a manned orbital flight)?

- Can we produce from a single location and distribute to our market competitively, or are multiple locations required (Joe's Garage or Circle K)?

- Can we use general-purpose machines, or do we need specialized, highly engineered machines to produce unique goods/services (standard auto repair shop or an automated assembly line that uses robots, conveyor systems, and computer-controlled quality)?

- Are there competitive substitutes for our goods/services that make them obsolete and that may preclude heavy investment in a production system (plastic grocery bags replacing paper bags)?

As we saw from our discussion of McDonald's, these questions just begin to scratch the surface of all those that need to be answered to design a production system. In this chapter, we cannot hope to answer all these questions—to do so is the purpose of a college major in operations management—but to present some of the tradeoffs that should be considered in a production system's design. The advantages and disadvantages of particular design alternatives should be uncovered in the course of a formal tradeoff analysis. It is then a manager's responsibility to use whatever analytic methods, judgment, and experience are necessary to choose the alternative that best serves an organization's strategic plan.

MANUFACTURING RESOURCE PLANNING

Producing a Big Mac requires planning for both manufacturing and service. To simplify our discussion, we will examine how the operations management process works in organizations designed solely for manufacturing, such as those that produce VCRs, motorcycles, and washing machines. Planning a production system in manufacturing organizations like these requires the integration of functional areas, such as marketing, finance, accounting, and engineering.

Suppose, for example, that you are the manager responsible for planning the production of a new line of sleeper sofas. For the production to proceed efficiently, you must ensure that there are enough parts in inventory (but not too many) to meet your output goal of 50 sofas a week. You must also determine how many employees you will need, what each will do, what machines will be required, and where the sofas will be shipped or stored upon completion. At the same time that the current week's sofas are being loaded into trucks, you should be monitoring in-

Specialized equipment and highly skilled employees are vital to the production of Mobil Chemical's "ultra performance" film that can stretch 300% to wrap pallet loads without breaking. In this picture, Tran Nguyen, an engineer at Mobil's Belleville, Ontario facility, shares his experience in the demanding film production process with personnel from Temple, Texas. On the platform at the rear, Belleville production specialist Stephen Davidson monitors a machine that blows resins into a bubble of film.

coming orders to see how many sofas you will need to produce next week, or 2 weeks from now, to keep up with demand.

This process is known as *production planning and control (PPC)*. It enables managers to plan and control production activities, as well as to feed back information, so new or revised production plans can be implemented as time unfolds.

In the past, the PPC process was called a *material requirements planning (MRP)* system, although it plans (and controls) much more than just materials. It aids in planning output capacities, inventory and workforce levels, work assignments, and the completion of customer orders. In addition, it monitors purchase orders placed with suppliers for component parts and raw materials.

In the early 1980s, the original MRP concept was expanded to include the planning and control of all resources required in an operations management process. The result is MRP II, which means *manufacturing resource planning.*

MRP II encompasses the planning and control of all the activities mentioned above, plus a more formal integration of PPC with marketing, finance and accounting, human resource management, and engineering than was the case with MRP. Figure 21.2 presents a simplified overview of an MRP II system. We will briefly introduce the basic elements shown in this figure.

STRATEGIC PLAN AND MASTER PRODUCTION SCHEDULE

As shown in Figure 21.2, the PPC process, as well as such support areas as marketing, finance/accounting, human resource management, and engineering, takes an active role in developing an organization's strategic plan (Chapter 6). An organization's strategic plan serves as input to a *master production schedule,* which is the key plan that determines how much of each final good/service an organization will make and when. Inputs from each support area must be considered and balanced, and their commitment to the goods/services being produced must be established.

Marketing, for example, must commit itself to selling goods/services; PPC to producing them; finance to financing them; engineering to designing them; and human resource management to providing the necessary employees. Once agreed upon, an organization's master production schedule is said to "drive" an MRP II system.

ROUGH CUT CAPACITY

Before a final master production schedule is agreed upon by an organization's support areas, the resources required to produce the estimated demand of goods/services must be compared in a "rough cut" manner with the available capacity of machines, labor, and other resources. If, in past experience, an organization's current capacity has allowed it to produce $10 million worth of goods/services a month, and the next year's master production schedule calls for $12 million in monthly production, the organization may have to choose whether to add capacity, reduce the output quantities in its master schedule, spread production over a longer time period, subcontract work out, or add a second work shift.

On the other hand, if an organization's master production schedule calls for only $8 million in production a month, it may have to reduce available capacity through layoffs, cancel subcontracts, or lower prices to increase demand. When this is done, then more detailed planning can begin to see if a proposed master production schedule can actually be met. This will involve considering the availability of raw materials, machine capacities, and labor.

FIGURE 21.2 SIMPLIFIED OVERVIEW OF AN MRP II SYSTEM

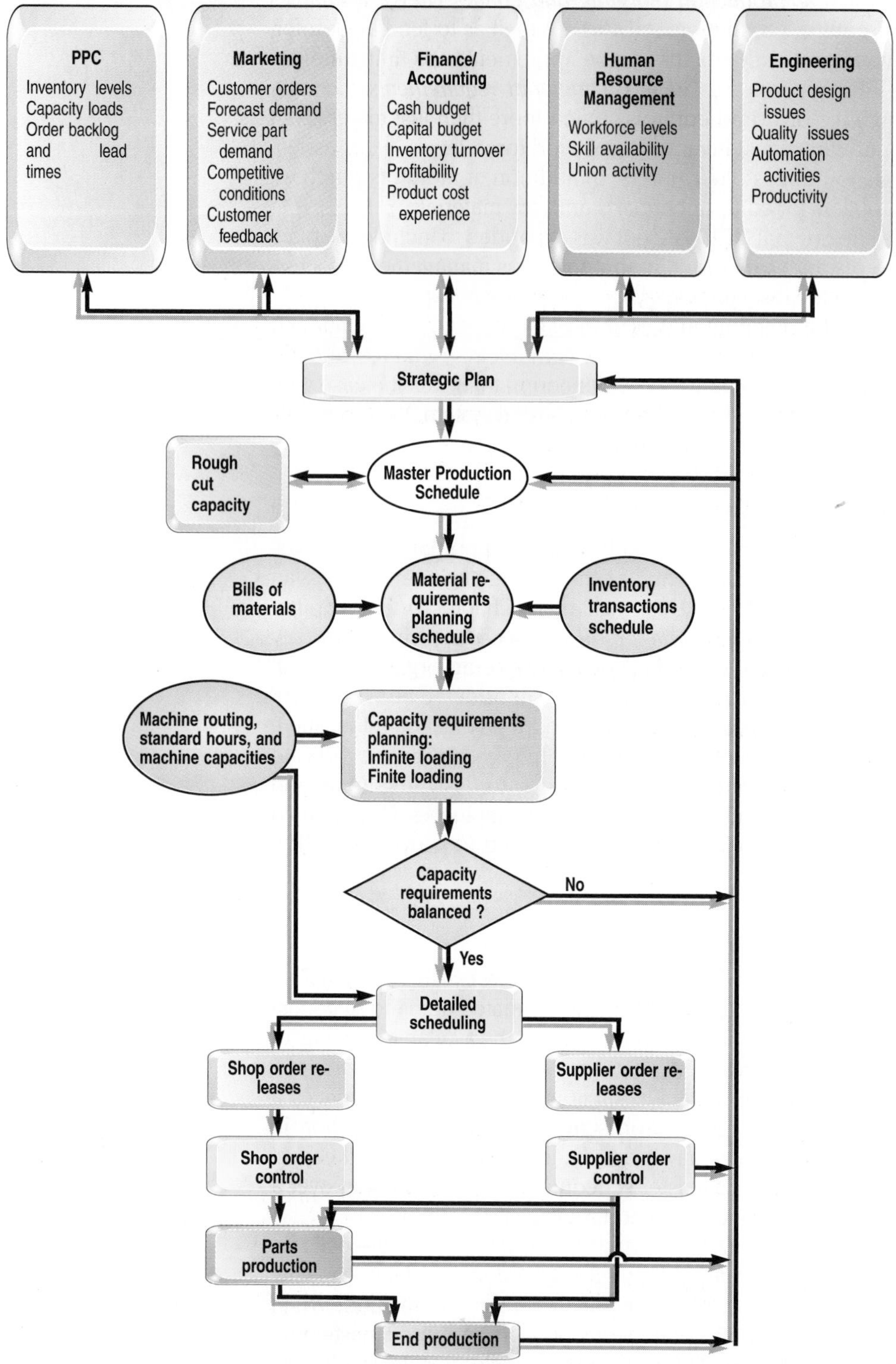

Source: Adapted from Thomas E. Hendrick and Franklin G. Moore, Production/Operations Management, 9th ed. (Homewood, IL: Irwin,1985),159; Thomas E. Vollmann, William L. Berry, and D. Clay Whybark, Manufacturing Planning and Control Systems, 2nd ed. (Homewood, IL: Irwin, 1988), 450; James B. Dilworth, Operations Management (New York: McGraw-Hill, 1992), 432.

BILLS OF MATERIALS

The manner in which a good/service is actually produced is defined by its *bill of materials*. A bill of materials is not simply a parts list. It also defines the sequence in which component parts must be assembled. A wagon needs four wheels, but before they can be attached, axles must be made, and rubber and steel must be subassembled into finished wheels. A bill of materials defines in explicit detail the component parts (wagon wheels) and the materials (rubber, steel, glue) that are required for each final product (wagon). It also specifies the sequence in which parts are to be assembled to produce a final good/service.

INVENTORY TRANSACTIONS SCHEDULE

Suppose we need 400 wheels to satisfy our master production schedule for, say, 100 wagons. Yesterday we had 50 wagon wheels in stock, and another 100 in the process of being produced. But since we have just shipped 25 wheels to replace faulty wheels for wagons previously sold, we now need to produce 275 wheels $(400 - 50 - 100 + 25)$. An *inventory transactions schedule* keeps track of the arrival and withdrawal of all parts, of on-hand balances, and of parts orders already placed but not yet received. An inventory transactions schedule ensures that a production planner will order or produce the correct number of component parts— not too many, not too few.

MATERIAL REQUIREMENTS PLANNING SCHEDULE

Information from each of these elements of an MRP II system feeds into a *material requirements planning schedule,* which calculates the total material and component part requirements needed to satisfy a master production schedule.

   The material requirements planning schedule then generates planned order releases for each part to be produced and for each part or material that must be purchased. *Planned order releases* specify exactly how much of a component part to make or buy, and when these orders should be released to an organization's shops or suppliers. These orders also form a basis for the scheduling of machines and labor.

CAPACITY REQUIREMENTS PLANNING

Before planned order releases can be finalized, machine and labor capacity must be closely checked. Machine loads are generally first planned as if there were no capacity restrictions *(infinite loading)*. Later, plans are tempered to meet actual machine capacity *(finite loading)*. To make these calculations accurately, managers must know the sequence of machines necessary to produce a part *(machine routing)*, the time required *(standard hours)*, and *individual machine capacities*. If severe capacity problems occur that cannot be solved with either overtime, an extra shift, or subcontracting, the master production schedule may have to be revised to match this lower available capacity.

SHOP ORDER AND SUPPLIER ORDER RELEASES

When capacity requirements are finally balanced with a master production schedule, *shop order* and *supplier order releases* are placed as "authorized" material and parts orders. Authorized orders are released to an organization's shops, materials

Beginning in 1989, Borden, Inc. launched an accelerated program of plant expansion, modernization, and consolidation in order to position itself as a high-volume, low-cost producer in each of its businesses. Borden invested over $100 million in expanding its pasta operations, consolidating the output of older, smaller, less efficient plants into a system of "hyperplants," such as this one located in St. Louis, Missouri. The plant is the largest in North America and is considered to be the most advanced in the world, with an annual capacity of 250 million pounds. The plant is also designed to be doubled in size in the future in order to meet the growing demand for Borden pasta.

are pulled from stock, and production begins. At the same time, any necessary authorized material and parts orders are released to suppliers. Ideally, this is done with enough lead time so materials arrive at the right time and in the correct quantities to be smoothly integrated into the MRP II system.

SHOP ORDER AND SUPPLIER ORDER CONTROL

Once material and parts orders are actually released to an organization's shops, an MRP II system monitors their progress as they move from work station to work station to see if they are behind, on time, or ahead of a master production schedule. For purchased parts, purchasing agents monitor the progress of orders that have been placed with suppliers to determine their status—on time, late, quality problems, threatened strike, and so on.

FEEDBACK

As time unfolds, the resulting information generated is captured and fed back to correct various MRP II system elements. As an organization's strategic plan is revised, an MRP II system recalculates production needs and repeats itself from day to day and week to week, continuously being updated. An MRP II system should likewise be updated with changes in bills of materials (as designs are revised by engineering), machine routings (as new machines are purchased), assembly sequences, standard hours, and other elements.

Corning Glass's experience in instituting an MRP II system is described in the accompanying "Smart Management" box.

SMART MANAGEMENT MRP II AT CORNING GLASS WORKS

Take an inventory of the typical U.S. household, and you're almost certain to find one refrigerator, two television sets, and three pieces of Corning Ware.

Surprised about the Corning Ware? Top management at Corning Glass Works wasn't. It was well aware of the world's appetite for cookware. But it *was* surprised to find that Corning Ware factories were having a difficult time filling orders. It wasn't that demand was simply outstripping supply. The problem was that coordination between many factories was so poor that, at any given time, there were often too many lids for too few bowls, or too few handles for too many coffee pots.

Top management went hunting for a better way to manage production. Its search took it right back to the shop floor. It was time, management decided, to begin balancing items on hand with the demands of a master production schedule. With 60,000 different kinds of goods to keep track of (including cookware, electronic components for computers, eyewear, and television tubes), and 29,000 workers in 63 plants around the world, the prospect seemed daunting. The solution: manufacturing resource planning (MRP II).

The switchover was anything but easy. For one thing, to begin installing an MRP II system has cost Corning more than $1 million a year for the past 4 years. In addition, some employees chose to leave Corning rather than accept the change. On several occasions, the entire project was nearly scrapped by an impatient board of directors.

To prevent panic in the ranks bred by "horror stories" about MRP II failures elsewhere, top management decided to disguise the project. They knew the term *MRP II* might send lower level managers and workers heading for the exits, so they christened their program EPIC (for *efficient production inventory control*).

Although fewer than half of Corning's 39 domestic plants have instituted EPIC, the returns are already impressive. Corning boasts savings of some $2 million a year directly related to MRP II. What's more, inventory accuracy has leaped from 69 percent to 86 percent, and schedule compliance—meeting internal deadlines—has improved from 71 percent to 90 percent.

Perhaps most important, EPIC has already helped Corning to salvage deteriorating relationships with two major customers. A few years ago, Corning knew that two major accounts, Sears and K mart, were unhappy with its performance. Only 50 percent of their orders were being delivered on time. "If we had continued at 50 percent customer service, we wouldn't have been doing business with them much longer," acknowledged R. Lee Bailey, master production planner for Corning's Consumer Products Division. But thanks to MRP II, customer service in the consumer division now exceeds 90 percent, and Sears and K mart still sell Corning Ware.

Source: Adapted from Bruce Horovitz, "Why Corning Is Sticking with MRP," *Industry Week*, January 25, 1982, 44–47.

Cyprus Minerals Company excels at providing a combination of quality products and services to its customers. The company defines its customer focus as a process of asking what customers want, listening to them and anticipating their needs; and building long-term, mutually beneficial relationships. As a result, the company has received awards for its performance as a supplier to organizations such as Promeon and Eveready Battery, U.S. Steel, John Deere, and Caterpillar.

CAPACITY PLANNING FOR SERVICE ORGANIZATIONS

Organizations whose output is a service (such as Federal Express) or a combination of a good and a service (such as McDonald's) undertake many of the same production requirements as those engaged in manufacturing. There are, however, some areas that pose challenges unique to service organizations and require different solutions.

The major difference between service and manufacturing organizations is in the area of inventories. In manufacturing organizations, inventories act as a buffer between variations in customer demand and available supply. Inventories, however, do not exist in a usual sense in service organizations. If a customer shows up for service and there is insufficient service capacity, the customer is likely to be irritated and a sale lost. If service capacity is high relative to demand, servers will be idle, and the resulting excess capacity cannot be put into inventory and used the next day. Thus, one of the major issues in designing a production system for service organizations is balancing capacity with customer demand.

One example of capacity planning for a service organization is described in the accompanying "Smart Management" box.

PRODUCTIVITY

We have noted that production systems should be designed to be highly "productive." What does this mean? **Productivity** is defined as the amount of output produced divided by the number of units of resources applied. As observed in Chapter 5, productivity measures an organization's ability to produce goods/services with fewer inputs (people, materials, money, information) and thus less cost. It thus indicates how well a production system is working. All organizations should be concerned about the relative productivity of their labor, materials, and energy.

Productivity.
The amount of output produced divided by the number of units of resources applied.

OUR "PRODUCTIVITY CRISIS"

The United States, is, without a doubt, the world's most productive nation. So why are we so concerned about productivity? We hear that other countries are beating us not in total productivity, but in *productivity growth* from year to year. Figure 21.3 shows this growth disparity.

Several reasons are thought to be behind this "productivity crisis." These include:

- A decline in the rate of investment in capital plant and equipment necessary to increase output.
- Heavy investment in antipollution devices and safety programs that do not contribute to output.
- Reduced expenditures on research and development.

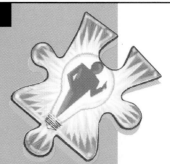

SMART MANAGEMENT CAPACITY PLANNING FOR THE DENVER FIRE DEPARTMENT

Although waiting to be served a Big Mac at a busy McDonald's can be annoying, waiting for a fire engine in a burning building can be deadly. Thus, when the City of Denver decided to look for ways to trim its fire department's costs, officials were concerned that such budget-cutting not result in a lower level of customer service.

A multidisciplinary team, consisting of fire department members, city officials, and operations researchers from the University of Colorado, was created to study the problem and determine if modern operations management techniques could be applied to solve it.

At the time of the study, the fire department had a $13 million budget, nearly all of which went to pay the wages of firefighters staffing 44 companies (each of which consisted of 17 firefighters and an engine or ladder truck). The objective of the study was to determine how many firehouses the city should have and where they should be located so that fires could be put out quickly and efficiently.

The research team began the study by having fire department members list existing fire hazards in the city and then evaluate them as to severity and to the maximum allowable travel time it should take for an initial vehicle to reach a fire scene. A list of potential new locations for firehouses was also developed.

The final piece of information required was prediction of the travel time from each existing fire station and each potential new firehouse site to each potential fire hazard. The information was arrived at through a detailed time-distance study of nearly 1,600 actual runs by fire department vehicles.

With this information in hand, researchers were able to predict the travel time from any firehouse location to any hazard. They could also analyze potential response times from a large number of alternative firehouse locations. An analysis of the information revealed a surprising discovery: One solution stood out as being much less costly than any of the others, but capable of maintaining approximately the same level of service with five fewer companies. This solution required that some firehouses be closed and others be built. But with the proposed solution in place, Denver could expect to save more than $2.3 million over a 7-year planning horizon, and more than $1 million annually thereafter.

But the best news was that even when the alarm rate was highest, there was no substantial increase in travel time between the existing 44 companies and the recommended 39 new companies. Even in the busiest periods, with five fewer companies, additional travel time was only about 11 seconds.

Although all the recommendations have not yet been implemented, the savings to date have been in excess of $4 million—a return thus far of more than 3,000 percent on the $117,000 cost of the study.

FIGURE 21.3 THE UNITED STATES VERSUS OTHER COUNTRIES IN PRODUCTIVITY GROWTH: OUTPUT PER HOUR IN MANUFACTURING, 1977–1990

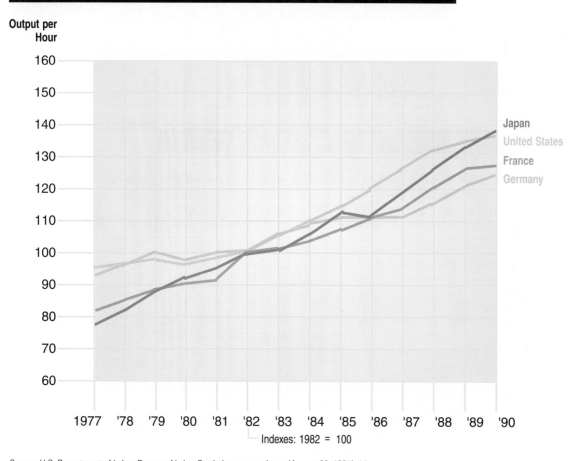

Source: U.S. Department of Labor, Bureau of Labor Statistics, press release (August 20, 1991), 14.

- More employees working in service occupations, which are inherently less productive.
- Labor unions' demands for higher wages and job security without commensurate increases in output.
- Economic recessions where output is reduced without proportional workforce reductions.

Although the picture may cause us concern, it is not disastrous. In recent years, we have continued to increase yearly productivity at a rate of about 2½ to 3 percent a year. And forecasters believe this rate will continue through the 1990s. Interestingly, however, U.S. manufacturing productivity alone (excluding the service sector) has been growing at about a 5 percent rate.

PRODUCTIVITY MEASUREMENT

One of the most important things an organization can do is measure its productivity. By doing so, it can gain a better understanding of its strengths and weaknesses, and thereby pinpoint less productive areas for improvement. The following discussion highlights some of the most common productivity measures.

Whenever economic tensions between the United States and Japan are discussed, the topic seems to center on the quality of manufactured goods and the productivity of the workers making them. U.S. companies have always prided themselves on high levels of quality and productivity and have had difficulty facing the fact that their progress in each of these areas has not matched that of the Japanese. Moreover, attempts to increase the quality of goods often results in a drop in productivity, and vice versa. Obviously we will not improve our competitive position unless we find ways of improving both quality and productivity.

One of the areas managers are concentrating on is *internal* quality—that is, the quality of operations within a company. No antagonism should exist between quality and productivity—they go hand in hand. Managers at the Chevron Oil Field Research Co. (COFRC) have made a major effort to improve the quality of research and development operations at their lab in La Habra, California. A large proportion of the employees working at COFRC are scientific professionals, who are generally individualists whose contributions depend on their ability to manage their own projects. They do not accept interference from upper management gracefully. Robert Heming, the laboratory's manager for quality and strategic planning, knew that he had to convince them that the quality program was not an attempt to speed them up in order to cut costs. Through a program aimed at reducing conflicts, increasing cooperation, and getting higher management to clarify the company's needs and priorities, COFRC has made some progress in improving both quality and productivity, but it will take time before the results can be quantified.

More dramatic results have been achieved in the field of high-technology manufacturing. Where enterprises have come close to the "automated factory," or computer integrated manufacturing (CIM), dramatic increases in quality are often accompanied by comparable improvements in productivity.

The aerospace industry has many companies that have come quite close to the ideal of computer integration. Northrop Corporation's development of the B-2 Stealth bomber is an example of the efficient, error-free design that is possible with intelligent use of high-powered computing tools and sensible changes in operations. The entire airplane was designed by computer, with the company's design and manufacturing departments working simultaneously.

Because the computer model was so intricate and precise, Northrop didn't even build a mock-up of the airplane as is usually done. And the precision of the model was so great that only 3 percent of the parts didn't fit perfectly the first time, compared to the usual 50 percent or more. There were only one-sixth the usual number of design changes, and when changes were made they took only one-fifth the usual time. But one of the most dramatic changes was to give the manufacturing department veto power over the design. Usually a manufacturing department has to take whatever the design department gives it, although it can request changes. The shift of power at Northrop eliminated a considerable number of change orders and made life easier for both departments while making the B-2 easier both to design and to manufacture.

Sources: "Smart Factories: America's Turn?" *Business Week,* May 8, 1989, 142–148; and Michael F. Wolff, "Quality in R&D—It Starts With You," *Research-Technology Management,* 34 (January-February 1991): 9–11.

TABLE 21.1 THREE WAYS TO DETERMINE LABOR PRODUCTIVITY

1. $\dfrac{\text{Sales per month (dollars)}}{\text{Labor costs}}$

2. $\dfrac{\text{Total number of goods/services produced}}{\text{Total labor hours expended}}$

3. $\dfrac{\text{Total dollar value of goods/services produced}}{\text{Total labor hours expended}}$

Labor Productivity

The relative productivity of labor is usually calculated by dividing sales per month (dollars) by labor costs (dollars) (see Table 21.1). Labor productivity may also be measured by either the total number of goods/services (for example, units, pounds, cases) produced divided by total labor hours expended, or the total dollar value of goods/services produced divided by total labor hours expended.

Raw Materials Productivity

The measurement of the productive use of raw materials centers on three areas: value analysis, scrap rates, and inventory control. *Value analysis* is the process of choosing a material of the appropriate quality, with the required characteristics, and the best price to be used in the manufacture of a good/service. Gold, for example, is a wonderful conductor of electricity for electrical connections, but copper is too, and it is much less expensive. However, gold is used in critical places where extreme reliability is important, such as in communication satellites, because its extra cost is justified when compared to the cost of failure. Productivity assessment of value analysis can be conducted through periodic management audits of bills of materials. This will help determine if value analysis guidelines are being followed by design engineers and purchasing agents.

A second way to measure the productive use of raw materials is to monitor *scrap rates.* High scrap rates may be caused by poor quality of raw materials, inadequately trained employees, or poorly performing machinery.

Inventory control is a final method to gauge the productive use. Raw materials, work-in-process, and finished goods that are idle (that is, sitting in inventory or waiting to be processed) may cost an organization a considerable amount of money. These costs are called *holding costs* and consist of the opportunity cost of the money invested in inventory, as well as the cost of storage space, insurance, inventory taxes, and the risk of obsolescence and spoilage (remember the Big Mac example). If improperly managed, these costs can mean the difference between a profit and a loss.

Energy Productivity

Energy, whether in the form of electricity, heat/cooling, or fuel for transportation, is an expensive input in many production systems. Ours is an energy-hungry economy, and much of our country's past rapid industrial growth and prosperity was aided by an abundance of cheap energy. However, the worldwide conservation movement has forever changed the way we think about and consume energy.

Measuring the productivity of energy has become more common and in large organizations is often under the control of an energy manager. Energy managers

Energy is an important and often expensive input in production systems. In this picture, a service representative for Cooper Energy Services confers with an operations supervisor at 3M's Central Utility plant in Texas. The Cooper-Bessemer® CleanBurn™ engines supplied to 3M by Cooper Industries are equipped with special igniters that allow for more complete combustion of both gas and diesel fuels, increasing engine efficiency and reducing air pollution. Waste heat from the engines is used to generate electricity and to provide steam and hot water for use in laboratories.

Source: Courtesy of Cooper Industries, Inc., Copyright © 1990, Michael Hart Houston, Texas.

periodically perform *energy audits* to determine where and how energy is being consumed and how its consumption might be reduced. Installation of computer-controlled energy management systems is becoming increasingly common.

The measure most commonly used to measure energy productivity is output quantity divided by units of energy consumed. That is,

$$\text{Energy productivity} = \frac{\text{Output quantity}}{\text{Units of energy consumed}}$$

Energy consumed may be in Btus (British thermal units) or kilowatt hours of electricity, tons of coal, gallons of oil or gas, or cubic feet of natural gas.

SUMMARY

This chapter has provided an overview of the operations management process. Additionally, the notion of productivity and its measurement were considered.

Learning Objective 1: Describe the kinds of organizations that have production systems.

All organizations, whether public or private, profit or not for profit, have production systems. This is because all organizations transform inputs into outputs.

Learning Objective 2: Outline the general nature of the operations management process.

As described in Figure 21.1, the demand for goods/services stimulates input (people, money, materials, and information), which is transformed (through facilities, machines, and methods) into outputs (goods/services). In addition, inputs, transformations, and outputs are revised by management as a result of feedback from an organization's environment.

Learning Objective 3: Identify various questions that must be considered before designing a production system.

Custom or standard goods/services or both? Capital intensive or labor intensive? What do we make? Buy? How stable is demand over time? What people skills are needed? Are good/service designs stable? Are our goods/services unique or copyright protected? Supplier reliability? Quality level desired? Single or multiple locations? General purpose or specialized equipment needed? Competitive substitutes available on the horizon?

Learning Objective 4: Understand the basic elements of a manufacturing resource planning (MRP II) system.

Figure 21.2 presents a simplified overview of an MRP II system's basic elements.

Learning Objective 5: Illustrate how an organization's strategic plan should influence the design of its master production schedule.

One illustration would be that of McDonald's versus Burger King. The McDonald's strategic plan involves selling standard products with few variations and thus producing burgers "to stock." This requires that it carry an inventory of finished burgers for quick distribution. Burger King's strategic plan involves selling a wide variety of burgers, which requires it to have a production system that quickly produces nonstandard items.

Learning Objective 6: Explain the major difference between service and manufacturing organizations.

The major difference between service and manufacturing organizations is in the area of inventories. In manufacturing organizations, inventories act as a buffer between the variability of customer demand and available supply. In service organizations, idle capacity is the buffer between customer demand and available supply.

Learning Objective 7: Define the term *productivity*.

Productivity is the amount of units of output produced divided by the number of units of resource applied.

KEY TERMS

operations management 616

productivity 624

THE MANAGEMENT EXPERIENCE A PRODUCTION SYSTEM

Look at the pen or pencil that you have in your hand. Based on what you have read in this chapter, and on your own creativity and experience, list ten things you would need to know before you could begin to design a production system for producing this good.

REVIEW AND DISCUSSION QUESTIONS

1. Do cities and banks produce outputs? What do they produce?
2. The slogan for McDonald's used to be "We do it all for you," while Burger King's was "Have it your way." What are the implications of these slogans for the design of their respective production systems?
3. Pick any organization with which you are familiar. Identify its inputs, transformations, and outputs following a format similar to that in Figure 21.1.
4. What are the main elements of an MRP II system?
5. It is often argued that "it's unfair to measure the productivity of the United States against that of Japan and Western Europe because they are still catching up with us." Do you agree? Why or why not?
6. Explain how a successfully implemented MRP II system is one way to improve raw materials productivity.

CASE 21.1   CENTRAL VALLEY UNIVERSITY

Central Valley University evaluates the productivity of its faculty members according to three factors: teaching effectiveness, research and publications, and service to the university and community. Each year these productivity evaluations are used as the basis for individual faculty salary increases, promotions, and tenure decisions.

Also, because Central Valley is a state-supported university, the state legislature is becoming more interested in faculty "productivity." It often complains that faculty teach only from 6 to 12 hours a week. "What do they do with the rest of their time?" one legislator complained. "I propose we require the university to provide us with productivity measures similar to those I get in my company," said another legislator, who was a manufacturing executive. Yet another legislator proposed that faculty productivity be measured by how successful their

graduates are at getting jobs—"After all, isn't that what education is all about?"

Problems

1. What difficulties might there be in measuring individual faculty productivity by the three factors that Central uses? What factors would you suggest?
2. What do you think of the legislature's desire to measure faculty productivity? Do you agree or disagree with the proposals and comments from the three quoted legislators?
3. How is productivity measurement likely to differ between manufacturing and service organizations?

Source: Thomas E. Hendrick, Arizona State University.

P A R T
S E V E N

CONTEMPORARY CHALLENGES

CHAPTER 22

LEARNING OBJECTIVES

Upon completing this chapter, you should be able to:

- Understand the nature of international business.
- Discuss what international management involves.
- Recount the different types of international business.
- Distinguish between a multinational corporation and a global corporation.
- Explain why an organization might enter the international business arena.

The Sara Lee Corp. is American as apple pie, but its recipe for success has international appeal. Sara Lee ranks among the top five U.S.-based consumer products companies in Europe and has a rapidly growing market share in Asia and South America—all thanks to a management team that knows how to adapt the product mix to satisfy diverse local tastes.

Sara Lee is best known in the United States as the maker of desserts that nobody doesn't like. But a major part of its revenue—both at home and abroad—comes from its collection of panty hose and underwear companies. The Chicago-based conglomerate owns such U.S. powerhouses as Hanes, L'eggs, Champion, Bali, and Playtex. And in recent years, Sara Lee has expanded globally by buying a multitude of foreign companies in related industries. Acquisitions completed since 1989 include Europe's leading hosiery maker, Dim; Spain's top underwear manufacturer, the Sans Group; Hungary's largest coffee roaster, Compack Trading and Packing Co.; and Australia's biggest apparel producer, the Linter textiles group. And that's just to name a few.

In every case, the strategy is the same. Sara Lee makes a quick entry into a new market by acquiring a product leader with a well-known brand name. It then builds on existing market share by expanding into a line of related products, creating what it calls a "megabrand." For example, after taking over the French hosiery maker Dim, Sara Lee sewed the popular label into a new line of un-

INTERNATIONAL MANAGEMENT

derwear, socks, and T-shirts. It then designed common packaging and advertising to build brand loyalty.

But there is another key ingredient to Sara Lee's international strategy. It keeps foreign nationals in its top posts abroad, reasoning that local managers better understand the culture and market. Take the 1992 acquisition of the Sans Group in Spain. Pedro Sans Llopart founded the company and built it into the leading underwear and knit products manufacturer in the country. Even after Sara Lee's acquisition, Sans stayed at the helm to continue building on the success of the last 40 years.

In the former Eastern Bloc it was even more important for Sara Lee to keep local managers in place, not only to overcome language barriers but to help ease the transition of acquired companies from government-owned bureaucracies to private corporations. "The most important thing is the industrial relations—motivating the people. Without an understanding of the feelings of the workers and a knowledge of the language, it would be difficult to manage this business," says Bogo Laszlo, general manager of both an acquired company and a new Sara Lee division.

Sara Lee's appetite for global expansion is far from satiated. Even though a recent buying spree added $1 billion in sales to the income statement, it is always looking for new opportunities. As chairman John Bryan puts it, "The world has literally opened up to do business." In this chapter, we will explore the nature of international business, its complexities and opportunities.

Source: Original article by Carol Cerulli.

The collaboration of George S. Vozikis, The Citadel, and Michael R. Czinkota, Georgetown University, in the preparation of this chapter is gratefully acknowledged.

THE NATURE OF INTERNATIONAL BUSINESS

We tend to think of international business in terms of the giants of particular industries—the Toyotas, the Exxons, the IBMs, or Royal Dutch/Shells. These mammoth corporations have high visibility the world over. Although such giants may dominate our view, in reality international business is composed of a thriving network of various kinds of organizations, large and small, well known and obscure, efficient and inefficient, whose activities span the globe. To appreciate the impact of international business on our daily lives, we need only look at the assortment of goods in many American households—Sony televisions, Volvo station wagons, Mexican floor tiles, French dinner wines, dhurrie rugs, Teenage Mutant Ninja Turtles (assembled in China), and good old American Calvin Klein jeans (made in Hong Kong, of course).

This globalization of world markets has had profound ramifications for today's managers. No longer can managers of domestic organizations think of their competition simply as a company in the next town or state. Foundry workers in Louisiana compete with foundry workers in Howrah, India. Not only that, but they are also competing with Japanese inventors searching for an improved steelmaking process, and chemical engineers in Germany who are developing plastics that can substitute for steel.

But as world competition intensifies, so do world opportunities. David's Cookies has outlets in Japan. Coca-Cola sells its soft drinks in China. American jeans are fiercely coveted in Moscow.

No one would deny that international trade has its hazards. But few ambitious organizations can long resist the siren call of the potential for trade on distant shores. In fact, world trade volume has increased in the last three decades more than twentyfold, from $200 billion to more than $4 trillion. Countries that were never considered leading world traders, such as Singapore, Hong Kong, Taiwan, and South Korea, have emerged as major economic powers. Moreover, the newly emerging democracies of Europe and the former Soviet Union are now beginning to enter the global market as both suppliers and markets for products. Clearly, both the opportunities and threats of world trade today are greater than ever before.

As a future manager in a world economy, you should be familiar with the various issues posed by international business. In this chapter, we will briefly consider how the management concepts we have explored apply to business on an international level.

INTERNATIONAL BUSINESS VERSUS INTERNATIONAL MANAGEMENT

There are nearly as many explanations of **international business** as there are tankers plying the waters between Kuwait and Galveston. Some writers explain it simply as business involving two or more nations. Others point out that international business may also include activities such as transfers of technology, infor-

International business.
A multifaceted system linking countries, governments, organizations, and people across national borders, involving all kinds of public and private business activities and sociocultural and political/legal processes.

Colgate-Palmolive is a global company that began expanding its international operations over 50 years ago. Colgate now serves over 3.5 billion customers, and continues to grow by carefully managing its international business activities, introducing new products, expanding product categories and acquiring complementary businesses. One of the more recent additions to Colgate's family of international products is Hill's Science Diet pet food line. In the last few years, the number of countries where Hill's products are available has grown from 2 to 22.

mation, or data. Still others see international business in terms of corporations that operate independently of fixed geographical boundaries.

For our purposes, we will view international business as being distinguished by the following features:

1. A multifaceted system linking countries, governments, organizations, and people.
2. A flexible definition of national borders that does not correspond directly to international political processes.
3. Participation in diverse public and private business activities.
4. Involvement of sociocultural and political/legal processes.

As this list implies, the scope of international business encompasses a wide range of activities. Although the management concepts to be discussed throughout the preceding chapters are equally relevant in an international context, environmental differences may greatly affect how they are applied. Differences in how nations and cultures conduct business can be dramatic or quite subtle. For example, the lack of a private business infrastructure and profit orientation in Russia will require new strategies in hiring, training, and motivating employees. On a less obvious level, subtle differences in language, even between the United States and England, need to be taken into account. For example, when an American says that negotiations have "bombed," he means that they have failed, while for a Briton, the same term indicates a major success. An effective manager must thus recognize that such differences may require learning new management practices to ensure an organization's survival and growth.

In keeping with our approach to management throughout this book, we can define **international management** as the process of achieving an organization's global goals through the efficient utilization of human and material resources. The challenge of international management is maintaining a dynamic equilibrium among the requirements of three areas:

1. *Managing international practices* in areas such as foreign licensing, export and import documentation, and the unique multinational aspects of support areas, such as finance, marketing, and production.

2. *Managing international business activities* in terms of investment, procurement, allocation, transfer, and utilization of an organization's human and material resources, as well as its technical and managerial skills. The diversity of the international environment, the wide scope of international business activities, and the unique character of each country's international infrastructure (its labor unions, distribution channels, capital markets, and so forth) require that an international manager keep vigilant watch over international business activities. Many managers have found that they cannot take things for granted when operating outside their home country.

3. *Managing sociocultural and political/legal processes* emerging from the interactions of a multinational organization with both its home country and its host country. International managers are responsible for monitoring sociocultural and political/legal developments and processes in the international business environment. They work to ensure swift and conflict-free interactions between home and host country environments. This invariably requires maintaining a flexibility in managerial practices to accommodate the special environmental requirements of different host countries.

Figure 22.1 presents a general outline of the elements of international management.

TYPES OF INTERNATIONAL BUSINESS

International business takes many forms. It is primarily composed of four main categories: international trade, portfolio investment, direct foreign investment, and services trade, such as licensing and franchising.

International Trade

The trading of merchandise is the oldest form of international business. **International trade** involves the buying and selling of goods and services among residents of different countries. From a global perspective, exports and imports always balance.

In overall international trade, the United States had a record deficit of $146 billion in 1987 (see Figure 22.2). By 1990, the gap was down to $70 billion, and by the close of 1991, the trade deficit was only $7 billion—a small amount relative to a $6 trillion economy. U.S. exports have been growing at an average 9.5 percent annually since 1985, much faster than the growth in imports. The current (1991) trade balance does show a $66.8 billion deficit in merchandise goods. This negative sum, however, is offset by a $49.5 billion surplus in services (including the sale of software, movies, insurance, and tourism) and a roughly $10 billion surplus in net investment income.

International management.

The process of achieving the global objectives of an organization through efficient utilization of human and material resources.

International trade.

The buying and selling of goods and services among residents of different countries.

FIGURE 22.1   THE ELEMENTS OF INTERNATIONAL MANAGEMENT

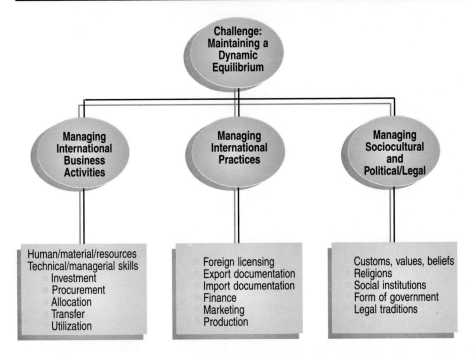

The recent boom in U.S. exports is attributable to three factors:

1. The value of the dollar has fallen by some 30 percent in trade-weighted terms.
2. U.S. productivity has risen sharply since 1982.
3. U.S. wages increased only 3 percent each year in current dollars between 1982 and 1990 as compared to, for example, an annually 9.7 percent increase in German wages and a 10.5 percent yearly increase in Japanese wages.

As a result of all three factors, U.S. labor costs have gone down while increasing sharply in other industrial economies.

U.S. competitiveness is most obvious in Europe. In 1991, the United States ran a $16 billion merchandise trade surplus with its European trading partners. This compares with a 1986 U.S trade deficit of $23 billion.

Portfolio Investment

The second main category of international business is **international portfolio investment.** It is the purchase of foreign securities in the form of stocks, bonds, or commercial paper to obtain a return on that investment in the form of dividends, interest, or capital gains.

U.S. investors consider adding foreign investments to their portfolios for several reasons:

1. By ignoring foreign markets for stocks and bonds, they reduce their choices to less than 50 percent of available worldwide investment opportunities.
2. The rates of return on non-U.S. securities have often substantially exceeded those on U.S. securities.
3. Diversification with foreign securities reduces portfolio risk.

International portfolio investment.
The purchase of foreign securities in the form of stocks, bonds, or commercial paper to obtain an investment return in the form of dividends, interest, or capital gains.

FIGURE 22.2   U.S. TRADE BALANCE

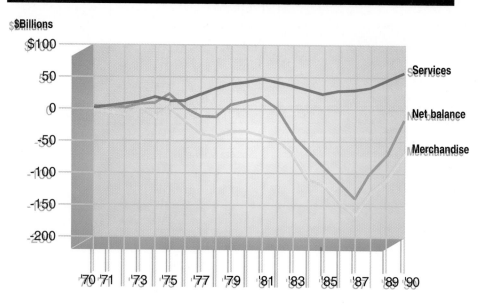

$Billions

Source: Based on Department of Commerce and Bureau of Economic Analysis data reported in Howard Banks, "The World's Most Competitive Economy," *Forbes,* March 30, 1992, 85.

The inability of the U.S. securities market to compete with other international securities markets is attributable partly to strict U.S. disclosure regulations, which, while ensuring investor protection, may discourage some foreign investors and move trading offshore, adversely affecting the ability of U.S. markets to compete.

Direct Foreign Investment

A third type of international business, **direct foreign investment,** involves the acquisition by domestic organizations of foreign-based operating facilities,

Direct foreign investment.

The acquisition by domestic organizations of foreign-based operating facilities, such as plants, factories, warehouses, and service centers, to enhance long-term profits.

Rolls of newsprint, bound for Pacific Rim markets, are inspected in the hold of one of Weyerhaeuser's Westwood Shipping Lines ships. Half of Weyer-haeuser's newsprint production is exported. Paper products and wood pulp are nearly 60 percent of the company's $1.9 billion in exports from North America.

CLOSE UP: INTERNATIONAL MANAGEMENT GETTING AROUND SOUTHEAST ASIA

The current emphasis on global thinking and global politics makes this a good time for expansion-minded U.S. companies to visit Southeast Asia—Singapore, Indonesia, Thailand, and Malaysia—with an eye toward joining in its economic growth. Southeast Asia is modernizing fast, and travelers should keep in mind the following:

Attire. Pack the same work clothes you would for a trip to Miami, Houston, or Los Angeles during warm weather. (Remember, you're near the equator.) Dress comfortably but conservatively.

Medical Needs. Generally, special shots are required only for travelers headed to a remote site. Consult your physician, however, if you have a special concern.

Getting There. Book well ahead—local holidays can fill flights at odd times. Plan on a 24-hour journey to the region.

Airline Pluses. Transpacific carriers, both domestic and international, are known for their service. You'll receive amenities kits, extended meals, two movies, and more.

Jet Lag. Air travelers are usually more affected by the change in time zones on their return from the East. (To ease some of the discomfort of jet lag, remember to drink plenty of water before, during, and after the long flight.) However, it's still wise to limit appointments in the area to a day or two after your arrival.

Hotels. Expect white-glove service. Hotels are the cities' business and social hubs.

Concierge Floors. Rooms on concierge floors are generally worth the extra cost with additional complimentary facilities like meeting rooms and lounges.

Secretarial Help. Top-notch business centers—fully equipped with copiers, faxes, computers, business reference books, and interpreters—are generally available at Asian hotels.

Fitness Facilities. At the region's hotels, health clubs and spas tend to be elaborate, with outdoor lap pools, workout machines, running tracks (or routes), tennis courts, and even golf. Some hotels, such as the Shangri-la in Singapore and Hilton in Jakarta, are more like resorts.

Transportation.

- In Singapore, use the superb new subway system or taxis. Car rentals are expensive and impractical (because of business-district driving restrictions).
- In Jakarta, most agencies require you to hire a driver with your car—and it makes sense because of confusing street signs. Rates are low.
- In Bangkok, take taxis but be prepared for slow progress through traffic jams.
- In Kuala Lumpur, where traffic is moderate except at rush hour, taxis are your best bet.

Business Breakfasts. Early-morning meetings are popular, and most upscale hotels serve sumptuous buffet breakfasts—which include local dishes.

Business Entertaining. Most entertaining is done in hotel restaurants. For instance, the Oriental in Bangkok has a half-dozen top restaurants, from French to Thai.

City-to-City. Allow only 60 to 90 minutes for flights between business capitals.

Etiquette. Have plenty of business cards on hand; you can arrange through your concierge for bilingual cards for a fee. Politeness is expected in Southeast Asia, but punctuality isn't.

Source: Adapted from "Getting Around Southeast Asia," *Travel & Entertainment* 9 (February 1992): 1–2.

such as plants, factories, warehouses, and hotels, and requires that managers consider the long-term potential for a country's political stability and profitability. Its advantage is that it gives an investor effective managerial control over the assets of an acquired company.

For decades, the United States was the world's leading direct foreign investor. U.S. multinationals sprouted everywhere. More recently, however, because the declining value of the dollar has made acquisitions in the United States more attractive, foreign investment in the United States has increased sharply. By 1990, total cumulative foreign direct investment in the United States totaled $401 billion, outpacing U.S. investment abroad by over $27 billion. For 1988 alone, the U.S. inflow of foreign capital totaled $42.2 billion, compared to U.S. foreign investment of $20.4 billion. Although some commentators have agonized over the "selling of America," there seems to be little cause for concern.

Direct foreign investment can take many forms. Among the most common are:

1. *Contract manufacturing,* in which a foreign producer manufactures an organization's output for sale in a foreign market.

2. *Turnkey projects,* in which an organization sets up an operation abroad involving the design and construction of a project, such as a dam or a refinery, in exchange for a fee. Upon completion of the project, the international organization turns over the operation to local people.

3. *Joint venture,* with a foreign organization or government in a facility abroad, to meet local demand or to be used as an "export platform" to boost that country's export sales.

SMART MANAGEMENT DIRECT FOREIGN INVESTMENT SURROUNDS US

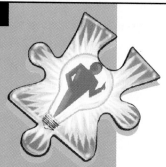

You don't need to be an international economist to understand how foreign money is transforming the United States. Take a typical day. You awaken and wash up with a bar of Dove soap. You dress in a Brooks Brothers suit or an outfit purchased at Bloomingdale's and hop into your car, which sports Michelin tires and parts supplied by Marada, Inc. At your office in the *U.S. News and World Report* building in Washington, you cozy up to a Fujitsu computer and use a Northern Telecom phone system. At lunchtime you pick up a business associate who is staying at the Embassy Suites Hotel. After work you shop at a Benetton Store or maybe Laura Ashley, paying for your purchases with money from a First American Bank cash machine. For a late snack, you eat Keebler cookies.

In each instance, foreign-owned companies with operations a few miles from the White House produced or marketed what you are eating, wearing, driving, and working on. Other foreign investors own your office building, the hotel, the stores, and the bank.

Most consumers know that Sony ships VCRs here from Japan and Hyundai brings over cars from South Korea. But less obvious is that a bar of Dove soap comes from a Baltimore factory owned by the giant Dutch marketer Unilever, whereas Brooks Brothers is owned by a British concern, Marks & Spencer PLC. And while General Motors makes its own cars in Baltimore, parts are produced by Marada, a Canadian-owned company.

Source: Adapted from Paul Farahi, "How Foreign Money Is Changing Washington," *Washington Post,* June 20, 1988, 1, 33.

In 1990 Alcoa and Kobe Steel Ltd. of Japan formed a 50-50 joint venture, KSL Alcoa Aluminum Company Ltd., to produce and market aluminum sheet primarily for the growing beverage can markets in Japan and other Asian countries. In 1991 Alcoa and Kobe agreed to form two more joint-venture companies, one in the U.S. and one in Japan, to serve the transportation industry.

4. *Wholly owned subsidiary,* in which a foreign organization holds 100 percent ownership of a foreign affiliate.

Services Trade

A final category of international business deals with services trade. Here an organization typically does not invest directly, but rather permits the use of its service capabilities by foreign firms abroad. While exposure to a foreign market is often small with such activities, the revenue derived and potential for growth may be large. The two most common forms of such activities are:

1. *Licensing,* in which an international organization, a *licensor,* provides another organization abroad, a *licensee,* with access to its patents and trademarks. The foreign organization pays the licensor a royalty or other form of fee for the use of these trade secrets.

2. *Franchising,* a form of licensing in which the supplier of a good or service, a *franchisor,* grants a dealer, a *franchisee,* the right to sell this good or service for a fee. Some examples of international franchises are McDonald's, Avis Rent-A-Car, and Hilton Hotels.

Tokyo Disneyland is owned and operated by a Japanese corporation unrelated to The Walt Disney Company. Disney licenses trademarked and copyrighted materials such as its names and characters to the Japanese corporation and earns royalties on revenues generated by Tokyo Disneyland.

MULTINATIONAL CORPORATIONS: THE VEHICLE OF INTERNATIONAL BUSINESS

MULTINATIONAL CORPORATIONS

The most active participants in international business are **multinational corporations.** Although their most visible activities abroad are foreign investment, they also often export, hold portfolio investments, or license and franchise. Table 22.1 lists the 40 leading multinationals. The United States is the host country for 19, with Japan a close second with 15.

Multinational corporation's take a worldwide approach to foreign markets and have an integrated global philosophy that encompasses all components of the international business description presented earlier:

1. It is a multifaceted system of domestic and foreign operating units called *affiliates*.
2. Its multicountry capacity generates international business relationships.
3. It engages in all kinds of business activities, including exporting, portfolio investment, and direct foreign investment, with different degrees of international involvement.
4. Its international business involves sociocultural and political/legal processes that stem from the many challenges associated with managing a wide range of environmental factors in many different countries.

Multinationalism is no longer the exclusive domain of one particular country or organization. The international marketplace has passed the point where any single multinational corporation or nation could expect to dominate the world market. We have entered an era that might be called the "New Globalism." Its hallmark is the increasing political and economic interdependence of nation-states.

THE EVOLUTION OF MULTINATIONAL CORPORATIONS

Multinational business is not a new phenomenon. The Phoenicians, for example, not only traded throughout their known world, but also established manufacturing

Multinational corporation.
A corporation that views each of its affiliates around the world as an independent entity, each on its own in serving the national market in which it is situated.

TABLE 22.1   THE 40 LEADING MULTINATIONAL CORPORATIONS

Rank in 1991	Corporation	Home Country	Market Value (Billions of U.S. dollars)
1	Nippon Telegraph & Telephone	Japan	103.00
2	Royal Dutch/Shell Group	Neth./Britain	72.91
3	Exxon	U.S.	72.81
4	General Electric	U.S.	67.45
5	Industrial Bank of Japan	Japan	64.18
6	Philip Morris	U.S.	63.33
7	International Business Machines	U.S.	60.77
8	Fuji Bank	Japan	58.68
9	Mitsubishi Bank	Japan	58.08
10	Dai-Ichi Kangyo Bank	Japan	57.38
11	Sumitomo Bank	Japan	56.39
12	Sanwa Bank	Japan	49.94
13	Mitsui Taiyo Kobe Bank	Japan	48.69
14	Wal-Mart Stores	U.S.	48.55
15	Merck	U.S.	46.01
16	Toyota Motor	Japan	44.01
17	Bristol-Myers Squibb	U.S.	42.45
18	American Telephone & Telegraph	U.S.	40.43
19	British Telecommunications	Britain	40.03
20	Coca-Cola	U.S.	38.26
21	Tokyo Electric Power	Japan	37.53
22	Du Pont	U.S.	33.16
23	Nomura Securities	Japan	30.80
24	British Petroleum	Britain	30.61
25	Johnson & Johnson	U.S.	30.18
26	Glaxo Holdings	Britain	30.02
27	Long-Term Credit Bank of Japan	Japan	29.79
28	Procter & Gamble	U.S.	29.49
29	Hitachi Ltd.	Japan	27.73
30	Mobil	U.S.	26.42
31	General Motors	U.S.	26.40
32	Amoco	U.S.	26.16
33	Allianz Holding	Germany	26.15
34	Tokai Bank	Japan	26.10
35	Chevron	U.S.	25.91
36	GTE	U.S.	25.91
37	Matsushita Electric Industrial	Japan	25.46
38	Pepsico	U.S.	24.89
39	Unilever	Neth./Britain	24.07
40	Bellsouth	U.S.	24.04

Source: *Business Week,* July 15, 1991, 56.

centers and facilitated the transfer of technologies such as metalworking, glass-making, and dyeing from one area of the Mediterranean to another.

During the American colonial era, trading companies such as the Dutch East India Company and the Hudson's Bay Company directed all colonial exports and imports through their home countries. They suppressed colonial goods that competed with those of the mother country. Such companies became extinct in the 1960s.

The early international ventures of U.S. business abroad were mainly prompted by technical inventions. The Singer sewing machine and the McCormick reaper had much to do with drawing attention to American industrial products. Samuel Morse's telegraph, Samuel Colt's revolver, and Charles Goodyear's vulcanizing process similarly enjoyed great international demand. At London's great Crystal Palace Exhibition in 1851, top medals were given to Goodyear for India rubber products, to Gail Bordon for a special meat biscuit, to Blodgett and Lerow for their sewing machine, and to Colt, to Palmer, and to Robbins and Lawrence for their firearms. American companies were not slow in turning these honors into diverse sales.

The Sherman Antitrust Act of 1890 provided another impetus to internationalization. The Sherman Act prohibited collusion among business firms in restraint of domestic trade, but it was quite indifferent about market sharing, price fixing, and competitive retaliation in foreign markets. As a result, American businesses rushed to acquire foreign companies, especially during the 1950s. Two decades later the pattern changed, and other nations' businesses found the United States a safe haven for direct foreign investment.

As a result, multinational corporations are now a global phenomenon. Even less developed countries have established their own multinational corporations.

MULTINATIONAL VERSUS GLOBAL CORPORATIONS

Although a global corporation is also a multinational one, the term *multinational corporation* is typically used to describe a corporation that views each of its affiliates around the world as an independent entity, each on its own in serving the national market in which it is situated. Thus, a multinational corporation may encompass many different types of organizations—a bottling plant in Peru, a trucking company in Belgium, a petroleum distribution firm in New Guinea. Each is a separate subsidiary, and the various subsidiaries do not necessarily work together.

A **global corporation,** on the other hand, will integrate its international operations such that they must work together. For example, a global corporation may buy components on three continents, ship them to be partially assembled in a country with inexpensive labor, and then put on the finishing touches in factories close to its customers. The result might be a Leica camera, an Epson printer, or a Canon typewriter. One part of a global organization could not exist without the others. Although such an approach will increase the short-term vulnerability of a global corporation, it also enables it to use the competitive advantage of each country to produce goods and services in the most efficient way.

Global corporation.
A corporation that integrates its international operations such that they must work together.

ENTERING THE INTERNATIONAL BUSINESS ARENA

What prompts an organization to go international? The specific reasons to go international differ for each organization, but the desire to find a larger market and achieve increased growth is typical. Confronted by global competitors, an organization may find that it needs an increased customer base to realize economies of scale and overhead. Other common reasons for international expansion are expense related. Increasingly, organizations are searching for countries where labor costs are lower and raw materials are less expensive. The attractiveness of foreign-investment climates and the desire to avoid trade restrictions are also other common reasons for international expansion. Table 22.2 identifies various other reasons.

When an organization goes international, its managers must take a global approach to long-term planning. This is especially true when an organization has to start from scratch to build a whole new industry within a country. The financial drain on all its operations can be considerable. Since the payback on such foreign investment can take years, organizations that go international must often plan well into the future to avoid any financial shortfalls.

ANALYZING THE INTERNATIONAL BUSINESS ENVIRONMENT

In Chapter 3 we discussed the many environmental factors that can influence an organization. In that chapter we principally dealt with factors that influence domestic organizations. Those organizations that decide to operate on an international scale must take into account not only domestic influences, but also environmental forces unique to the country in which they chose to operate. Because many countries have a less stable political and economic climate than ours, the decision to go international may pose sizable risks to any organization.

Political Risk

In the international sphere, multinationals face a major concern: **political risk.** Political risk exists in every nation, but the range of risk varies widely from country to country. In general, political risk is lowest in countries that have a history of stability and consistency. Political risk tends to be highest in nations that do not have this sort of history. In many countries, however, consistency and stability that were apparent on the surface have been quickly swept away by major popular

Political risk.
Risks such as nationalization, repeal of tax laws, political instability, and the like that may render the value of a corporation's investment in a foreign nation worthless.

Before investing in multinational operations, an organization must scan the environment in which it hopes to conduct business. Knowledge of a host country's economy, business and political structures, labor, and other resources is essential. The importance of the Asia-Pacific region as both a consumer and developer of advanced technology was a factor in Texas Instruments' decision to establish a new research and development center currently under construction in Tskuba, Japan. The center will help TI scientists to engage in collaborative research with its customers and the Japanese scientific community.

TABLE 22.2 REASONS FOR INTERNATIONAL EXPANSION

Marketing Factors

1. Market size
2. Market growth
3. Desire to maintain share of market
4. Desire to advance exports of parent company
5. Need to maintain close customer contact
6. Dissatisfaction with existing market arrangements
7. Export base

Trade Restrictions

1. Trade barriers
2. Preference of local customers for local products

Cost Factors

1. Desire to be near source of supply
2. Labor availability
3. Raw materials availability
4. Capital/technology availability
5. Lower labor costs
6. Lower production costs other than labor
7. Lower transport costs
8. Financial (and other) inducements by government
9. More favorable cost levels

Investment Climate

1. General attitude toward foreign investment
2. Political stability
3. Limitations on ownership
4. Currency exchange regulations
5. Stability of foreign exchange
6. Tax structure
7. Familiarity with country

General

1. Expected higher profits
2. Other

Source: *International Investment and Multinational Enterprises* (Paris: Organization for Economic Cooperation and Development, 1983), 41.

movements that drew on the bottled-up frustrations of the population. The rapid changes in Europe and the former Soviet Union serve as examples.

Three major forms of political risk can be encountered:

1. Ownership risk, which exposes property and life.

2. Operating risk, which refers to interference with the ongoing operations of an organization.

3. Transfer risk, which is mainly encountered when attempts are made to shift funds or operations between countries.

Political risk can originate from within governments or from sources outside the control of government, and can consist of a wide variety of actions, ranging from expropriation and sabotage to the repeal of current laws or introduction of new ones. In such instances, political risk can render the value of an organization's investment in a foreign country worthless in a matter of days.

Environmental Scanning

Managers must thoroughly examine several areas before making a foreign investment. As noted in Chapter 3, this process of examination is called *environmental scanning*. Government regulation, for example, can be an area of threat or opportunity. A country that holds a negative view of foreign investment may find numerous ways of limiting production and sales. Other countries may encourage foreign investment because of their own internal needs for economic or social advancement and may provide low-interest loans, land and capital grants, training and reconversion allowances, tax holidays, and government purchase orders. To prosper abroad, multinational corporations must attempt to anticipate and minimize the effects of negative governmental action, and take advantage of incentives that are offered. An up-to-date and accurate understanding of host country changes is therefore imperative.

PLANNING FOR INTERNATIONAL BUSINESS

Organizations that conduct business multinationally must realize that other countries are not just additional regions for production or marketing. Success in the international marketplace requires an appropriate state of mind that influences an organization's overall strategy. International planning must be tailored to an individual organization. Accurate information must be obtained and thoroughly evaluated to help an organization decide whether it can expect to operate safely and profitably in a given country.

The following information is essential:

1. Knowledge of the basic strengths and weaknesses of a country's economy.

2. An interpretative analysis of a country's commercial structure.

3. An accurate estimation of a country's investment climate, including an interpretation of current and pending legislation.

4. An understanding of the main factors affecting a country's commercial operations (for example, energy, labor, resources, market size).

An organization also should establish methods for obtaining information. These might include the following:

1. *Special consultants.* For example, Bechtel Corporation uses Richard Helms, a former director of the CIA and former ambassador to Iran.
2. *Advisory councils* of prominent foreign businesspeople and retired government officials. General Motors and Caterpillar Tractor Co. use this method.
3. *Private intelligence systems.* Gulf Oil Corp. has used this technique.
4. *Local managers.* These individuals can be held responsible for maintaining up-to-date information within their business community.

The information obtained by these resources will help match environmental strengths and opportunities with organization strengths and weaknesses. It also can provide a basis for top management to establish realistic goals for new ventures, to allocate resources, to curtail activities in some countries, and to initiate new activities in others.

SUMMARY

The globalization of world markets has had profound ramifications for today's managers. The current chapter has taken a brief look at how the management concepts we have explored apply in an international context.

Learning Objective 1: Understand the nature of international business.
International business is a multifaceted system linking countries, governments, organizations, and people across national borders, involving all kinds of public and private business activities and sociocultural and political/legal processes.

Learning Objective 2: Discuss what international management involves.
International management involves (1) maintaining a state of dynamic equilibrium for an organization within a multifaceted international system; (2) managing international practices; (3) coordinating international business activities in terms of procurement, allocation, transfer, and utilization of an organization's physical and human resources, as well as its technical and managerial skills; and (4) maintaining flexibility in managing sociocultural and political/legal processes emerging from the interactions of a multinational organization with both its home country and its host country.

Learning Objective 3: Recount the different types of international business.
There are four main categories of international business: international trade, portfolio investment, direct foreign investment, and services trade.

Learning Objective 4: Distinguish between a multinational corporation and a global corporation.
A multinational corporation views each of its affiliates around the world as an independent entity, each on its own in serving the unique demands of the national market where it is situated. By contrast, a global corporation integrates its international operations such that they must work together.

Learning Objective 5: Explain why an organization might enter the international business arena.
An organization's decision to enter the international business arena is often stimulated by the desire to get ahead of competitors. One way to do this may be to ex-

pand abroad where labor costs are lower or raw materials are less expensive. Or an organization might find that to grow and achieve maximum economies of scale, it must sell more than its home market can absorb. Organizations also might go international when impediments such as trade barriers or high transportation costs are removed.

THE MANAGEMENT EXPERIENCE THE WEALTH OF NATIONS: THE WORLD IS GETTING RICHER

The United States is no longer alone in terms of high standards of living. Other countries have made tremendous progress toward improving living conditions for their citizens.

Comparing countries is not easy. Per capita income ($19,789 for the United States in 1989 versus $16,419 for France) shows the size of a nation's gross domestic product but says nothing about income distribution or variations among countries in terms of local costs, such as the price of a house or movie. To account for these differences, two University of Pennsylvania economists, Alan Heston and Robert Summers, have come up with a complicated system of determining purchasing power parity (PPP) to compare the wealth of nations.

Against a U.S. index of 100, Switzerland fares well with a score of 86, which means that a Swiss person has 86 percent of the goods and services that an American has. A Japanese person scores 69 (up from 17 in 1950!), a French person scores a respectable 68, a British person 66, and an Italian 65.

A typical Japanese household fares well in comparison to a household in the United States. Fifty-seven percent of Japanese households have air conditioners, 71 percent have cars, and 99 percent have color television sets, compared with 60 percent, 87 percent, and 93 percent in the United States.

The most spectacular advances indicated in the PPP scale took place in Asia. In Hong Kong (PPP 71), Singapore (52), Taiwan (33), and South Korea (29), a broad middle class has developed to fill the tremendous gap between rich and poor that was the norm a few decades ago. This middle class enjoys indoor plumbing, electricity, telephones, and family vacations—simple, but at the same time extraordinary, conquests. In contrast, India scored a 4 on the PPP scale, while African nations, such as Zaire, scored a 2. In these countries, even a simple item, such as batteries for a flashlight, may be considered a luxury.

Despite the fact that the PPP scale is a better measure than per capita income, in reality it, too, has weaknesses. For example, Americans may own more homes, automobiles, and clothes, but Germans travel outside their country more, have 6 weeks of vacation a year, and are half as likely to get murdered as Americans, while the Japanese have a life expectancy of 78 years versus 76 for Americans.

Problems

1. What do you think about the fact that the world is indeed getting richer, but wealth is still relative?

2. What implications will these developments have for U.S. trade?

3. What implications will these trends have for a big, multinational hospital chain like Humana, Inc.?

Sources: Lee Smith, "The Wealth of Nations: The World Is Getting Richer," *Fortune,* September 14, 1987, 35; and Robert Summers and Alan Heston, "The Penn World Table (Mark 5): An Expanded Set of International Comparisons, 1950–1988," *Quarterly Journal of Economics* (May 1991): 327–368.

KEY TERMS

direct foreign investment 640

global corporation 646

international business 636

international management 638

international portfolio investment 639

international trade 638

multinational corporation 644

political risk 647

REVIEW AND DISCUSSION QUESTIONS

1. According to Ruben F. Mettler, former chairman of TRW, Inc., "Protectionism at best can only defer the inevitable day of reckoning and make it worse when it does come." What does Mettler mean?

2. The *Wall Street Journal* reports that foreign executives often arrive in the United States with fistfuls of cash and high hopes, only to leave with large losses and tarnished reputations. What mistakes might the foreign executives be making?

3. Commenting on a joint venture between General Motors and Toyota, one commentator has asked: "Just who is *us*? And who's *them*?" Respond.

4. "We haven't got any interest in Mr. Kendall's nose." So said Coca-Cola president Donald R. Keough in response to whether Coke was entering the Russian market to tweak the nose of former PepsiCo Chairman Donald M. Kendall, who got there first. Explain the Coca-Cola president's attitude and his company's international strategy.

5. "The global yuppie has arrived." As described by Kenichi Ohmae, a consultant for McKinsey & Co., "he awakes to music from his Sony radio, reaches for his Brazilian-grown coffee in a cup from Taiwan, rides down Otis elevators, climbs into his Porsche, turns on a Blaupunkt cassette player, and heads to work." Who is responsible for this globalization of trade?

6. How does strategic management differ between a domestic and a multinational firm?

CASE 22.1 GOING GLOBAL FUJITSU STYLE

The largest seller of computers in the world is IBM. Surprised? Probably not. However, the No. 2 seller of computers may be a surprise. Fujitsu Ltd., which is No. 1 in Japan by a small margin, is second to IBM in worldwide computer sales. Fujitsu is only about one-third the size of IBM, posting revenues of $21 billion last year, but it makes several products that are industry leaders: the world's fastest conventional supercomputers, the world's lightest cellular phones, and the world's largest memory chips. Fujitsu's lack of recognition results primarily from its

failure to become a major player in the PC market.

Fujitsu has captured the No. 2 position through investments in companies like Amdahl Corp. (currently owning 44 percent) and International Computers Ltd. (recently purchasing 80 percent). Amdahl is located in Silicon Valley, makes IBM compatible mainframes, and has annual revenues of $2.2 billion. ICL, with sales of $2.7 billion a year, is Britain's largest computer company. Of Fujitsu's $5.2 billion of overseas revenue last year, almost half came from Amdahl and ICL.

Why doesn't Fujitsu stand on its own or else completely take over the companies? First of all, these companies provide Fujitsu with needed technology. Amdahl was founded by IBM's former chief mainframe designer. Fujitsu supplied venture capital in exchange for technology to be used by Fujitsu in building mainframes in Japan. Also, Fujitsu recognizes the world's suspicion of Japan's industrial might. Fujitsu is becoming international by becoming local, almost neighborly. Amdahl and ICL operate autonomously, maintaining their Western management, developing their own strategy, and even competing against each other. Fujitsu views business as taking place in a borderless economy, but with an awareness of increasing nationalism.

Fujitsu has found a way to balance integration and autonomy. Within Fujitsu's basic structure, each division—telecommunications, computer, semiconductor—is managed independently. Cooperation takes place only on special projects.

Fujitsu has not always been successful when buying Western companies. In the mid-1980s, it attempted to buy Fairchild Semiconductor Corp. The Fujitsu proposal came when the United States was accusing Japanese chipmakers of dumping their products on U.S. markets below cost. The Commerce Department succeeded in pressuring Fujitsu to drop its offer, citing national security concerns. (Ironically, Fairchild was already foreign owned.)

Fujitsu has continued to pursue partnerships. The major strategy change has been to focus on smaller companies. Fujitsu is finding ripe fields among small, creative companies. In many cases, these companies are in the United States and are formed by engineers with an abundance of know-how and a shortage of capital.

Fujitsu is pushing for the lead held by IBM, but it is attempting to avoid the appearance of being another Japanese company out to dominate yet another critical world industry.

Problems

1. How has Fujitsu attempted to increase its global market share in the computer industry?

2. What is Fujitsu's basic strategy in its approach to its partnerships around the world?

3. Is Fujitsu justified in its belief that the fear of Japanese domination and increasing nationalism are threats?

Source: J. Michael Jenkins, Southeastern Louisiana University, Hammond, La., based on Brenton R. Schlender, "How Fujitsu Will Tackle the Giants," *Fortune*, July 1, 1991, 78–82.

CHAPTER 23

LEARNING OBJECTIVES

Upon completing this chapter, you should be able to:

■ Discuss the importance of quality in a globally competitive environment.

■ Trace the evolution of the quality movement in the United States.

■ Compare and contrast traditional control methods with total quality control methods.

■ List and discuss the four costs of quality.

■ Discuss the steps necessary to implement a quality improvement program.

■ List and discuss the seven basic tools of quality.

■ Discuss the Malcolm Baldrige National Quality Award and its effects on the quality movement in the United States.

et's assume that you run a package-delivery company. Because errors do occur, some customers will not be satisfied with your service. What is your target percentage for satisfied customers—90 percent, 95 percent, 98 percent? If you are Federal Express and you attain a customer satisfaction rate of 99 percent, you will still have 3.3 million dissatisfied customers each year. For Federal Express, the minimum acceptable percentage of satisfied customers is 100 percent.

Federal Express was founded with an eye to quality. From the start, chairman and CEO Frederick W. Smith knew that to ensure quality service you have to motivate and empower your employees to provide it. He structured his company accordingly.

People-Service-Profit (P-S-P) is Federal Express's corporate policy. This means that people—that is, employees—come first. By combining outstanding compensation policies and innovative structures for employee interaction and feedback with high levels of positive psychological reinforcement, Federal Express's management has shown that the company is people-oriented in deed as well as in word.

THE QUALITY IMPERATIVE

Internal communication at Federal Express goes through several formal channels. Its Open Door program, for instance, allows an employee with a question to direct it to an individual who can answer it, wherever that person may be in the company. The question must be answered within 10 days and accompanied by a list of reasons.

But even completely dedicated employees need something more than enthusiasm and skill to satisfy the customers who send 1.5 million packages through the Federal Express system every day. The company assists its employees by providing innovative, state-of-the-art electronic tracking. All packages are tracked from pickup to delivery by a central computer, and various possible errors are tracked and tabulated as well. A mathematical index, called the Service Quality Indicator (SQI), measures twelve possible errors and assigns each a value based on its severity in customers' eyes. This gives everyone a quantitative evaluation of how well the company is satisfying customers and keeps a record of problems for further evaluation.

Federal Express was the first service company to receive the prestigious Malcolm Baldrige National Quality Award, one of the most sought-after prizes in corporate America. In this chapter we will learn more about this award and about the concept of total quality control.

Sources: Nancy Karabatsos, "Absolutely, Positively Quality," *Quality Progress* 23 (May 1990) 25–27; "Federal Express Co.; Three Others Win Prize for Quality," *Wall Street Journal* 3, October 11, 1990, B8; Patricia L. Panchak, "How to Implement a Quality Initiative," *Modern Office Technology*, 37 (February 1992): 27–32; and "Federal Express Manager Knows Quality," *Kansas City Business Journal,* October 25, 1991, 15.
The contribution of Michael J. Savoie, University of New Orleans, in the preparation of this chapter is gratefully acknowledged.

IMPORTANCE OF QUALITY

The only sustainable competitive advantage any organization has is its reputation. In today's era of global competition, a reputation for **quality** cannot be overemphasized. Many U.S. organizations have fallen behind their international counterparts, however, because their goods/services do not provide acceptable levels of quality for their price.

It is virtually impossible for an organization to compete today solely on price and survive. It must provide a customer with an expected level of quality. "Delighting" customers is the current competitive advantage.[1] Organizations that delight their customers find those customers returning for future business. Those who do not delight their customers find themselves overrun by their competitors.

QUALITY DEFINED

Traditionally, quality has been defined as "conformance to requirements."[2] However, in the 1980s, quality came to be symbolized by customer satisfaction. David Garvin coined the phrase **"delighting the customer,"** and the quality movement in the United States assumed a customer focus.

The American Society for Quality Control (ASQC) is considered the leading authority on quality in the world. It defines quality as "a subjective term for which each person has his or her own definition. In technical usage, quality can have

Quality.
(1) The characteristics of a good or service that bear on its ability to satisfy stated or implied needs, and (2) a good or service free of deficiencies.

Delighting the customer.
Delivering a good or service that exceeds customer expectations.

SMART MANAGEMENT   WINNING BIG WHEN THE CHIPS ARE DOWN

One organization that has succeeded in the international marketplace is Motorola. CEO Bob Galvin provided insights into Motorola's success when he spoke recently at the American Quality Congress in Milwaukee, Wisconsin. When Motorola first sent computer chips to Japan, he said, they were well within the quality limits set by Motorola. However, when tested overseas, the chips failed to meet the standards set by Japanese industry. Engineers at Motorola discovered that although the mean value of the computer chips met the requirements of the Japanese contract, the quality of the chips fluctuated wildly, often approaching the control limits set by Motorola. Japanese chips, on the other hand, remained closely clustered around the mean value required by the customer. In performance testing, the tighter tolerances of the Japanese chips resulted in better overall performance.

Galvin and the Motorola team were determined to beat the Japanese at their own game and developed "six-sigma quality"—a goal that translates into only 3.4 defects per *million* chips produced. Many people scoffed at Motorola's effort, describing it as impossible for a U.S. company. Motorola, however, achieved six-sigma quality and is currently considered one of the top producers of computer chips in the world, competing with—and sometimes beating—its competition.

two meanings: (1) the characteristics of a good/service that bear on its ability to satisfy stated or implied needs and (2) a good/service free of deficiencies."[3] Quality can also be defined in terms of failures that occur either within or outside an organization.

Internal quality management involves establishing quality within an organization. Embracing concepts such as **employee empowerment** and **internal customers** allows employees to become involved in the quality process and to see the effects of improved quality on their fellow employees and on an organization's goods/services. Employee empowerment involves providing employees with the opportunity to implement their ideas and suggestions *even when management may not fully agree with them*.

Everyone who works in an organization is an internal customer. If someone within your organization is the recipient of a good you manufacture or a service you perform, then they are your customer and you should treat them as such. The use of the internal customer concept results in the assignment of responsibility for individual parts of the operations management process.

External quality is associated with a finished good/service after it is manufactured or performed. This quality relates to warranty, customer service, information on use, and so forth.

▲

Federal-Mogul's Van Wert, Ohio, oil seal plant is finding ways to work smarter by empowering employees. The set-up reaction team pictured here looks for ways to reduce machine set-up time. Cost of quality teams—organized by department—study ways to improve the plant's quality and the costs associated with it. Response teams focus on continuous improvement. This team approach to problem-solving involves employees in decision making and positively affects the plant's performance.

HISTORY OF THE QUALITY MOVEMENT IN THE UNITED STATES

BELL LABS

In 1924, Walter A. Shewhart of Bell Telephone Laboratories developed the statistical control chart concept, generally considered as the beginning of statistical quality control. Shewhart is often referred to as the "father of statistical quality control" because he brought together the disciplines of statistics, engineering, and economics. He described the basic principles of this new discipline in his book *Economic Control of Quality of Manufactured Product.*

Toward the end of the 1920s, Harold F. Dodge and Harold G. Romig, both of Bell Telephone Laboratories, developed statistically based acceptance sampling as an alternative to 100 percent inspection. By the middle of the 1930s, statistical quality control methods were in wide use at Western Electric, the then manufacturing arm of the Bell System.[4]

WORLD WAR II

World War II saw the widespread acceptance and use of statistical quality control concepts in manufacturing industries. Wartime experience made it apparent that statistical techniques were necessary to control product quality. The logistics of controlling troop movements and coordinating supplies, often from overseas, required tight control of operations management processes.

In 1946, ASQC was formed. What began as an association for specialists in the quality control field has expanded into the leading organization for quality management concepts, having over 100,000 members around the world. ASQC promotes the use of quality control techniques for all types of goods/services. It offers a number of conferences, technical publications, and training programs in quality assurance.

GROWTH OF ZERO-DEFECTS CONCEPT

The 1950s and 1960s saw developments such as quality costs and reliability engineering and the emergence of the viewpoint that quality is a way of managing an organization.[5] During the 1960s, the defense and aerospace industries made wide use of a quality concept called **zero defects.** Ideally, a zero-defects program has two aspects: a motivation aspect, aimed at stimulating employees to reduce their own errors, and a prevention aspect, aimed at encouraging employees to assist in reducing systematic controllable errors.[6] Unfortunately, most zero-defects programs did not create an environment in which these two aspects could thrive. As such, they have fallen out of favor with many quality professionals.

IF JAPAN CAN, WHY CAN'T WE?

In 1980, a documentary titled *If Japan Can, Why Can't We?* was aired on television in the United States. It highlighted Japanese industry's rise from the ashes of World War II to become a leader in the production of high-quality goods and is considered one of the most important events in the U.S. quality movement. It informed Americans of how and why the Japanese were producing better goods and credited W. Edwards Deming with Japan's success.

Internal customer.
The recipient (person or department) of another department's output (good, service, or information) within an organization.

External customer.
A person or organization that receives a good, a service, or information but is not part of the organization supplying it.

Zero defects.
A performance standard developed by Philip B. Crosby to address a dual attitude in the workplace: People are willing to accept imperfection in some areas while, in other areas, they expect the number of defects to be zero. Zero defects methodology states that if employers commit themselves to watching details and avoiding errors, they can move closer to the goal of zero defects. The performance standard that must be set is "zero defects," not "close enough."

Since 1980, U.S. organizations have studied and implemented the teachings of Deming and others in the quality field in an attempt to regain the reputation they had lost. Several of the key figures in the U.S. quality movement are discussed below.

W. EDWARDS DEMING

During World War II, Deming worked for the War Department and the Census Bureau. Following the war, he became a consultant to Japanese industries and convinced them of the power of statistical quality control. This commitment to *and use of* these methods has been a key element in the expansion of Japan's industry and economy, and today the world acknowledges Japanese products as the benchmark against which other goods are judged.[7]

Deming is considered the leading figure in the quality movement around the world. His 14 points of quality were discussed in Chapter 2.

JOSEPH M. JURAN

Next to Deming, Joseph M. Juran is probably the most widely recognized name in the field of quality. He has authorized 12 books and hundreds of papers in the quality field. His *Quality Control Handbook* is considered the gospel of the quality movement. Juran has focused most of his efforts on quality planning and analysis. It was he who coined the phrase **Pareto analysis** to describe the phenomenon whereby 80 percent of all defects are caused by 20 percent of the problems. Well into his 80s, Juran continues to publish, speak, and consult on quality around the world.

Pareto analysis.
A phenomenon whereby 80 percent of all defects are caused by 20 percent of the problems.

PHILIP CROSBY

One of the most prolific writers and outspoken proponents of the quality movement, Philip Crosby originated the zero-defects concept. Believing that the benefits derived from implementing a quality philosophy far outweigh the costs of implementing such a program, Crosby declared, "Quality is free," and developed a following built around the book by the same name.[8]

GENICHI TAGUCHI

Genichi Taguchi is the executive director of the American Supplier Institute, the director of the Japan Industrial Technology Institute, and an honorary professor at Nanjing Institute of Technology in China. Taguchi is well known for developing a methodology to improve quality and reduce costs, referred to in the United States as *Taguchi Methods*. These methods are an engineering approach to quality control. Taguchi calls for off-line quality control, on-line quality control, and a system of experimental design to improve quality and reduce costs.[9]

Taguchi is also credited with developing the **quality loss function.** The quality loss function is an approximation of the quality loss that occurs when a quality characteristic deviates from its target value. It is expressed in monetary units: The cost of deviating from the target increases quadratically the farther the quality characteristic moves from the target. The formula used to compute the quality loss function depends on the type of quality characteristic being used.[10]

Quality loss function.
An approximation of the quality loss that occurs when a quality characteristic deviates from its target value.

For example, a company that produces light bulbs tests random samples of the bulbs to make sure they meet quality control standards. Suppose a bulb is expected to burn for 2,000 hours. If the filament (the part of the bulb that produces light) is slightly off standard, the bulb may not burn as long, resulting in a calculatable loss to the consumer. If the filament is far enough away from standard, the bulb will not burn at all, resulting in a rejected lot and a cost to the company.

MASAAKI IMAI

Imai is best known as the director of the Kaizen Institute and author of the book *Kaizen: The Key to Japan's Competitive Success*. **Kaizen** is a Japanese term that means gradual, unending improvement by doing little things better and setting and achieving increasingly higher standards. Often referred to as **continuous improvement,** this philosophy is growing rapidly among American organizations.

TRADITIONAL VERSUS TOTAL QUALITY CONTROLS

Traditional quality control techniques involve keeping the production process going and the good or service flowing to the customer. Quality is treated as a feedback control, occurring at end-of-the-line stations where finished goods are tested to ensure that they perform as intended. Inspection, therefore, is seen as ensuring quality.

Modern quality control has evolved into a concept of total involvement by an organization with a goal of producing the best possible good/service for the price. It requires a continuous commitment not only from CEOs down to the lowest level employee, but also from an organization's suppliers and customers.

Total quality control involves continuous concern for quality. It is feedforward in the form of planning quality, design quality, and quality function deployment. It is concurrent in the form of statistical process control and employee empowerment. It is feedback control in the form of internal quality teams, sales and marketing quality, and customer service.

Modern quality control involves an entire organization, as well as its customers and suppliers. Cooperatively, their ultimate goal is to provide customers with the best possible good/service for the price.

FEEDFORWARD VERSUS FEEDBACK CONTROL

Quality cannot be inspected into a good or service; it must be designed and built in. At the same time, it is almost impossible to build a high-quality good from low-quality raw materials, or provide high-quality service with a low-quality (i.e., unmotivated, untrained) workforce. Feedforward controls examine incoming goods or services to determine if they meet quality standards. The traditional method of buying from the lowest bidder has been replaced with long-term buyer-supplier relationships designed to develop a win-win situation. Suppliers win by gaining steady, long-term customers, and buyers win by getting the highest quality raw materials for the price.

Feedback controls are not designed to help improve the quality of a good or service. Instead, they are designed to catch bad output before it leaves a factory or office (for example, comment cards at a restaurant). Unfortunately, the cost of manufacturing a good or providing a service has already been incurred. The best a company can hope for is that a rejected good can be reworked at additional cost and sold for the original price, often resulting in a loss. With a service, this often results in a refund, or a discount on future services (for example, the 30-minute delivery guarantee at Domino's Pizza).

Kaizen.
A Japanese term that means gradual, unending improvement by doing little things better and setting and achieving increasingly higher standards.

Continuous improvement.
The ongoing improvement of goods, services, or processes through incremental and breakthrough improvements.

A Thomasville Furniture process improvement team reduced the cycle time for the production of chair seats from 48 to less than seven hours—taking the seat department a significant step closer to its goal of total customer satisfaction. The reduction of the cycle time is a major contributor to increased customer satisfaction in the furniture business.

Source: Courtesy of Armstrong World Industries, Inc.

COST/BENEFIT

Armand Feigenbaum, General Systems Company CEO and a world-renowned quality expert, observed, "If all private and public organizations in the U.S. would adopt system-wide total quality processes, the nation would have nearly $300 billion to devote to further improving the quality of American society."[11] This is an astounding figure.

The **cost of poor quality** includes the costs associated with providing poor-quality goods or services. There are four categories of costs:

- **Internal failure costs** Costs associated with defects found before a good is shipped or the service is rendered
- **External failure costs** Costs associated with defects found after a good is shipped or the service is provided
- **Appraisal costs** Costs incurred to determine the degree of conformance to quality requirements
- **Prevention costs** Costs incurred to keep failure and appraisal costs to a minimum

Cost of poor quality. The costs associated with providing poor-quality goods or services. There are four categories of costs: internal failure costs, external failure costs, appraisal costs, and prevention costs.

IMPLEMENTING QUALITY IMPROVEMENT

TOP MANAGEMENT INVOLVEMENT

To produce a high-quality good or service, everyone in an organization must be committed to the operations management process. Because employees look to top

Top managers at the Halliburton Company, one of the world's largest engineering and construction companies in the energy industry, initiated a new quality program called the Environmental Quality Improvement Process (EQIP). EQIP applies the concepts of total quality to the protection of the environment. Each operating unit has developed a quality system of field environmental assessment to assure compliance with all environmental laws and regulations.

management for guidance, nowhere is this commitment more important than with an organization's managers. The top management of an organization represents its leadership. If employees perceive that top management is not committed to producing a high-quality good or service, they may not put forth the required effort, and a quality improvement program will fail.

Involvement by top management includes much more than simply saying "quality is job one." It involves backing talk with programs designed to help employees achieve that goal by improving the operations management process, not looking for scapegoats. Support includes empowering employees to make decisions regarding their jobs, management styles, and so forth *even when top management may not fully agree with the decisions*. By showing employees that they are part of a *team* and that their input is important, top management can put an organization on the road to achieving a philosophy of total quality and continuous improvement.

WHY PROGRAMS FAIL

If top management supports a quality philosophy, why do such programs sometimes fail? The first and foremost reason is that all the talk about quality is just that—talk. Without the commitment of each person in an organization, a quality improvement program will fail.

Another reason programs fail is that they are seen as one-time projects rather than a change in operating philosophy. If quality is perceived as a one-time project, many employees will treat it as "just another fad" top management is going through. They may play along but not actively involve themselves in the process. A commitment to continuous improvement is the only way to overcome this attitude. When employees recognize management's commitment to changing its operating philosophy, employees will more likely start integrating quality into their task performance.

A third reason quality improvement programs fail is due to lack of training. Quality is common sense. It does not require a college education. However, to be successful, it requires that employees understand the tools of quality and how these tools can be used to improve their jobs. Training employees in the proper ways to track and record defects, to make suggestions, to hold group discussions, and so forth, is critical to a quality improvement program's success. **Quality circles** are a perfect example of an excellent tool that has been misused due to lack of training. (See the accompanying "Close-Up: Quality" box.)

SUCCESSFUL IMPLEMENTATION STRATEGIES

There is no magic formula for successfully implementing a quality improvement program. There are, however, fundamental steps that must be taken for a quality improvement program to have a greater chance of succeeding.

First, top management must actively support the program. Without this support, the program cannot succeed. Second, employees must be trained in the techniques of quality control. These include not only the tools of quality, but the communication skills necessary to make the program succeed. Third, managers need to be trained to listen to their employees. No one knows better how to improve a job than the employee who works at it 8 hours a day. Finally, employees must be empowered with the authority to implement their quality improvement ideas. This does not require that managers give up control, but that managers and employees become partners in a process of continuous improvement.

CONTINUOUS PROCESS IMPROVEMENT

Continuous improvement is a critical component of a quality philosophy. It involves the ongoing improvement of goods, services, or processes through incremental and breakthrough improvements. The focus is not on putting together a team with the goal of developing a breakthrough or revolutionary good, service, or process, but on encouraging all members of an organization to continually look for ways to perform their job or the job of their co-workers better, thereby improving an organization's performance.

Quality circles.
Quality improvement or self-improvement study groups composed of a small number of employees (ten or fewer) and their supervisor. Quality circles originated in Japan, where they are called *quality control circles*.

CLOSE-UP: QUALITY THE ROLLER COASTER RISE AND FALL OF QUALITY CIRCLES

In the early 1980s, quality circles were the "latest fad." A quality circle is comprised of a group of employees on the same production or service line, project, and so forth, and a member of management who are brought together to discuss ways of improving the quality of the product or service being produced. Many companies began implementing quality circles without first training their employees and without fully understanding what quality circles really were. Needless to say, the results were not what top management expected, and quality circles often fell out of favor.

What failed was not the tool, but its implementation and application. Managers were not trained in employee empowerment, employees were not trained in the proper way to conduct quality control meetings or to prepare quality circle reports, and top management was not ready to implement the suggestions coming out of the meetings. As such, an excellent technique for improving the quality of an organization's good/service was wasted.

In the 1990s, quality circles are making a comeback under the name *quality improvement teams*. Whatever name is used, the suggestions that result from the techniques employed in such meetings are a valuable part of the quality improvement effort.

The continuous improvement approach to quality has involved the systematic re-engineering of key parts of the production process at the Mead Fine Paper division. For example, breaks in the web of paper running through a coating machine plagued operators and reduced capacity. Videotaped evidence pointed out trouble spots and operators corrected the problems. Improvements in productivity came quickly and breaks were reduced by 75%.

DOCUMENTATION/REPORTING

Another important aspect of quality programs is that they discourage the over-abundance of written communication. Many organizations have become overrun with paper and require a separate department to generate and print reports and other documentation. The tools of quality are graphics based. The intention is to present information in the simplest, easiest-to-understand format, using as few pages as possible.

Employees in a quality program generate their own documentation—from check sheets to control charts. Management collects these charts at the end of a predetermined period (shift, day, week, or longer) and generates Pareto analyses showing where improvements in a process can be made. Managers and employees come together as quality improvement teams and brainstorm possible courses of action. Communication is conducted in person whenever possible. Memos, reports, and so forth are used for documentation purposes, not for communication. In this way, an organization spends less time reading about its business and more time actually conducting it.

QUALITY IMPROVEMENT TECHNIQUES

The seven traditional tools of quality control are:

- cause-and-effect diagrams
- check sheets
- control charts
- information-flow diagrams
- histograms

Seven tools of quality.
Tools that help organizations understand their processes in order to improve them. The tools are the cause-and-effect diagram, check sheet, control chart, flowchart, histogram, Pareto chart, and scatter diagram.

- Pareto charts
- scatter diagrams

These tools represent the basis of a new management paradigm, one in which customers are provided the highest quality good or service for the price. They help organizations understand their operations management processes so that they can improve them. Each of the tools is discussed below.

CAUSE-AND-EFFECT DIAGRAMS

A tool for analyzing process dispersion, **cause-and-effect diagrams** are also referred to as *Ishikawa* or "fishbone" diagrams. Kaoru Ishikawa is the Japanese engineer credited with inventing the chart, which resembles the skeleton of a fish (see Figure 23.1). This kind of diagram illustrates the main causes and subcauses leading to an effect (problem).

Setting up a cause-and-effect diagram requires only that a problem be identified. The problem is noted in a box that forms the "head" of the fish. The "backbone" of the fish extends from the head. Off of the backbone are other "bones" representing possible causes of the problem. Each bone may have smaller bones that represent subcauses of the larger cause. A cause-and-effect diagram is an excellent tool for brainstorming sessions designed to identify the causes of problems within an organization.

CHECK SHEETS

A **check sheet** is a simple data-recording device custom designed by a user (see Figure 23.2). It allows users to readily interpret the results of a quality study. Users develop the check sheet by listing those items (problems, errors, failures, and so forth) that they want to track. Then, as each item on the list occurs, a user places a check or other mark next to that item on the check sheet. At the end of the day (or other time period decided by the user), the check sheet is examined to determine which item is occurring most frequently.

Cause-and-effect (Ishikawa or fishbone) diagrams. A tool for analyzing process dispersion. It is also referred to as the Ishikawa diagram, because Kaoru Ishikawa developed it, and the fishbone diagram, because the complete diagram resembles a fish skeleton. The diagram illustrates the main causes and subcauses leading to an effect (symptom).

Check sheet. A simple data-recording device custom designed by a user.

FIGURE 23.1 CAUSE-AND-EFFECT DIAGRAM

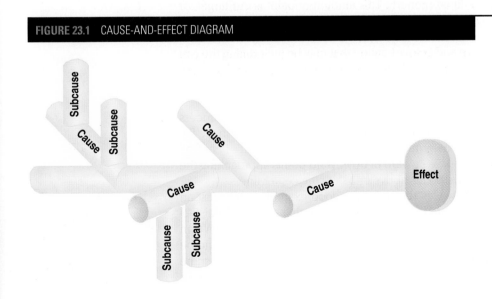

FIGURE 23.2 CHECK SHEET

Item 1	✔ ✔ ✔ ✔
Item 2	✔ ✔ ✔ ✔ ✔
Item 3	✔ ✔ ✔ ✔ ✔ ✔
Item 4	✔ ✔ ✔ ✔ ✔
Item 5	✔ ✔ ✔ ✔

CONTROL CHARTS

A **control chart** is a chart with upper and lower control limits on which values of some statistical measure, for a series of samples or subgroups, are plotted. The chart frequently shows a central line to help detect a trend of plotted values toward either control limit (see Figure 23.3).

Control charts are used to track processes, not goods or services. The focus is on determining whether or not a process is in control. If a process is in control, the product being produced will vary randomly about the center line (mean), with no products being produced above the upper control limit or below the lower control limit. If the process becomes out of control, a good will be produced that is outside of control limits and is unfit to be sold.

Let's look at the process of filling 1-gallon cans of paint. A 1-gallon paint can needs 1 gallon of paint to be filled properly. This amount of paint is our target, or mean, value. Because no process is without variation, management must decide on acceptable deviations from the mean. These upper and lower control limits represent the amount of paint above and below 1 gallon that may be included in the can and still meet the standards set for a gallon of paint. Remember, 1 gallon is our target amount, but it is unrealistic to expect that every can will have exactly 1 gallon of paint in it.

A control chart is used to monitor the filling process to ensure that the process stays within the upper and lower control limits. The chart will show trends in the filling process that may be used to determine if the process is headed out of control. Trends to look for include successive upward or downward points approaching the control limits, or eight successive points above or below the center line.

Control charts apply equally well to services. A good example is how fast an incoming telephone call is answered. Studies have shown that customer satisfaction with telephone business is directly related to how fast a call is answered. A firm may decide that on average (the center line of the control chart) a call should be answered by the second ring. Upper and lower control limits can be set (assume one and three rings, respectively) and the process plotted. By plotting over time, an

Control chart.
A chart with upper and lower control limits on which values of some statistical measure, for a series of samples or subgroups, are plotted.

FIGURE 23.3 CONTROL CHART

organization can determine if time of day is an assignable cause of the process being out of control. If so, adding more operators at that time may eliminate the problem.

INFORMATION-FLOW DIAGRAMS

Many students are familiar with **information-flow diagrams** from their computer classes. These diagrams are a form of flowchart, with a graphical representation of the steps in a process (see Figure 23.4). Flowcharts are drawn to clarify processes. Any process consisting of more than one step can be represented in a flowchart. What can be demonstrated on a single page using flowchart methodology and symbols may take several hundred pages of text to describe.

HISTOGRAMS

A **histogram** is a graphical summary of variation in a set of data (see Figure 23.5). The pictorial nature of a histogram allows people to see patterns that are more difficult to recognize in a simple table of numbers. If we were to draw an outline around the checkmarks in our sample check sheet, we would create a histogram. A histogram indicates the shape of a data distribution. A curve that is normally distributed about a mean is referred to as bell shaped. A curve that tails off in either direction is considered skewed.

PARETO CHARTS

A histogram rearranged so that the data are listed in descending order of occurrence is called a **Pareto chart** (see Figure 23.6). A *Pareto chart* is a graphical tool for ranking causes from most significant to least significant. It is based on the Pareto principle, which was first defined by Joseph Juran in 1950, and named after nineteenth-century economist Vilfredo Pareto. According to the principle, 80 percent of the effects in a process come from 20 percent of the possible causes. A Pareto chart

Information-flow diagrams.
A form of flowchart with a graphical representation of the steps in a process.

Histogram.
A graphical summary of variation in a set of data.

Pareto chart.
A histogram rearranged so that the data are listed in descending order of occurrence.

FIGURE 23.4 FLOWCHART

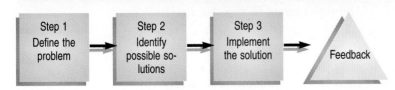

FIGURE 23.5 HISTOGRAM

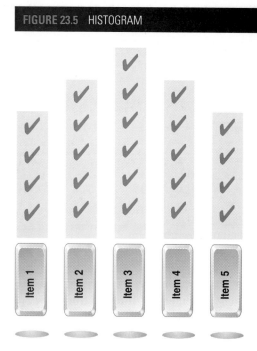

allows us to see which items are causing the most problems so we can then focus our attention on correcting those items.

SCATTER DIAGRAMS

A **scatter diagram** is a graphical technique to analyze the relationship between two variables (see Figure 23.7). Two sets of data are plotted on a graph, with the x-axis showing the independent variable and the y-axis showing the dependent variable. The graph shows possible relationships (although two variables might appear to be related, they might not be—those who know most about the variable must make that evaluation). A chart may appear to show a positive correlation between two variables, for example, sales of sundresses and inches of rain. In other words, as sales of sundresses increase, the amount of rainfall increases. The number of inches of rain is not dependent on the sale of sundresses. However, the two are both related to summertime.

Scatter diagram.
A graphical technique to analyze the relationship between two variables.

Recent research has added to these seven tools. To better understand this expanded list of quality tools available to the modern manager, we have divided them into four categories. The four categories and some of the tools associated with each are listed in Table 23.1.

Three of the more commonly used tools in this expanded list are *benchmarking, quality function deployment,* and *statistical process control.* Each is discussed briefly below.

BENCHMARKING

Benchmarking is an improvement process in which an organization measures its performance against industry leaders in areas such as quality control and proce-

FIGURE 23.6 PARETO CHART

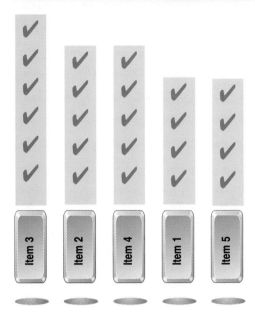

dures. An organization using this tool determines how other organizations achieved higher performance levels and then uses their information to improve its own performance.

Benchmarking can be carried out both internally and externally. Internal benchmarking occurs when processes are compared against themselves or against similar processes within the organization. External benchmarking involves comparison against an organization's competitors or against the **"best in class"**—a phrase referring to the industry leader in the area being benchmarked. One note of warning: When benchmarking against a competitor, an organization must compare

Best in class.
A term used to describe an organization recognized as outstanding in its field.

TABLE 23.1 CATEGORIES AND TYPES OF QUALITY IMPROVEMENT TOOLS

Concept Development Tools
Checklists
Brainstorming
Five whys
Visualization
Flowchart
Objective statement
Prioritizing
Quality function deployment

Quantitative Tools
Statistics/statistical process control
Theory of lines (queuing theory)
Ishikawa or cause-and-effect diagram
Pareto chart

Control or Tracking Tools
Control chart
Gantt chart
Critical path chart
Decision matrix

Appraisal Tools
Checklist
Benchmarking
The story

Source: Adapted from Harry I. Forsha, *The Pursuit of Quality through Personal Change* (Milwaukee: ASQC Quality Press, 1992), 55.

FIGURE 23.7 SCATTER DIAGRAM

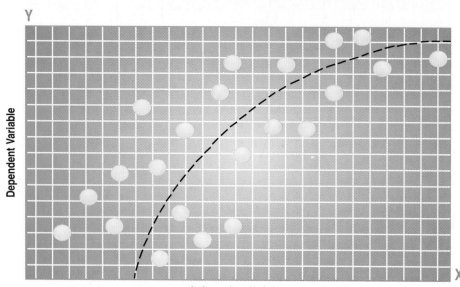

itself against its most successful competitor, or the comparison may be wasted. Speaking at the international conference of the Production Operations Management Society in New York, a Cadillac spokesperson stated that Cadillac benchmarks only against Lincoln. When asked about Lexus, Infinity, Acura, BMW, and Mercedes, the spokesperson said that Cadillac does not consider these automobiles to be direct competitors.

Benchmarking is not a marketing tool. You are not trying to make your organization look good; rather, you are trying to learn from the industry leaders how they achieved their level of performance.

QUALITY FUNCTION DEPLOYMENT

Quality function deployment is a structured method in which customer requirements are translated into appropriate technical requirements for each stage of product development and production. This process is often referred to as listening to the customer.

Customers can be involved in the process in several different ways. First, customer input can be used in developing the processes and goods or services an organization produces or provides. Second, customers can provide input as to the need for new or updated goods or services. Finally, by tracking customer use of, and satisfaction with, a good or service, an organization can better determine the life cycle of its goods or services and the effect quality improvement programs are having on customer satisfaction.

STATISTICAL PROCESS CONTROL

Statistical process control is the application of statistical techniques to control a process. It involves using control charts to track variables to determine if a process is in control or out of control. Control limits usually located at plus or minus 3 sigma

Malcolm Baldrige National Quality Award.
An award established by the U.S. Congress in 1987 to raise awareness of quality management and to recognize U.S. companies that have implemented successful quality management systems.

Quality function deployment.
A structured method in which customer requirements are translated into appropriate technical requirements for each stage of product development and production.

Statistical process control.
The application of statistical techniques to control a process. Often the term *statistical quality control* is used interchangeably with *statistical process control.*

(standard deviations) from the mean are used to differentiate between a process that is in control and one that is out of control. If a variable has a measured value that is above the upper control limit or below the lower control limit, the process is considered out of control. In those situations, the process should be stopped and the operator should look for an assignable cause for the variation. If one is found, the problem is corrected and the process restarted. If an assignable cause is not found, the process may have to be adjusted. Often the term *statistical quality control* is used interchangeably with *statistical process control*.

THE MALCOLM BALDRIGE NATIONAL QUALITY AWARD

ORIGIN AND SELECTION PROCESS

The **Malcolm Baldrige National Quality Award** was established by Congress in 1987 to raise awareness of quality management in the United States. Its purposes are to promote quality awareness, recognize quality achievements of U.S. organizations, and publicize successful quality strategies.[12] The award is divided into three categories: manufacturing, service, and small business. No more than two awards can be given in each of the categories.

The award is named after the late Secretary of Commerce, Malcolm Baldrige, a proponent of quality management. The award, conceived by Florida Power & Light Company, is administered and underwritten by a consortium of private

Preset quality control parameters, monitored by employees using computers, are part of Engelhard Corporation's statistical process control system. The system enables Engelhard to produce coating pigments and additives that consistently match the exact specifications of its customers in paint, plastics, paper, and other industries, Engelhard employs statistical process controls to insure high quality throughout the entire production process, including the monitoring of raw materials consistency.

companies and is managed by the Commerce Department's National Institute of Standards and Technology.

Award criteria deal with seven areas: leadership, information and analysis, planning, human resource utilization, quality assurance of products and services, quality of results, and customer satisfaction. The 1992 criteria also included financial performance and innovation considerations. A private-sector board of examiners makes the award selections based on a three-stage review process that includes (1) evaluation of written examinations submitted by applicants, (2) site visits to companies that score high on the written examination to review strengths and areas for improvement as revealed in the written examination, and (3) final judging of overall results.

Each application is evaluated by members from the board of examiners, and all applicants receive written feedback summarizing strengths and areas for improvement. High-scoring applicants are selected for site visits. The evaluation results in a point total for each area, with the highest totals indicating the winners in their appropriate categories. Of a possible 24 winners (two in each category over 4 years), only 12 have been named thus far.

WHY SHOULD AN ORGANIZATION COMPETE?

An organization should enter the Baldrige competition as part of a long-term quality improvement process that provides information for management to use in strategic planning. An organization should not enter the Baldrige competition for advertising purposes, or to prove it is the best company in the world, or for employee motivation, or because its competitors have entered the competition.

The award examination can be used for more than the evaluation of excellent manufacturing and service businesses. It is designed as a value system, an education and communications tool, a vehicle for cooperation, and a device to help evaluate quality standards.

The most significant uses of the award to date involve assessment—self-assessment, assessment of suppliers, and evaluation of candidates for awards. Because the award addresses the full range of quality issues, it can help those setting up new systems to get a complete, integrated picture of **total quality management.** As commonly defined, "total quality management" is an approach to quality that signifies a long-term success through customer satisfaction.

Total quality management.
An approach to quality improvement that signifies long-term success through customer satisfaction.

Additionally, the Baldrige Award examination can be used to support quality training and education, particularly at the management level. It represents a distillation of the major issues managers must understand and provides a convenient framework for describing quality management. Also, it can serve as a device for defining total quality management and for instruction in quality management principles. It can also serve as a framework for teaching problem-solving skills in professional disciplines and provide a guide for conducting workshops and symposia on quality. The award examination is well suited as an adjunct to curriculum development because it provides an overview of total quality management.

Winning the Baldrige Award is not the goal of the organizations that win it. (See Table 23.2 for a list of past winners.) Rather, it is a step along the path to total quality. As Ronald Schmidt, Zytec Corporation CEO, stated at the 1991 awards ceremony, "Winning this award is a double-edged sword. It validates for us that we are definitely on the right track, but I'm sure it will raise the aspiration levels of our existing and future customers. We will just have to plan to exceed those aspiration levels."[13]

TABLE 23.2	MALCOLM BALDRIGE NATIONAL QUALITY AWARD WINNERS	
Year	**Organization**	**Category**
1988	Motorola, Inc.	Manufacturing
	Commercial Nuclear Fuel Division, Westinghouse Electric Corporation	Manufacturing
	Globe Metallurgical	Small business
1989	Milliken & Company	Manufacturing
	Xerox Corporation, Business Products Systems	Manufacturing
1990	Cadillac Motor Car Division	Manufacturing
	IBM Rochester	Manufacturing
	Federal Express	Service
	Wallace Co.	Small business
1991	Solectron Corporation	Manufacturing
	Zytec Corporation	Manufacturing
	Marlow Industries	Small business

PROFILE OF PAST WINNERS

At the presentation of the first Baldrige Awards, President Ronald Reagan stated:

> The one trait that characterizes these winners is that they realize that quality improvement is a never-ending process, a company-wide effort in which every worker plays a critical part. They realize that customer satisfaction through better quality is the goal. And they know that America's economic strength and future depend more and more upon the quality of its products.[14]

Although describing winners of the 1988 competition, Reagan's words also characterize the 1991 award winners. The following sections profile these winners.

Solectron Corporation

Founded in 1977 as a small assembly job shop, Solectron now specializes in assembling complex printed circuit boards and subsystems for makers of computers and other electronic products. In addition, it provides system-level assembly services.

Solectron conducts customer surveys not yearly or monthly, but every week. About 90 percent of new business is additional work from established customers. These customers have benefitted from defect rates that have fallen to within 5 sigma, or 233 defective parts per million, and on-time delivery rates of 97.7 percent. Solectron has committed to achieving and then surpassing 6 sigma (3.4 defects per million) in critical processes over the next 5 years.

Zytec Corporation

The Zytec Corporation designs and manufactures electronic power supplies for original equipment manufacturers of computers and electronic office, medical, and testing equipment. It also repairs power supplies.

Six-sigma quality.
A term used generally to indicate that a process is well controlled (that is, $\pm$ 6 sigma from the centerline in a control chart).

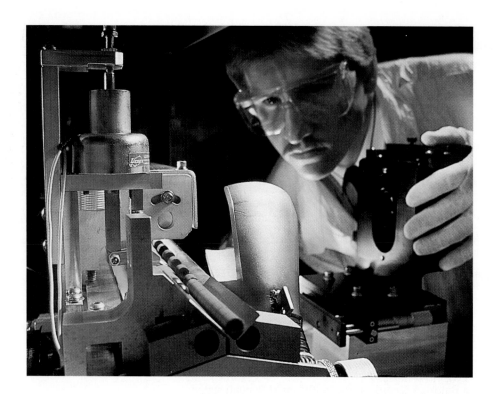

Westinghouse has created the Productivity and Quality Center (PQC) and the Science and Technology Center (STC) to further its commitment to quality. Here an engineer at STC uses an automated machine-vision inspection system to examine nuclear fuel to insure quality. The combined efforts of these centers and other quality programs have resulted in Westinghouse being selected as a finalist for the Malcolm Baldrige Award every year since the award was established.

Zytec first applied for the Baldrige Award in 1990. According to Ronald Schmidt, Zytec spent 767 hours and $9,000 trying to win the award. In 1991, the year it won the award, out-of-pocket expenses totaled $8,300, and total time was less than in 1990. The point is well made that you win with what you do everyday, not by performing for the judges.

At Zytec, customers join all levels of employees in refining the organization's long-range plans. Sales per employee are approaching $100,000, compared with an industry average of less than $80,000. At the same time, Zytec has realized a 50 percent improvement in manufacturing yields, a 26 percent reduction in manufacturing cycle time, and a 30–40 percent decrease in product costs—savings that are passed on to customers.

Marlow Industries

With 160 employees, Marlow Industries is one of the smallest companies to win the Baldrige Award. Founded in 1973, Marlow manufactures thermoelectric coolers, which are small, solid-state electronic devices that heat, cool, or stabilize the temperature of electronic equipment.

At Marlow, the customer feedback system has been described as exhaustive; it includes surveys and quarterly meetings with clients. Since 1987, employee productivity has increased at an average annual rate of 10 percent. In addition, the time between new product design and manufactured product has been trimmed, and the cost of scrap, rework, and other nonconformance errors has been cut nearly in half. Marlow's market share—better than 50 percent of the world market for customized thermoelectric coolers—continues to improve, even in Japan, where it has local competition.

FUTURE OF QUALITY MOVEMENT

The starting point in the design of the Baldrige Award was a customer needs assessment with the customer being the United States. This assessment provided the Baldrige Award Committee with the following facts:[15]

- Most organizations—businesses, government agencies at all levels, associations, schools, and health-care institutions—do not have systematic total quality improvement processes.

- Many organizations are just getting started in quality improvement and encounter disagreements over concepts, techniques, terminology, and emphasis.

- Only a small fraction of those organizations with systematic quality processes have a total quality focus; often there is a disparity in approaches and maturity among the quality processes in different departments and operating units.

- Most trade, business, and professional organizations have a minimal quality management focus, either in their headquarters operations or as a service to their members.

- Most accrediting, evaluation, regulatory, and procurement bodies have no process in place to foster systematic quality improvement efforts or standards in organizations under their jurisdiction.

- Most business schools devote minimal attention to quality management in curricula, and quality is not a major research area.

- More organizations are sharing information on quality strategies.

Many experts conclude that quality differences—real and perceived—are among the leading contributors to the U.S. trade deficit, and that quality-related market success stems from two major areas: production cost advantages and customer loyalty to brands that they perceive to be of higher quality.[16]

In remarks made at the 1988 National Quality Award news briefing, Secretary of Commerce C. William Verity quoted the Malcolm Baldrige National Quality Improvement Act of 1987 when he stated that "strategic planning for quality and quality improvement programs is becoming more and more essential to the well-being of our nation's economy and our ability to compete effectively in the global marketplace."[17]

Today, U.S. companies such as Ford Motor Company and Motorola are encouraging not only their employees, but their vendors to pursue quality excellence. Ford has implemented the Q1 award for vendors who meet or exceed Ford's rigid quality standards. The Q1 award carries major prestige and financial rewards for vendors who can claim it.

Motorola encourages its vendors to apply for the Malcolm Baldrige Award. Motorola's purpose is not so much to get its vendors to win the award, but to get the vendors to go through the same type of self-assessment that allowed Motorola to win the award.

By creating this type of atmosphere for quality, organizations can create a positive rippling effect around them. Companies such as Ford and Motorola will force their vendors to implement total quality programs. These vendors will in turn encourage their vendors to implement such programs, and so on. The goal is not only to make all American businesses aware of quality issues, but to cause every organization to strive to achieve maximum quality in its products or services.

Regardless of how an organization decides to go about it, an emphasis on quality must continue to increase in importance. A philosophy of continuous improvement will allow U.S. industry to regain its spot as the world leader in high-quality goods and services.

SUMMARY

In this chapter, we have looked at the quality movement in the United States and discussed its importance in terms of U.S. global competitiveness. For quality to succeed in an organization, management must adopt a new paradigm that includes employee empowerment, internal customers, and the use of quality improvement tools to bring about and evaluate quality improvement programs. The U.S. government is promoting quality through the Malcolm Baldrige National Quality Award, given to those organizations that exemplify the new paradigm of quality management. If the United States is to regain its role as a world industry leader, providing the highest quality products and services must become the norm, not the exception.

Learning Objective 1: Discuss the importance of quality in a globally competitive environment.
Today's business competition takes place on a global scale. It is not enough to produce a good or service and expect customers to line up at your door. By implementing a quality philosophy, an organization ensures that it will produce the best possible good or service. Only by doing this can an organization hope to survive in today's global marketplace.

Learning Objective 2: Trace the evolution of the quality movement in the United States.
Beginning with Walter Shewhart of Bell Labs, the quality movement in the United States has evolved into a corporate philosophy encompassing the works of W. Edwards Deming, Joseph M. Juran, Philip Crosby, Genichi Taguchi, and Masaaki Imai, to name a few. Founded in 1946, the American Society for Quality Control is considered the leading quality organization in the world, with over 100,000 members worldwide.

Learning Objective 3: Compare and contrast traditional control methods with total quality control methods.
Traditional methods did not focus on the quality of a good or service. Rather, they relied on feedback control mechanisms to inform management when a bad good or service was produced. Total quality control methods combine all forms of control into an organization-wide emphasis on producing the highest quality good or service for the price.

Learning Objective 4: List and discuss the four costs of quality.
The costs of quality include: Internal failure costs associated with defects found before a good is shipped or the service is rendered; External failure costs associated with defects found after a good is shipped or the service is provided; Appraisal costs incurred to determine the degree of conformance to quality requirements; Prevention costs incurred to keep failure and appraisal costs to a minimum.

Learning Objective 5: **Discuss the steps necessary to implement a quality improvement program.**

First, a commitment from top management must be secured. Without top management support, the changes necessary to create an environment for quality cannot exist. Second, employees must be trained in the techniques of quality control. These include not only the tools of quality, but the communication skills necessary to make the program succeed. Third, managers need to be trained to listen to their employees. No one knows better how to improve a job than the employee who works at it 8 hours a day. Finally, employees must be empowered with the authority to implement their quality improvement ideas. This does not require that managers give up control, but that managers and employees become partners in the process of continuous improvement.

Learning Objective 6: **List and discuss the seven basic tools of quality.**

The seven basic tools of quality are cause-and-effect diagrams, check sheets, control charts, information-flow diagrams, histograms, Pareto charts, and scatter diagrams. Each is a powerful tool for tracking and controlling processes to ensure the production of the highest quality good or service.

Learning Objective 7: **Discuss the Malcolm Baldrige National Quality Award and its effects on the quality movement in the United States.**

The Baldrige Award was created by Congress in 1987 to promote the application of quality improvement methodologies in U.S. industry. The award is given in three categories: manufacturing, service, and small business. The award is presented each year to as many as two companies in each category that have exhibited outstanding applications of quality in each of seven different categories.

KEY TERMS

best in class 669

cause-and-effect (Ishikawa or fishbone) diagrams 665

check sheet 665

continuous improvement 660

control chart 666

cost of poor quality 661

delighting the customer 656

external customer 658

histogram 667

information-flow diagrams 667

internal customer 658

kaizen 660

Malcolm Baldrige National Quality Award 670

pareto analysis 659

pareto chart 667

quality 656

quality circles 663

quality function deployment 670

quality loss function 659

scatter diagram 668

seven tools of quality 664

six-sigma quality 673

statistical process control 670

total quality management 672

zero defects 658

REVIEW AND DISCUSSION QUESTIONS

1. Discuss the four costs of quality.

2. What is the Malcolm Baldrige Award? Why should an organization compete for the award?

3. Discuss each of the following quality techniques:
   a. *Kaizen*
   b. Taguchi methods

    c. Internal customers
    d. Employee empowerment
    e. Quality function deployment
    f. Statistical process control
    g. Zero defects

4. Discuss the contributions each of the following persons has made to the quality movement in the United States and worldwide:
    a. W. Edwards Deming
    b. Joseph M. Juran
    c. Philip Crosby
    d. Genichi Taguchi
    e. Masaaki Imai

THE MANAGEMENT EXPERIENCE PARETO UP CLOSE

Any university (or organization, for that matter) is only as good as the people who live, work, and interact within its bounds. Examine your university and answer the following questions with a "yes" or "no."

1. Does your university offer student activities?
    _____No   _____Yes

2. Do you compete in intramural sports?
    _____No   _____Yes

3. Do you belong to a fraternity or sorority?
    _____No   _____Yes

4. Do you belong to student clubs other than a fraternity or sorority?
    _____No   _____Yes

5. Do you participate in student government?
    _____No   _____Yes

6. Do you vote in student elections?
    _____No   _____Yes

Now perform a Pareto analysis on the class's answers to these questions.

First, tally the "No" responses to each question using a check sheet. These "No" responses represent failures on the part of the student affairs office to involve all students in university activities.

Second, put the questions in order of descending number of "No" responses on a graph, and draw bars representing the number of "No" responses for each question.

You now have a Pareto chart that shows which activities students are least involved in. Such a chart can be used by student affairs personnel to focus their efforts to get more student involvement. It can also be used by you, the student, to determine your own involvement in student activities and as a guide to which activities could most use your help.

CASE 23.1   QUALITY FAILURE AT MED-X

MED-X, a small supplier of hospital products, is facing a major crisis. One of its boxes of medical supplies was rejected by HMR Hospital because it failed an incoming inspection. Bob Johnson, CEO of MED-X, was on the phone all morning with his friend Ned Jacobs, the inventory control manager at the hospital. Jacobs informed Johnson that hospital regulations prohibit the purchasing of supplies from a company whose products have failed inspection. Johnson explained to Jacobs that the products in question were not produced by MED-X, but by Hospital Supplies, Inc. (HSI), a major manufacturer of medical equipment. Johnson contended that HSI, not MED-X, is responsible for the bad product and that HSI should bear the punishment.

Jacobs agreed to contact HSI and request information on the shipment. However, HSI informed Jacobs that it does not deal directly with hospitals and that HMR should direct its complaint to the supplier (MED-X).

Feeling very frustrated, Jacobs typed a letter to Johnson informing him that, according to hospital policy, MED-X would be dropped from the hospital supplier list effective immediately. He also sent a memo to his staff requesting an inspection of all goods from HSI and encouraging the purchase of supplies from another manufacturer whenever possible.

Problems

1. From a quality standpoint, what could have been done to prevent the above scenario from occurring?

2. What could Bob Johnson have done differently to save his company's contract?

3. What suggestions do you have for each of the three companies involved to prevent this situation from occurring again?

NOTES

[1] David A. Garvin, "Competing on the Eight Dimensions of Quality," *Harvard Business Review* 65 (November–December 1987): 101–109.

[2] Harry I. Forsha, *The Pursuit of Quality through Personal Change* (Milwaukee: ASQC Quality Press, 1992), 3.

[3] Karen Bemowski, comp., "The Quality Glossary," *Quality Progress* 25 (February 1992): 20–29.

[4] Douglas C. Montgomery, *Introduction to Statistical Quality Control* (New York: Wiley, 1985), 13.

[5] *Ibid.*, 14.

[6] *Ibid.*

[7] *Ibid.*, 15.

[8] Philip Crosby, *Quality Is Free* (New York: McGraw-Hill, 1979).

[9] Karen Bemowski, "The Quality Glossary," 28.

[10] *Ibid.*, 26.

[11] Quoted in Ned Hamson, "TQM Can Save Nearly $300 Billion for Nation," *Journal for Quality and Participation* 13 (December 1990): 54–56.

[12] Chester Placek, "Baldrige Award as a Quality Model," *Quality* 31 (February 1992): 17–20.

[13] Karen Bemowski, "Baldrige Award Winners Pause to Celebrate Their Success," *Quality Progress* 24 (December 1991): 44–48.

[14] Ronald W. Reagan, "Remarks by President Reagan at Presentation of Malcolm Baldrige National Quality Awards, November 14, 1988," *Business America*, December 5, 1988, 5.

[15] Curt W. Reimann, "The Baldrige Award: Leading the Way in Quality Initiatives," *Quality Progress* 22 (July 1989): 35–39.

[16] *Ibid.*, 39.

[17] C. William Verity, "Remarks by Secretary of Commerce C. William Verity at the National Quality Award News Briefing, November 14, 1988," *Business America*, December 5, 1988, 4–5.

VIDEO CASE

L.L. BEAN

Despite the country's recent economic woes, more than 30,000 loyal fans from all over the country turned out to help L.L. Bean celebrate its 80th birthday and kick off a year long anniversary program. At the two-day anniversary celebration in Freeport, Maine, visitors joined L.L. Bean employees for several outdoor activities followed by a New England bean dinner and a fireworks show.

L.L. Bean has suffered from the recession in retailing in the last few years, and its Chief Executive Leon Gorman, grandson of founder Leon Leonwood Bean, has been working diligently to see that it withstands the downturn. In 1989, sales growth declined to 3 percent and in 1991 sales increased by only a modest 5 percent to reach $628 million. Merchandise returns also increased, and L.L. Bean has now begun to charge customers for shipping.

Some say L.L. Bean is a victim of its own success. L.L. Bean clothing is durable, and its high quality merchandise has motivated imitators and discount knock-offs. L.L. Bean's traditional generous return policy of taking anything back for whatever reason, no matter how long after the sale, has been both a strength and weakness. This has spawned a new management slogan at L.L. Bean: "Get it right the first time."

L.L. Bean was founded in 1912 by Leon Leonwood Bean and has become the largest outdoor specialty cataloger in the United States. Mention the name L.L. Bean and two images appear in most people's minds: the well-known and widely distributed catalog of the same name and the Maine Hunting Boot. Although L.L. Bean operates manufacturing facilities and a few retail stores, it principally relies on an expanding distribution channel for its sales: direct-response retailing through mail-order purchases or telephone orders. Eighty-eight percent of L.L. Bean's 1988 sales of $590 million were produced through catalog sales. Retail stores, the traditional outlet for consumer purchases, accounted for only $70 million.

Leon Leonwood Bean created his first handmade pair of hunting boots for himself. He made a few more, gave them to friends who raved about the boot's dry, lightweight comfort, and finally decided that anyone who enjoyed the outdoors should be able to acquire a pair of these boots. So, in 1912, he secured a mailing list of Maine hunting-license holders, set up shop in a basement, and prepared a three-page brochure that guaranteed "perfect satisfaction."

But the first 100 pairs of Bean's boots were far from perfect; 90 of them were returned to him after the bottoms fell off. The outdoorsman/entrepreneur had offered a 100 percent guarantee, and he was determined to live up to it. Bean borrowed the money to repair and return the boots, corrected the initial problem, and made more boots. Then he sent out more brochures.

This first experience taught Bean the value of personally testing his products, of honest advertising based on firm convictions, and of keeping the customer satisfied. He was determined to adhere to a simple business philosophy: Sell good merchandise at reasonable prices and treat customers like human beings; and they will always come back for more. The L.L. Bean Golden Rule remains a guideline even today.

Bean was also certain that mail-order marketing was the best way to reach his customers. The homespun catalogs mailed to his target markets continued to prove effective. By 1927, L.L. Bean had grown to a 25-person workforce; sales had increased to $135,000; and camping and fishing equipment had been added to the product line.

Most of the profits in the early years were funneled back into advertising to stimulate further growth. Bean ran ads promoting his free catalogs; he also began collecting information for use in market segmentation by developing a coding system for evaluating responses. He then used this information to analyze his customer base and make decisions on appropriate product-line additions and deletions. This type of information aided L.L. Bean in quadrupling sales even during the Great Depression. In fact, sales passed the $1 million mark in 1937.

The 1940s proved another growth decade for L.L. Bean as it acquired war contracts to manufacture boots and bags for the U.S. Armed Forces. As L.L. Bean's fame spread, it was the subject of major stories in mass-audience magazines like *Life* and the *Saturday Evening Post*. Bean's book, *Hunting, Fishing, and Camping* became a basic sportsman's guide.

In 1945, a special retail salesroom was opened in the middle of the L.L. Bean Freeport, Maine factory. The salesroom had an outside bell for the convenience of sports enthusiasts passing through town late at night. Six years later, the salesroom began staying open 24 hours a day, 365 days a year. In 1954, Bean took his wife's advice and opened a ladies' department to serve the growing number of women involved in outdoor sports. But Bean was getting older as the 1950s drew to a close and his energy was declining. L.L. Bean had grown old as well. The average age of its employees was over 60. Sales had stabilized between $2 and $3 million during the 1960s. Bean died in 1967.

Leadership passed to Bean's grandson, Leon Gorman, who had worked at L.L. Bean since 1961. Gorman's fresh leadership, combined with a growing interest in fitness and the outdoors, have produced steady annual sales increases. This was the era of President Kennedy's promotion of physical fitness programs in the public schools and a growing public interest in getting back to nature. Closely following this phase was the popularity of the 'preppy look'— rugby shirts, khaki-and-plaid materials, and the famous Main Hunting Shoe.

While sales climbed, Gorman revitalized L.L. Bean. Its entire product line was critically evaluated; its advertising budget increased; its mailing lists were computerized; its order-entry system was automated; and its manufacturing facilities and distribution centers were expanded. Improved training programs were added, and L.L. Bean continued to invest millions in automation in order taking and processing. L.L. Bean also increased its reliance on seasonal workers. Throughout his tenure, Gorman's efforts paid off, as L.L. Bean's sales quadrupled between 1975 and 1980, growing at an average annual rate of approximately 20 percent throughout most of the decade of the 1980s.

Through many changes and reorganizations the mail-order catalog has remained L.L. Bean's mainstay. It is through its catalogs that L.L. Bean communicates to its customers the value and quality of its products. The catalog provides time, place, and ownership utility for L.L. Bean customers with convenient services such as a toll-free telephone number for placing orders and a 100 percent return policy. Catalogs permit L.L. Bean to eliminate traditional intermediaries found in other marketing channels and directly market 6,000 different items to customers in their homes. Catalogs enable L.L. Bean to market its products abroad quite successfully. In 1991, sales to Japanese customers totaled $14 million and catalog distribution was initiated in the United Kingdom.

L.L. Bean's continuing reputation for superior customer service is evident in a recent Consumer Reports survey of 165,000 mail-order purchasers. L.L. Bean was the top-rated company in each of its seven merchandise categories; an outstanding 99.89 percent of the 11 million packages mailed were filled correctly.

The reasons behind these superlative ratings are many. L.L. Bean employees who take or check customer orders over the phone are unfailingly polite. They are trained to use the customer names, to say please and thank you, to be familiar with L.L. Bean's products; and to be ready to answer questions about product specifications, inventory, the customer's previous orders or even L.L. Bean history. Telemarketing employees are evaluated based on service quality rather than the number of calls they handle. Customers receive the best possible service through the use of telecommunication systems and computers that connect the L.L. Bean's own telephone system with customer records and its Freeport distribution center.

The distribution center encompasses 630,000 square feet. Workers who fill orders on the floor walk as many as twelve miles during a typical shift. Computers print out the sequence in which items should be collected from inventory, increasing warehouse efficiency by decreasing the time needed to assemble an order. The center can process more than 11 million orders a year, and it usually can deliver anywhere in the United States and Canada within 72 hours.

When Gorman speaks of the future, he emphasizes the fact that L.L. Bean's distribution channel has not been commonly used by U.S. marketers in the past. Approximately 90 percent of all customer purchases have typically taken place in retail stores. Even though L.L. Bean has increased its presence in traditional marketing by a recent agreement to provide merchandise to five Japanese retail stores, catalog sales will continue to be its bread and butter. Gorman explains that catalogs are in a unique position to combine research with product offerings targeted to specific markets. In his words, "Any consumer is a potential mail-order buyer if the offer is relevant to his or her lifestyle." And the L.L. Bean history continues to unfold.

Sources: Boone, Louis E. and David Kurtz, *Contemporary Business*, 6th Edition, The Dryden Press, Hinsdale, 1990. Ron Zemke, *The Service Edge* (New York: NAL Books, 1989), pp. 378–381; Rebecca Fannin, "Bean's Basics," *Marketing & Media Decision*, July 1987, p. 20; James A. Cooke, "Extending the Logistics Channel," *Traffic Management*, April 1988, pp. 69–71; Beverly Geber, "Training at L.L. Bean," *Training*, October 1988; and personal correspondence, February 23, 1989; Berman, Phyllis, "Trouble in Bean Land," *Forbes*, July 6, 1992, p. 42; "L.L. Bean Sets 5 Japan Stores," *Footware News*, March 9, 1992, p. 11; "Bean Bows East with Retail Unit," *Direct*, April, 1992, p. 5; Poirier, Mark, *Catalog Age*, April, 1992, p. 17; L.L. Bean Press Release, September 20, 1992.

Video Discussion Questions

1. What historical forces have shaped management practice at L.L. Bean?

2. What contributions of the Human Relations movement to management thought are illustrated in the video?

3. Describe various aspects of the Quality Improvement movement illustrated in the video.

4. Provide examples of the different functions of management as practiced by L.L. Bean.

5. Describe the relationship between L.L. Bean and its customers.

VIDEO CASE

ESPRIT DE CORP.

While many businesses fail because of a lack of sales, many more run into trouble because they grow too fast. One of the best contemporary examples of a entrepreneurial business that exploded into an international corporation and survived years of growing pains is Esprit de Corp.

Esprit began in 1968 when general partners and good friends Susie Tompkins and Jane Tise began producing clothing designs in their kitchen and marketing them under the label The Plain Jane Dress Company. They made deliveries from the back of Susie's station wagon with her two young daughters in the back seat. Their first showroom was located above a massage parlor. Three years later, Doug Tompkins sold his mountain-climbing equipment company, North Face, for $50,000 and joined his wife and Jane as a full-time partner.

Assisted by Doug's input and drive, The Plain Jane Dress Company manufacturer evolved from a trendy dress company to a wholesale apparel business featuring high-quality, moderately priced junior sportswear. In 1971, the partners changed the name of their company to Esprit de Corp. Translated, the name means a sense of union, common interests, and responsibilities among a group of persons associated together.

In the beginning, Tise and the Tompkins were self-taught entrepreneurs. Susie was something of a rebel growing up and earned what she calls a "non-academic" education. Susie attended the San Francisco Art Institute for a short time after graduation from high school, but she credits travel as the most important influence on her sense of style.

Esprit did not follow trends in high fashion or conduct any market research. Susie, as design director, worked with a small group of designers to produce loose-fitting, clean-lined clothes that she described as "timeless." Doug masterminded Esprit's ad campaigns and developed its image. As co-founders and owners, they enjoyed control of every phase of Esprit's development.

Their strategy was not typical. Instead of enticing retailers to carry the Esprit line, Tompkins mailed 850,000 catalogs directly to upper-income households across the country to generate sales and brand recognition. Consumer response to the catalogs was extraordinary; retailers began contacting Esprit in response to their customers' requests for Esprit clothing.

This consumer demand gave Esprit marketing clout. Department stores handling the Esprit line were required to provide specialized training for their salespeople. In addition, retailers were required to install specially designed store-within-a-store displays similar to the high-tech displays found in well-known outlets such as Bloomingdale's and Macy's. Esprit also refused to follow the common industry practice of reimbursing retailers for markdowns on slow-selling merchandise. They were able to implement these policies because demand for Esprit clothing was very high.

Although Jane Tise left Esprit in 1978, it continued its rapid growth under the leadership of Susie and Doug Tompkins. In 1984, in addition to wholesaling, the Tompkins expanded into direct retailing. Fifteen stores were opened in eight cities at a cost conservatively estimated at $50 million. One extravagant store in West Hollywood—a 30,000 square foot showplace—cost $16 million. In 1985, Doug launched Esprit's famous "real people" advertising, which solidly defined its image in customers' minds. The ads provided almost instant recognition, featuring customers and employees in natural poses and stark surroundings instead of professional models and typical fashion scenes. In the early 1980s,

Esprit became synonymous with a youthful California lifestyle.

By 1985, Esprit was generating annual sales of approximately $800 million in women's and children's apparel to customers in 23 countries. It embraced franchising to conserve capital and, by the late 1980s, Esprit franchise stores were operating in the U.S., Australia, Great Britain, Hong Kong, Singapore, and West Germany. Doug believed that franchising did not damage relationships with department stores within the same cities; claiming, "we have total proof that when we put an Esprit store in a market where a department store is carrying Esprit, it enhances our name."

As Esprit's original partnership arrangement became cumbersome, it was restructured as a closed corporation. Esprit began to resemble a federation of companies as it expanded into international markets. Its top two components included Esprit International, managed by Doug, and Esprit U.S., where Susie served as design consultant. Much of Esprit's actual manufacturing was contracted to foreign firms in countries including Italy, Mexico, New Zealand, Hong Kong, and Taiwan. The foreign manufacturers relied on Esprit designs and quality specifications. Licensing agreements with other companies expanded the Esprit product line to include bed and bath products, eyewear, socks, and tights.

Rapid growth is a double-edged sword. Rapidly growing companies frequently face common problems from escalating sales: lack of control, inadequate distribution outlets, continual pressures for additional funds to finance further growth, and an overburdened management team with limited time for making important business decisions. Esprit was no exception.

By 1987, sales had begun to sour for Esprit and other sportswear manufacturers. Costs were rising, especially in the Far East, where 70 percent of Esprit's product line were manufactured. Fashion-oriented shoppers began to reject rapid price increases and sales for Benetton, The Gap, Banana Republic, and Esprit, all dropped. For Esprit, the timing of this decline was especially unfortunate, arriving during a period of major and expensive expansion.

According to Doug Tompkins, "The rapid expansion created an infrastructure that wasn't really being supported by sales. A combination of many events really caused us to tighten our belts and change our focus from expansion and sales to reevaluating every department in the company—where our expenses were going and how we could keep spiraling expenses from just getting completely out of hand."

Esprit's young, enthusiastic workforce especially was proud of its San Francisco headquarters, dubbed "Little Utopia." There, employees felt like part of a family. There were sushi lunches, subsidized theater tickets, foreign language classes, and adventure travel. Esprit's recruitment brochure boasted of a "revolution in the workplace," where employees "have a meaningful job relationship." However, with a slowdown in sales, employees began to notice that they were not receiving their usual raises and bonuses. Company-subsidized pasta lunches and free coffee were phased out. Many people began to sense that Esprit was in trouble and began to leave. Other employees began to loose their team spirit.

This decline in employee morale was accompanied by an image crisis. Doug wanted to continue to produce and market the junior sportswear that had made Esprit famous; Susie wanted to design for baby boomers, a growing segment of the U.S. consumer market. This lack of a clear purpose and direction left buyers confused. According to an executive at another major retailing firm, Esprit needed to clarify its corporate-level strategy. A company that had found success with a well-defined public image seemed to be floundering over its identity.

Susie resigned as design director to become a design consultant; Doug resigned as president, but stayed on as head of Esprit International. Cost-cutting efforts resulted in layoffs for almost one-third of Esprit employees and plans for a $120 million corporate campus were postponed indefinitely.

The Tompkins turned over daily operations to an aide who had been with Esprit for many years. In addition, they recruited two veteran executives from Calvin Klein to oversee Esprit's consolidated apparel division, in hopes of turning its fortunes around.

Fortunately, foreign operations continued to perform well. An Italian-designed menswear line, introduced in late 1988, had been successful and sales for 1989 improved to about $1.2 billion. Even though direct catalog sales ended in 1984, Esprit continued to mail catalogs at least twice a year to 800,000 potential customers to encourage retail purchases. Despite its growing pains, Esprit's success, in a little over 20 years, is an admirable accomplishment for Doug and Susie Tompkins. So what went wrong?

According to one executive at a major department store, important business decisions were hindered by the Tompkins' independent personalities and their conflict over Esprit's image building. According to Doug Tompkins, their problems have been compared to the challenges of many growing companies: "Our banks [called] this textbook stuff. We wish we had read the textbook."

In 1990, the Tompkins ended their 25-year marriage. Instead of cashing in on Esprit, which they had started 23 years earlier, Susie bought her husband out, and is now one of the top women entrepreneurs in the U.S. She plans to maintain Esprit's idealistic vision, innovative management, and socially responsible policies.

Esprit is also returning to its roots. An increase in demand for junior apparel is providing new market opportunities. Esprit Kids is a response to the growing sophistication of children and increased importance of children's lines to retailers.

Today, Esprit has 27 stores in the United States. In addition to retail and franchise stores, Esprit operates a "shop-in-shop" program in over 100 major department stores across the country. International sales comprise more than two-thirds of Esprit's total worldwide volume.

Susie continues to generate social awareness on local and national levels through personal and corporate commitments to a many issues, including arts education, AIDS awareness, and environmental protection. The recently-released Susie Tompkins Collection reflects her values of simplicity and elegance. In the new Esprit showroom in New York City on Broadway, Susie launched her Susie Tompkins Collection in early March, 1992. According to Susie, "It's not about pretension and look-at-me clothes. It's simple."

Sources: Nadine Joseph, "Patching it up at Esprit," Newsweek, May 23, 1988, p. 69. Anne Ferguson, "Esprit: The Spirit Moves," Management Today, July 1987, pp. 59–61. Ralph King Jr., "How Esprit de Corps lost its Esprit," Forbes, March 21, 1988, pp. 91–94; personal correspondence, February 27, 1989; "Tompkins Gets Her Line," Women's Wear Daily, March 2, 1992, p. 12; Ellie McGrath, "Esprit the Sequel," Working Woman, September, 1991, pp. 66–69; Lee R. Bright, "Stepping Stones: Junior to Kids," Bobbin, July 1992, pp. 68–70; and, Esprit press releases received October 1992.

Video Discussion Questions

1. Many businesses fail because of rapid growth. Explain the factors that led to Esprit's growing pains.

2. What was Esprit's strategic plan in 1971? What was it in 1992?

3. How did Esprit achieve its original organization goals?

4. Discuss the changes in the way decisions have been made at Esprit over the past 25 years.

KIRK STIEFF COMPANY

Kirk Stieff Company, a Baltimore-based silversmith, continuously introduces innovative products. Jim Solomon, president, believes that the company is capitalizing on "a great opportunity with the casting of pewter," by introducing several new cast pewter products. According to Solomon, "pewter allows the firm to provide good prices and gives the firm the ability to expand the number of products." For example, Kirk Stieff recently introduced two new cast pewter groups: Getaway Gallery (a line of frames) and Cottage Glen (a line of silverware). In addition, the firm has product extensions in the Rhyme Time Designs and Stepping Stones collection of picture frames targeted to children. The Stepping Stones collection features three-dimensional sculptures in cast pewter highlighting recreational themes such as bicycling, skate boarding and roller blading. However, Kirk Stieff has not always been so innovative.

As one of the oldest and largest makers and marketers of silver and pewter products in the United States, Kirk Stieff has survived a long history of dramatic environmental fluctuations. Prior to 1990, small silversmiths produced pieces that were valued by an upper class market who appreciated quality and skilled craftsmanship. The market crash in 1929 damaged the silver business, and many silversmiths merged in order to survive.

Unfortunately, the national economic recovery during World War II did not greatly benefit silversmiths because of silver shortages. However, the period following World War II was a boom time for Kirk Stieff and other silversmiths. An enormous pent-up demand for silver flatware was released, and it took years for silversmiths to produce enough product to satisfy the market's needs. Demand tapered off in the 1960s, and by 1980, silver and pewter products were considered a mature market with only small incremental growth possibilities.

In the 1960s, consumers developed a taste for products other than traditional silver. In 1979, the Stieff Company acquired the Kirk Company in an effort to consolidate and survive in the declining market for traditional silver. The new Kirk Stieff Company had several strengths including 215 skilled employees, a tradition of quality, and numerous dealerships. However, instability in the external environment became a major problem. Silver prices skyrocketed to $50 on ounce, plummeted to $10 an ounce, rose to $25, and then plummeted again. The silver business became extremely unstable and, for Kirk Stieff, unprofitable. Kirk Stieff sales dropped 25 percent, and many valuable employees were laid off. The entire sterling flatware market dropped over 45 percent and Kirk Stieff lost one-third of its net worth in 1983 alone.

In 1984, a new president, Pierce Dunn, was hired from outside Kirk Stieff. His job was to develop a strategy that would enable Kirk Stieff to survive in an environment considered both stable and volatile. It was stable in the sense that favorite flatware patterns had been in demand for 100 years or more, and a segment of the population always desired silver. But so many other changes were taking place in consumer taste, in silver prices, and in the labor market that volatility seemed normal, and Kirk Stieff Company had to learn to adapt quickly to market changes.

Dunn's strategic plan was to innovate. He proposed that Kirk Stieff experiment with new products, weeding out those that did not work. A few new-product ideas were taken to a Tabletop Accessory Show, and retailers were delighted with the new upscale designs and sparkling jeweled flatware. This reaction reinforced Dunn's strategy to be customer-driven and market-sensitive. As Kirk Stieff diversified, it became stronger.

Kirk Stieff's strengths were its size, its industry position, and its excellent reputation. Flatware contributed about 60 percent and giftware nearly 40 percent of total sales. These products were sold in four areas: traditional products, awards, classic contemporary, and bridal. The traditional area was competitive and mature, but was a market in which Kirk Stieff had competitive advantage. Awards provided a market opportunity for pewter products. Classic contemporary was an emerging giftware market for young, upscale customers, which was important to Kirk Stieff's future business. The bridal market was a traditional, but important market for flatware products and silversmiths.

Johnna O'Kelly, director of marketing, was hired to help develop and market new products. Her initial efforts included stainless flatware, silverplated vases, silverplated goblets, and silverplated gift items and perfume atomizers. As an integrating manager, she coordinated the activities of several departments on a full-time basis to achieve specific product innovations. Her coordination between design, production, financing and marketing resulted in the introduction of products such as silver and precious stones kaleidoscope.

Kirk Stieff gradually decided to invest significantly in the market for highly crafted specialty goods that were expensive and unique, and to rely less on tableware as its primary product line. Its management invested $200,000 in a New York showroom to attract retailers to its product line, and built an on-site retail store to reach other customers. New, elegant giftware was also designed and marketed as corporate gifts for companies that wanted to give such presents to their clients.

Other innovations included the sourcing of raw materials from several new countries. A tele-marketing program was started to assist retailers. Kirk Stieff salespeople would call brides who had registered with retailers to answer questions on flatware warranties. In addition, they would help the brides plan how to complete their table services.

As Kirk Stieff shifted its strategic focus, it also began to modify its structure. It hired excellent people to complement the existing top-management team. For example, a new financial officer helped revamp Kirk Stieff's cost-accounting system. The new system allowed Kirk Stieff managers to identify the profitability of each product line, discovering that about 15 percent of their products did not sell well. These product lines were dropped as after products were introduced in response to changing market demand.

Another change at Kirk Stieff initiated by President Dunn, was a more decentralized decision-making process. Kirk Stieff changed its production system from specialized departments to production cells. In a production cell, a small group of individuals became responsible for the output and quality of the particular product that it produced. Within the cell, group members performed all the functions of polishing, welding, stamping, and engraving that were previously performed by different departments.

The system was more efficient in terms of time, labor, and inventory costs, and it also engaged the commitment of employees. The production cells also served as quality circles where employees meet to discuss problems and possible solutions. Production cells are the quality control mechanism at Kirk Stieff. Rather than maintaining a separate inspection department, the employees judge the quality of their own output.

As authority was delegated to those who actually did the work, Kirk Stieff relied more on its employees to uncover the best and most efficient means of making its products. The employees were able to take pride in their ability to produce more with fewer people and the fact that they have played an important role in making Kirk Stieff more successful. As one employee stated, "silver is a noble metal, and it deserves the best."

By 1989, a new spirit was infused throughout Kirk Stieff. It revived the innovative spirit that was initiated by the founder more than 100 years ago. The new leadership at Kirk Stieff appears to be committed to the strategy of innovation, illustrated by the wide range of innovative products recently introduced. As president Jim Solomon stated, "we think we can bring more to the (picture frame and tableware) categories, and that's what we're capitalizing on."

Source: "Kirk Stieff Casts its Lot With Pewter Products," *HFD-The Weekly Home Furnishings Newspaper,* Vol. 66, Issue No. 15, pp. 180–181; "Kirk Stieff Unveils Upscaled Designs," *HFD-The Weekly Home Furnishings Newspaper,* July 7, 1986, 60; "Group Launches Drive to Spur Pewter Demand," *American Metal Market,* February 1986, 4; and "Kirk Stieff Company" video produced for Growing a Business PBS series, copyright 1989 by Ambrose Video Publishing Inc.

Video Discussion Questions

1. What business-level strategy is illustrated by Kirk Stieff Company?

2. What type of organization design is illustrated by Kirk Stieff Company?

3. Describe the nature of authority and power at Kirk Stieff Company?

4. What techniques were used by Pierce Dunn to implement a new strategy and organizational culture? Was the resulting organization design appropriate? Explain.

VIDEO CASE

PATAGONIA

Yvon Chouinard is a fortunate entrepreneur who built his business around what he likes to do. The youngest of four children, Chouinard lived in the French-speaking town of Lisbon, Maine, until he was 8, when his father moved the family to Burbank, California. A rock-climbing legend, Chouinard is founder and chairman of Ventura, California-based Lost Arrow Corp., best known for its rugged and colorful Patagonia line of outdoor gear. He has created a people-oriented organization and in the process, has remained true to his own goals to (1) make money, (2) give money away, (3) be creative, (4) have pride, (5) eliminate hassles, and (6) have fun.

Lost Arrow traced its origins to one of Chouinard's own mountain climbing needs: He had been unable to buy an adequate molly, a spike used in scaling cliffs. Consequently, he designed his own version made from chromium.

Demand existed for molly spikes, and he found himself in the mountaineering hardware business from 1957 until 1970. In the early years, he distributed his climbing gear through retail stores such as those owned by his friend—and fellow mountain climber—Doug Tompkins of Esprit de Corps. But climbing equipment is a tiny market, and total sales amounted to only about $300,000 a year. When he started out, Chouinard picked up extra money by working as a private detective for Howard Hughes. Then, in 1974, fate intervened.

On a trip to Scotland, Chouinard purchased a supply of rugby shirts and expanded his business to sport clothing. The clothing was of the highest quality, covering activities such as climbing, skiing, sailing, flyfishing, and kayaking. Within a year, sales had more than tripled to $1 million.

Chouinard discovered that making money by offering high-quality products to avid, exclusive customers was easy. Controlling company growth was more difficult.

The $800 invested in Chouinard Equipment back in 1957 grew into today's Patagonia, Inc., a subsidiary of Lost Arrow. Patagonia's mail-order catalog has made it famous. Often called the best such catalog in the United States, it features a personal, familiar tone, with anecdotes and essays that are often unrelated to the catalog's products, real-life photographs, and a lavish, magazine-size format. About 75 percent of Patagonia's annual revenue comes from sales to 750 retail accounts (including EMS, L.L. Bean, and REI). Another 16 percent is generated from mail-order sales, with the remainder coming from Patagonia's nine retail stores on three continents.

Patagonia's growth has been supported by increases in human resources. It has more than 600 employees. Each was hired with one question in mind: "Would I want to have dinner with this person?" There is a strong commitment to Patagonia's organizational culture that is entrenched not only in the workforce but also in its customers.

Talking with some of Patagonia's employees reveals a lack of concern for many standard aspects of most businesses. Such worldly matters as sales, earnings, and inventory seem unimportant to many employees, who appear concerned only with producing the highest-quality product they can. It is important that employees fit into this strong, decidedly outdoorsy, organizational culture. At the spacious Patagonia headquarters, employees do not wear ties or suits; many, in fact, wear Patagonia clothes. Patagonia's top executives sit at simple wooden desks in an open room. Most are employees in their mid-thirties who are health conscious, stay in good shape, eat lots of yogurt and granola, and are exercise-oriented. During the day, employees can often be found outside, roller skating around headquarters or getting into their cars for a two-minute drive to the ocean.

Chouinard has a long-term attitude toward Patagonia and its employees: He wants them to stay with Patagonia and tries to ensure that they do. Part of achieving that goal is involvement. "We try to get the most intelligent people we can . . . But in the end, you really end up with fairly average people," Chouinard explains. "The secret is to try to get average people to do above-average work." He believes this is accomplished by giving employees a sense of responsibility and letting them see the direct result of their work as it affects the whole organization.

Among Patagonia employee benefits is an excellent on-premise child-care facility, Great Pacific Child Development Center, which further emphasizes Patagonia's family-like concerns. Patagonia recognizes an obligation to deal with employees' parental responsibilities, and believes that child care is everyone's concern. The Center helps integrate children and their parents' workplace into an everyday environment, relieving anxiety and frustration in both children and adults. Work satisfaction and productivity also increase. The benefit is total and mutual. Each staff member at the Center meets or exceeds all qualifications required by the state of California. The child-adult ratio allows individualized care and enhances the learning environment for the children.

Patagonia also provides excellent subsidized cafeteria facilities for its employees, specializing in healthful and nutritious foods. Rather than going out to an hour-an-a-half lunch, many employees eat in the cafeteria. They can conduct business there or take food back to their offices, thus remaining more productive throughout the day.

Keeping employees satisfied is important, but so is keeping customers happy, and at Patagonia this means keeping everyone involved. The customer relations established by Patagonia are unique in today's typical business world and envied by others. Says one L.L. Bean official, "Their customers are different." In addition to ordering at twice the rate of a typical L.L. Bean customer, these purchasers write to Patagonia. They even send pictures—about 25,000 a year. And how does Patagonia respond to its customers' communications? From about 1,000 new product suggestions received in 1987, approximately 60 percent were used, and their stories and pictures were included in Patagonia's biannual catalogs. The catalog is at the heart of Patagonia's corporate culture. While employees talk of quality, utility, and performance throughout the text and in charts and diagrams inside the catalog, there also are essays that create excitement with words and pictures that bring Kilimanjaro or rushing white-water rapids to the fingertips and minds of readers. The Patagonia catalog is for cultist, devoted sports enthusiasts.

But Patagonia does not stop with achievements in personnel benefits and customer relations—it is committed to keeping the earth's environment in its natural state for future generations. Patagonia far exceeds its social responsibility in this area by donating 10 percent of its net profit (or 1 percent of sales, whatever is greater) to worthy charitable causes, which the company calls its "earth tax." Patagonia also donates clothing and equipment to scientists, athletes, and astronauts, and to native American orphanages and needy families throughout the U.S. and Central America. Some of the 350 nonprofit organizations supported by Patagonia include Greenpeace, the Audubon Society, and the Cousteau Society. Marketing benefits also result from this generosity. "You give a few thousand dollars to a group with 50 volunteers," says Chouinard, "and you create 50 customers."

But Patagonia's growth path has not been without bumps. Like many retailers, Patagonia was caught with high inventories when the economy slowed in the late 1980s and early 1990s. By April 1991, sales were flat. Patagonia began a retrenchment in product lines, staffing, and marketing costs that culminated in a July 1991 layoff of about 20 percent of its workforce. Steps taken to tighten operations included keeping a closer eye on credit, producing fewer styles, using more local suppliers, and requiring dealers to purchase earlier, according to CEO Kris McDivitt.

And while the belt-tightening was painful, it appears to have left a trimmer, stronger organization that is moving forward against rocky terrain.

As a growing corporation (since 1981, Lost Arrow sales have increased from $5 million to $117 million in 1991), Patagonia is likely to be used as an example of the new face of contemporary business: a company concerned with its employees, its customers, and the environment of the world in which we all live.

Sources: Sidney A. Nachman, *Video Cases and Teaching Notes*. The Dryden Press, 1990. Fleming Meeks, "The Man Is the Message," *Forbes*, April 17, 1988, pp. 148–152; Gary Strauss, "Patagonia's Rugged Wear Leads the Pack," *USA Today*, January 11, 1989, pp. B1, B2; Paul Brown, "The Anti-Marketers," *Inc.*, March 1988, pp. 62–72; and personal correspondence, February 27, 1989; Edward O. Welles, "Lost in Patagonia," *Inc.*, August 1992, pp. 44–57.

Video Discussion Questions

1. According to Chouinard, the "secret [to Patagonia's success] is to get average people to do above-average work." Describe how this can be achieved.

2. Describe two motivational programs that demonstrate Patagonia' long-term commitment to its employees.

3. Describe how Patagonia develops its human resources.

4. Explain how Patagonia uses human resource planning and staffing.

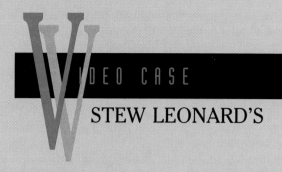

STEW LEONARD'S

Stew Leonard's retail outlet in Norwalk, Connecticut, is more than just "the world's largest dairy store." Back in 1969, it opened its doors by offering fewer than a dozen dairy items in a 17,000-square-foot store. Since then, the store has been expanded 27 times and today covers more than 100,000 square feet. Annual sales for the store, housed in an amusement park atmosphere, total more than $100 million—an amount equal to what the Food Marketing Institute estimates for a typical ten-store supermarket chain. Each year Stew Leonard's single store sells some 10 million quarts of milk, 8 million ears of corn, 5.6 million bananas, and more than 50 tons of Marianne Leonard's (Mrs. Stew Leonard's) meatloaf.

What makes this Connecticut store distinctive, in addition to being a cross between a supermarket and Disney World, is its volume—both in dollar sales and in inventory. Most supermarkets carry between 15,000 and 20,000 items in an attempt to provide everything the food and household goods shopper could want in a single location. But supermarket managers are all too aware of Pareto's Law, or the 80/20 principle: 20 percent of the items in inventory will account for 80 percent of total store sales. The typical supermarket loses money on heavy, bulky, low-margin items like sugar, but continues to stock them to offer one-stop service. Not Stew Leonard's. Stew has replaced Pareto's Law with "Leonard's Law." He gets 100 percent of his sales from less than 4 percent of those items sold in typical supermarkets. "The world's largest dairy store" limits its stock to about 800 fast-moving, high-margin items. Customers follow a winding pathway through the store's sections—bakery, dairy (milk is bottled on the premises), butcher (for meat and fish), produce, salad bar, deli with hot and cold food, and ice cream department. Customers must go to other stores for canned goods, spices, toothpaste, and household products. The average turnover on merchandise at Leonard's is 30 times a year, more than double that of a typical U.S. supermarket.

In a typical week, more than 100,000 shoppers will visit the Norwalk store, a total of over 5 million a year. This high volume of sales, combined with a significant percentage of the store's own private label merchandise and direct delivery of produce from West Coast suppliers, keeps prices down and profits up so that both Leonard and his customers are happy. These factors, along with the festive atmosphere (and a free ice cream cone for each shopper) attract shoppers from as far away as New York, an hour's commute.

To serve the customer as best he can, Stew Leonard provides a feedback mechanism in the form of an easy-to-locate suggestion box. More than 100 suggestions a day are received and all are given immediate attention by management. (They are typed and distributed to each department by 10 a.m. the following day.) Managers report weekly on what they have done about customers' suggestions and complaints. As a result of the suggestion box, English muffins are now stacked next to the bacon and eggs, strawberries are sold loose, and paper towels are on hand to wipe off rain-soaked shopping carts. The store uses its own customers as consultants. Focus groups, where managers hear criticism and suggestions from about 20 Stew Leonard's customers, are held every three weeks. Participants are served snacks and soft drinks and are given a $20 store gift certificate for their participation. Many of their recommendations are implemented.

Stew Leonard's is a family business. All four of Stew and Marianne's children work for the store. So do more than 700 full-time and part-time employees. More than half of Stew Leonard's team members (Stew dislikes the term employee) have relatives working in the store.

Many of the employees are young, more than half of them under 21. Starting pay is more than what other retailers pay for comparable work, and the store receives 15 to 20 applicants for every opening. "We don't look for skills or knowledge," Leonard says. "We look for attitude." First, he seeks people with positive, can-do dispositions, outgoing individuals who are likely to be genuinely friendly toward fellow team members and customers. "We can teach cash register. We can't teach nice," says Stew. New employees take an in-house Dale Carnegie course stressing attitude, people skills, and customer relations.

Stew is concerned with the selection, training, and motivation of team members because they represent a critical component of the Stew Leonard's promotional mix. Although the store does some advertising, its greatest emphasis is on sales promotion and personal selling. Predictably, in a self-service retail store, the selling that occurs is subtle, often consisting largely of advice on locating a particular item, suggestions from bakery personnel on the use of certain products, or just a smile.

Leonard's customer relations strategy is fairly direct. "It's five times easier to keep the customer you've got than to go out and find a new one." The store's motto is chiseled on a 6,000-pound boulder a the front entrance:

Rule #1: The customer is always right.
Rule #2: If the customer is ever wrong, reread Rule 1.

Happy customers, according to Leonard, are essential to long-term success. He reasons that because the average customer spends about $100 a week in the store, that amounts to $5,200 a year or $52,000 over the course of ten years. A single dissatisfied customer, then, represents a potential sales loss of about $50,000. This explains his comment that "When I see a frown on a customer's face, I see $50,000 about to walk out the door."

To determine what sells and what does not—which translates into what the customer wants and does not want—Stew Leonard's has one of the largest, most sophisticated computer systems of any single store in the world. With it, management can spot trends almost immediately from sales patterns and can quickly respond with inventory changes. The high turnover rates mean that customers are buying the freshest products possible. In addition, customers almost never have to wait in checkout lines—the bane of most supermarkets. Fifty-two checkouts are available and at least 27 of them are always in operation. Any time more than three customers have to wait in line, additional checkouts are opened and free cookies and ice cream are passed out to those waiting.

In addition to this kind of service, the "come to the fair" atmosphere makes Stew Leonard's a family place, particularly on weekends, when the 10-acre parking lot is filled with parents and children. Children and adults alike appear to enjoy the talking cows, the two robot dogs, the two 10-foot-tall mechanical bears, the "sheriff" who heads the security force, and the employees dressed as carrots walking the wide aisles singing country and western music. Store promotions include a $3 gift certificate given to customers who bring in a photo of themselves in some exotic local, holding a Stew Leonard's shopping bag. These photos, which come from such unlikely spots as the Kremlin, Stonehenge, the floor of the Pacific Ocean, and the North Pole, are displayed prominently at the front of the store. Each checkout counter has a light that periodically flashes to announce a randomly selected winner of a complimentary frozen yogurt cone. Any customer who purchases more than $100 worth of groceries receives a prize.

Behind the store is a petting zoo where children can find friendly animals, including goats, chickens, geese and cows. Inside the store, most departments are specially arranged. For example, shoppers feel like they are walking right into a kitchen when they enter the bakery section. This approach works: The bakery generates 20 times the sales of the average supermarket bakery.

There are samples everywhere: lemonade, horseradish cheese, cupcakes, nuts, ice cream, and chocolate chip cookies. As one shopper puts it, "You come in here just for milk and you walk out with a shopping cart full of food."

Leonard observes that sales increase 25 percent when he gives out samples.

For all this success, Stew has not really considered expanding his business into a chain, although a second store run by his son Stew Jr. opened in Danbury, Connecticut, in August 1991. The senior Leonard seems content to serve as master of ceremonies at his own store—greeting customers at the front door, serving them some of the various goods in the bakery, or stocking and adjusting displays. Like Walt Disney, Stew Leonard seems to have as much, if not more, fun as the more than 100,000 customers who visit him each week.

Sources: Feldman, Diane, "Companies Aim to Please," *Management Review*, Vol. 78, Issue, 5, May, 1989, pp. 89. "They Also Serve," *Adweek's Relate*, April 24, 1989, pp. 18–19; Tom Peters, *Thriving on Chaos* (New York: Alfred A. Knopf, 1987), pp. 98–99ff; Bruce Bolger, "Unconventional Wisdom," *Incentive*, November 1988, pp. 36–40; Lisa McGurrin, "Hillbilly Music in the Frozen Peas at Stew Leonard's," *New England Business*, February 17, 1987, pp. 38–41; Stew Leonard's, "Love That Customer!" *Management Review*, October 1987, pp. 36–39; and Ron Zemke, *The Service Edge* (New York: NAL Books, 1989), pp. 317–321; Everett T. Suter, "Stew Leonard: Soul of a Leader," *Executive Excellence*, June 1991, pp. 13–14; *Supermarket News*, Nov. 4, 1991, p. 12; Craig Steinberg, *Training and Development*, Vol. 46, No. 2, Feb. 1992, p. 9; Erika Penzer, "Secrets from the Supermarket," *Incentive*, Vol. 165, No. 8, August 1991, pp. 67–69.

Video Discussion Questions

1. Describe how Stew Leonard motivates his employees.

2. Is Stew Leonard an effective leader? Explain.

3. Describe the nature of communication, the nature of group dynamics, and how conflict is managed at Stew Leonard's.

4. What is the motto of Stew Leonard's store? What does it represent?

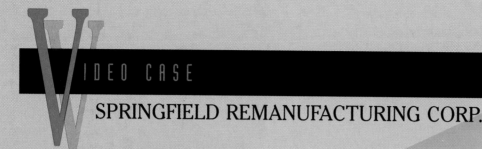

SPRINGFIELD REMANUFACTURING CORP.

"We teach them about finance and accounting before they turn a wrench." This statement by Jack Stack, president and CEO of Springfield Remanufacturing Corporation, a company that remanufactures and sells diesel and gasoline engines, transmissions, and related accessories, symbolizes the importance of effectively using management control systems. Springfield Remanufacturing Corporation (SRC), was generating sales of $26 million in 1983, but was also showing a loss of $2 million annually. Its ailing parent, International Harvester (now Navistar), was warding off bankruptcy and agreed to sell SRC to Jack Stack and twelve other employees in a highly leveraged buyout.

Stack and his partners acquired a formidable challenge. SRC's survival meant increasing sales and lowering costs to pay the interest on substantial new liabilities used to buy the company. Notes payable had become an additional burden on the new venture. Stack and the employee-owners of SRC rose to the challenge. By 1991, sales almost tripled to $70 million, the workforce grew to 650 people, and engines were produced for an expanded customer base in four industries: medium and heavy-duty trucks, agricultural equipment, heavy construction equipment, and automotive equipment. With a growth rate of 30 to 40 percent a year, SRC is ranked as one of the most successful small business operations in the United States.

Central to this growth has been SRC's open-door, open-book management control system and top-management support. When Stack and his associates purchased SRC from International Harvester, 115 of the original 171 employees continued with the company. Today, SRC is completely employee-owned through an employee stock ownership program (ESOP). Since SRC's rebirth, every year a portion of its earnings are used to buy unissued stock in the company. These purchases go into a trust fund for all full-time employees. Employee compensation is affected by the value of corporate stock, which is determined by company profits. Because of the direct link between financial rewards and profitability, SRC employees, encouraged by management, take an active interest in its financial status. The key to SRC's success has been in educating the employee-owners in the use of financial data—accounting statements, profit reports, cost control analyses, and quality measures—and giving them a stake in the financial outcome, good or bad.

Employees meet weekly to receive information on operating income, expenses, cash flows, and other relevant financial data. Employee training on how the numbers are determined and what they mean also occurs at these meetings; Stack and his management team believe that teaching employees about balance sheets, income statements, and cash flow statements is the most effective method to improve company financial performance—especially for an employee-owned company.

To overcome SRC employees' initial lack of enthusiasm toward learning about financial matters, Stack communicated his philosophy that business is basically a game—a game that anyone can learn to play. The first step is to teach employees the rules of the game. Next, they are given enough information to play the game. Ultimately, they must have the opportunity to win or lose. In Stack's words, "Winning the Great Game of Business has the greatest reward: continual improvement of your life and your livelihood. You get that reward, however, only by playing together as a team and by building a dynamic company." According to Stack, there are four primary reasons for management to play the game: to honor the employment obligation by ensuring that employees understand that they can influence their own job security; to eliminate jobs that are boring or demeaning and to create an environment where all employees can take pleasure in their work; to abolish the traditional employee mentality by giving employee-owners the information, understanding and confidence they need to make decisions; and to create wealth and distribute it to the people who created it.

SRC's extraordinary training program teaches employees the rules of business, including the importance of cash flow, and shows them how to "keep score" and "follow the action." Then they are given the information they need to do this. The entire SRC team—managers, supervisors, administrative personnel, and production workers—has access to the company's monthly financial reports. In small group sessions, supervisors review the figures, encouraging questions. In addition, the cost accounting department supplies daily printouts, detailing the progress of every job in each supervisor's area.

One of the most important aspects of SRC's training involves the use of the income statement. "For us," says Stack, "the income statement is the same as the daily racing form is to a guy handicapping a race, or the same as the tape is to a guy betting on the market. . . . it's addictive because SRC is an employee-owned company, beating the numbers means more profits and income for the employees.

The game starts every Wednesday, when top managers "huddle" with Jack Stack to produce a projection of SRC's income statement at the end of the current month. Employees are given blank income and projected cash flow statements. First, the sales department manager announces the sales forecasts for the coming month. Then, the other managers report the numbers for which they are responsible. When everyone has reported, the projected income statement is complete. The managers then return to their teams to discuss the income statement with them, and identify any adjustments that need to be made to the team's performance. This employee involvement in managerial decision making is encouraged with bonus programs tied to specific goals.

Mike Carrigan, an SRC vice-president, parallels these weekly updates to regular physical examinations: Employee rewards are linked directly to SRC's health. Because employees are aware of their performance standards, they can determine their contribution to SRC's overall productivity. For example, individual water-pump assemblers can see the impact of their efforts on costs. When a standard is met, rewards are given to the responsible employee. In addition to the productivity bonus programs, cash payments are made to employees who submit cost-saving ideas.

Delegation of cost-control decision making is visible at SRC. First-line supervisors are actively involved in not only reducing costs in their own departments, but also in helping reduce costs in other departments. Information is readily available, since there is one computer terminal in the plant for every three employees. Anyone can go to a terminal and retrieve information on incoming parts, costs, or engineering problems. Data on current labor, material and overhead costs—and comparisons with expected costs—are immediately available.

"You see, what happened here," says Carrigan, "is that now these people were in effect running their own small businesses. They had set their own budgets and they had to live with them. If they wanted to complain, they had to complain to themselves." More than being aware, the employees were now involved and responsible for their own future. At SRC, they realize that only people can make the numbers work, and they are the same people who set the numbers.

This company-wide sense of responsibility has helped SRC through some difficult problems. In 1988 SRC's health insurance premiums increased by almost 50 percent and pharmaceutical insurance premiums tripled. Sixty thousand dollars of the increase ended up coming out of SRC's bonus pool—directly affecting employee compensation. Jack Stack led an aggressive effort to identify the most costly claims with an eye to establishing preventive programs to reduce the number of claims at the source. Since many of the claims were childbirth related, SRC implemented prenatal classes on a variety of subjects. SRC negotiated reduced pharmaceutical costs with a grocery-store chain that agreed to provide prescription data to enable the company to purchase high-volume drugs in large quantities and in generic formulations. In addition, SRC offers wellness programs with prizes for improving one's weight, cholesterol and/or blood pressure.

Each employee at SRC shares in the risks and the rewards of the company by sharing in the vision championed by upper management. The employees focus on developing goals that will help them beat their common competitor—the numbers. Each employee devotes time and energy to learning the managerial accounting and budgeting system from compensation to finance. In addition, they enthusiastically assume authority that is happily delegated to them by Jack Stack. He has stated that his primary goal is to become obsolete by effectively delegating responsibility to employees and managers. The shared vision of creating and sustaining employment for employees is at the heart of self-management and control methods at SRC.

Sources: D. Keith Denton, and Barry L. Wisdom, "Shared Vision," *Business Horizons*, Vol. 32, July/August 1989, p. 67–69, Burlingham, Bo, "Being the Boss," *Inc.*, Vol. 11, No. 10, Oct. 1989, pp. 49–65, Denton, D. Keith, "SRC Uses Commodity Budgets to Boost Productivity," *Management Review*, Vol. 77, Issue 10, October 198, pp. 16–18, D. Keith Denton, "Appealing to Their Highest Level of Intelligence," *Supervision*, August 1988, pp. 3–6; Lucien Rhodes and Patricia Amend, "The Turnaround," *Inc.*, August 1986, pp. 42–48; D. Keith Denton, "an Employee Ownership Program That Rebuilt Success," *Personnel Journal*, March 1987, pp. 114–120; Jack Stack, "Crisis Management by Committee," *Inc.*, May 1988, p. 26; and personal correspondence, February 27, 1989. *Lammers*, Teri, "The Examined Health-Insurance Bill," *Inc.*, V. 14, no. 5, May, 1992, pp. 45–47; Greer, Olen L., Steven K. Olson and Marty Callison, "The Key to Real Teamwork," *Management Accounting*, V. 73, no. 11, May 1992, pp. 39–42; Stack, Jack "The Great Game of Business," *Inc.*, V. 14, no. 6, June, 1992, pp. 52–56.

Video Discussion Questions

1. Explain how SRC employees use financial statements to play the "great game of business."

2. How is employee involvement implemented at SRC?

3. Is budgeting top-down or bottom-up at SRC? What are the benefits of their budgeting system?

4. What type of control methods are used at SRC? Explain the impact on SRC's employee morale, production efficiency, and product quality.

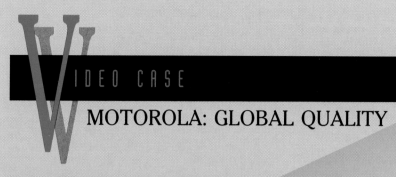

VIDEO CASE

MOTOROLA: GLOBAL QUALITY

Imagine the scandal if U.S. pharmacists gave out 24,000 wrong drug prescriptions a year. Suppose surgeons annually performed 26,000 bad operations and, every year, ob/gyn doctors and nurses accidentally dropped more than 15,000 newborn babies. This would occur if these professionals had done their jobs correctly 99.9 percent of the time. This success rate sounds almost perfect but in reality could drive you out of business.

In the global marketplace, quality is viewed as a means of continual improvement, a way to organize manpower and machines successfully. The current quality revolution is as powerful and influential as the Industrial Revolution. Due to changes in transportation and communication, the quality revolution involves every person on the face of the earth.

Every technical advance has had an economic effect that we have not fully appreciated. Competition and modern technology have refocused attention from quantity to quality.

Traditionally, whoever could make the most would win. Now, the winner is whoever can make the best. Customers want quality, although people do not always agree on what quality means.

What is quality? There are many definitions. According to Neil Dial, Manager of Paging Division at Motorola, "to use Webster's definition of quality, it's the meaning of excellence." Earl Conway, of Procter & Gamble, says, "Quality is the unyielding and continuing effort by everyone in an organization to understand, meet, and exceed the needs of its customers."

As defined by Michael Maccoby, President of the Maccoby Group, in the past "you could have any car you wanted as long as it was black. Quality meant making the same thing the same way, over and over again, in a way that wouldn't break down and would be durable." Maccoby

also believes that quality is "not only satisfying customers, delighting them, innovating, creating—and that's a whole new game . . . Now we're moving into a post-industrial, post-modern world in which the key is customization and continual innovation." As depicted by Carol Griffin, Material Handler at Motorola, "quality is the best product that you can produce with the materials that you have to work with." According to W.G. Mulder of Romac Industries, quality involves "continuous good products which a customer can trust." James Jones, Hines VA Hospital, states that "quality is producing a product or service that meets the needs or expectations of the customers."

All economies were local until the 19th century when railroads and the telegraph helped make them national or regional economies. It was not until the 1950s that fiber optics were invented, the first satellite orbited the earth, improved transistors made modern computers possible, and the first jet airline service was started. For business purposes, the world began to shrink and continues to shrink today. Geographic distance is irrelevant.

Daniel Yankelovich, President of the Public Agenda Foundation, agrees, stating that "Now the integration, the crossfertilization, the joint ventures and the breakdown of lines of culture are creating a truly global marketplace." Robert B. Reich, Professor, Harvard University, has stated, "the only factor of production that is relatively immobile internationally and, therefore, upon which our standard of living and the standard of living of every country depends are the nation's people . . . . If you don't have an infrastructure that's state-of-the-art, your people are not going to have a high standard of living. It's as simple—but as complicated as that."

According to George Fisher, Motorola Chairman

and CEO, to remain competitive, the U.S. must focus on five key elements to ensure strong economic leadership. Those key elements proposed by a non-partisan Council on Competitiveness report, include the following: The U.S. must commit to achieve leadership in critical generic technologies, which are the drivers of economic growth; the U.S. must create a national infrastructure that will keep the country competitive into the 21st century; it must develop an environment that ensures investment in people, capital, and technology to compete globally; the U.S. must use trade and foreign investment tools to prevent its major foreign rivals from protecting home markets, subsidizing competition in third-world markets, or dominating U.S. markets based on nonreciprocal access; and, private industry must encourage U.S. firms to implement best practices for quality and cycle time improvement and workforce training and education. Fisher also supports a long-term commitment to quality management to achieve and maintain the United States' global competitiveness.

This kind of commitment enabled Motorola to win the prestigious Malcolm Baldrige Award in 1988. The Malcolm Baldrige Award was created in 1987 to help companies increase their quality standards. Applicants for the award are evaluated on five key quality determinants: customer focus, meeting commitments, process management and elimination of waste, employee involvement and empowerment, and continuous improvement.

The Malcolm Baldrige Award was accepted by Robert Galvin, Motorola's Chairman of the Executive Committee. Galvin sees successful quality improvement as an act of faith by an organization, and has stated that it "will never cost money to have a quality program" because companies will always "have lower costs and better products when [they] have a quality program."

One important component of any quality program is benchmarking. Although benchmarking has existed for many years, it has enjoyed a recent rebirth as a result of an expanded scope pioneered by Motorola and other companies. Benchmarking provides a powerful capability for firms to efficiently and effectively implement dramatic improvements in process and project management. Process management helps companies prepare to benchmark their critical processes, products and services. Project management assures that improvement ideas generated from benchmarking will be effectively implemented and monitored. Motorola uses a Six Sigma program, which is a defect prevention system that allows no more than about three defects per million opportunities. Using Motorola as the benchmark, IBM adopted a similar defect reduction program.

At a conference on benchmarking sponsored by *Industry Week* and the International Quality and Productivity Center, Brenda Sumberg, director of quality at Motorola University, said that "benchmarking exercises must not overlook internal operations." Managers at the conference discussed two benchmarking truisms: (1) no two benchmarking strategies are identical, with the consequence that organizations need to tailor their efforts to their own specific situations, and (2) top-management support is always vital.

According to George Fisher, Motorola "identified people who are the very best in the world in each of the elements of our business although, perhaps, not all in one company." Galvin supported this strategy, stating that "we learned that they did some things better and we copied some of their processes." He continued, "I think the single most important thing is that the Chief Executive Officer has to decide that it is his [or her] uncompromising objective to accomplish the highest quality standards for that business and that his personal involvement will be ever evident and he [or she] will be the role model."

At Motorola, quality is not just a buzzword or a fad. As Fisher explained, "you can't just talk about quality one day a month, or one day a week. It's got to be a way of life and you had better walk the talk, as they say, or your people will see right through it."

While a quality program will not cost money, some investment is required. When Motorola built an automated production line at its pager plant in Boynton Beach, Florida, the money invested was recouped by a faster and more efficient production process. It used to take Motorola 30 days to build a pager, usually called a beeper. The new process builds the same beeper in 30 minutes. That's revolutionary.

To plan and build a similar new production line normally requires three years. Motorola cut that in half by taking the best of what was already available, including Japanese Sako robots. People maintain the robots and do what the company calls a "cosmetic" inspection. Does the pager look right? Is there anything the customer would not like?

According to Neil Dial, "it's more than just the factory force in this. It's the five things that the customer wants. He wants the right product, right service, right time, right quality, and right cost. They can actually, today, build a pager radio from order entry to the time they ship it in about 28 minutes."

As stated by Fisher, "the designer can't design a product and throw it over a wall and expect the manufacturing organization to simply make it . . . The solutions to get there cannot be conventional solutions. People really have to think quite differently about how they approach their processes."

Quality also involves human resource development. An employee who has been with Motorola for ten years can be fired only with the permission of Chief Executive Officer Fisher. Every Motorola employee must be able to make a bottom-line contribution. This requires training. Motorola has classes for all employees to upgrade their skills in courses from Basic English to Advanced Statistics. Every Motorola employee at every level must take a minimum of 40 hours of training each year. According to Fisher, "today, to get the quality and the cost you need, you really have to have an integrated team effort starting with the customers and suppliers and across all the organizations."

Dial agrees, "when we were chasing cheap labor, we did it around the world and we went to places where labor was cheaper. Now, as we start to upgrade our manufacturing processes and reinvest in our factories, we're finding that we also have to reinvest in our people skills. Manual dexterity used to be the most important factor in recruiting. Today, we want people who can make

decisions and communicate with the engineering group, the business people, and the managers."

Predictably, competition will become more severe in the global marketplace as more companies and more countries adopt a Quality Management philosophy and begin to produce better goods for less cost. That is not so much a threat as it is an opportunity.

The global quality competition has improved some multi-national firms. It would be a mistake to think that a quality program is easy to do. It is not. A quality system is demanding and time consuming. Continuous improvement never ends and quality requires constant attention. Ultimately, there is only one reason to pursue a quality program—survival.

Sources: George Fisher, "Competing and Cooperating in a New, Market-Driven World," *Quality*, April, 1992, p. 20 and p. 22; William D. Schulte Jr., "An Interview with David Cheney," *The Competitiveness Review*, Spring, 1991, p. 1–2; Leonard M. Fuld, "Achieving Total Quality Through Intelligence," *Long Range Planning*, Feb. 1992, p. 109–115; Gerald J. Balm, "Benchmarking—Nicety or Necessity?," *Tapping the Network Journal*, Spring 1992, p. 6–8; Charles R. Day, Jr., "Benchmarking's First Law: Know Thyself!," *Industry Week*, Feb. 17, 1992, p. 70; Robert Mason, CC-M Productions, "Quality or Else," a video production, rights obtained by the Dryden Press, Fort Worth, Texas, 1992.

Video Discussion Questions

1. What are the key quality determinants for selecting the Malcolm Baldrige Award winner? What factors helped Motorola win the Malcolm Baldrige Award?

2. What are the key elements for global competitiveness according to Fisher and the Council on Competitiveness? Is Motorola a global economic leader? Explain.

3. What is quality? How does Motorola define quality?

4. What is benchmarking? How did benchmarking affect productivity and quality at Motorola? Explain.

Acceptance theory of authority. Authority stems from below because subordinates can always reject a directive.

Accommodation. A conflict-resolution option that involves one party maintaining harmony by giving in to another.

Achievement-oriented leadership. A type of behavior in which a leader sets challenging goals, expects subordinates to perform their best, and shows confidence that subordinates will perform well.

Activity ratios. One of several ratios used to gauge how efficiently an organization uses its resources.

Adaptive strategy. A type of business-unit-level strategy which holds that an organization should formulate strategies for each of its SBUs that are congruent with their task environment.

Adjourning. A stage of group development exemplified by task completion.

Administrative management. An approach to management pioneered by Henri Fayol.

Analyzer strategy. A type of adaptive strategy that seeks to maintain stability while selectively responding to opportunities for innovation.

Arbitration. The final step in the union grievance procedure. A neutral third party is selected to render a final and binding decision on a grievance between labor and management.

Artificial intelligence. Efforts to make computers perform the duties and the actions of people.

Aspiration level. A subjectively defined performance goal.

Asset turnover ratio. The ratio between an organization's sales and total assets. Used to indicate how efficiently an organization is using its assets.

Authority. The right to perform on command.

Autocratic I method. A decision-making method in which a manager solves a problem alone, using whatever information is available at the time.

Autocratic II method. A decision-making method in which a manager obtains necessary information from subordinates before making a decision alone.

Autonomy. The extent to which employees are free to act.

Auxiliary storage. Devices such as magnetic disk and tape and optical disks that store data and programs for later processing.

Avoidance. A conflict-resolution option that involves withdrawing from or suppressing a conflict.

Avoidance learning. A type of reinforcement that strengthens behavior by teaching individuals to respond in ways to avoid undesirable consequences.

Backward integration. When an organization undertakes to supply some or all of its own inputs.

Bankruptcy. A means whereby an organization that is unable to pay its debts can seek court protection.

Behavioral model. A decision-making model that focuses on how managers actually behave.

Behaviorally anchored rating scales. A performance appraisal technique in which specific behaviors are related to varying levels of performance.

Benchmarking. An organization rating its own practices against the world's best and then emulating those practices.

Benchmarking. An improvement process in which an organization measures its performance against that of best-in-class organizations, determines how those organizations achieved their performance levels, and uses the information to improve its own performance.

Benefits. Noncash forms of compensation that employees customarily receive in addition to a salary.

Best in class. A term used to describe an organization recognized as outstanding in its field.

Binging. A practice whereby one group member expressed displeasure with the actions of another by hitting him as hard as possible on the upper arm.

Bogey. Daily output expected of a worker.

Bona fide occupational qualification (BFOQ). A permissible job-related exception to the fair employment requirement that all human resource decisions be made without regard to race, color, age, gender, national origin, religion, and mental or physical impairment.

Bonus. Compensation received in addition to one's regular salary.

Bounded rationality. A situation that reflects not only the limited capability of the human mind and emotions to grasp the full complexity of managerial decisions, but also the uncertainty of future events with which organizations must cope.

Brainstorming. A creativity technique that involves the identification of alternatives by individuals interacting spontaneously in an unrestrained setting.

Break-even analysis. A method of visualizing the relationship between costs and revenues.

Break-even point. Number of units that must be produced and sold for total costs to equal total revenues.

Budget. A single-use plan that deals with the future allocation and utilization of various resources for different organization activities over a given period.

Bureaucracy. A system of management pioneered by Max Weber.

Business cycle. A period of economic activity consisting of recession, recovery, growth, and decline, lasting from one peak (high point of expansion) or trough (minimum point of contraction) to the next.

Cafeteria benefit plan. A plan that allows employees to choose from a menu of benefit options.

Career. A sequence of work-related experiences that span a person's work life.

Career gridlock. A problem created by an organization's structure that leaves little chance for employees to move up.

Career plateau. A point in someone's career when further advancement is unlikely or impossible.

Cash cows. Strategic business units with a relatively large share of a slow-growth market.

Cause-and-effect (Ishikawa or fishbone) diagrams. A tool for analyzing process dispersion. It is also referred to as the Ishikawa diagram, because Kaoru Ishikawa developed it, and the fishbone diagram, because the complete diagram resembles a fish skeleton. The diagram illustrates the main causes and subcauses leading to an effect (symptom).

Central processing unit (CPU). The control, arithmetic, and logic unit of a computer.

Central tendency error. The tendency to steer away from assigning extreme performance ratings.

Centralized/decentralized. Terms denoting the degree to which authority is delegated in an organization.

Certainty. Decision-making condition in which the available alternatives and the benefits (or costs) associated with each are known.

Chain of command. A systematic ordering of positions and duties that define a managerial hierachy.

Charisma. A special quality of leaders that reaches people on an emotional, nonrational level, motivating them to extraordinary efforts.

Classical view of authority. Managers derive their authority from the right of private property.

Closed system. A system that does not depend on other systems for its input.

Coercive power. Power based on a manager's ability to punish for not complying with orders.

Collaboration. A conflict-handling option that involves reaching an agreement that permits all parties involved to achieve their desired outcomes.

Collective bargaining. The process by which labor and management establish and administer conditions under which employees will work.

Committee. A group assembled to consider, investigate, take action on, or report on some matter.

Communication. The process of transmitting understood information among two or more people.

Comparative method. A performance appraisal technique that compares subordinates with one another rather than using abstract standards.

Comparative standard. A kind of standard based on the experience of others.

Competition. A conflict-resolution option that involves attempting to win a conflict at the expense of another.

Compressed workweek. A shortened workweek in which employees work more than 8 hours a day.

Compromise. A conflict-resolution option that involves reaching an agreement that gives all parties at least some of what they want.

Computer hardware. A broad term to denote the physical components of a computer system.

Concentration. A type of growth strategy that focuses on increasing the growth of a single product line.

Conceptual skill. The ability to see an organization as a whole.

Concurrent controls. Controls that monitor the transformation of inputs into outputs to ensure that they conform to set standards. Also known as screening or yes/no controls.

Conflict. A situation in which two or more parties are in opposition.

Conglomerate. An extremely diversified company.

Connectivity. The compatibility of hardware components to be linked into a network.

Consideration. A dimension of leader behavior oriented toward developing mutual trust, two-way communication, respect for subordinates' ideas, and concern for their feelings.

Consultative I method. A decision-making method in which a manager shares problems with subordinates *individually*, getting their ideas and suggestions before making a decision.

Consultative II method. A decision-making method in which a manager shares problems with subordinates as a *group*, getting their ideas and suggestions before making a decision.

Consumer movement. Groups of consumers joining together to exert pressure on specific firms and even entire industries in an effort to see that the public gets a "fair shake."

Content approach to motivation. An approach to motivation concerned with what motivates people.

Contingency approach. An approach to management that holds it is impossible to specify a single way of managing that works best in all situations.

Contingency planning. Planning that involves identifying alternative courses of action that might be followed if various developments occur.

Contingency theory of leadership. A leadership theory which holds that work group performance is contingent upon the match between a person's leadership style and the "favorableness" of the leadership situation.

Continuous improvement. The ongoing improvement of goods, services, or processes through incremental and breakthrough improvements.

Continuous reinforcement. When a desired behavior is always followed by a specific result.

Continuous-process production. A production system in which raw materials are transferred into finished products using a modern system in which the composition of raw materials is changed.

Control. The process of ensuring the efficient accomplishment of organization goals.

Controlling. The process of ensuring the efficient accomplishment of goals.

Coordination. The process of integrating various individual and work group activities to efficiently achieve a common goal.

Cost leadership strategy. A competitive strategy that involves aggressively pursuing operating efficiencies so that an organization is the low-cost producer in its industry.

Cost of poor quality. The costs associated with providing poor-quality goods or services. There are four categories of costs: internal failure costs, external failure costs, appraisal costs, and prevention costs.

Craft union. A union that organizes employees only in particular occupations or skills.

Creativity. Using knowledge and imagination to generate new ideas.

Credibility. The perceived characteristics of an information source as related to four distinct elements: honesty, competence, enthusiasm, and objectivity.

Critical path. The largest path or sequence of activities in a PERT network.

Current capacity to act. The extent to which an organization can respond to major challenges in its environment, including changing social issues.

Current ratio. The ratio between an organization's current assets and current liabilities. Used to judge an organization's liquidity.

Customer departmentalization. A method for organizing activities according to customer needs.

Cybernetic system. A self-regulating system.

Debt-equity ratio. The ratio between an organization's total liabilities and total equities. Used to indicate the extent of an organization's debt financing.

Decision. A choice made between two or more alternatives.

Decision support system (DSS). A system for providing information to help managers with new, unstructured decision making.

Decision tree. A visual display of the benefits or costs likely to result from alternative courses of action.

Decoding. A step in the communication process wherein the receiver of a message interprets it.

Defender strategy. An adaptive strategy that seeks stability by emphasizing a limited set of products directed at a narrow market.

Delegation. The process by which authority passes from one organization level to another.

Delighting the customer. Delivering a good or service that exceeds customer expectations.

Delphi technique. A creativity technique intended to overcome the undesired effects of group interactions while retaining the positive effects of interactive group judgments.

Differentiation strategy. A competitive strategy that involves attempting to develop goods or services that are perceived industrywide as unique.

Direct foreign investment. The acquisition by domestic organizations of foreign-based operating facilities, such as plants, factories, warehouses, and service centers, to enhance long-term profits.

Directive leadership. A type of behavior in which a leader informs subordinates what is expected of them and provides specific guidance.

Discipline. Action taken against an employee for violating work rules.

Discretionary responsibilities. Responsibilities that exceed ethical responsibilities and lead to truly proactive actions on the part of an organization.

Disparate impact. The result of an employment practice that appears fair, but has an adverse effect on protected group members.

Disparate treatment. Using race, color, national origin, religion, or gender as a basis for treating people unequally in employment practices.

Diversification. A type of growth strategy that focuses on affecting an organization's strategic direction by adding new goods or services.

Divestiture. A type of retrenchment strategy that involves a multiunit organization selling off or divesting one or more of its units.

Dogs. Strategic business units with a relatively small share of a slow-growth market.

Downsizing. Elimination of employees and activities to reduce costs and increase revenues.

Driving forces. Forces that direct behavior away from the status quo and facilitate change.

Electronic data interchange. Set of standards as well as hardware and software designed to permit the transfer of data between computers in different organizations.

Electronic mail. Instantaneous transmission of written messages via computers that are linked by telephone lines. Also known as e-mail.

Employee associations. Groups that represent employees in the public sector (federal, state, or local government) and negotiate for professional employees (such as engineers, lawyers, and professors).

Employee empowerment. The pushing of authority down to lower organization levels.

Employee empowerment. A condition whereby employees have the authority to make decisions and take action in their work areas without prior approval.

Encoding. A step in the communication process wherein a sender translates the message to be conveyed into a set of symbols, which it is believed an intended received will understand.

Engineering standard. A kind of standard based on technical analyses.

Environmental scanning. Monitoring and evaluating environmental forces and trends.

Equality. When an individual's perceived outcomes are equal to outcomes received by another person.

Equifinality.   Achieving the same outputs in multiple ways, with different inputs and different transformation processes.

Equity.   When the ratio of an individual's perceived outcomes to inputs equals the ratio of another person's outcomes to inputs.

Essay appraisal.   A written commentary of a subordinate's performance.

Esteem needs.   The needs for a personal feeling of achievement or self-esteem, as well as for recognition or respect from others.

Ethical responsibilities.   Responsibilities that exceed legal responsibilities on the part of an organization.

Executive information system (EIS).   A system designed to meet the information needs of top managers through direct hands-on contact with a computer.

Expectancy 1.   The belief that effort will lead to performance.

Expectancy 2.   The belief that performance will lead to rewards (outcomes).

Expense center.   A unit whose criterion of control is service provided.

Expert power.   Power based on possessing valued knowledge or special skills.

Expert system (ES).   An information system that uses special symbolic reasoning to solve problems.

External customer.   A person or organization that receives a good, a service, or information but is not part of the organization supplying it.

Extinction.   A type of reinforcement that weakens behavior by withholding a desirable consequence when an undesirable behavior occurs.

Fair employment.   Nondiscriminatory employment practices.

Feedback.   A step in the communication process which allows a sender to determine if an intended message has been accurately received.

Financial ratios.   Control guidelines commonly used to express relationships between single or group items on an organization's balance sheet and income statement.

First-line managers.   Managers responsible for directly managing operating (nonmanagerial) employees and resources. Management's first line of contact with labor.

Fixed costs.   Costs that do not vary with levels of output.

Fixed-interval schedules.   Reinforcement applied on the basis of time elapsed, with the amount of time specified in advance.

Fixed-ratio schedules.   Reinforcement applied on the basis of number of behaviors performed, with the number specified in advance.

Flextime.   Allowing employees, within certain limits, to determine their own work schedules.

Focus strategy.   A competitive strategy that involves an organization concentrating its attention on a specific segment of an overall market.

Forced distribution method.   A procedure that requires managers to assign their subordinates to predetermined performance categories.

Force-field analysis.   A depiction of the status quo as an equilibrium locked between two opposing forces—driving and restraining.

Formal group.   A group deliberately created by an organization to achieve a specific goal.

Forming.   A stage of group development characterized by orientation and testing.

Forward integration.   When an organization undertakes to distribute some or all of its own outputs.

Free-rider problem.   The tendency for some individuals to seek the benefits of group membership without contributing their fair share of the costs involved.

Functional authority.   An arrangement that enables staff managers to exercise limited line authority over other units in matters related directly to staff expertise.

Functional departmentalization.   A method for organizing activities into separate units or departments, each of which undertakes a distinctive function—production/operations, marketing, finance/accounting, engineering, and so on.

Gantt chart (bar chart).   A control method that depicts across time the occurrence of those activities comprising a project.

GEMS.   An acronym for global employees, mobile and skilled.

General environment.   All factors external to an organization.

General union.   A union that organizes employees in any industry, occupation, or skill.

Global corporation.   A corporation that integrates its international operations such that they must work together.

Goals.   Those ends that an organization seeks to achieve by its existence and operation.

Grapevine.   An informal channel of communication that develops between employees who have no reporting responsibility to one another but nevertheless share information.

Graphic rating scale.   A scale that requires a manager to appraise a subordinate's performance on a variety of specific factors.

"Greatman" theory of leadership.   The view that a person is born with or without the necessary traits to be a successful leader.

Grid OD.   A copyrighted OD technique based on the *Leadership Grid*.®

Grievance.   An employee charge alleging a labor contract violation.

Group.   Two or more people who interact regularly to achieve a common goal.

Group cohesiveness.   The degree to which group members form a strong collective unit reflecting a feeling of "oneness."

Group decision support system (GDSS).   An information system that supports collective decision making by managers working as a group on unstructured problems.

Group Participation method. A decision-making method in which a manager shares problems with subordinates as a group and together they make a decision.

Groupthink. A phenomenon that occurs in situations where the drive to achieve consensus among group members becomes so powerful that it overrides independent, realistic appraisals of alternative actions.

Growth strategy. A grand strategy that involves an organization attempting to expand its relative market share.

Halo error. The tendency to generalize about all of a person's characteristics based on knowledge of one or a few characteristics.

Harvesting. A type of retrenchment strategy that entails minimizing investment in a product line while attempting to maximize short-term profits and cash flow.

Heroes. An organization's lead players.

Heuristics. Intuitive or unconscious methods of structuring, understanding, and solving problems.

Historical standard. A kind of standard based on past experience.

Horizontal integration. A grand strategy that involves combining two or more organizations operating at the same stage in the production-marketing chain.

Human relations. An approach to management originating with the Hawthorne Studies.

Human resource planning. The process of providing an adequate mix of employees for achieving organization goals.

Human skill. The ability to work with other people effectively.

Hygienes. Factors that produce job dissatisfaction.

Ideation. A step in the communication process wherein a sender has information for, or needs information from, another person.

Image advertising. Advertising used to sell ideas as well as products.

Industrial Revolution. A rapid major economic change occurring around 1776, marking the transfer of work skills from craftworkers to machines.

Industrial union. A union that organizes workers along industry lines regardless of skill or occupation.

Informal group. A group that is independent of an organization's structure and created for its members' purposes.

Information system. A mechanism for collecting, analyzing, and disseminating data in the form of usable information.

Information system (IS). A system of people, computer hardware, software, and procedures to provide an organization with required information.

Initiating structure. A dimension of leader behavior oriented toward structuring subordinates' activities for the purpose of goal attainment.

Inputs. People, materials, money, or information.

Intergroup intervention. An OD technique aimed at improving the effectiveness of two or more interdependent groups by allowing them an opportunity to discuss relations with one another.

Intermittent reinforcement. When a desired behavior is rewarded on an intermittent or periodic basis, as opposed to every time it is performed.

Internal customer. The recipient (person or department) of another department's output (good, service, or information) within an organization.

International business. A multifaceted system linking countries, governments, organizations, and people across national borders, involving all kinds of public and private business activities and sociocultural and political/legal processes.

International management. The process of achieving the global objectives of an organization through efficient utilization of human and material resources.

International portfolio investment. The purchase of foreign securities in the form of stocks, bonds, or commercial paper to obtain an investment return in the form of dividends, interest, or capital gains.

International trade. The buying and selling of goods and services among residents of different countries.

Inventory turnover ratio. The ratio between an organization's cost of goods sold and inventory. Used to measure the number of times an organization's inventory has been sold during a period.

Job analysis. The process of collecting and studying information pertaining to a job.

Job description. A list of important duties to be performed on a job.

Job design. Designing the content of jobs to enhance intrinsic outcomes.

Job enlargement. Extending a job's range so that the number and variety of different activities an employee performs is increased. (Also known as horizontal loading.)

Job enrichment. Extending a job's depth so that employee control is increased. (Also known as vertical loading.)

Job posting. The posting of job openings on bulletin boards and in organization publications.

Job rotation. Periodically shifting employees from one job to another to increase skill variety and task identity.

Job sharing. One job being shared by two or more people.

Job specialization. The narrowing of activities to simple, repetitive routines.

Job specifications. The knowledge, skills, and abilities, as well as physical characteristics, experience, and other qualifications, necessary for successful job performance.

Joint venture. A type of growth strategy that involves an ownership arrangement between two or more organizations that results in the creation of a new managerial entity.

Just-in-time (JIT) inventory. Having suppliers deliver materials to a factory on the day they are needed.

Kaizen. A Japanese term that means gradual, unending improvement by doing little things better and setting and achieving increasingly higher standards.

Key result area. A result area vital to an organization's existence.

Law of effect. Behaviors resulting in desirable consequences will likely recur; and those resulting in undesirable consequences will be less likely to recur.

Law of heavy laboring. Fatigue is cumulative.

Law of the marketplace. Organizations that are unable to compete successfully will soon be confronted with the uncomfortable prospect of either changing their product line or being eliminated.

Law of the situation. The necessity of acting in accord with the unique requirements inherent in any situation.

Leader position power. The right to reward and punish, hire, or fire with organization backing.

Leader-member exchange theory. A theory which holds that leadership is a one-on-one exchange in which leaders behave differently with different followers rather than behaving the same across the board.

Leader-member relations. Relations between a leader and work group members.

Leadership. The process of influencing others toward accomplishing goals.

Leadership style. A leader's manner of acting in a work situation.

Leading and interpersonal influence. The process of inducing individuals (peers, superiors, subordinates, and non-subordinates) or groups to assist willingly and harmoniously in accomplishing goals.

Least preferred co-worker (LPC) scale. A scale that asks respondents to think of all the individuals with whom they have ever worked and, using the scale, describe the one person with who they worked *least well.*

Legends. Stories about a true event or person.

Legitimate power. Power based on an individual's position in a managerial hierarchy.

Leveling. The tendency for a message to become shorter, less detailed, and more easily grasped and repeated as it is passed from one person to another.

Leveling effect. When individual thinking is brought into line with the average quality of a group's thinking.

Leverage. The increased rate of return on stockholders' equity when an investment earns a return larger than the interest paid for debt financing.

Leverage ratio. One of several ratios used to identify the source of an organization's capital—stockholders or outside creditors.

Line authority. Authority that follows an organization's direct chain of command.

Line unit. A unit that contributes directly to accomplishing an organization's goals.

Linear programming. A quantitative tool used for optionally allocating limited resources among competing uses to maximize benefits or minimize losses.

Liquidation. A type of retrenchment strategy that entails terminating an organization's existence through the sale of its assets.

Liquidity. A measure of an organization's ability to pay its short-term debts.

Local area network (LAN). A group of computers and terminals that are interconnected in a small geographic area.

Malcolm Baldrige National Quality Award. An award established by the U.S. Congress in 1987 to raise awareness of quality management and to recognize U.S. companies that have implemented successful quality management systems.

Management. The process of achieving desired results through efficient utilization of human and material resources.

Management by exception. The notion that controls should concentrate on significant exceptions from planned performance.

Management by objectives (MBO). A goal-setting approach based on the belief that joint subordinate-superior participation in translating overall organization objectives into individual objectives will have a positive influence on employee performance.

Management process. A phrase used to collectively refer to the five functions of management: (1) planning, (2) organizing, (3) staffing and human resource management, (4) leading and interpersonal influence, and (5) controlling.

Manager. An individual in an organization who holds a position of authority and makes decisions about the allocation of resources.

Managerial ethics. Valued-based reflection and choice concerning the moral significance of individual and organization actions.

Manufacturing automation system. An information system that supports manufacturing scheduling and planning activities as well as the automation of machines and product transportation in an organization.

Mass production. A production system in which large batches of standard products are manufactured in assembly-line fashion by combining component parts in a specified manner.

Matrix departmentalization. A method for organizing activities that crosses product departmentalization with functional departmentalization.

Mediation. The process in which an outside, neutral person assists in reaching a settlement.

Mentoring. An arrangement whereby a higher level manager acts as an adviser, counselor, and role-model for a lower level employee.

Middle managers. Managers occupying roles positioned above first-line management and below top management.

Midlife crisis. An unstable and troubled period in many persons' lives occurring between their mid-30s and late-40s.

Modems Two devices used to transform the digital electrical signals into an analog-transmittable system that connects two computers via telephone lines.

Motion study. The study of the motions necessary to perform a task.

Motivation. The will to achieve.

Motivators. Factors that produce job satisfaction.

Multinational corporation. A corporation that views each of its affiliates around the world as an independent entity, each on its own in serving the unique national market of where it is situated.

Net profit ratio. The ratio between an organization's net profit and sales. Used to measure an organization's short-term profitability.

Network. A diagram showing the interrelationships between the events and activities that compromise a PERT project.

Network departmentalization. A method for organizing that temporarily ties together resources required to achieve specific tasks.

Networking. Using personal connections as a source of job information.

Noise. Any factor that disturbs or distorts a message.

Nominal grouping technique. A five-step technique useful in situations where individual ideas need to be tapped, but where a group consensus is desired.

Nonprogrammed decision. A decision that is novel and ill structured and for which there can be no established methods for handling it because it has never occurred before or because it is too complex and elusive.

Normative theory of leadership. A leadership theory that offers normative guidelines for how decisions ought to be made in a specific situation.

Norming. A stage of group development characterized by a sense of heightened solidarity.

Norms. Standards of behavior accepted by a group's members.

Office automation system. An information system that supports the varied activities and work requirements of office and white-collar employees.

Ombudsperson. Representative who investigate customer complaints.

On-the-job training. Assigning a trainee to an experienced supervisor or senior co-worker for training.

Open door policy. A policy that permits employees free access to higher level management so that they can speak out on organization affairs.

Open (versus closed) system. A system that depends on other systems for its inputs and thus cannot exist in isolation.

Operations management. The design and implementation of a production system that transforms inputs (people, money, and information) into outputs (goods and services) with a high rate of productivity.

Organization chart. A diagram of all the positions in an organization and their formal relationships to one another.

Organization design. The creation or modification of an organization's structure.

Organization development (OD). A long-range program that focuses on changing employee attitudes and behavior, thereby improving organization performance.

Organization structure. Segmented or departmentalized activities and connections established within and among departments according to some logical pattern.

Organizational culture. The common set of beliefs and expectations shared by members of an organization.

Organizing. The process of dividing work among groups and individuals and coordinating their activities to accomplish goals. Organizing also involves establishing managerial authority.

Orientation. The process that introduces new employees to their new work environment.

Outputs. Goods and services.

Paired-comparison method. A procedure in which all subordinates are compared one at a time with each other, with a final performance ranking determined by the number of pairings in which an individual is rated the better performer.

Pareto analysis. A phenomenon whereby 80 percent of all defects are caused by 20 percent of the problems.

Parity of authority and responsibility. No one should be expected to shoulder responsibility without commensurate authority.

Participative leadership. A type of behavior in which a leader consults with subordinates and asks for their suggestions before making a decision.

Path-goal theory of leadership. A leadership theory that describes how leader behavior affects a person's beliefs that effort will lead to performance and that performance will lead to rewards that are valued, which in turn affect subordinate outcomes.

Payoff matrix. A tool for calculating the benefits or costs likely to result from alternative courses of action.

Performance appraisal. The process of determining the extent to which an employee is performing a job effectively.

Performance feedback. The extent to which employees are provided with information about how well they are doing their jobs.

Performing. A stage of group development heralded by increased cooperation, problem solving, and task performance.

Perquisites. An extra, noncash form of compensation.

Person specialization. Individuals with a high degree of training who have power because their ability makes other people dependent on them.

Physiological needs. The needs for food, water, rest, air, and so forth.

Planning. The process of establishing goals and selecting a future course of action for their accomplishment.

Planning. The process of establishing organization goals and selecting a future course of action for their accomplishment.

Poka-yoke. A method for making the workplace mistake-proof.

Policy. A general statement that serves to guide decision making.

Political risk. Risks such as nationalization, repeal of tax laws, political instability, and the like that may render the value of a corporation's investment in a foreign nation worthless.

Pooled interdependence. A situation in which work units render a discrete contribution to an organization and, in turn, are supported by the organization.

Position blockage. Employees not being promoted because the positions above them are filled.

Positive reinforcement. A type of reinforcement that strengthens behavior by providing a desirable consequence when a desirable behavior occurs.

Postaction controls. Controls that monitor outputs to ensure that they meet set standards. Also known as feedback controls.

Power. The capacity to influence others.

Precontrols. Controls that monitor inputs to ensure that they meet the standards necessary for successful transformation. Also known as feedforward or preventive controls.

Proactive behavior. Actions taken in anticipation of social challenges.

Probability analysis. A quantitative tool used under conditions of risk or uncertainty.

Problem. A discrepancy between an existing and desired state of affairs.

Procedure. A series of related steps that are to be followed in an established order to achieve a given purpose.

Process approach to motivation. An approach to motivation concerned with how people are motivated.

Process consultation. An OD technique in which a change agent helps employees to understand and act upon process events in their work environment.

Product departmentalization. A method of organizing activities into separate units or departments according to product line.

Productivity. A measure of an organization's ability to produce more goods/services with fewer inputs (people, materials, money, information) and thus less cost.

Productivity. The amount of output produced divided by the number of units of resources applied.

Profit center. A unit whose criterion of control is comprised of both revenues and expenses.

Profitability. The gain resulting from an activity.

Program evaluation and review technique (PERT). A control method that depicts the interrelationships across time among those events and activities comprising a project.

Programmed decision. A decision that is repetitive and routine and for which a definite method for its solution can be established so that it does not have to be treated anew each time it occurs.

Programs. Single-use plans intended to accomplish a specific goal within a fixed time.

Projects. Usually a subset or component of a specific program.

Prospector strategy. An adaptive strategy that continually seeks market opportunities and regularly experiments with innovations.

Protected group. Specific groups identified by race, color, national origin, religion, gender, age, or impairment who are "protected" from unfair employment practices by the 1964 Civil Rights Act.

Prototyping. A shortened software development procedure that relies on advanced software development tools to quickly provide a working system for users to examine.

Punishment. A type of reinforcement that weakens behavior by providing an undesirable consequence when an undesirable behavior occurs.

Quality. (1) The characteristics of a good or service that bear on its ability to satisfy stated or implied needs, and (2) a good or service free of deficiencies.

Quality circles. Quality improvement or self-improvement study groups composed of a small number of employees (ten or fewer) and their supervisor. Quality circles originated in Japan, where they are called *quality control circles*.

Quality improvement movement. An approach to management that integrates quality into every department within an organization in an effort to improve productivity.

Question marks. Strategic business units with a relatively small share of a rapidly growing market.

Queuing theory. A quantitative tool for analyzing the costs of waiting lines.

Quick asset ratio. The ratio between an organization's net profit and total assets. Used to measure an organization's ability to meet its financial obligations.

Quick assets. Highly liquid assets such as cash, short-term securities, and accounts receivable available to cover a sudden organization emergency.

Rate of return on assets. The ratio between an organization's net profit and total assets. Used to measure an organization's efficiency in generating profit.

Rater pattern error. The tendency toward either excessive leniency or strictness in assigning performance ratings.

Rational model. A decision-making model that focuses on how managers should behave.

Reactive behavior. Actions taken in reply to social challenges.

Reactor strategy. A type of adaptive strategy that entails responding to competitive pressures by doing whatever is necessary to survive.

Receive. A step in the communication process wherein an intended message is perceived by a receiver.

Recency error. The tendency for managers to remember events that occurred most recently rather than considering a subordinate's performance over time.

Reciprocal interdependence. A situation in which outputs from one work unit serve as inputs for another *and* vice versa.

Recruiting. The process of attracting job applicants who have knowledge, skills, and abilities needed to achieve an organization's goals.

Referent power. Power that attaches to specific managers because people admire them, want to be like them, or are impressed by their integrity, charisma, or charm.

Reinforcement. A consequence of a response.

Relationship-oriented leadership. A leadership style in which good interpersonal relations are seen as a requirement for task accomplishment and satisfaction is derived from establishing close personal relations with fellow workers.

Replacement chart. A chart indicating the various positions in an organization, the jobholders and their present performance, and the readiness of different candidates for promotion into each position.

Response. A unit of behavior that follows a stimulus.

Restraining forces. Forces that direct behavior toward the status quo and hinder change.

Retrenchment strategy. A grand strategy that is used when an organization seeks to reverse a decline in performance.

Revenue center. A unit whose criterion of control is revenue generated.

Reward power. Power based on a manager's ability to provide various kinds of rewards for complying with orders.

Rolling plans. Plans of future operations updated on an annual basis.

Rule. A statement that either prescribes or prohibits action by specifying what an individual may or may not do in a given situation.

Rumors. Information without a factual base.

Safety needs. The needs for security and stability, as well as freedom from fear or threat.

Satisficing. Settling for an alternative deemed "satisfactory" rather than searching for the optimum choice.

Say's Law. Supply creates its own demand.

Scenario planning. A type of contingency plan that examines "critical uncertainties" and then proposes ways for an organization to meet its goals under whatever developments occur.

Scientific management. An approach to management pioneered by Frederick W. Taylor.

Selective perception. A phenomenon wherein people reject or inaccurately perceive information that is inconsistent with their previously established expectations.

Self-actualization needs. The needs for a feeling of self-fulfillment, or the realization of one's potential.

Self-managing teams. A group of employees who have the day-to-day responsibility for managing themselves and the work they do.

Sequential interdependence. A situation in which the outputs from one work unit are the inputs for a following work unit.

Serial transmission effect. The change that a message undergoes as it is successively communicated from one management layer to another.

Seven tools of quality. Tools that help organizations understand their processes in order to improve them. The tools are the cause-and-effect diagram, check sheet, control chart, flowchart, histogram, Pareto chart, and scatter diagram.

Sharpening. The tendency for certain details to become relatively more prominent or central to a message's main theme as a consequence of leveling.

Simulation. A quantitative tool involving the use of several different methods, all with the common objective of imitating a set of real conditions so that the likely outcomes of alternative courses of action can be compared.

Situational favorableness. The degree to which a situation enables a person to exert influence over a work group.

Six-sigma level. A statistical measure expressing 3.4 defects per million parts.

Six-sigma quality. A term used generally to indicate that a process is well controlled (that is, $\pm$ 6 sigma from the centerline in a control chart).

Skill variety. The extent to which a job requires employees to perform a wide number of activities.

Skills inventory. A list containing information on various characteristics and skills possessed by an organization's employees.

Slack time. The difference between the total time required by the critical path and any other path in a PERT network.

Social needs. The needs for friendship, affection, acceptance, interaction with others, and so forth.

Socialization. The process by which new employees are made part of an organization's culture.

Soldiering. Working slowly while at the same time trying to make it appear that one is working fast.

Span of control. The actual number of subordinates that report *directly* to a manager.

Stability strategy. A grand strategy that is used when an organization seeks to pursue a "steady as it goes" approach to growth.

Staff authority. Authority to provide advice and expertise to assist line staff units in achieving their goals.

Staff unit. A unit that contributes indirectly to accomplishing an organization's goals.

Staffing and human resource management. The process of ensuring that employees are selected, developed, and rewarded for accomplishing goals.

Standard. A criterion against which actual performance can be compared.

Standing plans. Plans that are used again and again, focusing on situations that recur repeatedly.

Stars. Strategic business units with a relatively large share of a high-growth market.

Statistical process control. The application of statistical techniques to control a process. Often the term *statistical quality control* is used interchangeably with *statistical process control.*

Stereotyping. The tendency to attribute characteristics to a person based on certain observable traits, such as race, gender, or appearance.

Stimulus. An event that leads to a response.

Storming. A stage of group development marked by intragroup conflict and interpersonal differences as members vie for group and task roles.

Strategic business unit. A segment of an organization with a distinct objective, product market, and strategy for dealing with that market.

Strategic planning. The process of focusing on an organization's continuing relationship with its environment.

Strategic window. An untapped opportunity that fits an organization's strengths.

Strategy. A plan of action that will develop an organization's competitive advantages and compound them.

Stress. The body's total response to any stimulus.

Structured interview. A job interview in which an applicant is asked a predetermined set of questions.

Succession planning. The identification of likely candidates for future vacant positions.

Supportive leadership. A type of behavior in which a leader is friendly and approachable and shows concern for the status, well-being, and personal needs of subordinates.

Survey feedback. An OD technique in which survey results are fed back to employees for analysis and interpretation so that necessary changes can be designed by the employees themselves.

SWOT analysis. The assessment of an organization's internal strengths and weaknesses in relation to its external opportunities and threats.

Symbols. Objects or events that convey meaning.

Synergy. The creation of a whole that is greater than the sum of its parts.

System. A set of interdependent parts that relate in the accomplishment of some purpose.

Systems approach. An approach to management that draws on systems theory.

Systems development life cycle (SDLC). A procedure for proposing, analyzing, designing, and implementing computer software.

Task environment. Those elements of the general environment *directly* relevant to an individual organization.

Task identity. The extent to which a job allows employees to perform a "whole" piece of work and to clearly identify the outcome of their efforts.

Task significance. The extent to which a job has a substantial impact on the lives of others.

Task structure. The degree to which a group assignment can be programmed and spelled out in a step-by-step fashion.

Task-oriented leadership. A leadership style in which satisfaction is derived from successfully completing a task and interpersonal relations are given a much lower priority.

Team building. An OD technique that combines survey feedback and process consultation to build cohesive and successful work groups.

Technical skill. The knowledge and ability necessary to perform a specific task.

Technology. The means by which an organization transforms inputs into outputs.

Telecommunications. The electronic transmission of data from one computer device to another.

Territorial departmentalization. A method for organizing activities according to geographic location.

Therbligs. A system for classifying hand motions into 17 basic divisions ("Gilbreth" spelled backwards with the "th" transposed).

Time study. The study of the time necessary to perform a task.

Top managers. Managers who determine the form of an organization and define its overall character, mission, and direction.

Total costs. The total of fixed and variable costs.

Total quality management. An approach to quality improvement that signifies long-term success through customer satisfaction.

Total revenues. Income computed by multiplying selling price per unit times number of units sold.

Training. The process of developing knowledge, skills, and abilities so as to improve present and future performance.

Trait. A distinctive physical or psychological characteristic that accounts for a person's behavior.

Transaction-processing and reporting system. An information system that gathers, stores, and processes transaction data.

Transformational leadership. A theory which holds that leaders can motivate followers to perform beyond expectations through charisma, inspiration, individualized consideration, and intellectual stimulation.

Transmission. A step in the communication process wherein a message is sent.

Turnaround. A type of retrenchment strategy that attempts to "restructure" or streamline an organization's operations to reestablish previous performance levels.

Understanding. A step in the communication process wherein mutual understanding results.

Union. A group of employees who join together to bargain to improve their wages, benefits, work hours, and conditions.

Unit production. A production system in which either one or a small number of finished goods are manufactured according to customer specifications.

Unity of command. The notion that no subordinate should report to more than one superior.

Unstructured interview. A job interview in which there are no predetermined questions or prearranged sequence of topics for discussion.

Valence. The value placed on an outcome (reward).

Validity. The relation between test results and actual job performance.

Values. An organization's beliefs about what is good or bad, desirable or undesirable.

Variable costs. Costs that vary with levels of output.

Variable-interval schedule. Reinforcement applied on the basis of time elapsed, with the amount of time varying.

Variable-ratio schedule. Reinforcement applied on the basis of number of behaviors performed with the number varying.

Vertical integration. A grand strategy that involves an organization entering one or more additional stages in the production-marketing chain.

Wide area network (WAN). A group of computers and terminals that are interconnected in a large geographic area.

Working to the rules. Performing exactly what is required by prevailing work rules and nothing more.

Zero defects. A performance standard developed by Philip B. Crosby to address a dual attitude in the workplace: People are willing to accept imperfection in some areas while, in other areas, they expect the number of defects to be zero. Zero defects methodology states that if employers commit themselves to watching details and avoiding errors, they can move closer to the goal of zero defects. The performance standard that must be set is "zero defects," not "close enough."

Zone of acceptance. A conditional range within which subordinates will accept their superiors' orders.

CREDITS

PART OPENERS

PART 1 Photo, P. 1: © Bruce Bishop

PART 2 Photo, P. 121: Copyright 1991, COMSTOCK.

PART 3 Photo, P. 235: George Haling ©.

PART 4 Photo, P. 337: Copyright 1992, COMSTOCK.

PART 5 Photo, P. 435: © David Madison 1992.

PART 6 Photo, P. 557: Wolf Von Dem Bussche/The Image Bank.

PART 7 Photo, P. 633: Copyright 1991, COMSTOCK.

CHAPTER 1

Photo, P. 3: © 1991 Theo Westenberger.

Photo, P. 5: © Pioneer HiBred International, Inc. Photo: Scott Sinklier.

Photo, P. 10: Courtesy of Santa Fe Pipeline and Power.

Photo, P. 14: Courtesy of Apple Computer, Inc.

Photo, P. 17: © Kim Steele for The Square D Company.

Photo, P. 18: © Kim Steele for The Square D Company.

CHAPTER 2

Photo, P. 27: © Marvullo/Photomontage

Photo, P. 30: Smithsonian Institution Neg. No. 81–192.

Photo, P. 30: Courtesy of Stevens Institute of Technology, Samuel C. Williams Library, Frederick W. Taylor Collection.

Photo, P. 32: Courtesy of Bethlehem Steel Corporation.

Photo, P. 34: Courtesy of Stevens Institute of Technology, Samuel C. Williams Library, Frederick W. Taylor Collection.

Photo, P. 37: Courtesy of Ronald G. Greenwood.

Photo, P. 39: Courtesy of Ronald G. Greenwood.

Photo, P. 42: Courtesy of Centre National de l'Organization Française.

Photo, P. 44: Courtesy of the German Information Center.

Photo, P. 46: Courtesy of AT&T.

Photo, P. 47: Courtesy of Manuscript & Archives, Baker Library, Harvard Business School.

Photo, P. 48: Courtesy of AT&T.

Photo, P. 50: The making of Scientific Managements, Vol. 3, by Colonel L. Urwick and Mr. E.F.L. Brech. Reprinted by permission of Pitman Publishing Ltd., London.

Photo, P. 55: Courtesy of Morrison Knudson Corporation.

Photo, P. 57: © Kim Newton/Woodfin Camp & Associates.

CHAPTER 3

Photo, P. 69: Bruce Maxwell/Fort Worth Star-Telegram.

Photo, P. 72: © Robert Semeniuk/FIRST LIGHT, Toronto.

Photo, P 74: © Joseph C. Unitas.

Photo, P. 76: Courtesy of Hershey Foods Corporation.

Photo, P. 79: Courtesy of Sonoco Products Co./Photo by Terry Parke.

Photo, P. 86: © 1991 Arthur Meyerson. All Rights Reserved.

CHAPTER 4

Photo, P. 101: Copyright Andy Freeberg.

Photo, P 104: Courtesy of Union Electric Co.

Photo, P. 106: Courtesy of H. J. Heinz Company.

Photo, P. 107: Courtesy of Xerox Corporation.

Photo, P. 111: Courtesy of The Promus Companies.

Photo, P. 113: Courtesy of New United Motor Manufacturing, Inc.

CHAPTER 5

Photo, P. 123: Copyright © Patricia M. Doty 1992.

Photo, P. 128: Courtesy of Temple-Inland, Inc.

Photo, P 132: Courtesy of American Electric Power Co.

Photo, P. 137: Courtesy of Herman Miller, Inc.

Photo, P. 139: Courtesy of The Neiman Marcus Group.

Photo, P. 142: Courtesy of Browning-Ferris Industries, Inc.

CHAPTER 6

Photo, P. 155: Courtesy of Ford Motor Company.

Photo, P. 158: Courtesy of Motorola, Inc.

Photo, P. 165: Photography by Ken Reid. © 1991 Hallmark Cards, Inc.

Photo, P. 167: Courtesy of Chicago Bridge & Iron Company.

Photo, P. 175: Courtesy of Hewlett-Packard Company.

CHAPTER 7

Photo, P. 201: © Steve Elmore/Tony Stone Worldwide.

Photo, P. 204: © 1992 Warner Bros. Inc.

Photo, P. 207: Courtesy of Hudson's Grill of America, Inc.

Photo, P. 211: © Steve Niedorf/3M Company.

Photo, P. 213: Courtesy of TRW Inc., © 1992.

Photo, P. 219: Courtesy of Ford Motor Co.

Photo, P. 226: Courtesy of Ford Motor Co.

CHAPTER 8

Photo, P 237: Copyright © Patricia M. Doty 1992.

Photo, P. 241: Courtesy of Apple Computer, Inc. Products mentioned are trademarks or Registered trademarks of Apple Computer, Inc.

Photo, P. 247: Courtesy of The Aerospace Corporation.

Photo, P. 255: Copyright © Patricia M. Doty 1992.

Photo, P. 258: © Brian Smith, Miami Beach, FL.

CHAPTER 9

Photo, P. 265: Courtesy of GE. Photo by Brownie Harris.

Photo, P. 269: © Steve Niedorf/3M Company.

Photo, P. 275: Courtesy of John F. Johnston, Humana, Inc.

Photo, P. 277: Courtesy of Springs Industries, Inc.

Photo, P. 281: © Alen MacWeeney for ALCOA Co.

CHAPTER 10

Photo, P. 291: Courtesy of Saturn Corporation.

Photo, P. 297: Courtesy of U.S. Shoe Corporation.

Photo, P. 298: Courtesy of Bristol-Myers Squibb Company.

Photo, P. 301: Courtesy of Whirlpool Corporation.

CHAPTER 11

Photo, P. 311: Courtesy of Corning Incorporated/Robert Barker, Photography.

Photo, P. 314: Courtesy of BP America, Inc.

Photo, P. 315: Used with permission of Pacific Telesis, Kathy Madlem, and Apple Computer, Inc. Apple and the Apple logo are registered trademarks of Apple Computer, Inc. Photographer, © Robb Kendrick.

Photo, P. 323: Courtesy of Goulds Pumps, Inc.

Photo, P. 324: Courtesy of The Perkin-Elmer Corporation/ William Taufic, photographer.

Photo, P. 327: Courtesy of The Timkin Company.

CHAPTER 12

Photo, P. 339: Courtesy of BP America, Inc.

Photo, P. 345: T. Michael Keza/NATION'S BUSINESS.

Photo, P. 349: Courtesy of Walgreen Company.

Photo, P. 353: © Jim Pickerell/Tony Stone Worldwide.

Photo, P. 355: Courtesy of The Psychological Corporation.

CHAPTER 13

Photo, P. 369: © 1991 Dennis Brack/Black Star.

Photo, P. 373: © 1991 Richard Howard.

Photo, P. 375: Courtesy of Newport News Shipbuilding.

Photo, P. 384: Courtesy of Varian Associates, Inc.

Photo, P. 388: © Jeff Smith for The Southern Company.

Photo, P. 393: UPI/Bettmann.

CHAPTER 14

Photo, P. 405: © Peter Gregoire.

Photo, P. 413: © Mark Richards.

Photo, P. 419: Photographer, Greg O'Loughlin for Southern California Edison Co.

Photo, P. 424: © Barbara Ries, 1990.

Photo, P. 425: Courtesy of Genentech, Inc.

CHAPTER 15

Photo, P. 437: © Richard Mitchell.

Photo, P. 440: Courtesy of Longs Drugs.

Photo, P. 442: Courtesy of John F. Johnston, Humana, Inc.

Photo, P. 450: Jackson Hill/Southern Lights.

Photo, P. 455: Courtesy of United Airlines.

CHAPTER 16

Photo, P. 469: © Steven LaBadessa.

Photo, P. 470: Courtesy of Beech Aircraft Corporation.

Photo, P. 479: © 1992 Steven Pumphrey. All Rights Reserved.

Photo, P. 481: © Michael L. Abramson.

Photo, P. 486: © Russ Kennedy.

Photo, P. 487: Courtesy of Chrysler Corporation.

CHAPTER 17

Photo, P. 497: Courtesy of Canon and Luciano Salio, architecte, president of STA Computer Grafica.

Photo, P. 498: © Ed Wheeler, Reprinted by permission of Philip Morris Companies, Inc.

Photo, P. 500: Courtesy of Tyson Foods, Inc.

Photo, P. 505: Courtesy of Santa Fe Pacific Pipeline and Power Partners.

Photo, P. 507: © 1991 Jay Brousseau.

Photo, P. 511: Courtesy of Penton, IPC, Inc.

Photo, P. 516: Courtesy of J. P. Morgan & Co. Incorporated.

CHAPTER 18

Photo, P. 523: © 1992 Steven Pumphrey. All Rights Reserved.

Photo, P. 526: Courtesy of Rockwell International/David Perry.

Photo, P. 532: Steve Smith/Onyx.

Photo, P. 535: © Steve Niedorf 1988. All Rights Reserved.

Photo, P. 542: Courtesy of Hoffmann-La Roche, Inc.

Photo, P. 548: © David Kluth.

CHAPTER 19

Photo, P. 559: Copyright © Patricia M. Doty 1992.

Photo, P. 562: Obata Design, St. Louis, Mo.

Photo, P. 563: Courtesy of Pall Corporation, East Hills, New York.

Photo, P. 566: © Davis Freeman.

Photo, P. 571: Courtesy of Stew Leonard.

Photo, P. 572: © 1992 Steven Pumphrey. All Rights Reserved.

CHAPTER 20

Photo, P. 595: Courtesy of Ryder System, Inc.

Photo, P. 597: Laura Resen © 1992.

Photo, P. 600: Courtesy of Fleming Companies, Inc.

Photo, P. 601: Courtesy of GM Hughes Electronics.

Photo, P. 604: Photo by Jeff Crain, Southwestern Electric Power Company.

Photo, P. 607: Mark Joseph Photography Inc., Chicago.

CHAPTER 21

Photo, P. 615: Courtesy of McDonald's.

Photo, P. 618: © Sheryl Rossum 1991 for Mobile Corporation.

Photo, P. 622: Borden, Inc. Columbus, Ohio. © Borden, Inc. 1991.

Photo, P. 624: Courtesy of Cyprus Minerals Company, Bob Lynn Photographer.

Photo, P. 629: Courtesy of Cooper Industries, Inc., Copyright 1990, Michael Hart Houston, Texas.

CHAPTER 22

Photo, P. 635: Copyright © Patricia M. Doty 1992.

Photo, P. 637: Courtesy of Colgate-Palmolive Company.

Photo, P. 640: © John A. Gallagher for Weyerhaeuser.

Photo, P 643: Courtesy of Aluminum Company of America.

Photo, P. 644: Courtesy of The Walt Disney Company.

Photo, P. 647: Courtesy of Texas Instruments.

CHAPTER 23

Photo, P. 655: Courtesy of Federal Express Corporation.

Photo, P. 657: Compliments of Federal-Mogul. Photo by Lou Kulikaukas.

Photo, P. 661: Courtesy of Armstrong World Industries, Inc.

Photo, P. 662: Mark Green for Brown & Root, Inc., a subsidiary of the Halliburton Company.

Photo, P. 664: Mead Corporation. Photographer: D. Altman Fleischer.

Photo, P. 671: Courtesy of Engelhard Corporation.

Photo, P. 674: Courtesy of Westinghouse Electric Corporation.

Adams, J. Stacy,   449–454, 466
Ailes, Roger,   433
Akers, John F.,   528
Albanese, Robert,   521
Alexander, Larry D.,   233
Alexander the Great,   472
Alger, Horatio,   491
Allaire, Paul,   14, 237
Allen, Robert F.,   509
Alter, Allan E.,   603n, 612n, 613n
Amerman, John,   532
Ancona, Paula,   538
Ankerson, Robert S.,   408
Apple, Howard P.,   263
Appleby, Robert,   586
Arkwright, Richard,   28
Armstrong, Larry,   67
Ash, Mary Kay,   315, 323, 335
Atwater, Bruce,   122, 123
Austin, Nancy,   98
Austin, Wanda,   247
Axley, Stephen R.,   555n
Ayers, David,   327

B

Bach, Johann Sebastian,   441
Bacon, Francis,   286
Bailey, Earl L.,   198
Bailey, R. Lee,   623
Bailey, Ronald,   432
Baldrige, Letitia,   374
Baldrige, Malcolm,   671
Barham, James,   367
Barnard, Chester I.,   267, 288
Barnes, Ralph M.,   66
Barnett, Peter,   67
Barth, Carl G.,   32, 35
Bass, Bernard M.,   495
Bateman, Thomas S.,   423
Bauer, Harald,   19
Baughman, James P.,   13n
Bedeian, Arthur G.,   67, 263
Beech, Olive A.,   470
Beech, Walter & Olive,   470
Beer, Michael,   403
Beethoven, Ludwig van,   441
Bemowski, Karne,   679n
Benson, Tracy E.,   25, 185
Bentsen, Lloyd,   90
Berenbeim, Ronald E.,   108n
Berry, William L.,   620n

Beyer, Janice M.,   467
Binns, W. Gordon, Jr.,   390
Bird, Barbara J.,   495
Black, Arthur,   546
Blair, John D.,   101, 103
Blake, Robert R.,   328, 329, 335
Blue, James,   98
Boesky, Ivan F.,   91, 112
Bonaparte, Napoleon,   471, 472
Bovard, James,   98
Bowen, David E.,   495
Boyne, John et al,   263
Bradshaw, Francis F.,   232
Brandeis, Louis D.,   35
Braude, Jacob M.,   335
Breeze, John D.,   67
Bretz, Robert,   433
Brock, William,   97
Brodie, Morris B.,   66
Brokaw, Leslie,   279n
Brooks, Lester,   590n
Brown, Louise,   189
Brown, Peter A.,   358n
Bryan, John,   635
Bryant, John,   97
Buford, James A., Jr.,   339, 369
Burch, John C.,   402
Burden, Larry,   333n
Burgess, Carter,   15
Burke, James E.,   16
Burns, M. Anthony,   594
Bush, George,   14, 16, 85, 256
Bush, Vannevar,   47
Bushardt, Stephen C.,   521
Bylinsky, Gene,   567n

C

Caesar, Julius,   471
Calloway, Wayne,   278
Caminiti, Susan,   232
Campbell, Donald T.,   555n
Cannella, Albert A. Jr.,   184
Carey, Ernestine Gilbreth,   66
Carley, William M.,   89n
Carnegie, Andrew,   29, 470
Carroll, Archie B.,   103, 105
Carroll, Paul,   263
Carter, Jimmy,   491
Cartwright, Dorwin,   521
Cartwright, Edmund,   28
Case, John,   437, 439
Catherine the Great,   472
Cerulli, Carol,   635n

ORGANIZATION INDEX